William Trent
Factor of Ambition

Jason A. Cherry
with a Foreword by Marcia Balisciano, Ph.D.

Mechanicsburg, PA USA

Published by Sunbury Press, Inc.
Mechanicsburg, PA USA

www.sunburypress.com

Copyright © 2024 by Jason A. Cherry.
Cover Copyright © 2024 by Sunbury Press, Inc.

Sunbury Press supports copyright. Copyright fuels creativity, encourages diverse voices, promotes free speech, and creates a vibrant culture. Thank you for buying an authorized edition of this book and for complying with copyright laws. Except for the quotation of short passages for the purpose of criticism and review, no part of this publication may be reproduced, scanned, or distributed in any form without permission. You are supporting writers and allowing Sunbury Press to continue to publish books for every reader. For information contact Sunbury Press, Inc., Subsidiary Rights Dept., PO Box 548, Boiling Springs, PA 17007 USA or legal@sunburypress.com.

For information about special discounts for bulk purchases, please contact Sunbury Press Orders Dept. at (855) 338-8359 or orders@sunburypress.com.

To request one of our authors for speaking engagements or book signings, please contact Sunbury Press Publicity Dept. at publicity@sunburypress.com.

FIRST SUNBURY PRESS EDITION: February 2024

Set in Adobe Garamond Pro | Interior design by Crystal Devine | Cover by Lawrence Knorr | Edited by Lawrence Knorr.

Publisher's Cataloging-in-Publication Data
Names: Cherry, Jason, author.
Title: William Trent : factor of ambition / Jason A. Cherry.
Description: First trade paperback edition. | Mechanicsburg, PA : Sunbury Press, 2024.
Summary: In this new riveting biography, comes the rise and fall of William Trent, one of the most influential backcountry merchants of the eighteenth century. With newly discovered primary sources, author Jason A. Cherry brings to light a brand-new saga of Trent's life, never told in such vivid detail, until now.
Identifiers: ISBN : 979-8-88819-185-9 (paperback) | ISBN : 979-8-88819-186-6 (ePub).
Subjects: HISTORY/ United States/ Colonial Period (1600-1775) | BIOGRAPHY & AUTOBIOGRAPHY / Historical | HISTORY / United States / State & Local / Middle Atlantic (DC, DE, MD, NJ, MY, PA).

Designed in the USA
0 1 1 2 3 5 8 13 21 34 55

For the Love of Books!

Front cover painting *Sign of Friendship* by Robert Griffing used with permission.

Dedicated
to the memory of

"Captain" Jack Oelschlager
(May 14, 1940 – September 20, 2018)

Corey "Cyber" Mitchell
Umass Football #79
(May 15, 1979 – June 18, 2020)

Vance Kennedy
(May 18, 1923 – August 17, 2023)

Contents

List of Illustrations vii
Foreword by Dr. Márcia Balisciano xi
Acknowledgments xiii
Descendant Chart of Major William Trent xv

PRELUDE: A Scandalous Beginning 1

CHAPTERS
1. An Uncertain Life 7
2. The Fight for a Different Path 16
3. A Taste of Ambition 32
4. A Brush with Death 49
5. Prosperous Expansion 65
6. Justice and the Proclaim of Liberty 85
7. A Perilous Opportunity 112
8. The Indian's Eyes are Fixed upon You 132
9. Race to the Western Country 147
10. Darkness Before the Light 170
11. The Fall of Fort Duquesne 188
12. Profit and Victory 212
13. The Desired Effect 230
14. A Monumental Presence 250
15. A New Colony 267
16. Restlessness and Mutiny 295
17. The Internal Struggle 315
18. Choosing Sides 331
19. A Feverish Attempt 347
20. The Poorest of Circumstances 365

POSTLUDE: One Last Chime 381

APPENDICES
- A. 1710 Marriage Certificate of Judge William Trent and Mary Coddington 385
- B. Captain William Trent's Return of his Company in September of 1746 and the Narrative of the Captivity of Nehemiah How in 1745-1747 386
- C. Hockley, Trent, and Croghan Tanyard Accounts 1752 391
- D. Commission of William Trent and Official Orders on January 26, 1754............................... 396
- E. Expense Account of the Government of Virginia to William Trent April 8, 1754........................... 399
- F. Baptism Records found in the Trent Family Bible............ 401
- G. Commission to William Trent to be Assistant Superintendent of Indian Affairs dated September 3, 1758..... 402
- H. Roll of the Militia at Fort Pitt 1763 404
- I. Ledger of the Crown to Levy, Trent & Company 1763........ 410
- J. First Will of William Trent 1775 414
- K. Schedule of Indiana Company Losses and Shares [1776]................................... 417
- L. William Trent's Oath of Allegiance 1778 419
- M. Second Will of William Trent 1782 420
- N. Last Will and Testament of William Trent 1784 and Trent's death announcement in 1784 Letter............. 422
- O. The Inventory of a Black Trunk, belonging to the Estate of William Trent................................ 425

Bibliography...................................... 428
Index 439
About the Author.................................. 457

Illustrations

Original bell of Christ Church 9
1719 William Trent House 12
Dutch delft tiles in William Trent House 20
Old Barracks Museum 28
Silhouette of Edward Shippen III 32
Site of First Presbyterian Church in Philadelphia 35
Mary Coddington signature 37
Site of Slate Roof House in Philadelphia. 38
Site of Penn Square in Lancaster 42
George Croghan's cabin c. 1745 45
Map of Pennsylvania, New Jersey, New York, and the three
    Delaware counties by Lewis Evans c. 1749 46
Site of the St. George and the Dragon Inn in Philadelphia 50
Site of the ambush of Trent's men on April 7, 1747, near
    Schuylerville, New York 62
Site of George Croghan and William Trent's tannery. 67
Site of Shannopin's Town 70
Trademark of Hockley, Trent and Croghan firm c. 1748–1752 74
Site of the Royal Exchange in London. 75
Site of Swiegly Old Town 87
Original room of Carlisle's first courthouse in Shippensburg. 89
Wax seal of Major William Trent. 90
Trent family crest from Scotland 90
William Scull, a map of Pennsylvania c. 1770 92
Widow Piper's Tavern 95
Path Valley region 96
Site of Burnt Cabins 96
Site of George Croghan's barn 98
White Horse Tavern c. 1721 100

Original staircase at White Horse Tavern c. 1721	101
Carlisle town square	105
Pennsylvania State House	107
Tall case clock owned by Major William Trent c. 1750s	109
State House Bell	111
Portrait of Robert Dinwiddie	115
Daniel Leet, 1785 Survey of Depreciation Lands	116
Sketch of Tanarisson by Fred Threlfall	119
Governor's Palace in Williamsburg	129
Site of the New Store tract and Trent's house	131
View of Fort Hill and the prehistoric mound	135
Spelling of John Fraser by Trent	137
The Great Hall at Stratford Hall c. 1735	143
Site of the Forks of the Ohio	146
Site of the Frederick County (VA) courthouse	148
View of Monongahela River from the mouth of Redstone Creek	151
"Trent and Half-King at the Forks" by Robert Griffing	157
Join or Die cartoon on May 9, 1754, in the *Pennsylvania Gazette*	169
A Plan of the Fort and Barracks at Mount Pleasant in Maryland c. 1755	179
View from the New Store Tract to the former site of Fort Cumberland	180
House of Evan Watkins c. 1741	182
Site of the Wolgemuth Mill	184
Timothy Horsfield House c. 1749	189
House of lawyer Robert Carter Nicholas in Williamsburg c. 1720s	197
Portrait copy of John Forbes by unknown artist c. 1751	199
Parnell Knob	200
Reconstruction of Fort Loudoun in Pennsylvania	201
Chalk drawing of William Pitt the Elder by William Hoare c. 1754	211
Burial marker of General John Forbes	213
Flag Bastion of Fort Pitt	234
Copy of original 1761 plan of Fort Pitt by Bernard Ratzer	235
House of William Trent in Carlisle c. 1760	238
Portrait of Colonel James Smith by unknown artist c. 1800–1810	247
Site of the Indian Queen Tavern in Philadelphia	248
Wood engraving of Samuel Wharton c. 1770s	248
Print of Burn's Coffee House in Lower Manhattan	259

"Johnson Hall" by Edward Lawson Henry 260
Aerial view of Fort Stanwix in Rome, NY 265
Advertisement for the Betsy on March 23, 1769, in the
    Pennsylvania Gazette. 267
Signatures of Trent and Croghan for the Burlington Company
    c. 1769. 269
"Charing Cross, with the Statue of King Charles I and
    Northumberland House" by Joseph Nickolls c. 1750 270
Benjamin Franklin House on Craven Street in London. 271
Villiers Street in London. 273
St. Paul's Cathedral in London 275
Site of the Crown & Anchor Tavern in London 278
Eighteenth-century print of the Crown & Anchor Tavern in
    London 279
Portrait of Wills Hill, the Earl of Hillsborough by Pompeo
    Batoni c. 1766 281
Margaret Stevenson's parlor at 36 Craven Street in London. 283
Site of former New Suffolk Street in London now called
    Nassau Street 284
Uppark House in South Harting c. 1690 286
Fournier Street in Spitalfields 288
Trent court waistcoat c. mid-1770s. 289
Close-up of pocket on Trent's court waistcoat c. mid-1770s 289
Print of William Legge, 2nd Earl of Dartmouth c. 1777. 293
Hopewell Church Burial Ground in Trenton 294
Portrait of Sarah Lethieullier, Lady Fetherstonhaugh by Pompeo
    Batoni c. 1751. 296
Portrait of Sir Matthew Fetherstonhaugh by Pompeo Batoni
    c. 1751. 296
Portrait of Queen Charlotte of Mecklenburg-Strelitz by Allan
    Ramsey c. 1762 300
Site of the former Norton Street, now called Bolsover Street in
    London 301
Portrait of General John Burgoyne by Joshua Reynolds c. 1766 311
Portrait of Sir Henry Clinton by John Smart c. 1777 311
Print of Sir William Howe by engraver Charles Corbutt c. 1777. . . . 311
"View of the Attack on Bunker Hill with the Burning of
    Charles Town, June 17, 1775" by engraver John Lodge 317

Ruins of Thomas Cresap's house c. 1740 319
Map showing Indiana and Vandalia boundaries 321
View from the site of Trent's Continental Ferry on the
    Delaware River. 326
Proprietary House in Perth Amboy c. 1764. 327
Portrait of William Franklin by Mather Brown c. 1790. 327
Signature of Sarah Trent, wife of Major Trent c. 1776. 328
St. Michael's Episcopal Church in Trenton 330
Survey of Major Trent's property in Trenton by John Watson Jr.
    c. 1777. 335
Carpenter's Hall in Philadelphia c. 1775. 337
Reconstructed Capitol Building in Williamsburg, Virginia 342
Bronze Statue of General Greene in Greensville, South Carolina. . . . 349
Shippen-Wistar House in Philadelphia 355
Site of the Trenton School Company 357
Grave tablet of George Croghan in Philadelphia. 358
Grave of Edward Shippen III in Lancaster. 359
Portrait of John Paul Jones by Charles Wilson Peale
    c. 1781–1784. 364
Drummonds Bank in London. 366
Willings Alley in Philadelphia. 368
Site of the office for notary Assheton Humphreys on Black
    Horse Alley in Philadelphia 370
Advertisement placed by Elijah Bond for selling Trent's
    plantation in Trenton that appeared on July 14, 1784, in
    the *Pennsylvania Gazette*. 371
Site of the house of schoolmaster John Todd in Philadelphia. 375
Site of New Street, formerly Key's Alley in Philadelphia 376
"A Portraiture of the City of Philadelphia in the Province of
    Pennsylvania in America" by surveyor-general Thomas
    Holme c. 1683. 378
Site of possible burial ground for Major Trent in Washington
    Square Park in Philadelphia 379
Tomb for the Unknown Soldier and Eternal Flame at
    Washington Square Park in Philadelphia 380

Foreword

JASON Cherry first discovered William Trent as a child when his family joined a local history group. It sparked a long-standing quest to uncover the story of this 18th-century military commander and trader who reached great heights yet died in poverty. We, his readers, are the beneficiaries of his commitment and scholarship in presenting a rich portrait of the 'real' Trent and the tumultuous times in which he lived.

The pages ahead color in Trent's life from challenging beginnings to serving as a merchant's apprentice and captaining colonial troops during campaigns before, during, and after the French and Indian War, where he engaged with George Washington.

Cherry details Trent's dynamic frontier mercantile career and his exploits as a land speculator, which provided initial success and marked the first concerted colonial attempts at westward expansion. He invested in Vandalia, a proposed colony south of the Ohio River, which he pursued with Benjamin Franklin and others during six years in London. Trent predicated his and his family's future on its realization, but war with England sabotaged his plans. Age and ill health made starting over improbable, and when reparations claims proved unsuccessful, his life ended in the precarious financial circumstances with which it had begun.

So what of Trent's legacy? *William Trent: Factor of Ambition* reexamines his relationship with the Indigenous peoples with which he traded. He involved Native leaders in mutual protection, and the book shows how Trent's counsel urging tolerance among colonial leaders helped involve Native populations in efforts that led to the end of the Seven Years War.

Trent deserves Cherry's thoughtful re-evaluation. In addition to colonial scholars who will benefit from this contribution to the study of early American history, it will bring Trent to wider recognition among all those interested in America's past. Lucky for us, Cherry parlayed a childhood interest into a seminal work.

Dr. Márcia Balisciano, Director, Benjamin Franklin House, London

Acknowledgments

TELLING William Trent's story has been an incredible journey and not a short one by any means.

It began first with joining my eighteenth-century living history group, Captain William Trent's Company, over thirty years ago in 1990. They have always been my second family and my first trip back in time. This is where my research began on William Trent and piecing together his complete life, along with the great assistance of so many historic places, museums, and repositories.

I must first acknowledge the great staff and resources found at the Historical Society of Pennsylvania in Philadelphia. Their vast boxes and folders truly make the archives there the greatest collection pertaining to Trent's life.

Next, I must also thank the assistance by the staff at the William L. Clements Library at the University of Michigan in Ann Arbor for pulling the specific boxes from the papers of Thomas Gage and Jeffrey Amherst for me to do some in-depth research. It was in both collections I found valuable information about Trent's role at Fort Pitt during Pontiac's Rebellion, including the newly discovered evidence regarding who else may have conspired to "gift" smallpox blankets to the Indian nations. The Amherst Papers also listed, for the first time, the complete return of Major Trent's militia, including his officers, during the attack on Fort Pitt in the summer of 1763, some of whom became rather infamous in their own right.

The same could be said for the British Library in London, allowing me to research the Miscellaneous Grand Ohio Company Papers that connected the dots of Trent's stay in London from 1769 to 1775.

Further acknowledgments go out to the Victoria and Albert Museum in London (U.K.), the Pennsylvania State Archives, the State Archives of New Jersey, Cumberland County (Pennsylvania) Historical Society, Winterthur Museum, Library of Congress, University of Illinois at Urbana-Champaign, American Philosophical Society, and the Jacob Rader Marcus Center of the American Jewish Archives.

Special recognition goes out to the Colonial Dames of New Jersey, whose headquarters at Historic Peachfield is the home for the Trent clock, a significant piece of Trent's history. I also cannot forget Dr. Samuel Stephens and Shawn Carney at the 1719 William Trent House Museum in Trenton, New Jersey, whose fine interpretation of Trent's original boyhood home is why I chose to assist them in bringing the Trent family to life.

In July of 2022, I visited the Benjamin Franklin House in London, and it was another extraordinary place that immediately transported me back to the eighteenth century, thinking about the important figures of Franklin's time, including Trent, who came through that door on Craven Street, which is why I was very honored for Dr Márcia Balisciano, founding director of the Benjamin Franklin House to write my foreword.

The same goes for Alexander Patho Jr and my good friends Gerald Seymour of Paramount Press Inc. and artist Robert Griffing, who once again allowed me to use Griffing's fantastic artwork for the cover and bring realism to Trent's story.

As for my friends and colleagues Dr. David Preston, Andrew Masich of the Heinz History Center, Mike Burke of Fort Pitt Museum, and fellow authors Brady Crytzer and Stephen Brumwell, much appreciation goes out to these men whose knowledge and wisdom helped me along the way in completing the journey that became Trent's captivating story. That being said, so much gratitude also goes to Sunbury Press for their advice and acceptance to allow me to share Trent's life with the world.

Finally, so much appreciation goes out to my extended family for their love and support. This extends graciously to my parents, Ken and LuAnn Cherry, for their love of history that three generations now share. I must also show much gratitude to my brother Justin of Half Crown Bakehouse, who was always there for me when I needed historical advice or feedback to move the story forward. You will always be my partner in crime when it comes to keeping the eighteenth century alive. Then, most importantly, to my wife Emily and my two girls, Penny and Charlotte, who always supported me during our "research" trips and endured the countless hours I spent working on this project. I could not have done this without you all.

Jason A. Cherry
2024

Descendant Chart for Major William Trent (c. 1722 – Dec 1, 1784)

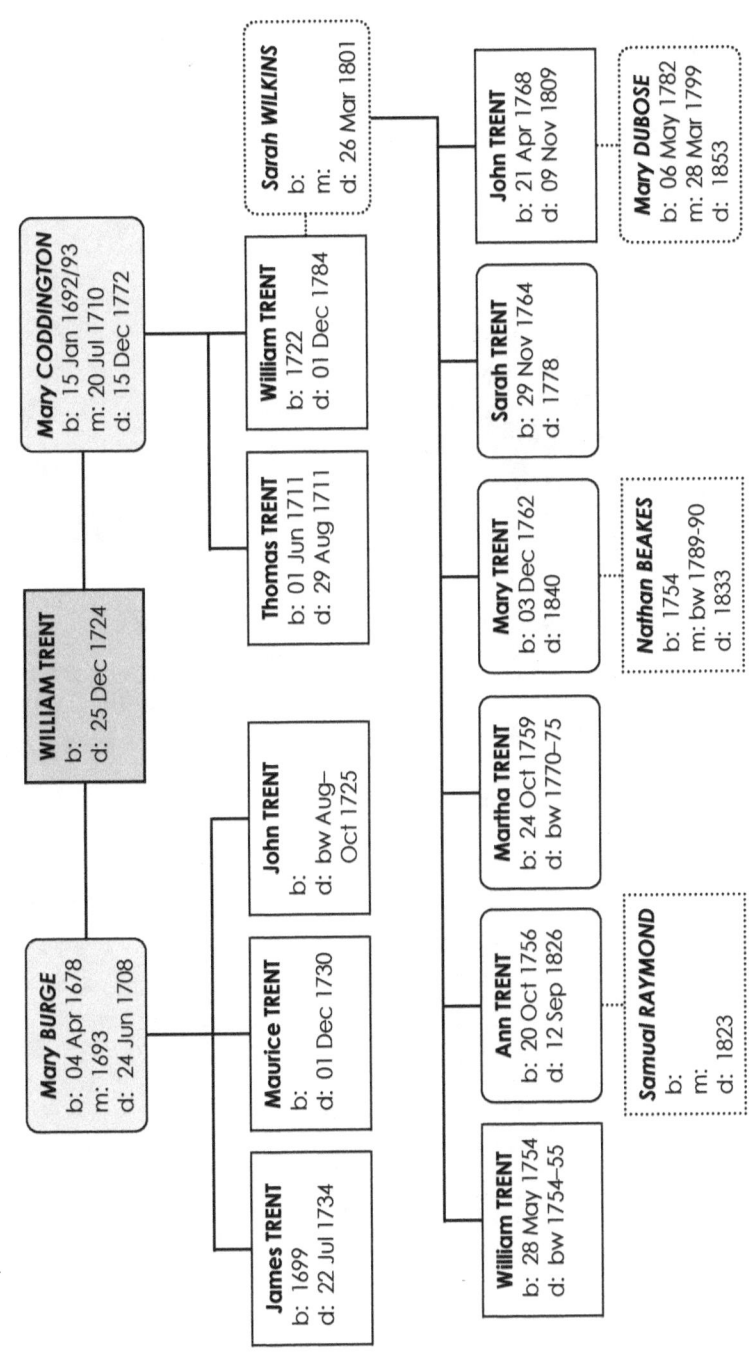

Prelude

A Scandalous Beginning

It was late Sunday afternoon in February when Peter Evans, the High Sheriff of Philadelphia, heard the boisterous yells in the distance and began loading his pistol. The year was 1715, and it was almost five o'clock[1] when he left the half-naked prisoner sulking in his jail cell under the watchful eye of his deputy, buttoned up his woolen coat and stepped through the doorway outside.

Almost a year ago this day, the trees were already sprouting buds, but now, as he gazed up High Street[2] at the large group of people approaching from Second Street, frost covered the once quiet street like an icy blanket. But even on the Sabbath, Sheriff Evans had good reason to be concerned about the growing mob.

Gossip amongst the twenty-year-old congregation of Christ Church[3] tainted the air so heavily that it finally reared its ugly head last night with the sudden arrest of the church's "steward' rector, Reverend Francis Phillips.

The mob, consisting of the church's congregation and numbering in the hundreds, voiced their displeasure as to why the church's doors were locked for this morning's service. Evans held up the notarized documents he received last night from Ralph Assheton, the town clerk and Recorder of the City, amidst the belligerent threats to free Rev. Phillips, or they planned to remove him from the jail themselves.

According to the affidavits,[4] Reverend Phillips was allegedly heard boasting of having "lain" with two distinguished women of the church and impregnating

---
1. Fulham Papers Volume VII, Folders 45–46.
2. High Street was the main east-west street in Philadelphia and was originally named by William Penn. It held that name until 1800, when it was changed to its current name, Market Street.
3. Before alterations in 1711, the original Church of England structure along with the congregation began in 1695.
4. Fulham Papers VII, Folders 45–46.

a servant girl. The first writ marked for one thousand pounds was issued by John Moore in accordance with his daughter Mary, who coincidentally had "personal" ties to the very man currently wielding the document to the raucous crowd.

In fact, when he dragged Phillips barefoot from the parsonage house down Second Street late last night in the shadow of Pewter Platter Alley,[5] Evans was reminded of the previous writ he sent himself to Phillips just a month earlier on January 21, 1714/5.

> *To Mr. Francis Phillips,*
> *Philadelphia*
>
> *Sir, You have basely scandalized a gentlewoman that I have a profound respect for. And for my part shall give you a fair opportunity to defend yourself tomorrow morning on the west side of Joseph Carpenter's Garden, [the present Arcade, I believe,] betwixt seven and eight, where I shall expect to meet you gladio cinctus[6] in failure whereof, depend upon the usage you deserve from.*
> *-y'r ever-*
> *Peter Evans at the Pewter Platter Inn[7]*

Phillips never accepted the duel, but the second writ Evans carried in his possession was issued for an even larger sum of two thousand pounds. The other "person of distinction of unblemished reputation and rank" named in the affidavit with Miss Mary Moore was the wife of a merchant of credit and a chief man of the church.[8] Her former name was Mary Coddington, twenty-two years old[9], a stepchild of brewer Anthony Morris and niece of the former mayor of Philadelphia, Edward Shippen I.

Unfortunately for the accused, she was also the wife of William Trent, a member of the Pennsylvania Provincial Council and eventual father of her only adult child, William Trent Jr. The elder William Trent was born in Inverness, Scotland, to a Scottish father, William Trent, and a mother, Issobel Stewart. He

---

5. Pewter Platter Alley was named for the tavern that stood there and had a pewter platter for its trade sign. Today in Philadelphia it is the Church Street 100 block across from Christ Church and running east-west from Second to Front Street.
6. *Gladio Cinctus* was a gentleman's duel where the two men used swords to defend their honor.
7. Fulham Papers Volume VII, Folder 33.
8. Ibid., Folders 45–46.
9. According to the Rhode Island Friend's Records, Mary Coddington was born in Newport, Rhode Island on January 15, 1692/93, Vital Records of Rhode Island 1636–1850, 51.

arrived in Philadelphia in the early 1690s as a merchant for he was listed on the very first tax list of Philadelphia in 1693.[10]

His brother James joined him later, after joining the Swedish army as a quartermaster in Wismar, Germany, on May 5, 1689.[11] Later, James finished his military career in the Swedish Navy as a sub-lieutenant and joined his brother William in Philadelphia in the mercantile business. Captain James or "Jacob" Trent, though listed as a mariner, had an infamous reputation for using his thirty-six gunship, the *Charles* or *Carl XI*,[12] to not only transport goods but also the illegal cargo of Scottish children. In the court records of Chester and Philadelphia Counties, it was James who sold off kidnapped children of Scotland as indentured servants he acquired from their uncle Maurice, who resided in the seaport of Leith, Scotland.[13]

The eldest Trent married first Mary Burge, the half-sister of Sarah Eckley and brother-in-law of Daniel Coxe. They obtained property and resided along the Delaware River on Front Street in Philadelphia,[14] where they had only three children: Maurice, John, and James.

It must also be pointed out that previously, a daughter named Mary was also listed by historians Sewell A. Slick and Hamilton Schuyler as a fourth half-sibling of William Trent Jr, but this has been proven through vast research by the author to be false. This Mary who married Nathaniel French of Antigua in 1729 was not a Trent, however, and had the surname Streate. Mary Streate was the sister of Abigail Streate[15] and daughter of Leonard and Mary Streate.

Tragically, Mary Burge, the first wife of William Trent, the Elder, died from "childbed fever" on June 24, 1708,[16] resulting in Trent selling the Slate Roof House he owned on Second Street and Norris Alley in Philadelphia to Isaac Norris. He continued to lease it until he moved to New Jersey.

On July 22, 1710,[17] William Trent married his second wife, seventeen-year-old Quaker Mary Coddington, formerly of Newport, Rhode Island. Witness and S.P.G. missionary George Ross officiated it, the eventual assistant rector of Christ Church. Reverend George Ross coincidentally oversaw the scandal at Christ Church and sent his report to the Bishop of London in the spring of 1714/15.

---

10. *Pennsylvania Magazine of History and Biography* (PMHB) Volume 8, No. 1, 82–105.
11. Biografiska Anteckninjer om Officerare vid Orlogsflottan 1600–1699, 391.
12. Captain James Trent's ship was the *Carolus XI* or *Carl XI* and his thirty-six-gun ship was named in honor of Karl or Charles XI Rex, the King of Sweden from 1675–1697.
13. Browne, 567.
14. Philadelphia County Pennsylvania Deed Book C, 142–44.
15. National Archives of United Kingdom Prerogative Court of Canterbury and Related Jurisdictions: Will Registers PROB 11 Will of Mary Bullock, 22 January 1784.
16. Penn and Logan, 275.
17. HSP, James Hamilton Collection, Box 43, Folder 6. For full wedding certificate, see Appendix A of this book.

This same congregation Ross so eloquently saw divided now refused to disperse from the High Street Jail.[18] Evans, not wanting to have his small brick jail on High Street vandalized, stepped aside as Phillips was released and taken back to the parsonage house on Second Street. His supporters surrounded him so he wasn't accosted by the angry onlookers along the way, but the next few days were not without incident. On the following Monday and Tuesday, John Moore's house at the corner of Garden Alley and Second Street and Trent's house on Second Street were defaced by unknown vandals who broke a few windows with rocks.[19]

Several months later, in August of 1715, the servant girl Elizabeth Starkey recanted her story, saying disgruntled members of the congregation coerced her to speak against Francis Phillips. The pregnancy was real, however, but she admitted openly a John Phillips, a mariner of the ship the Hopewell, fathered the child.[20]

To add a twist to this controversial tale, once Starkey confessed to lying, she was ordered to join the father of her child, John Phillips, on the *Hopewell* and leave Philadelphia. The *Hopewell* was partially owned by not only merchant Isaac Norris but also ironically, the husband of one of the accused, William Trent.

This ripple effect stemming from the alleged scandal at Christ Church stretched across the ocean to the Anglican Diocese in London. Despite the charges being dropped by Moore and Trent, Reverend Phillips never conducted another sermon at Christ Church again and sailed back to England.

William Trent became Speaker of the Pennsylvania Assembly and Justice of the Supreme Court,[21] but his name became forever shadowed by the cloud of allegations involving his wife, Mary Coddington Trent, having supposedly lain with the rector of Christ Church.

Fortunately, as the Trent name became obscure in Philadelphia due to the scandal and eventual financial losses, a son was born to William and Mary, who finally survived infancy and honored his namesake. For the latter half of the eighteenth century, this young Trent's savvy reputation was as notable as his father's, but sadly, his story has slowly been forgotten. Since his story was told through brief narratives of his life from authors Alfred T. Goodman,[22] Charles

---

18. The High Street Jail was twenty feet by fourteen feet wide, made of brick and stood just east of Second Street in the middle of High Street.
19. Fulham Papers Volume VII, Folders 45–46.
20. Ibid., Folders, 61–64.
21. MacKinney, 216. Martin, 19 and 60.
22. Alfred T. Goodman, secretary for the Western Reserve Historical Society edited the "Journal of Captain William Trent from Logstown to Pickawillany A.D. 1752" and they published it for the first time in 1871.

Landis,[23] and Sewell E. Slick[24] in the early half of the twentieth century, I can now continue his legacy through recently discovered firsthand accounts told by the remarkable man who carved his own path, a man known simply throughout history as Major William Trent.

---

23. Judge Charles I. Landis was President of the Lancaster Historical Society and in the "Papers Read Before the Lancaster County Historical Society" published a biographical sketch "Captain William Trent, An Indian Trader" in 1919.

24. Mentoring under Dr. Alfred P. James at the University of Pittsburgh, Sewell E. Slick pioneered his graduate work into the first complete biography of William Trent. His book "William Trent and the West" was published in 1947.

Chapter 1

An Uncertain Life

The exact year when Judge Trent and his young bride, Mary Coddington, heard the first cries of their young William fill the room remains a matter of debate. Most scholars suggest the birthyear of 1715 since Alfred T. Goodman first theorized it in his biographical sketch of Trent,[1] but unfortunately, no sufficient primary evidence has been found to support this. The author did discover, however, several contributing factors as to why no baptism or birthdate of the young Trent is known and, by doing so, helped narrow the window of Trent's suggested birth year to a single year.

It began first with the tragic loss, only three years after the death of Judge Trent's first wife, Mary Burge. The elder Trent had been married less than a year to his new bride, Mary Coddington, when she gave birth within a half hour to a baby boy on June 1, 1711.[2] They did not name the boy after his father but instead named him after hers, the late Thomas Coddington of Newport, Rhode Island. Mary's father, Thomas, was the son of Rhode Island Governor William Coddington and his third wife, Anne Brinley. Thomas married her mother, Mary Howard, on January 22, 1689, in the Friends Meetinghouse in Newport, Rhode Island.[3] Mary was the sister of Rebecca Howard, who married merchant Edward Shippen I, the first elected mayor of Philadelphia. Thomas, on the other hand, died in Newport, Rhode Island, on March 4, 1692/93,[4] when young Mary was barely two months old.

---

1. After Alfred T. Goodman edited the 1752 journal of Trent, he also wrote a short biographical sketch of William Trent in the back. Unfortunately, many of Goodman's initial assumptions about Trent's life including the presumed year of birth and death have been now discredited.
2. Hildebarn, 99.
3. Arnold, 10.
4. Moon, Volume 1, 59

The infant Thomas Trent was baptized in Christ Church, the Anglican church in Philadelphia on Second Street, whose small brick structure had already stood for sixteen years. They chose this church because the elder William Trent was possibly a founding member of the congregation and served the vestry, purchasing land in 1719 for a burial yard that today holds the interments of several founding fathers like Benjamin Franklin and Dr. Benjamin Rush.[5]

It was right before young Thomas's baptism when the members began to enlarge the belfry and gable ends with over 37,000 bricks to accommodate the expanding congregation that arose above the original forty-two pews adorning the original structure.[6] For what should be a joyous occasion to celebrate the church's first major renovation and the new addition to the Trent family became quite the opposite soon after. On August 29, 1711, Judge Trent stood in his finest black linens along with Reverend Evan Evans and the rest of the somber attendees who paid their respects to his young Thomas, who was being interred in the Christ Church burial ground outside the church, days short of his three-month birthday.[7]

Rev. Evans was called to England in 1714, and Francis Phillips became the steward rector at Christ Church in his absence. The eventual scandal (detailed in the prelude) between Phillips and the Trent family in 1715, combined with the death of their firstborn became the precursor as to why young William's birthdate was always in question. With the Trent name and reputation publicly tarnished in lieu of the ambiguous outcome of Phillip's leaving for England, this could be the reason why his actual baptism was never listed in the records kept in the archives of Christ Church.

However, the elder Trent being a possible founder and active member, it seems unlikely he baptized young William elsewhere instead of Christ Church at this time unless two things happened:

First, the Trent family opted to perform young William's baptism in the privacy of their residence, or he was not born in the theorized birthdate assumed by most scholars in 1715 and it was conducted later when they left Philadelphia. Private baptisms were not uncommon practice in the early eighteenth century and were usually sought because the family had suffered sudden losses of their children before their first year. It seemed likely then since the elder Trent had lost a child (and his first wife back in 1708)[8] and now young Thomas in August of 1711, that they summoned the acting rector of their neighboring Anglican

---

5. Vestry Minutes of Christ Church, Volume 1, 16.
6. Dorr, 14.
7. Hildebarn, 220.
8. Penn and Logan, 275.

Original bell of Christ Church in Philadelphia dated 1702. This 350-pound bronze tenor bell was hung in the belfry of the original building of Christ Church and was hanging during the death of infant Thomas Trent in 1711 and the arrest of Rev. Francis Phillips. (Author photo.)

church. If it were before 1720 or earlier, then the young William was born in Philadelphia and most likely baptized at Christ Church since the elder Trent was a member and eventual vestryman there.

The author wants to point out he said *most likely* since the elder Trent had also been acquaintances with the Rev. John Talbot of St. Mary's Anglican Church in Burlington, New Jersey and gave money to this society's foundation.[9] However, since no evidence supports this earlier birthdate, we must keep

---

9. Hills, 216.

in mind the primary evidence that supports a later birthdate than 1720 after the elder Trent moved his family to the province of New Jersey. Despite the ten-year gap since the last known birth, we can also assume that, quite possibly, there were other failed births before young William was finally conceived and were just never recorded.

When the elder Trent wished to expand his mercantile business from Philadelphia, he looked to the land near the falls of the Delaware River in western New Jersey. In August of 1714, Judge Trent purchased eight hundred acres of land from Quaker Mahlon Stacy Jr. that was found along the north and south sides of the Assunpink Creek.[10]

Unfortunately, the cost of keeping up appearances began to take its toll on the elder Trent. Since he purchased the land in New Jersey in 1714, he also had to contend with boarding school expenses overseas for his other son, James. James was attending St. Peter's College (today known as Westminster School) at Westminster Abbey as the American Colonies' first Queen's Scholar at the age of fourteen.[11] On October 20, 1714, he became a King's Scholar as his acceptance allowed him to attend the coronation of George Ludwig of Hanover, aka King George I.[12] Later, tuition payments were needed in January 1717/18 as James attended Balliol College at Oxford and was accepted as a barrister to learn law at the exclusive Middle Temple.[13]

Judge Trent also watched his partnership with Philadelphia merchant Isaac Norris dissolve over the years. Trent still owed debts when he and Norris lost one-third of their ships to a storm in 1704 and in 1718 when pirates near Barbados took his primary ship, the *Charles*.[14] The *Charles* was the ship his brother James left him via his will upon his death in 1698 and was named after the Swedish King Carolus or Charles XI.[15] The debts were mounting, and the elder Trent barely kept his business out of the "red" in Philadelphia despite all the opportunities.

The same could not be said for his mills in New Jersey. His first endeavor to prosper on his newly acquired New Jersey property, he expanded onto Mahlon Stacy Sr's grist mill along the southern bank of the Assunpink Creek, adding two more grist mills, one sawmill, one fulling mill,[16] one baking house,

---

10. (BBB (WJ). Folio 122) land deed from Mahlon Stacy to William Trent, August 16, 1714.
11. Westminster School (U.K.) Archives.
12. George Ludwig was born on May 28, 1660 in Hanover, Germany and was King of Great Britain and Ireland from August 1, 1714 until his death on June 22, 1727.
13. Westminster School (U.K.) Archives.
14. Isaac Norris Letter Book, Volume 8, letter to William Trent on February 1, 1721/22.
15. Charles XI was born on November 24, 1655, in Tre kroner, Sweden and was King of Sweden from 1660 until his death on April 5, 1697.
16. A fulling mill was a water operated mill that stretched and pounded woolen fabrics.

and one dye house.[17] This became known as Trent's Mills and, by 1717, had the highest tax assessment of any mill in New Jersey at four pounds for the first eighteen months.[18] In other words, the elder Trent was assessed four times higher than any mill in West Jersey and was considered the best gristmill in the entire province.

Soon after, he also began construction of a two-story Georgian-style brick dwelling house on the three hundred acres south of the Assunpink Creek, lying in the Nottingham township boundaries of what was then Burlington County, New Jersey. Completed in 1719, the Trent house rivaled William Penn's residence "Pennsbury Manor" in Bucks County, Pennsylvania, with its forty-foot by forty-eight-foot foundation and an alleyway of cherry trees down to his dock on the Delaware River.[19] In the last few days of 1718 in March, he also purchased an additional two hundred acres courtesy of Samuel Atkinson and Ruth Beakes, whose property and dwelling house called the "Ferry Plantation" adorned just south of the Trent property line near present-day Ferry Street in Trenton.[20]

By the late summer of 1720, the elder Trent had finished his term as a vestryman[21] at Christ Church in Philadelphia and began frequenting his new house and mills that were now transforming into a settlement. A portion of this property he donated this same year to the young county of Hunterdon and a courthouse was built.[22]

Though just referred to as the "Falls of the Delaware" by Mahlon Stacy Sr., the founder, the settlement was renamed "Trent's Town" in honor of its newest and most extravagant resident, Judge William Trent. Coincidentally, the elder Trent finished his last term as a member of the Provincial Council of Pennsylvania in October of 1721[23] and soon after moved his wife Mary and sons Maurice, James, and John to his house in Trent's Town.

Since the move, it seemed the elder Trent had not set foot in the city of Philadelphia except for when his armed merchant sloop delivered bread and bolted wheat flour from his new mills along the Assunpink.[24] His former business partner Isaac Norris attested to this sudden absence by declaring that Trent

---

17. The specific description about the Trent Mills is found in the New Jersey State Archives under the Supreme Court Case file Mary Trent vs. James Trent in 1728.
18. Bush, 217.
19. Kimball and Henson, 271.
20. State Archives of New Jersey, DD:Folio 225.
21. Christ Church Vestry Minutes, Volume 1, 26.
22. Lee, 35.
23. Judge Trent's last appearance on the Provincial Council was October 4, 1721. Minutes of the Provincial Council of Pennsylvania Volume 3, 139.
24. Judge Trent's letter dated May 17, 1721, mentions delivering flour and bolting the wheat. It is found in the New Jersey Historical Society.

Judge Trent's house was completed in 1719 and is the oldest standing structure in Trenton, New Jersey. This was where the young William Trent was born and lived until his teenage years. (Author Photo.)

was trying to merely escape his financial obligations in Philadelphia by moving to another province where debt collectors by law could not follow to seek payments. Norris's anger can be felt in a letter dated February 1, 1721/22, by the Julian Calendar, where he expresses it from his dwelling house just north of Philadelphia called "Fairhill."[25]

> I chose rather, frankly, to shew my thoughts & apprehensions just as I cannot forbearing having them. ___ & I should appear too tumerous it is thy power to abate it & set me right. There is when ye ground rents are Compleatley conveyed to me Above four hundred pounds due to me____thou art not only long Absent which (with thy others avocations when here) make it very difficult (Especially to me who am out of Town& Cannot give daily attendance to obtain any point of Business with ye. But thou art also moved with ye Greater part of they Visible Estate into another province__where thou should be taken of lands pay no Debts.[26]

---

25. Isaac Norris Letter Book Volume 8. Letter to William Trent on February 1, 1721/22.
26. Ibid.

An Uncertain Life

The elder Trent, it seemed, had not only left Philadelphia behind but also fled from outstanding balances and his partnership with his former neighbor on Second Street,[27] Isaac Norris. Trent's Town was a place where he could wipe the slate clean financially and provide better for his family.

It is assumed then, that between the time the Trent family began life in Trent's Town and the following spring of 1722, that young William was born. The assumption can only be proven by the evidence that young William completed his Philadelphia apprenticeship in the early spring of 1743 (discussed in Chapter 3), recognizing the Pennsylvania law pertaining to finishing contracted apprenticeships by the age of twenty-one years.[28] This can also be supported that the young William also began witnessing land indentures away from Philadelphia in Lancaster County, more than validating his completion of a mercantile apprenticeship in Philadelphia.[29]

Young William's baptism, though lost over time, was conducted at only two places during this suggested timeline. Since their change of residence to a new province, the Trent family joined a new Anglican congregation. The property where their church resided was previously part of the Thomas Hutchinson tract in Hopewell Twp, a few miles to the north of Trent's Town.

Back in April of 1705, a royal license to build a church was issued by Richard Ingoldsby, Lieutenant Governor of New York and New Jersey, and it was named Hopewell Church.[30] Today, only a small brick-enclosed burial yard remains from the church, located on the current grounds of the Trenton Psychiatric Hospital off Sullivan Way and across from the Trenton Country Club. So, if young William were baptized at Hopewell Church, it was conducted by Reverend William Harrison, a missionary for the Society for the Propagation of the Gospel in Foreign Parts (S.P.G.) and the Church of England. He was assigned as not only the acting rector of Hopewell Church on the outskirts of Trent's Town but also at the church in Maidenhead (now Lawrenceville, New Jersey) from late 1721 until 1723.[31]

According to the S.P.G. records, Rev. Harrison arrived in Lewes, Delaware, during the early winter of 1721, but due to Hopewell Church being "out of repair" and the conditions making the roads impassable, he proceeded on his journey to Mr. Trent's House with a letter from the Honorable Sir William Keith Baronet Governor of Pennsylvania. He stayed at the Trent house until the

---

27. In 1703, William Trent had purchased from Samuel Carpenter a large red brick mansion that stood on the 100 block of Second Street between Walnut and Chestnut Street in Philadelphia. It was known as the "Slate Roof House" and stood near the historic Norris Alley, the home of his business partner, Isaac Norris.
28. Purdon, 98–99.
29. Lancaster County Deed Book B pages 102–104, Deed from James Dinnen to Edward Shippen dated July 13, 1743.
30. Schuyler, 26.
31. Ibid., 36.

beginning of the Lenten season, which was observed on Wednesday, February 25, 1721/22, in accordance with the Julian Calendar.[32]

The letter from Governor Keith was for Judge Trent and stated:

> Ye Mr. Wm. Harrison Missionary for the parish of Hopewell did at ye earnest request of the Revd Mr. John Vicary Minister of Philadelphia accept a letter from ye Governor of Pennsylvania to Wm Trent Esq. whereby he obtained leave there from ye sd Mr. Trent to officers, his parishioners & all Hopewell to come to Philadelphia to attend the Service of ye Church there during the late Season of Lent and the Easter Holydaies the Rev. Mr. Vicary being by a Severe& tedious fit of Sickness rendered miscapable to officiate in his own parish at that time.[33]

With Rev. Harrison preaching temporarily at Christ Church in Philadelphia for the ill Rev. John Vicary, one can argue young William could have been baptized in Philadelphia at this time. However, in the Anglican Church, baptisms were forbidden during the Lenten Season. Therefore, the baptism of William Trent could have only taken place before this time at the recently completed Trent house while he stayed as a guest since Hopewell Church was closed temporarily.

It was also the reason why no church had archived his baptismal record since only the rector, his parents, and possibly a voluntary witness viewed it. The private baptism was recorded by Judge Trent in a family Bible[34] and by the Rev. Harrison himself. (Unfortunately, both documents are presumed to be lost over time).

Young William had the world at his feet and his future well aligned. He was the only surviving child of Judge William Trent and Mary Coddington, lived in a grand house, and was destined to follow in his mercantile father's footsteps. Then, it all came to a tragic halt.

On Christmas Day in the year 1724, Judge William Trent, father of four and "universally beloved by all,"[35] was dead from apoplexy.[36] To make matters worse, he left his family without a will and, most importantly, for young William's poor mother, a questionable dower or share of her deceased husband's estate.[37]

---

32. S.P.G. Records 1679–1750 Volume XII American Colonies: New Jersey, letter of Governor William Keith to William Trent April 2, 1722.
33. Ibid.
34. Normally the Bible or Book of Common Prayer was used to record the births of the family on the inside cover.
35. Whitehead, 77.
36. Apoplexy was the term used for suffering a stroke.
37. A dower was a provision agreed upon by the husband at the time of their wedding in the event she should become widowed. By law, the widow received rights or shares to certain property and interests of her deceased husband's estate.

It was best described in a letter from Trent's former business partner Isaac Norris to London merchant John Askew in January of 1724/25: William Trent died suddenly of an Apoplexy on Christmas Day, left no will much involved and has not been in Philade these 3 or 4 Years past.[38]

Sadly, those words spoken by Norris were the only ones worthy of a possible eulogy for someone whose legacy was as one of the most respected merchants and businessmen in Pennsylvania and New Jersey. For young William, he was without a father at a very young age, and unfortunately, the foreseeable path that once led to his possible education overseas and bright future was now in a cloud of uncertainty.

---

38. Isaac Norris Letter Book, Volume 8. Letter to John Askew from Isaac Norris 11th Month (January) 1724/25.

Chapter 2

The Fight for a Different Path

Word of his father's death spread throughout the newspapers from the *American Weekly Mercury* in Philadelphia on January 29, 1724/25, to the northernmost newspapers in the colonies, the *Boston Gazette*. The week of January 11th to 18th, the *Boston Gazette* echoed the announcement in Philadelphia but added that "he was one that was universally Beloved and is as much lamented."[1]

For such a respected figure, there should not have been a question as to where the elder Trent was buried, but his gravesite remains a mystery today. Author Eli F. Cooley[2] gives his theory with confidence, declaring that "his mortal remains found their resting place on the banks of the Delaware, in the graveyard of the Friends, consisting of the old portion of what is now known as Riverview Cemetery,"[3] but unfortunately no sufficient evidence exists to support this claim. In fact, the old section of the Thomas Lambert Burying Ground or the Friends Burying Ground that Cooley refers to, was a site for Quaker interments only and forbidden for these non-Quakers who worshipped in the Church of England like William Trent.

So, where do the remains of Judge Trent have their final resting place? Truthfully, his gravesite is not exactly known.

However, the author can say with certainty his final resting place has been narrowed down to two possible locations. To the north of Trenton, the first locations have been suggested by many historians, including Hamilton Schuyler, author of *A History of St. Michael's Church*, that Judge Trent was buried at

---

1. Nelson, 89.
2. The Rev. Eli F. Cooley along with his son William wrote the book, "Genealogy of Early Settlers in Trenton and Ewing, Old Hunterdon County, New Jersey."
3. Cooley, 282. Riverview Cemetery is located near 870 Centre Street in Trenton, New Jersey.

Hopewell Church burial yard.[4] This was where the Trent family joined the congregation of Hopewell Church after they moved permanently to Trenton and whose acting rector, Rev. William Harrison, had been entertained at the Trent residence in 1721 and 1722.

Yet after Rev. Harrison's services were recalled to St. Andrew's Church on Staten Island in 1723,[5] the parish was once again without a S.P.G. missionary. So, in 1724, the Rev. John Talbot of St. Mary's Church in Burlington, New Jersey, conducted sermons there when he was able. Which now could also explain why the elder Trent may have been buried in the churchyard adjacent to St. Mary's Church in Burlington. Trent was not only a good friend of Rev. Talbot's but also, before his untimely death on Christmas Day, worked upon the S.P.G. house in Burlington down the street on October 24, 1724.[6] Burial records for St. Mary's also show that his former brother-in-law from his first marriage, Daniel Coxe, and his wife's sister were buried on the grounds.[7] Regardless of the exact site, Rev. Talbot no doubt conducted the funeral rites and sermon for Judge Trent after Christmas.

By the spring, young William accompanied his mother, Mary and his three half-brothers, James, John, and Maurice, to the courthouse in Burlington to see who the surrogate court appointed as administrator of his father's estate. Since Judge Trent died intestate,[8] the court was obligated to select an administrator who acted on behalf of his father's estate, pay off his outstanding debts, or, if needed, hire legal counsel.

The widow was usually chosen in this case of intestate succession, but on March 12, 1724/25, when Ordinary Samuel Bustill selected Mary Trent, she immediately swore this disclaimer, renouncing her rights and titles to do so:

> Known all men by these presents that I Mary Trent Widow of relict of William Trent Esq. Deceas'd for good causes &consideration me thereto moving, having renounced &disclaim all my right, title & Interest, of in & to the Administration of the Estate of ye sd deceas'd & every part thereof, in Witness Whereof I have hereunto set my hand & seal the 12th Day of March anno domini 1724/5
>
> Sealed& delivered in ye presence of Sarah Higbee James Trent Mary Trent[9]

---

4. Schuyler, 341–42.
5. Burr, 609.
6. S.P.G. Records at the Library of Congress-New York and New Jersey Papers, 1724, 229.
7. Hills, 255.
8. Intestate means the person died without having made a will.
9. Trenton Free Public Library, 1724 Mary Trent Disclaimer.

Though it was not uncommon, Mary refused her right as administrator because she was preserving the future of young William. Being an administrator meant she exhausted the potential earnings of her dower to pay off her husband's debt, and his mother was fully aware of his father's accumulated losses, especially in Pennsylvania. So, by refusing this title, there was no worry of depleting her dower rights or one-third of his estate throughout her lifetime. This included any equity, rents, or income held in trust for her, meaning any additional property her name was listed upon throughout their fourteen-year marriage.

With the death of both her uncle John Howard of Philadelphia in 1711 and now her husband, it also meant his mother could reclaim the Rhode Island property and monetary trust of fifty pounds placed upon her in accordance with her mother Mary's will in 1699.[10] His mother could now provide for her son's future education, and by law since she was a widow and William no more than three or four years old, the two of them could stay in their brick dwelling house in Trenton if they desired or until he reached the age of twenty-one years.

Just four days later, the surrogate allocated the oldest heir-at-law of Judge Trent, his eldest son James, a newly appointed administrator. The attestation read as follows:

> The 16th day of March, Anno Domini one thousand seven & Twenty-four, personally appeared before me Samuel Bustill, Surrogate and Ordinary of the Northern Division of the Province of New Jersey duly commissioned and appointed, James Trent Esq'e one of the Witnesses within subscribed on his solemn oath which he took on the holy evangelist of almighty God, he doth dispose that he was present and said the within named Mary Trent, Sign and Seal & as her Voluntary Act & Deed Deliver the within instrument to uses is therein Mentioned James Trent
>
> Sworn before me
> Samuel Bustill[11]

The court also acknowledged that day the administrator bond paid by James was received, and two other fellow bondsmen were appointed in case James could not manage his duties or died before performing them. The two bondsmen named were former Hopewell constable Alexander Lockhart and his father's former brother-in-law Daniel Coxe.[12]

---

10. Philadelphia Will Book A, 516.
11. Trenton Free Public Library, 1724 Mary Trent Disclaimer.
12. Daniel Coxe married Sarah Eckley the half-sister of Judge Trent's first wife, Mary Burge.

As an administrator, James managed their father's 1000-acre estate in its entirety, including the four dwelling houses adorning the properties, the five mills along the south bank of the Assunpink Creek and the eleven enslaved people consisting of nine Africans and two Indian men.[13] This also included the land in Hunterdon County on the north side of the Assunpink Creek within the town limits of Trenton, where his two other half-brothers resided. His brothers John and Maurice became Clerks of the Common Pleas courts in the old Hunterdon County courthouse that once stood near present-day 23 South Warren Street in Trenton, New Jersey.[14]

James eventually joined his stepmother Mary and young William in his father's brick dwelling house, for he wrote he was residing there in the deed of the property later conveyed to his uncle William Morris in 1729.[15] This also explained later, after the appraisal of his father's inventory of the house, why his mother (or Madam Trent's room as it was listed in October of 1726) had her room up on the second floor and down the hall. She had a four-posted bedstead flanked on all sides by blue curtains made of silk and worsted wool called camlet.[16] It can also be assumed a small black armchair listed amongst the contents of her room was where young William came and practiced his reading.

It is believed the first room just up the white pine-boarded staircase belonged to young William. His corner room held a small fireplace encased by imported Dutch Delft tiles that depicted scenes of small children playing games like flying kites and walking on stilts.[17] An adjoining door led to his former parent's room, and after they conducted inventory in 1726, probably the room where his brother James eventually stayed. The evidence further suggests from the inventory later conducted in 1734 at his eldest brother's house in the city of Trenton that James possessed the very same field or tent bed with calico quilts and curtains from this room.[18]

In the summer of 1725, James joined his brother John in the court system and, with his law background, was elected as a judge for the Court of Common Pleas in Hunterdon County.[19] He also served as a vestryman at Saint Mary's Church in Burlington,[20] which was also where William and his mother probably attended service each Sunday.

---

13. Office of Superior Court, bound volume 1211–1216C 1433–1448C New Jersey State House, Inventory of William Trent 1726.
14. Trenton Historical Society, 79.
15. D(WJ). Folio 382–386 (SSTSEO23) Land Deed from James Trent to William Morris dated March 29, 1729.
16. Inventory of William Trent 1726. Pernot, 17.
17. Pernot, 18.
18. Inventory of James Trent 1734.
19. Snell, 197 and 257.
20. Hills, 208–209.

These original Dutch Delft tiles adorn the fireplace in what is believed to be Major Trent's room as a young boy at the 1719 William Trent house. (Author photo.)

Being the eldest heir-at-law of Judge Trent and according to intestate succession, James was set to inherit the bulk of their father's estate once the appraisal of his father's household inventory could be conducted. This proved to be rather problematic since inventory could not be appraised legally until his father's outstanding debts were paid off.

Like every wealthy landowner and proprietor of a mercantile business, his father obtained loans with the intention of repaying them and gaining significant profit to increase his wealth. He was also heavily taxed from his five large mills on the Assunpink to the wide "Kings boards"[21] he flaunted to esteemed visitors and businessmen he entertained in the room called the "best" parlor of his extravagant New Jersey home.

Unfortunately for James, this was just debt from New Jersey. It was no secret their father escaped creditors from Pennsylvania by moving to another province, but that did not mean Trent's estate was completely protected from it. Creditors who were owed a significant amount filed a grievance or writ with

---

21. The British government enacted the White Pine Act of 1711 making it llegal to harvest any timber more than twenty-four inches in diameter. These old growth white pines were marked with a broad arrow and prohibited from being felled. Among the wealthy it was popular to flaunt this "superior" timber in their house despite paying heinous fines for doing so.

the Supreme Court or Governor's office of the supposed province where the person currently resided if they wished to pay the bond fee it cost to file. For some whom Trent owed in small amounts, it was usually ignored since the fee was more than the debt itself.

However, with the news of his death, some began to seek repayment of these debts finally. From the city of Perth Amboy and the office of New Jersey Royal Governor in Middlesex County came a suit by lawyer James Alexander. The former attorney general was alleging he was never paid for £14.00 he lent to William's brother Maurice and an additional 9 pounds, 1 shilling 10 pence of goods sent to his father that he had never received payment for.[22] Eventually, the plaintiff, Alexander, was awarded the suit, and he purchased Yaff,[23] one of the enslaved Africans listed on the inventory that was finally conducted on April 9th, 1726, by Peter Bard and Nathaniel Leonard. Their father's estate was valued at 1,083 pounds, 9 shillings, and half-pence,[24] but the suits against their father's estate kept coming. This came just in lieu of the sudden death of young William's brother John, who died in his 20s in the fall of 1726.[25] He was immediately replaced as Clerk of the Common Pleas courts in Hunterdon County by his older brother Maurice.[26]

On February 7, 1726/27, James patented a Trenton ferry granting him exclusive ferry rights for the transportation of goods and passengers over the River Delaware within two miles above and below the falls of the Delaware River near Trenton.[27] The ferry he built was at the foot of present-day Ferry Street in Trenton and was the ferry the Continental Army and the French detachments used on their march to Yorktown in August and September of 1781.[28]

This extra source of income came at a most opportune time for James because another suit came from the Royal Governor's office in Middlesex County. Their father's former business partner and neighbor, Isaac Norris, was seeking repayment on debt for a bond worth 1,296 pounds.[29] To put into perspective, the specified amount owed to Norris in Philadelphia was almost two hundred pounds more than the total appraisal of the Trent estate that now included his mother's room when it was appraised again in October of 1726.[30]

---

22. State Archives of New Jersey, Suit of James Alexander v. James Trent 1725.
23. *New York Gazette*, June 9, 1729.
24. Inventory of William Trent 1726.
25. Hunterdon County Miscellaneous Court Records (1713–1860).
26. Ibid.
27. Trenton Historical Society, 49.
28. The owner of James Trent's former ferry was Hugh Rankin in 1781. It had resided at the foot of present-day Ferry Street in Trenton on the Delaware River.
29. State Archives of New Jersey, Suit of Isaac Norris v. James Trent 1726.
30. Inventory of William Trent 1726.

Those emerging debts were exactly what his mother feared could possibly happen when she renounced her role as administrator. Mary, though many years her husband's junior, had no doubt gained adequate knowledge of her husband's business since her name accompanied his on several indentures like the former Williamstadt manor along the Schuylkill River on January 8, 1723/24, and the use of an iron forge on the Assunpink Creek on July 11, 1723.[31]

The reality was that only two years after his father died, the Trent estate was slowly shrinking in the hands of his brother James. At this time, James was occupied frequently by his newly established transportation, and it could be assumed he was staying in the ferry plantation he owned now, whose dwelling house by no coincidence lay exactly near where he built his new ferry. It was also just a few hundred yards south of his father's house, where Mary and young William resided.

By the early fall of 1727, evidence also suggests James had been neglecting his administrative duties. He hadn't repaid the loss of the James Alexander suit[32], and the Norris suit was threatening to ruin the Trent name financially. However, the most important person he neglected from the beginning had been living under his same roof. On November 28th, 1727, his mother, Mary, traveled twenty miles south to Burlington to see Chief Justice Thomas Farmer and demand compensation for her dower promised to her by law.[33] The common law stated as a widow, his mother was entitled automatically to 1/3 of her husband's estate upon death including any joint tenancy or settlements made before. She declared that since her husband's death (on Christmas in 1724), she had asked her stepson James to render the dower to her, and he had since refused to give it to her.[34]

In other words, while James oversaw any of his father's five mills, iron works, bakehouse, or pasture of sheep and milk cows, his mother had received nothing financially from the profits for her or young William. When the complaints went unresolved into the following fall season of 1728, his mother took legal action.

On the 1st of November 1728, James received a writ from John Kinsey, his stepmother's attorney for her dower rights and damages for detention of them.[35] He was to appear in court in Burlington and give his statement as to the alleged detainment of these rights unto her. Kinsey, a Quaker attorney in Philadelphia,

---

31. Cassel, 169. Nelson, 8.
32. In the suit James Alexander v. Samuel Burge dated 1745, it gives mention of a previous suit from 1725 that was listed as won by James Alexander.
33. State Archives of New Jersey, Case 41804, Mary Trent v. James Trent 1728.
34. Ibid.
35. Ibid.

listed all the appurtenances and messuages (dwelling houses) owned by her late husband. It was described as follows:

> 4 messuages, 3 grist mills, one Saw mill, 1 fulling Mill, one bakehouse, one Dyehouse, one ferry-house, half an Iron Work, one Barne, three Gardens, two Orchards, thirty-acres of meadowland, three hundred Acres of pasture land And two hundred-Acres of woodland with the Appurtenances Situate lying and being in Burlington.[36]

She was to receive one-third or third part of all the above mentioned. In response, his brother James arrived at the courthouse with Henry Vernon, a leading barrister from New York City.[37] Vernon produced the following statement from James that:

> At the time of the death of the said William his father hath allaies been ready to render & hitherto have been ready & this he is ready to Verify wherefore pray & Judgment if the said Mary any damages by Occasion of the Determining of the Dower aforesaid against him.[38]

James, it seemed, was willing to swear an oath he had always been ready since his father died to give his stepmother Mary her dower, including damages supposedly suffered by her. Based on the evidence associated with the suit entitled *Trent v. Trent*, the law favored his mother, since his brother James couldn't produce any evidence as to why he precluded the dower from her in the first place.

Unfortunately, the court files found in the State Archives of New Jersey do not provide the outcome of the ruling, but based on a land conveyance, there is sufficient evidence that his mother won the suit and rightfully received her dower. The source of this favorable ruling for his mother is found in the State Archives of New Jersey but under a land discharge from her to George Thomas of Antigua. According to her deposition on September 26, 1735, in the presence of Samuel Bustill Jr and John Sober, his mother received a full sum of 1,000 pounds from George Thomas for the remiss release and quitclaim to him for the several messuages, two tracts of land, the mills, and ferry lying in Nottingham Township of Burlington County.[39] This above-mentioned land she

---

36. Ibid.
37. Goebel and Naughtan, 363.
38. State Archives of New Jersey, Case 41804, Mary Trent v. James Trent 1728.
39. State Archives of New Jersey, Burlington County Clerk's Office, Box 50.

deposed was the very same land of her late husband and what she had sought for her dower rights in the previous suit from her stepson. His mother gave mention to receiving a previous sum of 1000 pounds mortgage to her from her half-brother William Morris when he purchased this estate from James in 1729.[40] By law, the only way she received this large sum from her half-brother William Morris and sold off her final interest in the estate was if she had won her suit and received her dower.

For his brother James, however, the insurmountable debts of his father and the loss of the suit forced him on March 28, 1728/29, to sell off the three hundred acres he inherited in Burlington County, including the new ferry he had just established on the Delaware.[41] He lived on the remainder of his father's property in Trenton Township in the city limits, selling off the rest in parcels to anybody who was buying lots in Trenton, including land for the use of an iron forge, on June 20, 1729.[42]

The next buyer of that Trent estate and mills was previously mentioned as William Morris. He was the son of Philadelphia brewer Anthony Morris and his third wife Mary Howard Coddington (Mary's mother), making him half-brother to Mary Trent and uncle to James, Maurice, and young William. Their mercantile uncle had married an heiress from Speightstown, Barbados, named Sarah Dury[43] and had little issue paying the 2,800 pounds to his nephew for it.[44] By the summer of 1730, his aunt and uncle had both joined William and his mother in his father's brick dwelling house along with their three children, ten-year-old William Morris Junior, seven-year-old Sarah, and two-year-old Anthony.[45]

Young William, now almost seven or eight years old presumably, possibly welcomed the chance to interact with cousins around his age since his eldest half-brothers were at least twenty years older. Around this age it was also when he learned to read and write, no doubt learning from his mother or his brother James when he still lived in the house. His mother was raised in an upper-class Quaker household before she married his father, an Anglican, and no doubt earned an equivalent of a valuable Quaker education for young girls of Philadelphia. She learned to read, write, and possibly do needlework and other household duties. Her signature as a thirteen-year-old attendee of the Quaker wedding of Thomas Story and Ann Shippen was a fine example of this.[46]

---

40. Ibid
41. D(WJ) Folio 382–386 (SSTSE023) Deed James Trent to William Morris March 28, 1729.
42. Nelson, 3–4.
43. Sarah Dury married William Morris on February 14, 1718/19 in Speightstown, Barbados. She died on June 20, 1750, and is buried in the Trenton Burying Ground that resides today on 180 East Hanover Street in Trenton, New Jersey.
44. D(WJ) Folio 382–386 (SSTSE023) March 28, 1729 Deed James Trent to William Morris.
45. Moon, Volume 1, 197.
46. Library of Congress, Shippen Family Papers, Box 15.

It is quite possible she benefited from her stepfather, Anthony Morris, and her legal guardian, Edward Shippen I, with both men being trustees or overseers of the Friends Public School. The school, created by Pennsylvania province founder William Penn in 1689, educated at first young Quaker boys and girls and then, after 1711, any young children of non-Quakers who wished to attend.[47]

It was not out of the question to assume (since records do not exist currently before 1746) that young William may have been taught at his residence privately by tutors from this school that his mother or Uncle William hired for him and possibly his cousins. A schoolmaster jumped at the chance to make additional income since the employment at the Friend's School was not a considerable salary[48], and most of their neighbors were Quakers on the western side of New Jersey.

William learned to read by the book they carried to service each Sunday under Reverend Talbot, "The Book of Common Prayer and Administration of the Sacraments and other Rites and Ceremonies of the Church, according to the Use of the Church of England"[49] or from the age-appropriate book that could teach him the basics of reading and religious instruction with the Church of England. This book, dated 1719 and found at the State Archives of New Jersey, was once in possession of the Trent family. It was entitled *A Key to the Church Catechism*[50] and had a meaningful dedication to his late father, who was once called a "chief man of the church."

To Mr. William Trent
Merchant in Philadelphia

Sir,
As your singular Humanity and Good-will to all men do justly recommend you to the Esteem and Love of all; so the Instances thereof, that you have applied to me particularly, do particularly require of me my most thankful Acknowledgment. And as much I desire you to accept of his New and Small Essay for the more effectual Promoting of Catechetical Instruction; and to vouchsafe it your Patronage. For as it design'd in part For the Use of a poor Countrymen, who are dispersed up and down in your vast and spaced Regions; so your honored and

---
47. William Penn Charter School Archives at Haverford College.
48. Ibid.
49. Hills, 183.
50. A copy of the book dated 1719 can be found at the New Jersey State Archives in the Rare Books and Manuscripts Collections from the William Trent House.

worthy Name prefixed hereunto, may recommend it very much to their Acceptance and Use. For I know not any Gentlemen, in all the country round about you, that is either better known, or more beloved than yourself: And particularly by him, who in really is,
Sir,
Your most obliged, most humble, and most respectful servant
Philo-delphus[51]

Once he gained adequate knowledge of reading and writing, William probably began to seek knowledge outside the walls of his father's house. Since the summer of 1729, he could visit the house of his brother James in town and peruse the various folios that garnered his interest. In his brother's household inventory conducted in Trenton in 1734, it came to light that James had a rather impressive collection of books accumulated since his school days at Westminster, Oxford, and the Middle Temple. Books like *the Iliad*[52], the epic tale of Achilles during the Trojan War, played wonders with a young boy's imagination, only influencing William's sense of adventure when he decided to lead an expedition into Canada in 1746.

He also learned arithmetic or ciphering so he could decide to follow the career of law like all his brothers or become a merchant like his father. If he was ambitious enough, it could even be both since his father was not only a shipping merchant but also a former judge in two different provinces. Though it seemed cumbersome for a boy his age, eventually, he had to choose one before his mother or brothers could arrange an apprenticeship. That came later as he reached his teenage years.

He had not reached the age of double-digit years when the winter of 1730 was once again the setting for another loss in the Trent family. Maurice, William's brother, died soon after he wrote his will on December 1, 1730, while recovering from an unknown illness.[53] There was not much known about his brother but only that he was young in his years, around his late 20s or, at the very most, the age of 30. Maurice had succeeded his late brother John as Clerk of the Court of Common Pleas of Hunterdon County in Trenton and was unmarried, with no children.

Judging by the meager inventory of his sundries in Trenton, Maurice didn't have much in his possession except for items that were used to display his appearance. There was no mistaking him as he rode through town on his

---

51. *A Key to the Church-catechism* by Philo-Delphus dedication page.
52. Honeyman, 488.
53. Hunterdon County Wills and Inventories Reel 714, Will of Maurice Trent December 1, 1730.

reddish-brown horse with a white blaze across its face.[54] In his finest clothing with gold buttons, he sat upon the saddle or imported velvet housing or saddlecloth with his brightly colored holster cap and a silver-hilted sword hanging from his waist.[55]

It was also the first death in the family, that William could probably dictate with a strong remembrance. Though no personal letters exist in Maurice's hand, one can assume the siblings had an amicable relationship. In Maurice's will, he indicated his younger brother in the following manner:

> I give and bequeath unto my dear and beloved brother William Trent and to his heirs, executors, administrators, and assigns forever all that lots of land lying between Joseph read and Joseph green containing about half an acre.[56]

It is the earliest known document with his name on it, and the land was later sold to his Uncle William Morris without him ever using the property off present-day Hanover Street in Trenton.[57] That lot, along with several others, was once part of the larger tract formerly owned by their father, who had around five hundred acres north of the Assunpink Creek in Hunterdon County. The current owner of this acreage in Trenton was James, and with the recurring debts of his father and now his brother Maurice, James began selling off small parcels to those wishing to settle or prosper in Trenton. Since the summer of 1729, James lived just northeast of a small tributary of the Assunpink Creek named after the neighboring Quaker plantation owned by Nathaniel Pettit.[58] Petty's Run, as it was known, became the western boundary of what was becoming the city limits of Trenton. He had already sold property along King Street to James Neilson on January 29th, 1729, that was bought by John Coxe for forty-eight pounds, ten shillings, in a sheriff's sale in 1742.[59] Coxe deeded the land to "the Church of Trenton," which was called later in 1761 "St. Michael's Church."[60] Today King Street is now known as Warren Street.

From the lots adjoining the fence of his own residential house, James sold a lot to blacksmith Isaac Harrow on January 26, 1731/ 32, along the east side of Petty's Run.[61] This, along with another parcel purchased in 1734, became

---
54. Ibid., April 1731 Inventory of Maurice Trent.
55. Ibid.
56. Ibid., Will of Maurice Trent December 1, 1730.
57. Nelson, 50.
58. Lee. 34.
59. Schuyler, 44–45.
60. Ibid.
61. Nelson, 9.

Today the Old Barracks Museum (c. 1758) along 101 Barracks Street in downtown Trenton, New Jersey sits on a portion of Judge William Trent's original one-thousand-acre tract in West Jersey. (Courtesy of Public Domain.)

the site of Trenton's plating mill that made items from dripping pans to casts for bell making. Recent archaeological work by Hunters Research Inc. has pinpointed not only the location of the former Petty's Run but also the location of Harrow's plating mill right along today's Wilson Street.[62]

On March 10th of the same year, he sold a lot of thirty-six acres to Joseph Peace, the miller who oversaw his father's grist mill, for one hundred and seventy pounds.[63] A portion of this tract became the Old Barracks, the site ordered to be built by the New Jersey Assembly on April 15, 1758.[64] A block from Barrack Street is Peace Street, which is named in honor of this Trenton citizen.

Despite the prosperous land conveyances, the following winter in 1733 continued the misfortunes of the Trent family and their relations. Western New Jersey had been hit hard with snow and ice accumulations, and as the temperatures rose, the Assunpink Creek watershed transformed into a massive flood plain. As a result, the freshets or melted snow and ice lasted several weeks, and it was reported by several newspapers in March of 1733/34 that:

> The Freshets it's have done much damage at Trent town, that it carried away the dam of the Iron-work and the Dam of the Grist Mill Bridge

---

62. Burrow and Hunter, 3–6, 7–92.
63. Hall, 310.
64. Ricard and Nelson, 576.

& Dying-house with a large Copper was carried down the Stream & abundance of other damage.[65]

This meant William's brother James, who owned a 1/4 share[66] in the ironworks on the north side of the Assunpink, after seven years, plummeted into financial ruin. His uncle William Morris fared no better. The significant damage to both dams hit him very crucially. The ironworks of which he also owned a 1/4 share had to be rebuilt or transplanted upstream, and now the five former mills of his brother-in-law had to be inventoried for damage estimates to run again. It is theorized that this was the main factor as to why William Morris sold the five hundred acres in Nottingham Township and the mills on the south side of the Assunpink to George Thomas of Antigua on October 12, 1733.

The recent purchase of the house and property to a non-relative didn't affect Mary and William's tenancy, however. George Thomas was still handling his mercantile business in Antigua for at least a year and lived sparse or perhaps not at all in the brick dwelling house despite the next nineteen years of ownership there.[67]

It seemed, based on the evidence, that Mary was timing their stay based on the age of young William to learn his trade in an apprenticeship. Of course, there was one setback with the spring flood damaging the mills and affecting her yearly dower payment, which ultimately extended their stay a few more months.

But in the summer of 1734, William was forced to start growing up. That July, his thirty-four-year-old brother James died suddenly at his house in Trenton.[68] His cause of death was unknown, but like his previous brothers had died relatively young. In fact, since James was the eldest of three from Judge Trent's first marriage to Mary Burge, the mean age of his half-brothers was about twenty-nine years of age. All three causes of death were unknown but an eventual article in the *Pennsylvania Gazette* conspired an interesting story involving them.

The article dated February 28, 1738/39, read:

We hear from Trenton, That two Negroes were last Week imprisoned on the following Occasion. 'Tis said that they were about to persuade

---

65. Nelson, 11.
66. Ibid., 7.
67. While owning the Trent House, George Thomas was elected Deputy Governor of Pennsylvania from 1738 to 1747 and resided on Chestnut Street in Philadelphia. He also leased the Trent House to Lewis Morris from 1742 to 1746.
68. Since James Trent died intestate, his administrator of his estate was named on July 23, 1734. It was presumed he died some day in July before that.

another Negro to poison his Master; and to convince him of the Efficacy of the Drug which they presented him for that purpose and the Security of giving it, let him know that Mr. Trent and two of his sons, Mr. Lambert and two of his Wives, and sundry other Persons were remov'd by their Slaves in that manner.[69]

The article went on further to say lastly that one of the enslaved people arrested was carrying arsenic and an unknown kind of root. So, could this be possible? Were two of William's brothers, the youngest two, John and Maurice, poisoned by their servants? Unfortunately, autopsies were not performed in the early half of the 18th century, so we will never know. It is interesting to note that one side effect of ingesting arsenic or a poison root, such as hemlock, is a sudden fit of apoplexy or suffering a stroke, which was coincidentally what William's father died of on Christmas Day in 1724.[70]

Conspiracies aside, William was the man of the Trent household now. His brothers died childless, and sadly, James died drenched in debt like his father. His financial situation was so bad his principal creditor, Nathaniel French, had to become administrator since his outstanding debts outweighed his estate value.[71] This town of Trenton had seemingly left her husband and stepsons in nothing but financial misery, and it was not a place for William to make his way in the world.

So, Mary knew it was time to leave the place young William had called home for fourteen years. On September 26, 1735, in Burlington, before witnesses Samuel Bustill Junior and John Sober, she extinguished her final interest, land and title from her dower to the current owner, George Thomas, for 1,000 pounds.[72] William said goodbye to his boyhood home and crossed the Delaware River to start a new life in Philadelphia. The very next day his mother acquired a country house[73] with a considerable amount of property so that William could adjust to life in Pennsylvania before he entertained the prospects lying in Philadelphia for his career. The brick farmhouse she acquired was originally built by Peter Cock, a Swede, near the mouth of the Schuylkill River in the colony once known as New Sweden.[74] Later, as it became part of Philadelphia County,

---

69. *Pennsylvania Gazette*, February 28, 1738/39.
70. Isaac Norris Letter Book, Volume 8, 89.
71. In certain circumstances like this one, the administrator was only given to a principal creditor like Nathaniel French when none of the next of kin assumed the role as administrator due to large financial debt. It was assumed Nathaniel French was owed the most.
72. Hunterdon County Miscellaneous Court Records (1713–1860).
73. Today even by car, the former site of the Cannonball Farm bought by Mary Trent was twenty minutes to the southwest of Philadelphia.
74. Before William Penn established the colony of Pennsylvania, New Sweden was a Swedish colony from 1638 to 1655 residing on the lower reaches of the Delaware River.

it was sold to Quaker merchant Samuel Carpenter and the land flanked by Boon's Creek, Eagle Creek, and the Delaware River was nicknamed Carpenter's Island.[75] His son Samuel Carpenter Jr mortgaged it to Mary Trent to pay off mill debts he owed Trent's former miller, Joseph Peace, and was income Peace still owed to Mary by her previous dower rights.[76] The house was described later as a "brick house with a garden and a large orchard of the best Cyder-Apples and a young Orchard, of the same sort."[77] All while sitting on six hundred and seventy-five acres, and they could live on the respectable plantation for at least fifteen years rent-free. The house, when it was later put up for sale, was valued at nine hundred pounds down Pennsylvania currency,[78] almost fifty pounds more than the Slate Roof House her late husband had once purchased on Second Street in Philadelphia in 1703.[79]

For Mary and young William, they were off to a prosperous start, and now her teenage son could focus on his future. It's possible he had already. Perhaps even taking the pair of money scales and the sundry sorts of money weights from his late brother's house.[80] It was decided William was going to be a merchant, like his father.

His mother, all too familiar with the turbulent life of his late father, had seen too many family members die so young because of this chosen career path. If this was what life he chose, she made sure he learned the right way. So, she arranged an apprenticeship with her cousin and arguably one of the wealthiest merchants in Philadelphia, Edward Shippen III. If William Trent wanted to carve his legacy, it began now with the Shippen family in Philadelphia.

---

75. Philadelphia County Deed Book F, Volume 7, 68.
76. Ibid.
77. *Pennsylvania Gazette*, January 22, 1741, 4.
78. Ibid.
79. Philadelphia County Deed Book E, Volume 3, 32.
80. Inventory of James Trent, July 25, 1734.

Chapter 3

A Taste of Ambition

On Saturday, the twentieth of May 1738, Edward Shippen III likely stared out the window of his residence and office at the corner of the side alley and Second Street. His account books needed balancing, and the constant writing probably made his eyes hurt. He was a partner in the mercantile firm of Logan and Shippen and didn't wish to be ridiculed by his partner James Logan, who micromanaged from his country house on the outskirts of town in Stenton.[1]

Just a short distance away, up on a small hill overlooking a small stream called Dock Creek, was his grandfather's former residence. The extravagant home was once the temporary home to the governor and founder of the Pennsylvania province, William Penn. It stood on two hundred and sixty acres and stretched as far east as the Delaware River. His grandfather had passed almost twenty-six years this upcoming fall season.[2]

This silhouette of Edward Shippen III (1703-1781) is the only known portrait of him known to exist. (Courtesy of Winterthur Museum Garden & Library: Joseph Downs Collection of Manuscripts and Printed Ephemera.)

The thirty-five-year-old merchant furiously scribbled in his account books. For seven years now, he was an active partner in the firm of his former master, James Logan. Logan, a former schoolmaster at various Latin schools in Lurgan,

---

1. "Stenton" the home of James Logan was built between 1723 and 1730 and still stands today, nine miles north of Philadelphia on 4601 North 18th Street.
2. Edward Shippen I died in Philadelphia on October 2, 1712.

Ireland and London, had his career linked more than often with the Shippen family. After he taught at a Latin school in London, he began a career in the shipping trade near Bristol, England, in 1697. It was there that fate allowed him to meet renowned landowner William Penn, who had just fifteen years earlier begun his new colony named "New Wales" and that King Charles renamed "Pennsylvania" in honor of William's late father, Admiral William Penn.

When Penn returned to Philadelphia in December of 1699 on the *Canterbury*, Logan sailed with him as now his new Provincial Secretary. It was in Philadelphia at Penn's residence where he began courting Ann Shippen, the daughter of the first mayor of Philadelphia, Edward Shippen I. After Edward Shippen I, chose the mature Thomas Story as a more suitable spouse for his daughter; he continued life as a clerk and secretary for Penn.

When Ann Story died in the same year as her father,[3] he began his mercantile life at the very same house of his one-time girlfriend, once Thomas Story moved to England. By 1720, he began to expand his business, and he took on a young apprentice named Edward Shippen III, the son of Joseph Shippen Sr., who had once approved of the match between Logan and his sister Ann. The apprentice and potential junior partner Edward Shippen III was looked upon as consolation for his acclaimed loss in 1706. Unfortunately, in 1727/28, Logan took a fall on ice that left him incapacitated and bedridden for three months with a broken hip.[4]

In 1730, Logan realized the internal damage that left him hobbling was permanent, and he gave his power of attorney for his business to his new partner, Edward Shippen III. He relegated Shippen to his house along Second Street while he spent the rest of his days in the country at his house in Stenton, conducting business as the colony's land agent.

Currently, in early summer, the firm's trading business was exponentially rising due to a recent boost from essential proprieties in 1737. The first was a large acquisition of land from the Penn family in 1733,[5] what was then Lancaster County, which he named "Shippensburgh." The goal was to establish a trade depot that allowed traders a final supply post before heading into the Western country. The other came on September 17, 1737. This day, notoriously known as "The Walking Purchase," was a treaty arranged by Logan that claimed land from the Lenape Indians based on how far west a man could walk in a day and a half. The chiefs of the Lenape had the assumption the longest distance consumed was forty miles, but Logan hired the three fastest runners

---

3. Ann Shippen Story died in Philadelphia on December 6, 1712.
4. Klein, 60.
5. Ibid., 73.

or "walkers" in the colony. One of these participants, Edward Marshall, covered almost seventy miles, resulting in a total area consumed equivalent to the size of Rhode Island to Penn's original claims.[6] The Lenape moved west after vacating their ancestral lands and began towns in what was called the "Ohio country."

With the sudden surge in business, Shippen decided to take on another apprentice after Hugh Parker, his current apprentice from Bucks County, who was almost finished. The apprentice he acquired was none other than William Trent, a bright teenager from New Jersey, the son of the former Supreme Court Judge and shipping merchant William Trent Sr. Judge Trent had not only served with Shippen's grandfather and his partner James Logan on the Pennsylvania Provincial Council but had been 1/3 partners with Logan, and Isaac Norris for the Brigantine called the *Robert and Benjamin*.[7]

There was still probably much lobbying done by his mother, Mary, to begin her son's future, and she reminded Shippen that his grandfather was once her legal guardian[8] and promised to take care of her and her potential heirs. After confiding with his partner James Logan, who had once commended Trent's father for his thorough skill and insight into trade,[9] the agreement was mutually made for young William to learn the mercantile business.

Though the apprenticeship contract has not been found, it followed the standard agreement made between the "master craftsman" or supervisor of what trade he was learning and the legal guardian. In this case, it was between Edward Shippen III and his mother, Mary Trent. William also signed the indenture, which listed the length of his term that was agreed upon to learn the said trade of becoming a merchant.

According to the Pennsylvania laws at the time, the said apprentice "worked" out his term until the age of twenty-one years.[10] So, if young William were born in the dual date months of 1721/1722, then at that current time in 1738, he was sixteen or seventeen years of age, giving him at least four or five years to learn under Shippen.

It was also amongst the written terms that Trent wasn't to embezzle his master's goods on cards, dice, or unlawful games. He was also not allowed to frequent taverns or alehouses and could only depart his assigned residence if given permission, which meant that Trent, for the next four or five years, was a temporary member of the Shippen household on Second Street. He also

---

6. Sipe, 112.
7. Penn and Logan, 288.
8. Philadelphia County Wills Book A, 516.
9. Penn and Logan, 106.
10. Purdon, 98.

Today this is the present site of where the First Presbyterian Church once stood in Philadelphia, at the corner of Market Street (formerly High Street) and Bank Street (formerly White Horse Alley). (Author photo.)

attended Sunday service with the Shippen family at First Presbyterian Church,[11] whose house of worship stood facing High Street on the east corner of White Horse Alley.

Trent not only sharpened his skills with reading and writing but also learned to cipher or do arithmetic, which was instrumental in dealing with money and understanding account books. It was a tremendous enterprise for Trent, who realized the firm handled accounts in parts all over the world. Logan and Shippen owned brigantines that transported goods from the wharves in Philadelphia to islands of the West Indies like Antigua or Barbados and to European ports like Bristol, England and Malaga, Spain.[12]

---

11. Edward Shippen III married Sarah Plumley on July 20, 1725 at First Presbyterian Church in Philadelphia. He joined the church in 1730. Klein, 52.
12. Ibid., 122.

The fur trade, though, was becoming the future for the mercantile business. With proprietors expanding to the west, the firm that claimed most of the traders' market could become a powerful conglomerate.

Trent understood that his master's firm acted as a "middleman," taking from Indian traders various skins like deer, bear, and beaver, then selling to prospective merchants across the ocean in London at a suitable price to obtain a nice profit.

Being a second-generation merchant did have its advantages. He had grown up around merchants for most of his young life, either visiting his brother James along King Street in Trenton or at the mills with his Uncle William Morris near Queen Street. He could read and write well before even beginning his apprenticeship, so Shippen began educating him a step further. The legal terminology was key to understanding indentures or legal agreements, so he chose next to teach Trent Latin or what was considered then "the language of the educated elite." Becoming a merchant meant interactions with the wealthy class, and excelling in a language beyond "Old English" was beneficial for business and lifestyle.

That very day, as Shippen kept writing in his books, Trent's mother, Mary, traveled to Philadelphia from her country house to assist in his next step of learning. Just a few blocks north, she strolled east down the main thoroughfare of the city, which was bustling on a Saturday afternoon.

High Street, as it was originally named over half a century ago, was as wide as the streets in William Penn's London and rivaled its market days as well. The citizens who resided along its street called it "the Market" because of the fruits and other sundries that came fresh off the ships that constantly arrived at the wharfs every day on the river.[13] Trent's mother weaved herself around the vendors selling wild poultry and through the people making their way across the crowded cobblestones. Only two blocks from the water, she could see the shadows of the large brigantines cascading across the wooden wharf as she headed to her destination a few doors just passed the intersecting Second Street. The shop at 139 Market Street[14] she entered on the north side of "the Market" bore the name "B. Franklin" on the sign above the door. In the front room of "Benjamin Franklin's New Printing Office" was his stationary store that sold ink-powder, sealing wax, and a large variety of books.

Just two days earlier, Trent's mother had seen the advertisement[15] in Franklin's *Pennsylvania Gazette* for the books just imported from London and

---

13. Jackson, 3.
14. Roach, 139 and 173.
15. The advertisement first appeared in the *Pennsylvania Gazette* on May 18, 1738.

A Taste of Ambition

A copy of the signature by a young Mary Coddington (Trent), then thirteen years old at the Quaker wedding of Thomas Story and Ann Shippen. (Courtesy of the Library of Congress.)

visited the shop to make her necessary purchase. Franklin's common-law wife, Deborah Read, who assisted her husband by running the stationary store, recorded the purchase in Franklin's Account Ledger for his shop as follows: Widow Trent Dr. For Clark Intreyduckshon for Latin 5.0.[16]

After his mother exited the shop, she crossed the cobblestones to the southern side of the street and took the first left, going south on Second Street. Just off the southwest corner of Second, the Friends Meetinghouse stood on her right as she walked past. The "Great Meetinghouse," as it was known, was very familiar to Trent's mother. She was just thirteen years old when she accompanied her stepfather, Anthony Morris, to the wedding of her cousin Ann Shippen to merchant Thomas Story. Over one hundred Quakers attended that celebratory day, and she was amongst one hundred and thirty signatures that witnessed the union on July 10, 1706.[17] Sadly, the marriage lasted only six years, and her cousin Ann died of consumption, being interred with her father, Edward Shippen I, in the Friends Burying Ground on Arch Street.[18]

She continued down Second Street, crossing over Chestnut Street and finally seeing the dormer window tops of Shippen's townhouse.[19] The entrance was double-fronted and hugged Second Street just off the corner of the Norris Alley Extension (known by some as Logan's Alley and later after 1754, known as Lodge's Alley). Trent's mother remembered this section well, for the house stood directly across the street from her former residence the "Slate-Roof house" that she and her late husband lived in for almost ten years.

Trent's father had sold the "Slate Roof house" to his business partner Isaac Norris in 1709 after his first wife died but continued to reside there until his New Jersey house was completed at the Falls of the Delaware. Although the house was torn down in 1867, the "open air" museum Welcome Park on present-day Sansom Street commemorates its location.[20] Sadly, the townhouse of

---

16. Franklin's accounts for 1738, Print Shop Books.
17. Shippen Family Papers at Library of Congress, Box 15 Reel 10.
18. Today the Friends Burying Ground lies beneath the Arch Street Meeting House on 320 Arch Street in Philadelphia.
19. Watson, 476.
20. Welcome Park is named after the ship that brought William Penn to the mouth of the Delaware River in 1682 and stands today across Second Street from City Tavern Museum.

Today the present site of Judge Trent's former "Slate Roof" house, now found in Welcome Park at the corner of 2nd Street and Sansom Walk in Philadelphia. (Author photo.)

Edward (or "Neddy" as his kinsmen knew him[21]) Shippen and its tiered steps met the same fate when the Bank of Pennsylvania was built. Today, it once resided on the property adjoining the City Tavern Museum and the Philadelphia Passport Agency.

Trent's mother dropped the Latin book off, but it wasn't the only one her son used. In lieu of his fast-learning apprentice, Shippen returned three weeks later to "Franklin's New Printing Office" on June 9, 1738, to purchase "Baileys Exercises," a book of "English and Latin Exercise for School Boys methodically digested for the more Speedy attaining the Latine Tongue."[22]

Trent continued his education with Latin and ciphering under Shippen for almost two and half years, for it wasn't until October 31, 1740,[23] that his signature first appeared on a document for the Logan and Shippen mercantile firm. It appeared his apprenticeship followed the same path as his predecessor Hugh Parker, who first signed his name as early as 1738, but by late in 1741,

---

21. Most letters addressed to Edward Shippen III at Philadelphia from his brothers or other family members began their letters as "brother Ned" or "My dearest Neddy."
22. Franklin's Accounts for 1738, Print Shop Books.
23. Wainwright, 348.

had begun to work for the firm as a clerk, traveling to specific clients who held or requested Logan and Shippen accounts.

For a financial transaction from visiting Lancaster County trader James Hendricks to Shippen[24], Trent was a witness the next month, on November 26, 1740. The "Donnagiel" Township native paid thirty pounds of Pennsylvania currency for dry goods such as "pewter plates" and "sixty yards of cloth" he had purchased from the firm's store located at Front and Walnut Street near the river.

Trent, without question, spent most of his daylight hours there assisting Shippen and other employees with the accounts and indentures. A year later, he signed two more land indentures as a witness between his master, Edward Shippen, and his physician brother, William Shippen Sr. The first one drafted on July 1, 1741, was a deed from Doctor William Shippen Sr. to his brother Edward for land on the east-west running Cedar or South Street in Philadelphia.[25] Today, Cedar Street is just called South Street, and the lots purchased were just east of the north-south running Passyunk Avenue.

It adjoined the tripartite or three-person deed on March 10, 1742,[26] between the Shippen brothers Edward, William Sr, and Joseph Jr, that Trent witnessed along with Shippen's other apprentice Hugh Parker and newly assigned apprentice William Coxe. (Extensive research in the Philadelphia County deeds shows that this tripartite deed was the last deed Parker signed in the city before traveling as a clerk for Shippen to the neighboring counties).

William Coxe was a relation by marriage to the Trent family, the son of Daniel Coxe and Sarah Eckley[27] of Burlington, New Jersey, an attendee of Saint Mary's Church of Burlington and a boy just a year or so younger than Trent. Coxe also followed the familiar pattern of a Shippen apprenticeship. After Hugh Parker became a traveling clerk and official employee, Trent appeared more frequently on Shippens' transactions.

Further proof suggests Trent still was an apprentice in 1742 based on the small receipt found in the Shippen Family Papers at the Library of Congress. It read:

> Received this 5 of April 1742 of Mr. John Shere and the hands of Mr. Sanderson four pounds on accot of my Master Edwd Shippen.
> William Trent[28]

---

24. Lancaster County Miscellaneous Papers, 23.
25. Shippen Family Papers at Library of Congress, Box 16.
26. Ibid.
27. Daniel Coxe's wife the former Sarah Eckley was half-sister to Judge Trent's first wife Mary Burge.
28. Shippen Family Papers at Library of Congress, Box 16.

The receipt was also a strong testament to the improving quality of Trent's penmanship as a young man. The difference can be seen in the capitalization of the letters W and T of his name. The letters began to highlight his strength in "round hand," which originated from the Latin alphabet. Six months later, Trent also displayed his hand in a hybrid of "italic proper and "round hand." His next signature on a Shippen deed suggests that he was nearing the conclusion of his mercantile apprenticeship. The deed dated January 1, 1742/43, between partners Edward Shippen and James Logan for lots and messuages in Germantown was not only the final signature for the Shippen firm in Philadelphia but presumably written in its entirety by Trent himself.[29]

By July 13, 1743, Trent had joined fellow clerk Hugh Parker and traveled to the city of Lancaster to witness a land deal between their employer, Edward Shippen and Pennsborough Indian trader James Dinnen (Dunning).[30] Based on the primary evidence of this specific deed and in accordance with Pennsylvania laws, Trent completed his mercantile apprenticeship with Shippen not much after he wrote the deed in January of 1742/43. It also meant that somewhere in the six months before he left the city in July, Trent reached the age of twenty-one years. Like it was discussed in the previous chapter, Trent had to complete his apprenticeship by the time he reached twenty-one, so the signature on the Lancaster County deed meant he was no longer an apprentice but was now a respected clerk in the firm of Logan and Shippen. Like his traveling companion Hugh Parker, he handled the firm's indentures in neighboring counties and balanced the accounts of their clients. One of these clients brought Trent to Chester County in the fall of 1743. In November of 1743, he signed off on a small tract of land for James Hamilton,[31] the son of Scottish lawyer Andrew Hamilton, who served on the Governor's Council in Philadelphia in 1720 with Trent's father.[32]

When he eventually returned in 1744 to his temporary residence in Philadelphia, Trent found the city in disarray over news from across the Atlantic. On the 29th of March, 1744, King George II of Great Britain met with his council at the Royal Court of Saint James and declared war officially on France and its ruler, King Louis XV. It formed part of the "War for Austrian Succession" that had begun in Europe in 1740, but now the conflict was affecting North America. On May 23, 1744, the British port at Canso, Nova Scotia, was attacked by French forces, as were several Acadian settlements with English families.[33]

---

29. Shippen Family Papers at Historical Society of Pennsylvania (HSP), Box 5. Wainwright, 348.
30. Lancaster County Deed Book B, 102.
31. James Hamilton (1710–1783) was a Philadelphia lawyer like his father, who lived on an one hundred and fifty acre country estate north of Philadelphia called "Bush Hill."
32. Colonial Records of Pennsylvania Vol. 3, 14.
33. Ibid., Vol. 4, 766.

Weeks later, the colony of Massachusetts began supplying British forces to fend off the attacks, and now the major seaports in the colonies began sending their ships north to support the conflict known as "King George's War." Unfortunately, mercantile ships going to New England in Nova Scotia instead of Europe were bad for business and even worse for the Logan and Shippen firm. The goods and skins were still coming in at their stores in Shippensburg and Philadelphia, but their buyers in England had no way of receiving them. For every one or two ships that landed in Bristol or near London, the brigantines couldn't be overloaded with goods due to customs officials checking each ship for proper documentation of cargo.

The future seemed promising, however, as Trent returned to Lancaster in the summer of 1744. The city square itself was clamoring since early June with the expected arrival of important out of town visitors. One such visitor who arrived in the afternoon of June 21st was Witham Marshe, a representative for the colony of Maryland who joined commissioners from neighboring colonies of Virginia and Pennsylvania.

Their large congregation was to meet peacefully with the deputies of the Haudenosaunee Confederacy (also called the "Six Nations" or "People of the Longhouse") and the Lenape tribe. Marshe kept a descriptive journal of his two weeks in Lancaster and at the treaty held at the courthouse in the center of town. He mentioned that around six in the evening, Governor (and owner of Trent's former residence in New Jersey) George Thomas of Pennsylvania, along with Virginia commissioners Thomas Lee and William Beverly, accompanied him to dinner along with some gentleman from the city of Philadelphia.[34] Although Trent or Shippen was not mentioned by name specifically by Marshe, one can assume both men were amongst the "gentlemen" of Philadelphia who accompanied Pennsylvania Governor George Thomas.

A land indenture between trader Henry Smith and Edward Shippen can confirm their presumed whereabouts in Lancaster. The document found in the Lancaster County deeds is dated July 4, 1744, and bears the two signatures of Shippen's two clerks, John Mackarall and William Trent.[35] This meant on the same day the treaty ended in the square, Trent and Mackarall emerged from the hundreds leaving the treaty and walked into the two-story brick courthouse to witness the draft of this document. Trent also witnessed the Indian nations up close for the first time, outside of the eight paintings of them once listed in his late father's inventory.[36]

---

34. Marshe, 12.
35. Lancaster County Deed Book B, 158.
36. Inventory of William Trent 1726.

The present site of Penn Square in Lancaster, Pennsylvania and just a few yards from where the Treaty of Lancaster took place in the summer of 1744. (Author photo.)

Further proof of their attendance at the treaty can be proclaimed forty years later in 1784 by the contents of a large black trunk accredited to William Trent's estate.[37] According to its alleged inventory, Trent once held three different documents from those two weeks in 1744. In his possession at the time of his death were "Remarks on the Treaty held at Lancaster 1744, A paper containing parts of a Deed at the Lancaster Treaty," and a "Copy of a letter from Mr. Nelson concerning the Treaty of Lancaster." Except for a copy of William Nelson's letter, the other two documents could only be held by a person who attended this treaty.

---

37. HSP, John A. McAllister Collection, Box 1, Folder 31. For a complete inventory of Trent's black trunk, see Appendix O of this book.

For Shippen and his associates, this treaty was the first step toward expanding their business domestically while the war raged in New France. On July 2, 1744, the Haudenosaunee and their Native allies signed a deed of cessation to commissioners from Virginia and Maryland for what they understood were lands in the Shenandoah Valley east of the Allegheny Mountain range.[38]

The Virginia commissioners interpreted their claim rather differently, however. They understood this claim as lands that reinstated their colony's charter in 1609,[39] meaning Canassatego, the council speaker, had signed over all lands north of Virginia's southwestern boundaries. This land, rich and unsettled, made up present-day parts of Ohio, Kentucky, West Virginia, and western Pennsylvania and was known as the "Ohio country." Months after the council in Lancaster, the Shenandoah Valley was exactly where Trent and fellow clerk Hugh Parker traveled first to witness the power of an attorney of their firm client, Captain Elias Cotting, to Frederick County, Virginia farmer Lewis Stevens. The document, dated September 4, 1744,[40] took place at the courthouse in the infant city of Winchester, formerly named Frederick Town.

The following month, Shippen was elected mayor of Philadelphia[41] and found most of his obligatory duties to the city kept much of his time occupied from his new residence on Fourth Street across from Willing's Alley.[42] For now, Trent ceased his traveling for the firm and established a temporary residence where Logan and Shippen needed him the most, at the settlement of Shippensburg.

The frontier depot owned by Logan and Shippen's firm stood as the gateway to the western frontier. Since the 1730s, it was the last stop for traders and backcountry merchants needing mercantile goods before the roads became less traveled paths into the upper Ohio country. Since the colony of Virginia self-proclaimed the lands just west of the Allegheny Mountain range and essentially the eastern region of the Ohio country, the frontier depot flourished under Trent's watch. Not only was he overseeing the arrival and departure of furs, deer skins, and dry goods, but he was recording the letters of credit and cash payments for all the accounts opened under the Logan and Shippen firm.[43]

In the summer of 1745, one such down-on-his-luck client of the firm arrived somberly in the city of Philadelphia. A former associate of another

---

38. Marshe, 6.
39. The Virginians believed the Treaty of Lancaster in 1744 meant the Haudenosaunee Confederacy had relinquished to the English Crown any claim the Six Nations had within the boundaries stated under the Second Virginia Charter of 1609.
40. Frederick County (VA) Deed Book 1, 134.
41. Martin, 94.
42. Sellin, 337.
43. Letter from Joseph Shippen to John Wood dated May 18, 1745, University of Pittsburgh Archives, Series III, Folder 63.

Shippen client, Peter Tostee,[44] the twenty-something George Croghan (pronounced Crow-han)[45] arrived in the city after being evicted from his contraband trading house along the shores of Lake Erie at the mouth of the Giahaga River (called today the Cuyahoga River). Croghan's lucrative business began as early as 1739[46] on the shores of Lake Erie, but according to the deposition he made to Mayor Edward Shippen, the French had tried to seize him, and when that failed, they had taken forty-eight horseloads of deer skins, four hundred pounds of beaver pelts, and six hundred raccoon skins.

Croghan was offered a line of credit to start anew and was urged to start a new base of operations from Shippen's depot at the westernmost settlement in Shippensburg. He arrived probably at the end of summer at the depot and met for the first time young William Trent, the bookkeeper and clerk who oversaw the operations of Shippen's trading post. The encounter with Croghan blossomed almost immediately into a friendship, for in the fall of 1745, Trent took his very first leap into forming his own firm outside of Shippen and Logan's.

Originally, Trent had applied for a land warrant in Hopewell Township of then Lancaster County in August of 1745.[47] But if he was to maintain ownership of his potential purchase or garner a profit, he needed a business partner to help him begin. So, forgoing the two hundred acres north of Shippensburg, he decided (or was possibly suggested by Shippen) to purchase jointly three hundred and fifty-four acres[48] in Pennsborough Township with his new business partner George Croghan. The tract, previously owned by yeoman William Walker, hugged the meandering southern banks of Conodoguinet Creek just a few miles west of a settlement called Harris's Ferry.[49] Today, the Hampden Elementary School and Good Hope Middle School sit on the southern border of the specific oxbow once owned by Trent and Croghan.

It was an excellent location for the experienced Croghan to show Trent the potential of their new trading firm, but the first couple of months were rough on them financially. On December 24, 1745, it was agreed by both to mortgage the acreage they divided between them to supersede the original cost of one hundred and fifty pounds of Pennsylvania currency.[50] So, Abraham Mitchell, a hatter from Philadelphia, paid in hand to them the full amount plus fifty pounds extra for their own to pocket. This was Trent's first attempt at becoming

---

44. Wainwright, 5.
45. Croghan phonetically spelled his own name on several letters as "Crohan." See Endnote 93, 146 in the author's previous work "Pittsburgh's Lost Outpost: Captain Trent's Fort."
46. Trent's Remarks 1757, 8.
47. Pennsylvania State Archives, Lancaster County Warrant Registers, Box RG-17, 220, Warrant No. 107.
48. Cumberland County Deed Book S, Volume 1, 262.
49. In 1733, trader John Harris Sr. obtained a patent to operate a ferry across the Susquehanna River from land known as "Paxtang." Today the city is known as Harrisburg, the state capital of Pennsylvania.
50. Lancaster County Deed Book B, 299.

This is part of the original cabin structure built by George Croghan in 1745 during he and Trent's partnership in East Pennsboro Township. The cabin today is found along 401 Skyport Road in Mechanicsburg, Pennsylvania. (Author photo.)

a successful merchant, which he gladly boasted after each signature with the abbreviation Esq. for Esquire.

The upcoming winter was a slow season, but as he and Croghan prepared for their first prosperous spring, Trent couldn't ignore the alarming reports that were on every Philadelphian's lips walking the streets and alleys. From their northern neighbor, Indians burned a settlement in New York called Saratoga, and the few surviving inhabitants had fled thirty miles east, seeking protection in Albany.[51] When the warm spring finally opened the roads and business resumed, they immediately began to expand their firm's property while keeping a close eye on Pennsylvania's next move.

On May 2, 1746,[52] they jointly purchased an additional one hundred and seventy-one acres that stood adjacent to the western side of the previous tract they bought in October. Now, the combined purchase granted them exclusive

---

51. *Pennsylvania Gazette*, December 6, 1745.
52. Pennsylvania State Archives, Lancaster County Warrant Registers, Box RG-17, 36, Warrant No. 276.

The 1749 Map of Pennsylvania, New Jersey, New York, and the three Delaware counties by Lewis Evans shows the cabin marked "Croghans" just west of Harris's Ferry and the Susquehanna River. (Courtesy of Public Domain.)

access for use of Conodoguinet Creek's southern shoreline. The original house built by Croghan and Trent stood on the border of these two properties, a log cabin that was labeled as just "Croghans" on Lewis Evans's map in 1749.[53] Today, the house still stands in Cumberland County along Skyport Road in Silver Spring Township.

Meanwhile, in Philadelphia, a couple weeks later, on May 21, 1746,[54] the discussion between the governor and his council was now about Pennsylvania's role going forward due to an important express that arrived from London via Boston. The letter to Governor George Thomas came from Thomas Pelham-Holles, 1st Duke of Newcastle, who was the Cabinet Secretary of State for southern Europe.

It was a message from King George II declaring that:

> It was the King's intention that the troops to be raised should consist of Companies of one hundred Men each and that these that shall be raised in several provinces of New York, New Jersey, Pennsylvania, Maryland & Virginia.[55]

It seemed he, too also been concerned with the French presence in North America. The king wanted to reinforce the captured garrison at Louisbourg on Cape Breton Island and begin a campaign for the "immediate reduction of Canada."[56]

---

53. Library of Congress, A Map of Pennsylvania, New Jersey, New York, and the three Delaware Counties (1749).
54. Colonial records of Pennsylvania Vol. 5, 37.
55. Ibid., 38.
56. Ibid., 37.

He concluded that:

> You will appoint such Officers as you think proper to command them; and assuring all those that shall engage in this service, as well Officers as Soldiers, that they will immediately enter into His Majesty's pay___ the Officers from the time they shall engage in His Majesty's Service.[57]

Pennsylvania's role was made clear by King George II. Independent companies were to be raised immediately under the pay of the king, meaning they were not militia paid by their county's levy but first raised troops or volunteers that were paid directly from London. Governor Thomas immediately sent letters to these private persons whom he wished to fill the blank commissions as commanders of these companies of one hundred men.

One such letter arrived at the trading house of the Croghan and Trent firm on the Conodoguinet Creek in Pennsborough Township. The two men had established a business presence by namesake alone in Philadelphia for their recent success and expertise in the fur trade, so it wasn't a surprise. However, it was more likely Governor Thomas remembered the Trent family and the highly reputable Trent from when he was a young teenager, living in the former house of his late father on the Assunpink Creek in Trenton when Thomas purchased the house and property in 1733.[58] The son of a wealthy gentleman and respected man of the church, it seemed was an ideal candidate to be an officer. Unfortunately for Croghan, Trent must have been rather captivated by the offer and surprisingly accepted the commission. Now, there's never been a letter from Croghan or even Trent himself as to why he chose to leave his successful trading firm rather abruptly for military service, but the eventual Provincial Secretary Richard Peters did describe this decision secondhand in a letter to Thomas Penn on November 24, 1748:[59]

> Before he engaged in the King's service, he carried on the Indian trade successfully in partnership with George Croghan who is one of the most reputable & sensible traders and Trent might by this time have made a fortune but ambition seiz'd him so violently that he broke up the partnership in hopes to be a man of figure in the conquest & settlement of Canada.[60]

---

57. Ibid., 38.
58. State Archives of New Jersey, October 13, 1733 Deed from William Morris to George Thomas.
59. Richard Peters Letterbook, Richard Peters to Thomas Penn, November 24, 1748.
60. Ibid.

For the twenty-something Trent, ambition meant his successful business was not enough for him. He wanted more than what his brothers or father ever achieved. An honorable military career in the King's service could do just that by potentially boosting his social standing from esquire to a gentleman.

So, by dissolving the fateful partnership with Croghan, he instead chose to risk both his life and his legacy, hoping that history one day remembers the name, Captain William Trent.

Chapter 4

A Brush with Death

After Trent sent his reply to join the expedition to Canada, it left him just over a week to put his affairs in order. He was now one of four captains commissioned in His Majesty's service on June 4, 1746. The other three captains commissioned for these proposed independent companies of Pennsylvania were John Shannon, John Diemer, and Samuel Perry.[1]

Five days later, when Governor Thomas issued a proclamation across the colony for the "want of able-bodied men" for an expedition to Canada, Trent decided to leave the banks of the Conodoguinet Creek and head east along the old Peters Road[2] just a few miles from their firm's trading house. The old Indian path was the fastest route to Philadelphia from the nearest settlement of Paxtang[3] and its ferry operator, John Harris Sr.

A few days later, he arrived back in the capital city just before the 25th of June, confident and eager to prove he was worthy of the commission. There was barely a trace now of that teenage apprentice who once stared wide-eyed at the endless streets and alleyways. His tall physical presence over six feet tall[4] alone stood out from the other officers.

Yet it was the initial task that worried him as he rode east down Arch Street.[5] The orders were made clear by the governor. Trent was to raise a com-

---

1. Montgomery, 6.
2. An old wagon road named for trader Peter Bizellion who frequented this road from the Susquehanna River near present-day Harrisburg to Philadelphia.
3. Originally purchased by colony founder William Penn, the settlement of "Paxtang" or "Paxton" was near the ferry patented by John Harris Sr. and today is part of the city of Harrisburg.
4. William Trent's sleeveless waistcoat is at the 1719 William Trent House Museum in Trenton, New Jersey and the author took measurements of the specific garment. It is estimated Trent stood between six feet and six foot two inches tall.
5. The east-west street was named Mulberry Street in William Penn's original plan of Philadelphia in 1682 but was always referred as "Arch" Street because of the arch that rose over the intersection at Front Street. After 1854, it changed permanently to Arch Street and is presently known by that name today.

Today the present site of the former "St. George and the Dragon Inn" or "Sign of the George" at the corner of 2nd Street and Arch Street in Philadelphia. (Author photo.)

pany of one hundred men, "of which he was to Enlist none but healthy, abled body'd men, not exceeding forty-five years of Age, good stature, nor under any other bodily disorder which may be an impediment to their Marching."[6] The last phrase was the most important because as soon as he and the other three officers reached one hundred men each, they eventually set off for the long two-hundred-mile march to Albany, New York.

The twenty-something Trent pulled on the reins just by the intersection of Second St. and Arch and dismounted. He had reached the destination to start his recruitment along with his Lieutenant Daniel Byles and Ensign William Rush. He was at 200 Arch Street, where a wooden sign displayed the picture of patron Saint George atop his white horse while slaying a dragon. The public house was run by cartographer Nicholas Scull[7] and was known as the "Saint George and the Dragon Inn." Most men who frequented there called it the "Sign of the George."[8]

---

6. Hazard, 688.

7. Nicholas Scull II (1687–1761) was a mapmaker or cartographer, innkeeper of the "St George and the Dragon Inn" and served as the Surveyor General of Pennsylvania from 1748 to 1761. He was most known for his map of Philadelphia called, "A Map of Philadelphia and Parts Adjacent 1752."

8. Despite being called the "St. George and the Dragon Inn," the advertisements throughout Franklin's *Pennsylvania Gazette* referred to the tavern as "Sign of the George" in the 1740s.

It was here that Captain Trent began filling the roster for his company, recording their name, age, occupation, and date of their enlistment. On June 26th, he enlisted five. Six more on the 27th. Then an additional five by the last day of June.[9] Sixteen total before he could send the official word out about the expedition and its rewards.

In accordance with his instructions that were replicated to the other three officers, the men who volunteered to join his muster were to be given living quarters and "promised a Dollar upon enlisting, and Three Pistoles in Gold for the support of their families in their Absence."[10] The latter, worth about fifty-four shillings,[11] was the most appealing, for by the end of July, Trent had garnered an additional seventy-eight men to sign or make their mark upon his muster book.[12]

It also helped that the "Sign of the George" was also in the shadow of Christ Church, the large Protestant congregation that provided several prospects for his company. The Anglican church had recently finished the pews on the interior, and a plan to build a spire or steeple was in the works, though it wasn't constructed until the fall of 1755.[13]

These men were not all just Protestants but people of different backgrounds and occupations. The average age of his men was twenty-eight years,[14] some if not mostly older than their recently commissioned captain. They were laborers, sawyers, and colliers, and some were born outside the colonies like England, Ireland or even Saint Christopher.[15] Captain Diemer had even enlisted William Franklin, the teenage son of *Pennsylvania Gazette* editor and printer Benjamin Franklin, as an ensign in his company.

Trent, on the other hand, chose the "able-bodied" description too literally, enlisting runaways[16] and criminals who wish to escape the city. He assumed that these individuals were just satisfied with their monetary advance upon enlisting because they feared worse punishment by the law if they deserted and were returned to Philadelphia.

As for Trent, if he had any early doubt about his own decision to boost his social status, it disappeared when he placed his signature upon a deed conveyed

---

9. Montgomery, 9–11.
10. Hazard, 688.
11. A pistole is worth about eighteen shillings in English currency.
12. Montgomery, 9–11.
13. Dorr, 17–18.
14. Montgomery, 8–11.
15. St. Christopher's Island was an island in the West Indies, now known today as St. Kitts.
16. Advertisement of William Trent and a runaway servant from his company named Patrick Linch. *Pennsylvania Gazette*, September 4, 1746. Advertisement of William Trent and a runaway servant from his company named Robert Beard. *Pennsylvania Gazette*, September 11, 1746.

to George Croghan on July 4, 1746.[17] It was no secret that his ambitious impulse to join the expedition to Canada had put a strain on his friendship with Croghan, so Trent made sure his former partner was better off financially. He wanted no bad blood between them, especially since it could be months or years before he might resume his mercantile business. So out of respect for Croghan, Trent, "presently residing in the city of Philadelphia," sold off to Croghan his half parts and conveyances of the three hundred fifty-four acres they jointly purchased on October 7th, 1745, and the one hundred seventy-one acres on May 2, 1745.[18]

Now, he could focus on his biggest challenge in Philadelphia yet, teaching his men the manual of arms. When the bulk of their respective companies were enlisted by the end of July, the four captains took their companies to the bordering settlements outside the city to finish their recruitment. Captain Shannon went seventeen miles to the settlement of Chester along the Delaware. Captain Perry took his men just west of the city to Derby (Darby), and Captain Diemer finished his recruitment in Germantown, near Logan's "Stenton" house.

As for Trent, he took his men northeast a few miles outside of the city on a path known then as the "Kings High Road or Kings Highway." The road ran over 1,300 miles and connected Charleston, South Carolina, to Boston, Massachusetts, since the year 1650. Today, Frankford Avenue is the road now leading out of Philadelphia, and Trent followed it about five miles north of the city to where Frankford Creek emptied itself into the Delaware River. It was there at the small settlement of Frankford that Trent and his men encamped until they received marching orders. It was also where Trent followed his original orders to practice the manual of arms, trying to "be very diligent in Teaching them the Facings, Wheeling and Firings, that they may load and Fire quick and regular."[19]

Unfortunately, this was not so simple. The latest handbook of drill exercises, called "The New Manual Exercise," had just been published in London, and it didn't arrive in Philadelphia until July 10, 1746.[20] The drill manual was written by the military commander of the Scottish Highlands, Lieutenant General William Blakeney and Trent couldn't obtain a copy for 6d or six pence from Franklin's print shop until after that time.

By the end of August, Trent divided his company into four platoons of twenty-five, with each platoon having one sergeant and corporal to echo the command. He wanted to make sure their facings or turns together were precise. Once they did that, Trent had them march forward as one line, shifting as

---

17. Lancaster County Deed Book B, 445–47.
18. Ibid., 447–49.
19. Hazard, 688.
20. *Pennsylvania Gazette*, July 10, 1746.

one line left or right in formations called wheelings or wheels. Like Governor Thomas said, he was not granted sufficient time to perfect it. This was all for now. Finally, during their daily exercise, Trent ordered them to load with gunpowder and a lead ball. Once loaded, he barked the first command.

Cock your firelock!

The men put their thumbs on the cock, then held the flint and clicked it back as far as it could go.

Present!

The muskets and rifles that were once upright and pointing to the sky fell parallel to the ground.

Fire!

Their fingers drew briskly on the trigger, and when the flint struck the iron hammer stall, the powder in their pans ignited the rammed ball and powder in the long barrels. Smoke exploded from the barrels and the one hundred or so musket balls fell harmlessly across the pasture, a football field length away.

That day, Trent's commands were loud and stern. The loading and firing had to be regular and fast. The men had to realize that this expedition was nothing like hunting game birds or deer. If it came to it, swiftness on the battlefield meant life or death. It was also why he had been firing his two pistols alongside his men. Trent had probably acquired them in Philadelphia, and he wanted to feel comfortable discharging them with ease. Even if the situation never called for him to use them. The pistols were the Queen Anne's model and concealed nicely within his coat, which was why they were called "gentlemen coat pistols" or "pocket pistols."[21]

In September,[22] the final muster roll was submitted to Governor Thomas. Trent's company was around one hundred sixteen men, not including the two commissioned officers on his staff, Lieutenant Byles and Ensign Rush. (See Appendix B for a complete roster of names). Over four hundred men[23] embarked on leaving Pennsylvania for the expedition into Canada. For innkeepers Joseph Lewis, James McVeigh and James Claxton, their departure wasn't soon enough.

After Trent arrived in Frankford, he chose McVeigh's "Old Inn"[24] at the corner of Kensington and Frankfort Avenue (now Womrath Park), Lewis's Inn

---

21. New Jersey Historical Society, Manuscript Group 7, New Jersey Manuscript Collection 1669–1840, Item 39.
22. Montgomery, 9–11.
23. Ibid., 6–16.
24. *Pennsylvania Gazette*, August 12, 1772. MacKinney, 3125.

near Waln Grove (at Tacony and Church Street)[25] and Claxton's "Sign of the Bear"[26] for accommodations for he and his men. When Claxton initially refused to provide this luxury, Trent showed him official orders and promises of reimbursement by the Governor of Pennsylvania to use his establishment. A few weeks after Trent's men departed for New Jersey, Claxton petitioned the Pennsylvania Assembly for seventy-eight pounds and seventeen shillings due to him for feeding or "dieting" the soldiers of Captain Trent's Company.[27]

Unfortunately, the innkeepers that housed the soldiers and officers outside Philadelphia were not the only ones with outstanding balances. The officers and the men had not received their promised pay since the day of their respective enlistments. At the previous August 22, 1746, meeting[28] between Governor Thomas and the Assembly, he addressed this lack of funding once more, warning those present in Philadelphia that these men might desert if these promises could not be fulfilled from London. Thomas mentioned the bounty of three pistoles and the much-needed freight to transport the baggage and necessaries. Wagons were essential not only for these provisions but also for the carriage of the four hundred soldiers assembled.

During the first week of September, Trent received specific orders to meet the other three Pennsylvania companies in Brunswick, New Jersey, so they could assemble to head from there to Albany, New York.[29] Trent and his large detachment traveled on the King's Highway into New Jersey, crossing the Delaware River near Trenton. As they marched up the road toward the banks of the Assunpink Creek, it is probable to assume Trent didn't abstain from noticing the familiar cupola atop his boyhood home still standing near the river. The house in 1746 had been called "Kingsbury House"[30] by the now-deceased Lewis Morris, who had died a few months back in office as Governor of New Jersey. Morris had been leasing the house from its owner, Pennsylvania Governor George Thomas, the very same individual who not only purchased the house from his uncle William Morris but who commissioned him a Pennsylvania captain in the King's service.

The house also looked larger now, for when Morris began leasing it in 1742, he built a "handsome paved gangway" from the house to a large two-story brick kitchen that stood twenty feet by thirty feet.[31] Trent and his company traveled on Queen Street (now Broad Street) past his father's mills and above the

---

25. MacKinney, 3125.
26. *Pennsylvania Gazette*, August 14, 1746. MacKinney, 3123–3125.
27. MacKinney, 3123.
28. Minutes of the Provincial Council of Pennsylvania, Volume 5, 53.
29. Colonial Records of Pennsylvania, Vol. 5, 53.
30. Papers of Lewis Morris 1738–1746, 303.
31. Butchko, Burrow and Hunter, 2–3.

main borough of Trenton, taking a right at the Y-shaped intersection of roads Pennington and Brunswick.

When the four Pennsylvania companies eventually arrived in Brunswick, they were met with disappointment. The necessary funds from London had not arrived. Governor Thomas had been forced to withdraw from the province's treasury, rounding up what little provisions and wagons he could muster on an already depleting account.

When Trent and the rest of the Pennsylvania men began their trek north up the Hudson River, Governor Thomas wrote a letter to New York Governor George Clinton for additional aid.[32] Thomas hoped by the time the companies journeyed the one hundred eighty miles to Albany, the province catered to their needs.

It was a remarkable sight for Trent as he marched on the King's Highway (the corner of Cornbury Place and Eagle Street) within the defensive walls of the city of Albany. On the hill overlooking the Hudson, he saw a large stone fort the garrison named "Fort Frederick"[33] in honor of the Prince of Wales, Frederick Louis, the son of King George II of England. This also marked the first time Trent saw a fort. The square-structured outposts could maintain at least three hundred men inside and mounted up to ten cannons along its walls. There was also a two-story brick house called the "Governor's House" which the current governor stayed when he visited from New York City.[34] On September 16, 1746, it was also where New York Governor Clinton addressed his letter to Indian agent William Johnson as the men of Pennsylvania arrived outside the fort. Clinton wrote from the Fort that "Five Hundred troops from the Jerseys and Four Hundred from Philadelphia arrived here, besides several more companies from New York which amount to above two thousand men."[35]

After the rendezvous in Albany, they were to travel to Montreal and drive the French from their settlements on the upper Saint Lawrence River.[36] The only problem was their commander of the expedition, Virginia Lieutenant Governor William Gooch, declined the position, leaving the two thousand troops to reside in Albany until further orders. Clinton appointed Lieutenant John Roberts, the former Cornet of Horse member under King George I, as Gooch's successor.[37]

In the meantime, Trent and the Pennsylvania troops began constructing their encampments with the wooden poles and tents provided by Clinton.

---

32. Colonial Records of Pennsylvania, Vol. 5, 132–33.
33. Lake Champlain Weekly, September 17, 2003 issue.
34. Ibid.
35. Sullivan, 64.
36. Paltsits, 10.
37. O'Callaghan, 314.

Provisions such as peas, rice, and smoked thighs of a hog called gammons[38] were also rationed, but the cold wintry breeze and weather off the river were chilling his men at night and day during their daily exercise. It was barely October, and his men were freezing. The conditions were miserable and were only going to get worse as the months went by.

So, he and the other captains requested an audience[39] with Governor Clinton to explain to him their current dilemma. The men needed covering over their snuff-covered jackets and leather leggings[40] since they had been refusing to drill in the cold. Some had even deserted during the night over the last few days.

Clinton, who had seen troops in Albany from New Jersey and New York arrive properly equipped, secured one hundred fifty blankets for the Pennsylvania men. He also suggested to those officers that they could seek the goods of the local merchants and citizens if they needed more.[41]

The blankets were barely sufficient to supply his men, let alone the rest of the Pennsylvania soldiers. So, by October 21, 1746, Trent ventured up to what is now Steuben Street and visited the house of Cornelius Cuyler, a fur trader, Indian agent, and the recent mayor of Albany. There Trent was supplied with some blankets by Cuyler for credit of twenty-four pounds sixteen shillings of Pennsylvania currency. He charged the remaining blankets for his men under local merchant James Stevenson, who resided on upper State Street by the fort. The bill for Stevenson amounted to fifty-one pounds four shillings. The total bill of credit accumulated by Trent, along with his fellow officers, was drawn up in Governor Thomas's name with the hope he would pay this balance once the necessary funds reached Philadelphia.[42]

Trent wrote to Governor Thomas about these specific amounts but voiced concern about desertion in the ranks, saying, "Considering the circumstances we were in, we had received orders to march, the weather very cold and nothing to cover the men, the consequences of which must have been the desertion of the whole Company."[43]

Trent cited such an example as the returns of the Pennsylvania men, stating to Thomas that of the original four hundred men that arrived in Albany, only three hundred thirty remained effective. Which meant almost seventy men had deserted their ranks in the last few weeks. Of the other regiments, Shannon's

---

38. DeValinger, 52.
39. University of Michigan, William L. Clements Library, George Clinton Papers, October 7, 1746.
40. *Pennsylvania Gazette*, September 4, 1746.
41. University of Michigan, William L. Clements Library, George Clinton Papers, October 7, 1746.
42. Linn and Egle, 586.
43. Ibid., 585.

company had lost thirty men, while around twenty each had deserted from Diemer's and Perry's units.[44]

Surprisingly, Trent had only reported one single deserter from his regiment, and it demonstrated that despite his selection of questionable characters, his gamble of enlisting runaway servants and fugitives proved to be a wise one.

While his men were complacent with their current conditions, the others, as Trent described, were not saying, "They say they had better perish by trying to make their escape, or a few days will determine their fate and to stay where they are."[45] Trent described a man of Captain Shannon's that "when crossing the mountains trying to make his escape, where the snow was knee deep, one of them got frostbit,"[46] suffering a terrible fate since they were forced to leave him to freeze at the foot of the nearby Catskill Mountains.

All four captains were self-aware of the quantity of provisions, specifically stating they only had enough bread and rum to last those encamped until about the 19th of January. They needed more provisions in the next few weeks, for when the Hudson was frozen, it was impossible to freight the provisions north by water.

By December, the men at Fort Frederick were not only squabbling with themselves but also with a brand-new foe, disease. With the men drawn to tight quarters in and around the fort, typhoid and smallpox ravaged Albany and the outpost in the north. This constraint forced the Governor of Massachusetts, William Shirley, to refrain from sending his Massachusetts troops and relief to New York, citing "it would be extremely dangerous to the health of the New England troops."[47]

It was alarming news for Captain Henry Livingston, the garrison commander at Fort Clinton just South of Fishkill Creek near the banks of the Hudson. The wooden fort, named after its colonial governor, was rebuilt in 1746 on the site of the previous Fort Saratoga that was burned on November 17, 1745, by Lieutenant Paul Marin de la Mague and his regiment of Troupes de la Marine.[48]

The newly built Fort Clinton held just a small garrison, and being New York's northernmost outpost, it was the most vulnerable to attacks by French and Indians. Now, with Shirley's men not coming, Livingston sent immediate

---

44. Ibid.
45. Ibid., 586.
46. Ibid., 585.
47. Preston, 65.
48. Paul Marin de la Malgue (1692–1753), a French officer who led a successful raid against the British outpost and its settlement of Saratoga on November 17, 1745. He was later promoted a captain and in 1752, helped France seize the Ohio River valley by building outposts in present-day western Pennsylvania. Marin died at the outpost along Le Boeuf called Fort de la Rivière au Boeuf on October 29, 1753 in present-day Waterford, Pennsylvania.

word to Fort Frederick requesting detachments to not only patrol the road north to "Saraghtogue"[49] but also join his garrison along the west bank of the Hudson River. So, it was Captain Trent and his Pennsylvania troops that were sent north up the wintry fifty-mile road along the frozen Hudson to Fort Clinton.

To accommodate Trent's men, the carpenters at the Fort, who had already built blockhouses and floured the guard houses, began "building barracks for Captain Trent's detachment"[50] to house them inside the Fort. Trent and his men were probably gracious to leave Albany, anxious to distance themselves from the sickness and the smell of fires burning the infected clothes. For Trent, he saw not another similar outbreak of smallpox until he became the militia commander at Fort Pitt in 1763.

But at Fort Clinton, Trent and his men found a post demoralized by lack of supplies and constant harassment by French and Indians. His Pennsylvania detachment could not escape the wild stories they heard when they first arrived in February of 1746. Back in June, when Trent was first commissioned, Indians killed one and captured another.[51] When he and his men marched on the King's Highway in September, another eight soldiers were attacked from this garrison, leaving four killed and the remaining captured.[52]

Then, soon after they arrived at Fort Clinton on February 22, 1746/47, a raiding party struck again. This time, attacking a dozen from the fort who, when searching for firewood, strayed too far off the road.[53] After a relief column was sent out for support, they returned with only four of the original party. Of the remaining four, only one went unscathed and told what happened. Four men were killed on the spot. Four others were taken captive. Three more had been wounded and brought back to the fort surgeon. It was at this time the garrison buried two of these men who died of their wounds, including the one soldier found alive with a tomahawk stuck in his skull.[54]

For Trent, it seemed his ambition had gotten the better of him. Their proposed plan to capture the French outpost Fort St. Frederick, built on the future site of the English outpost Crown Point, had been postponed indefinitely due to the lack of supplies and the delay of New England troops. Now, there was no planned expedition to take Montreal, so therefore, his status remained either unchanged unless disease or the enemy killed him first while he was stationed at a seemingly miserable outpost on the New York frontier.

---

49. The pronunciation of Saratoga originated from the Mohawk word "Se-rach-ta-gue" which means "the hillside country of the quiet river." Today this area is near present-day Schuylerville, New York.
50. University of Michigan, William L. Clements Library, George Clinton Papers, Folder 39, May 21, 1747. Preston, 79.
51. Preston, 65.
52. *Pennsylvania Gazette*, September 18, 1746, 3. Ibid.
53. *Boston Post-Boy*, April 20, 1747. Ibid., 66.
54. Ibid.

This was not the prestige he originally desired when he chose to leave the mercantile scales and account books behind for the life of a soldier. Perhaps it was why, in early spring, he didn't hesitate to help deliver supplies south to the smaller post at Half Moon (presently Waterford, New York) along his way to Albany. On the morning of April 7, 1747, Trent, along with his subordinate Lieutenant William Proctor, gathered what provisions the fort could spare. Amongst his baggage and personal correspondence were a dozen blankets, twenty-three deer skins, fifteen knives, two cooking glasses, two waistcoats, leather, thread, and some chocolate.[55] The spare ammunition was even more scarce, leaving just five ct. of gunpowder and four ct. of musket balls.[56]

Trent's guard consisted of only forty-four able-bodied men, a mixture of his Pennsylvanians and Proctor's New Yorkers, who were fit and effective for the trek south along the Hudson. Before they left the gates of Fort Clinton, Trent made sure his men utilized the quire of paper, issuing sixteen or seventeen cartridges[57] per man. He had hoped with the limited ammunition, they only used them if necessary.

The twenty-five-mile journey to the outpost at Half Moon however, already hit a snag before they could put the walls of Fort Clinton behind them. Sentries reported the Fishkill had risen over the banks just a few hundred yards southwest of the Fort and made the road south impassable.

The fort lying on the flatlands between the tall banks of the Fishkill and the Hudson was now murky swampland, leaving Trent with a tough decision. Should he wait a few days for the road to clear for his traveling caravan? This meant the provisions arrived later at Half Moon. It also meant the garrison of Fort Clinton was not receiving their much-needed clothes and supplies that had just arrived in Albany until much later than expected. Or should he just take the path north and cross the water near the site of the old Phillip Schuyler house[58] and head south that way?

With most of the men at Fort Clinton weak or sickly, Trent chose the latter. He needed to leave immediately, especially if the French arrived down from Fort St. Frederick to attack the garrison, now that the weather was improving. So, they headed up north into narrow, uncultivated lands known as "Sarachtogie." The area, including the fort, was once part of the large tract purchased from

---

55. New Jersey Historical Society, Manuscript Group 7, New Jersey Manuscript Collection 1669–1840, Item #39.
56. Ibid.
57. *Pennsylvania Gazette,* April 16, 1747. *Boston Post-Boy,* April 20, 1747.
58. On November 17, 1745, French and Indians burned the house of Philip Johannes Schuyler and killed him when he tried to protect his house. Today the remnants of the house lie today on the present-day site of his nephew's General Philip Schuyler's country estate near Schuylerville, New York.

the Mohawk Indians, formerly known as the "Saratoga Patent."[59] By 1708, the land was divided among seven Dutch patentees and stretched twenty-two miles long by six miles wide.[60] The Hudson River ran through the center of this tract, starting at its southernmost border on the Anthony Kill near present-day Mechanicsville, New York, until it stretched north at the Batten Kill, a mile north of present-day Schuylerville, New York.[61] The town (which lies along the north bank of the Fishkill today) was named for the prominent Schuyler family whose surname also was amongst the original seven signatures of the Saratoga Patent. This patentee, Johannes Schuyler, was given the lot[62] found on both banks of the Fishkill, whose mouth flowed into the west side of the Hudson just below where Schuylerville resides today.

Opposite the current town, Johannes's son Phillip built a house along the southern shoreline of the Fishkill and was killed defending it when the French and Indians attacked there in November of 1745.[63] The remnants of the Schuyler estate were within sight of Trent and his men when they passed through the crude pastureland currently owned by Albany's current mayor, Dirck Ten Broeck.[64]

The land near the road narrowed here and sunk the path between the steep shorelines of the Fishkill and the Hudson. It echoed what Swedish naturalist Peter Kalm described later in his 1749 journal of this specific region as he canoed up the Hudson towards Canada. Kalm described that the "Thuya occidentalis" (northern white cedar) appeared along the shores of the river there for the first time.[65] These trees were probably the same ones disguising the hidden ambuscade as they lay in wait, watching the front of Trent's convoy march through. Just off the road, shots bellowed at them from the thicket. Before Trent could react, a dozen of his men lay dead or wounded from the first volley of shots.

    Take cover!

His men were scrambling to find any tree or rock that could protect them from the ensuing cascade of musket fire.

    Cock your firelocks!
    Present!
    Fire!

---

59. In 1684, New York Provincial Governor Thomas Dongan granted the petition of Pieter Schuyler, Robert Livingston and others to purchase a large tract of land from the Mohawk people. This became known as the "Saratoga Patent."
60. Stevens, White, Graswold, and Brown, 26.
61. Ibid.
62. Schuyler's lot was Lot 1 and half of 6 in the original patent.
63. Preston, 5–6.
64. Dirck Ten Broeck succeeded Cornelius Cuyler and served as mayor of Albany from 1746 to 1748.
65. Kalm, Vol. 2, 288.

Their return volley was sporadic and did little damage to their seemingly invisible foe. Some of their guns clicked without even a hint of smoke.[66] Quickly, he made them reload and fire again. In between the enemy shots and the rising hillside, Trent heard the war cries echo from the river. Indians ran out after their last volley and began scraping their knives under the hair of Trent's men, who lay helpless amongst the scattered baggage on the road. An eyewitness to the battle said he saw six of them scalped right in front of them.[67]

More shots came from the opposition, but Trent and his men held their ground. He probably fired his pocket pistol a few times while his men directed their shots at the shadows that moved throughout the mist caused by the musket smoke. An hour[68] had passed when Trent surveyed the ammunition of his men. Most had already fired the sixteen or seventeen rounds they had carried. Some of them used their final cartridge or took some off the dead. When each man fired his last cartridge, Trent told them to leave the baggage behind and retreat to the nearby swamp.[69] By now, he hoped the garrison of Fort Clinton heard the distant shots, and Livingston hopefully sent more men in relief. It was their only chance of survival. Because of the high waters, he and his men could retreat no further. They were pinned with no ammunition, as one soldier later described, "no way to prevent the enemy's falling on our men with their hatchets."[70]

The area was a chaotic hell, something Trent had never witnessed firsthand before except maybe reading about war and Greek tragedies from his brother's library.[71] Men lay lifeless, scattered across the road. Wounded were being carried away or crying out before a tomahawk made them silent. When he watched the Indians, and now the French Troupes de la Marine led by Lieutenant Frederick Louis Herbin,[72] loot the baggage and the dead, Trent prepared for the worst. Then, a barrage of musket fire erupted from across the water, and he watched several French fall to the ground.

It was the help they had hoped for. Livingston had heard the shots and sent a relief force under Ensign Bratt from the fort.[73] The raiding party was repulsed across the Fishkill and eventually retreated almost eighty miles to Fort Saint Frederick.

---

66. *Pennsylvania Gazette*, April 16, 1747.
67. New Jersey Historical Society, Manuscript Group 7, New Jersey Manuscript Collection 1669–1840, Item #39.
68. *Boston Post-Boy*, April 20, 1747.
69. Ibid.
70. *Pennsylvania Gazette*, April 16, 1747.
71. Inventory of James Trent 1734.
72. Frederick Louis Herbin (1711–1792) was stationed at the French Fort Saint-Frederic on Lake Champlain that later became the English outpost at Crown Point. After many successful raids in the area of Saratoga, he became commandant at Fort Michilimackinac from 1754 to 1759. In 1759, he was also awarded the Cross of Saint Louis for being an exceptional officer.
73. *Pennsylvania Gazette*, April 16, 1747.

Today the present site of the ambush of Trent's Pennsylvania regiment on April 7, 1747, just north of Fort Clinton in what is now known as Schuylerville, New York. (Courtesy of Dr. David Preston.)

Trent took the first count of surviving effectives. Nine of his men were killed. Nine more were wounded or missing. Another six were taken captive in addition to the complete loss of his correspondence and baggage, including one of his pocket pistols.[74]

Lieutenant Herbin eventually arrived back at their fort overlooking Lake Champlain and reported intel amongst the capture correspondents in which Fort Clinton's commander Livingston had described the garrison "in miserable condition and all the soldiers as ill."[75]

It was a garrison he believed was further weakened with the loss of one of their officers, Captain Trent, who Herbin believed had died in their April 7th raid near the Fishkill. This assumption came from one of the most recent English captives, a soldier in Trent's convoy who had mistakenly thought Trent had died at the battle.

Later, after being taken to Montreal, this captive announced Trent's presumed death to another prisoner named Nehemiah How.[76] Despite the false

---

74. New Jersey Historical Society, Manuscript Group 7, New Jersey Manuscript Collection 1669–1840, Item #39.
75. Preston, 81.
76. How, 54. For the entry in How's Account, see Appendix B in this book.

report of his death, Trent was fortunate to be alive. He and Lieutenant Proctor returned quietly with their small party to Fort Clinton but were commended by Livingston for their bravery and exertion of great courage.[77] So, Trent was branded a hero for his gallant actions as an officer, but the expedition for Canada was at a standstill. Weeks later, he and his men were ordered to return to the fort at Albany.

In June, Trent saw the men's morale reach the lowest point of their campaign. Every day he had men desert, something he never thought might happen. He couldn't blame them for what the four Pennsylvania captains described to Governor Clinton as "vile Insinuations that has from time to time been put in the heads of our men."[78]

There were many reasons their men were deserting. They were tired of idleness around the fort and the delays in receiving their full pay. The men even feared disease since the New York Governor had issued a proclamation banning inoculations of smallpox in the city.[79]

The four Pennsylvania captains feared a mutiny amongst their own might transpire unless their situation improved, but in August, news from London dealt them all a full final crushing blow.[80] The expedition for the reduction of Canada was over. The levies of men from the northeast colonies finished their enlistment and returned home. The conflict with France, or what became known as "King George's War," continued, but Trent's stint as a Pennsylvania officer in His Majesty's service concluded. Trent served from June 4, 1746, until the 31st of October 1747.[81] Five hundred and fifteen days of His Majesty's service and long enough to learn of the abandonment and burning of his former post, Fort Clinton on October 6, 1747.

Trent had not risen in social status, but he was going to be forever addressed as Captain William Trent or Captain Trent. It was also a title he began to place before his signature on his correspondence and receipts.

After his return to Philadelphia, Trent's first mission was to seek out his former partner George Croghan on the Conodoguinet Creek. They had parted on questionable terms, and he wanted to show Croghan his plans now that he was a civilian once again. More importantly, he wanted back into the fur trading firm and, with his captain's pay soon arriving, had enough capital to boost their mercantile business financially.

---

77. *Pennsylvania Gazette*, April 16, 1747.
78. O'Callaghan, 376.
79. With numerous outbreaks in Albany and New York City in the summer of 1747, Governor Clinton banned the issuing of smallpox inoculations, fearing it was the cause of the recent spread between soldiers and citizens.
80. O'Callaghan, 384–85.
81. Severns, 178.

Croghan had just freshly arrived at his house in Pennsborough from the mouth of the Cuyahoga River with news of the Ohio Indians wanting presents of powder and lead.[82] Trent knew supplying the Indians on this side of Lake Erie was key to their expansion into the Ohio country. He and Croghan just didn't realize the territory of future western Pennsylvania was also in the crosshairs of the colony of Virginia.

While Trent was still in Albany, twelve men from Maryland and the Northern Neck region of Virginia petitioned the Virginia governor for 200,000 acres of land "from ye Branch called Kiskimanetts and Buffalo Creeks on the south side of the river Alligany"[83] (near present-day Freeport, Pennsylvania) to where it met the Monongahela River (present-day Pittsburgh, Pennsylvania). Their spokesperson on this petition was the proprietor of Stratford Hall,[84] Thomas Lee, the former Virginia commissioner who, in July of 1744, had dined several nights with Trent and John Mackarall at the Lancaster meeting of the Six Nations.[85]

So, the winter of 1747/48 became the dawn of a new age in land speculation. For Trent, it was another chance to revive the promising mercantile career he once left behind. Meanwhile, for Thomas Lee and eleven others, the petition, successful or not, became a rough draft to not only exert their proposed authority in the colonies but also to showcase the efforts of westward expansion. The news of this plan hadn't yet reached Trent or Croghan, but their paths were destined to cross someday and soon, all of them heard of the land group aptly named the "Ohio Company."

---

82. O'Callaghan, 122 and 213.
83. James, 10.
84. The plantation was built by Thomas Lee, the former resident manager of the historic Northern Neck proprietary in the later 1730s. The house called "Stratford Hall" housed four generations of the Lee family including Richard Henry Lee, Francis Lightfoot Lee, "Light Horse" Harry Lee, and his son General Robert E. Lee. Today the property and house still stand today in Westmoreland County, Virginia along the Potomac River near the town of Stratford.
85. Thomas Lee (1690–1750) was a former resident manager of the Northern Neck proprietary for Lady Catherine Fairfax, who oversaw five million acres of her family's vast land grant until her son Thomas 6th Lord Fairfax of Cameron was of age. After attending the Treaty of Lancaster in 1744, he founded the renowned land speculation agency, the Ohio Company in 1747. Lee served as acting Governor of Virginia in 1749 and 1750 before his death in 1750. Two of his sons, Richard Henry Lee and Francis Lightfoot Lee later signed the Declaration of Independence in 1776.

Chapter 5

Prosperous Expansion

In the early hours of August 12, 1748, William Trent probably awoke abruptly and rubbed his eyes. For the past six months, he had been trying to transition back into the life he had left behind. It hadn't been easy for him, especially at night. While at Fort Clinton, Trent and his men only slept sparingly in their newly customized barracks due to the constant fear of being attacked by French and Indians. When an alarm was raised in the pitch of night, the outpost felt more like a snare for whomever wished to pounce from beyond the waters of the Fishkill and the Hudson. Over a year and a half in the service of his province and his king, yet nothing seemed to be gained for his efforts.

It had been six months since his honorable discharge, and he still received no compensation from across the ocean. The only such response from London came by the words forwarded by his grace the Duke of Newcastle from His Majesty King George II. The king, making no mention of pay for the Pennsylvania companies, only offered his minuscule gratitude about their past service:

> And We do also Thank them in His Majesty's Royal Name for their readiness to engage in their Country's Cause against the common Enemy; and though they are prevented at present of revenging themselves on a cruel perfidious Enemy, it cannot be doubled but the same Zeal and Spirit will always animate them to serve whenever they are called upon.[1]

---

1. Colonial Records of Pennsylvania, Vol. 5, 143.

Truthfully, this same zeal and spirit almost got him killed and seemingly left his return to the mercantile business in peril. Fortunately, his partner in Pennsborough, George Croghan, had prospered remarkably in his absence. After failed negotiations on the Cuyahoga River, Croghan moved his operations for trade from the shores of Lake Erie to the Great Miami River at a village called Pickawillany or Pick's Town.[2] Pickawillany (near present-day Piqua, Ohio) was the home of the Miami or Twightwee people, an Indian nation of the Great Lakes region, who previously lived along the Wabash River[3] in the present-day state of Indiana.

The chief of the Twightwee town was of the Piankashaw nation and called himself Memeskia. He was also known by the English traders as "Old Briton"[4] for his loyalty to the English, and it was he who permitted Croghan to build a trading house there.

Croghan also built a trading house on the Allegheny River in the upper Ohio country just north of where it joined the Monongahela to form the Ohio River. That specific area to the south was called the "Forks of the Ohio" and became a strategic area during the conflict known as the French and Indian War. Croghan's house, however, was about five miles north of the Forks (and the future site of Pittsburgh), lying near the mouth of Pine Creek, where the town of Etna resides today.

For now, the Pennsborough plantation on the Conodoguinet Creek, west of Harris's Ferry, still acted as their main distribution center and residence. From Pennsborough, Croghan and Trent received, distributed, purchased, and sold dry goods and animal skins to and from wealthy clients. They could also utilize the new tanning yard[5] down by the creek to transform the scraped raw animal hides into leather goods like saddles, harnesses, or even boots.

Waking up that morning to the familiar pungent smell of decaying animal hides and hemlock bark wafting up the bluff from the creek, Trent realized this was probably where he belonged. As he stepped out the cabin doorway, hooves sounded up the path from the east just as the sun emerged through the trees. It seemed the convoy he and Croghan were waiting on had finally arrived from the region of the Tulpehocken,[6] lying just west of the present-day city of Reading,

---

2. Most of the English traders or firms who traveled to Pickawillany referred to the village as "Pick's Town." It was located about two miles from modern day Piqua, Ohio where the mouth of Laramie Creek meets the Great Miami River.

3. The Wabash River runs near five hundred and three miles from its headwaters in Fort Recovery, Ohio to the mouth in Shawneetown, Illinois where it joins the Ohio River.

4. Trent records his name with the spelling "Old Briton" though some contemporaries spell it "Old Britain, "similar to Great Britain.

5. HSP, Cadwalader Family Papers, Box 202, Hockley, Trent and Croghan Account of Skins.

6. The homestead of Conrad Weiser built in 1729 is still standing today and is located in Womelsdorf, Pennsylvania in Berks County.

Today the present site of Croghan's Pennsborough property along Skyport Road in Mechanicsburg and where the tannery was located along the Conodoguinet Creek. (Author photo.)

Pennsylvania. This region was home to the convoy's leader, fifty-one-year-old Johann Conrad Weiser, the official interpreter of their proposed expedition to visit the Ohio country. He signed his letters usually as just "Conrad Weiser," and it was his language expertise that Trent witnessed at the meeting of the Six Nations just four years earlier in Lancaster.[7]

Weiser was also known to the Indian nations as "Tarachiawagon" or "Holder of the Heavens" and had brought with him £200[8] worth of presents from the Pennsylvania Assembly and Executive Council of Virginia (mainly because they did not attend), such as vermilion, blankets, skins, and beads of wampum. The latter were the most important, the white beads being made from the inner spiral of a whelk shell. For the "black" or purple wampum beads, the inside of quahog shells was used. Strung together, they formed a large belt and were offered to the Ohio Indians as a token of peace or friendship.

Weiser and Croghan had already gifted some strings of wampum to the Twightwee tribes last month in Lancaster,[9] but this was different. This was the

---

7. Conrad Weiser was the official interpreter at the treaty in front of the Lancaster courthouse that lasted from June 22, 1744 to July 4, 1744.
8. Colonial Records of Pennsylvania, Vol. 5, 257.
9. Pennsylvania Archives First Series, Vol. 2, 11.

first treaty of Pennsylvania in the Ohio country and their ideal opportunity to establish commerce with the Ohio Indians and expand into the uncarved wilderness.

This meant exponential profits if the partnership of Croghan and Trent could network a chain of trading posts from Pennsborough to Pine Creek to Beaver Creek[10] to as far west as Pickawillany in present-day western Ohio. It was also a chance to regain the Lenape's favor who had frequented the land near Croghan's plantation on Pine Creek ever since they were "exiled" after the Walking Purchase of 1737.

Traveling with Weiser was also seventeen-year-old William Franklin, the son of Philadelphia printer Ben Franklin. The young Franklin, a former Pennsylvania soldier stationed with Trent in Philadelphia and Albany,[11] probably volunteered himself to Weiser and Croghan as a fellow acquaintance of Trent. It seemed even after being discharged from His Majesty's service, his sense of perilous adventure still called to him from the drafty confinements of his father's printing office.[12]

Weiser's convoy was joined by Trent, Croghan, and a half dozen or so of their hired hands or "servitors" that resided in Pennsborough like Thomas Cowper and Croghan's clerk, Roger Walton.[13]

Several Ohio Indians that stayed with Weiser since last month's treaty in Lancaster, had also tagged along but initially refused to go no farther than Croghan's house. Amongst these Indians was Scarouady,[14] the Oneida chief who was anointed as one of the speakers for the Ohio Indians and who had finally recovered from the unfortunate fall that forced him to be absent from Lancaster last month.[15] Scarouady stayed behind at Pennsborough for a few days to inquire about the intentions of a few families[16] that were settling in the region. Weiser noted in his letter to Provincial Secretary Richard Peters on August 15th that Scarouady was still at Croghan's house as they were crossing the intersection of the Tuscarora Path and were twenty-four miles from Standing Stone (Huntingdon, Pennsylvania) on the Juniata River.[17]

---

10. Croghan's trading house was located along the Beaver River (called Beaver Creek in the eighteenth century) near Kuskusky, where the town of New Castle lies today.
11. William Franklin was an ensign in the company of Captain John Diemer.
12. Franklin's printing office was located on 139 Market Street in Philadelphia.
13. Thomas Cowper was mentioned in several letters written by Croghan and Trent. He also assisted Trent when he became a district justice later in Frederick County, Virginia in 1753, (December 10, 1753 Thomas Cresap v. Richard Pearis, University of Pittsburgh Archives). Roger Walton was the bookkeeper for Croghan and Trent's tanning yard, (Letter of Thomas Cookson to Croghan and Trent, November 23, 1751).
14. Scarouady or Scaruneate was also known as Monacatootha or Monacatoocha. Monaca, Pennsylvania is named for him.
15. This specific treaty took place in Lancaster on July 19, 1748.
16. One of the head of these families was a man named Jacob Pyatt.
17. Pennsylvania Archives Series One, Vol. 2, 15.

On the twentieth, they arrived at the abandoned village of Asunepachla (Frankstown, Pennsylvania), where the Lenape and Shawnee moved on, "leaving no Houses or Cabins."[18] Here, they left behind four of Croghan's servitors because of an unknown illness before moving west on the Kittanning Path.[19]

Trent traveled over one hundred more miles on this path before he reached the Ohio for the first time. According to Weiser, the convoy crossed the Kiskiminetas River at the future site of Saltsburg, Pennsylvania and traveled twenty-six miles to leave their supplies at Chartier's Old Town on the Allegheny on the 25th.[20] Chartier's Old Town is today known as Tarentum, Pennsylvania.

It must also be noted that prior to settlers coming to the Ohio country, the Allegheny River was frequently called the "Ohio." This was not a case of mistaken identity by the Indian nations but rather their belief that the Allegheny and Ohio Rivers were one river, not two separate branches. This was why the Forks of the Ohio was also being referred to as the "mouth of the Monongahela"[21] and the shortened "Ohio" name given to this river as high as above Venango or Franklin, Pennsylvania, when referring to the Allegheny River.[22]

When Weiser bartered a canoe for one thousand black wampum beads, they paddled almost twenty miles down the Allegheny River and stayed the night about three miles north of the Forks of the Ohio in a Lenape village called Shannopin's Town.[23] The village was named for the chief who lived in the region and held about twenty families,[24] most of whom came west after being forced out by the Walking Purchase. The river was extremely wide near Shannopin's Town. On his journey in 1750, surveyor Christopher Gist estimated the river was seventy-six poles wide[25] or about 1,254 feet wide.

The next morning, on the 27th,[26] the convoy paddled south in the rain about six or seven miles to the mouth of Chartier's Creek that flowed into the Ohio River just below the Forks. Here was a large prehistoric Native mound[27] and a town of Seneca Indians who were a member of the "Six Nations."

---

18. Thwaites, 22.
19. The Kittanning Path ran east-west from the town of Frankstown, Pennsylvania on the Juniata River to the village of Kittanning on the Allegheny River (called the Ohio).
20. Thwaites, 23.
21. Wainwright, 38. Cherry, 46 and 93.
22. Galbreath, 99–100.
23. Shannopin's Town was located about three miles above the city of Pittsburgh (Forks of the Ohio) near Thirtieth Street along the Allegheny River. Cherry, 62–63.
24. Darlington, 34.
25. Ibid.
26. Thwaites, 24–25.
27. The mound stands about sixteen feet high and eighty-five feet wide. It was believed to be built by hand by the Adena people between 200 B.C. and 100 A.D. Today a blue historic sign marks the spot in McKee's Rocks at the end of Sproul Street near the Ranger Field ballpark.

View from the 31st Street Bridge, just a few miles north of the "Point" in Pittsburgh. Immediately to the left along the Allegheny River was the site of the Lenape village of Shannopin's Town. (Author photo.)

When they landed ashore, they were all greeted by "a great many guns"[28] and spent the day in their company. Weiser described the encounter as they greeted the self-proclaimed authority on the Ohio, who might have been upset had they decided to paddle past her village.

> We dined in a Seneka Town, where an old Seneka Woman Reigns with great Authority.[29]

The Seneca woman he was referring to was known as Queen Aliquippa. The French explorer Céloron also met her on his "lead plate" expedition the following year in 1749 and said, "She looks upon herself as a queen, and it is entirely devoted to the English."[30] She lived later on the Forks of the Youghiogheny and Monongahela Rivers near the future town of McKeesport when a young George Washington and guide Christopher Gist visited her in 1753.[31]

---

28. Thwaites, 24.
29. Ibid.
30. Galbreath, 28.
31. Journal of George Washington 1753–54, 22.

Later that evening, they finally arrived at Logstown (near Baden, Pennsylvania) on the northern shore of the Ohio River, about eighteen miles below the Forks of the Ohio. The village was composed of about fifty cabins[32] of several Indian nations, including the Shawnee and all six members of the Haudenosaunee Confederacy composed of the Seneca, Cayuga, Mohawk, Onondaga, Oneida, and Tuscarora people.

The neighboring Lenape and Wyandots (Huron) also made an appearance at Logstown, joining the others in their customary salute of firing their guns to show approval of their arrival. Weiser or Trent witnessed about one hundred guns firing.[33]

While some of the Indians journeyed back to Chartier's Old Town to fetch the goods they left behind with Croghan's servitors, Trent and the others followed Weiser to the large Native town of Kuskuskies[34] to have wampum belts made and to request the presence of the inhabitants there to Logstown for a council.[35] Kuskuskies were found along Beaver Creek, where the present town of New Castle stands today.

In September, the council began with His Majesty's flag[36] raised above the village and a renewal of friendship between all those in attendance. For the Wyandots, they gave them a quart of whiskey and a roll of tobacco[37] for becoming brethren with the English. The Seneca were given a large string of black and white wampum beads[38] to show the wounds were healed from past transgressions, including most recently when they attacked the English and took prisoners in Carolina.

Like the Seneca Queen Aliquippa, Weiser, Croghan, Franklin, and Trent paid their respects to the "King" of the of the Shawnees next. Their leader was Kakowatcheky,[39] the elderly sachem who removed his people from the Delaware Water Gap area to Logstown in the early 1740s. Trent described his age as about one hundred fourteen years in 1748.[40] The sachem was gifted a woolen cloth for trading called a stroud, a blanket, a shirt, a pair of stockings, a large twist of tobacco, and a match coat which was a loosely made coat of deer skins.[41]

---

32. Galbreath, 36.
33. Thwaites, 24.
34. Croghan and Trent both called it Kuskusky in 1748, while Christopher Gist called it Kuskuskies in 1753.
35. Thwaites, 29.
36. His Majesty's flag was the King's colors or the flag of Great Britain. Since 1707, it was a combination of the red cross of St. George from England and the white cross of St. Andrew from Scotland. It wasn't until after 1801 did the red cross of St. Patrick from Ireland come onto the flag in present-day.
37. Thwaites, 30.
38. Ibid., 31.
39. Trent pronounced the Shawnee chief's name as "Caw-caw-wi-chaw-kee."
40. Trent's Remarks 1757, 2.
41. Thwaites, 32.

Kakowatcheky thanked them but took no other part in the rest of the council. It seemed he left his vocal counterpart to speak for the Shawnees and the Six Nations. Trent explained later that this orator's close association with the old Shawnee king was why the English called him the "Half-King."[42] The Six Nations, however, called the Seneca speaker by his birth name, "Tan-a-riss-on" or "Tannar- iss-on."[43]

The author must note that the spelling Tanacharison, though widely used by most contemporaries, is probably incorrect. Weiser, in his journal to the Ohio, recorded his name like Trent as "Thanayieson" and "Tannghrishon."[44] The German-born Weiser was spelling his name phonetically so it can be stated with much certainty that there was no "ch" sound found in his name. The silent "g" sounded also like the pronunciation of Croghan's surname (Crow-han).

Tanarisson's speech declared that it was not their intention to break the friendship because "by the Instigation of the Evil Spirit, struck their Hatchet into our own Body like for our brethren the English & we are of one body."[45] Tanarisson wanted to make it clear that animosity displayed by a few did not mean they all had changed their ways. The Six Nations and the others at this council always thought of the English as friends and wanted to keep it that way.

Tanarisson explained the wounds had healed, and it was time to move on. He explained "that the Chain of Friendship which is of so long standing may be preserv'd and unhurt."[46] This was good news for those men like Weiser, Trent, and Croghan. The Indian nations were pleased with the presents from Pennsylvania and Virginia (Weiser recorded he gave them ten thousand grains of white and black wampum)[47] and even more so with their vow to honor the proclamation to stop traders from selling liquor to them.

The chain of friendship continued, and it opened trading routes for not only Pennsylvania but possibly Virginia, too.[48] As a result, these provinces could now send their traders west into the Ohio country to the Great Lakes region. The council was a success and was the last such council or treaty. Trent played such a supporting role by just being in attendance.

After they returned home, Trent and Croghan were paid a visit by John Hayes on October 19, 1748,[49] who gave them some alarming news. At Kuskuskies, Trent's acquaintance and former Shippen employee Hugh Parker

---

42. Trent's Remarks 1757, 2.
43. Ibid.
44. Thwaites, 42.
45. Ibid., 34.
46. Ibid.
47. Pennsylvania Archives Series One, Vol. 2, 17.
48. Sipe, 107.
49. Pennsylvania Archives Series One, Vol. 2, 16–17.

had escaped capture by the Indians after Parker had also one of his hands killed when the Indians thought the person leaving his house was him. Apparently, Hayes told Trent that Parker had escaped from being tied up and rode bareback thirty miles to Logstown.[50]

Trent was probably relieved his friend was alive, but he seemed more concerned as to his questionable whereabouts in that part of the Ohio country. Parker had left the service of the Shippen and Logan firm before Trent to pursue the fur trade in Maryland but wondered why Parker had been heading to Lower Shawnee Town[51] with a wagon of liquor when he was captured.

Trent wrote to Provincial Secretary Peters to voice this concern while proposing to head to England to seek reimbursement for the pay certificate voucher from his military service for the King. He was still owed two hundred and fifty-seven pounds and ten shillings[52] and wanted to use his income, along with Croghan's, to attract a third partner from Philadelphia's mercantile elite. Trent also requested that Peters write a letter of introduction[53] to the brainchild of the Walking Purchase and current chief proprietor of Pennsylvania, the English-born Thomas Penn, who now resided in London.

Peters immediately reached out to Richard Hockley, who ran a mercantile store on Water Street[54] across from Fishbourne's Wharf[55] that stored various dry goods such as men's and boy's caster felt hats and worsted damask. "Dickey,"[56] as the Penn family called him, was also a "protege" of the same person that Trent wished to be introduced to. So, a plan was drafted and quickly presented to Croghan and Trent. Hockley had Trent, when he sailed for England try and borrow one thousand pounds sterling from his mentor Penn to purchase goods in London in exchange for becoming their third partner. He even agreed to advance Trent the one thousand pounds.[57]

It was a good deal, but Trent wanted to make his trip worthwhile. Plus, he was thinking of the firm's future seasonally. So, he counteroffered to borrow two thousand pounds[58]; that way there were one thousand pounds worth of goods for the upcoming summer and one thousand pounds of goods for the fall. The deal was mutually accepted, and the articles of partnership began on

---

50. Ibid.
51. Lower Shawnee Town was located in Portsmouth, Kentucky at the mouth of the Scioto River. Trent's mention of Lower Shawnee Town in his October 20, 1748 letter was considered by many, one of the first references of this Indian village.
52. Colonial Records of Pennsylvania, Vol. 5, 178.
53. HSP, Richard Peters Letterbook, Richard Peters to Thomas Penn, November 24, 1748.
54. *Pennsylvania Gazette,* May 27, 1742.
55. Fishbourne's Wharf was on the Delaware River just below Walnut Street.
56. Jenkins, 135.
57. HSP, Cadwalader Family Papers, Articles of Partnership, November 24, 1748.
58. HSP, Richard Peters Letterbook, Richard Peters to Thomas Penn, November 24, 1748. Articles of Partnership, November 24, 1748.

November 14, 1748.⁵⁹ The partnership between them was obligated to last five years, and each man additionally was responsible for putting up three hundred and sixty-nine pounds nineteen shillings⁶⁰ for the purchase of horses and goods to keep the firm active until Trent's return from England.

It was also agreed that Hockley himself handled any business concerning the firm in Philadelphia. All other business dealings outside the city, accounting, bookkeeping etc., were run by Croghan and Trent, with Trent handling most, if not all, the bookkeeping.

Despite his obvious interest, Peters was excluded as a potential investor because of his prejudicial stature as Provincial Secretary. The trio of Hockley, Trent, and Croghan finally agreed to share equally any profits they received. The shipments were stamped with the trademark HTC inside a rhombus.⁶¹

The original HTC trademark of Hockley, Trent and Croghan from 1748 to 1752. (Author photo.)

With their partnership finalized, Trent traveled to Philadelphia and bought passage on the *Beulah*, a new one-hundred-and-sixty-ton ship that was docked near Arch Street at the wharf of Samuel and Benjamin Shoemaker. Captain James Child commanded the ship and was to set sail by the 20th of November.⁶²

It was a dangerous time to travel across the cold Atlantic Ocean with the uncertain weather, but Trent must have felt a small bit of comfort knowing the *Beulah* even though carrying freight for London also had "extraordinary Accommodation for passengers."⁶³ He arrived successfully in England sometime in January 1748\49.

The initial meeting with the son of William Penn, however, did not fare so well. Trent learned when he arrived that Thomas Penn had already invested his time and money prior to another firm owned by Thomas Hyham and his son. The Hyam firm also dealt with Indian goods, so Penn did not share Hockley's excitement about the venture as his "protege" did. It was too risky to invest more into westward trade, which he probably felt was a gamble in its infancy. Penn was impressed by Trent's character, though and did offer five hundred pounds to him for Hockley's advance, saying, "Notwithstanding what I've now wrote, I am unwilling to disappoint your scheme, and let Capt. Trent who has merit go back disappointed."⁶⁴ Trent probably saw this as a partial win with Penn since the door had now been opened to London's mercantile elite.

---

59. HSP, Cadwalader Family Papers, Hockley, Trent and Croghan, May 20, 1752.
60. HSP, Cadwalader Family Papers, Hockley, Trent and Croghan, Case & Articles of Agreement 1748–1749.
61. Ibid., October 20, 1750 Account.
62. *Pennsylvania Gazette*, November 17, 1748, 3.
63. Ibid.
64. Wainwright, 25. Penn Letterbook Volume II, Thomas Penn to Peters February 20, 1749/50.

Today the present site of the former Royal Exchange where Trent visited both times when he journeyed across the Atlantic. Though this current building is still called the "Royal Exchange", it was completed around 1844 in the Cornhill Ward of London and is now home to thirty-three stores and five restaurants and cafes. Author photo.

So he went first to see Elias Bland, the silent partner and co-owner[65] of the *Beulah* with the Shoemakers of Philadelphia. Bland was around the same age as the late twenty-something Trent and had done his apprenticeship with Philadelphia Quaker merchant John Reynell[66] while Trent learned under Edward Shippen III. It was probably Bland who personally introduced Trent to the mercantile world of London. If Philadelphia once made his teenage eyes widen, the exchange building in England's bustling metropolis made him stand in awe. Trent spent the next three months networking and even hooking in a few potential investors for their new firm. Merchant John Samuel advanced the firm five hundred pounds worth of goods,[67] as well as the firm's potential London liaison, Elias Bland.[68] The London trip, though, wasn't a total success. Trent still failed to receive his pay for military service under the King, so he left

---

65. Pennsylvania Magazine of History and Biography (PMHB), Vol. 24, 500.
66. John Reynell (1708–1784) was a Quaker merchant who had a mercantile firm with his nephew Samuel Coates, the future treasurer of the Library Company of Philadelphia.
67. HSP, Cadwalader Family Papers, Hockley, Trent and Croghan, Account of John Samuel 1748–1749.
68. Ibid., Account of Elias Bland 1748–49.

his task under the watchful eye of Elias Bland. He hoped that Parliament finally honored the pay certificate and Bland could send the sum he was owed.[69]

Trent left London via the port of Gravesend, almost thirty miles to the southeastern tip of England. On March 20, 1748/49[70], he sailed for Philadelphia aboard the *Myrtilla*, a large two-hundred-and-fifty-ton ship with ten guns captained by Richard Budden and owned by Jewish merchants Moses Franks and Nathan Levy.[71] The consignment of goods provided by Thomas Hyam and his investor Thomas Penn was also aboard this ship, accompanying Trent. The five hundred pounds worth of goods consisted of knives, looking glasses, calicos, linens, vermilion, and twenty barrels of cannon and pistol powder.[72] Trent and the goods arrived at the sizable Hamilton Wharf near Dock Street in Philadelphia just before the 25th of May 1749.[73] The passengers and cargo were met by fair weather and intermittent rain as they arrived.[74] Trent unloaded the firm's cargo, probably storing the casks of gunpowder in a powder magazine to keep dry near Hockley's store and taking the remaining trade goods to Croghan's plantation on the Conodoguinet Creek.

He traveled west through another storm of "flying clouds"[75] that spewed rain on him and arrived back eventually at Pennsborough. Unfortunately, both Trent and Croghan didn't realize the rain-soaked barrels carried a dark secret along with their contents. In June of 1749, only a few weeks after Trent returned by way of Gravesend, England, he contracted intermittent fever.[76] Intermittent fever, or malaria as it was more commonly known later, was believed to have been contracted in the eighteenth century by ingesting vapors from brackish areas or swamplands, hence "malaria" being Italian for "bad air." A person could only contract malaria if they were bitten by a mosquito carrying the disease from stagnant, brackish water or marshland. One could argue Trent might have contracted it living near the marshes along the Conodoguinet, but this water was not brackish or stagnant, so it had to be brought from somewhere else, i.e., the barrels. The wooden barrels were soaked with seawater from the *Myrtilla* and now, after the recent storm, from rainwater. This dampness became prime breeding grounds for mosquitoes and their larvae to thrive, from the estuarine waters of the Thames River to the confinements around Croghan's plantation.

---

69. Trent was still owed 257 pounds 10 shillings for his captaincy in the King's service.
70. *Pennsylvania Gazette*, September 22, 1748, 3.
71. Ibid.
72. Wainwright, PMHB Vol. 72 No. 4, 355.
73. *Pennsylvania Gazette*, May 25, 1749, 3.
74. Kalm, Vol.2, 754.
75. Ibid.
76. HSP, Cadwalader Family Papers, Elias Bland to William Trent July 9, 1749.

It was also why his partner Croghan was also stricken with that sickness.[77] Trent, along with his partner, suffered chronic distempers, cold shivers, and finally sweating due to the high fever in the June heat. It might have even left him with a dusky, yellow complexion or "jaundiced."

Both were weakened immensely, and it was not how they wanted to begin season one of their new firm. The business had been booming, and now they both spent the month bedridden or sickly, hoping that Peruvian Bark from a South American cochina tree possibly arrived in the stores along the Philadelphia waterfront[78] to reduce their ailments. It wasn't until July when either of them had been well enough to conduct business around the plantation or with their contacts in London.

Croghan seemed to have been feeling better to garner a reply to the express he received from Pennsylvania Governor James Hamilton on the night of July 2nd. Hamilton had been inquiring if there were any intentions of the French to interfere with the Indian trade in the Ohio country, and Croghan concurred that "It was assumed ye French Desinge to hinder the English from Makeng a setlement on Ohio."[79]

Croghan knew it was probably inevitable that the French made every opportunity "to make use of their unfair Methods to bring over all ye Indians they can to their Interest,"[80] so he sent one of his servitors to ask the half-Indian Andrew Montour if "the French were on Lake Erie or there Abouts."[81] He also was going to visit Logstown within the week to reassure the interests of the Indian nations there, but for Croghan, the French were not the current problem.

After Trent had told Peters and Croghan about his friend Hugh Parker being captured near Kuskuskies and before he left for England, Croghan asked around his trading house on Beaver Creek about Parker's intentions.

It seemed Parker was doing more than just transporting liquor to the Lower Shawnee Town. Both Trent and Croghan were told that Parker and fellow Maryland trader Thomas Cresap were conducting business for Virginia and "spread amongst ye Ingans last Fall that ye Virginians was going to Setle a Branch of Ohio called the Yougagain & that then they would supply the Indians with goods Much Cheaper than they Col'd be suplyd from Pensilvania."[82]

The proposed undercut of the Pennsylvania trade was a power move, but according to Croghan had little effect on the Ohio Indians. He seemed to think

---

77. Wainwright, 29.
78. *Pennsylvania Gazette,* July 26, 1739.
79. Pennsylvania Archives Series One, Vol. 2, 31.
80. Ibid.
81. Ibid.
82. Ibid.

the Virginians were more interested further west toward the Wabash River, but that "vile fellow Cresap," as Peters once called him[83] and Parker, were a part of something bigger. Trent apparently had just cause for his suspicions about his friend Parker back in October. Both Parker and Cresap were now both members and agents of the sixteen-person Ohio Company,[84] the land speculation group that was continuing to rise in power and causing quite a stir for those in the province of Pennsylvania.

While Trent had been stricken with malaria in June, the Ohio Company had gathered for a meeting at the Stafford Courthouse in Virginia. On June 21, 1749, the committee named Hugh Parker their 'factor,"[85] in charge of their accounts, credits, and supplies. His former co-worker under Edward Shippen III had done well for himself, especially since the Ohio Company had been granted a royal charter for their 200,000 acres near the Forks of the Ohio.

About a week later, their London liaison Elias Bland sent his empathetic wishes to Trent on July 9th, 1749, to "congratulate thee on thy Recovering from thy Intermitting fever and also to heartily wish the Long life of Good Health & every Desirable Comfort."[86] Bland also gave Trent a promising update on the status of his military reimbursement saying that "Payments Ordered of the Bills & Certificates soon after the Parliament meet after the 16th Inst."[87]

With the summer almost over, the firm needed to make up for lost time. While Croghan traveled with supplies to the Ohio to find out more about the Ohio Company's interest for Governor Hamilton, Trent remained at the Pennsborough plantation to handle the firm's bookkeeping, process, and send the shipments of skins to Hockley in Philadelphia, and co-manage the tanning yard. Three enslaved individuals assisted Trent[88]: Croghan's clerk, Roger Walton; Croghan's kinsman, Thomas Smallman[89]; and the younger half-brother of Croghan, Edward Ward. It was believed Croghan's father died when he was a boy, so his mother eventually remarried a trader who frequented Logstown and the Lower Shawnee Town named Thomas Ward.[90] Young Edward was the result of this union.

Trent was thankful for all the help while his business partner was away in the Ohio country. The opportunity for considerable gain was endless and

---

83. James, 13
84. Mulkearn, 23.
85. Ibid., 24.
86. HSP, Cadwalader Family Papers, Elias Bland to William Trent July 9, 1749.
87. Ibid.
88. Ibid., Hockley, Trent and Croghan Accounts of Skins.
89. Philadelphia County Wills, Book S, 164.
90. Philadelphia County Wills, Book S, 164.
that Thomas Ward was one of the English traders who had dinner with Céloron in his tent at the Lower Shawnee Town.

was probably why they kept balances open and remittances on hold for their Philadelphia and London creditors. Trent described the situation as leaving no stone unturned, saying, "We have been obliged to buy a great many goods in order to fit out our hands."[91]

Their first season had yet to garner a profit, but Croghan and Trent were confident the fall yielded the necessary financials to guarantee a bonafide successful season. It began first when Croghan mortgaged his property on the Conodoguinet Creek and a few other tracts to Richard Peters for one thousand pounds.[92] The Pennsylvania currency was used then to purchase the following goods for the Indians of the Six Nations:

> 476 pieces of strouds, 800 Duffield blankets, 919 pairs of half thick stockings, 400 shirts, 40 pieces of calico, 32 pieces of calamanco, 40 pieces of embossed surge, 100 pounds of Vermilion, 82 gross of gartering, 100 pieces of ribbon, 100 dozen of knives, 1000 pounds of gunpowder, 2000 pounds of bar lead, 5000 gun flints, 100 pounds of brass kettles, 406 pounds of thread, 2000 needles, twenty dozen Jew harps, thirty dozen tobacco tongues, and 200 pounds of tobacco.[93]

When Croghan finally returned to Pennsborough the following spring, Trent, as well as Governor Hamilton, was pleased to find it led to a solid investment. In August of 1749, Croghan acquired 200,000 acres of land in the vicinity of the Forks of the Ohio. The deed dated August 2, 1749, was probably composed before Croghan left Pennsborough, leaving the possibility its terms of legality were drawn up and penned by the better scribe, Trent.[94] The first tract was 100,000 acres on the south side of the Monongahela River from opposite Turtle Creek and then down the River Monongahela to its junction with the River Ohio, thence to the mouth of Raccoon Creek[95] and up that Creek ten miles. The second tract was fifteen miles long and was about 60,000 acres on both sides of the Youghiogheny River, including the Native village of Swiegly Old Town[96] at the mouth of Big Sewickley Creek between present-day Sutersville and West Newton, Pennsylvania. The last tract was 40,000 acres, beginning on the east side of the River Ohio to the northward of Shannopin's

---

91. HSP, Cadwalader Family Papers, Trent to Elias Bland October 8, 1749.
92. Lancaster County Deed Book A, 56. Mortgage of George Croghan to Richard Peters June 27, 1749.
93. Hanna, Vol. 1, 360.
94. Trent having written legal documents such as land indenture agreements since 1742 or 1743, probably more than likely drafted this specific deed to the Six Nations dated August 2, 1749.
95. The mouth of Raccoon Creek is along the Ohio River about six miles south of Rochester, Pennsylvania.
96. Swiegly Old Town also became the future site of a George Croghan plantation with fenced fields and planted grains in 1754.

Town, several courses onto the Monongahela, then up to the mouth of Turtle Creek adjoining the previous first tract.[97]

It was a monumental acquisition for all parties involved, and all it took was the wagon loads of goods previously purchased with Peter's mortgage payment for the chiefs of the Six Nations, Tanarisson and Scarouady. This also offset the rumor of the half a million acres[98] the Ohio Company was granted from King George II once they began settlements and outposts in the Ohio country.

Yet even as more reports came about the Ohio Company agents skulking in the west, Croghan and Trent's benefactor Richard Peters was more concerned about another rival, threatening from the north. According to Peters, "The Indian trade is in the most flourishing condition and I know of but one thing that can hurt it, that is the French governor of Canada."[99] Peters was, of course, referring to the French detachment sent recently by Governor General of Canada, Roland-Miche Barrin de La Galissoniere[100], to the Ohio country during the past summer of 1749. While Trent and Croghan were stricken with malaria, La Galissoniere ordered an expedition from Lachine, a borough of Montreal, to rekindle the trade relations with the Indians of the Ohio Valley and the traders of New France. On June 15, 1749, this expedition led by the former commandant of Fort St. Frederick and Detroit, Pierre Joseph Céloron de Blainville, left the region of Montreal and traveled south across Lake Erie with a detachment of two hundred men to the villages of Logstown, Lower Shawnee Town, and Pickawillany. On this trip, Claude-Pierre Pécaudy de Contrecoeur, the future commandant of Fort Duquesne, was his second-in-command.[101]

Croghan arrived in Logstown probably on the 15th or 16th[102], only a few days after Céloron and his men left on the morning of August 12th. The accounts about Céloron's visits were told to Croghan by the residential Indian nations, and Trent recorded them at Pennsborough in the following spring.

They turned up in a later document dated 1757 that Trent wrote after a council fire at Easton in July of 1757.[103] The ten-page memorandum[104] focused on the events Trent heard or witnessed from 1749 to 1757 and was personal commentary against the French propaganda scattered throughout Europe and

---

97. This third tract had included the eventual residence of John Fraser in the summer of 1753 at Turtle Creek and Croghan's trading house on Pine Creek near present-day Etna, Pennsylvania. Hanna, Vol. 1, 360–61.

98. The Ohio Company was given a royal grant of 200,000 acres from King George II and was promised an additional 300.000 acres if one hundred families settled on this land within seven years.

99. HSP, Penn Correspondence IV, 245, Richard Peters to Thomas Penn October 26, 1749.

100. Roland-Michel Barrin de la Galissonière (1693–1756) was the French Governor of New France from 1747–1749.

101. Galbreath, 14.

102. Trent in his remarks said Croghan arrived at Logstown a few days after Céloron and his men. Céloron wrote he left on the morning of the 12th, so we can assume it was the 15th or 16th of August 1749.

103. Numerous references throughout the document suggest Trent wrote these remarks in the early fall of 1757.

104. The ten page manuscript was acquired in 2002 by the William L. Clements Library at the University of Michigan in Ann Arbor, Michigan.

the colonies. Since the author had pages of this memorandum previously published for the first time in book form, the document is referred to by the author as "Trent's Remarks 1757."[105] Trent spent the first few pages speaking about "Monsieur Céloron,"[106] as he referred to him.

In retrospect, most historians agree the expeditionists' inability to change the Ohio Indians' sympathies to the English and to evict the English traders led to this mission being called a failure. The French had even tried to claim the territory by marking it for King Louis XV, but that had little or no effect. Trent described their attempt to "take possession of that country for the French king,"[107] saying that every "remarkable Creek & river & nailed Tin Plates on the Trees and sunk some at the mouth."[108] At Logstown, the Indians told Croghan those were the "same many of which Iron and Tin plates on the Indians found as they had spies watching the French all the way."[109] One such lead plate was eventually presented to Colonel William Johnson at his limestone residence at Mount Johnson in New York. On December 4, 1750, a Cayuga sachem presented Johnson with a "piece of writing which the Senecas our Brethren got by some artifice from Jean Cour."[110] The plates like that one were about eleven inches long, seven and a half inches wide and about one-eighth of an inch thick.[111] It bore the date 1749 and the inscription of Louis XV. This plate given to Johnson was taken from near the Niagara River where it was originally buried by Phillipe-Thomas Chabert de Joncaire, interpreter and advisor for Céloron. Later, Joncaire dined with the young Major George Washington in the former John Fraser house at Venango in December of 1753.[112]

The "removal" of the plates was not the worst encounter the French experienced. At Logstown, when Céloron appeared in sight, "The Indians would immediately hoist the English Colors and the Shawnee king Kakowatcheky (whom Trent saw with Weiser) about 114 years of age Set his back against the Flag Staff with his Gun in his hand and desired the young man to kill them all."[113] Their lives were spared, however, by the English traders residing there intervening. The inhabitants only proceeded to shoot at their feet and through the French flag and the French encampment along the shoreline of the Ohio. It

---

105. A portion of the Trent manuscript was first published in the journal "Pennsylvania History" Vol. 74, No. 3 called "The Shot Not Heard Round the World: Trent's Fort and the Opening of the War for Empire" by Douglas MacGregor in July of 2007. It was also completely transcribed for the author's previous work, "Pittsburgh's Lost Outpost: Captain Trent's Fort" in 2019. It was in that book, the manuscript was called "Trent's Remarks 1757."
106. "monsieur" is the French word for Mr. or Sir. It was a form of address as in "Mr. Céloron."
107. Trent's Remarks 1757, 2
108. Ibid.
109. Ibid.
110. Jean Cour was the phonetic spelling of Phillipe-Thomas Chabert de Joncaire. O'Callaghan, Vol. 6, 608.
111. Galbreath, 110.
112. Journal of George Washington 1753–1754, 13.
113. Trent's Remarks 1757, 2.

was the English traders who told Croghan that "the English had pity on them seeing Monsieur Céloron and his people much dejected & trembling with fear as they were sure of Certain death, should the traders advise them."[114] They faced similar treatment at the Lower Shawnee Town. The residents there forced the French party to camp along the floodplain on the opposite side of the Scioto River from the main village and were only allowed to use driftwood[115] to burn for their fires.

When Céloron traveled further west to Pickawillany in September, they faced further hostility from the Piankashaw king, "Old Briton," and his people of the Miami Confederacy. Céloron had not reached the outskirts of town when "the Twightwees or Miamis killed two or three of them & came out of town into the open field & challenged the French to fight."[116] Despite the violence against their party, Céloron was still granted an audience with Old Briton around the council fire. After five days of presents and speeches, Old Briton thanked them for journeying to see them.

Céloron and his detachment arrived back in Montreal almost two months later, on November 10, 1749[117] having made a strong opinion about the Indian nations in the Ohio country. He knew for certain it was going to take solid establishments or outposts in those parts of the country if they were to attract their interest. In his report, he did not mention the specificity of the hostilities shown by the Natives but rather summarized his trip: "All I can say is, the nations of these localities are badly disposed towards the French and are entirely devoted to the English."[118]

It was also at about this time in the late fall that Croghan arrived at Pickawillany from Logstown. Not only did he hear the French's attempt to remove the Twightwees back to their ancestral lands, but Old Briton informed him that the Confederacy there had received an invite to visit the Governor of Maryland.

On November 25, 1749, Croghan wrote to Provincial Secretary Peters, voicing his dismay over once again the two constituents behind the suggested arrangement, Ohio Company agents Thomas Cresap and Hugh Parker.

"Perhaps maybe a determent to the tread of Pennsylvania," Croghan wrote, "As they went to enter into the tread. I could put a stop to thire going down, if you think itt convenient."[119]

---

114. Ibid., 2–3.
115. The limited access to only the damp, wilted woody debris that adorned the shoreline was clearly meant to show the French were not welcome at Lower Shawnee Town.
116. Trent's Remarks 1757, 2–3.
117. Galbreath, 57.
118. Ibid.
119. Wainwright, 30.

Prosperous Expansion

Croghan's assumption had some merit. The Ohio Company committee had met on January 29, 1749/50, and approved "the purchase made by Parker and Cresap of an Entry for a Tract of Land and improvement on the North Branch of Potomac opposite the mouth of Wills Creek."[120] The land originally belonged to Scottish peer Lord Thomas Fairfax,[121] along what was then the Maryland-Virginia border, specifically lots one, five, fourteen, fifteen, and sixteen of his grants. The land is found today just across the tied arch Blue Bridge in Ridgeley, West Virginia, near the Fort Ohio historic sign.

Once Parker obtained the grant from Lord Fairfax, he was ordered: "that he do with all possible Expedition build convenient houses & Stores for the reception of the Goods thereon."[122] After it was purchased, the lots became known as the "New Store Tract."[123]

Then came more bad news. At the mouth of Scioto River near the Lower Shawnee Town, a private shipment of trade goods owned by Croghan and Trent, along with traders Robert Callender and Michael Taafe, was en route to some Wyandots when a party of French attacked them.

Among them was Louis Coulon de Villiers, who traveled on the Céloron lead plate expedition, and he was known later on July 4th, 1754, as the only opponent to accept surrender terms from George Washington at a place known as the "Great Meadows." The raiders seized three hundred and twenty-nine pounds, ten shillings[124] in valued goods, including five hundred buckskins and seven horses. The hired hands Luke Irwin, Joseph Faulkner, and Thomas Burke were taken prisoner and sent to the outpost of Ponchartrain du Detroit or Fort Detroit.[125]

This was probably why, in late fall and during the winter of 1749/50, Croghan helped strengthen their defenses in the Ohio country by building a stockade fort[126] at Pickawillany. After Céloron's report spread throughout Canada and Europe, the French were showing more aggression now to any English traders who encroached upon the Ohio Valley near their outposts at Fort Miami (Fort Wayne, Indiana) and Fort Detroit.

---

120. Mulkearn, 171.
121. At one time, Thomas Fairfax, 6th Lord Fairfax of Cameron (1693–1781) owned over five million acres in the Northern Neck Proprietary of Virginia. He is buried at Christ Episcopal Church in Winchester, Virginia.
122. Mulkearn, 171.
123. The New Store Tract or "New Store" became the main base of operations and warehouse for the Ohio Company. On October 25, 1754, Ohio Company treasurer George Mason finally secured the patents for the New Store Tract from Lord Fairfax.
124. Bailey, 36.
125. Ibid., 37.
126. The stockade was built around the main epicenter or warehouse for supplies and the trader cabins with a high wall of split logs. Christopher Gist described four hundred Indian families living at Pickawillany in 1751.

Unfortunately, with almost fifty or more English traders passing through Pick's Town and some who resided there permanently,[127] the village, even with a fort, stood out like a vulnerable lamb that had strayed from its pen. Trent and Croghan knew the raids and harassment were not going to stop, and if this recent robbery near the Scioto was any indication, from now on, this could clearly be bad for business.

---

127. Two permanent residents of Pickawillany at that time, were trader Andrew McBryer and blacksmith Thomas Burney.

Chapter 6

Justice and the Proclaim of Liberty

Trent stared intently at the blank sheet on his desk that he had retrieved from a fresh ream of paper. A lot had changed in the last few months. The Provincial Assembly of Pennsylvania voted on January 27, 1749/50[1], to take lands in western Lancaster County and create a sixth county in the province, joining Chester, Philadelphia, Bucks, York, and their previous Lancaster County. The county was named Cumberland, and from Lancaster County, they took "westward of Susquehanna River (including the land where both he and Croghan's houses were at Pennsborough) and northward and westward of York County for its geographical outline." Now, the borders themselves were meaningless to already established inhabitants, but now, with a recognized county, by law, applications were needed to apply for the unimproved land that fell under this new jurisdiction.

On February 13, 1749/50,[2] Trent applied with the appropriate fee for two hundred acres of land just over a mile south of Pennsborough near the Yellow Breeches Creek to the Provincial Secretary Richard Peters. This land, lying in the East Pennsboro Township now, was then issued on order of a survey to current Surveyor General Nicholas Scull, who owned the "St. George and the Dragon Inn" where Trent previously recruited his company during King George's War in 1746. The final step in the process was obtaining the patents that gave him all exclusive rights to the land in question. According to the warrant process, the patentee for this tract was instead Robert Sterrett (or the guardian), meaning Trent transferred ownership to Sterrett.

---

1. Hain, 185.
2. Pennsylvania State Archives, RG-17, Warrant Registers of Cumberland County, 178.

With more potential settlers (some, including Trent and Croghan, called them squatters) trickling past Pennsborough since last summer, the firm was busier than ever. All hours of the day the plantation of Pennsborough had visitors. There were Indian nations concerned about the recent emigration. There were hired hands like Samuel Arsdale or Robert Roberts[3] going west or returning with trade goods from there. They also had express riders such as James Foley[4] with reports from the Ohio country and Philadelphia, where correspondence came from their London agents.

About a week before, Deputy Surveyor Thomas Cookson passed through and told Trent and Governor Hamilton one of the most suitable places for the "county town" or county seat was the land adjoining the stream called Letort Spring just beyond the few settlements on the said creek. Cookson recorded his plan on March 1, 1749/50, "That there were about two thousand acres of tolerable well-timbered land that may be serviceable to accommodate the Town."[5] Trent was familiar with this territory, having passed it along the Great Road or Frankstown Road and knew how valued the area was or could be once a town square for this seat of the new county was quickly blueprinted out. It was also the reason he and Croghan were considered one of the first applicants for land in Cumberland.

By now there wasn't a person in the Ohio country or Philadelphia that didn't mention Trent and Croghan by name or reputation. The rhombus trademark H, T + C was also everywhere. Either stamped on sold goods or by their established trading posts in the Ohio Valley. There were now seven additional trading houses under Croghan and Trent's name beyond their main center of operations at Pennsborough. Most of them were considered locations for Trent and Croghan's private transactions because they excluded their Philadelphia partner Hockley from the profits and later only claimed their losses from these houses as their own.[6]

From Pennsborough, there was the village of Swiegly Old Town, also referred to as Youghiogheny Big Bottom or "Oswegle Bottom"[7] on the Youghiogheny River. The house there was about twenty-five miles from the Forks of the Ohio and held fenced-in fields and grain in the ground. Near the mouth of Pine Creek, their base five miles above the Forks, there were ten acres

---

3. Bailey, 63–64.
4. It appears James Foley witnessed the termination of the Hockley, Trent and Croghan partnership, signing as a witness to dissolve on May 20, 1752. It was probably Foley that delivered it to Trent from Richard Hockley.
5. Pennsylvania Archives First Series, Vol. 2, 43.
6. Bailey, 61.
7. Several letters involving the Ohio Company including Trent call the area where the mouth of Big Sewickley Creek (near West Newton, Pennsylvania) meets the Youghiogheny River by all three of these names.

Today the present site of Swiegly Old Town owned by George Croghan is found between towns West Newton and Sutersville, Pennsylvania where the Big Sewickley Creek meets the Youghiogheny River. (Author photo.)

of corn surrounded by fencing.[8] When they visited the chiefs of the Six Nations, like the Half-King or Scarouady, a house was used within the village of Logstown on the northwest bank of the Ohio River eighteen miles below the Forks.[9] The same could be said for the storehouse at the mouth of the Beaver Creek (called the Beaver River today)[10] near present-day Rochester, Pennsylvania and at the mouth of the Muskingum River near present-day Coshocton, Ohio. The latter storehouse in the Wyandot town was where Christopher Gist, an agent for the Ohio Company, saw the English colors flying on December 14, 1750.[11] At the Lower Shawnee Town, Croghan described their trading post as "a large storehouse on the Ohio opposite to the Mouth of the River Scioto, where the Shawnees had built their new town."[12] It was also like their large two-story trading house at Pickawillany that sat inside the stockade that Gist aided other hired hands in repairing the fort, by "bringing Loggs to line the Inside."[13] All these places transformed their firm into a frontier conglomerate with skins in such

---

8. Cherry, 45–46. Mouth of Pine Creek is where town of Etna, Pennsylvania lies today.
9. Bailey, 61.
10. Thwaites, 26–27.
11. Darlington, 37.
12. Bailey, 61.
13. Darlington, 49.

high demand it consumed both Trent and Croghan to manage the fluctuating productivity.

Their first full season was a wondrous success, but there were still unpaid balances and outstanding letters of credit or remittances forwarded to them from merchants like John Carson in Philadelphia for nine hundred and thirty-seven pounds ten shillings and Elias Bland in London for six hundred and sixty-four pounds twelve shillings eight pence.[14] Several mercantile firms needed to pay the remaining balances before they requested an extension of credit. Edward Shippen III and Thomas Lawrence's firm in Philadelphia owed two hundred and ninety-five four pence[15], and just about a week ago, on March 3, 1749/50, they received a letter for goods from the London firm Thomas Hyam and Sons. Hyam had received word from Stephen Mesnard, the master of the sloop the *Carolina*[16] they frequently used to transport shipments, "that there was a fair prospect of a good trade & that some skins were intended to be shipped off before winter"[17] which unfortunately for Trent had either still not arrived in London or were intended for another firm before them. Whatever the reason, Trent decided the agents and their accounts across the water had to wait. For now, he had more pressing matters locally. Trent removed the goose quill from his pewter standish[18] resting on his desk, dipped the point in the center and began writing.

With a new county came new laws and certain individuals to enforce the said laws. So, a commission selected thirteen inhabitants[19] within the boundaries of Cumberland County who were leading men of property and title in the region and resided close to the proposed county seat to become magistrates or justices of the peace and common pleas. Trent and Croghan naturally were both selected to fill two of these positions, and on March 10, 1749/50[20] they became official justices of the peace and common pleas for Cumberland County. Though it was one of the lowest-ranking positions in the judicial system, the job was by no means without any respective duties. A justice of the peace handled local criminal arraignments such as misdemeanors or infractions of the county ordinances and approved licenses to trade and conduct civil marriages.

Trent finished his letter of acceptance and signed his name at the bottom. Then he held a crimson wax stick to a candle until the wax began to melt and drip, forming a dark red blot next to his signature. Before the wax dried,

---

14. HSP, Cadwalader Family Papers, Hockley, Trent and Croghan Folders.
15. Ibid., Shippen v. Trent Case 1758.
16. *Pennsylvania Gazette*, November 8, 1750.
17. HSP, Cadwalader Family Papers, Thomas Hyam to William Trent March 3, 1749/50.
18. Ibid., Account with Abraham Mitchell ye 2 Month (April) 19, 1749.
19. Colonial Records of Pennsylvania, Vol. 5, 436.
20. Ibid.

Today this original room, the desk and the chair were all used by the justices of peace or district justices including Trent on the second floor of Widow Piper's Tavern in Shippensburg, Pennsylvania until a second building was built in Carlisle in the summer of 1751. Author photo.

he pressed the brass mold of his signature seal[21] firmly into the blot and then removed it. Trent's seal paid homage to his ancestry in Scotland and the family name. An escutcheon or shield was holding three roses and two swords crossing in a saltire design. Above the shield on the seal was a small, knighted arm holding a scimitar, the crest for the Trent name.[22] When he was finished, he sprinkled pounce[23] all over the letter to have it dry quicker and then he sealed it closed. With his new position, he conducted his "civic" duties in Shippensburg until the proposed county seat and town square was built on Letort Spring.

Around this same time, the Ohio Company began their construction on March 29, 1750, authorizing their factor, Hugh Parker, to build a warehouse to store the company's goods and skins.[24] Since last fall, the Ohio Company's lead-

---

21. Trent's wax seal was found fully intact in three different decades, all sporting the exact same design, verifying his personal seal.
22. This scimitar and three roses can also be found on the seal of William's older half-brother James Trent in the 1720s. For details about the seal see "History of St. Michael's Church" by Hamilton Schuyler, 339.
23. Pounce in the eighteenth century was usually made from pumice or the bones of a cuttlefish ground into a fine powder.
24. Mulkearn, 507, Endnote 182.

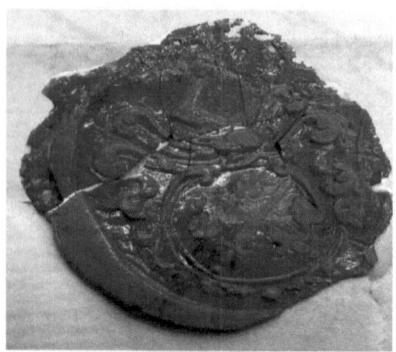 

The original wax seal of Major William Trent used on several documents throughout his life showing the family crest on top with a saltire of swords and three roses in the middle of the shield. (Author photo.)

A copy of the Trent family crest in Scotland, the knighted arm holding a scimitar. (Author photo.)

ing shareholder and newly appointed president of Virginia's Executive Council, Thomas Lee, made quite clear his intentions to the Pennsylvania government.

> His Majesty has been graciously pleased to grant to some Gentleman and Merchants of London, and some of both sorts Inhabitants of this Colony, a large Quantity of Land West of the Mountains, the design of this Grant and one condition of it is to Erect and Garrison a Fort to protect our trade (from the French) and that of any of the neighboring Colonies.[25]

Like Croghan and Trent, Lee believed the French were the biggest threat to their trade in the Ohio country, but he also had complaints pertaining to those men who conducted business in the Ohio country under the Pennsylvania banner. These men, who were no doubt employees under the Croghan-Trent firm, had left Lee with no choice but to voice his frustrations to Governor Hamilton in Philadelphia:

> I'm sorry that's so soon I'm obliged to complain to You of the insidious behavior, as I am informed of some traders from your Province, tending to disturb the Peace of this Colony and to alienate the Affections of the Indians from Us.[26]

---

25. Colonial Records of Pennsylvania, Vol. 5, 423.
26. Ibid.

In the eyes of Thomas Lee and the rest of the Ohio Company committee members, the sooner a warehouse could be built on their recently purchased land along the North Branch of the Potomac in Frederick County, Virginia, the sooner they could protect their royal grant and begin a fort in the Ohio country. For the time being, goods and skins affiliated with the Ohio Company were stored at member Thomas Cresap's house[27] at Shawnee Old Town[28], about fifteen miles away, until the new warehouse was built on the land tract that Hugh Parker had bought from Lord Fairfax.

Meanwhile, in Cumberland County, Trent obtained two more warrants (no. 2 and no. 3) for tracts of land that totaled five hundred acres.[29] Warrant No. 2 was for two hundred acres along Mountain Creek, a branch of the Yellow Breeches Creek, the natural boundary of the outskirts of Cumberland County and at the foot of South Mountain. Warrant No. 3 was three hundred more acres along the Cumberland and York County border near the region called "Chestnut Hill."[30]

It is not known whether he ordered surveys for either of these particular tracts, but Warrant No. 2 was where Trent assisted Thomas Cookson in erecting a sawmill along Mountain Creek in the summer of 1751.[31] This could also be why the South Mountain was called locally "Trent's Hills or Trent's Mountains"[32] and the pass through the mountain was nicknamed "Trent's Gap"[33] after this period. Today, the town of Mount Holly Springs sits at the foot of the South Mountain or "Trent's Mountains." Both tracts were found within the newly formed Middleton Township, whose boundaries began in the north at "Croghan's Gap"[34] in the Blue or Kitochninney Mountain range to almost twenty miles south to just past "Trent's Gap" over South Mountain.

Trent, listed as a resident of Middleton Township on the tax list in 1751,[35] had probably already begun construction of a larger dwelling house by this time in the spring of 1750 along Letort Spring and closer to the proposed county seat area. He still resided temporarily at Pennsborough but moved eventually when the house was completed in the late spring or early summer of 1751. Renovations on the new house or even business, however, were put aside when Provincial Secretary Richard Peters requested his civic obligations and presence.

---

27. Mulkearn, 507, Endnote 182.
28. Shawnee Old Town was called "Skipton" after the birthplace of Cresap in England. Today it is known as just Oldtown, Maryland.
29. Pennsylvania State Archives, RG-17, Warrant Registers of Cumberland County, 178.
30. Ibid.
31. HSP, Cadwalader Family Papers, Thomas Cookson to William Trent June 1, 1751.
32. See Library of Congress, Map of Pennsylvania 1770 by William Scull, Map 10 E7.
33. Ibid.
34. Ibid. Croghan's Gap was a pass through the North or Kittatinny Mountain. Today it is on Route 34 and known as Sterret's Gap.
35. Cumberland County Pennsylvania Archives, Tax Books 1751, Middleton Twp. List.

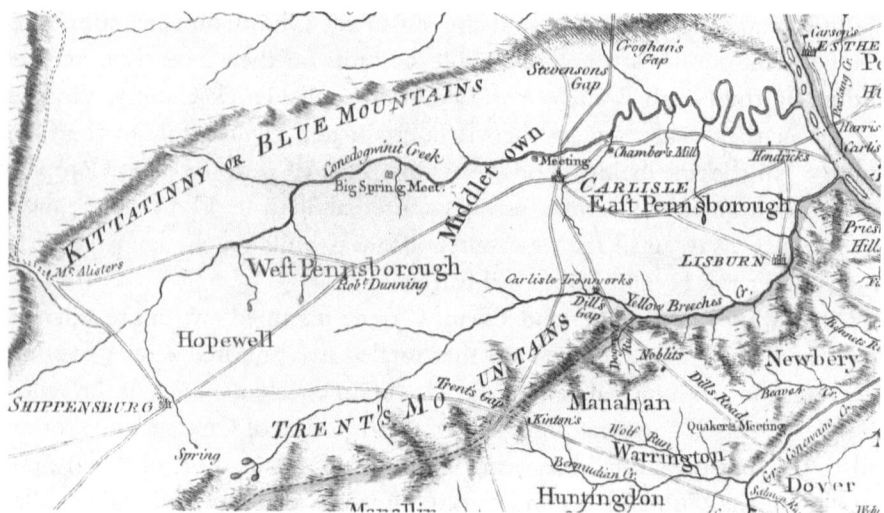

The 1770 map of Pennsylvania by William Scull shows "Trent's Mountains" and "Trent's Gap". Today both were near the present town of Boiling Springs, Pennsylvania just south of Carlisle. (Courtesy of the Library of Congress.)

The Six Nations had come forward to address their concerns that various inhabitants had settled west of the Blue Hills without their permission and, by refusing to leave, violated the agreement between them and the government of Pennsylvania. His partner Croghan held a council with the Provincial Secretary Peters, Conrad Weiser, Andrew Montour, and several deputies of the nearby Six Nations to discuss these matters on May 17, 1750.[36]

It was agreed that not even a year had gone by before these inhabitants had breached the proclamation issued by Governor James Hamilton and the Six Nations on July 18, 1749. According to Hamilton's proclamation, "They were not to settle, or seat themselves and their families on lands not purchased of them, lying westward of the Blue Hills."[37] However, these same families had ignored the province's ordinance and settled in the valley past the Kittochtninny or Blue Mountain ridges along the Juniata River and Little Aughwick Creek.

So, Secretary Peters suggested to the Six Nations that "the Magistrates were come together to go and remove the People off the land at Juniata and other Places by Direction from the Governor, agreeable to the Promise His Honor made the Deputies of the Six Nations last Summer."[38] The deputies of these local Indian nations were pleased by the suggestion but still were worried that

---

36. Colonial Records of Pennsylvania, Vol. 5, 431.
37. Ibid., 394.
38. Ibid., 435.

these evictions were only temporary "Because they believed even after leaving, they will put off now and come next year again."³⁹ They felt it was best if only a few of their own go along with some magistrates to show this came mainly from the Proprietary's government. "We recommend it to the Governor," they stated, "To place two or three Faithful persons over the mountains who may be agreeable to him and Us, with commissions impowering to them immediately to remove every one who shall presume after this to settle there, until the Six Nations shall agree to make sale of their Lands."⁴⁰ The men in attendance gifted the Six Nations with wampum and replied, "With strangest Assurances that they would do their duty."⁴¹

All the justices or magistrates of Cumberland County, like Trent, were then put on notice or alert until orders were given. Five days later, Croghan, Weiser, Peters, and four other justices, Thomas Wilson, Matthew Dill, James Galbraith, and James Finley, along with Sheriff John Potter,⁴² were sent up the north side of Big Juniata River (about twenty miles above the mouth) and ten miles north from the Blue Hills, inside the current boundaries of today's Walker Township in Juniata County. Trent and the remaining nine justices were told to await word from their exploits in the north before meeting them in a few days.

On the 26th or 27th of May, Trent was sent word for him and the other justices to meet in Shippensburg, the temporary seat and site of the Cumberland County courts, by the 28th. By the morning of the 27th of May 1750, Trent put on his beaver hat with "dressing lace" he bought from Philadelphia Hatter Abraham Mitchell⁴³ and saddled his horse. Peters had also informed him and the other justices that along the Juniata River and near the mouth, they had faced some resistance from the squatters. Settlers George and William Galloway resisted when they were ordered to leave immediately and tried to flee before they were arrested. To Sheriff John Potter, they said, "You may take our Lord and houses and do what you please with them, we deliver them to you with all our hearts, but we will not be carried to gaol."⁴⁴

Near the mouth of the Juniata, there was even further resistance when Andrew Lycon presented a loaded gun to the magistrates and Sheriff, saying, "He would shoot the first man that dar'd come nigher."⁴⁵ After even more arrests

---

39. Ibid.
40. Ibid., 436.
41. Ibid.
42. Ibid., 441.
43. The store of Abraham Mitchell was at the corner of Pewter Platter Alley (now the 100 block of Church street running from Second Street to Front Street) in Philadelphia.
44. Colonial Records of Pennsylvania, Vol. 5, 443.
45. Ibid.

along nearby Sherman's Creek, including one such man, Simon Girty Senior,[46] the father of nine-year-old Simon Girty, the controversial figure during the American Revolution, there was great deliberation as to what to do with the cabins once they were emptied of tenants and possessions.

Weiser suggested that "in his firm Opinion that if all the Cabbins were left standing the Indians conceived such a contemptible Opinion of the Government that they would come themselves in the winter, murder the people and set the Houses on fire."[47] They didn't want another Walking Purchase where the Six Nations resented the men of Pennsylvania like the Lenape, so a decision was made. On these conditions and to prevent these families from returning, cabins along the Juniata, the mouth of the Juniata, and Sherman's Creek were burned until nothing remained.

Trent grabbed his pocket pistol and a newly acquired brass blunderbuss,[48] fastening them to his horse. Just in case he faced similar resistance in the Path Valley on or near Aughwick. Then he climbed atop his horse, grabbed the reins, and rode off on the Raystown Path[49] to Shippensburg. On the 28th of May, he and ten other justices[50] arrived at the two-story Widow Piper's Tavern to discuss the proposed plan. The stone tavern, originally built in 1735 by Trent's fellow Pennsylvania captain Samuel Perry from King George's War and later sold to William Piper and his wife, was also the first courthouse of Cumberland County, receiving cases upstairs from 1750 until April of 1751.[51]

In the large room on the bottom floor, the justices Samuel Smith, William Maxwell, George Croghan, Benjamin Chambers (founder of Chambersburg, Pennsylvania), Robert Chambers, William Allison, John Finley, John Miller, Hermanus Alrick, John Galbraith, and Trent informed Richard Peters they planned to evict those squatters on the Tuscarora Path, in the Big Cove area and at Aughwick because they were not leaving without aggression or "submit" to them.[52]

The justices slept upstairs for the next two nights at the tavern until the heavy rain subsided, but on the morning of the 30th, Trent and the others led their horses over the Kittochtinney Mountains or Blue Hills and onto the north-southerly Tuscarora Path[53] near present-day Fannettsburg. Nestled

---

46. Ibid.
47. Ibid., 442.
48. Trent bought four brass blunderbusses on May (3rd Month) 7, 1749.
49. The Raystown Path went east-west from Paxtang (present-day Harrisburg) to the settlement of Raystown (present-day Bedford). It was the southern branch of the Allegheny Path with the Frankstown Road being the northern branch. Wallace, 142–43.
50. Colonial Records of Pennsylvania, Vol. 5, 443.
51. Durant and Fraise, 139.
52. Colonial Records of Pennsylvania, Vol. 5, 443.
53. Wallace, 168.

The outside of Widow Piper's tavern built by Samuel Perry in 1735 and found today in Shippensburg, Pennsylvania at 6 South Queen Street. (Author photo.)

between the West Branch of the Conococheague Creek and Tuscarora Creek, this valley known as Path Valley was a settlement of at least eleven houses or cabins, including the cabin of Jacob Pyatt,[54] whom Scarouady had been suspicious of on Weiser's expedition to the Ohio country in August of 1748.

Trent and the others arrested eighteen men who confessed to trespassing beyond the Blue Hills and were fined a penalty of one hundred pounds[55] and ordered to appear in Shippensburg to hear their case. Eleven houses in all were burned that day by Trent and the others, and according to Peters, "The Trespassers, most of them cheerfully, and a very few of them with reluctance carrying out all their Goods."[56]

This specific settlement just five miles west of the Tuscarora Path was renamed Burnt Cabins in 1758, and it's still known as that today as a remembrance of this day on May 30th, 1750. They did the same to two more

---

54. Colonial Records of Pennsylvania, Vol. 5, 444.
55. Ibid., 443.
56. Ibid., 444.

This region called the "Path Valley" lies in present-day Fannettsburg, Pennsylvania and was the route the justices of peace like Trent traveled on during the Burnt Cabins expedition in 1750. (Author photo.)

This historic sign near McConnellsburg, Pennsylvania marks one of the regions where Trent and others evicted those families who settled illegally on Native land in 1750. (Author photo.)

cabins along the Little Aughwick Creek,[57] where four men were convicted of trespassing, including another individual whom Trent knew personally. How awkward it must have been having to arrest his friend and fellow Pennsylvania Captain Samuel Perry from the 1746-7 Canada expedition and have to try his

---

57. Ibid.

case of trespassing in the very same house once built for Perry's residence in Shippensburg. Before they returned to Shippensburg, they destroyed the final settlement, arresting twenty-three more men in the Big Cove region[58] just above present-day McConnellsburg.

So, by June 1st, their mission was fulfilled. All new settlements lying west of the Blue Hills were destroyed or burned, and inhabitants were removed and arrested. To prevent further squatting in these areas, it was suggested by Governor Hamilton to "get some proper persons to reside there at convenient distances & to give them orders to inform the magistrates ye moment they observe any body."[59] Hamilton was pleased with Trent and the other justices, sending him his gratitude for carrying out their duties and personally thanking them "for the commendable zeal showed by you in the execution of this necessary and serviceable work."[60]

On June 7, 1750,[61] at Croghan's plantation in Pennsborough, the Six Nations also expressed their satisfaction in hearing about removing settlers from their hunting grounds. The conference, held by Secretary Peters, included several chiefs of the Six Nations like Caha-ja-chanah, also known as Broken Kettle, and several of the justices from Cumberland County. Along with Trent and Croghan were Hermanus Alrick, Matthew Dill, the future namesake of present-day Dillsburg, and George Stevenson,[62] the builder of an iron furnace on Mountain Creek, later called Pine Grove Furnace.

Broken Kettle had said he'd heard "that the Secretary had been turning the White People off and was at Mr. Croghan's, whereupon we came here to inquire if this be true and as we find it is, We return to the Government Thanks for their Care of our Lands."[63]

As it put Trent and Croghan in good design with the local Indian nations and over in the Ohio country, it still left them in a tight spot with those who had pending accounts with the firm, both privately and with Hockley, Trent, and Croghan. Specifically, the tanning yard suffered without standing debts and open lines of credit linked to several of the nearby inhabitants like Jacob Pyatt and John Martin,[64] whose cabins they destroyed last month. Most of them couldn't pay their bond for trespassing, let alone settle their accounts now.

By the end of June, business resumed as usual, with shipments of skin sent to their London merchants, some of whom finally received the skins they

---

58. Ibid.
59. Pennsylvania Archives First Series, Vol. 2, 49.
60. Ibid.
61. Colonial Records of Pennsylvania, Vol. 5, 438.
62. Ibid.
63. Ibid.
64. HSP, Cadwalader Family Papers, Hockley, Trent and Croghan Account of Skins.

Present-day site of where George Croghan's barn resided on the Pennsborough property and where the council took place with the Six Nations, Lenape and Shawnee after the Burnt Cabins expedition was over. (Author photo.)

demanded from the previous fall. Trent also had time to indulge himself in buying some expensive appurtenances on the firm's account for his house in Middleton Township. On the 30th of June, he purchased from London merchant John Samuel "Two large gold frames and glasses carved and gilt for sixteen pounds twelve shillings" and "A large Peer Glass with a Walnut Tree frame & Gold edge Carv'd & Guilt for seven pounds."[65] The latter was a long-standing mirror that Trent hung between two windows (a pier in architecture was the upright walls between openings), probably in the parlor of his plantation house where he hosted acquaintances or travelers passing nearby. Pier glass, along with its frame made from English walnut, was clearly meant to display his social status, for Trent paid additionally for packaging of the items in cases, wharf fees for loading and unloading the glass and frames called wharfage, insurance on said items if damaged, and fees for custom men to assess the ship's cargo called searchers.[66]

While he was already in the city, Trent made sure his shipment of skins was loaded on their departing ships. By July of 1750, three different ships

---

65. Ibid., June 30, 1750, Hockley, Trent and Croghan.
66. Ibid.

sailed for London with back orders of fall skins that were supposed to be sent before January. With master Peter Reeve, 1,371 skins were sent on the New York built *Lydia*[67] that Elias Bland and James Pemberton owned. On July 12, more skins were sent on the ship the *Forest* under the tutelage of master Patrick Ouchterlony.[68] Yet after the two ships departed from Plumsted's Wharf near Pine Street, the patience of a few merchants was growing thin.

A letter written on July 9, 1750, by John Samuel arrived, and Trent immediately saw his displeasure in his writing. Interest had accumulated greatly on the current balance with their account with Samuel and his brother, and they wished he or the firm finally paid it. Samuel was growing angry at Trent personally, writing "You wrote me for more goods, but your returns are so slow that Quite Disheartens me not knowing when to depend upon my money."[69] It was apparent Trent had acquired a large amount of credit, and instead of paying it, he asked for even more goods. Samuel indicated that "it had been just over a year since he have had a remittance."[70]

When the third ship, the *Macclesfield*,[71] departed Hamilton's Wharf near Dock Street on July 21st, Trent quickly wrote a letter to Elias Bland that he gave to master Alexander Stupart. It was a follow-up to his friend Bland about a previous shipment he sent in early summer, and since his reprimand from John Samuel, he didn't want other merchants like him requesting immediate remittance for lines of credit that he or the firm couldn't pay now.

"I hope the skins which Mr. Hockley shiped you on the company Acct are come safe to hand," Trent wrote, "and the next proceeds passed to my Credit."[72] Trent also responded to Bland hearing about an update on his military backpay by also declaring "I'm glad to hear there's some hope of the Certificates being paid."[73]

He left the city the same day on the 21st, heading back to his house in Cumberland County, but only rode about twenty-five miles west along the Great Conestoga Road (now Swedesford Road in Malvern, Pennsylvania) before night fell. Then he walked his horse into the stables, grabbed his portmanteau and proceeded into the two-story stone dwelling house of public entertainment known as the White Horse Tavern or "the White Horse"[74] for the night. On

---

67. PMHB, Vol. 26, 134.
68. *Pennsylvania Gazette*, July 12, 1750.
69. HSP, Cadwalader Family Papers, John Samuel to William Trent July 9, 1750.
70. Ibid.
71. *Pennsylvania Gazette*, July 19, 1750.
72. HSP, Cadwalader Family Papers, William Trent to Elias Bland July 21, 1750.
73. Ibid.
74. The White Horse Tavern was originally built by James Thomas of Whitland Township in Chester County before he purchased a tavern license in 1721. The stone house and the barn are still standing today in addition to the newer part that was built in 1790. Today it lies at 606 Swedesford Road in Malvern, Pennsylvania.

This is the original 1721 White Horse Tavern that survives today and is found at 606 Swedesford Road in Malvern, Pennsylvania. (Author photo.)

the bottom floor, Trent indulged himself with beef, oysters, and some spirits.[75] Then he walked up the narrow, spiraling plank steps and slept the night on the second floor.[76]

The next morning, he had ridden almost through Lancaster when he wrote to Richard Peters,[77] realizing he had forgotten to ask his mother if Peters had sent more marriage and trader licenses for him to sign and approve for the county of Cumberland. Apparently, the visit to see his mother never rendered a conversation about Secretary Peters dropping them off to her. Trent wrote, "I'm afraid my Mother has forgot to tell me if you have sent them, please to send them to my Mother's for them."[78]

He also alerted Peters about trouble again in the Ohio country. Ironmaster John Potts (and future founder of Pottsgrove, Pennsylvania) had met Trent that morning, telling him about two hired hands of trader James Young who were presumed missing or dead ever since they arrived at Hockhocking, a Native village near present-day Lancaster, Ohio. After Young sent for them, "They found

---

75. Recent archeological studies were conducted outside the area of the original kitchen and turned up broken bottles, bones from cattle and various oyster shells. This suggests the tavern probably served beef from the grazing cattle on the property and oysters in barrels from Philadelphia and the Lower Counties of Pennsylvania.
76. Like the most taverns, lodging was purchased and spent on the upper floor. Today the original planked staircase and second story floorboards still are intact.
77. Pennsylvania Archives First Series, Vol. 2, 50.
78. Ibid.

This is the original staircase Trent took to his room for the night at the White Horse Tavern. (Author photo.)

the horses and saddles, although Buckles cut from the saddles, but the Men were gone, either killed or taken by the French or Indians, supposed to be done by the Ottoways."[79] Once again, this was most alarming to those like Trent and Croghan, who invested their businesses solely in goods and skins acquired in this territory.

This robbing of goods and possible murder of English traders had little effect on those working diligently along the North Branch of the Potomac River, however. On the newly purchased land in Frederick County, the Ohio Company continued to prepare for the onset of a trading enterprise by building their main warehouse or center of operations. Their factor Hugh Parker had

---

79. Ibid.

hired carpenter John Hammer for "work done in the storehouse making a door cutting out of joice and making a post."[80]

The Ohio Company warehouse was narrowing completion, and soon the "New Store" and the land surrounding it were referred to in letters as the "New Store Tract." It was most likely completed in the early fall of 1750.[81] It was also by this time in October that Hockley shared frustrations with the London merchants began to boil over.

After all, his surname also adorned the trademark label. So, when the skins and goods were so slow to arrive in Philadelphia, and he saw the accumulation of unpaid remittances of so many open accounts, Hockley went to Secretary Peters to complain of his co-partners. Peters, who felt just as frustrated because he influenced Hockley to invest, wrote to Trent on November 13, 1750, and gave him and Croghan an ultimatum: "You and Mr. Croghan should put an end to your own private trading and in lieu thereof that the capital should be augmented."[82]

Peters accused Trent and Croghan of forming a larger trade between the two of them and even asked if the horses were used for personal business instead of what they were intended. He used to describe these intentions as "promiscuous."[83] The letter ended with him pleading with Trent "to send him the true state of all the accounts."[84]

Unfortunately, if he or Croghan thought they could recover or offset these debts in the winter of 1750/51, they were wrong. Winter in the Ohio country was the harshest on record for them financially and so much so that he reported this from one of his hands who returned from the Ohio country: "The winter has been the hardest ever known in these parts and Provisions so scarce that a Peck of Corn will fetch five shillings."[85]

He also suffered the loss of many horses used to transport these said provisions. To make matters worse, even the London merchants were refusing to advance them any anymore credit until their outstanding balances were paid. On February 15, 1750/51, merchant John Samuel wrote to Trent asking for the two hundred and ten pounds, eight shillings, eleven pence[86] he was still owed. He was quite angry and had little patience for any more excuses; it seemed: "I thought instead of letting it increase, you would have lessened long before this

---

80. James, 199.
81. Ibid., 38.
82. PMHB, Vol. 72, 365.
83. Ibid.
84. Ibid.
85. Lancaster Historical Society of Publications, Vol. XXIII, 175.
86. HSP, Cadwalader Family Papers, John Samuel to William Trent February 15, 1750/51.

& beg if not already done you will forward me Remittance & first opportunity."[87] Samuel wrote further, his words seemingly more demanding and bitter as he finished. Their business relationship had already reached the breaking point not even two years after forming it: "Mr. Hockley has paid me on the partnership account 230 pounds, which he says is all he can do at present. I'm in great want of money and I hope you will not disappoint me."[88]

When the end of 1750 drew near, Trent's situation fared no better. He wrote on March 7, 1750/51, to Secretary Peters, concerned over the threats posed by the French that spread at each trading house lying deep in the west. Trent had "Word that a body of French & French Indians intended for the Twightwee Country to destroy the English traders there as soon as the season would permit."[89] These threats had been incessant since the Céloron expedition in 1749, but both he and Croghan could not afford any further losses if their business were going to survive.

In the meantime, an opportunity arose in the early part of 1751 when applications were accepted for three hundred and twelve lots of land[90] in the new county seat of Cumberland County. The settlement, formerly inhabited and founded by trader James Letort, was a new county seat and settlement in Cumberland County called Carlisle. It was no doubt another name for the Scot-Irish influence like its sister counterpart and county Cumberland,[91] named for Cumbria, England, adjacent to the Scotland border. The large emigration of Scot-Irish to this area stemmed most likely from the rebellion of the "Forty-Five,"[92] which forced many Scottish exiles to flee to the colonies in the summer of 1746.

Some of their early houses were collateral damage in their previous summer evicting those settlers west of the Blue Hills. But even that seemed to be in vain. Trent also heard at Pennsborough that "several hundred families intended to remove or emigrate over the hills."[93] He knew this had not sat well with the Six Nations who already had begged his partner Croghan to convince the Pennsylvania government to build a fort in the Ohio country.

---

87. Ibid.
88. Ibid.
89. Ibid., William Trent to Richard Peters March 7, 1750/51.
90. Ridner, 50.
91. Cumberland County in England (now called Cumbria) was the northwestern most county bordering the Scottish counties of Dumfriesshire and Roxburghshire. Carlisle was the county seat of Cumberland and now Cumbria County.
92. The "Forty-Five" was the nickname of the Jacobite Uprising of 1745 in which Charles Edward Stuart or "Bonnie Prince Charlie" failed in his attempt to regain the British throne for his father James Francis Edward Stuart also known as the "Old Pretender". After a disastrous defeat at Culloden on April 16, 1746, it became the final confrontation of the rebellion. Charles Stuart escaped to France and most of Stuart's army headed home or fled to the American Colonies soon after to avoid capture.
93. HSP, Cadwalader Family Papers, William Trent to Richard Peters March 7, 1750/51.

When the Pennsylvania Provincial Assembly decided not to make an official request to build a strong house upon the Ohio,[94] the Six Nations next sought out the Ohio Company and those shareholders from Virginia and Maryland who no doubt wished to build a fort and settlements. At this point, the Six Nations supported any province, foreign or domestic, that protected them and sold them cheap goods.

With the Quaker-run government refusing to finance an outpost that may induce a global conflict, this was the opportunity for the Ohio Company to invoke its power on the Ohio country. They already had hired trader and surveyor Christopher Gist[95] to explore the land of their royal grant, but in the late spring of 1751, the Ohio Company suffered another loss of an influential shareholder, the second one since back in November of 1750, when President of the Ohio Company and Executive Council of Virginia, Thomas Lee succumbed to consumption or tuberculosis.[96] Now, between April 3, 1751, and May 21st, 1751,[97] factor for the Ohio Company and good friend of Trent, Hugh Parker, met his somber fate. For the moment, Lawrence Washington (older half-brother of George Washington) became the current president of the Ohio Company, while a new candidate was needed to replace Parker.

After the loss of his friend, Trent applied for a lot in Carlisle (he was application No.3)[98] and assisted Deputy Surveyor Thomas Cookson in supplying a newly built sawmill on Mountain Creek near the South Mountain. The proposed town of Carlisle began taking shape, with a church and a courthouse being constructed in the center of town. Trent heard disputes or approved trader and marriage licenses in Shippensburg until April of 1751. Then, from July 23, 1751[99], he rode only a short distance to the Carlisle courthouse, a temporary log building that stood in the northeast corner[100] of Carlisle town square and epicenter. It was also at this time Trent's name appeared on the 1751 taxables of Middleton Township in Cumberland County.

His partner George Croghan appeared on the tax list for East Pennsboro but on September 17, 1751, paid less taxes for Pennsborough when he decided

---

94. Colonial Records of Pennsylvania, Vol. 5, 547.
95. Christopher Gist was hired as a surveyor by the Ohio Company on September 11, 1750. His first expedition to observe the Ohio Company lands he left on October 31, 1750, and didn't return to his house upon the Yadkin River in North Carolina until May 19, 1751. He was hired a second time on July 16, 1751, and left to explore the other part of the Ohio Company grant on November 4, 1751. He did not return to the Ohio Company warehouse on the North Branch of the Potomac River until March 29, 1752.
96. Thomas Lee died on November 14, 1750 at his home at Stratford Hall in Virginia. His successor as president of the Ohio Company was Lawrence Washington and he died of consumption (tuberculosis) on July 26, 1752.
97. Maryland Prerogative Court Records, Will Book Volume 28–29, 128. Parker's will was proven on June 19, 1751. His death was confirmed by the Ohio Company committee meeting on May 21, 1751.
98. Ridner, 49.
99. Durant and Fraise, 139.
100. Ibid.

The present site of Carlisle's town square and where a log house was built for the justices of peace like Trent to perform their civic duties in the new county seat of Cumberland County in Carlisle, Pennsylvania. (Author photo.)

to "sell" his tanning yard to his half-brother Edward Ward and clerk Roger Walton for two thousand pounds.[101] This "gift" was obviously to pay off several debts and keep creditors from confiscating it. Along with the tanning yard, he sold four enslaved servants, goods from the trading house and all the cows, sheep, and horses that grazed near the Conodoguinet Creek.[102]

For Trent and Croghan, it was all they could do to keep the firm afloat. After Hockley returned from England in October 1751, he was able to see in London firsthand the balances that remained unpaid from those merchants

---

101. HSP, Cadwalader Family Papers, George Croghan to Edward Ward and Roger Walton September 17, 1751.
102. Wainwright, 58. For a list of these tanyard debts in 1752, refer to Appendix C of this book.

who clearly wanted their money upfront since it had been months and possibly more than a year since Trent or Croghan discharged their accounts.

When Hockley wished to learn the "exact state of their affairs," it was already too late for some creditors. Secretary Peters, to whom Croghan had mortgaged his plantation at Pennsborough, decided to foreclose on the property with several other tracts Croghan owned on October 15, 1751.[103] This included the tanning yard now owned by Ward and Walton, whose bill of sale was deemed invalid by Peters. By law, Croghan could no longer set foot on the property again since now it was repossessed by the mortgagee, Richard Peters. With the loss of his home Croghan moved his residence near Aughwick Creek and traveled to the Ohio country to tend to his trading houses.

Trent was set to join him in the Ohio country, but on September 27, 1751,[104] he officially was elected along with fellow Middleton Township resident Daniel Williams to appear in Philadelphia as the two representatives or delegates of Cumberland County for the Pennsylvania Provincial Assembly. Delegates appeared on returns from five counties of Pennsylvania according to the sheriffs or constables that help organize the elections for the leading vote-getters and report to the State House on Fifth and Chestnut Street in the Quaker city.

Daniel Williams appeared first on October 14th,[105] but Trent was delayed until the next day, arriving on October 15, 1751.[106] He joined fellow delegates such as Griffin Owen and Benjamin Franklin, who represented Bucks County and Philadelphia, respectively, among others.[107] His friend William Franklin was Clerk of the House, and Isaac Norris Jr, the son of his father's former business partner, led the Provincial Assembly as Speaker of the House.[108]

The day Trent arrived was probably different than his usual trips to the city. He still wore his hat dressed in lace but more than likely wore a fancier coat, fine stockings, a silk handkerchief,[109] and instead of riding boots, probably the lavish shoes he bought from Abraham Mitchell. These shoes had buckles with close-set paste stones[110] that were made of high-end glass and mimicked diamonds or fine gemstones.

With his one partner exiled to the Ohio country because of creditors and the other near those angered over their private dealings, Trent had to find some

---

103. PMHB, Vol. 72, 369.
104. Statutes at Large of Pennsylvania, Vol. 5, 155. *Pennsylvania Gazette*, October 10, 1751, 2.
105. Pennsylvania Archives, Eighth Series, Vol. 4, 3467.
106. Ibid., 3468.
107. Ibid.
108. Ibid., 3317. Ibid., 3466.
109. HSP, Cadwalader Family Papers, Account of William Trent to Abraham Mitchell 1751. Trent also listed previously one and half yards of "Brown Broad Cloth" on an earlier 1749 receipt from Mitchell, which presumably was meant for a coat he had used for this meeting.
110. On the account, Trent wrote the paste stone buckles as just "stone buckles."

Justice and the Proclaim of Liberty

The Pennsylvania State House on 529 Chestnut Street is where the Pennsylvania Assembly met in 1751 and is now known as Independence Hall in Philadelphia. (Author photo.)

way to expel the rumors at the London Coffeehouse[111] in the city and to quiet the gentlemen in the State House who already suspected something was amiss. For now, Trent knew his days were numbered, especially if creditors became aware that Croghan's partner and co-signer was somewhere in the city.

So, before the Provincial Assembly adjourned, the delegates from the five counties needed to be in the majority that funding be allowed so the superintendents of the State House could "provide a bell of such weight and dimensions as they shall think suitable."[112] The bell was to be hung and rung in the

---

111. The London Coffee House or "Old Coffee-House" was located near Chestnut Street and Front Street. A second coffeehouse was opened later by printer William Bradford in 1754 and named after the First London Coffee-House. Both were public vendues where traders, merchants, and mariners conducted business, listed advertisements for employment and runaway servants, and purchased passage on ships while drinking imported coffee.

112. Pennsylvania Archives, Eighth Series, Vol. 4, 3470.

proposed bell tower being constructed above their heads in the State House, a gift to honor the fiftieth anniversary of William Penn's Charter of Privileges,[113] the colony's first constitution of laws. Ironically, it was written in the Slate Roof House on Second Street, where Penn resided before the house was sold to Trent's father in 1704.[114]

After Trent and the others cast their vote, Norris and two other superintendents of the State House sent a letter to London agent Robert Charles that they wished to purchase a bell for the State House steeple.[115]

The meeting adjourned and before Trent left the city, he probably at this time purchased another item of luxury, a tall case clock from Philadelphia. Though the exact year of the clock has not been presently known, it has, however, been determined Trent had the clock made in Philadelphia during the early part of the 1750s based on its maker and Trent's availability before most of his time was spent in the Ohio country from 1752 to 1763. The tall case or Queen Anne style grandfather clock stood almost nine feet tall and was handmade from tropical timber native to the West Indies called mahogany.[116] The brass dial face had a silvered ring with engraved Roman numerals (I through XII at intervals of 5) and Arabic numerals for the minutes (5 through 60 at intervals of 5) that were varnished in resins and oils to imitate Asian lacquer work called japanning.[117] Trent also had a moon dial arched above the face to display the different phases of the moon during a given lunar month. A lunar month consists of one complete lunar phase cycle that is equivalent to twenty-nine days, twelve hours, forty-four minutes, and three seconds. Across the gold, five-pointed stars in the sky painted with the color Prussian blue,[118] the moon dial accurately indicated what nights Trent could ride safely on horseback under the light of a full moon, to Philadelphia or the Ohio country for the firm. Eventually, he also used this same moon dial to show when he could harvest crops on his new plantation. Finally, engraved across the silvered arch was the name of its Philadelphia maker, John Wood.[119]

---

113. The Charter of Privileges effective on October 28, 1701 was written by the province's founder, William Penn and used as a frame of government in Pennsylvania. It functioned as Pennsylvania's Constitution until the end of the American Revolution.

114. See previous endnote 51 for information about the Slate Roof House.

115. The three superintendents were Isaac Norris, Thomas Leech, and Edward Warner. The letter was dated November 1, 1751. HSP, Norris Family Papers, Isaac Norris II Letter Book.

116. According to British shipping returns, mahogany came from Jamaica, Bahamas, and the Mosquito Coast (Hondoras). Historic Peachfield Collection.

117. Historic Peachfield Collection.

118. Ibid. Prussian Blue was a dark blue pigment similar to the uniform color worn by infantry and artillery regiments of the Prussian Army.

119. The arched moon phase according to the recent appraisal was undoubtedly the signature handiwork of John Wood Sr. (d. in 1761). John Wood Jr, continued the Philadelphia clockmaking from his father for over thirty years, meeting his fate during the outbreak of yellow fever in the city in 1793.

Justice and the Proclaim of Liberty

The original clock purchased by Trent from Philadelphia clockmaker John Wood Sr in the early 1750's. Today it is owned by the National Society of The Colonial Dames of America in The State of New Jersey at Historic Peachfield in Westampton, New Jersey. (Author photo and courtesy of the NSCDA of New Jersey.)

John Wood Sr. was one of the most significant clock and watchmakers in Pennsylvania, if not the entire colonies. His house and shop were purchased from the late Peter Stretch, another early renowned clockmaker, and it was at this corner of Front and Chestnut Street[120] in Philadelphia where Trent visited to have his clock made. This block, lined with residential clockmakers, became known locally as the "Sign of the Dial."[121]

After John Wood Sr. finished the clock, it was believed the clock was transported to Trent's plantation in Middleton Township, but if weather or transportation became problematic (after all, it was almost nine feet tall), the clock

---
120. Stretch, 228.
121. *Pennsylvania Gazette*, July 12, 1753.

might have stayed temporarily with Trent's mother Mary at her country residence just outside Philadelphia or at her house in the city only a couple blocks away from Wood's shop. Either way, Trent left Philadelphia and stopped briefly at his house near Letort Spring before heading to join his partner Croghan in the Ohio country.

Perhaps they could garner more profits before winter, but himself, being thousands of pounds in debt, was probably unlikely to make up for this deficit. On November 23, 1751, Hockley sent Thomas Cookson near Pennsborough to look for either Croghan or Trent, but to no avail. Both had already left for the Ohio country.

Hockley, now a principal creditor seeking past reimbursement for private funds used under the firm's name, hoped just to receive some compensation for his losses. Hoping Cookson at least saw Trent, he passed this message to Cookson, who wrote to him, "We think therefore it would be best to collect what skins and furs you can and keep them together till you are ready to come down with them."[122]

Meanwhile, in London, Robert Charles chose the firm of Thomas Lester and Thomas Pack, who owned the Whitechapel Bell Foundry, to cast the State House bell. The bell weighed just over two thousand pounds and held the inscription, "Proclaim LIBERTY throughout all the land unto all the Inhabitants Thereof." from the King James Bible in the book of Leviticus Chapter 25: Verse 10.[123] The irony in that verse was not lost on Trent, for he had heavily borrowed money and for almost two years, left unpaid balances. His debt was too much to overcome, and with the price of skins dropping in value in London, he was branded an outlaw if he did not show his presence in the province come spring of 1752.

The State House bell (later called the Liberty Bell)[124] proclaimed liberty, yet here, he was unable to return safely to the province of his residence without being arrested. Hopefully, with the change of the Julian Calendar to the Gregorian Calendar after December 31st,[125] Trent's luck changed in 1752.

---

122. HSP, Cadwalader Family Papers, Thomas Cookson to William Trent letter, November 23, 1751.
123. Whipple, 111.
124. The bell during the eighteenth century was simply known as the "State House Bell." It wasn't referred as the "Liberty Bell" until 1835 when it was given that nickname by a New York journal called the *Anti-Slavery Record* during the anti-slavery movement.
125. The Calendar Act of 1750 introduced the British Empire (including the thirteen American Colonies) to adopt the Gregorian Calendar called the "New Style" from the Julian Calendar or "Old Style." This meant the year 1751 was only two hundred and eighty-two days long because the New Year on the Julian Calendar previously on March 25, was now on January 1st. The year 1752 then began on January 1st.

Liberty Bell

Today this State House Bell is actually the second one made, since the original cast by the White Chapel Foundry cracked at its inaugural ringing. It was melted down and recast by John Pass and John Stow in 1753, which after 1835 was nicknamed the "Liberty Bell". (Courtesy of Public Domain.)

Chapter 7

A Perilous Opportunity

The water from the Allegheny River sprayed the side of Trent's face as he and his hired hands, John Owens and James Foley,[1] paddled their canoes past the high-timbered embankments that formed a rocky point at the confluence of the Ohio River. It was the early morning of June 3rd, 1752,[2] and in a way, the irregular shoreline of that large triangular-shaped bluff commonly known as the Forks of the Ohio resembled the ups and downs of his mercantile career.

Since November of 1751, he and Croghan had spent the usual winter trading season in this backcountry accumulating skins at their various trading houses, but this time felt different. This time he and Croghan were mainly in the Ohio country because they were trying to evade Pennsylvania creditors who sought their immediate arrest for unpaid debts.

But as spring approached, Trent realized there was no way to ship the skins from Philadelphia or store them at his house in Middleton Township if he was arrested the moment he crossed the realm of what was then the borders of Cumberland County, Pennsylvania.[3]

So back on February 28, 1752,[4] Trent wrote to the one person who could help him and his firm in their time of need. This letter of inquiry arrived on Fourth Street in Philadelphia[5] at the residence of his mentor, Edward Shippen

---

1. Both of these names appear as witnesses on the document dated May 20, 1752, that terminated the partnership of Hockley, Trent, and Croghan. They both appeared alongside Trent at Logstown, the Ohio Company warehouse along the North Branch of the Potomac River and around the Forks of the Ohio. Foley later served as an itinerant for Trent and Owens, who had horses at the Forks of the Ohio and at Murdering Town in 1753 and 1754.

2. Trent was first mentioned in the Treaty of Logstown minutes on June 3, 1752.

3. In 1752, the farthest western borders drawn officially within the province of Pennsylvania were found in the township of Peters in Cumberland County which after 1784 became part of Franklin County.

4. HSP, Shippen Family Papers, Edward Shippen to William Trent letter, March 9, 1752.

5. Edward Shippen III lived on Fourth Street across from Willing's Alley in Philadelphia from 1745 to his eventual move to Lancaster, Pennsylvania in May of 1752.

III. Shippen, who currently owned a mercantile firm with merchant Thomas Lawrence,[6] was also presently one of the district justices of Philadelphia County.[7] So he knew most of Trent's creditors in the city and, most importantly, the laws of Pennsylvania (he was later named a judge on November 22nd, 1752)[8] that could protect Trent. Almost immediately, Shippen began knocking on doors along the waterfront and throughout the city at the residence of merchants and creditors who owed sizable sums from the Hockley, Trent, and Croghan firm. On Trent's behalf, Shippen showed every one of them a "Letter of Lycense"[9] that if they produced a signature upon it, this pardoned him and Croghan temporarily.

By the time trader Robert Callender[10] delivered the license to him, he had several signatures written at the bottom. The letter from Shippen enclosed with the license warned Trent that it only gave him safe passage in Philadelphia. Outside the city, he may not be so lucky. "I hope your other creditors in the country will also sign it," Shippen wrote, "It was with much difficulty I got ye Letter Signed by So many."[11] Shippen concluded his letter to Trent by saying his mother was doing well in the city.[12] A letter of license pardoned him from arrest for four months, meaning he had until July in his home province to pay off these debts by conducting his business and continuing his civic duties as justice of the peace.

In the early spring, Trent did manage to convince his account holders to forward him a small parcel of goods but drastically failed to repair his and Croghan's dysfunctional relationship with their Philadelphia partner and now principal creditor for those London merchants for whom they owed thousands of pounds. In fact, word of Trent's sudden emergence from the Ohio country due to Shippen's influence was probably the last straw for Richard Hockley. He sent word to Trent and Croghan from Philadelphia that "yet as we have found that our carry on the said Trade does not answer our expectations; we do therefore hereby mutually agree to dissolve and we do by those present actually dissolve, anul, and declare our said Copartnership absolutely void."[13]

---

6. Merchant Thomas Lawrence was elected to six one-year terms as mayor of Philadelphia between the years of 1729 and 1754 and was a founder of the Academy and College of Philadelphia with Benjamin Franklin. This secondary school eventually became part of the University of Pennsylvania in 1791. Lawrence is buried in the Christ Church Burial Ground on Fifth and Arch Streets in Philadelphia.
7. Martin, 32–33.
8. Ibid., 7.
9. HSP, Shippen Family Papers, Edward Shippen to William Trent letter, March 9, 1752.
10. Robert Callender was a trader partnered with Michael Teafe or Taafe and had joint ventures with Croghan and Trent. He later served on the Kittanning expedition in 1756, became wagonmaster general on the Forbes Expedition in 1758 and constructed the building in Bedford, Pennsylvania that became the Jean Bonnet Tavern. He was buried in the Old Graveyard, in Carlisle, Pennsylvania.
11. HSP, Shippen Family Papers, Edward Shippen to William Trent letter, March 9, 1752.
12. Ibid.
13. Ibid., Cadwalader Family Papers, Hockley, Trent, and Croghan May 20, 1752.

So, on May 20, 1752, while Trent sat inside the log building[14] of Carlisle's courthouse in the town square, he and Croghan signed and sealed their names at the bottom of the document next to Hockley's to officially terminate the three-and-a-half-year-long[15] mercantile firm of Hockley, Trent, and Croghan. Despite the firm's failure, Trent and Croghan were not idle for long. The pounce powder had barely dried the ink upon their signatures before an express arrived requesting them to join representatives from Virginia in the Ohio country.

Robert Dinwiddie, the newly appointed Lieutenant Governor of Virginia (and member of the Ohio Company), hired commissioners to represent Virginia to meet with the Indian nations to "enter into a treaty for polishing and strengthening the Chains of Friendship,"[16] warn them against the influence of the French and help them recognize the ceding of land in the Ohio country to Virginia during the Treaty of Lancaster in 1744.[17]

Since December of 1751, Dinwiddie appointed three Virginia commissioners to facilitate this treaty. He first appointed James Patton, a former ship captain who settled near present-day Blacksburg, Virginia (now part of the campus of Virginia Polytechnic Institute and State University) at an area known as Draper's Meadow.[18] Dinwiddie appointed next Joshua Fry[19] of Albemarle County, Virginia, a renowned cartographer and surveyor and Virginia House of Burgesses member. It was also he, along with Peter Jefferson (father of Thomas Jefferson), who surveyed the colony's disputed boundaries with the neighboring Maryland colony and sketched a highly regarded map of Virginia in 1751.[20] Currently, he was a professor of mathematics at the College of William and Mary in Williamsburg, Virginia. The third and final commissioner named was Lunsford Lomax of "Portobago," a plantation in Caroline County, Virginia, along the Rappahannock River, where he too was a member of the Virginia House of Burgesses for the said county in 1742 and 1750.[21]

All three had requested Trent and Croghan's presence at the Ohio because they had not only attended previous conferences with the Indian nations at Lancaster and Logstown but had interacted previously with several chiefs of the Six Nations, like the Half-King and Andrew Montour. Montour, known as Eghnisara,[22] was Virginia's appointed interpreter for Ohio Company agent

---

14. The building also served as the temporary church until a permanent structure replaced it in the 1760s and became the official site of St. John's Episcopal Church in Carlisle.
15. The Hockley, Trent, and Croghan mercantile firm began on November 14, 1748.
16. Mulkearn, VMHB Vol. 59, No. 1, 14.
17. Ibid.
18. Shackleford, VMHB Vol. 82, No. 2, 194.
19. VMHB Vol. 8, No. 3, 251.
20. Library of Congress, Georgraphy and Map Division 1751.
21. VMHB Vol. 8, No. 3, 249 and 251.
22. The Six Nations and other tribes at Logstown called Montour "Eghnisara" at the treaty. He was sometimes called Sattelihu and French Andrew.

A Perilous Opportunity

Portrait of Robert Dinwiddie (1693-1770) by an unknown artist c.1760-1765. (Courtesy of the National Portrait Gallery and Public Domain.)

Christopher Gist, a former resident of the Yadkin River Valley[23] in North Carolina.

After the invitees had been given word to the conference, Dinwiddie allowed the location to be left up to wherever best suited the Indian leaders. The chiefs of the Six Nations preferred the treaty to be at Logstown along the banks of the Ohio River, and it was Croghan who left immediately for it.[24] Trent and his hired hands followed soon after, traveling west and now, almost two weeks later, paddling below the Forks of the Ohio to the shores near Logstown. When they finally came within view of the houses on the hill,[25] the residents fired the customary salute into the air to welcome their arrival.

Today, the site of "Old Logstown" can be determined by the surveys conducted by Major Daniel Leet of one hundred and forty-three lots in the area

---

23. Gist and his family lived on the northern side of the Yadkin River just west of the Reddies River and Tucker Hole Creek (Saw Mill Creek in 1750) within a few miles of present-day Wilkesboro, North Carolina.
24. According to the minutes of the Logstown Treaty, Croghan was there on June 1, 1752.
25. Darlington, Mary C., 29.

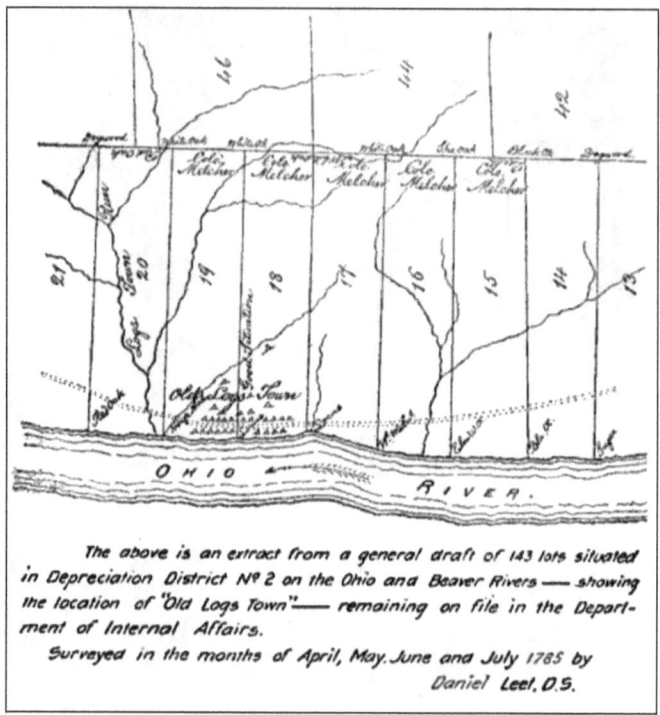

1785 Survey map by Daniel Leet showing "Old Logstown" within the property lines of Old Economy Village today. (Author photo.)

from April to July 1785[26] that were given to Pennsylvania's Revolutionary War soldiers. On Leet's map of the Second District of Depreciation lands dated 1785, he places "Old Logstown" at lots 18 and 19, which will later become under the ownership of the Harmony Society of Economy.[27] So, as Trent's canoe landed, he approached the steep embankments of what now lies in the vicinity of Old Economy Village Museum.

A week later, on June 10th, Trent joined the three Virginia commissioners, Christopher Gist and his partner George Croghan, as they addressed the Half-King and the various sachems and warriors who came to sit at the council to hear their speeches. The Virginia commissioners wasted little time in idle chatter, offering a string of wampum and addressing Virginia's claim to all the Indian lands agreed upon in accordance with the treaty signed in Lancaster previously on July 2, 1744.[28] Trent recalled that before the Six Nations agreed that day, the proposed settlements upon these certain lands not only promised

---

26. Bausman, 973–74.
27. Ibid.
28. Robinson, 137.

reasonable trade with the neighboring settlers but also protected them against those not considered their brethren.

The commissioners pointed out the previous present brought by Conrad Weiser, Croghan and Trent to the village in the summer of 1748, and the presents they brought now were to verify this promise.[29] Which was "A large present of goods to be divided among you and your Allies, which is here ready to be delivered to you, and we desire that you will confirm the Treaty of Lancaster."[30] The commissioners assured that Virginia's purchase in 1744 was "never to take their lands from them" but instead to "live together as one people and keep them from the French, who would be bad neighbors."[31] The commissioners said, "It is Design of the King, our Father, at present, to make a settlement of British subjects on the South East side of the Ohio" and reminded those present of how bad the French intentions were in the Ohio country.[32] They talked once again of the past expedition under French Captain Céloron in 1749 and how the English King "is not the French King who calls himself your Father and endeavored about three Years ago with an armed force to take Possession of your Country by setting up Inscriptions on Trees, and at the Mouths of Creeks, on this River, by which he claims the Lands, tho at the time of their Coming and for many Years before, a Number of your Brethren, the English were residing in this Town, and had several other places on this River."[33]

When the commissioners finished their speeches, they delivered the presents from Governor Dinwiddie to the Half-King and other chiefs of the Six Nations. They also set aside a small present of goods for the Twightwees, who had sent no representatives to the council and a set of "Indian clothing"[34] for Kakowatcheky, the old Shawnee King, who was sickly and bedridden.

Trent and the others watched the chiefs accept the gifts graciously and quietly, for they said after it was distributed, they did so "without the least Noise or Disorder."[35] After much listening, it was the Half-King's turn to speak. With a ten-row wide wampum belt clutched in his hand, he called out George Croghan by his new Indian name, "the Buck," and explained that Croghan, after much business with the province of Pennsylvania, the Half-King explained, "We understand he does not intend to do anymore."[36] He said Croghan was

---
29. Ibid.
30. Ibid.
31. Ibid., 138.
32. Ibid.
33. Ibid., 140.
34. Ibid.
35. Ibid.
36. Ibid.

"one of our people"[37] now and helped them further in the Onondaga Castle instead of his own province.

According to the Half-King, it was the false promise by Conrad Weiser after "he delivered us this Belt of wampum" that summer of 1748 that this relationship crumbled. He explained that with the arrival of too many quantities of spiritous liquors and "no Notice taken to prevent it, we believe Mr. Weiser spoke only from his mouth and not from his heart, and without the Governor's Authority, so we think proper to return the Belt."[38] Then he laid this belt at the feet of George Croghan. The return of wampum, it seemed at least to Trent, meant that Pennsylvania's role in the Ohio country and dealings with the Six Nations was all but over.

The next day, on the 11th, after such a shocking conclusion the night before, the Half-King accepted more gifts of wampum and clothing but first addressed the Lenape or Delaware nation. The Lenape were without a leader, and the Half-King wished to choose one of their "wisest counselors"[39] to assume this position. So, he, along with the commissioners, chose Shingas as the new Lenape King.

Now, because Shingas was absent from this council, "The Half-King put a laced hat on the head of the Beaver, who stood proxy for his brother Shingas and presented him also with a rich Jacket and a suit of English Colours, which had been delivered to the Half-King, by the Commissioners for that Purpose."[40] Surprisingly, the Half-King countered next with his opinion of the French. After hearing the Virginia commissioner speak earlier that the French were "a designing people," the Half-King agreed and said they now realized "they designed to cheat us out of our lands."[41] He added how the French design was "nothing else but mischief,"[42] especially since they had constantly harassed their friends, the Twightwees, so protection was definitely needed if more French came to the Ohio.

It was also during this talk of protection when the Half-King gave his blessing on behalf of the Six Nations and Lenape that "we therefore desire our brethren of Virginia may build a strong house, at the fork of the Monongahela, to keep such Goods, Powder, Lead and necessaries as shall be wanting and as soon as you please."[43] For those in attendance, the Six Nations' approval to build a "strong house" or fort on the Ohio was exactly what they hoped to hear.

---

37. Ibid.
38. Ibid., 141.
39. Ibid., 142.
40. Ibid.
41. Ibid.
42. Ibid.
43. Ibid.

"The Half King" by Fred Threlfall. The sketch shows the gifts the chiefs received like a rich jacket and a suit of English Colors as described at Logstown in 1752. (Courtesy of Fred Threlfall.)

Their only condition was to acknowledge Shingas as King of the Lenapes when and if they began construction because it was his village that resided near this proposed site on the Ohio River.

Shingas's village was a location two miles below the Forks that Céleron referred to as "Rocher e´crit"[44] or the Written Rock village on the Ohio. The village was near the mouth of Chartier's Creek (present-day McKees Rocks), where a few English traders had scrawled their names on the rocks with charcoal. It used to be the home of the Seneca Queen Aliquippa (who now resided on the opposite bank) and was where Trent, Weiser, and Croghan stopped on their way to Logstown in the summer of 1748.

Unfortunately, this small victory was short-lived. When the Half-King met in private with the Virginia commissioners, he clarified that he and the Six Nations did not approve, however, of an English settlement on the southeast bank of the Ohio. When the commissioners argued, "the trade could never be

---

44. Montgomery, 640.

carried on with them to their Advantage, unless we had a settlement of people near to raise provisions,"[45] the Half-King still answered no.

Two days later on the 13th, he explained to Trent and the others his reasonings. The Half-King and the chiefs wanted to sign the commissioner's instrument of writing to confirm the deed ushered by those at Lancaster in 1744 to build a Fort but said he and the others "have not the full power in our hands here on Ohio."[46] At Lancaster in 1744, it was the Onondaga Council for the Grand Council of the Haudenosaunee Confederacy that conducted the cessations of land in the Ohio country to Virginia, so according to the Half-King, it was only "they" who could make the final approval now for a fort and a possible settlement by Virginia.

This deferral of answering was like when Trent and Croghan constructed trading houses as far west as Pickawillany, meaning they could conduct trade there but had no ownership of the land the cabin was built on. In other words, the Six Nations believed that if Virginia was asking permission to build a fort upon the Ohio, then despite the deed made at Lancaster, they never "owned" it in the first place.

The Half-King, Andrew Montour, and other sachems still signed that said deed along with Trent and the others confirming their consent, but not before making one last request. Their allies, the Twightwees, had traveled from the west to attend the previous council in Lancaster in 1748, but we're notably absent from this one. So, the Half-King wished the commissioners to deliver a belt to them along with the gifts from Governor Dinwiddie. As he explained, he and the others "desire they may hold fast by the Chain of Friendship, & not listen to any but their Brethren, the English & us, the Six Nations, Delaware and Shawnees, as we will stand by them; We expect they will come down and confirm the friendship they have engaged in with the English."[47]

The commissioners of Virginia agreed and to show their loyalty to the Six Nations and their allies, immediately chose William Trent to complete this task. His orders, dated June 14, 1752, were as follows: "We desire to proceed to the Picts Town with Expedition in there to deliver to the Piankashaw King a Hat cloak and vest a shirt and stockings for his own use and the other part of His Majesty's Present to be divided as the said King and his Chief men shall think fit and that you will endeavor to promote his interest there."[48]

Over the next five or six days, Trent rounded up the necessary horses and baggage, having his "hands" James Foley and John Owens load up His Majesty's

---

45. Robinson, 143.
46. Ibid., 144.
47. Ibid., 145.
48. HSP, Frank M. Etting Collection, Revolutionary Papers.

presents brought from Williamsburg. The commissioners also selected Métis[49] interpreter Andrew Montour to accompany Trent. Like his mother, Mrs. Montour, better known as Madame Montour,[50] Andrew could speak several Native languages and was well respected amongst the Onondaga Council. His appearance, along with Trent, gave some assurance to the Twightwees that the English were serious about their continued friendship if they traveled over three hundred miles[51] to see them.

Trent began a journal of this mission with the intention to give this account personally to Virginia Lieutenant Governor Robert Dinwiddie when he was done, saying, "In pursuance to instructions which I received from the honorable Colonel Joshua Fry, Colonel Lunsford Lomax, and Colonel James Patton your Honor's commissioners, appointed to deliver His Majesty's present to the Indians at Logstown, to proceed with the present to the Twightwees. An account of that whole affair I begged leave to lay before you which will appear in the following sheets."[52]

Then he and the others left Logstown on June 21, 1752, traveling west along the Ohio River, passing through the mouth of Beaver Creek (today called the Beaver River and near the town of Rochester, Pennsylvania) in the direction of their first stop of inhabitants, the Native town of Muskingum.[53] Trent wrote that from the Logstown, it was about one hundred and fifty miles to the Wyandot town of Muskingum.

Four days into their journey, they spoke to a passerby who, after seeing their pack horses, probably questioned Trent and the others about their expected destination. When Trent told him, the traveler seemed to indicate that the trek to Pickawillany or "Pick Town" was currently hopeless. This man had all had been almost two weeks from Pickawillany, and according to Trent, he had "informed us the French Indians had been there and that twenty-five families of the Picks or Twightwees had gone back with them to the French."[54]

Trent, not one to listen to a single rumor, continued until he met a man named "Powell"[55] on June 27th, who had just come off the route called the "Great Trail," or "Great Path." This path was the main route from the Forks of

---

49. Métis were Indian nations that were a mix of Indian and European. Montour was of Oneida, Algonquin and French ancestry.
50. Madam Montour and her husband Carandawana lived at Otstonwakin, a village along the Great Shamokin Path at the confluence of Loyalsock Creek and the West Branch of the Susquehanna River. Today it is named for her son Andrew and known as Montoursville, Pennsylvania.
51. According to Lewis Evans's map in 1755, the distance from Logstown to Pickawillany was three hundred and twenty-six miles.
52. Goodman, 83–84.
53. Ibid., 85.
54. Ibid., 84.
55. Ibid., 85.

the Ohio that led northwesterly to the French outpost erected on the west bank of the Detroit River called Fort Ponchartrain du Détroit.[56]

This man Powell told Trent that he had been at Fort Detroit "and ten days before he left the fort, three hundred French and Indians had set off either to persuade the Twightwees back to the French, else to cut them off."[57]

Since neither man could confirm what became of Pickawillany, Trent pushed on, finally reaching Muskingum on the 29th. He had hoped to find answers there and immediately questioned two men in the town who lived to the south at a place called Hockhocken.[58] They told Trent they heard that Pickawillany had been captured by the French and all the English in the town had been killed. This, unfortunately, was confirmed by the young Shawnee king, Lapechkewe (Loapeckaway). Lapechkewe was the son of Opessah, the Shawnee King whose former town was now the "Skipton" residence of Ohio Company member and Maryland trader Thomas Cresap. It was once called "Opessah's Town" or "Shawnee Old Town." Today, it is known as Old Town, Maryland, about fifteen miles southeast of Cumberland, Maryland.

Lapechkewe arrived at Muskingum and met Trent at probably Croghan's trading house, wearing the laced hat and "rich suit"[59] the commissioner sent to him from Logstown during the treaty. He corroborated the unfortunate news because he had made his escape after the force of French and Indians (That Powell had seen leaving Fort Detroit) attacked Pickawillany.

The same was said in the Lenape village of Hockhocken, or French Margaret's Town,[60] named after a relation of Andrew Montour, the chief resident until her death. There, on July 2nd, a man named William Ives told Trent he passed through Pickawillany during the night and saw "the white man's houses were all on fire and that he heard no noise in the fort, only one gunfire, and two or three hollows."[61] This was most troubling to Trent. He always knew that Pickawillany was dangerously vulnerable and isolated in the west, but that was why his partner Croghan lined and repaired the stockade for it around their trading post during February 1749/50.[62]

It was also necessary since that same month rumors circulated from Canada there was a bounty for Croghan and Montour's heads. It had been speculated the

---

56. Fort Ponchartrain du Détroit was built by Antoine de la Mothe Cadillac, a Canadian explorer who served as its commandant until 1710. It was later ceded by the French to the British on November 29, 1760, where it stayed in their possession until the American Revolution. Fort Detroit was given to the newly formed United States under terms negotiated in the Jay Treaty, on July 11, 1796. Today the Crown Plaza Detroit Downtown Riverfront hotel sits on the fort's original location.
57. Goodman, 85.
58. Ibid.
59. Lapechkewe's hat and suit were sent to him from Logstown on June 12, 1752. Robinson, 143.
60. Hockhocken or French Margaret's Town is today located at the present-day town of Lancaster, Ohio.
61. Goodman, 85.
62. Darlington, Christopher Gist Journals, 49.

bounty was one thousand pounds or more. According to the report, "Canada brought news that the French offered a large sum of money to any person who would bring to them the said Croghan and Andrew Montour the interpreter alive or if dead, their scalps."[63] Now, two years later, if this latest report about an attack on Pickawillany was true, then their trading post and the "nervous system" of the Twightwee town were also in jeopardy.

Trent sadly heard much of the same when they came about fifteen miles to the Lenape town of Maguck (near present-day Circleville, Ohio) the next day on July 3rd.[64] That night, he met in council with Andrew Montour on what they should do with His Majesty's presents from Governor Dinwiddie. After careful deliberation, it was decided that if the report were true, he sought the whereabouts of the proposed recipients of the gifts, the Piankashaw chiefs, Assapausa, the Turtle and the leader of the Piankashaws, Old Briton.

Trent said that this news "made us go to the Lower Shawnees town with the goods that we might know the certainty."[65] The town Trent was referring to was not along the way to Pickawillany but rather about seventy miles to the south of Maguck. Trent had agreed with Ohio Company agent Christopher Gist that though the Shawnees were not part of the Haudenosaunee or Six Nations, they were friends of the English and the Twightwee nations, so they were helpful nonetheless in finding out what happened at Pickawillany.

Lower Shawnee Town was a much larger village, the main houses found opposite the mouth of the Scioto (sigh- O- toe) River (Creek) just across the Ohio River near the present-day site of South Portsmouth, Kentucky. It was also opposite the mouth where Trent and Croghan had "a large Store House where the Shawnese had built their new Town."[66] This storehouse was also near the town's council house, "a kind of State-House" that was about ninety feet long with a light Cover of Bark in which they hold their councils."[67]

On the 6th of July,[68] after the Native population greeted them with the customary yells and guns firing, it was the same council house that Trent and Montour entered and explained their reasoning for a visit. It was soon interrupted by more whooping and guns discharging outside. Then, two familiar men entered the council house with soiled clothes and looked ragged from traveling all night. Trent recognized trader Andrew McBriar and blacksmith Thomas Burney and asked them what had happened.

---

63. Ibid., 48.
64. Goodman, 86.
65. Ibid.
66. Bailey, 61.
67. Darlington, Christopher Gist Journals, 44.
68. Goodman, 86.

According to Burney, when Pickawillany was attacked, "About 240 French and Indians on the 21st of June about 9:00 o'clock in the morning surprised the Indians in the cornfields and that they came so suddenly on them that the white men who were in their houses had the utmost difficulty to reach the Fort."[69] Burney was referring to the traders' houses that dwelled within ten yards of the outer stockade walls, whose tall upright logs protected the house of Old Briton, Burney's forge for blacksmithing and the trading post owned by Trent and Croghan.[70] From the houses inside the stockade, he told Trent he watched "the French and Indians keep a smart fire on the fort till the afternoon."[71] Then the French and their Native allies traveling with them said if "they would deliver up the white men that were in the fort, they would break up the siege and go home."[72]

Old Briton and the others, after much discussion, agreed to give up the English traders along with beaver pelts and belts of wampum, but they soon learned it was a false promise by the French and their allied nations. Burney explained a trader wounded in the belly was immediately stabbed and then scalped. Then he watched from his hiding place as they cut out his heart and ate it in front of everyone.[73]

Trent inquired about who else was killed. It was known they killed one Englishman and took six others prisoner. They also killed one Mingo warrior, one Shawnee, and three Twightwees.[74]

And the Piankashaw leaders? Trent asked.

The statuses of the Turtle and Assapausa were unknown to either of the men, but everyone witnessed Old Briton's unfortunate fate. For his loyalty and attachment to the English, the old Piankashaw King was taken prisoner from the fort, led to an open fire, and while the resident families and English prisoners watched, was boiled in the fire and eaten.[75] This horrific murder of Old Briton and the burning of the English houses in and around the fort was a message that was expressed loud and clear. The French were trying to flex their muscles and regain their control over the region.

Trent found out this party was from the French-controlled outpost Ponchartrain du Detroit and was led by Charles Michel de Langlade,[76] a French cadet who was fluent in both French and the Ojibwe dialect called Ottawa or

---

69. Ibid., 87.
70. Ibid.
71. Ibid.
72. Ibid.
73. Ibid., 87–88.
74. Ibid., 88.
75. Ibid.
76. Trap, 18–19.

Odawa. What Trent didn't know at the time was that Langlade's actions were ordered by the Commandant of Detroit, who had waited three years to exact his revenge and finally drive the English traders from the Twightwee town.

The French commandant was none other than Pierre Joseph Céloron de Blainville, the commander of the lead plate expedition in the Ohio country in 1749, who had expressed his frustrations then with his lack of influence to persuade the loyalties of the Miami Confederacy.

By destroying Pickawillany, Céloron could once again reclaim the road and territory from Detroit to the Great Miami River. But it was his ordered destruction of the English trading houses in and around the stockade that was even more devastating. Burney and McBriar, whose supplies were hit during the attack and escaped in the night, estimated to Trent that over three thousand pounds of goods were lost after plundering.[77] Burney, who was employed by business partners Robert Callender and Michael Taafe, lost over three hundred pounds alone, losing bars of lead, linen and various amounts of coarse woolen fabrics called duffels and strouds.[78] McBriar lost almost three times that, losing knives, embossed flannels, half-thicks, and thousands of wampum beads.[79]

Trent probably realized he should cut his losses and return the presents to Logstown. The next day, on the 7th, however, Oneida chief Scarouady and others from the Six Nations arrived and requested Trent to join them in order "to bring the remaining Twightwees this way."[80]

He agreed and set off northwest. His traveling party had increased now by twenty-two more men[81], including the blacksmith Burney, as they crossed the Little Miami River and followed it to where it joined the Great Miami River. By the 19th of July, they were heading north of the Great Miami River, just twenty miles south of Pickawillany, staying the night near the present-day town of Vandalia, Ohio.[82]

Trent must have had flashes back to his nights at Fort Clinton in New York, when he and the others heard several guns sound in the darkness followed by hollering and whistles. He noted they all laid awake, clutching their guns on alarm until the sun appeared from the horizon.[83]

When it was morning, Trent sent two of his party to scout Pickawillany and report back. Then he led the loaded horses up the river closer to the Twightwee town. His scouts joined them as they were about five miles from Pickawillany,

---
77. Bailey, 37–38.
78. Ibid.
79. Ibid.
80. Goodman, 89.
81. Ibid., 90.
82. Ibid., 91.
83. Ibid.

saying the town was deserted, and there were French flags still flying[84] over the burnt remnants of the trading post and the house of Old Briton.

While they continued into the deserted remains of Pickawillany, Trent sent two scouts out again to track where the surviving residents had fled. Meanwhile, Trent raised the King's colors,[85] brought water to the fort and posted guards near two of the gates of the stockade. Here, Trent wisely made camp as darkness fell, being very cautious after more guns sounded in the distance. It must have been a long, somber night for Trent and his party, while the charred remains of a once bustling village still produced smoke and ash a month later.

The next morning, on July 21st, scouts informed Trent that the tracks from the town led two different directions. One fresh trail went north up the "French Road"[86] that went to the French outpost Fort des Miamis, rebuilt by Captain Céloron and was the stockade at the site of a large village of the Twightwees called the Kekionga. It was the previous residence of the late Old Briton before he built Pickawillany and stood where the future city of Fort Wayne, Indiana, is today.

The other tracks went south down the Great Miami River and through the thickets and what Trent estimated was toward the direction of Lower Shawnee Town.[87] If they needed any other reason to turn back, the scouts laid the items they found on the path of Trent's feet. Both were articles of clothing and according to Trent, "A blue jacket and a shirt stabbed in six or seven places, all bloody, which we suppose belonged to some of the Indians that were killed."[88] After seeing the town that rivaled the jaws of Hell and now the reeking, bloodied clothes, Trent didn't want to make more of the Six Nations and their children uneasy. So, despite the hot weather, he decided to lead them back to the mouth of the Scioto at the Ohio River.

The seven-day journey back to Lower Shawnee Town was the highest temperatures he and the others had experienced thus far. By now, Trent had traveled almost seven hundred miles with goods in the sweltering heat, witnessing the dogs the Six Nation used for hunting along the way drop dead from dehydration.[89] There had been little water in the creeks or rivers to replenish their drinking containers, and Trent said they traveled almost twenty-two miles before they were able to find a drop.[90]

---

84. Ibid.
85. Ibid. For a detailed description of the King's colors, see Endnote 323.
86. Ibid., 92.
87. Ibid., 91.
88. Ibid., 92.
89. Ibid.
90. Ibid.

But when they finally arrived exhausted and thirsty at Lower Shawnee Town, good news came in the appearance of their friends, the Piankashaws. On August 4, 1752, they saw their rival Cherokee Chief Blue Shadow and some others from the south[91] who must have received the news of the attack on the Twightwee village of Pickawillany.

Yet before they could all sit together in the council house, Trent had to remedy the problem that stood waving in the wind. The Shawnees had hoisted the French colors[92] to show what the French had once given them, and Trent immediately lobbied to take it down.

After what happened at Pickawillany, he didn't want the Piankashaw chiefs and Cherokees to misinterpret why he and the others had returned there. So, through his interpreter Montour, Trent told the Shawnees and Blue Shadow that he "looked upon the hoisting them colors as an affront to His Majesty the King of Great Britain, and as I was doing the King's business, I could hear no councils under them."[93]

Then he and Montour proceeded to walk away from the entrance of the council house, but the message had already struck a nerve with Blue Shadow, who abruptly brought down the flag and threw it as far as he could.[94] Trent and Montour, realizing their ruse had worked, were gestured back through the council house, and the speeches began. Trent watched as the Cherokees laid black and white wampum to show their grieving with the Miami nations. Then Scarouady and the Six Nations did the same.

But then Scarouady laid a belt of just white wampum and advised the Piankashaw chiefs "to not listen or hear what the French say to you."[95] He also pointed to the goods that were lying beside Trent and said, "King of Great Britain, your father has now sent a very large present of goods to Logstown to be divided amongst his children. As you could not come thither, we have taken care to send you parts. We joined with the Six United Nations of Indians and advised you to stand fast in the chain of friendship, which you have taken hold of and assure you of the friendship of the government of Virginia, under the direction of the great King, your father, on the other side of the water."[96]

The young Piankashaw chief named Assapausa responded by laying a large beaver blanket on the ground at their feet with a green spot painted in the center. This was to signify the English were smooth like this blanket, and

---

91. Ibid., 93.
92. The French colors had been given to them by Nucheconner, another "King of the Shawnees" who along with Kakowatcheky spoke for the Shawnees at several early treaties.
93. Goodman, 93.
94. Ibid.
95. Ibid., 96.
96. Ibid.

the dwellings of each colony's governor were like the green spot, "Which represents the spring and its bloom."[97] Trent understood their message, realizing that although Virginia Lieutenant Governor Robert Dinwiddie was called a bright flower in full bloom, Piankashaw chiefs representing the entire Miami Confederacy knew it might not last for very long.

So, before the council ended, Trent gave a scarlet cloak to Ellanagea Pyangeacha,[98] the young son of Old Briton, a hat and jacket with a shirt and stockings to Assapausa, clothing for Old Briton's wife and the rest of the goods to "the Turtle" and the Twightwees that came with them.[99] After the distribution of his goods was finished, Trent was somewhat relieved. His Majesty's presents had all been given out, and he could eventually stand before the Governor of Virginia with confidence that some of the chiefs of the Miami Confederacy continued their friendship and loyalty with the English.

However, he knew Dinwiddie was very concerned when he received word about the attack on Pickawillany. So, he sent Thomas Burney on the northern path to Pennsylvania to depose his account of Pickawillany to trader Robert Callender at Carlisle on August 29th[100] while he delivered the report of the Twightwees and the French to Williamsburg himself.

Trent arrived in the Virginia capital the first week of October,[101] riding down the main street of the city known as Duke of Gloucester Street[102] and then veering off past the brightly colored foliage adorning each side of the long palace green[103] in front of the Governor's house.

After he gave Dinwiddie his "sheets,"[104] the news of his expedition and attack on Pickawillany next appeared in published type from the building on Lot 48.[105] This was the location of "the Post-Office"[106] and printing house of Williamsburg printer and editor of the *Virginia Gazette*, William Hunter. Though it had not appeared in time for the week of October 6th, the second page of the *Virginia Gazette* instead teased a small snippet or headline that read "Extract of a letter from a gentleman in the back Parts of the Country" in the October 20th edition.[107]

---

97. Ibid.
98. At the Treaty of Carlisle on October 3, 1753, the wife of Old Briton called her son by his name "Ellangoa Pyangeacha."
99. Goodman, 104.
100. Hanna, Vol. 2, 289.
101. *Virginia Gazette*, October 6, 1752.
102. Kimball and Hanson, 71.
103. The palace green was about a quarter mile long before it reached the Governor's palace. Ibid., 72.
104. Goodman, 84.
105. William Hunter paid one hundred sixty-three pounds, fifteen pounds for "House in Williamsburg No. 48 on June 21, 1751.
106. *Virginia Gazette*, October 6, 1752, 4.
107. *Virginia Gazette*, October 20, 1752, 2.

A Perilous Opportunity

Today the reconstruction of the Governor's Palace in Williamsburg, Virginia replaced the original that burned in 1781. (Courtesy of Public Domain.)

The small headline became so popular with subscribers that a full description was requested from Trent for the front page on the week of October 27, 1752.[108] This article was not only longer but printed a more vivid portrayal of the horrific acts of the French and French Indians, which no doubt augmented its relevance to the numerous subscribers from the House of Burgesses.[109] It also made Trent somewhat of a local celebrity or hero for being a witness to such atrocities in the wilderness, so he probably took advantage of his stay in the city.

In fact, his timing could not have been better. Trent's published account came coincidentally a week and a half before the New Calendar's celebration of King George II's birthday, which was observed on the following Friday,

---
108. *Virginia Gazette*, October 27, 1752, 1.
109. Hunter was the "public printer" for the House of Burgesses in the colony of Virginia from 1751–1761.

November 10, 1752.[110] That night Governor Dinwiddie hosted the biggest celebration in the city, inviting his guests to see the play "The Tragedy of Othello" and then afterward utilize his latest addition to his residence, a new large ballroom for games and dancing.[111] This extravagant room was built on the ground floor of the Governor's Palace, which extended to almost the Palace gardens.

Now, since there is no definitive proof Trent attended the Governor's ball, he probably still watched the "several beautiful fireworks that were exhibited in the Palace Street."[112] Either way, Dinwiddie himself paid his expenses in Williamsburg for four pounds one shilling ten pence. Trent was also given an additional gratuity of sixty-two pounds ten shillings[113] by the Receiver General Phillip Grymes for his service and expedition under the Virginia banner.

Yet the most important news of all came to Trent before he left the streets of the colonial capital. Unbeknownst to Trent, previously, while he journeyed from the western backcountry in September, the Ohio Company met in Alexandria, Virginia, for their annual fall meeting on September 17, 1752.[114] With the recent loss of their two founders, Thomas Lee on September 4, 1750, and now Lawrence Washington on July 26, 1752, the discussion focused on the company's next resolution:

> To survey the first 200,000 acres, from the Kiskiminetas down the Southeast side of the Ohio to the mouth of the Big Kanawha where it was thought absolutely necessary to have some fort or place of security.[115]

According to Dinwiddie, the Ohio Company had already sent for goods valued at two thousand pounds sterling[116] for this specific undertaking from Tower Street merchant and company member John Hanbury,[117] so they needed to employ a "factor" to replace the late Hugh Parker of Maryland. This person then carried on the company's mercantile trade and business from their newly constructed warehouse on the North Branch of the Potomac River in Frederick County, Virginia.

---

110. According to the New Calendar, King George II's birthday was now on November 10 instead of October 30. They observed it that Friday in Williamsburg. *Virginia Gazette*, November 17, 1752.
111. *Virginia Gazette*, November 17, 1752.
112. Ibid.
113. Ibid., 411.
114. George Mercer Papers (GMP), Mulkearn, Case of the Ohio Company, 7.
115. Ibid.
116. Ibid. Ibid., 235.
117. The Hanbury family of John, Capel, and Osgood were original members of the Ohio Company in 1747/48. It was John that submitted the Ohio Company's original petition in for 500, 000 acres in the Ohio Country to His Majesty on January 11, 1748/49.

A Perilous Opportunity

The present site of Trent's former house on the New Store tract when he served as factor for the Ohio Company in what was then Frederick County, Virginia. It is now found in Ridgeley, West Virginia. (Author photo.)

Although it was not made official until their next meeting on November 22, 1752,[118] at the Stafford County Courthouse, the future of the Ohio Company rested squarely on the shoulders of who they decided to select as their next candidate. Their newly appointed factor was William Trent.

---

118. GMP, Mulkearn, Case of the Ohio Company, 8.

Chapter 8

The Indian's Eyes are Fixed upon You

By the beginning of 1753, Trent had moved to Virginia on the North Branch of the Potomac River to begin his duties as "factor" for his new employer, the Ohio Company. He had a new two-story house with a dry cellar for storing skins, a kitchen and a stable for a dozen horses, not to mention the boat built by joiner John Hammer[1] for company business on the Potomac. The house was on the hill near the company warehouse, and although smaller than the plantation he still owned in Middleton Township, Pennsylvania, it was also described as "with proper conveniences for a family to live in."[2] This last detail was most important because, by spring, Trent had found a wife formerly named Sarah Wilkins. Her surname suggested her father may have been a trader or person of mercantile background,[3] but unfortunately, their marriage record, according to Trent (later in a will drafted in 1775),[4] had been destroyed and lost.

So, Trent began to hopefully accomplish what his deceased predecessor, Hugh Parker, could not. From the second company warehouse and headquarters called the "New Store" (The original Ohio Company storehouse was built at the mouth of Rock Creek[5] near the present-day town of Georgetown, Maryland.), Trent began the Ohio Company's expansion onto their half-million acres in the upper Ohio country where they began a town and a fort to protect these potential settlers and neighboring Indian nations.

---
1. "July 1750 Account of John Hammer," James, 199.
2. *Maryland Gazette,* February 17, 1763, 3.
3. The Wilkins's surname was linked to a few traders that resided in Donegal Township of Lancaster County, Pennsylvania. Unfortunately, little is known of Sarah Wilkins's parents or siblings, to confirm she was from that specific area.
4. HSP, Simon Gratz Collection, William Trent Will April 14, 1775. The 1775 will is found in Appendix J of this book.
5. GMP, Mulkearn, 146.

The only problem was the French had their own ideas of expansion from Canada. Trent had already heard that "15 or 16 French are come to Loggstown and are building Houses"[6] by the time he arrived at the New Store Tract. He and Thomas Cresap had written to Virginia Lieutenant Governor Dinwiddie to voice this concern, but in response, Dinwiddie had "hope these people are only French Traders and they have no other View but Trade."[7]

In the same letter dated February 10, 1753, Dinwiddie hoped, "there is no great army of French among the lakes,"[8] but for those men like Trent who had witnessed atrocities and lost goods at Pickawillany, it was only a matter of time. This proved true when he received word from George Croghan about their hired hands that were attacked near Eskippakithiki (pronounced S-kip-pa-key-tahkey) or what the traders called "Little Pict Town." (Today, a historical marker along Route 15 and Ironworks Road in Clarks County, Kentucky, marks the vicinity where Eskippakithiki was.)

Although, it happened only a few days after Trent warned Dinwiddie[9] about the French building houses at Logstown in January, he wasn't notified officially of what happened until he received Croghan's letter in April. According to the account told to Croghan by James Lowrey (who escaped after three days as a prisoner), almost £400[10] worth of their goods, such as wampum, calimanco[11] bed gowns, and robed strouds were taken by fifty Ottawas, Piscataways (called by Trent Conewangos)[12] and a Dutchman named Phillip Phillips, allied to the French. The goods owned by Trent and Croghan were under the care of David Hendricks, who, along with four others, were sent to Montreal. Eight prisoners in all were taken,[13] including three employees for the Lowrey trading firm.

On April 10, 1753, Trent wrote to Deputy Governor of Pennsylvania James Hamilton to make him aware it wasn't just Virginia or the Ohio Company facing aggression from the French, but also those licensed to trade from Pennsylvania. One such person from Pennsylvania he mentioned was his good friend John Finley (whose whereabouts currently were unknown), of Lurgan Township[14] from Cumberland County. Finley, along with Trent, was elected as a justice of the peace for Cumberland County in 1749 and, in May of 1750, protected

---

6. R.A, Brock, Vol. 1, 22.
7. Ibid.
8. Ibid.
9. The attack on Trent's employees occurred on January 26, 1753.
10. Bailey, 39.
11. Calamanco is a thin fabric of worsted wool yarn and in this case used for morning attire like a bedgown.
12. Piscataway's or Conewango's were an Algonquin speaking tribe from Maryland to the south.
13. Hanna, Vol. 2, 230–31 and 253.
14. Cumberland County (Pennsylvania) Archives, 1751 Tax Lists, 27.

local Indian nations in the Blue Hills during the Burnt Cabins expedition.[15] Finley also later, in 1755, joined the Braddock expedition as a teamster, where he first met North Carolina waggoner Daniel Boone.[16]

The friendship between them lasted over twenty years as it was Finley in 1769 who came to Boone's home in the Yadkin River Valley[17] and persuaded him to see the land up the Warrior's Path[18] and beyond the Cumberland Gap.[19] His territory near the Red River was where Trent described in his letter dated April 10, 1753, where Finley originally had three of his men killed defending his and Croghan's goods "at a place called Kentucky."[20]

Though the "Cuttawa" or Cuttaway River[21] was frequently used by traders in the region (Christopher Gist's exploration of present-day northern Kentucky in 1751 comes to mind), Trent's exact spelling of the word "Kentucky" is credited to him as being the first use of the modern-day word we identify today to describe the "Bluegrass State."

Meanwhile, by the 26th of April,[22] his neighbor near the New Store, Christopher Gist, had begun identifying boundaries of the Ohio Company's grant using the help of Marylander Thomas Cresap and Virginian George Mercer, son of company member John Mercer of Marlborough. Surveyor George Mercer began across the Potomac near the mouth of Will's Creek or the "Inhabitants"[23] and ran a course the whole way to the two hundred acres set aside where they proposed to build a town on the Ohio. He sketched a map[24] of their surveying route, where it reached near the mouth of Redstone Creek (near present-day Brownsville, Pennsylvania) and toward the "Indian towns" where the Ohio Company committee had decided their initial site for a town and building a fort.

For this "initial site," Mercer sketched a dark mound labeled A and marked it "Fort Hill" upon his map, noting at the bottom that:

> This hill is a very Fine Situation for a Fort, being very steep on the North and South Side, the River running at the Front of it on the

---

15. Colonial Records of Pennsylvania, Vol. 5, 436, 441 and 443.
16. Hanna, Vol. 2, 234.
17. Boone lived just west of the present-day town of Wilkesboro, North Carolina where Ohio Company surveyor Christopher Gist once lived until Gist moved near the mouth of Will's Creek in Virginia in 1752 or 1753.
18. The Warrior's Path or Great Warrior's Path was a network of footpaths that ran from present-day New York to Alabama through the Great Appalachian Valley.
19. Cumberland Gap is a pass through the Cumberland Mountains (part of the Appalachian chain) that lies near the junction of modern-day states of Kentucky, Virginia, and Tennessee.
20. Darlington, Christopher Gist Journals, 192–93.
21. Ibid., 59.
22. L.A. Brown, George Mercer Map 1753, No. 17.
23. The land across the Potomac River from the Ohio Company warehouse in Virginia had several houses in Maryland near the mouth of Will's Creek. This became known as "the Inhabitants" by Trent and others.
24. LA. Brown, George Mercer Map 1753, No. 17.

Present view of Mercer's "Fort Hill" and the prehistoric mound at the mouth of Charter's Creek where the Ohio Company originally wanted to build an outpost in 1753. Today it lies in McKees Rocks, Pennsylvania. (Author photo.)

North Side as it does at the East End, which is inaccessible being near 100 feet high and large Rocks jutting one over the other to the top. The West End has a gradual Descent down to the River.[25]

The "hill," or proposed site of the fort Mercer described, was a prehistoric Indian mound dated between 200 B.C. and 100 A.D.[26] and was at the mouth of Chartier's Creek (spelled Shurtees on Mercer's map) on the Ohio River. (Today, it lies near a baseball field called Ranger Field in McKee's Rocks, Pennsylvania).

It was also near the Lenape town where Trent, Croghan, Weiser, and William Franklin visited in 1748 and was now the home of the Lenape chief Shingas. The town was proposed to be called Saltsburg[27] to no doubt favor the influx of Protestants who were emigrating from Germany looking for new property to settle with their families and also to fill the quota of one hundred families needed to settle on the 200,000 acres within seven years.[28]

Another interesting item on George Mercer's map was the survey plot of Colonel William Russell, a land agent employed by the company of John Blair

---

25. Ibid.
26. Western Pennsylvania Historical Magazine, Stotz, Vol. 52, 333.
27. GMP, Mulkearn, 147.
28. James, 75.

Sr. and several others. Mercer noted in the margins that he saw Russell and his party on "Thursday 26th of April in my way to the Indian Towns."[29] Russell, in a rival land company, was finally surveying the 100,000 acres granted to them "westward of line of Lord Fairfax on the Waters of the Potomack and Youghyanghgane"[30] on November 4, 1745, and which had been renewed in 1751[31] for four years so they could settle on this land.

According to the Mercer map, the Blair Company grant (the survey done by Colonel Russell) was between the Monongahela and Youghiogheny Rivers just north of the mouth of Redstone Creek. The corners of this plot were so close to Ohio Company land; in fact, they were within 1/8 of a mile from Christopher Gist's new plantation house "Monongahela"[32] and about ten or twelve poles (165 feet or 198 feet) from Gist's son-in-law William Cromwell's house,[33] who resided on the same property.

This posed a problem since Russell and his company had not been welcoming since they spied Cresap and Mercer trying to lay off a town near "Shurtees" Creek. George Mercer's father, John, filed a caveat or former notice against Russell[34] to the Virginia courts to desist their activities until the Ohio Company completed their official survey, but apparently, the rival land company continued being a thorn in their side for the rest of the summer.

On May 1, 1753, Trent added another title to his name, being selected by the Governor's Council of Virginia as a justice of the peace for Frederick County along with John Funk.[35] Like in Pennsylvania, Trent conducted his public service and duty in Virginia by traveling to the seat of the residential county. In Frederick County, the county seat was in Winchester, about sixty miles away, but alarming company business delayed him getting sworn in officially until early September.

Less than a week later, on May 7th, he was back again in the upper Ohio country when the alarming news arrived. He and trader Robert Callender were at the mouth of Pine Creek, where Croghan had built a house on the northwest side of the Ohio (Allegheny River) with large fields and ten acres of corn[36] when an express arrived from Scottish gunsmith John Fraser, who lived at the mouth of French Creek (Franklin, Pennsylvania) since 1741.[37]

---

29. L.A. Brown, George Mercer Map 1753, No. 17.
30. James, 76.
31. Ibid., 75.
32. On their return from Fort Le Boeuf, Major George Washington and Christopher Gist arrived at his new plantation on January 2, 1754 and Washington referred to it as "Monongahela" in his journal.
33. William Cromwell married Violetta Gist, the eldest daughter of Christopher Gist. They were one of the fifty families Gist invited to come settle on the Ohio Company grant.
34. GMP, Mulkearn, 425.
35. Executive Journals of the Council of Virginia, Vol. 5, 422.
36. Bailey, 61.
37. Ibid., 83–84.

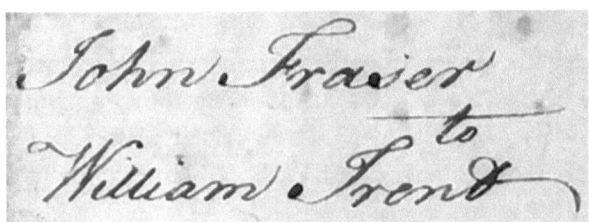

A picture of the original spelling of John Fraser's name written in Trent's hand. (Author photo.)

Fraser reported to Trent, Croghan, and Callender that "since March last, one hundred and fifty French and Indians were at a carrying place which leads from Niagara to the Heads of the Ohio, building canoes and making other preparations."[38] He also told them that the French had eight pieces of brass cannon and intended to "build a Fort at Monongahela."[39]

After receiving confirmation of this report, the next day, on the eighth, Trent wrote to the son of one of his former mentors, William Logan, who now served in his late father's seat on the Governor's Council in Pennsylvania. He also wrote to Governor Dinwiddie and requested an audience with the Half-King. Hopefully this time, the governments of Pennsylvania and Virginia took the threats of the French more seriously. This confirmed assembling of a French army and preparations to invade the Ohio country was not just squabbling between English and Canadian traders as both provincial leaders had described the previous attack on Pickawillany.

Trent made sure this message was blatantly clear. According to the messengers sent by the Onondaga Council in New York, the French had one goal and "intended to strike the governments of Pennsylvania and Virginia."[40] Trent himself had heard enough. Now is the time to respond and strike back if necessary. Since he fought in King George's War, the French had robbed, murdered, and inched their way closer to the Ohio country. His first mercantile firm had dissolved because of this aggression, and now they were once again posing threats to the region and employer that held his future. A part of him hoped the French did invade the region and raid the Indian towns because, as he told Logan and the rest of the Governor's Council: "We are in hopes five or six hundred will come while we are here and we may have the pleasure of helping the Indians kill a few of them which will be some satisfaction."[41]

---

38. Colonial Records of Pennsylvania, Vol. 5, 614.
39. HSP, Shippen Family Papers, William Trent to William Logan May 8, 1753.
40. Ibid.
41. Ibid.

The message did finally strike a nerve with Governor Dinwiddie's Council in Williamsburg. There was much discussion based on Trent's reports in the Ohio, but they shifted their focus to supplying the Ohio Indians with arms and ammunition. On May 31, 1753, Dinwiddie expressed his concern for "the present situation of the Indians and friendship with us"[42] by writing to another council member at his home in "Belvoir,"[43] Colonel William Fairfax, and having him arrange these gifts at Winchester. It was there the cases or chests of firelocks, flints, powder, ball, and duffels[44] were transported by trader John Owens[45] to Trent at either Cresap's house at Shawnee Old Town or the mouth of Patterson's Creek, then taken to the New Store. Dinwiddie added he hoped "the Half-King would give a good account of the French and their Indians and prevent their taking possession of land on the Ohio."[46] Like Trent, Dinwiddie knew if the Half-King and the Six Nations changed their loyalties to the French, then the Ohio Country and company land were lost. It was the Half-King's voice that controlled their interests in the Ohio Valley, so they didn't come this far to lose their interest now.

Dinwiddie claimed he had total confidence that Trent made sure their "firm attachment to their interests"[47] continued. He admired how Trent could "frame of speech to the Indians, in their style better than he could."[48]

So, he told Trent to "assure them of my sincere friendship and readiness; at all times to assist them, deliver the present to them, as from this colony and tell them it is intended for the Six Nations and the other nations of Indians, and amity with us and them."[49] Dinwiddie also told Trent to gather information about the French, most specifically being "inquisitive as possible of the number of the French and their Indians of their designs and situation of the Picts and Twightwees are now in."[50]

Unfortunately, while Dinwiddie entrusted him to be his personal emissary from this transportation of goods and gather French intel, he never told Trent that the council had already ordered someone before him to travel to Logstown

---

42. GMP, Mulkearn, Case of the Ohio Company, 10.
43. "Belvoir" plantation completed in 1741, was built by Colonel William Fairfax on his 2,200-acre tract that was in Fairfax County, Virginia. The house was decimated by a fire in 1783 and later destroyed by British forces during the War of 1812. Today the ruins are found on Fort Belvoir Army installation, outside of Washington D,C, and just four miles from George Washington's home at Mount Vernon.
44. Duffel was a coarse woolen fabric, sometimes used as a heavier blanket or coat and to make a bag to carry supplies.
45. In the memorandum from the treasurer for the Ohio Company George Mason, he wrote to John Mercer in March of 1767, listing the accounts and receipts of the Ohio Company. It was listed that John Owens received six pounds eleven shillings, four pence for helping Trent deliver presents to the Indian nations at Logstown in July of 1753.
46. GMP, Mulkearn, Case of the Ohio Company, 11.
47. Ibid.
48. Ibid.
49. Ibid.
50. Ibid.

and "desire admittance to the commandant of the French forces and to demand by whose Commission and Authority he acts."[51] This individual who was given instructions to gather information at Logstown was none other than Colonel William Russell and was no doubt chosen due to the influence of his partner John Blair, who sat on the Virginia Governor's Council.[52] This was why now, in June at his Virginia house on the Potomac, Trent could barely contain the emotions from his newly received message. An express had arrived from Barnaby Curran at the Ohio. Curran had reached Logstown, but apparently, along the way, he was robbed of the 125 grains of white wampum[53] Trent enclosed with his letter to the Half-King. The letter Trent sent with Curran informed the Half-King and others of the Six Nations that he was to arrive at the Ohio in twenty days as soon as the arms and ammunition arrived at his house from Winchester.

But Curran alerted Trent of another disturbance. There had been another run-in with Colonel Russell, and it appeared Russell tried to sabotage any dealings Curran and Trent had with the Ohio Indians. When Curran informed them all that Trent was arriving soon with arms and ammunition, "Colonel Russell went up and told the Indians it was a lie, there was no powder nor lead coming for them."[54] Curran announced on June 15th and 16th[55] to the Native council at Shannopin's Town not to listen to Russell's drunken misbehavior, but later Trent's employee John Finley deposed that he was also at Shannopin's and " the said Russell was sober all time he was in his company."[56]

It was Curran's word against Russell's but did not irritate Trent any less. Numerous rival land companies since James Patton had been petitioning for land in the upper Ohio country opposing the Ohio Company, so like his predecessor Hugh Parker, he knew what to expect. Yet it was the last part of Curran's message that made Trent's blood boil. According to Curran, Russell had a commission "to negotiate affairs with the Indians, relating to the troubles with the French,"[57] and it was written entirely in Colonel William Fairfax's hand. He felt betrayed. Dinwiddie himself had personally ushered upon Trent to transmit business at the Ohio and gather intel in His Honor's name, yet for some reason, Russell was on the same mission going to Shannopin's Town and Logstown before Trent could leave Virginia.

---

51. Executive Journals of the Council of Virginia, Vol. 5, 433.
52. Ibid.
53. Virginia Historical Society, On the reverse side of Trent's letter to the Half-King dated June 8, 1753, he wrote, "125 Grains white Wampum in the Strings."
54. Bailey, 21.
55. Calendar of Virginia State Papers, Palmer, 248.
56. Ibid.
57. Ibid.

Trent probably wondered if it was all a ploy. If the arms and ammunition had arrived precisely from Winchester, then he could be at the Ohio already and could have halted Russell and his company from spreading lies about him and the Ohio Company. But he wasn't. It was almost July and he waited three weeks for the presents and the horses to transport them. It was more than enough time for those in the Governor's Council to delay his Ohio Company business on the Ohio. Or at least time for Colonel William Fairfax (who was not a member of the Ohio Company) to order Russell to find out about the French moving from Canada while he "organized" presents for Trent's excursion.

At this point, Trent didn't know what to think. So, he expressed his anger and frustrations in the only way he knew how: through written words. He wrote to Governor Dinwiddie on June 28th and voiced his concerns boldly by going right to the main cause of his trouble after speaking about his estimated arrival at Logstown on the following Sunday, the 8th of July:[58]

> I cannot help concerning myself right much hurt by the Gentleman who undertook to send Colonel Russell (who at any time is but little better than a Madman) to interfere in a Business, which I had undertaken to transmit for the Govt of Virginia at your request.[59]

Trent knew Fairfax commissioned Russell but for the council to make it official, Dinwiddie had to give his approval. Perhaps Dinwiddie was naive again like he was about the attack on Pickawillany or even his employees that were captured in Kentucky and taken to Canada. Either way, Trent was fed up with Dinwiddie's latest actions. In Trent's eyes, the disgraceful commission with Russell was the last straw, and he gave Dinwiddie an ultimatum: "But you must excuse me, Sir, if I decline transacting any further Business for the Government of Virginia."[60]

He sealed the letter and handed it sternly to itinerant Thomas Burney, telling him to verify "in Regard to Colonel Russell's behavior on the Ohio."[61] Burney headed to Williamsburg with the letter while Trent and John Owens led the pack horses to the Ohio, mindful of the dark clouds forming in the sky. Trent did not arrive at Logstown until the 11th of July, delayed by almost three days, having "stopped on the road by great rains & high Waters."[62]

---

58. Bailey, 22.
59. Ibid.
60. Ibid.
61. Ibid.
62. Trent's Account with the Proceedings of the Six Nations of Indians and Allies, 29.

The next day, after spending most of the day talking to the Half-King, Trent was told he knew what the French were up to once Monacatootha (Scarouady) returned in four days from the north.[63] Halfway to Monacatootha's arrival, a Conewago messenger appeared from the newly built French trading houses near Logstown and gave Trent an update on the French near Lake Erie. He said the French army consisted of at least twelve hundred soldiers[64] besides the canoe men who brought the provisions, and they were more on their way, eager to assist with the recent construction. The French had already begun construction on two forts near the shores of Lake Erie.

The first was built upon the rising banks of Lake Erie, described later as being "very strong of hard timber about six-foot apart fill'd in between with dirt with four bastions, a Ditch it stands close upon the Edge of the Lake."[65] There were also about one hundred houses surrounding the fort. This was later named upon completion, Fort Presque Isle, where the present-day East Bayfront Parkway runs past Sobieski Street in Erie, Pennsylvania. The second fort, described only as a "Pallisaded Fort," was being built "on a little lake about three or four hundred yards wide & about the same distance from the French Creek; the Fort stands between the Lake & the Creek."[66] The second fort, which only began construction on July 11, 1753,[67] by previous Presque Isle engineer Francois Le Mercier, was later called Fort de la Rivière au Boeuf or Fort Le Boeuf and stretched near High Street and First Street in present-day Waterford, Pennsylvania. In addition, eight pieces of cannon had already arrived on the shores of Lake Erie, and more were coming once the French soldiers came up the Mississippi from the Illinois country.

That night, when a few Lenape arrived from near John Fraser's house at Venango,[68] they told him most of the village had left to aid the French at the "Carrying Place" (the waterway between Lake Ontario and Lake Erie), and Trent realized the magnitude of the situation had grown exponentially. The loyalties of the Ohio Indians were casually drifting away from them, and they remarked on the 14th that he "didn't like the Behavior of the Delawares."[69] So, Trent called Shingas to a council before he left so they could rekindle their chain of friendship between Virginia and the Lenape. After all, it was near Shingas's village up the Ohio from Logstown where the Ohio intended to build a fort and lay out the town of Saltsburg on Shurtees Creek (Chartier's Creek). But if

---
63. Ibid., 30.
64. Ibid.
65. Ibid., 37.
66. Ibid., 36.
67. Hunter, 68.
68. Trent's Account with the Proceedings of the Six Nations of Indians and Allies, 30.
69. Ibid., 31.

his suspicions about the Lenape were warranted, they had to move the location of their town and fort. The Pro-French (Francophile) Lenape never allowed an English town to be established there.

Trent revealed two twists of tobacco and placed some in a pipe tomahawk, saying, "Brothers, Smoke one from your Brothers, the English."[70] Then, he allowed the Half-King to convince Shingas and the Lenape people where their loyalty should lie. He first spoke with the French's intentions to take possession of the Forks of the Ohio and to "build as low as the Mouth of Beaver Creek."[71]

Then the Half-King told them, "Now cousins, you see what sort of people the French are, put no belief in them; their words are as sweet as Honey, but they don't come from their Hearts, only from lips."[72] He held up a tomahawk and then let it fall from his hand to the ground.

> The French say they have no Hatchet with them, but its all one to us if we are killed whether we are Knocked in the Head with a Hatchet or Poisoned by drinking a dram.[73]

Trent watched as there was little expression or change in Shingas after hearing the bold statement. He and the Lenape left the next day without a justified response, and he understood why. On the 21st of July, news came from Venango by a Conewago messenger. A French force led by Canadian fur trader Pierre Louis Boucher de Niverville Sieur de Montizambert[74] captured trader John Trotter with his servant James McLaughlin and forced resident gunsmith John Fraser and his employee William Wilson[75] to flee south toward the Forks of the Ohio. (Fraser later wrote that Niverville had previously built a house at Logstown back in January). The French's intention was now to build a third fort using the former Fraser house as a temporary supply depot that lay on the mouth of French Creek at Venango and then build one at the Forks and the other at the mouth of Beaver Creek.[76]

Meanwhile, as the French finished their construction of forts and Trent organized another council in Logstown, The Ohio Company met at Stratford Hall in Westmoreland County, Virginia, over three days from July 25th to 27th, 1753.[77] Stratford Hall was now the residence of Philip Ludwell Lee, the eldest

---

70. Ibid., 31, part 2.
71. Ibid., 32. (This is where present-day Rochester, Pennsylvania lies today.)
72. Ibid.
73. Ibid.
74. Pierre-Louis Boucher de Niverville Sieur de Montizambert was considered one of the first French traders to frequent the area of Logstown which they called Chiningué. He later built a house there by January of 1754. Hunter, 99.
75. Steele, 50.
76. Trent's Account with the Proceedings of the Six Nations of Indians and Allies, 33.
77. GMP, Mulkearn, 178.

Today the Great Hall at Stratford Hall (completed in 1738), where the Ohio Company members met from July 25-27, 1753. (Author photo and courtesy of Stratford Hall, Stratford, Virginia.)

son of the Ohio Company's co-founder Thomas Lee, and he called the meeting inside his house so they could finalize their plans for the Ohio Company fort on Chartier's Creek.

The Ohio Company treasurer, George Mason, announced to these members in attendance that he had written to their London liaison[78] and member John Hanbury and ordered twenty brass swivel guns as well as other arms and ammunition. Once they arrived in the colonies, they were to be transported to "factor" William Trent at the New Store to take to the new fort once it was constructed. The Ohio Company fort itself was still proposed to be located (at least to the company members in attendance) on the southeast side of the Ohio at Shurtees Creek, and blueprints were shown to the committee. Though the sketch of this proposal was probably lost over time, a description of it was recorded in the minutes of the meeting on July 25, 1753, and was described as follows:

> The walls of the said Fort shall be twelve feet high to be built of sawed or hewn Loggs and to enclose a piece of ground Ninety feet Square,

---

78. Ibid., 149.

besides the four Bastions at the Corners of sixteen feet square each with houses in the middle for stores Magazines.[79]

The committee then suggested three supervisors of the laborers, carpenters, and workmen for this outpost. They were willing to authorize and appoint Thomas Cresap, Christopher Gist, and William Trent to supervise the construction "and employ hunters to supply them with provisions."[80] The supervisors also oversaw the layout of the town proposed on an adjacent two hundred acres of land with streets and lots or squares of two acres each.[81] The settlers who bought these lots were required to build upon them within three years. One square was even designed for a school to be built primarily for the education of Indian children.[82]

Yet while the Ohio Company members sat and probably dined in the early evening at the Lee residence, Trent sent messages throughout the Ohio country to announce an important council to hear the message from Christopher Gist and seduce any chiefs whose support remained questionable.

They gathered on August 10th, and in attendance at this council were many who sat with Trent one year earlier with Virginia commissioners at Logstown and at the Lower Shawnee Town. There was Shingas, King of the Lenape and his brother Tamaqua or "the Beaver," Nucheconner the King of the Shawnees and the young Shawnee chief Lapechkewe, the Half-King and Scaruneate (Scarouady or Monacatootha), a Wyandot (Huron) chief, and Assapausa the young Piankashaw chief with "the Turtle."[83]

The message Thomas Burney brought from Christopher Gist was an invitation for all in attendance at this council to come to Winchester next month and meet with the Governor of Virginia, Robert Dinwiddie. It was also at this council where Trent described the Ohio Company settlement and fort plans organized to brighten the chain of friendship, which he "assured I would build a trading house on that Piece of Ground you appointed the commissioners last spring which House still serve as a Nursery for you and at the same time be a Place of Defence where you may defend yourselves from your Enemies & Shelter your Women & Children in Time of Danger."[84] After letting that message sink in with the various leaders, he offered a final plea towards their questionable loyalties. Trent figured they weren't all attending to hear what he

---

79. Ibid., 147–48.
80. Ibid. 148.
81. Ibid.
82. Ibid.
83. Trent's Account with the Proceedings of the Six Nations of Indians and Allies, 37–38.
84. Ibid., 38.

had to say if they didn't trust him. But if the "Shurtees" Creek fort and settlement were going to work, he needed to find out what they all planned to do next. So, he asked them while presenting a string of wampum:

> And I expect each Nation will open their Hearts & Minds, tell me what you intended to do? Whether you intend to let the French finish this Fort & take your whole country away from you & make slaves of you all; Or whether you intend to drive them off.[85]

Unfortunately, he didn't receive many answers from them before the council ended, but he gave his own opinion about the council in a letter to Dinwiddie on August 11th. Until now, Dinwiddie had not garnered much credibility to Trent's reports from the Six Nations about the French, but Trent warned him in his letter that was read aloud at Dinwiddie's council and Williamsburg:

> The eyes of all the Indians are fixed upon you. You have it now in your power with a small expense to send this whole country for His Majesty, but if the opportunity is missed it will never be in the Power of the English to recover it but by a great Expense & the United Force of all the Colonies.[86]

The Governor's Council was pleased to find the Six Nations' interest was still with them, but Trent said the many chiefs were only going to Winchester next month if they saw Dinwiddie there, "whom they chiefly depended for immediate assistance."[87]

Trent still assumed the Shawnees and Lenape dictated their own decisions based on the next move of the French. He told Dinwiddie the French were already "repairing" Fraser's former house as a third outpost,[88] so in those months, the French had three forts in the Ohio Valley. Colonel Fairfax's suggestion was to award Trent a commission "to command a body of Rangers"[89] to aid in this purpose, but until they received directions from London, none could be appointed at this time.

By the end of August, the Half-King, as promised to him, had headed north to see the French commandant to warn the French off their land entirely,[90] as

---

85. Ibid., 40.
86. HSP, Frank M. Etting Collection, William Trent to Robert Dinwiddie August 11, 1753.
87. Executive Journals of the Council of Virginia, Vol. 5, 440.
88. It was still just called "Venango" until the fort was completed near the mouth of French Creek. Then it became later known after 1755 as Fort Machault.
89. Executive Journals of the Council of Virginia, Vol. 5, 440.
90. Colonial records of Pennsylvania, Vol. 5, 660.

Today the present site of the Forks of the Ohio now the site of Point State Park in the city of Pittsburgh, Pennsylvania. (Author photo.)

Trent arrived at John Fraser's new house, built near the mouth of Turtle Creek upon the banks of the Monongahela River. It was apparent Trent did not express confidence in the support from Shingas and the Lenape people, so he left Fraser's house and began to reconnoiter an alternative location for the fort and adjacent settlement.

On August 25th, Andrew Montour (called French Andrew by Fraser) and Trent viewed[91] the familiar triangular piece of land that stood in the middle between the neighboring Lenape towns: Shannopin's Town to the north on the Allegheny and Shingas's village to the south on the Ohio River. The truth was, Trent hadn't forgotten about this place when he paddled past it five years earlier.[92] This area had much potential and be much more appreciated by the Half-King (since he had once suggested it)[93] and the Six Nations. As he left for his house in Virginia, he couldn't help but feel optimistic about choosing the Forks of the Ohio for the new site of the Ohio Company fort.

---

91. Ibid.
92. Almost exactly five years to the day, August 27, 1748, Trent, Croghan, William Franklin and Conrad Weiser paddled from Shannopin's Town past the Forks of the Ohio and stopped at Queen Aliquippa's "Written Rock" village on the Ohio River.
93. Thwaites, 78.

Chapter 9

Race to the Western Country

Since September of 1753, the whirlwind of events Trent encountered made him feel like he was soaring through an endless dream. After he stopped at his house on the North Branch of the Potomac, Trent finally arrived in Winchester, Virginia, on the 4th of September. It was there before the entire county court consisting of several justices, including Thomas Bryan Martin,[1] Morgan Morgan (the father of the future founder of Morgantown, West Virginia)[2] and the colony's lone resident peer[3] Lord Thomas Fairfax, did Trent finally take the oath as justice of the peace with the Bahamas born George William Fairfax.[4] Almost a week later, he stood on the same grounds at the courthouse, listening to the local militia volley-fire their guns to salute the ninety-eight individuals, who consisted mostly of Indian chiefs, wives, and children that arrived to the beat of a militia drum cadence.

Unfortunately, this promising treaty with Governor Dinwiddie, discussed at Logstown back in July, soon unraveled before the council even met in Winchester. They already knew the Half-King could not attend because he was still at the French forts on Lake Erie to give the French their third and final notice of trespassing in the Ohio country, so this also meant Dinwiddie did not attend as well. The governor stayed in Williamsburg since he only promised to

---

1. Thomas Bryan Martin (1731–1798) was a land agent for the Northern Neck Proprietary of Virginia and nephew of Lord Thomas Fairfax. He served two terms in the Virginia House of Burgesses from 1756–1758 and 1758–1761. Later the city of Martinsburg, West Virginia was named in honor of him by founder, General Adam Stephen.
2. Morgan's son Zachquill Morgan founded Morgantown in 1767.
3. Thomas Fairfax, the 6th Lord Fairfax of Cameron (1693–1781) came into possession of the vast Culpeper family estate in 1719 and at one time owned about 5,282,000 acres in Virginia. He was also the only Scottish peer or nobleman of hereditary title who resided in the colonies.
4. George William Fairfax (January 2, 1723/24–April 3, 1787) was born on the island of New Providence in the Bahamas to Colonel William Fairfax and Sarah Walker. He served two terms in the Virginia House of Burgesses for both Fairfax County (1752–1755) and Frederick County (1756–1758).

The present site of the former Frederick County courthouse and the 1753 Treaty of Winchester in Winchester, Virginia. Today it's the entrance to the Shenandoah Valley Civil War Museum on 20 N. Loudoun Street.

travel to Winchester if the Half-King made an appearance. His last-minute absence did not sit well with those sachems in attendance like Monacatootha and Delaware George.[5] They had come to Virginia to see Dinwiddie and hoped to address their concerns personally, but now, through interpreter Andrew Montour, they could only have Trent and Colonel William Fairfax deliver the message to him.

The physical presence now of a large French army from Canada invading their lands was making them uneasy and they were tired of waiting. To them, while the French had almost built three forts, the English had done essentially nothing. So, the Six Nations decided to handle this conflict internally instead of waiting for assistance and according to Monacatootha: "Our Kings have nothing to do with Our Lands, for we, the Warriors, fought for the Lands, and so the Right belongs to us, and we will take Care of them."[6]

Trent had warned Dinwiddie the Ohio Indians might act sooner rather than later if he didn't act accordingly to please them. Now, as the days progressed, Trent watched his expansion plans at the Forks of the Ohio crumble right in front of his eyes.

On the twelfth, Monacatootha addressed his words to everyone but looked directly over at Trent and Croghan:

> You told us you would build a Strong House at the Forks, after bidding us take care of Our Lands; we now request you may not build that Strong-House for we intend to keep Our Country clear of settlements during these troublesome Times.[7]

It was exactly what Trent feared might happen. Without the voice of the Half-King and their biggest supporter of an Ohio Company fort and settlement, the present council didn't support the English presence in the Ohio country. Governor Dinwiddie, on the other hand, did not discourage very easily. He assumed the Half-King did eventually return and support them, but he still needed somebody to reconnoiter the newly built French outposts.

Fairfax's mission to send out his man William Russell to see the Commandant of the French forces was nothing short of failure. Russell had gone no further than Logstown, so intel of the northern outposts was bleak except for Trent's account from the Six Nations, and Dinwiddie had not accepted

---

5. Delaware George also known as "Nennatchehan" was present at the Treaty of Logstown in 1752 and Carlisle in 1753 as well as others. He was a member of the Turkey clan of the Lenape (or Delaware) and was the brother of Pisquatomen, Tamaqua (the Beaver), and Shingas, King of the Delawares.
6. Vaughan, 185.
7. Ibid.

that as valid. (It was, in fact, proven costly because he hadn't sent Trent's account and journal with the Six Nations dated July 11th until November 17th). When Trent wrote to Dinwiddie that "the Half-King who was returned from the French army much displeased with the treatment he received from the Commander,"[8] he pleaded with the governor to listen and accept the Half-King's word as viable intel.

"The Half-King is the best friend the English have," Trent wrote, "But fears a great part of the Six Nations favor the French and doubts all the settlers on the Ohio Company's' Lands will be obliged to move off if the Governor didn't fall on some method speedily to stop the progress of the French."[9]

Trent must have also felt proud when he told Dinwiddie that the Half-King still was "desiring two forts to be built, one at the Forks, and the other at the old French Town."[10]

It left a short window to begin this Ohio Company fort at the Forks of the Ohio, so Dinwiddie needed a volunteer more than ever "to grow properly commissioned to the Commandant of the French Forces, to learn by what Authority he presumes to make Incroachments on His Majesty's Lands on the Ohio,"[11] so he could learn what the French's next move was in the Ohio country. Dinwiddie could have sent Trent; however, his duties as factor for the Ohio Company were too important to risk if he received hostile treatment by the French. They needed somebody ambitious enough to ignore the lurking dangers. This person also had to be expendable, so if, barring all diplomacy, he was killed, the Half-King then mustered all the Six Nations to pledge their full support behind the English.

On October 27, 1753, the governor and his council found such an individual when a young twenty-one-year-old adjutant of the Southern District[12] named George Washington "offered himself"[13] for such a perilous task. Washington not only took surveyor Christopher Gist along on this journey but also hired away four employees of the Ohio Company to act as his "servitors"[14] for the baggage he had carried since Winchester. One such servitor was Barnaby Curran and Trent was probably none too pleased Washington had "stole" away his best itinerant.

---

8. Executive Journals of the Council of Virginia, Vol. 5, 443.
9. Ibid.
10. Ibid., 447.
11. Ibid.
12. Washington was commissioned as adjutant of the Southerrn District on December 13, 1752. The Southern District was made up of the counties of Princess Ann, Norfolk, Nansemond, Isle of Wight, Southampton, Surry, Brunswick, prince George, Dinwiddie, Chesterfield, Amelia, and Cumberland.
13. Executive Journals of the Council of Virginia, Vol. 5, 444.
14. "Servitors" were servants or hire hands that guided the horses, traded with the local Indian nations, and helped hunt for food.

Present-day view of the Monongahela River near the mouth of Redstone Creek near Brownsville, Pennsylvania. (Author photo.)

So now it was just a few days ago when Curran returned ahead of Washington and Gist from the French forts to report the French intentions were to take the Forks of the Ohio before the English did. Trent himself had just returned from Winchester after overseeing a case[15] involving a debt owed between Thomas Cresap and Richard Pearis[16] when Curran arrived.

So, in response on January 5th, 1754, under the care of John Faulkner,[17] Trent sent nineteen carpenters to drive seventeen pack horses[18] and supplies he gathered at Cresap's to build a third Ohio Company storehouse at the mouth of Redstone Creek with the hope to have orders to begin a fort. Where Redstone Creek emptied itself into the Monongahela, Trent estimated, was only about thirty-seven miles from the Forks of the Ohio and "being the first convenient place for laying stores to be transported by water"[19] instead of traveling the one hundred thirty miles in its entirety from the New Store Tract. The men he sent

---

15. The case was a declaration of Thomas Cresap for a debt involving Richard Pearis on December 10, 1753.
16. Richard Pearis (1725–1794) was a trader that formed a partnership with Nathaniel Gist, the son of surveyor Christopher Gist. Later he lived in South Carolina where he became a Loyalist officer during the American Revolution and eventually resided in the Bahamas for his final years.
17. Bailey, 65.
18. Journal of Major George Washington 1753–1754, 39.
19. Trent's Remarks 1757, 3.

out were also to scout the road ahead of the Cromwell relations[20] that were traveling a day or two after them to settle near Gist's new plantation, and then Trent's men were to begin construction of their company storehouse until he could join them shortly.

Trent finally slept through the night of the 5th, but early the next morning, he woke to dictate a letter to Governor Dinwiddie about the men he sent to Redstone. He justified this motivation to send men to Redstone Creek without any official orders that he "could stop the French this winter if properly empowered to do so."[21] Before he could seal his letter, he heard a loud whinnying of a horse outside Christopher Gist's house. Trent put on his breeches and a coat over his new cambric shirt,[22] then quietly put on his boots so he didn't wake his sleeping wife Sarah, who was now with child. When he stepped outside, he recognized Christopher Gist immediately, but at first almost couldn't identify the individual traveling with Gist. Major George Washington looked nothing like the clean shaven and surefooted emissary he saw back in November[23] when he came to the New Store to recruit "servitors."

He looked tired and ragged, dressed in leggings and moccasins while tied in deerskins[24] to protect himself from the cold. Washington also seemed agitated; he had to stay a night to rest. The "necessary papers"[25] he carried were a response from the French commandant Jacques Legardeur de Saint Pierre, and it meant Trent's account from the Six Nations had been right all along. The French weren't leaving the Ohio country, and now their sights were set on the Forks of the Ohio once spring came. By the 15th of January, French militia and regulars left Montreal and headed to the outpost below Lake Erie.

Washington left the next day for Williamsburg on the same horse and saddle he purchased at Gist's plantation,[26] but not before taking the letter Trent wrote to Governor Dinwiddie, he dated the 6th instant.[27] As Washington was set to arrive in Williamsburg around January 16th, Trent prepped the remaining horses and supplies to join those Ohio Company men at the mouth of Redstone Creek. He loaded up his horse, packing at least a quire[28] of paper,

---

20. Journal of Major George Washington 1753–1754, 39.
21. Brock, Vol. 1, 55.
22. HSP, Frank M. Etting Collection, Ohio Company Papers, Trent and Croghan Account for the Ohio Company 1753–1754.
23. According to Gist, Washington came to his house at the mouth of Will's Creek on November 14, 1753.
24. On his April 8, 1754 account to Governor Dinwiddie, he refers to pieces of deer skins as "matchcoat pieces" so we can assume Washington's matchcoat was made of deer skins. For complete list of expenses, see also Appendix E of this book.
25. Journal of Major George Washington 1753–1754, 36.
26. According to Washington, he purchased a horse and saddle at Gist's "Monongahela" on January 2, 1754. (Journal of Major George Washington 1753–1754, 39).
27. Brock, Vol. 1, 55.
28. A quire is 1/20th of a ream of paper. A ream is 480 or 500 sheets (depending on the region) so a quire is approximately twenty-four or twenty five sheets of paper.

quills, ink, and red sealing wax. Then he filled the empty holsters on either side of his saddle with his pistol and brass blunderbuss.

On January 21, 1754,[29] Trent loaded up the fourteen horses with powder lead and flints he acquired in Winchester, some presents for the chiefs of the Six Nations from Governor Dinwiddie and left his house on the Potomac for the mouth of Redstone Creek. He arrived nine days later, on January 30th.[30] There at the mouth of Redstone, Trent's "artificers"[31] he sent out at the beginning of January had already built a fortified cache or storehouse on a nearby bluff with loopholes to use as musket portals if defense was necessary. (It is believed today the site of the Ohio Company storehouse lies on the grounds of Assad's Iron Metals Inc. just off Brownsville Road).

The Ohio Company storehouse was (according to Louis Coulon de Villiers Journal on June 30, 1754) about thirty feet in length and twenty-two feet in width or breadth,[32] and like the previous building at Rock Creek and the New Store Tract, probably had a joiner[33] cut out a joist to support the door. This fine craftsmanship later only lasted six months, for after the battle of the Great Meadows, the French burned this same storehouse on July 6th, 1754.[34] The French referred to this as "Le Hangard" and is not to be confused with Redstone Old Fort or Fort Burd, which was built almost two miles to the south on Nemacolin Creek (now Dunlap Creek) in 1759 near the prehistoric burial mounds in present-day Brownsville, Pennsylvania.

Upon Trent's arrival, he immediately sent messengers out to the Ohio Indian nations that he had brought arms, ammunition, with other presents for them once they met him at the Forks of the Ohio or mouth of the Monongahela. Trent also wrote to his partner George Croghan (who since the 12th of January had been near the mouth of Turtle Creek and Logstown) to come and be his interpreter there once the Indians sent word they were coming. Croghan wrote to Governor Hamilton of Pennsylvania on February 3, 1754, referring to Trent's request, saying:

> Mr. Trent is Just come outt with the Virginia goods, and has brought a quality of Toules and workmen to begin a fort, and as he Can't talk ye Indian languidge, I am obliged to stay and assist him in Delivering them goods, which is Mr. Montour's advice.[35]

---

29. Trent's Remarks 1757, 3.
30. Ibid.
31. Artificers were "skilled craftsmen", so Trent's men were skilled at carpentry, the Indian languages, and surveying.
32. Papiers Contrecoeur, 198.
33. "Account of John Hammer," James, 199.
34. Papiers Contrecoeur, 202.
35. Pennsylvania Archives First series, Vol. 2, 119.

At the same time in Williamsburg, Governor Dinwiddie addressed his council on January 21st with the letter from Trent and the French letter from the commandant St. Pierre that Washington had delivered. After much consideration and as French forces were expected down the Ohio in the spring, Dinwiddie suggested that:

> I think it is for His M'y's service and the Protection of settlem'ts of this Dom'n to do all in our power to prevent their building any forts or making any Settlem'ts on that river, and more particularly so nigh us that of the Logstown.[36]

So, it was agreed with all those council members that "the chief command be given to Major Washington and a Captain's Commission to Mr. William Trent to raise what traders and other men he can to annoy the enemy; That Mr. John Carlyle be appointed Commissary of Provisions."[37] Washington was commissioned on January 25, 1754, with Trent's official commission the next day on January 26th and Carlyle's a day later than Trent's on the 27th.

Dinwiddie also wrote separately to Colonel James Patton and Lord Thomas Fairfax requesting them "to send immediately out 200 men to protect those already sent by the Ohio Comp'a to build a Fort in to resist any attempts on them,"[38] with Patton told to "make a draft of 50 men to be at Alexandria, the head of the Potomac River by the 20th of next Mo."[39] Colonel Patton and Lord Fairfax were both commanders of their Virginia county militias in Augusta and Frederick Counties, respectively.

However, with Trent currently at the mouth of Redstone Creek, Dinwiddie sent Thomas Cresap to deliver the commission and orders personally to Trent. Cresap arrived almost two weeks later at the mouth of Redstone Creek on the 10th of February[40] and handed him the packet from Governor Dinwiddie. Trent looked at the sealed packet of letters.

> Com. to William Trent commander of a company of men intended to the Ohio.[41]

He broke the seal and read the orders:

---

36. Brock, Vol. 1, 49.
37. Executive Journals of the Council of Virginia, Vol. 5, 460.
38. Brock, Vol. 1, 49.
39. Ibid., 50.
40. Trent's Remarks 1757, 4.
41. This was how Dinwiddie addressed the packet of papers he sent to Trent.

> I do hereby constitute and appoint you Wm Trent Esq'r to the Com'd'r of such and so many of His My's Subjects not exceeding 100 men as You can immediately raise and enlist.[42]

Trent was also ordered to find a "suitable Lieutenant" to be his second-in-command.

His orders also stated that:

> Major Washington has a Com'o to raise 100 men with them he is to join you and I desire you to March your men out to the Ohio where a Fort is proposed to be built. When You are there, you are to protect and assist them in Finishing the Fort and be on your guard against any Attempts of the French.[43]

When he finished reading, he realized what Dinwiddie had failed to enclose along with his packet of letters. The governor had sent no advance wages from the Assembly or even letters of credit to pay his eight shillings a day wages for his captaincy[44] and wages for his province's first raised troops or "volunteers." As Trent understood it, the men enlisted for this expedition were to be the "first raised" troops of Virginia, independent companies like when he raised men of Pennsylvania during King George's War in 1746. So, by law, these "volunteers" were to be paid two shillings each day for their service, and just like in 1746, he needed to raise 100 of them.

Trent also realized Dinwiddie's intentions were for him to pay his own wages and those one hundred men he recruited with funds he managed from the Ohio Company funds. It was with confidence then that Dinwiddie paid the balance in full plus possible interest after the expedition was completed. This also included the blunderbusses, cutlasses, and other short arms[45] he took from the New Store and stored in the newly built storehouse at Redstone.

After paying Cresap four pounds[46] for delivering the packet to him, Trent sent itinerants to every trading house, cabin, and Indian town with the message that for two shillings a day, any trader who had sufficient knowledge of paths to and from the Forks and willing to build a fort for the Ohio Company should meet him in a few days either on his march or at the Forks of the Ohio.

---

42. Cherry, 110. Brock, Vol. 1, 56–57. For Trent's commission and orders, see Appendix D of this book.
43. Ibid., 110–11. Ibid., 55.
44. Brock, Vol. 1, 112.
45. Ibid., 106, 125.
46. Library of Virginia, Expense Account of Government of Virginia to William Trent, April 8, 1754. For complete list of expenses, see also Appendix E of this book.

Then he used the rafts they had built[47] in the last week to float the deer and bearskins and work tools next to their canoes down the Monongahela. The deer skins were most important to keep dry because he used these "matchcoat pieces"[48] he purchased as skin wrappers around the gunpowder so it didn't dampen inside the purple half-thick bags.[49]

The presents for the Ohio Indians he took himself as he marched up the Sewickley Old Town Path[50] to the mouth of Turtle Creek and the new residence of gunsmith John Fraser. Trent arrived at Fraser's house on February 14th,[51] waiting not only for word from the Half-King and Monacatootha but also to fill the blank commission he had drafted before he left Redstone Creek.

John Fraser was his lieutenant and second-in-command of his men at the Forks of the Ohio but had one stipulation before he accepted. Fraser became lieutenant if he could continue to conduct his trading business with James Young[52] at his house on Turtle Creek and only traveled to the Forks if deemed necessary. Trent accepted his conditions but had an idea to enlist another officer as an ensign and third-in-command to be present along with him just in case Fraser couldn't be. For this position, he sent for Edward Ward, the half-brother of his partner Croghan and a former employee of their Conodoguinet Creek tanning yard a few years ago.

His timing for recruitment was perfect because the next day, on the fifteenth, twenty-one men[53] arrived at Fraser's house to enlist in Trent's company. So far, they were already to half of what was required of him, but he still had to wonder if two hundred men were enough to defend the Forks if the French and Indians became hostile towards them. This, of course, depended on Dinwiddie and his meeting on February 14th with the House of Burgesses at the Capitol in Williamsburg. The Assembly wasn't supposed to meet again until April, but Dinwiddie called an emergency meeting to speak about "the welfare of all the colonies on this continent, and more especially of this Dominion."[54]

He talked about how the French were "instigators of robberies and murder" with the Indians and "that they had 220 canoes made and many more rough hew'd to be made in order to transport early this spring, a great number of regular forces not less than 1500 men."[55] This report was not even dramatized

---

47. History of Colonel Henry Bouquet, Darlington, 65.
48. Library of Virginia, Expense Account of Government of Virginia to William Trent, April 8, 1754.
49. Ibid.
50. The path began at the mouth of Sewickley Creek near West Newton, Pennsylvania and ventured northwest two miles above Herminie, then the remaining four miles to Fraser's house at Turtle Creek.
51. Cherry, 79.
52. Bailey, 122–27.
53. GMP, Mulkearn, 83.
54. Brock, Volume 1, 73.
55. Ibid., 74.

"Trent and Half King at the Forks" by artist Robert Griffing. (Courtesy of Paramount Press Inc.)

or exaggerated. Dinwiddie had received this account from Washington when he returned from the French fort and the news of recent pillaging and murder from Trent. Years later, he reported the murder of a German family in January of 1754 "between the Ohio and the Appalachian Mountains,"[56] and it wasn't wrong to assume they were one of the several German families moving to settle on the Ohio Company tract after hearing about the proposed town of Saltsburg.

When Trent finally received word from the Half-King and chiefs of the Six Nations to meet him at the Forks of the Ohio, he, Ward, and the others traveled the last eight miles to the Forks. They arrived on February 17th[57] and joined up with Andrew Montour, Christopher Gist, George Croghan, and other traders who had answered the call to join Trent's company. There was Jacob Arrants, "a master of any language and perfectly acquainted with all the way and mountains between this and ye Fork."[58] Samuel Arsdale (also spelled Asdill, Easdale or Isdale), the thirty-two-year-old, five-foot-seven trader from Frederick County, Virginia[59] and Robert Roberts, a former employee of James Dunning that lost goods when the French and Indians attacked Pickawillany on June 21, 1752.[60] Roberts probably arrived with Paul Peirce (Pearce), who also lost goods at Muskingum when the French attacked in the summer of 1752.[61]

---

56. Trent's Remarks 1757, 5–6.
57. *Maryland Gazette*, March 14, 1754, 2.
58. Toner, 181.
59. Clark, 484. Cherry, 75.
60. Bailey, 145.
61. Ibid.

It was Peirce and Joseph Campbell,[62] a frequent trader with the Half-King, who were present at the Forks because both owned trading houses[63] near the Forks of the Ohio.

It wasn't just former acquaintances or employees of Trent and Croghan like James Foley or John Owens that arrived either. Three employees of the Lowrey trading firm appeared as well. Their names were Nehemiah Stevens, John Kennedy, and a woman named Elizabeth Williams.[64] All three, along with trader Andrew McBriar, were captured on April 23, 1754, near Gist's plantation[65] and taken as prisoners back to the eventual Fort Duquesne.

His company, it seemed, was all coming together nicely. When he and Christopher Gist wrote to Washington on February 19th, it was said by them that "in two or three days, they expected down all the people, and as soon as they came, were to lay the Foundation of the Fort, expecting to make out for the Purpose about 70 or 80 men."[66]

When all the neighboring chiefs of the Six Nations and Lenape arrived, Trent began a council to give them their presents from the government of Virginia. It began by distributing powder, lead bars, and flints to those in attendance, even gifting a musket, pistol, and a match coat to one of the chiefs of the Six Nations who came down from the towns above Venango. Through interpreters Croghan and Montour, the chief told Trent, "As he Came upon Business he bought brought no Arms with him, he said it was hard for him to go home without arms as he should run a great Risque as he was obliged to go through the French to warn their people from Amongst them."[67]

Trent also did the same for the Half-King and Monacatootha. He not only gave each a case of "neat" pistols,[68] a ruffled shirt and a plain shirt[69] but also made sure their wives received the same despite not being present. Then, while they sat admiring their gifts, Trent held up a wampum belt made of three thousand black or purple beads and three hundred white beads.[70] The combination of the light and dark colors symbolized togetherness despite being a contrast to each other. This belt then he handed to Monacatootha was visible proof of when Trent told him at Logstown last summer this house was not just for the English but might "serve as a Nursery for you and at the same Time be a Place

---

62. Journal of Major George Washington 1753–1754, 35.
63. Bailey, 145.
64. Memoirs of Robert Stobo, 91. Steele, 51, 91–92.
65. Steele, 51.
66. *Maryland Gazette*, March 14, 1754, 2. *Pennsylvania Gazette*, April 2, 1754, 2.
67. Library of Virginia, Expense Account of Government of Virginia to William Trent, April 8, 1754.
68. Neat means they are plain with no patterns carved into the barrel or stock.
69. Library of Virginia, Expense Account of Government of Virginia to William Trent, April 8, 1754.
70. Ibid.

of Defense where you may defend yourself from your Enemies and shelter your Women and Children in Time of Danger."[71] Monacatootha eventually carried this belt from Trent with him everywhere, and he later presented it to Governor Robert Hunter Morris at a council on December 19, 1754:

> This belt was sent by the Governor of Virginia and delivered by Captain Trent. You see it in the Representation of the Hatchet. It was an invitation to us to join with and assist our brethren to repel the French from the Ohio. At the same time it was given, there were but four or five of us, and we were all that knew anything about the matter; when we got it, we put it in a private pocket on the inside of our garment. It lays next to our breasts.[72]

The belt seemed to make an impression on them more than the governor's presents. Looking at each other momentarily, they spoke through Croghan and Montour, telling Trent what exactly should be done next.

> The chiefs of the Indians insisted that I should set the Indian traders that I had enlisted & the workmen that I had brought out with me to work and begin a Fort against the troops from Virginia should arrive.[73]

At that notion, Trent wasted no time.

> At the request of the Indians, I set the carpenters to work & layed out a Fort.[74]

So, Trent's hired laborers began immediately sawing and chopping at the red and white oak trunks[75] that peppered the large point of land between the Monongahela and Allegheny Rivers. When there was a large enough clearing, a circumferentor or surveyor's compass was mounted upon a tripod called a Jacob staff. This was probably operated by Thomas Cresap or Christopher Gist who both had previously surveyed the Ohio Company tract. Swiveling it around to find the flattest terrain to lay out the fort's square, Trent took out the measuring wheel that he brought from the New Store and was purchased by Gist[76] last

---

71. Trent's Account of Proceedings with Six Nations of Indians and Allies, 38.
72. Colonial Records of Pennsylvania, Vol. 6, 195.
73. Trent's Remarks 1757, 4. Cherry, 54.
74. Ibid.
75. Darlington, Christopher Gist Journals, 34.
76. GMP, Mulkearn, 149.

summer. The measuring wheel or waywiser was a wooden framed wheel with brass spokes that someone pushed, calculating the distance between two specific points.

While Gist previously calculated furlongs or miles to establish the large boundaries of the Ohio Company grant, Trent used the dial to approximate feet or rods. Two full revolutions of the wheel equaled one rod or 16 1/2 feet, so after ten full turns, Trent had a long upright stake pounded in the corner. He did this four times until he had the fort's square marked.

Trent no doubt referred to the previous blueprint the Ohio Company comprised in July,

> To enclose a piece of ground ninety-foot square besides the four bastions of the corners of sixteen feet square each with houses in the middle for stores, magazines.[77]

After the fort with bastions was marked with stakes across the "Point," Trent pointed to a piece of timber and motioned for the Half-King to place the log in the middle of the square. It was at that time Trent christened the outpost "Fort St. George"[78] and recorded it in the account books dated 1753 and 1754 for the Ohio Company. As acting "factor," Trent chose not to take Dinwiddie's suggested name of the outpost after the Prince of Wales and future King George III, calling it Fort Prince George.[79] He chose instead to name it after the patron saint that adorned the King's colors as a red cross and gave homage to the public house in Philadelphia; he recruited men for the King's service 1746-47 called "St. George and the Dragon Inn."[80] His reasoning behind independently naming it was because Virginia did not pay him, and later, according to his Ensign Edward Ward, "It was no matter so the country was secured for His Majesty, which was his view which was at the expense of the Fort, as he had orders from the Ohio Company to build a Fort and none from the Government to build any."[81]

After the Half-King laid the first log of Fort St. George, he declared to Trent and the others his loyalty to the English, saying: "That this Fort belonged to the English and them. With the English they would defend it against any Nation that should attack it."[82]

---

77. Ibid., 147–48. Cherry, 54.
78. HSP, Frank M. Etting Collection, Ohio Company Papers, Thomas Cresap to James Tilghman May 20, 1767.
79. Brock, Vol. 1, 343.
80. See Endnotes 209 and 210.
81. History of Colonel Henry Bouquet, Darlington, 46. Cherry, 120.
82. Trent's Remarks 1757, 4. Cherry, 54.

The log laid by the Half-King was "the First Log of one of the Storehouses."[83] By the time the first storehouse was built to lodge the blankets, powder, skins, and flints and a second building was almost completed, it was around the first week of March.

The treaty and business with the Ohio Indians were over, but a new concern came to light. Despite hearing that Washington might be coming in a few days, Trent still was waiting for him and his men to arrive. Reports came daily since they arrived at the Forks that the French were coming soon down the river, so each day that came and went without Washington's men worried Trent immensely.

On the 3rd of March, he wrote to Washington to speed up him and his detachment but had heard nothing. Three days later, spies from Logstown were spotted from across the river. Ensign Michel Chauvgnerie sent these men,[84] and after returning to Logstown, they gave a report that corroborated Trent's status of the outpost at the Forks:

> The scouts arrived at the village of the Loups having no hope of finding a carriage to cross the river. The Scouts made to cross to an island opposed to the establishment where they took notice an advanced house almost made which is to serve as a Magazine, because of the distance they could not know in what manner they were constructing their fort, since it was still only marked out.[85]

With all the transactions done with the Indians, there was obvious unrest amongst them. The Lenape had already returned to their towns in the Ohio, questioning before they left "while the English did not intend to assist them."[86]

Trent wrote to Washington with more haste on March 7th, pleading with him to hurry because with more Ohio Indians threatening to leave and the French rumored to be down soon, he could not rationally hold the Forks with about seventy, including Indians. Despite the gossip of a large French army appearing down the river, the force had only reached Fort Presque Isle on March 8th. The rivers had only begun to thaw, so it was weeks or months until they could be properly equipped to head down the Ohio.

---

83. Ibid.
84. Ensign Michel Maray Sieur de La Chauvignere (January 24, 1704/5–August 10, 1778) was a Canadian military officer who spoke many Indian languages and replaced Phillippe-Thomas Chabert de Joncaire as commander of the future outpost known as Fort Machault. It was he and Francois de Lignery who left Fort Machault trying to support the garrison of Fort Niagara in the summer of 1759 and were defeated at the Battle of La Belle-Famille where Chauvignere was taken prisoner and de Lignery was killed.
85. Papiers Contrecoeur, 108.
86. Trent's Remarks 1757, 4.

Meanwhile, Washington had received both of Trent's letters but could not decide how to respond. The truth was, he had spent over a month recruiting in Alexandria and had rather minuscule results. Originally, it forced Dinwiddie back on February 19th to declare a proclamation that any man who enlisted for the province of Virginia be rewarded land within the 200,000 acres "on the East Side of the River Ohio over and above their pay to all who shall voluntarily enter into the said Service."[87]

Even with that initiative in place, it only helped Washington reach about twenty-five men by March 9th and he wrote to Dinwiddie to complain how they were of the lowest quality.

> We find the generality of those who are to be enlisted, are of those loose, idle persons that are quite destitute of house and home.[88]

He continued about their lack of garments or footwear, saying, "There is many of them without shoes, others went stockings, some are without shirts, and not a few that have Scarce a Coat or Waistcoat, to their Backs."[89] The complaints were warranted, but for Dinwiddie, there was no time for the soldiers to be in "uniform dress" or "not time to get them made."[90] So, while Dinwiddie sent three sloops[91] up the Potomac River with tents, weapons, and more recruits to complete Washington's detachment, he advised Washington on March 15th to march what men he did have and "I recommend to you dispatch to be with Capt. Trent, if possible before the French come down the river."[92] Enclosed in the letter dated March 15th, Washington also received a lieutenant colonel's commission[93] and a notice that five more companies have been raised[94] to join Trent at the Forks. The supreme commander and Colonel of the Virginia Regiment was surveyor and College of William and Mary professor Joshua Fry, who had previously commissioned Trent's expedition at Pickawillany in the summer of 1752.

Unfortunately for Trent, this progression was not fast enough. Their provisions at the Forks were scarce and what game he did barter a deal to acquire, the Lenape charged outrageous prices such as seven shillings six pence for a turkey.[95] So they used what was left of the Indian meal and corn without powder.[96]

---

87. Executive Journals of the Council of Virginia, Vol. 5, 462.
88. Brock, Vol. 1, 92.
89. Ibid.
90. Ibid., 106.
91. Ibid., 107.
92. Ibid.
93. For his promotion to lieutenant colonel, Washington received twelve shillings, six pence.
94. Brock, Vol. 1, 86.
95. History of Henry Bouquet, Darlington, 43.
96. Ibid.

With his men coming and going as they pleased and hearing a report from Christopher Gist that "a Chickasaw Indian had seen a force of 400 French coming up the river from the Falls of the Ohio,"[97] Trent devised a plan with the Half-King, Monacatootha, and Ensign Ward. He had little hope Washington was coming in a few days and if the French arrived instead, Trent wanted to "have timber ready to raise the Fort against troops that they might immediately have a place of defense."[98]

He made sure to tell only the three he wanted to know this plan because he didn't want those men leaving to forward this information to the French. Trent had told his second-in-command Fraser as well, but Fraser had been too busy in the past few days to leave his house and come to the Forks.

Over the next few days, Trent supervised the men in implementing this plan, acquiring more timber for their use and digging entrenchments of piling dirt around their constructed buildings and fort layout. According to Trent, "I constantly attended the work from daylight in the morning till night as everyone worked, and everyone seemed to have the good of the country at heart; there was an incredible deal of work done in time."[99]

Croghan also echoed this observation, writing to Pennsylvania Governor Hamilton that before he left the Ohio, he left Trent "and his men at the mouth of the Monongahela building a Fort which seemed to give the Indians great pleasure and put them in high spirits."[100] It was at this time Trent took advantage of the current morale and utilized his equestrian skills. He had to go to Washington and gather more provisions and men himself.

So, on the Half-King's urging, Trent stated it was "insisted I would immediately set off for the Inhabitants & hurry out Coll. Washington with the Troops."[101] It was the soldiers that were needed to hold this outpost, according to the Half-King, because Trent and his Ohio Company employees were always considered one of them "because we chiefly lived in that country and from the long time, we had lived amongst them they looked upon us as Indians."[102]

After Trent went to Fraser's house to gather some provisions for Ward and the remaining company, he quickly journeyed back to his house and the New Store on March 17th.[103] He left Ward in temporary command with the understanding he could seek assistance from Fraser just eight miles away.

---

97. *Maryland Gazette*, March 14, 1754, 2.
98. Trent's Remarks 1757, 9.
99. Ibid.
100. Colonial Records of Pennsylvania, Vol. 6, 21.
101. Trent's Remarks 1757, 9.
102. Ibid.
103. Ibid.

With snow still in the mountains, Trent didn't arrive back at the North Branch of the Potomac until the 27th of March.[104] When he crossed the river and arrived at the New Store, he found a letter dated March 19th waiting for him from Washington. Washington had written Trent, letting him know, "He had received orders to March and Convoying the Arms and that in seven or eight days, the wagons would be ready."[105]

Trent saw Washington wrote this from Alexandria, which still worried him because it was, as Trent estimated, "Not less than 150 miles the Waggon Road."[106] Even if he left Alexandria on the 19th, he couldn't arrive at the New Store until at least sometime in April. It just angered him that after much delay, "there was no account from the Regiments nor any Detachment from it or any provisions."[107]

In the meantime, Trent spent over two weeks at his house recruiting more men in the vicinity and gathering provisions to take back on the Ohio. Since April 8th,[108] he listed an account of all his expenditures and items he purchased with pistoles[109] since he brought back the presents from Winchester in December of 1753. (See also Appendix E for the 1753/1754 expenses).

As he finalized packhorses for the return trip, an urgent express arrived with a copy of trader John Davidson's letter dated April 12th at Logstown. Ensign Ward sent these letters. Since Ward traveled[110] to see Lieutenant Fraser for advice and counsel, they were preparing for the worst. The French were believed to have arrived at Venango and now were disembarking in their bateaus and canoes made of pine and birch down the Ohio (Allegheny). That meant at least by Trent's estimation, the French might be at the Forks by the 19th or 20th. Quickly, Trent dispatched an itinerant to Washington desiring him for "Reinforcement with all Speed" to the Forks as he (meaning Ward) hourly expected a Body of Eight Hundred French."[111]

By the morning of the 20th, the arrival of itinerant James Foley confirmed this when he arrived at Trent's house to give the "Account that the French with nine pieces of cannon and seven hundred men had obliged Mr. Ward my Ensign to abandon the Work."[112]

---

104. Ibid.
105. Ibid.
106. Ibid.
107. History of Colonel Henry Bouquet, Darlington, 44.
108. Library of Virginia, Expense Account of Government of Virginia to William Trent, April 8, 1754.
109. A pistole was a Spanish coin worth eighteen shillings.
110. Ward traveled to Lt. Fraser's house on April 14, 1754 accompanied by Robert Roberts, Thomas Davison, Samuel Arsdale and an Indian.
111. Toner, 26.
112. Trent's Remarks 1757, 10.

Trent sent him along to Washington, who received the bad news along the road after he left Cresap's house at Shawnee Old Town. Later that day, Washington and his three companies in Virginia arrived over one hundred and fifty soldiers strong, with one surgeon, James Craik, and two wagons of provisions,[113] camping near the mouth of Will's Creek across the Potomac. Trent watched them from his house, beginning to set up the encampment. He decided he wasn't going to rush to greet them. It had been almost three months since he and Washington had been first commissioned, and only now was he just arriving at the Inhabitants.

On April 22nd, Ensign Ward finally arrived with two Indian warriors[114] sent by the Half-King and gave both Trent and Washington his account. Apparently, when the French landed on the afternoon of April 17th,[115] "the French commander Claude-Pierre Pecaudy de Contrecoeur sent to the fort ordering them to surrender immediately; otherwise, they (the French) would cut them to pieces, having a piece of cannon leveled at the Fort and one thousand French men."[116]

Ward told the French he only complied with such terms if "they should march out of the fort walls with all their arms and colors flying."[117] The "walls" Ward referred to were the small upright logs called palisades; he had them put up after "laying one log all around four days before the French came."[118]

The terms were accepted, but not before Contrecoeur warned Ward about any other persons coming to support him or any of the fifty individuals remaining at the Forks that if they had arms or supplies, "that they were determined to secure them in all their effects and every Englishman they could find."[119] They proved this by taking trader Hugh Crawford[120] that day and threatening to do the same to Robert Callender and others[121] who came near the Forks.

Ward added there was still uplifting news to come from this. He handed a belt of wampum to Washington and a letter dated April 18 from the Half-King. The Half-King, who had "told the French they had no business there on their hunting grounds pushing the French officer with his hand" and "upon

---

113. Toner, 20.
114. Ibid., 30.
115. Ibid., 39.
116. Pennsylvania State Archives, Burd-Shippen Papers, April 30, 1754.
117. Ibid.
118. Trent's Remarks 1757, 10.
119. Pennsylvania State Archives, Burd-Shippen Papers, April 30, 1754.
120. Hugh Crawford was a trader and hired hand of Trent and Croghan, who was taken prisoner after the French captured the Forks on April 17, 1754. Later in 1756, he served as a lieutenant in Captain James Patterson's Company of Conrad Weiser's Pennsylvania Battalion, and in 1758 on Forbes's expedition. He also resided at Fort Pitt in 1760 with Trent, Croghan and Thomas Smallman, where he was one of the first militia captains at Fort Pitt in 1761.
121. Pennsylvania State Archives, Burd-Shippen Papers, April 30, 1754.

which ensued a Scuffle,"[122] wanted them to know "that ye Indians are not yet afraid and willing to strike as soon as ye English is ready."[123] Which is why two Mingoes had accompanied Ward. They wanted to see for themselves the English army that was forming and then visit Governor Dinwiddie.

When Ward's report was finished, he wished to leave immediately for Williamsburg. Strangely, he showed some slight animosity to Trent by not seeking transportation from the Ohio Company stables. Instead, Ward paid Lt. Col. Washington two pounds ten shillings to use his horse, saddle, and bridle[124] and then rode off with his two companions on the road east.

The next day, on the 23rd of April, Washington invited Trent across the river for a council of war to discuss and consult what needed to be done next until Colonel Fry and his detachment arrived from Winchester. With the account by Ward, Washington seemed hesitant to advance until Colonel Fry and his remaining two companies arrived. As Washington suggested, "It was thought a thing impractical to march towards the Fort without sufficient strength."[125] It was also why he informed Trent that he already sent expresses to Pennsylvania and Maryland when they heard the disagreeable news about the Ohio several weeks after Dinwiddie did.

Trent reminded Washington of their newly constructed storehouse that his artificers had built in the name of the Ohio Company at the mouth of Redstone Creek. The building had loopholes and could be fortified further since it sat on a small bluff. This suggestion highly appealed to Washington. Not only was it thirty-seven miles from the Forks of the Ohio and the first convenient place for laying stores on the Monongahela, but Washington could also provide "clearing a road broad enough to pass with all our artillery and our baggage and there to wait for fresh orders."[126] In fact, Washington approved of his plan so much that he hoped to have Trent and the rest of the forty-odd men scout for this detachment and show them the best road to Redstone Creek once his men finally returned from the Forks.

Unfortunately, on April 25th, when Trent's men sparsely appeared on the road into the Inhabitants, they were in no mood to receive further orders from anyone. Since January, they had directed packhorses, cleared bramble and brush, felled trees and erected wooden buildings at Redstone Creek and the Forks. They were weary, their bellies aching of starvation, and most of all, frustrated with the young lieutenant colonel who never arrived to help them.

---

122. In *Braddock's Defeat* by David L. Preston, Appendix E in back of his book explains this account by an unknown Iroquois warrior. P.R.O. Colonial Office (CO) 5:15, 194–95.
123. Pennsylvania State Archives, Burd-Shippen Papers, April 30, 1754.
124. Toner, 181.
125. Ibid., 41.
126. Ibid., 42.

When Washington requested an audience with them and Trent, he wished to exploit their mastery of Indian languages and how most of them were "perfectly acquainted with all the way and mountains between this and ye Fork."[127] This had their attention, but first, they asked Washington by which daily rate did all of them receive if they joined the Virginia Regiment? Washington scoffed at the question. There's only one rate he was aware of, and it was the soldierly rate of eight pence per day. After all, Washington believed Trent's men had been listed as militia troops by Dinwiddie, so what rate had they received from Trent?

It's probably then when Trent stepped in and defended his men. Washington was right; they were technically militia, but "the Virginians had altered the scheme"[128] since the proclamation was established in February. Trent pointed out they had always been volunteers or "first raised" troops like his stint as a Pennsylvania captain during King George's War, and by Virginia law, the daily rate was two shillings per day. So, they needed to be treated as such. Washington, insulted, abruptly shook his head. He did not pay any of these men three times what he was paying his own detachment, not unless he wanted a mutiny amongst his men. He stood his ground and, slightly irritated, offered these conditions to Trent and his men. "First raised" troops or not, they were now under the command of Colonel Fry and himself, so they needed to accept the eight pence per day without further argument. Furthermore, they did not camp with his men[129] but instead at the New Store until he gave them further orders. Washington was fed up and didn't want the grumblings and complaints of grizzled traders causing dissension amongst the men already in want of more pay and clothing.

Trent, like the others, left the meeting in disgust and angrily crossed the river to the New Store Tract. After failing to come to their aid at the Forks because he was too experienced to garner recruits, what authority did he have to dictate what they must do next? When they stood outside the company warehouse, Trent noticed they were a few less. Three of his men, Jacob Arrants, Edward Lucas, and Samuel Arsdale,[130] had stayed behind to offer their services to Washington. The rest of them, however, wished to return home, and Trent agreed with their misgivings. They had all done all they could for the Ohio Company and still were ridiculed for it. Trent did not stand for the disrespect anymore. As he wrote later, "The Government used me ill, not paying my men agreeable to the footing I raised on so they had neither me nor my men with

---

127. Ibid., 181.
128. Trent's Remarks 1757, 9.
129. Brock, Vol. 1, 170.
130. Clark, 484. Toner, 181. Cherry, 75.

them."[131] So, he dismissed his men and sent them home, disregarding the expected backlash from those just across the Potomac.

Meanwhile, a week later, on Friday, May 3rd,[132] the express sent from their April 23rd council at Will's Creek finally arrived in Philadelphia at the door of the editor of the *Pennsylvania Gazette* and joint postmaster of the colonies. Ben Franklin adjusted his spectacles as he read the first paragraph:

> That Mr. Ward, Ensign of Captain Trent's Company was compelled to surrender his small Fort in the Forks of the Monongahela to the French, on the 17th past who fell down from Venango with a fleet of 360 Battoes and Canoes, upwards of 1000 men and 18 pieces of Artillery, which they planted against the Fort; And Mr. Ward having about 44 men and no cannon to make a proper defense was obliged to surrender on Summons, capitulating to march with their arms.[133]

After meeting with Governor Hamilton and his council, it was agreed that Franklin wrote to London agent Richard Partridge to express their concerns that "the confidence of the French in this undertaking seems well grounded on the present disunited state of the British Colonies."[134]

The letter dated May 8, 1754, to Partridge also had the following postscript:

> Sir,
>
> With this I send you a Paragraph of News from our Gazette, with an Emblem printed therewith, which it may be well enough to get inserted in some of your most publick Papers.[135]

This emblem, inspired by hearing of Trent's men surrendering at the Ohio to the French, was also published the next day in the *Pennsylvania Gazette* along with the letter. It showed disjointed parts of a black snake with each colony name (except Georgia) assigned to a piece, starting with the New England colonies N. E. on the head. Using it again later to present his Albany Plan of Union in the summer of 1754,[136] the snake emblem became the future nation's first political cartoon, mostly in part due to the three bold black words printed

---

131. HSP, Shippen Family Papers XV, 119, William Trent to James Burd, July 7, 1754.
132. *Pennsylvania Gazette*, May 9, 1754, 2.
133. Ibid.
134. P.R.O. Colonial Office 5:14, 156.
135. Ibid.
136. The Albany Congress began on June 19, 1754 and after much delegation, seven colonies that were present adopted the proposal suggested by Benjamin Franklin that the colonies should be run by one centralized government.

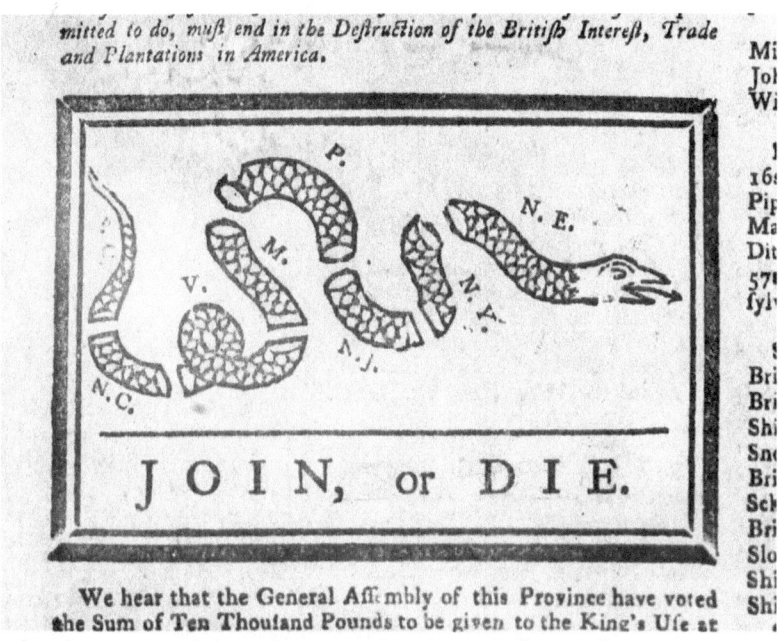

The Join or Die cartoon as it appeared in the Pennsylvania Gazette on May 9, 1754. (Author photo and courtesy of the Library of Congress.)

directly beneath it. Seemingly, this motto beckoned loudly to those willing to protect His Majesty's lands at all costs in the early summer of 1754.

JOIN, or DIE.

Chapter 10

Darkness Before the Light

Trent bowed his head and closed his eyes as he listened to Chaplain John Hamilton's words: "Lord have mercy upon us."[1] It seemed his men surrendering the Forks of the Ohio to the French and allowing them to disperse to their homes had proven to be a bad omen last month. By the first instant of May, Washington and his detachment of 160 effectives[2] had left without them on the road to Redstone Creek and Governor Dinwiddie was displeased to hear Washington's report about Trent's men, who he "found them rather injurious to the other men than serviceable to ye Exp'n till they could be upon the same Establishment with us and come under the reg't of Martial Law."[3]

Washington didn't mince words either when he pointed out to Dinwiddie *who* was responsible for their delayed advance to the Ohio.

> The want of proper Conveyances has much retarded this Expedition, and currently, unfortunately delay'd the Detachment I have the Honour to command. Even when we came to Will's C'k, my disappointments were not less than before, for there I expected to have sufficient pack Horses provided by Capt. Trent, conformable to his promise [in reply to] Major Carlyle's and my own (that I might prosecute my first intention with light expeditious Marches) but inst'd of th't there was none in readiness nor in any expectation that I could perceive which reduced me to the necessity of waiting till Wagons c'd be procured from the Branch (40 miles distant).[4]

---
1. Book of Common Prayer 1753, Baskett, 226.
2. Brock, 152.
3. Ibid.
4. Ibid., 151.

Never mind the fact that Washington's poor recruitment was the main reason he was never able to reach Will's Creek in under two months, let alone the Forks of the Ohio, where Trent had been laboring since February.

When Trent's Ensign Edward Ward gave his deposition about the Forks before Dinwiddie and his council on May 7, 1754, the governor had heard enough. The province of Virginia already looked bad enough to the other neighboring colonies and London with their failure to maintain the Forks of the Ohio, so Dinwiddie shifted blame to certain individuals hoping to overshadow their failures to heed Trent's' warnings in 1753. He wrote to Commander Joshua Fry and called out those supposed scapegoats, stating: "I'm advised the Captain Trent and his Lieut. Fraser had been long absent from their duty."[5]

He mentioned Ward's account of having only twenty-three men to guard the workmen and noted that Fry should establish a suitable punishment for both, suggesting, "Which conduct and behavior I require and expect you inquire into at a Court Martial and give sentence accordingly."[6] Fry's investigation into Trent's supposed negligence and "dormancy" from his duties took a backseat, however, to the misfortune that fell upon his arrival at the Inhabitants on the 28th of May. Fry had fallen from his horse near the mouth of Will's Creek and suffered injuries that resulted in a mild illness or indisposition.[7]

During this time, while the detachment waited a day or two for Fry's recovery, Trent and his wife Sarah had their first child baptized by the Virginia Regiment's chaplain, John Hamilton[8], on the morning of May 28, 1754. The child was named William, the fourth generation to be named such on Trent's paternal line.

While young William's cries filled their house on the 28th, an express arrived on the 30th from itinerant William Jenkins, former "servitor"[9] for Washington on his 1753 trip. The letter dated May 29, 1754, from Washington's camp at a place called the Great Meadows urged Fry to put himself and his detachment on the march to their camp. The reason was that on the day before, according to Washington, "I engaged a party of French, where of 11 were killed and 20 taken, with the loss of only one of mine killed and two or three wounded among which was Lieutenant Waggoner."[10]

---

5. Ibid., 147.
6. Ibid.
7. Washington referred to this "indisposition", Fry suffered in a letter he wrote to Fry on May 29, 1754. Brock, 183.
8. Trent recorded this baptism in his 1755 family bible. A copy of the original baptismal page for all six of Trent's children is found at the Historical Society of Pennsylvania in Philadelphia, Pennsylvania under the Family bible records (Br Tr). The entirety of this page is also found in Appendix F of this book.
9. Jenkins was one of four "servitors" or servants that traveled with Major George Washington and Christopher Gist. The other three were Henry Steward, Barnaby Curran, and John MacQuire (McGuire).
10. Brock, 183.

What he failed to disclose to his superior was that one of these eleven killed on the French side in the rocky bower was a French ensign and commander of the party named Joseph Coulon de Villiers, Sieur de Jumonville. (Today, the infamous skirmish location is named for the slain officer and called Jumonville Glen).

Washington had assumed the French might retaliate to counter this skirmish, so he ordered Fry with haste to march immediately, for he boldly stated, "If there does not come sufficient reinforcements, we must either quit and returned to you or fight very unequal numbers, which I will do before I give up one inch of what we have gained."[11]

Washington even urged Fry to send an officer of the detachment, Major George Muse, the former adjutant of the Middle Neck,[12] to lead the column ahead if Fry hadn't recovered, which was why on May 31st, Trent and the soldiers listened to Chaplain Hamilton's final sermon from the Book of Common Prayer. Colonel Joshua Fry was dead.[13] He had succumbed to his injuries that morning and was buried near the mouth of Will's Creek. He was sadly joined by Trent's infant son William, who did not survive soon after his birth and baptism.[14]

At this point, Trent had taken losses both personally and financially. He and Sarah had lost their firstborn, and now, if the French controlled the Ohio country, merchants and employees of the Ohio Company could not conduct any kind of business with the neighboring tribes. So, Trent sent all the gunpowder and horses[15] he could spare with Major Muse to take to the Great Meadows with the understanding he would be paid later for this service.

Now, with Fry's death, the chain of command also faced some drastic changes. Dinwiddie selected North Carolinian Colonel James Innes[16] to replace Joshua Fry as the commander of all the raised forces and then promoted Washington and Muse to the ranks of colonel and lieutenant colonel,[17] respectively. Washington became the temporary commander, with Muse his second-in-command until Innes arrived from North Carolina.

Dinwiddie also let Washington know that the company of South Carolina Independents led by Captain James MacKay had landed in Alexandria and

---

11. Ibid.
12. George Muse was appointed adjutant on November 6, 1752. The Middle Neck District was found between the Rappahannock and James Rivers.
13. According to the diary of Colonel James Wood of the Frederick County (VA) Militia, Joshua Fry died in Will's Creek or the Inhabitants on May 31, 1754.
14. The record of this baptism is the only primary evidence that William and Sarah Trent's first born was named William. It is assumed since the next five children were baptized at their residences by the area's rector, young William died soon after his baptism on May 28, 1754.
15. HSP, Shippen Family Papers, Letter from Edward Shippen III to Thomas Penn, November 25, 1754.
16. James Innes replaced Joshua Fry as Commander-in-Chief of the Provincial forces on June 4, 1754.
17. Brock, 193.

were on the march to join Washington at the Great Meadows. Trent viewed their arrival across the Potomac on June 9th,[18] one hundred men in scarlet red uniforms with Popinjay green facings,[19] highly disciplined and paid exclusively by His Majesty King George II. It reminded him of his service in 1746, and the mere mention of these men was probably why Washington sought his advice on receiving volunteer pay independent from the daily wages governed by the province.

Despite Washington's original hostility geared towards Trent or his men's conduct last April, he realized Trent was right to seek certain compensation. Both of them had just cause to be paid as volunteers if officers like Captain McKay or his second-in-command Lieutenant Peter Mercier did already without conflict.

Currently, the officers were being paid less than the ones in charge of British troops, officers who deserved such pay if, as Washington explained, "Had those gentlemen been as knowing of this Country and as Sensible of the difficulties that would attend a campaign here."[20] Washington even used Trent's former Canada expedition in 1746 as an example to support his argument. Like Trent had said earlier at their council on April 23rd, "First raised" troops in the province should always receive pay as volunteers.

Unfortunately, Governor Dinwiddie dismissed his abdication of pay in exchange for British service, calling them "ill-timed complaints."[21] He even disagreed with the comparison with the previous Canada expedition, declaring it "a mistake to say that those who served in it were found with wine and beer at the Public Expense and that their Wages were higher, or even so high as Yours."[22] The discrepancy with pay continued even after McKay and his Independent company arrived at Washington's camp with sixty beeves[23] and other provisions, and this internal fighting proved costly in their eventual defeat by the French at the Great Meadows.

On the 7th of July, Trent witnessed an advanced party of Washington's detachment return across the Potomac, and the news they brought was alarming. The five Virginia companies, along with Captain Mackay's South Carolinians and Andrew Montour's company of traders, were attacked and defeated by an overwhelming French force of one thousand men and Indians led by

---

18. Toner, 105.
19. Popinjay green originated from the German word Pappelgrün that meant poplar (as in tree) green or a yellowish green.
20. Brock, 177.
21. Ibid., 172.
22. Ibid.
23. Ibid., 199.

Louis Coulon Sieur de Villiers,[24] the half-brother of previously slain Ensign Jumonville. According to the advanced party and what Trent wrote that day to James Burd, the French appeared about 10:00 a.m. on July 3rd, and they attacked continuously in the pouring rain until "our guns got wet so that they found themselves not in a fit condition to renew the fight."[25] The initial report to Trent was that on the English side, there were many wounded and sixty killed, including the second-in-command of the South Carolina Independents, Lieutenant Peter Mercier. During the battle, Mercier was disabled by two musket balls, and while being carried to surgeons James Craik and Maurice Anderson,[26] a "third put an end to his life."[27]

There were also Articles of Capitulation signed by Washington and his officers that night, for they marched out with honors the morning of the 4th, but the French could do nothing to prevent plundering by their Native allies. The Indians destroyed the chests of the surgeons inside the stockade "to prevent our wounded from being dressed,"[28] confiscated baggage and correspondence of certain importance, and killed cattle, dogs, and horses, including the ones Trent loaned them from the stables near the New Store. The worst atrocity that occurred, according to Trent, was the desecration of Lieutenant Peter Mercier's body. After he was given a makeshift grave during the night of the 3rd, that morning, as the troops retreated from the Meadow,

> They (meaning the French) suffered Indians to raise Lieutenant Mercier the King's troops after he was buried & Scalp him without interfering in the least to prevent it.[29]

This was also joined by a report to Trent about a particular man in Captain George Mercer's Company. As Washington led his detachment from their hastily made "Fort Necessity," they encountered more Indian warriors painted for war who preyed upon the wounded and took any stragglers as prisoners. One such prisoner presumed missing in Captain Mercer's Company was Jacob

---

24. Louis Coulon Sieur de Villiers was one of six brothers, including Ensign Jumonville, who all were veteran soldiers in New France and/or in the American Colonies.
25. HSP, Shippen Family Papers, William Trent to James Burd, July 7, 1754.
26. Maurice Anderson was a surgeon from South Carolina who also probably served with Captain McKay and Lt. Mercier in James Oglethorpe's regiment in Georgia before being commissioned in the South Carolina Independents in the summer of 1754 to capture Fort Duquesne. He was one of three individuals whose occupation were doctors, joining Dr. James Craik and Major Adam Stephen at the Great Meadows. Later he served as the surgeon at Fort Loudoun (TN) on the Little Tennessee River in present-day Vanore, Tennessee and was killed on June 2, 1760, leaving the fort with a packhorse and a man named Thomas Smith.
27. *Virginia Gazette*, July 19, 1754, 2–3.
28. Trent's Remarks 1757, 4.
29. Ibid.

Arrants[30] (one of Trent's former interpreters for the Six Nations at the Forks of the Ohio), who was one of the eight captured and marched naked to Fort Duquesne.[31] Later, he was transported to Fort Niagara[32] on Lake Ontario until he was eventually sent to Montreal.

As the French returned to their canoes and batteaus lying along the shoreline of the Monongahela River at the mouth of Redstone Creek, Commandant de Villiers left behind a path of destruction. He ordered the ransacking and burning of Gist's house, "Monongahela," and its outbuildings, including the neighboring houses of Gist's relatives who settled on Ohio Company land and, finally, the new Ohio Company storehouse[33] built by Trent's men (the French called Le Hangard). The French removed all the stores and items of private persons[34] from this log building before setting it ablaze.

This news of their admonishment was devastating to both Trent and the Ohio Company. The campaigns in the spring and summer of 1754 to reclaim the Ohio country had been complete failures, and now the unprotected Ohio Company families were fleeing back to the Inhabitants. As panic and fear reached the Inhabitants and the New Store, the conditions worsened with the arrival of Colonel James Innes at Trent's house. The new chief commander had been given orders to reorganize their strategy to reclaim the Ohio country, and his first order of business was to "take possession of the Ohio Company's warehouse at Will's Creek"[35] and use it as a magazine to store the army's provisions and ammunition. It was a shocking development, and before Trent could ask who sent the orders, Innes showed him the letter dated August 30, 1754, signed and sealed by Governor Dinwiddie. The letter also included that sheds or temporary barracks[36] were also be built in case of bad weather for those soldiers arriving from Virginia and New York, so Trent was ordered to accommodate them all at his earliest convenience.

Dinwiddie was punishing Trent for his refusal to obey Washington's orders, and with business in the Ohio country on immediate hiatus, Trent pushed back as any merchant might do when the want of certain supplies became in high demand. Plus, until the government or the Crown could reimburse him, Trent was facing considerable private business losses at the hands of the French.

So, he began to charge higher rates[37] for the rent of cabins or houses near the New Store until the barracks could be built and for the price of timber

---

30. Cherry, 101. Toner, 181.
31. Memoirs of Robert Stobo, 90.
32. Publications of the Buffalo Historical Society, Vol. 9, 238.
33. Trent's Remarks 1757, 7.
34. Papiers Contrecoeur, 202.
35. Brock, 297, 307.
36. Ibid., 321.
37. Ibid., 321 and 460.

since the danger arose in the neighboring forest after the defeat of the Great Meadows on July 3, 1754. Innes, having no choice but to accept Trent's current prices to begin a fortification across the Potomac, also requested that Trent help him talk to the Indians who were arriving in a few weeks and whose support they needed to proceed next to destroy the cornfields near Fort Duquesne and at Logstown.[38]

Unfortunately, even before the defeat in July, the Ohio Company and Virginia had lost their biggest supporter in the Six Nations, thanks to Washington. After Trent had earned the Half-King's full support by giving him presents and choosing him to lay the first log of the Ohio Company fort, Washington seemingly unraveled this trust and friendship. The young colonel had done so by his inexperience and his inability to build a suitable fortification of his liking at the Great Meadows.

The Half-King viewed this small "palisaded" fort and left weeks before the battle, moving his family to Aughwick near George Croghan's house (present-day Shirleysburg, Pennsylvania). It was there he described Washington's behavior as being "good natured" but that "he took upon him to be as his Slaves and would have them every day upon the Out Scout and attack the Enemy by themselves, and that he would by no means take Advice from the Indians that he lay at one place from one full Moon to the other and made no fortifications at all, but that little thing upon the Meadow."[39]

The voice of the Half-King was also something Trent never heard again. In late October of 1754, as he and Andrew Montour served as interpreters for Colonel Innes at the newly fortified Inhabitants (now known as Fort Mount Pleasant), they learned from those Indian nations in attendance that the Half-King had died of an illness on the 4th of October on John Harris's farm near Paxtang.[40] They also said for this sudden sickness, they "blame the French for his death by bewitching him, as they had a conjuror to inquire into the cause a few days before he died."[41] This "bewitching," according to Conrad Weiser, was a result of the Half-King's heavy drinking of alcohol.[42]

The members of the Six Nations who arrived at the camp at Mount Pleasant were clearly on edge, and without their principal orator, the Half-King, an unknown chief warrior who traveled with Monacatootha, spoke instead. On the 5th of November,[43] this speech was in a private council between Innes,

---

38. Ibid., 263–64.
39. Colonial Records of Pennsylvania, Vol. 6, 151–52.
40. The early settlement of "Paxtang" was later part of a plan for a town by trader John Harris Jr. that he named for his father John Harris Sr. Today it's the capital of Pennsylvania and known as Harrisburg.
41. Rupp, 250.
42. HSP, Richard Peters Letterbook, Conrad Weiser to Richard Peters October 12, 1754.
43. Preston, Appendix E, 351.

Captain John Rutherford of the New York Independents, Monacatootha and others of the Six Nations, including this chief warrior and Trent, who, by this time, could finally speak their language or at very least understand it. The Six Nations announced originally they all had an open mind but were angry at the English for their refusal to listen with both ears and the lack of willingness to take the blame for their incompetence. This warrior, who was not familiar to Innes, said he began at the Forks of the Ohio with Trent but warned Innes now to not "be foolhardy" or "rely on your strength as Col. Washington did" for this overconfidence was why most of their fellow allies went to the French.[44]

He also echoed the last speech of the Half-King about how Washington did not stop at Logstown on his return trip from Fort Le Boeuf in 1753 to inform them about the French initial intentions in the Ohio country or, more recently, listen to them a few months back at the Great Meadows when they told Washington "An Account of how strong the French were."[45] This happened previously on June 3rd, when Washington addressed one hundred or so Native families and wrote to Governor Dinwiddie bragging about his newly finished stockade in the meadow and boasted that regardless of his little force, he declared, "I shall not fear the attack of 500 men."[46]

Yet, according to the chief warrior, the cause for this conflict between the French and the English Kings in the meadow all began because of what materialized with the looming discovery of a French party encamped beneath the ridge. The chief warrior admitted it was they who tracked the French where they encamped that night at the end of May; however, he explained carefully that the eventual skirmish began the morning of May 28th because "When they came near the top of the hill, Colonel Washington begun himself and fired and then his people, which the French returned, two or three fires as many Pieces as would go off, being rainy Weather and then run off."[47]

This shocking revelation suggested firsthand that Washington himself instigated the attack before either party fired upon each other and ironically came to light after Washington's plausible deniability that he assassinated a French ambassador when he "mistakenly"[48] signed the French drafted Articles of Capitulation that rainy night of July 3rd.

---

44. Ibid.
45. Ibid., 353.
46. Brock, 193.
47. Preston, Appendix E, 352.
48. After Washington signed the French written Articles of Capitulation he was later accused of "assassinating" Jumonville who was described as an ambassador sent from Fort Duquesne. He then stated with the wounding of his initial French interpreter Ensign William Le Peyronie and the poor translation by Dutch Lt. Jacob Van Braam, Washington had no idea what he was signing and thus admitting to murdering a French ambassador.

It was a cautionary tale of one's sketchy past coming back to haunt them, and by the beginning of 1755, Trent found himself being caught in the same web. Correspondence arrived from his on-again/off-again partner Croghan at Aughwick and alerted Trent that James Burd had visited him in September[49] on behalf of his father-in-law and busy Lancaster Prothonotary, Edward Shippen III.[50] On the eastern side of Pennsylvania, the pending status of the western fur trade hit the pockets of those investing firms especially hard and now they requested the attention of the man who had previously helped Trent and Croghan evade debtor's prison in Pennsylvania.

It's been over two years since Shippen's letter of license[51] for them expired and now several of these men still wished compensation for goods they placed on credit plus interest for the former mercantile firm of Hockley, Trent, and Croghan. Credit that, unfortunately, both he and Croghan had used on private business transactions instead of what was intended. Which was why the said problem came to light. The Pennsylvania creditors were now led by Trent and Croghan's former partner Richard Hockley, who, like Shippen, was done being a scapegoat for their risky business ventures and wished repayment as well.

Back in September, Burd had warned Croghan that his new residence at Aughwick was vulnerable to those arresting creditors if they didn't pay them as soon as possible, but Croghan instead pursued another option. He'd been offered to bring the Ohio Indians (most of them the remaining families that left the Great Meadows in June) and other nations he could gather to the outpost at the mouth of Will's Creek.[52] The former fortified camp at Mount Pleasant was now a fully completed fort, four hundred feet long, standing on the hill with twelve feet high walls about two hundred yards from Will's Creek[53] and named for His Majesty's youngest son, Prince William Augustus the Duke of Cumberland.[54]

The decision by Croghan to join the newly proposed Ohio expedition was based on two reasons: one, traveling to Maryland and Virginia kept him from being arrested, and two, he hoped his assisting with the Indian nations might, in turn, forgive him and Trent's outstanding debts that by the end of 1754 had reached almost six thousand pounds.[55]

---

49. Burd visited Croghan at Aughwick on September 25, 1755.
50. Edward Shippen III was a prothonotary, an elected civil clerk of the Court of Common Pleas in Lancaster. He served this position from 1753 until 1778.
51. The letter of license acquired by Edward Shippen III was dated March 9, 1752.
52. Wainwright, 96.
53. Preston, 107.
54. Prince William Augustus, Duke of Cumberland (April 15, 1721–October 31, 1765) the youngest of three sons of King George II of Great Britain and Ireland and his wife Caroline of Ansbach. He is best known for his success at ending the Jacobite uprising at the Battle of Culloden on April 16, 1746. It also earned him the nickname "Butcher" Cumberland.
55. Papers of William Johnson, Vol. 1, 497.

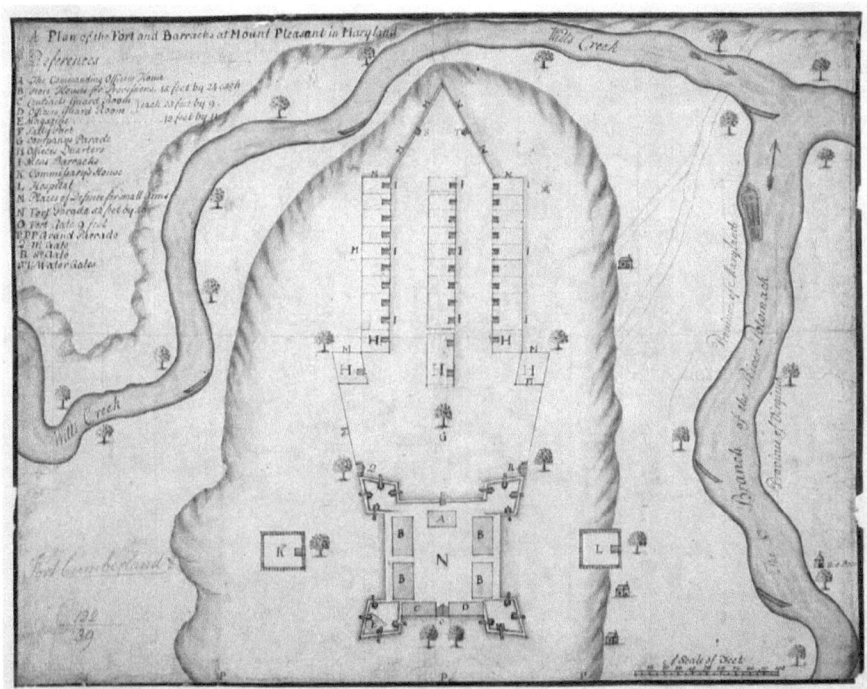

Plan of Fort Mount Pleasant later named Fort Cumberland. The New Store tract is shown in the bottom right corner across the North Branch of the Potomac River. (Map reproduction courtesy of the Norman B. Leventhal Map & Education Center of the Boston Public Library.)

When Croghan arrived at Trent's house during the first week of May 1755 with individuals from various Six Nations, he asked the factor for the Ohio Company for any stores or presents he could give them for the expedition. Trent was at an impasse on his end. For the time being, he had little to offer Croghan since the Ohio Company warehouse had already been seized and used as a magazine for Fort Cumberland and the expected arrival of the new Commander-in-Chief of His Majesty's forces, Major General Edward Braddock.

The sixty-year-old Braddock, a former Coldstream Guard, had landed at Hampton, Virginia, in February of 1755 and, after staying in Alexandria, arrived at Fort Cumberland on May 10, 1755.[56] He was followed by two regiments of British regulars fresh from their garrison duties in Ireland,[57] joining both independent and provincial troops from some of the neighboring thirteen colonies.

---

56. Wainwright, 86.
57. The British regular troops were stationed at various outposts in Ireland and left Cork harbor for America on January 9, 1755.

Present-day view from the New Store tract in Ridgeley, West Virginia toward Emmanual Episcopal Church (the steeple in background) and site of Fort Cumberland. (Author photo.)

Unfortunately, on May 22nd,[58] also arriving at Fort Cumberland was Provincial Secretary Richard Peters accompanied by an unexpected visitor, Richard Hockley. Trent, along with Croghan, had no choice but to see him and reach a satisfying accord. On May 24, 1755, they both signed a letter of agreement that declared "that those Goods (except an article of several grosses of gardening which he desired the said Hockley to purchase) were bought without the privacy or knowledge of said Richard Hockley" and which Trent added "that he took up the said Goods from the said Mr. Shippen and desired him to leave the Invoice at Mr. Hockley's to be forwarded to him in the Country."[59]

Croghan settled Shippen's balance by sending him "one wagon load of skins" in accordance with said debt. He also promised Hockley as his power of attorney[60] to collect his accumulated losses once the government reimbursed him. This confident assurance was influenced by the opinion of General

---

58. Wainwright, 87.
59. HSP, Penn Manuscripts Official Correspondence, May 24, 1755.
60. Wainwright, 87.

Braddock, who, upon hearing the case of Croghan's recent losses, all but assured Croghan further restitution once they retook Fort Duquesne and drove the French from the Ohio.[61]

Trent, on the other hand, did not share in Croghan's optimism about Braddock's promise, especially since their seizure of the New Store and the arrival of over 2,500 troops of the British Army who had seemingly damaged the houses and properties[62] on both sides of Potomac River including his own. The Maryland officers had also wreaked havoc upon the land surrounding the river, rendering it devoid of timber[63] they needed for public buildings at the fort and used by the coopers to make provision barrels for the army.

After Braddock's large army left Fort Cumberland on the 29th of May, the New Store Tract was no longer the sustainable land it once was. Trent could not continue his duties efficiently as factor for the Ohio Company, so he and Sarah loaded their belongings (possibly floated some down the Potomac with the Ohio Company boat) and took a new residence near where the mouth of the Conococheague Creek met the Potomac River (present-day Williamsport, Maryland).

At this time, it is not known whether Trent and his wife lived on the Virginia or Maryland side since the few letters he endorsed at the "Mouth of the Conococheague," could be referring to either side of the Potomac. However, it is quite possible he lived near the new Ohio Company storehouse built on the Virginia side near the ferry established by Evan Watkins in 1744[64] since he still had to finish his term as Frederick County District Justice at a Virginia residence. Later, the storehouse was fortified and called "Maidstone"[65] in late 1755 and 1756. Here Trent waited to hear the news of Braddock's victorious conquest of Fort Duquesne so he and the Ohio Company could resume activities in the Ohio country. Sadly, he did not have to wait long. Shocking news arrived at Fort Cumberland from waggoners who fled the apparent battlefield and retreated to the fort by noon on July 11th.[66]

According to one of these waggoners, a "sober young man" who arrived at the mouth of the Conococheague on July 9th, 1755, just past the charred remains of John Fraser's former cabin at Turtle Creek,[67] the army was "beaten"

---

61. Ibid.
62. Ohio Company of Virginia and the Westward Movement, Bailey, 323.
63. Ibid.
64. Evan Watkins built a single pen loghouse around 1741 and established a ferry patent from the Virginia House of Burgesses in 1744. The farmhouse and ferry stood opposite the mouth of the Conococheague in Maryland and is now in present-day Falling Waters, West Virginia.
65. GMP, Mulkearn, See Note 58 on 472. Also Bockstruck, 58–59.
66. Preston, 275.
67. Colonial records of Pennsylvania, Vol. 6, 481.

Present site of the original 1741 house of ferryman Evan Watkins known as "Maidstone-on-the-Potomac" in Falling Waters, West Virginia. (Author photo.)

after being surrounded on both sides by French troops, Canadian militia and several hundred of their Native allies. As Trent described this account in a letter dated July 16, 1755, to Pennsylvania Deputy Governor Robert H. Morris, there was optimism, however, in his tone describing their return, saying, "That the General (Braddock) with the rest of the army are marching a good retreat"[68] back to Fort Cumberland.

After the letter was sent, that afternoon he rode west to Fort Cumberland to see for himself what happened to Braddock's army before they reached the Forks of the Ohio and the French Fort. When he arrived at Fort Cumberland, Trent discovered first-hand the atrocities of what these men truly encountered. What wagons did make it back occupied their space with the dying and seriously wounded. The fort was now a large makeshift trauma hospital, with over two-thirds of Braddock's army killed, wounded, or missing. Worse yet, of the eighty-five commissioned officers, approximately seventy percent were killed or wounded,[69] including their commander, General Braddock. Braddock, mortally wounded on July 9th, was supposedly carried with his long red sash acting as

---
68. Ibid.
69. Preston, 276.

a litter into a retreating cart until he died the night of July 13th.[70] It was within the shadow (about one mile west) of the Great Meadows they buried him with honors beneath the road to prevent desecration by which the remaining wagons and army passed over the unmarked grave on their sullen retreat.

The aftermath of horrors that Trent witnessed at the fort signified anything but a "good retreat," as the young man earlier described, and this must have stayed with him over the years. In late 1757, he remarked again about the army's somber march after the Battle of Monongahela when he heard the badly wounded were "left on the field to the next day when the Indian boys came out from the towns and shot them with their bows and arrows and knocked others in the head putting them to death."[71]

The French were even victorious in the spoils of battle, capturing various important papers of the general's baggage, including instructions from London, private correspondence, and a few strategic maps or plans. One such map was the plan of Fort Cumberland,[72] and this was a dangerous foreshadowing of terror that reigned upon those residing unprotected along the Potomac, a few miles outside the walls.

This vulnerability was put into motion after Colonel Thomas Dunbar (the interim commander)[73] made the controversial decision to not only leave Fort Cumberland in the hands of the Marylanders but also pull out all His Majesty's troops and establish "winter quarters" in Philadelphia by late August. Within a few weeks after their withdrawal, alarming reports came pouring in near Trent's new house as the French and Indians unleashed their wrath on settlers neighboring Fort Cumberland. Trent heard the reports about two miles north of the mouth of the Conococheague at the mill and house of Joseph Wolgemuth on Friday night, the 3rd of October 1755. The express reported that "Jenny McClane[74] girl (and eventual wife of John Fraser), that lived with Fraser, was taken first by the Fort"[75] as John Fraser worked at Fort Cumberland mending and repairing guns. Today, a white historic sign along Route 51 in Allegany County, Maryland, about three and a half miles southeast of Cumberland, commemorates where she was captured.

---

70. Ibid., 273.
71. Trent's Remarks 1757, 5.
72. Preston, 267.
73. With deaths of General Braddock and Colonel Halkett, Dunbar became the acting commander of the entire detachment.
74. "Jenny" or Jane McClane (McClean) married trader John Fraser. After her husband's death in Bedford, Pennsylvania in 1773, she drafted a petition for losses suffered during the French and Indian War including an amount of 2,252 pounds four shillings for goods lost at the Great Meadows in July of 1754. The petition was signed Jane McClane Fraser, widow & Administratix of John Fraser.
75. Pitt Archives, Burd-Shippen Papers, William Trent to James Burd, October 4, 1755.

The original site of the Wolgemuth Mill today found along the Conococheague Creek at the intersection of Kemps Mill Road and Rock Hill Road in Williamsport, Maryland. (Author photo.)

The report also said that near the mouth of Patterson's Creek between Fort Cumberland and Thomas Cresap's house, there were at least forty killed or captured, including "one whole family was burnt to death in a house."[76] The fort later estimated at least one hundred families[77] had been murdered or captured since the summer.

The next day, on the 4th, Trent composed a letter to James Burd and alerted him of these attacks, warning him that more might be heading his way in Pennsylvania toward the town of Shippensburg. These raids on settlers were only the beginning, and Trent vented his frustrations at the bottom of the letter by blaming the provincial governments for not acting to protect them all in the first place. "How long will those in Power by their Quarrels suffer us to be massacred? Its time for every Body to Provide for the Safety of their families that can?"[78]

When the terror continued to Penns Creek on October 16th with fourteen men, women, and children murdered,[79] the Pennsylvania Provincial Council

---

76. Ibid.
77. Colonial Records of Pennsylvania, Vol. 6, 643.
78. Pitt Archives, Burd-Shippen Papers, William Trent to James Burd, October 4, 1755.
79. Ibid.

finally responded. By the first week of November and on orders from Deputy Governor Morris, blank commissions were being sent for those individuals and "the most respectable persons in the several Counties of Cumberland, York, Lancaster, and Chester."[80] They were to organize local inhabitants into a county militia and protect our neighboring residents until a fortification could be built nearby.

Naturally, Trent was chosen as one of these captains. Even though he currently resided at the mouth of the Conococheague, he still possessed a house in Cumberland County,[81] nonetheless, to be selected. George Croghan joined him at Aughwick, Charles Foulk and Jacob Arndt at Gnadenhutten and several others.[82] Their superiors were Lieutenant Colonel James Burd at Shippensburg, who was building the future outpost Fort Morris,[83] Benjamin Chambers (the former justice of the peace with Trent)[84] at Falling Spring (the future town of Chambersburg), Conrad Weiser at Womelsdorf, and Timothy Horsfield of Bethlehem.[85]

Before Trent and Croghan could proceed with their provincial duties, however, they both needed assurance their appearance in the Pennsylvania province was safe from prosecution or arrest. The pipe dream of restitution from London had died temporarily with General Braddock that fateful day on July 9th, so the principal creditors were still wishing for their money plus interest.

So, Trent and Croghan presented a bill in Trent's hand to the Pennsylvania Assembly, asking for an exemption from a simple letter of license (which lasted only a few months), and it was virtually impossible anyway to acquire hundreds of signatures due to so many traders and merchants spread throughout the province. They pleaded that because "distressed circumstances forced them to continue remote, so they cannot transact any business nor put themselves in a condition of retrieving their affairs, and in such their situation they cannot exert themselves either in the service of themselves their creditors or their country, and there is no probability of there being ever able to satisfy their just debts by any other means than by permitting them to transact their business and affairs without molestation."[86]

---

80. Colonial Records of Pennsylvania, Vol. 6, 670.
81. This house was his plantation in Middleton Township where he was found on the tax lists of Cumberland County in 1751.
82. Pennsylvania Archives, Fifth Series, Vol. 1, 44.
83. After the defeat of Braddock's army on July 9, 1755, plans were made to build an outpost to protect the settlers who resided in or near the town of Shippensburg, Pennsylvania. The fort was later described by General John Forbes as "a regular square with four bastions and one gate in that curtain which faces due east towards the town." The fort resided today near Burd Street in Shippensburg.
84. Chambers accompanied Trent on the Burnt Cabins expedition in May of 1750 when he was a justice of peace of Cumberland County (Pennsylvania).
85. Pennsylvania Archives, Fifth Series, Vol. 1, 44
86. Mitchell and Flanders, Volume V, 212–13.

The submitted bill, dated November 28, 1755, had fifteen signatures[87] in addition to their own and requested a space for ten years from being arrested, imprisoned, or sued by said creditors to whom Trent and Croghan were indebted. Their reasoning for such a lengthy period was for them to try to regain those losses suffered by "the defection of our allies from their former friendship and amity with this province and the invasion of conquest by the French on the Ohio and the adjacent country."[88]

The application for the bill was presented at the State House in Philadelphia (where Trent was once a part of the assembly in 1751) on November 29, 1755, and received one last endorsement from Isaac Norris Jr, the Speaker of the House.[89] Norris wrote along with this document that "The Bill has already laid before him above two weeks and we fear if something of the kind is not immediately gone into we shall lose our few remaining Indians on Susquehannah."[90]

So, three days later, on December 2nd,[91] Speaker of the House Norris and the rest of the Pennsylvania Assembly presented the bill to the governor, who enacted it into law and allowed Secretary Richard Peters to authenticate with the Great Seal of the Pennsylvania colony upon it. This Indian trade bill, newly titled "An Act for the Relief of George Croghan and William Trent,"[92] was also sent to the clerk at the Privy Council of London, where all laws enacted in the colonies were presented before the King. Trent, along with Croghan, had once again saved themselves from financial ruin by boosting their status and notoriety despite their business at a standstill in neighboring provinces ravaged by the colonies' self-proclaimed "French and Indian War."

This bill also set a precedent in Pennsylvania and once it became a law, was announced as soon as Pennsylvania printers could publish them.[93] As word spread, more traders and merchants voiced their recent depredations suffered by the French in the Ohio country and began itemizing their losses. This lobbying by Trent and Croghan sparked a movement, and as the group increased its members, a plan of restitution was drafted to His Majesty in April of 1756.[94] Though King George II largely ignored the petition, it was the first fight of many by Trent to reimburse those individuals (like himself) who tried

---

87. The fifteen signatures were: David Franks for Levy & Company, Jeremiah Warder, Samuel Neave, William and David McIlvaine, Buckridge Sims, Benjamin and Samuel Shoemaker, James Wallace, James Benezet, Thomas Campbell, William West, Adam Hoops, John Potter, and Joseph Morris.
88. Mitchell and Flanders, Vol. V, 213.
89. In 1751, Isaac Norris Jr. was elected Speaker of the House for the Pennsylvania Provincial Assembly and held that position until his death in 1766.
90. Colonial Records of Pennsylvania, Vol. 6, 743.
91. Ibid., 744.
92. Mitchell and Flanders, Vol. V, 212.
93. *Pennsylvania Gazette*, December 4, 1755, 2.
94. Bailey, 34.

at one time to transform their business firms into a mercantile conglomerate in the Ohio Valley. Even with the conflict in the colonies spreading globally now and soon to be called the "Seven Years War,"[95] Trent made sure those officials across the ocean learned about the group known simply as the "Suffering Traders of 1754."[96]

---

95. Despite the conflict between England and France subjects happening in the thirteen colonies as early as 1754, the conflict did not officially begin across multiple continents until 1756. In 1756, the conflict became global, expanding across five continents and lasted until the Treaty of Paris was signed on February 10, 1763. Which was why in Europe it was nicknamed the "Seven Years War."

96. Bailey, 34–35.

Chapter 11

The Fall of Fort Duquesne

When was it all ending? It was the mystifying question Trent likely asked himself as he stared out the window of his house on the misty morning of May 12, 1757. After the annihilation of Braddock's army, the gates to destruction across the upper cusp of the frontier had seemingly been opened. The outposts in Pennsylvania, Maryland and Virginia were defenseless, which left the neighboring settlements between these posts susceptible to ambushes and raids. It was why he and Sarah were now living in Lancaster, Pennsylvania, their third residence in four years after he became factor for the Ohio Company. That and for the safety of their almost seven-month-old daughter, he was rocking back to sleep.

Ann Trent was born in Lancaster on the 20th of October 1756.[1] Her birth was recorded in the Trent family bible, and her baptism (as the record stated) was done by the minister for the borough of Lancaster, the Rev. George Craig, who was also the Anglican rector at St. James Church in town. Since the death of young William at their home on the New Store Tract, the Trent family opted for a private baptism at their residence to be cautious. They eventually did the same for their next four children.

His return home was short-lived, however. With the war raging on and the danger increasing further outside the Ohio country, negotiations with the Indian nations to side with the English were more than necessary in these dark hours.

Most importantly for Trent, it wasn't just the continued loyalty of the Six Nations they needed, but the loyalty of the Shawnee and Lenape, too. It was why, back on the 28th of April, Trent had traveled to the Moravian town of

---

1. HSP, Family Bible Records, BrTr.

The Fall of Fort Duquesne

The house of Timothy Horsfield built in 1749 still survives today in Bethlehem, Pennsylvania. (Author photo.)

Bethlehem to meet Teedyuscung, the self-proclaimed "King of the Delawares,"[2] and escort him back to Lancaster.

But when Trent returned to Lancaster on May 5[3] with just four Lenape men and one woman and no Teedyuscung, questions were raised about his absence. Speculation at Timothy Horsfield's house in Bethlehem[4] was that he left to plant his fields, but others traveling with Trent told him the truth as they made their way back to Lancaster. More white settlers had been killed in the region, and he was afraid he or his people were blamed for the incident. Either way, it didn't bode well for those arriving that evening on May 11th at the treaty in the town square.

---

2. Teedyuscung was born on Lenape land in New Jersey that later became part of the settlement called Trent's Town in 1720 and then became a spokesperson for the Lenape people after moving to Pennsylvania. After being forced from his land in Northampton County because of the Walking Purchase of 1737, he proclaimed himself "King of the Delawares" when he lived in the Wyoming Valley.
3. Colonial Records of Pennsylvania, Vol. 6, 513.
4. The original house built in 1749, still stands today and is located at 42 West Market Street in Bethlehem, Pennsylvania.

Trent knew how important Teedyuscung was to the negotiations. Perhaps he wondered if his name was even the reason for the Lenape sachem's absence. After all, Trent was just a boy on the Assunpink Creek when the booming expansion of his father's Trent's Town settlement led to Teedyuscung and the Lenape losing their ancestral lands there.[5] Later, Teedyuscung lost his home again in the Lehigh Valley after the Walking Purchase Treaty of 1737, and Trent knew after these past English discretions, they had to tread lightly with him and his people, or they might go to the French.

This time, when the treaty was called again in Lancaster instead of the new smallpox-stricken Philadelphia, however, Trent's name came up in a conversation[6] between Superintendent of Indian Affairs William Johnson and his former business partner and friend George Croghan, the new Deputy Agent of Indian Affairs for the Northern District. They were discussing who might record the minutes of the treaty, and they both agreed on Croghan's recommendation of Trent for his superior skills in penmanship. In Croghan's letter to Pennsylvania Governor William Denny,[7] he endorsed his choice, saying, "There should be any one secretary and proposed Mr. William Trent which was agreed to."[8]

So, after incessant rain delayed their meeting until that morning of the 12th, a little before 10:00 a.m., Trent left his house to join the others, like Speaker of the House Isaac Norris Jr. and Governor Denny, outside the courthouse. It was hard to believe it was almost thirteen years since he traveled with men from Philadelphia to attend the Treaty of Lancaster in the summer of 1744. This time, however, Trent wasn't just a spectator. For ten days as secretary, he wrote down what was said and gave his presents, including several wampum belts of nine rows or more,[9] to the deputies from all the Six Nations, the Nanticoke,[10] and Lenape people. Sadly, there was one deputy and chief missing from the Six Nations. Trent's friend Monacatootha, who helped him plan defensive trenches at the Forks in March of 1754, was dead from smallpox[11] before the treaty began.

Unfortunately, without the appearance of Teedyuscung, the treaty to get the Lenape's allegiance to favor the English made no leeway. Governor Denny

---

5. Around 1730, the settlement of Trent's Town in western New Jersey expanded and the Lenape were forced to move west into Pennsylvania and the Ohio country.

6. Papers of William Johnson, Vol. 2, 658.

7. William Denny (March 9, 1709–1765) was an Oriel College (Oxford) graduate and a member of the Society of Dilettanti that studied ancient Greek and Roman art. He also served as the Deputy Governor of Pennsylvania from 1756–1759.

8. Colonial Records of Pennsylvania, Vol. 6, 517.

9. Ibid., 519.

10. The Nanticoke's were a member of the Algonquin nation and who primarily resided in the Chesapeake Bay and present-day Delaware region.

11. Alberts, 273.

didn't lose hope, however. A message was sent with a Lenape named William Sam[12] back to Teedyuscung in the Wyoming Valley, and the governor hoped this time, the Lenape king would join them with even more of his people. Trent also agreed, writing to Timothy Horsfield on May 25, 1757, saying, "As I look upon the bringing about the peace with Delawares & Shawnees to be of the greatest Consequence to this Government."[13]

While they waited on word from Teedyuscung, Trent rode to Virginia, arriving in Winchester on the 12th of June. He joined Croghan and Colonel John Armstrong as they arrived at the northern outskirts of town (near North Loudoun Street), just below the gates of the outpost set atop the hill. The fort (if it could be called one), named for John Campbell, the 4th Earl of Loudoun,[14] was not even half completed. Though judging by the sentries posted along the double defense walls and twelve-pound and four-pound cannons decorating the bastions,[15] Washington and his garrison still believed the threats of a large French force attacking Fort Cumberland and then Fort Loudoun were true. Even Trent himself believed these rumors as well. On June 16, 1757, he wrote to merchant and Philadelphia relation William Coxe that word from Captain Dagworthy was that six Cherokees lay about Fort Duquesne "where they saw a large Body of French and Indians and a great number of Carriages & Horses."[16]

But on June 20,[17] when about sixty Cherokee and Edmund Atkin,[18] Superintendent of Indian Affairs for the Southern District, arrived at Fort Loudoun with a captured French ensign, those (including Trent) inside the fort learned the actual truth. The prisoner's name was Francois-Marie Picote sieur de Belestre,[19] and he was taken prisoner when he and nine others were attacked on the 30th of May halfway between Fort Cumberland and Fort Duquesne.

Colonel Washington inquired if a large force had left the Forks of the Ohio, and Belestre replied, "That when he left Fort Duquesne, he heard nothing of an Expedition intended on any of the Frontier Settlements or the Out Forts, they having no Artillery to enable them to conduct such an Expedition, the whole

---

12. Trent's Remarks 1757, 1.
13. American Philosophical Society, Timothy Horsfield Papers, William Trent to Timothy Horsfield, May 25, 1757.
14. John Campbell, 4th Earl of Loudoun (May 5, 1705–April 27, 1782) took part in the Jacobite uprising in 1745 for the Hanoverian government, serving at Prestonpans and at Culloden in Scotland. He also served as the Commander in Chief and Governor General of Virginia in 1756 where the county of Loudoun was named after him in 1757. Later he was made Governor of Edinburgh Castle in Scotland in 1763 which he held till his death in 1782.
15. Papers of George Washington, George Washington to Robert Dinwiddie, June 27, 1757.
16. Colonial Records of Pennsylvania, Vol. 7, 601.
17. Documents Relative to the Colonial History of the State of New York, Volume VII, 282.
18. Edmund Atkin (1707–1761) was a former merchant in Charleston, South Carolina and the first Superintendent of Indian Affairs for the Southern Department. He served in this role from 1756–1761.
19. François-Marie Picoté, Sieur de Belestre (November 17, 1716–March 30, 1793) was first promoted to the rank of ensign in the Troupes de la Marine in 1754 and led a detachment at the Battle of the Monongahela in 1755 to defeat British forces under General Braddock.

they have being eight six-pounders and six four-pounders which was mounted at Fort Duquesne."[20] This was a relief, for those stationed at Cumberland must have misunderstood the Cherokee's original report.

"How many soldiers at the fort?" Washington asked next.

Belestre didn't hesitate. He estimated that "when he left Fort Duquesne, there was a Garrison of 300 men one half which were Regulars and the other half Militia."[21] However, he did add that three hundred more men were expected from Montreal and almost 1,500 Indians "to annoy the Frontier of the three Neighboring Colonies."[22]

The only question now was if their prisoner was telling the truth. Ensign Belestre confirmed his intel wasn't false by concluding with one more piece of vital information. "The commanding officer's name at Fort Duquesne is Delignery,"[23] he said.

Despite the valuable intel, the potential number of French and their Native allies was quite troublesome. Trent estimated Washington's men at about two hundred thirty Virginians, with maybe an additional eighty warriors[24] that came to their aid. So, unfortunately, if they wanted more allies and to keep the frontier safe, their fate rested on the loyalty of the neighboring nations and the future appearance of their main voice and influencer, Teedyuscung.

After Atkin and Croghan finished their business with the southern nations, the Native party eventually followed Croghan to Carlisle to meet Colonel John Stanwix[25] and receive more presents from the Pennsylvania government. Later, when Croghan returned to Philadelphia on July 7th, he saw an express[26] that Teedyuscung and about two hundred Lenape men and women were on the move. Governor Denny informed Croghan that just three days earlier, they had already spent the night on the Lehigh River at Fort Allen and arrived in Easton by the 18th of July.

It was also at this time the Pennsylvania government requested Trent's services to be acting secretary once again and record the minutes of the meeting. From his house in Lancaster, Trent rode beyond Bethlehem, this time along the Maxatawny Path[27] till he reached the town of Easton, a place the Lenape once called "Lechauwitank" or the "Place at the Forks" in the recently formed

---

20. Documents Relative to the Colonial History of the State of New York, Volume VII, 282.
21. Ibid.
22. Ibid.
23. Documents Relative to the Colonial History of the State of New York, Volume VII, 282.
24. Colonial Records of Pennsylvania, Vol. 7, 601.
25. On January 1, 1756, Stanwix was colonel-commandant of the First Battalion of the 60th Royal American regiment and set up headquarters at Carlisle, Pennsylvania in 1757.
26. Colonial Records of Pennsylvania, Vol. 7, 634.
27. The Maxatawny Path in Pennsylvania ran from the present town of Kutztown (then called Maxatawny meaning "bear's path creek") to Easton, also known as the "Place of the Forks."

Northampton County, Pennsylvania.[28] This meeting was the first of two important treaties in Easton (the second was a year later, on October 7, 1758), and it was clear the moment Trent arrived with the others, which they all suspected controlled the narrative of the upcoming meeting.

To their dismay, the "Friends" or Quakers had "crashed" the treaty, and now they began to coerce with Teedyuscung and one hundred fifty-nine of his company[29] before it even began. This was bad, very bad. The "Friends" were not invited for a reason. Those attendees experienced in negotiations with the local Indian nations like Weiser, Croghan, or Trent knew what might happen if the "Friends" spoke of the Walking Purchase or land fraud. Now was the time to discuss peace, not open wounds from the past.

The Lenape king, unfortunately, wasted no time announcing Lenape John Pumpshire or Cawkeeponen[30] as his interpreter. Then, it was declared through Pumpshire that Trent and his assistant, inaugural College of Philadelphia grad Jacob Duché (the future rector of both St. Peters Episcopal and Christ Church in Philadelphia), had an additional secretary joining them. Teedyuscung, it seemed requested a personal clerk to record his own minutes of the treaty.

Trent placed his quill in his pewter standish and closed his marble-covered book. Another secretary? Something was amiss. This last-minute development was unprecedented, and when Teedyuscung refused to see Governor Denny without one, Croghan and the others had no choice but to comply. So, as the treaty officially got underway on July 25th, Trent saw who Teedyuscung chose as his secretary.

He was Charles Thomson, a Quaker schoolmaster in Philadelphia and no doubt recommended to him by "Friends" attendees Joseph Galloway and Israel Pemberton. Thompson later became Secretary for the Continental Congress (1774-1789), editing the Declaration of Independence and composing the Great Seal of the United States, where the three colors adorning the emblem, red, white, and blue, eventually symbolized America.

Like Trent, Croghan didn't understand why Teedyuscung needed a personal secretary, but he had a theory. "As to his having a clerk or not having one," Croghan later wrote, "I think it is a matter of little consequence, but the having a clerk was not the thing. Those people [the Quakers], by having a clerk, they had a counsellor for themselves to put Teedyuscung in mind what they had

---

28. Northampton County, Pennsylvania was formed in 1752 from the county of Bucks and named for Northamptonshire, England.
29. There were fifty-eight men, thirty-seven women, and sixty-four children traveling with Teedyuscung. Colonial Records of Pennsylvania, Vol. 7, 649.
30. John Pumpshire was a Lenape missionary who also spoke English. Throughout the late 1750s he was acting interpreter for Teedyuscung, wearing a ruffled shirt, stockings, and a waistcoat. He was said to be originally from West Jersey.

wanted him to say, and it appeared very clearly one day when he had got his speech drawn up in writing and desired his clerk to read it off as a lawyer would put it in a plea at the bar."[31]

A week later, as the treaty progressed into August, Croghan's theory was not so far-fetched. The exchange of words shifted from peace negotiations to previous fraudulent land transactions orchestrated by the Penn family and now the need for two million acres of land around Teedyuscung's town near Wyoming for compensation to him and his people of the Ten Nations. Clearly, the "Friends" were whispering their demands in his ear.

In response, Trent recorded that Governor Denny informed Teedyuscung through Pumpshire that neither Croghan nor Crown interpreter Thomas McKee held the authority to settle previous land claims. Those specific complaints had to be brought directly to the Superintendent of the Northern District, William Johnson.

As for the two million acres near Wyoming, the land was theirs to claim outright if they wanted it. This pleased Teedyuscung, but when Denny diverted the council back to peace negotiations, the Lenape king seemed insulted at the suggestion. He didn't get to speak more about this disapproval because one of the Shawnee sachems had heard enough. Trent recognized the Shawnee king Lapechkewe, who still wore his laced hat and jacket gifted to him by Virginia commissioners at the Treaty of Logstown on June 13, 1752.[32]

Lapechkewe stepped forward to direct his opinion at the Lenape king and wanted to hear no more talk of just land:

> Why did you bring us down? We thought we came down to make peace with our brethren, the English, but you continue to quarrel about the land affair, which is dirt.[33]

This bold statement was followed by more boisterous yells and voices in agreement. It was obvious now that the "Friends" bad influence on Teedyuscung had led him astray and forced him into a corner with his own people. If he continued to balk at peace, then the rest of the Ohio Indians might leave. So, rather unexpectedly, the Lenape king nodded amongst the loud opposition towards him and through Pumpshire and announced his support with the English. According to Teedyuscung, "The confirmation of the peace with our brethren, the English," took up about three or four months from the last day of the treaty

---

31. Wainwright, 130.
32. GMP, Mulkearn, 64, 561.
33. Wainwright, 132.

on August 7th.[34] For those veterans of such previous councils like Croghan and Trent, they were less than optimistic that Teedyuscung's immediate change of heart helped end hostilities across the ravaged frontier. At best, the treaty ended with a truce between them all, but they still were far from forming an official alliance with the Ohio Indian nations.

In the meantime, Trent's recorded minutes from the treaty and external notes from his assistant Jacob Duché were sent for publication at the new printing office south of "The Jersey Market"[35] in Philadelphia to David Hall and his semi-retired partner Benjamin Franklin. It was published in September as the pamphlet *Minutes of Conference held with the Indians at Easton in the months of July and August 1757*.

The pamphlet proved to be an engaging read but there was another circulating publication overshadowing across the colonies. In fact, this publication was so popular with subscribers that it was advertised every month by Hall and Franklin since its first printing by James Chattin on June 9, 1757.[36] Trent even purchased a copy before his return to Lancaster. The book, published in Paris by order of King Louis XV, was written by his historiographer Jacob Nicolas Moreau and was finally translated into English with the title, *A Memorial containing a Summary Account of Facts, with their Authorities in Answer to the Observations sent by the English Ministry to the Courts of Europe*.

After reading it completely through, Trent saw it covered the years 1749 to 1756. It featured captured English trader depositions in 1749, the journal of Major Washington in 1754 and 1755, and General Braddock's "secret" orders.[37] The book was clearly published to propagate how the English started these hostilities in the Americas, and after the mention of contraband traders and his "little Fort," Trent felt personally attacked. Most of these statements were exaggerated or taken out of context, not to mention damaging to his reputation for future endeavors. So, almost immediately in response, he brought a quill to paper and began furiously writing. For those misleading assertions, Trent made sure to point out specific pages and lines of each discrepancy and then used his first-hand experience to explain what occurred. When he finished, he had written almost ten pages, with most of his remarks or reflections directed towards the inconsistencies of his months from January to April 1754, attempting to build a fort at the Forks of the Ohio. He followed this up with a

---

34. *Minutes of Conferences held with the Indians at Easton 1757*, University of Michigan, William L. Clements Library.
35. The "Jersey Market" was a public market located between First and Second Street of Philadelphia right in the center of High Street (later called Market Street). It was called the "Jersey Market" because the sheds were exclusively from those individuals bringing produce from the province of New Jersey.
36. *Pennsylvania Gazette*, June 9, 1757, 4.
37. *Pennsylvania Gazette*, March 3, 1757, 4.

letter to Governor Denny and William Johnson, listing to the best of his memory the traders and their employees who had been murdered or robbed by the French and their allied nations.[38] He wanted to make every effort to discredit this French propaganda, spreading lies in the colonies and Europe.

For now, though, he needed to rest. He was beyond exhausted. At first, he thought it was the tedious ride from Easton and Philadelphia or writing for thirteen days until his hand hurt. But after the aching in his body lasted for a few days, he thought otherwise. In his letter dated September 5, 1757,[39] he even described himself as being "unwell" in the first sentence. Unfortunately, this "aching" of the body or head continued to appear intermittently for the rest of his life. (It was quite possible this began when he was stricken with malaria back in 1749). This illness was also the reason this ten-page manuscript of *Trent's Remarks* in 1757 was never found or obtained until over two hundred and forty-five years later in 2002.[40] Today, this manuscript lies in the Native American History Collection at the William L. Clements Library at the University of Michigan in Ann Arbor. It was transcribed completely for the first time and mostly used in the author's previous work, *Pittsburgh Lost Outpost: Captain Trent's Fort* published in the March of 2019.

After Trent recovered from his illness, good news appeared in early November with a surprising letter from his good friend John Mercer of "Marlborough Plantation."[41] For the past six months, Mercer, the acting attorney for the Ohio Company, had teamed up with treasurer George Mason to prosecute any person who owed debts to the Ohio Company. While being meticulous with the list of debtors, one name caught their eye. Robert Dinwiddie still had an outstanding balance owed directly to factor William Trent for goods purchased at Thomas Cresap's house and at the Ohio Company warehouse (the New Store) since Trent paid for the previous 1754 expedition to the Forks the Ohio in its entirety from Ohio Company funds. The amount totaling six hundred and sixty-five pounds sixteen shillings[42] included not only pay for himself, his officers, and his men but also for items like lead, powder, flints, wampum, deerskins, and purple half-thick bags. Plus, the cost of carriage of these items from these places to the Forks of the Ohio in January of 1754.

But here was their predicament. Dinwiddie, though still active as Lieutenant Governor of Virginia, was coming to the final month of his term. His health had also been poor, and he was looking to sail to England before the winds

---

38. Library of Congress, Marian S. Carson Collection 1656–1995, Box 28.
39. Ibid.
40. The William L. Clements Library at the University of Michigan acquired this ten-page document in 2002.
41. "Marlborough" plantation resided near the present town of Fredericksburg, Virginia in Stafford County. A historical marker today lies on 1050 Emancipation (formerly Jefferson Davis and Route 1) Highway commemorating its location.
42. HSP, Cadwalader Family Papers, George Mason and John Mercer to James Tilghman, March 1, 1767.

Original house of lawyer Robert Carter Nicholas who defended Robert Dinwiddie in Trent's trial and who resided in the house from 1753-1761. The house is along the Palace Green in Williamsburg, Virginia. (Courtesy of Justin Cherry.)

on the eve of winter became unfavorable. Time was running out, and if they wished to collect this debt, Trent had to act now. With Dinwiddie already believed to be in "York"[43] ready to sail out with his family, Trent had Mercer issue a warrant and have Dinwiddie arrested. Later in 1767, Mercer described the initial decision by Trent, saying, "He offered me any part of what I could recover it, and I realy believe it would have been lost, if I had not by a good fee procured Mr. Dinwiddie to be arrested at York."[44]

The warrant stipulated that unless the debt was paid, Trent might take the Lieutenant Governor to court for the unpaid amount plus compensation for malicious attacks against his character. Governor Dinwiddie must have likened his chances because his refusal to pay the amount and hiring of Council Treasurer Robert Carter Nicholas as his attorney[45] meant the dispute was now brought to the courthouse in Williamsburg. After Dinwiddie sailed on the HMS *Baltimore* back to England on January 12, 1758,[46] the long, intricate case of William Trent versus Robert Dinwiddie began.

---

43. It was called "York" for York, England from 1691 when it was founded in Virginia until after the American revolution when it became known as Yorktown.
44. James, 240.
45. Colonial Williamsburg Foundation, Corbin Family Papers, Robert Corbin to Robert Dinwiddie, November 11, 1760.
46. Papers of Henry Bouquet (BP), Vol. 1, 277.

That same January, Trent also pursued another debt. Twenty-year-old French Mason left his cousin's house in Dogue's Neck[47] on January 4th for Mount Vernon and collected the one hundred and sixty-five pounds, twelve shillings, two and three-quarters pence[48] from a dysentery-stricken George Washington that was owed to Trent.

The year 1758 had become pivotal in the war and after almost three years since the failed Braddock campaign, a larger western expedition to the Ohio country was finally being planned. On April 18, 1758, Brigadier General John Forbes arrived in Philadelphia and began his strategy to accomplish hopefully what his predecessors could not. They used the road opened by Colonel James Burd[49] to Rea's Town (Bedford)[50] in 1755 and extended it beyond the mountains to capture the Forks of the Ohio and Fort Duquesne. This time, however, the army was over six thousand strong, consisting mostly of provincials from the colonies of Pennsylvania, Virginia, North Carolina, and Maryland. The rest were British regulars, such as independent companies from South Carolina, Scottish Highlanders, and Royal American Regiments.

The goal by summer was to assemble in Carlisle and eventually join those regiments from Fort Cumberland along the way while building outposts and redoubts a day's march apart to supply their expedition until they were within striking distance of Fort Duquesne. But before the army could begin their trek west, Forbes hoped to obtain the services of the southern Indian nations who arrived in Winchester, wishing to show their support to the English for the right price.

Over six hundred warriors[51] came by the end of April and conferred with Captain Abraham Bosomworth[52] of the Royal American Regiment, the veteran Indian agent hired by Forbes to oversee the affairs and transactions. Bosomworth wrote that although the southern Indian nations anticipated joining Forbes's army, they were growing impatient. He said they wished for "an early campaign and plenty of goods."[53] This was why, hoping to put their minds at ease, he

---

47. Dogue's Neck was named for the Dogue nation who held a Native village in the region that was marked on Captain John Smith's map of Virginia dated 1608. It was where George Mason built his plantation known today as Gunston Hall, about twelve miles from George Washington's Mount Vernon.

48. Papers of George Mason, Vol. 1, 41.

49. The road Burd constructed was the old Raystown Path and ran from his residence in Shippensburg to Raystown (Bedford) hoping to join the other road built by General Braddock's men. Eventually the plans developed too slowly but his road was used again for the expedition in 1758 led by General John Forbes.

50. Rea's Town or Raystown got its name from the trader John Rea or Wray who had a residence in the area with a few other settlers. Before troops under General Forbes arrived, it was called (and spelled) Rea's Town (Raystown).

51. In Christopher Gist's "A Return of the Southern Indians Winchester April 21, 1758," Gist listed 652 total Indians.

52. Abraham Bosomworth was first an ensign in James Oglethorpe's regiment in 1747 and spent the next eleven years in South Carolina amongst the Indians. On January 20, 1756, he was commissioned into the Royal American 60th Regiment. In 1758, John Forbes acquired his services on the expedition to take Fort Duquesne and he was promoted to Superintendent of Indian Affairs for the Western Department.

53. University of Virginia Library, Headquarter Papers of John Forbes, George Washington to John Forbes, April 23, 1758.

The Fall of Fort Duquesne

Copied portrait of General John Forbes from the possession of the Royal Scots Greys Regiment in Aldershot, England. (Courtesy of the Darlington Digital Library at the University of Pittsburgh and Public Domain.)

sent those Catawba and Cherokee warriors still left in town to Pennsylvania to meet his latest liaison, whom some of these warriors had met just last year in Winchester with Edmund Atkin.

In mid-May, Bosomworth requested Trent personally to meet this arriving party at Shippensburg and escort them to receive their presents at Fort Loudoun. On the 20th of May,[54] Trent sent out the wagon carrying the goods ahead with an escort on Burd's Road (Raystown Path) toward the fort while he and Carlisle resident (and future Revolutionary War general) Captain William Thompson prepared to face the dark clouds gathering with both the Cherokee party and across the sky.

The head of the Cherokee contingent, Captain Bullen (The son of an Irish father and Catawba mother),[55] wasn't the initial problem but rather his constituents, who Trent described "had blacked themselves and were going off in a

---
54. Ibid., William Trent to John Forbes, May 23, 1758.
55. Myers, 187.

View of Parnell Knob from Fort Loudoun Historic Site in Fort Loudoun, Pennsylvania. (Author photo.)

bad humor."[56] The party wanted to see this large army the English were boasting about and, more importantly, the presents Trent was to distribute.

The next morning, as Trent, Thompson, and the warrior party followed the wagon along the dilapidated road, Bullen and a Cherokee warrior galloped ahead the remaining twelve miles to the fort. Trent, feeling their impatience growing, knew they had a strong task once they got to their destination.

By that afternoon, thunder rumbled above Parnell Knob,[57] and the dark clouds poured rain upon them when they arrived at Fort Loudoun. The square fort of about one hundred and twenty feet[58] itself stood as a suitable redoubt (despite the lingering rats) to shorten the journey and bad roads between Shippensburg and the next outpost on the Raystown Path at Fort Lyttleton, whose site today lies in Fulton County.[59]

As Trent posted a sentry outside that evening and carried the goods into the fort's commissary store, he was immediately approached by one of the head warriors. The Cherokee warrior wanted his goods now because he was setting

---

56. University of Virginia Library, Headquarter Papers of John Forbes, William Trent to John St. Clair, May 22, 1758.
57. Parnell Knob was the ridge where Front Mountain and Broad Mountain meet in southcentral Pennsylvania, near the village of St. Thomas, Pennsylvania in Franklin County.
58. Myers, 174.
59. There is a historical marker along Route 522 (Great Cove Road) just a one-tenth mile east of Sinoquipe Road that commemorates the site of the fort in the town of Fort Littleton.

Today's reconstruction of Fort Loudoun that was the first stop of the 1758 expedition to the western country led by General John Forbes. (Author photo.)

off for home in the morning. Trent knew what might happen if he gave some goods to one and not to all of them, so he refused. He motioned to the warrior to look outside. It was just night, and it rained hard that it was too late to open them.[60] But Trent's interpreter, Anthony, failed (whether purposefully or not) to communicate the message. More of the warriors came in and, ignoring the sentry, grabbed two bales of goods and tried to walk back to their barracks. The sentry tried to go after them, but Trent stopped him and just called out to them to bring the goods back. These words were not lost in translation. No sooner had they come back into the store and Trent told them to wait till morning, did they react in anger. The warriors began running and raising their tomahawks and knives, whereas Trent described, "They broke open the cases and ripped open the bales & began to divide the Goods."[61]

His hand touched the handle of his pistol as he demanded Anthony to tell them to stop breaking into the King's goods and act like "good brothers."[62] When this had little effect on them, Trent took the sentry and called in officers Captain Ward (His former ensign at the Forks in the spring of 1754)[63] and

---

60. University of Virginia Library, Headquarter Papers of John Forbes, William Trent to John Forbes, May 23, 1758.
61. Ibid.
62. Ibid.
63. Edward Ward was commissioned a captain in the First Battalion of Pennsylvania under Colonel John Armstrong in 1758.

his superior, Captain Thompson, for advice. Thompson immediately ordered the drummers to beat the call to arms. Soldiers grabbed their muskets and rifles and assembled in the middle of the fort. They were not going to be bullied into giving them the goods. Unfortunately, when the thirty-seven Cherokee and Catawba's saw them do this, they grabbed all their belongings and tried to leave out the gate. Trent called out to them, then ordered Thompson and his men to retire to the barracks. When the Pennsylvanians began to disperse and return their arms, the warriors stopped and walked back toward Trent by the store.

In what seemed harsh language they spoke to Anthony, then back to their barracks. They all waited till the morning. For now, all had settled down, but Trent wasn't so sure. He expected to receive this same kind of treatment in the morning. After consulting with Thompson and Ward, he dispatched Lieutenant Henry Geiger[64] ahead to Fort Lyttleton during the night with an express for Cherokee Chief Wahatchee. The letter requested his presence immediately here at the fort because he needed to speak with those of his nation who had just tried to take the King's goods by force.

Something had to be done. Trent knew if the southern nations became their enemy, then it would ruin their western expedition. To his surprise, though and after a sleepless night, Trent found them either sleeping or in "good temper" the next day. He did remark to Quartermaster John St. Clair that this previous night, "I never was engaged in so difficult and interesting affair in my Life, nor did I ever spend a Night with so much anxiety."[65] Surprisingly, these were strong feelings and words coming from the same person who barely survived an ambush at Saratoga, witnessed the aftermath of Pickawillany and spent weeks expecting an attack from the French at the Forks of the Ohio.

One thing that also bothered him was the behavior of his so-called Indian interpreter. After much attitude from the Cherokee party, he realized this Anthony was part of the problem by not telling them what he said, but instead, what pleased them. It was also the reason he took Wahatchee and the twenty-five in his party to Shippensburg. Trent wanted to get away from this "scoundrel"[66] Anthony and have Wahatchee, who they described as "a great warrior and a very leading man in the nation,"[67] meet the Superintendent of Indian Affairs in the Western District, Abraham Bosomworth. Then, they received tierces[68] of

---

[64]. Lt. Henry Geiger emigrated to Pennsylvania from Germany. He resided in Northampton County and served with the First Battalion during Forbes's expedition in 1758. During the American Revolution, he was commander of the Northampton County militia with the rank of colonel.
[65]. University of Virginia Library, Headquarter Papers of John Forbes, William Trent to John Forbes, May 23, 1758.
[66]. BP, Vol. 2, 37.
[67]. Ibid., Vol. 1, 397.
[68]. 1 tierce was equivalent to forty-two wine gallons.

rice with the promise of other goods once Forbes second-in-command Colonel Henry Bouquet met them at Fort Loudoun.

Wahatchee and the others returned with him to Fort Loudoun, but on June 5th, Trent found little to their satisfaction. When Wahatchee informed him that with nothing available for him or his party, they all intended to go home in three days, Trent showed them a letter that Lieutenant Colonel Adam Stephen and six hundred Virginians[69] were just six miles away, and when they arrived in the morning, they might, at the very least, have necessary goods. They all seemed pleased but warned Trent that if he "would not make them a large Present to Carry home with them, they would rob all the English Houses they met with on their way home."[70] One of the warriors even mocked the absence of the goods and Colonel Bouquet by throwing a shirt at Trent's feet. Trent thanked him "jocosely," but the warrior said it was not for Trent that he "desired me to get it washed and give it to you,"[71] meaning Bouquet. It was followed up by them throwing bundles of goods near the shirt and telling Trent "To keep them" and to give them to Bouquet since "he loved goods."[72] Trent also added that this supposed hostility all was because of his interpreter Anthony (called a Rascal by Bouquet), who had told him when they first arrived Bouquet was to give them all nothing. When Trent reassured them that Bouquet's arrival was delayed only because he was waiting on arms and munitions (some of which he was giving them among other goods), they opted to stay a few days more.

Bouquet was in Shippensburg by the 9th but remarked the way was almost impassable due to the rain softening the already damp road. His assumption proved correct when several wagons became stuck along the way, and it took them over three days to reach Fort Loudoun.[73]

He finally arrived at Fort Loudoun on June 11th, but it wasn't until after meeting with the Cherokee that he realized what Trent had been complaining about all along. Like Lieutenant Colonel Stephen, he agreed that "Trent has used all possible endeavors to please them"[74] and recognized this main issue with the "infamy of the conduct of that rascal Antoine."[75]

In the end, it was Trent's "method" of negotiations that kept them at bay until they could see Bouquet. For on June 16th as he and Bouquet traveled the

---

69. BP, Vol. 2, 41.
70. Ibid., 37.
71. Ibid.
72. Ibid.
73. Ibid., 47.
74. Ibid., 52.
75. Ibid., 49.

freshly repaired road twenty miles to Fort Lyttleton, twenty Catawba traveled with them.[76]

Although the expedition was finally taking shape with supplies and troops being sent out along the road across the ocean, a particular act of relief appeared under the new business agenda at the meeting of the Royal Court at Kensington in the Western District of London. His Majesty King George II, after reviewing the "Act of Relief of George Croghan and William Trent" (since the Privy Council clerk failed to disclose this earlier), declared his disallowance of the said act and had it repealed or void.[77] This meant after only two and a half years (and not ten),[78] Croghan or Trent were no longer protected from arrest or being sued in a court of law for their said debts from all the creditors in question. This repeal eventually plagued both men for the rest of their lives, but Trent did not hear of this news until later in the year.

Meanwhile, just over a week later, Trent and Bouquet traveled the mountainous road past their completed fort to Juniata Crossing (near Breezewood, Pennsylvania)[79] and, fourteen miles later, set up their next encampment along the Juniata River. Here, Bouquet and engineer Captain Harry Gordon[80] chose the elevated terrain adjacent to the river for their next fortified outpost called Rea's Town (Raystown) and then later, by December of 1758, after the Duke of Bedford, which it's still called today.[81] As most letters were addressed temporarily as the "Camp at Rea's Town," men from Pennsylvania and Virginia began clearing the area to begin construction of a fort, working for a gill (pronounce Jill)[82] of rum per day. By mid-July, storehouses were built along with eighteen outdoor ovens for baking bread and charcoal was made to burn in these ovens.[83]

The outpost was eventually a star-shaped Fort with five bastions[84], becoming the first major supply base of their western expedition along with what was their final one, the eventual fort constructed at the camp at the Loyalhanna. Eventually, when all the troops arrived at Rea's Town, it became the second most inhabited "city" or area next to Philadelphia. Trent spent the next two months

---

76. Ibid., 95.
77. Mitchell and Flanders, Vol. 5, 576–77.
78. The relief bill when passed in 1755 was originally for ten years until it was repealed.
79. A historical marker to commemorate this outpost is along Route 30 about three-tenths of a mile west of Dell Road in Bedford County, Pennsylvania.
80. Harry Gordon was an engineer who came over to the American colonies from Scotland and constructed Braddock's Road before the Battle of the Monongahela on July 9, 1755, where he was wounded. He was also the designer of Fort Pitt, probably using the original plans he carried during the failed Braddock expedition. Later after the French and Indian War, he was employed in Canada and the West Indies as an engineer.
81. Bedford, Pennsylvania.
82. A gill is ¼ of a pint or four fluid ounces.
83. BP, Vol. 2, 217.
84. Norman B. Leventhal Map Collection, "Fort Bedford on Juniata Creek." Outpost of the War for Empire, Stotz, 115.

at Fort Rea's Town amongst the initial eight hundred and eleven men[85] in the garrison, helping Colonel Bouquet with keeping their Indian allies happy.

On the very same day (August 23, 1758) that Colonel Burd with his Second Battalion of Pennsylvanians marched with five companies of Montgomerie's Highlanders[86] and four pieces of artillery to the camp at the Loyalhannon to begin a fort, Trent left for Fort Cumberland to bring all the Indian nations that had resided there with Colonel Washington back to Rea's Town. He brought back two less, however, when Catawba Captains Bullen and French were killed[87] by the enemy lurking outside the fort.

The journey down the Warrior's Path to the mouth of Will's Creek was most welcoming for Trent, as the last two months at Rea's Town were stricken with the spread of smallpox and the outbreak of the flux.[88]

Both Archibald Montgomerie, the highlander commander and General Forbes had become its latest victims of this "flux." Though the latter had persisted much worse, violent constipation that Forbes described as being so taken by it, it left him feeling as "weak as a newborn infant."[89] It was said the flux originated from the limestone water consumed near their respective outpost, so those who could afford it purchased shrub punch or rum[90] from the local sutlers to prevent it. Fort Cumberland, it seemed, had also been affected by it, for his former house and warehouse on the Potomac was now a makeshift hospital.[91]

When Trent returned to Rea's Town, he found the camp in extreme jubilation. News came on the 26th[92] that the British troops under General Jeffrey Amherst had been victorious in Nova Scotia, seizing the large French fortress of Louisbourg on Cape Breton Island. This major British victory was a large blow to French forces in New France and made this expedition key to ending the war if they could seize Fort Duquesne and control the Forks of the Ohio.

Trent also had a reason for celebration. His efforts to help the cause didn't go unnoticed. General Forbes ordered Colonel Bosomworth to fully commission Trent as his Assistant Superintendent of the Western District.[93] He received twelve shillings per day for his Pennsylvania service in "keeping the Indians under proper Regulations."[94] The celebration was short-lived, however, be-

---

85. BP, Vol. 2, 148.
86. The 77th Highland Regiment was commanded by Archibald Montgomerie (May 18, 1726–October 30, 1796) who in 1769 became the 11th Earl of Eglinton then the Governor of Edinburgh Castle in 1782.
87. Myers, 187. BP, Vol. 2, 424.
88. BP, Vol. 2, 337.
89. Ibid., 344.
90. BP, Vol. 2, 352. Shrub punch refers to a drink compound of fruit, vinegar, and rum or brandy.
91. Myers, 196.
92. BP, Vol. 2, 461.
93. Trent was commissioned on September 3, 1758. For details of Trent's 1758 commission, see Appendix G of this book.
94. Cadwalader Colden Papers (1755–1760) Vol. 5, 259.

cause that night, he received orders to take what Catawba's, Nottaway's, and Tuscarora's he could from Rea's Town and join Colonel Dagworthy with three hundred men from Maryland, North Carolina, and the Lower Counties[95] to take possession of an advantageous post toward Fort Duquesne.

This was the site first known as Dagworthy's Camp, and it was about nine miles past the camp Colonel Burd and Major James Grant had set up along the Loyalhanna Creek (where the present town of Ligonier is today). Both officers preferred the advanced post (about a mile southeast of Latrobe, Pennsylvania), but since the road conditions were bad and Bouquet already had a small fort marked out around their storehouses, a breastwork was planned instead at where Trent and the others were going.

Bouquet which described Dagworthy's Camp as "well entrenched" and "naturally very strong,"[96] felt a French force could not overtake it without artillery. The entrenchment of Dagworthy's Camp, when constructed, stood about seven feet high[97], and it wasn't completed until days later. This being because the road beyond the "Loyalhanna" outpost was atrocious, with only trees felled to clear a way mixed with the continual rains that Trent and the rest experienced getting there.

Once they arrived, loud musket fire could be heard[98] in the distance and they began work rather quickly until it was finally completed on September 8th. Though they spent the next two days on alert, nothing came of it until Major Grant arrived with over seven hundred troops under his command on the morning of September 10th.[99] Apparently, a hunting party was attacked, which was why Trent and the others heard the shots. Grant was consented by Bouquet to find the perpetrators of this attack and, if possible, reconnoiter Fort Duquesne at night. He was not to engage any of the enemy from the French garrison. Beyond that, the mission was secretive and although Bouquet agreed it was a "good lesson,"[100] he nor Dagworthy knew Grant's full intent of the mission. When he left Dagworthy's Camp, now called "Grant's Paradise," for the proposed mission on the 11th, Grant told Bouquet he returned with solid reports on the 16th.

Three days later, Trent and those at Grant's Paradise received their report, but rather an alarming one from the front. According to a ragged Ensign James

---

95. Before it separated from Pennsylvania on June 15, 1776 the region known today as the state of Delaware was known as "the Lower Counties."
96. BP, Vol. 2, 493.
97. Hanna, Vol. 1, 285.
98. BP, Vol. 2, 493.
99. Ibid., 519.
100. Ibid., 493.

Grant of the 77th Highland Regiment and eight others[101] whose white shirts over their coats were stained with blood and soil, they had an engagement within sight of Fort Duquesne. Most, if not all, in the black of the night, were cut off and surrounded, including Major Grant himself and none of them could know for certain if he was alive or not.

On the 15th, fifty more men appeared, giving the same account: "The enemy were chiefly Indians, with French to an upwards of Two Thousand."[102] A return suggested there were almost three hundred[103] presumed missing or dead. Bouquet, not wishing to panic, countered with a physical response almost immediately. First, he sent out Ensign Archibald Blane of the Royal Americans[104] with an escort until Grant's Paradise. Then he and two sergeants, one drummer and thirty privates were on their own to conduct a parlay at Fort Duquesne and learn the fates of Grant and his detachment's whereabouts.

Then, on the 22nd of September, he ordered Trent with a detachment of Cherokees and Catawba towards Venango if agreeable to them: "Where you are to reconnoiter the enemy and endeavor, if possible, to take a prisoner as in your power the Indians from committing an attack on the French that may fall into your hands."[105] The last thing Bouquet needed was another Major Grant disaster with no intelligence, so he warned Trent also to be aware of the French party escorting Ensign Blane with a letter from Fort Duquesne.

> In case you meet with the escort of French which is expected with Mr. Blane who went to Fort Duquesne with a flag of truce, you already use all your endeavors to prevent the Indians with you from falling upon a Detachment or offering any violence to them whatever.[106]

Trent probably slung his blunderbuss behind his back and made sure the powder in his pistol was dry. His orders were clear, but with all the incidents, insults, and struggles to keep them with the British Army, he could make no promises. At the very least, he made sure Ensign Blane returned safely to deliver the "Governor of Fort Duquesne's"[107] response.

A week later, he did just that, writing to Colonel Bouquet from the "Loyalhannah" that he did encounter the French party and "had great difficulty

---

101. Ibid., 499.
102. Ibid., 511. (Later, it was estimated around 800 to 900, but nonetheless more than assumed by their recent intelligence on the road).
103. Ibid., 520.
104. Archibald Blane was commissioned an ensign on December 6, 1756 in the 60th Royal American Regiment.
105. Auction letter from Henry Bouquet to William Trent, September 22, 1758, "At the Camp at Lawillhammer."
106. Ibid.
107. The "Governor" or commander was Captain Francois-Marie Le Marchand Sieur de Lignery.

in preventing the Indians attacking them."[108] But Blane and his French escort Philippe Francois de Rastel de Rocheblave returned to the "Loyalhanna" safely. The same was not said for a party of Lenape and French soldiers whom Trent admitted, "They had killed and wounded some others."[109]

Trent presented the prize of this aftermath to Colonel Burd by having the Indians "gift" him a French scalp they took near Fort Duquesne. He also informed Burd that he did, in fact, find "a good road from the Breastwork to Turtle Creek."[110] This road he spoke of was the southern fork of the old trader's path or the Raystown Path, close to where General Braddock's army engaged the French and Indians, about eight miles from Fort Duquesne.

Before he was sent to deliver this intelligence to General Forbes at Rea's Town, he did note to Burd that although he and his men traveled the same path from Fraser's former cabin at the mouth of Turtle Creek to the Forks of the Ohio in February of 1754, he did not know the condition of the road beyond that. Trent also assumed the enemy party the Indian scouts had seen lurking near the breastworks at Grant's Paradise had taken this very road from Fort Duquesne.

So, while Trent delivered this report to sickly General Forbes in October, Burd and his post at the Loyalhanna faced an assault from the main body of this party of French and Indians on October 12th. With the fort already on alarm, Burd silenced the enemy harassment with his cannons and coehorns[111] that roared across the creek at them, proudly announcing that "Captain Gordon's Musik from the Great Guns far Exceeded the Indian solos."[112] By the 14th, the French and Indians had all but retreated.

Despite Trent's valued intel and the most recent attack, officers Forbes and Bouquet were at a crossroads. Bouquet agreed with Forbes that "the path discovered by Capt. Trent seems to be the best,"[113] but there was one problem with it. Trent had no idea if the path beyond Turtle Creek could withstand artillery trains or supply wagons since "as he could not go to the end of it, there is a little dependency upon it."[114] Plus, the Monongahela River was too swollen to ford it twice to get past Braddock's Field.

With Forbes's health barely satisfactory (he had to be carried in a litter between two horses) on his way to Rea's Town and the soldier's morale beginning to be hindered, a decision needed to be made about the expedition. It was then,

---

108. Auction letter from Henry Bouquet to William Trent, September 22, 1758, "At the Camp at Lawillhammer."
109. Ibid.
110. BP, Vol. 2, 546.
111. A coehorn is a lightweight mortar that could fire a shell up to one thousand yards.
112. BP, Vol. 2, 556.
113. Ibid., 546.
114. Ibid.

The Fall of Fort Duquesne

on November 11th, the ailing Forbes called in his officers for an important council of war at the Loyalhanna he now temporarily called "Pittsborough."[115] If they were to withhold their attack on Fort Duquesne until spring and go into winter quarters, they needed more clothes and more food. To feed an army of over 4,000 men for four months, they needed almost 1,500 beeves.[116] Of course, that was only possible if smokehouses could be built to keep the meat from spoiling before winter came.

Nonetheless, after discussing all risk factors, it was still decided they were not proceeding to attack Fort Duquesne without proper supplies this late in the year. Fortunately, this decision was not final. Two days later, a scouting party captured three individuals, and they informed the officers at the Loyalhanna that for months, the garrison at Fort Duquesne was without adequate provisions and was now in an indefensible position.[117] They also learned that after "their" victory over Major Grant in September and the peace reached with the English at the Treaty of Easton last month, the French Indian nations (who numbered almost one thousand) had chosen to leave the fort and their alliance to the French army altogether.

So now, with this sudden turning point reversed in their favor, General Forbes ordered the quick advance of the fifty miles or so to try and take Fort Duquesne and undoubtedly the Forks of the Ohio. Over two thousand five hundred men, including Trent, left the outpost at the Loyalhanna with just a blanket, knapsack[118] and their weapons. They were followed by a light train of artillery, proceeding on the road west to meet the French, as Bouquet described, "determined by a battle who should possess this Country."[119] They covered fifty miles in about five days, taking the northern fork of the Raystown Path opposite from the southern one of the former Braddock Road and halting on the 24th at a place later called Bouquet's Camp (along Davidson Road just west of Boyce Park in Plum, Pennsylvania)[120] about twelve miles from Fort Duquesne. It was there Trent was joined by his former partner Croghan and three Indians arriving straight after their Congress at Easton to scout ahead that evening of the enemy numbers at the Forks of the Ohio. Later that night they returned to report that "a very thick smoke from the Front extending in the bottom along the Ohio."[121]

The next day, on the 25th, as the troops marched within sight of the French fort, they found this report true. The enemy had abandoned their post, taking

---
115. Ibid., 600.
116. Ibid., 449.
117. Washington in the Forbes expedition, Toner, 22.
118. Stewart, 72.
119. BP, Vol. 2, 610.
120. The historic sign commemorating this location is found on 6106 Saltsburg Road, Verona, Pennsylvania 15147.
121. BP, Vol.2, 610.

their batteaus down to the Ohio to the mouth of Beaver Creek, eventually north to Fort Machault,[122] the French outpost at Venango on French Creek. Fort Duquesne, or what remained, lay in burnt, smoldering ruins. Before they left, the French had set fire to their fortifications, houses, and ovens and destroyed their magazine.[123] Pennsylvania and Lower Counties officer John Haslet further added to this description by saying thirty chimneys[124] were standing with all the houses burnt. Sadly, he also noted that amongst the rubble and within a mile of the Forks were those who were left unburied[125] from the defeat of Grant's detachment back in September.

Apparently, those on the night of September 14th who didn't meet their end on the present-day Grant's Hill were taken to the fort to either be burned in the fort or tomahawked by the warriors who captured them.[126] Haslet, along with fellow Pennsylvania officer Hugh Mercer, eventually faced their ends almost twenty years later in 1777 as Continental officers at the Battle of Princeton in New Jersey.

The capture of Fort Duquesne was bittersweet for men like Trent and even Pennsylvania Captain Edward Ward, who both in the spring of 1754 had their incomplete outpost "Fort St. George" replaced by this one. Now, on November 26, 1758, after a long, arduous expedition, they could feel proud to reclaim the Forks of the Ohio as they joined the others for a "Day of Public Thanksgiving to Almighty God for our success,"[127] led by a public sermon conducted by Rev. Charles Beatty. Before Trent bowed his head in prayer, he looked all around the "Forks." Everything was going to change for the better, including this place. No longer was it called Fort Duquesne. As the general had once temporarily named the advanced post at the Loyalhanna (now called Fort Ligonier), the English camp at the Forks of the Ohio was named in honor of British Secretary of State William Pitt the Elder.[128] Pronounced "Pitts- borough" like the city of Edinburgh from the general's beloved homeland,[129] the city still retains the name despite being pronounced "Pitts- berg" today.

---

122. The French fort or supply post near the mouth of French creek and the Allegheny River (near present-day Franklin, Pennsylvania was named in honor of Jean-Baptiste Machault d' Arnouville, the current French Minister of the Marine.
123. BP, Vol. 2, 610.
124. Stewart, 72.
125. Ibid.
126. Stewart, 72.
127. *Pennsylvania Gazette*, December 14, 1758. BP, Vol. 2, 614.
128. William Pitt (November 15, 1708–May 11, 1778) was known as William Pitt the Elder to distinguish from his son William Pitt, who also served as Prime Minister of Great Britain. The son was known as William Pitt the Younger. The elder Pitt served on Parliament from 1755 to 1766, Secretary of State for the Southern Department 1757–1761 and Prime Minister of Great Britain from 1766–1768.
129. Forbes was born in Dunfermline, Scotland and grew up at Pittencrieff House whose building still stands today inside Pittencrieff Park, a public park located on the outskirts of Dunfermline, Scotland in Fife.

An original black and white chalk drawing of William Pitt the Elder (circa 1754) by artist William Hoare. (Courtesy of the Elisha Whittelsey Collection and Public Domain.)

As 1759 loomed near, the French and Indian War was nearing its end, and Trent hoped all these changes meant he could resume mercantile operations once again. Though he felt optimistic, for now, Trent had to wait and see what his future held.

Chapter 12

Profit and Victory

In Lancaster, the cold February wind likely stung Sarah Trent's face outside as she raised the axe over her head and split the piece of wood in two. Quickly, she picked up the chopped logs and wrapped them in her apron. Inside, she threw two logs on the small flame and watched the moisture make the fire hiss.

Suddenly, the door creaked open, and there he was, covered in fresh snow and wrapped in a deerskin match coat. He barely had time to brush himself off before they immediately embraced. After Trent left Shippensburg in May, his letters home had stopped coming and so she had no idea where he was or what happened until now.

He informed her for now he was home until the spring. It was by then his exceptional penmanship was needed again when the Indian nations wanted to meet at Pittsborough. By that time, a suitable defense could be constructed that hopefully impressed their latest allies.

Though, by spring, the Ohio Indians wanted to meet their newest Brigadier General, John Stanwix, who relieved General Forbes. Forbes, still suffering from his ailments, left the Forks on December 3rd and finally arrived in Philadelphia on January 17, 1759. From the city, he continued to hear the progress of the Pittsborough outpost until he succumbed to what was most likely stomach cancer on March 11, 1759.[1] Forbes was interred in the chancel of Christ Church in Philadelphia, where a tablet marks this location today.

By the time Trent left the Forks in late January, the commander of Pittsborough, Colonel Hugh Mercer of the Pennsylvania Battalion, had already constructed a considerable defense. He and about three hundred and fifty

---

1. BP, Vol. 3, 156. *Pennsylvania Gazette*, March 15, 1759.

Profit and Victory 213

In the wall of the chancel of Christ Church in Philadelphia and just behind the pulpit, lies the tablet marking where General Forbes was interred in March of 1759. (Author photo.)

men[2] began an outpost that kissed the Monongahela River shoreline, with barracks raised and roofed adjacent to enclosed bastions with a gate and a magazine.[3] It was sufficient for protection but not to withhold a siege. Delaware George had sent one of his runners to Fort Machault and reported that the French intend "to make a Descent on this place & Loyalhanning, they have two pieces of cannon and about 300 men at Wenango and expect a Reinforcement of both from Priscisle."[4]

If this were true, then Mercer had no intention to repel such a superior force but rather "pass over the Monongahela in ye night and Keeping a continual firing ye Fort to mask your retreat and as soon as the whole is over, burn the

---
2. Stewart, 350.
3. BP, Vol. 2, 635 and 640.
4. Ibid., 640.

Fort having for that Purpose Wood ready within for it."[5] Trent, like Mercer, knew the French were not launching an attack until the Ohio was clear of ice, so until then, it was time he returned home until Croghan needed his services again. While he was home in Lancaster, he could ride to his other lands and country plantation house in Carlisle, making sure the soil was fertile before the planting season began.

Trent hoped that the forthcoming spring meant he was getting closer to resuming his mercantile business once more. He figured if they maintained their stronghold of the outpost at Pittsborough, then for the first time in almost six years, the fur trade could safely resume in the Ohio country. This was also good news for his employer, the Ohio Company, who began the year 1759, settling litigations and collecting debts before the committee could meet and resume their business in the summer. One such litigation was the pending case of Trent versus Robert Dinwiddie. Still active since November of 1757, John Mercer wished Trent to send him any documents now that could preserve his character and help with the prosecution of this high-profile suit.

Trent opened his large black trunk[6] and removed a dozen documents[7], such as his original captain's commission on January 26, 1754, and several letters from Colonels George Washington and William Fairfax. Then he bundled them together and placed them in his document portmanteau below his saddle on his horse. He arrived in Philadelphia by April 11, 1759, and that night composed a letter to John Mercer that he brought the enclosed documents and sent them with Captain Robert Stewart[8] to take to Mercer or any other affiliate of the Ohio Company staying in Williamsburg. Trent also included a list of potential individuals who could testify on his character and behalf to serve as witnesses for the prosecution.

A few months later, as no outcome of his suit had been determined before the summer, Trent left Lancaster to record the minutes with the chiefs of the warriors of the Six Nations, Lenape, Shawnee, and eight nations of Wyandots (Huron) at Pittsburgh from July to October 1759. Trent, along with Thomas McKee,[9]

---

5. Ibid., 643.
6. HSP and Library Company of Pennsylvania, "Books & being the contents of a Black Trunk, belonging to the estate of William Trent, deceased." For a complete inventory list of Trent's black trunk, see also Appendix O of this book.
7. James, 231–32.
8. Robert Stewart (1729–1809) was a friend of George Washington and became a captain of the light horse in the Virginia Regiment that served during the Braddock expedition in 1755. He also served near Fort Loudoun in Winchester, Virginia and be stationed at Maidstone, the stockade built opposite the mouth of the Conococheague that today lies in Falling Waters, West Virginia. Later Stewart served at Fort Pitt and the English outpost built at Venango in 1760.
9. Thomas McKee was an Irish trader and assistant to deputy agent George Croghan who conducted business from the Susquehanna River to the Ohio country. He was licensed in Pennsylvania to trade as early as 1742 and held a trading post near the mouth of the Juniata River on a place now called Haldeman's Island near present-day Duncannon, Pennsylvania. He was also the father of trader and Indian agent Alexander McKee, the eventual loyalist and namesake for the town of McKee's Rocks.

were acting assistants to Deputy Agent of Indian Affairs George Croghan and his interpreter Andrew "Henry" Montour. Croghan acted on his superior's behalf for the northern department since William Johnson was now busy with troops under General John Prideaux laying siege to Fort Niagara on Lake Ontario.

The first meeting began on July 4th, with those invitees extending their greetings by discharging their pistols and muskets in the air. As they walked to the gate, the fort fired its cannons across the river to answer their greeting. For a week until the 11th, Croghan presented gifts and a belt to about one hundred warriors from all those nations to ratify the peace between them that was agreed upon at Easton last October. He even extended to confirm it by traveling with them to Philadelphia, but the Beaver, the main voice of the council and "King of the Delawares," refused, saying they weren't going to Philadelphia while the English and "French were at War in their Country."[10] Croghan replied it was fine because "while the Enemy are in Possession of your Country, we cannot Trade safely with you as formerly."[11]

The treaty ended on the 11th with the Beaver agreeing to take the discussion of peace at Pittsburgh and tell the rest at a general council of all nations over the lakes. He added before he left that "you may depend on a large Body of our people being here in about two Months, in order to Confirm the Peace on our parts."[12]

With the talk of resuming trade in the Ohio country, it was rather ironic that at this very same time as the conference at Pittsburgh, the committee of the Ohio Company met to discuss the future of their enterprise at the Stafford County Courthouse in Stafford, Virginia on July 6th, 1759. Their chief concern was applying to London to extend their original grant, whose seven years had expired three years ago.[13] With the French and Indian War reduced to Fort Niagara and those remaining strongholds in Canada, this was the best opportunity as any to build their settlements and forts again while controlling the Ohio country.

So, it was voted upon at this meeting for John Mercer to draft a pamphlet for London that covered in meticulous detail the years of the company's activities and why they should be granted an extension for their original land tract from 1749. This time, however, there wasn't a Virginia Lieutenant Governor throwing his full support behind them. Denny's replacement, Francis Fauquier,[14] made his

---

10. Colonial Records of Pennsylvania, Vol. 8, 385.
11. Ibid., 389.
12. Ibid., 390.
13. The original royal grant was given to the Ohio Company on May 19, 1749, for them to settle one hundred families and build a fort within seven years. This expired in May of 1756.
14. Francis Fauquier (1703–March 3, 1768) served as acting Lieutenant Governor of Virginia from 1758 until his death in 1768. He was a close friend of Thomas Jefferson and Fauquier County is named for him.

feelings about the Ohio Company's ventures known when he spoke to the Board of Trade back on January 30th.

"It is supposed that all the Great Grants are actually forfeited; if so, and the Crown should think proper to resume them, I apprehend it will be best not to renew them, for great and extensive Grants are destructive to the well-settling and peopling a Colony."[15] Nonetheless, Mercer had to quickly draft their resolutions as soon as possible if they wanted to protect them now.

Meanwhile at Pittsburgh, Trent and the rest of their garrison did receive some good news from two Indian runners who arrived back from Fort Machault. On August 4th, they explained to them in the fort that the French who left Venango to reinforce Niagara were "repulsed with the loss of Twenty-Eight Officers killed & taken, a great number of Soldiers killed and taken and twelve Indians killed, amongst the prisoners is Mr. Delinery who commanded at this place, shot through the thick of the thigh."[16] It came on the night the Beaver and another group of warriors were eager to sit with them inside the garrison and declare peace with each other. This time came Chippewas and Twightwees, who, according to Croghan, were there so the Beaver and eighty Indians could "take the French Hatchett out of the hands of some few of their People."[17] By the next day, on the 8th, the Beaver gave two belts, one to the Wyandots and one to the Twightwees. He concluded the treaty by saying, "We will as soon as possible comply with the Engagements our Deputys entered into with our Brethren the English on confirming the Peace."[18]

Croghan also informed him to come next month, but they finally requested an audience with General Stanwix, who arrived at the end of August with a wagon of goods. Both he and Croghan also hoped the large council coming next month also saw the new progress of the proposed fortification in Pittsburgh, whose plans had been engineered by Captain Harry Gordon when he arrived before the previous treaty in August. Originally, Gordon scouted the location around Fort Hill (where the Ohio Company once proposed to build at Chartier's Creek)[19] but, as Trent had once observed in 1753, thought it too difficult "getting up materials on the Ridge as the access is not easy."[20]

So, with the Forks chosen as the primary location for the new fort, Gordon next began plans for a sawmill. He started first with building the clogs and wheels[21] that they transported a mile from the fort, where they built the mill

---

15. James, 112.
16. BP, Vol. 3, 493.
17. Ibid., 502.
18. Ibid., 511.
19. See Endnote 682.
20. BP, Vol. 4, 13.
21. Ibid., Vol. 3, 569.

along a small tributary[22] on the south side of the Ohio River. With the arrival of General Stanwix and several Indian nations on September 2nd, it was announced before the treaty that Gordon and his artificers officially began a large pentagonal outline made of earth[23] rather than logs. The next day, on the 3rd, General Stanwix addressed the council of warriors and how he appreciated the new chain of friendship established from the previous treaties of Pittsburgh the last couple of months. Then he handed them a wampum belt to confirm the peace. The Ottawa chief then lit a large pipe with eagle feathers[24] and passed it around for everyone in attendance to smoke. He declared this was to show the peace between all those Western nations and their brethren, the English.

The Twightwee chief also spoke at the end, showing the tomahawk given to them by the French and how they were carrying it no longer. With the same purpose as the Ottawa chief, they both said, "We have thrown away the French & must now depend upon you for Supplies & hope you will consider our Necessities at this Time."[25] Then the treaty ended, and after four pages of recorded minutes, Trent signed at the bottom, "William Trent, Assistant to Geo. Croghan Esq."[26]

At this time, Trent had grown accustomed as acting secretary for both Croghan and Johnson, but by late October, he relinquished those duties after one final council. After hearing the account of the siege of Niagara by Captain Charles Lee[27] of the 44th Regiment of Foot on October 4th,[28] then over a week later,[29] the confirmed capture of Quebec in September,[30] Trent must have decided. With his wife expecting a child this month, this was his last council in Pittsburgh before he returned home.

On the 25th of October, General Stanwix addressed first those not at last month's treaty and declared how they continued to abide by the original boundaries established at the Treaty of Easton a year ago between the English and the Six Nations. He also acquainted them that "the English had the city of Quebec

---

22. Today this tributary is called Saw Mill Run, just below the West End Bridge just south of downtown Pittsburgh.
23. BP, Vol. 4, 71.
24. Friendly Association Papers, Minutes of Conference held at Pittsburgh September 1759.
25. Ibid.
26. Ibid.
27. Charles Lee (February 6, 1732–October 2, 1782) was a British officer who was first a lieutenant in the 44th Regiment of Foot that served during the 1755 Braddock expedition. He also was at the failed capture of Carillion (Fort Ticonderoga) in 1758, but recovered to help capture Fort Niagara, and the capitulation of Montreal in 1760. During the Revolutionary War he became a major-general despite being in the running for Commander-in-Chief that went to George Washington. This resentment toward Washington continued to be worse even after being captured by the British in New Jersey and released in 1778. Later he was relieved of his command after a disagreement at the Battle of Monmouth Courthouse with General Washington and was suspended from the Continental Army for a year. He died in Philadelphia and was interred at Christ Church in the city.
28. BP, Vol. 5, 134–39.
29. At Pittsburgh they heard about the capture of Quebec on October 13, 1759.
30. The British captured Quebec after the Battle of the Plains of Abraham on September 13, 1759.

and that we captured soon to drive the French out of America."[31] The next day the Beaver spoke that he had taken the belts they received months ago to the nations over the lakes and hoped that "they would come next Spring and take fast hold of the chain of friendship."[32] When they all finished speaking, General Stanwix gave the chiefs in attendance each a medal. Then, they all were poured a drink and raised their glass to the King's health.

Trent left the next morning, heading east, but along the road, he noticed the number of wagons he saw heading toward Pittsburgh. Word had spread, it seemed, of the British control of the Ohio country, so more and more inhabitants left the east using the Forts Loudoun to Ligonier along Forbes's Road to settle in the west. These people were what Trent and the others feared might happen again after the Burnt Cabins expedition in 1750. Now, they were crossing the Allegheny Mountains and settling further west, ignoring not only the marked surveys of the Ohio Company land but also violating boundaries that the general had promised they were never breaching from the Treaty of Easton. It was only a matter of time before problems with settlers arose again.

Trent returned home to Lancaster in November and discovered his wife had given birth to their second child on October 24, 1759.[33] They named her Martha, and she was baptized at their house by the minister of the borough of Lancaster and the former chaplain on the Forbes expedition, Rev. Thomas Barton.

A few months later, it was there in Lancaster in the spring of 1760 when, once again, a business venture seized him. Just a few blocks from his house at the southeast corner of Penn Square[34] was the mercantile store co-owned by three Jewish merchants who wished to reboot their enterprise in the Western country by somewhat "interrogating" Trent about the new fortification being built in Pittsburgh. Though he had never conducted business with the trio, he was well familiar with their firm and connected to them rather indirectly. Merchant David Franks's spouse was Margaret Evans, the daughter of Mary Moore and sheriff Peter Evans, who, along with his parents in 1715, were "people of interest" in the Christ Church scandal with Rev. Francis Phillips.[35] Franks was also formally partnered with the late Nathan Levy (the founder of the Jewish community in Philadelphia), and it was both who owned the ship the *Myrtilla*, which Trent sailed back on from London in the spring of 1749.

---

31. Early History of Western Pennsylvania, Rupp, 140.
32. Ibid., 142.
33. HSP, Family Bible Records, BrTr.
34. Now the present site of the Lancaster County Convention Center on South Queen Street in Lancaster, Pennsylvania.
35. See the Prelude of this book that focuses on the Christ Church scandal in 1715.

Frank's sudden interest in Trent came about when he and William Plumsted[36] were appointed agents or contractors for the army, hired by Colonel Henry Bouquet. For now, he and Plumsted supplied the army in the Western country, so a side venture at Pittsburgh only boosted his firm.

The second partner was Joseph Simon,[37] who, after settling in Lancaster, owned several properties in and around town. One such property was most likely the house Trent and his family resided in currently since the spring of 1756. Finally, the third merchant was Simon's nephew Levi Andrew Levy,[38] who, since he came to Lancaster from England, had started as Simon's clerk and since become a partner in their fur trading firm.

Now, we don't know the conversation beyond their meeting at the store in Lancaster, but all four saw an opportunity they could not pass up. The fur trade business in the Western country was soon on the rise again, with the Ohio Indians being open to it in Pittsburgh, so an established mercantile store there faced few rivals outside the Provincial Store or King's Store already inside the fort. In addition, the forts along the Forbes Road all eventually needed goods or supplies from either contractor Franks or their store, and now word from Croghan was houses and magazines were being constructed across the perimeters of the new fort at Pittsburgh. The "earthen" fort was engineered to be so large it was designed to have two towns or villages attached to it. The first one was called the Lower Town, closer to the Allegheny River shoreline and planned gardens, while the other was called the Upper Town, nestled near the Monongahela River shoreline on the outskirts of the fort toward Ayer's Hill.[39]

It was no secret that Simon, Franks, and Levy needed Trent's connections at the fort, and if he could get them to set up a store, then this conglomerate prospered exponentially with Frank's latest contract with the army. The three also knew about Trent's notorious ambition, so there was no doubt he wanted in. It also made him forget about the Hockley investment failure and, more importantly, support the vision he always dreamt of when he and the Half-King chose the site of the Forks for an outpost in the late summer of 1753.[40]

---

36. William Plumsted (1708–1765) was the son of prominent merchant Clement Plumsted and was the mayor of Philadelphia in 1750, 1754, and 1755. It was he and David Franks who were ordered to supply the army and various outposts of the Western country in 1760. Plumsted also was a founding trustee of the Academy and College of Philadelphia (later the University of Pennsylvania) and founder of St. Peters Church until his death in 1765.
37. Joseph Simon (1712–January 24, 1804) was a leader of the Jewish community who immigrated to Lancaster, Pennsylvania from England by 1740. He was a successful merchant and owned large tracts of land in the Western country from the 1740s on. Later he owned several lots in Lancaster and a mercantile store he ran in downtown Lancaster. In 1804 he was interred in the Shaarai Shomayim Cemetery which he and Isaac Nunes Henriques purchased the land for in 1747.
38. Levi Andrew Levy's mother was the former Mary Simon, sister to Joseph Simon.
39. Stotz, Diagram on 137.
40. See "Trent's Account with the Proceedings of the Six Nations of Indians and Allies," at the University of Pittsburgh Archives (ULS).

So, on May 16, 1760,[41] merchants Joseph Simon, David Franks, and Levi Andrew Levy added Trent as a fourth partner to their articles of agreement for the western fur trade. The agreement was unlike his previous one in 1748 with Hockley and Croghan and was an "adventure" agreement where each person could pursue other business "interests" outside the firm if they wished. The firm's headquarters remained at the store in Penn Square under the management of Joseph Simon, while Franks handled the shipments coming to the docks in Philadelphia and then sent them west to Lancaster.

Trent and Levy, along with an enslaved servant,[42] handled the new store in the fort at Pittsburgh. Evidence shows by the census conducted at Pittsburgh by Colonels James Burd and Henry Bouquet, they resided and probably operated this store by July 22, 1760.[43]

Levi Levy was not listed as an inhabitant of Fort Pitt, but probably because he traveled as a liaison or distributor of goods between Fort Pitt and the English outposts. Three of these outposts were newly acquired below Lake Erie and being rebuilt that late summer. Since July, Colonel Bouquet marched troops to establish British outposts to garrison at Venango, Fort Le Boeuf and Presque Isle. It was why Trent and Levy's store at Pittsburgh became the largest mercantile store at Fort Pitt to acquire furs and goods other than the King's Store.

Then, even better news arrived at the fort in October. The French had capitulated Montreal,[44] so Canada now belonged to Great Britain. Rum and other spirits were probably opened in the name of the King from both stores to celebrate this conquest. This all came soon after an order was passed down that sutlers and traders were not to offer a sale or trade of rum to local Indian nations in exchange for furs.

Meanwhile, in Williamsburg, Virginia, the Ohio Company met to discuss and sign John Mercer's "Case of the Ohio Company."[45] After many drafts, it was finally ready to be sent to London solicitor Charlton Palmer[46] for royal approval. At this same time, it was also decided to repair the "old" Ohio Company warehouse[47] on the New Store Tract since its abandonment and use as a hospital and barracks since the construction of Fort Cumberland.

---

41. Byers, 47.
42. PMHB, Vol. 37, No. 1, 16.
43. Fleming, 467–68.
44. The capitulation of Montreal was signed on September 8, 1760.
45. The Ohio Company committee met in Williamsburg, Virginia on October 17, 1760.
46. Charlton Palmer was a solicitor for the Ohio Company from 1760–1764 and a lawyer in London that studied at the Middle Temple. He also assisted in the merger of the Indiana Company with London merchants that became the Grand Ohio Company by 1770. He replaced the late John Hanbury of Tower Street in London in being the liaison for all London activities after the French and Indian War ended in the American Colonies.
47. GMP, Mulkearn, 179–80.

Less than three weeks later, more specifically Ohio Company business became known for Trent when a letter dated November 8, 1760,[48] arrived at Fort Pitt from Williamsburg. It was from his good friend and Ohio Company member George Mercer, who brought important news for him about the deliberation of the jury and the final verdict of his suit against former Lieutenant Governor Robert Dinwiddie. Mercer, as well as Colonel George Washington (who Trent recommended as witnesses), attested to Trent's good nature at this trial, opposing those made by Dinwiddie as Mercer wrote, "Where I may assure you that all his malicious Attempts & Aspersions agst your Character & Credit were sufficiently cleared up both to the Court & Jury."[49]

So, following three long years of deliberation, Trent won his suit versus Robert Dinwiddie, and in return, a verdict of eight hundred pounds[50] besides costs was awarded for character defamation and reimbursement for money used from Ohio Company funds for the Fort St. George expedition in 1754. Later, on April 9, 1761, it was reported in the Virginia House of Burgesses that only about two hundred and ninety-one pounds five shillings were paid via public levy with the remaining amount attributed to a personal agreement and interest constituted between Trent and Dinwiddie that they voted not to raise.[51]

After Trent's highly regarded victory, he was riding high for the first time since the fighting began in 1754, and business was thriving. He and Levy's store was benefiting greatly from not only being one of the "first" stores in the Lower Town but also offering different services the King's Store at the fort could not provide. One obvious advantage they held over the King's Store was that they offered an alternative means of payment with credit as well. So those soldiers, inhabitants or Indians who wished for goods such as powder, bullets or even clothing but had no money or trade item to exchange for it could be listed on credit (Cr) with the promise to pay off the debt plus interest later. This was even more beneficial when Levy or fellow longtime assistants Alexander Lowrey[52] and James Foley traveled to the Indian towns to the north and further west down the Ohio River.

Now, despite the ordinance at Fort Pitt that no trader or merchant could travel or sell their goods outside the fort to other outposts or Indian towns

---

48. Bailey, 348–49.
49. Ibid.
50. Ibid.
51. Journals of the House of Burgesses 1758–1761, 255.
52. Alexander Lowrey (1723–1805) was an Indian trader in the Lancaster County/ Donegal region of Pennsylvania and part of the Lowrey trading firm that included his brothers James and Daniel, and his father Lazerus. It was their firm who sent traders and hired hands to the Forks of the Ohio in February of 1754 when Trent conducted a treaty to begin building Fort St. George. Later he was a good friend of Lancaster merchant Joseph Simon and traveled with Trent to Detroit and Sandusky in February of 1761. He continued to conduct business at Fort Pitt, Carlisle, Lancaster, and Fort de Chartres in the Illinois country.

without a designated pass, this did not hinder Trent and Levy. Permission could be granted by the commanding officer or His Majesty's Deputy Agent. Thankfully, this Deputy Agent was, of course, Trent's former partner and friend George Croghan, who had a house in the Lower Town and a large plantation house built on the opposite shore of the Allegheny River[53] from his previous one along Pine Creek. It also wasn't odd to suggest that Trent and Levy also promised Croghan a small percentage of the profits in exchange for business directed toward them from those Indian towns that needed supplies.

The other reason was Trent and Levy also did not refuse or limit any goods to any Indian man or woman who came to the store or sent word from afar before the fort's cannon thundered in the evening.[54] Business was booming, and their relationship with the local Native population was stronger than ever, so why should he abide by a quantity limit on goods? After all, the Ohio Indians trusted him to supply them, so how could he not fulfill the demands of his best customers?

Sure, it was breaking the rules, but not exactly forbidden, at least not like selling alcohol. For example, rum and spirits were forbidden to be exchanged for skins or sold to any Indian man or woman. This was respected by most of the traders or merchants like Trent because a repercussion was their "Houses pulled down, their stores plundered & themselves turned out of camp."[55]

The word "most" was used because the keeper of the King's Store, Quaker John Langdale (a man jealous of Trent and Levy's store), had not been following this general order. Apparently, this Langdale sold a quality of rum to an Indian woman[56] despite receiving no permission from His Majesty's Agent (meaning Croghan) and after others before him had been refused "liberties" to do so.

Trent knew Langdale had been envious of their large store from the beginning, so this was clearly an attempt to undermine their "high in demand" business. In fact, his feelings were so strong on this matter that he persuaded three other traders and a servant[57] to sign his "memorial" or grievance to Colonel Bouquet about Langdale's misdeeds as shopkeeper of the King's Store that February.

Before this eventually was sent to Bouquet, word of their highly reputed business spread even to the Great Lakes where British Deputy Agent and commander for Detroit Donald Campbell requested Croghan send them a supply

---

53. This plantation house was known as "Croghan Hall" by 1763.
54. On February 21, 1761, an ordinance was issued that traders, merchants and sutlers were only allowed to trade or sell their goods up until a fort's cannon was fired in the evening hours. BP, Vol. 5, 2.
55. BP, Vol. 5, 62.
56. Ibid., 315.
57. In addition to Trent's signature, there were three traders: Hugh Crawford, Ephraim Blaine, Thomas Mitchell and one servant to William Thompson named James Harris.

of goods. When they loaded up their horses, Trent and Alexander Lowrey left on February 15th, 1761, to sell goods along the way of the "Sanduskee" outpost (present-day Sandusky, Ohio) and then at Detroit. Right as they left, however, Croghan issued them selected prices "and to be careful to dispose of your goods at the prices agreed on and be careful to cultivate a good understanding with the Indians."[58] According to Captain Campbell, the Indians around Detroit had always been loyal to the French until the capitulation, so they were not as friendly or loyal as at Pittsburgh.

By the time he and Lowrey arrived at Detroit and started their journey back, Langdale received a discouraging letter from Bouquet on February 28th and garnered an angered response and memorial of his own on March 5th, respectively. Bouquet expressed his disappointment of receiving these complaints, "Charging you with Selling Liquor to Indians,"[59] but hoped this accusation by Trent was only just that and that Langdale could "therefore answer the said charge whereof I hope you will be able to clear yourself."[60]

If this letter Langdale received from Bouquet was cordial, the response back to him was not. In a letter dated March 5th,[61] Langdale pleaded his case that he did, in fact, give this Indian woman two quarts of rum but only because she promised not to touch it until she returned home and, therefore, did not think it violated this ordinance by General Monkton and Colonel Bouquet.

He then spent the rest of the letter in its entirety to Bouquet complaining about Trent's store and His Majesty's agent's abuse of power, saying, "Whatever was in former orders, there was no such dispensing powder given to Croghan nor is he mentioned to referred to in any shape or Character in the Generals last order on that head,"[62] and the complaint that "the draught and demand was now proportionately greater at Trent and Levys Store by means of Croghan or McKee still assuming that director thereof."[63]

He continued his rant about Croghan and Trent's store, calling it a "Prostitution of Power or partiality,"[64] especially when it came to other goods such as powder and lead. Truthfully, Croghan and Trent were just competition for Langdale and the King's Store, which he ran with entitled authority he believed was higher than those merchants and sellers in the Lower Town. Unfortunately for Trent, this resentment from the Quaker storekeepers was only the beginning.

---

58. BP, Vol. 5, 282–83.
59. Ibid., 317.
60. Ibid.
61. Ibid., 329.
62. Ibid.
63. Ibid.
64. Ibid.

When he returned from Detroit, he came back just in time as Colonel Bouquet ordered all the dwelling houses to be numbered in the Upper and Lower Towns[65] so he could conduct an updated census of the inhabitants (men, women, and children) on April 14, 1761. Trent was recorded as the owner of three houses in the Lower Town, one of which was their store, which he shared with Levi Andrew Levy, who no doubt resided in one of the other houses, as well as his loyal itinerant from his Hockley firm, James Foley. All three buildings were given #34.[66] These houses were located by Croghan's house at #35, several artificers or craftsmen such as German baker Leonhard Jung at house #43, John Finley (his former hand and fellow justice of peace of Cumberland County) at house #26 and near John Ormsby at house #41[67] who later was interred in 1805 not far on present-day Sixth Ave. in the Trinity Church burial ground in downtown Pittsburgh.

On May 4, 1761, a few of these artificers began raising a storehouse and cleared the ditch of one of the protective curtains of the Fort.[68] This was no doubt in response to the Lenape and Shawnees nearby stealing horses from the traders in the Lower Town, who mostly let them free graze at night between the fort and the newly constructed sawmill, a mile down the river.

Trent and Levy, who already had horses stolen back in February when he went to Detroit, kept theirs in a stable in the Lower Town. But as the horse stealing became more frequent each night, Bouquet ordered all the free grazing horses to be kept in the stable with theirs. Unfortunately, it only gave the free-lancing perpetrators nearby a larger population of horses to take back with them. Within a few days of Bouquet's order, Croghan and Trent were both down the Ohio River trying to round up their stolen property. Croghan lost all four of his horses, finding one shot along Chartier's Creek while failing to retrieve the rest almost sixty miles down the Ohio.[69] Trent fared much better, it seemed. While retrieving ten horses stolen by several warriors, he also captured a French deserter lurking about from the outpost at Detroit.[70]

After this latest adventure, their commanding officer had seen enough. At the end of June, on the 29th, Bouquet organized two companies of militia (one from each Lower and Upper Town)[71] and appointed trader Hugh Crawford as captain of the militia from the Lower Town and Robert Pearis[72] from the Upper Town.

---

65. PMHB, Vol. 37, No. 1, 29.
66. BP, Vol. 5, 408.
67. Ibid.
68. Ibid., 461.
69. Ibid., 482–83.
70. Ibid.
71. Ibid., 594.
72. Robert Pearis was a fur trader and brother of trader Richard Pearis of Maryland. He was a captain in the Frederick County (VA) militia since 1756 and resided in a a fortified house (known as Pearis's fort) just west of Winchester along Hogue Creek.

It was in Bouquet's best interest and the Crown's to form these troops better to protect the inhabitants and the merchants of Fort Pitt. He informed Crawford and Pearis to keep a daily role of those mustered in the militia and have guards placed on both banks of the Allegheny and Monongahela Rivers.[73] The behaviors of the Ohio Indians had been of bad design of late, and now, with talk of a plot against several garrisons (including Fort Pitt), Bouquet managed every effort not to be surprised by them.

This "call to arms" was also considered mandatory to those residing in either town, whether merchant or inhabitant, but Trent, for the time being, was not mustered in Crawford's militia. It appears since his partner Levi Andrew Levy is listed on the first militia roll dated June 30, 1761,[74] Trent excluded himself due to running his large store and being acquaintances with Captain Crawford, one of his artificers who was previously with him at the Forks in the spring of 1754. Though, according to Langdale's replacement at the King's Store, this was not a viable excuse in his opinion. Quaker clerk James Kenny[75] had not only arrived to replace Langdale in May of 1761 to oversee the King's Store but also joined Crawford's militia.

So, in his opinion, why was Trent exempt even though the "said inhabitants who does not chuse to enter himself in one of the Said Companies of militia, is ordered to quit this Place in two days?"[76] Kenny, like his predecessor, wanted to know his reasoning and expressed his strong feelings toward Trent and Levy's store. He did not like how their chief rival at the fort was allowing credit for an advance of goods and how "they draw on all ye Custom to that Store; this a Point they have ye advantage of the Province Store in at cent."[77]

The resentment grew progressively worse when he witnessed how, despite the alarm raised through the early fall and the proclamation issued, Trent or his friend and agent Josiah Davenport had refused Captain Crawford's summons to join his militia. Davenport, a former Philadelphia baker, was a nephew of Benjamin Franklin.[78] Kenny just did not understand how Trent was not reprimanded for his refusal or that he and Davenport were eventually "dispute ye point thinking themselves above it."[79]

---

73. BP, Vol. 5, 598.
74. Ibid., 606.
75. James Kenny was a Quaker from Chester County, Pennsylvania who came to replace John Langdale as a clerk of the King's Store at Fort Pitt.
76. BP, Vol. 5, 594.
77. PMHB, Vol. 37, No. 1, 13.
78. Josiah Franklin Davenport was the son of Sarah Franklin and baker James Davenport. By 1749, he operated a bakery in Gray's Alley in Philadelphia and in 1757 taught at a singing academy. After he became secretary to the Indian commissioners of Pennsylvania, he was also ordered to replace John Langdale (and also James Kenny) as Indian agent and storekeeper of the King's Store at Fort Pitt in 1761. Later, he was an officer in the Fort Pitt militia in May of 1763 during the attacks on Fort Pitt that summer. In 1768, he operated a genteel tavern on Third Street in Philadelphia called the "Bunch of Grapes."
79. PMHB, Vol. 37, No. 1, 23.

By the end of August, Trent had his reasons for not joining the militia. First, his partner Levy had been ordered daily to stand on sentry duty, and now, with Levy's enslaved servant disappearing (he ran away earlier in August to join the Six Nations),[80] Trent was forced to run the store and handle shipments completely by himself. Even at night, he barely slept, keeping watch on the goods till morning with all the recent robberies.

This was a crucial time to conduct business with the Ohio Indian nations because, as Croghan expressed last month from his previous observations at Sandusky, the Six Nations were declaring themselves ill-used by General Amherst and "resting uneasy." It was their belief Amherst was hindering them of trade and ever "Sence ye Reduction of Cannada from which they are of opinion that you Gineral by Distresing them in this Manner Intends to Inslave them."[81]

After the treaty conducted a Detroit by Croghan and Johnson in September helped smooth over these grievances, Bouquet made sure this threat to their way of life did not continue in the Western country either. On the 30th day of October, Bouquet declared that it was of the highest importance to the Crown that after a "good understanding with the Indians to avoid them any Just Case of complaint, this is, therefore, to forbid any of His Majesty Subjects to settle or hunt to the west of the Allegheny Mountains on any pretense whatsoever."[82]

Stating precedence with the Treaty of Easton in October of 1758, the order was like when Trent, in the summer of 1750, helped the other Cumberland County magistrates evict or set fire to cabins of those selling west of the Blue Mountain. Those guilty of this were not tried in their previous counties, however, according to Bouquet, but brought to Fort Pitt by these officers at the western garrisons to be "tryed and punished."[83] This attempt at the disallowance of settlers to their hunting grounds was praiseworthy, but one major issue remained unresolved.

After all, to the Native people, what good was land with valuable resources if they had no sufficient powder and ammunition to hunt game? The word had spread from Detroit to Fort Pitt, and the Indian nations let it be known they had a desperate want of powder.[84] It was why they were originally frustrated at the council at Detroit. Usually, they were permitted by the commanding officers to purchase or trade for powder from the garrison stores, but by the late fall of 1761, there were little or none to spare. The Ohio nations all knew "who"

---

80. Ibid., 16.
81. BP, Vol. 5, 664.
82. Ibid., 844.
83. Ibid.
84. Ibid., Vol. 6, 29.

was responsible for this scarcity of powder, and it wasn't Croghan, Johnson or even merchants like Trent.

Honestly, their assumptions were correct. Amherst was visibly disappointed by "the greatness of the sum" or expenditure of the presents previously given at Detroit and felt they must deal more "sparingly."[85]

Clearly, by his letter to William Johnson on December 26, 1761, he had no intention to supply them sufficiently any longer:

> I can see very little reason for bribing the Indians or buying their good behavior, since they have no enemy to molest them, but on the contrary Every Encouragement & protection they can Desire for their Trade.[86]

Meanwhile, at Fort Pitt, Trent watched the heavy snow come down and blanket the Fort. Snow was almost two feet deep[87] now, and he probably wished he had left on the 5th of December 1761[88] with Burd and the provincials, whose enlistments were up, to get more supplies in Lancaster. Levy had just sold a cousin of Delaware George a pair of half-thick leggings and French blankets[89], but business this month had been rather slow due to the weather.

When the temperature turned mild, it looked like things were looking up, but on the 8th of January, it started to rain. Those traders and merchants watched from the Lower Town as the Monongahela and Allegheny Rivers (once frozen over just less than a month ago) were breaking into large chunks and drifting with the current up over the banks.[90] Trent and Levy, with the help from others, spent all hours of the night preparing to utilize what things they could to blockade their spare barrels of powder and salted meat from rising waters. Like clerk James Kenny, Trent began loading up a few canoes to move to the higher ground in the Upper Town.[91]

The next morning, their efforts were literally washed away from rising waters that even Colonel Bouquet described in his journal: "The water came upon us through the Drains, Gates and Sally Ports and boiled in large springs out of the ground in Several Parts of the Fort."[92]

Trent watched the cold, icy water reach their doors by almost noon as he put as many goods as he could before the water became dangerously high.

---

85. Papers of William Johnson, Vol. 10, 348.
86. Ibid.
87. PMHB, Vol. 37, No. 1, 33.
88. Ibid., 29.
89. Ibid., 34.
90. Ibid., 35–36.
91. Ibid.
92. BP, Vol. 6, 36.

Quickly, he closed the doors to his three buildings, grabbed his blunderbuss and pistol, and made his escape in a canoe before he had to swim in the chilling waters to safety like Josiah Davenport.[93]

The next day, on the 10th, dogs and horses ran past them as they tried to see the Lower Town from the high points of the Upper Town.[94] The river currents continued as strong as ever and were still rising. Not even building Fort St. George in the early spring of 1754 did he see such detrimental flooding. (In reality, this one and the one in early 1763 were the worst floods Pittsburgh had ever seen until March of 1936). It was not until the morning of the 11th could Trent and Levy returned to their store and houses to assess the damage.

The cold, murky waters had risen so high it stained the buildings just below the shutters,[95] and they were the fortunate ones. Most of the Lower Townhouses close to the river's edge had been destroyed or carried away by the floodwaters to almost below Chartier's Creek.[96] According to clerk James Kenny, the waters crested at almost forty feet high,[97] leaving the cellars of those mercantile stores like Trent's full of water and free-flowing sod from the nearby curtains made from earth. All of Trent's powder and flour were probably wet and damaged[98] beyond use when the waters rose over the top of the barrels. Even any meat that was preserved in the cask was going to have to be salted again if they were even manageable to be salvaged. Their losses were unfavorable and now left them in financial ruin if he didn't resume operations soon. Especially since the overwhelming traffic to the King's Store, he saw now after the flood.

Perhaps he could borrow temporary supplies up to Youghiogheny River from Colonel William Clapham[99] who bought Colonel Croghan's former plantation at Swiegly Old Town,[100] but it was still wise to return finally to their Lancaster headquarters and see his family. His employers, Simon and Franks did not take the news lightly of their potential loss from the flood, but since Trent and Levy had been successful up to this point, all could be forgiven if they had a good spring and summer. It was also at this time that Trent moved

---

93. Ibid.
94. Ibid.
95. PMHB, Vol. 37, No. 1, 36.
96. Ibid., 39.
97. Ibid., 37.
98. Ibid.
99. William Clapham was the former lieutenant colonel and colonel of the Third battalion of Pennsylvania provincials, commissioned on March 29, 1756. During his tenure, he ordered the construction of Fort Halifax (near Halifax, Pennsylvania), Fort Hunter (near Harrisburg, Pennsylvania), and the larger Fort Augusta in Sunbury, Pennsylvania. He later served under General Forbes in 1758 and then purchased the former property and plantation of George Croghan on the Youghiogheny River. He was murdered on this property in May of 1763.
100. Swiegly Old Town and Croghan's plantation sat where the mouth of Sewickley Creek emptied into the Youghiogheny River between the towns of Sutersville and West Newton, Pennsylvania. It was about twenty-five miles from Fort Pitt.

his family of three (wife Sarah, five-year-old Ann, and two-year-old Martha) closer to him that spring of 1762 in a house in Carlisle, free from rent with his employer Joseph Simon and potential creditors seeking payment for their latest investment in Fort Pitt.

Trent still owned and ran (when he was able) the plantation along Letort Spring outside of Carlisle but had his family live on a large corner lot of East Street and High Street in Carlisle, a two-story stone house with an attached kitchen and log stable.[101] Sarah probably went back between both the country plantation and their new house in town. Today, the outside structure of the house lot still stands at 7 North East Street in downtown Carlisle.

His change in residence was not the only big change happening by the fall of 1762. By November, also came a change of command. While Trent and Levy's store resumed operations and sent shipments of goods again (including what limited powder they could spare) to towns like the Lower Shawnee Town and those along Lake Erie, a new commanding officer arrived to replace Colonel Bouquet at Fort Pitt. His name was Simeon Ecuyer, a Swiss born officer in the Royal American Regiment.[102] Ecuyer immediately wished to speak with the garrison's Deputy Agent and inquired upon the status of the local Indian population after his latest return from treaties at Easton and Lancaster.

Croghan, who arrived at the end of November 1762, described it best to Ecuyer and in a letter to Colonel Bouquet:

> They Interprett the Gineral's Frugality in lesing ye Expence of presents In a Designs of Revenging what has past being Couriouess they Deserve to be punished how itt May End ye Lord knows Butt I ashure you I am of opinion it will not be long before we Shall some Croyles (Quarrels) with them.[103]

Regrettably, seeing how this new policy by Amherst was going to be bad for business, Trent couldn't agree more.

---

101. Schaumann, 167–68.
102. Simeon Ecuyer (pronounced Equi-yay) was a Swiss born British officer who was commissioned as a lieutenant in the 62nd Regiment of Foot on January 25, 1756. Four years later he was Captain Lieutenant of the 60th Regiment on February 14, 1760, and then captain on April 27, 1762. Later he arrived at Fort Pitt to relieve Colonel Bouquet as commander in November of 1762.
103. BP, Vol. 10, Frontier Forts and Trail's Survey, 177.

Chapter 13

The Desired Effect

After the final gun was sounded on the evening of the 28th of May 1763, the commander of Fort Pitt, Simeon Ecuyer, summoned Trent to his quarters. With recent reports of the Mingos and Lenape selling off all their peltry and then abandoning their towns,[1] the battalion was to be on alarm the next morning at 6 o'clock. The problem was Hugh Crawford had not returned from delivering goods to the Twightwees, so he needed Trent to command the militia. (Which was why the orderly book of William Trent begins the night of May 28th). Ecuyer knew Trent being a former veteran officer naturally made him an obvious choice, and his years of a long-standing relationship with the Ohio Indian nations were impeccable. It was also a relationship that was strained now because of the recent policies implemented by General Amherst. One such policy had the biggest impact where Amherst (despite the recent squabbles at Fort Pitt) had suppressed all presents that had been normally customary for any of the nation's requesting it.

"As to Appropriating a particular Sum to be laid out yearly, in Presents to the Warriors and that I can by no means Agree to," Amherst wrote to Bouquet, "Nor can I think it necessary to give them any Presents, by way of Bribes for if they do not Behave properly, they are to be punished."[2]

It was also a policy that George Croghan expressed his sarcastic concern by saying, "I wish itt may have its Desird Effect, but I take this opportunity to acquaint you I Dread the event as I know Indians can't long persevere."[3]

---

1. BP, Vol. 6, 193.
2. Ibid., 147.
3. Papers of William Johnson, Vol. 10, 965.

In response, Trent's Indian customers on credit refused to settle their accounts with him and Levy. It forced Trent to not only stop accounts on credit but also send his partner Levy with Croghan's kinsman Thomas Smallman[4] to collect these current debts below Lake Erie. Trent made his feelings known by writing to the general himself about his recent losses[5] at Lower Shawnee Town and other towns but heard no response.

The only express he received was two days ago when word arrived that Levy and Smallman had been taken prisoner by the Wyandots on May 20, 1763, within four miles of Detroit.[6] Worse yet, it was believed after both were sold to the Shawnees and Chippewas, they were put to death.

This brought business to a screeching halt and was probably why Trent didn't refuse to become the militia commander at Fort Pitt. He was commissioned a major (a title he was addressed as till his death in 1784) officially on May 29th[7] over one hundred and eight men along with his second-in-command, Lieutenant (and eventual captain) Josiah Franklin Davenport and other subalterns. Ironically, it was the second time fighting alongside a relation of Ben Franklin, having fought years before in New York with Ensign William Franklin (Ben's son) during King George's War.

That night, Ecuyer also gave the parole or word code to address the sentries around the fort in the morning. The word George was the parole.[8] Hearing it probably reminded Trent of the funeral of Delaware George he attended previously outside the fort, as they interred him[9] over the Allegheny River and then, that night, traditionally fired guns to ward off evil spirits and bad luck. It seemed (at least for Trent) that he had suffered nothing but bad luck since that night.

Unfortunately, it was about to be worse. As the sun broke from the horizon the next morning, three men arrived at the gate from Swiegly Old Town with a horrific account of the murders of his friend Colonel William Clapham and four others at the hands of a Lenape warrior named the Wolf. Trent, upon hearing the report, excluded the grisly details in his daily marble-covered journal and told storekeeper James Kenny about the loss of Davenport's horse, writing that "The women that were killed at Colonel Clapham's, were treated in such a brutal manner that decency forbids the mentioning."[10]

---

4. Hanna, Vol. 2, 29.
5. General Amherst indicated in his reply letter to Trent on June 25, 1763, that Trent had wrote him on May 16, 1763. The losses can be found in the Historical Society of Pennsylvania under the account of Alexander Lowrey, Trent and Levy and Company 1763.
6. Steele, 531. BP, Vol.6, 412–13. *Pennsylvania Gazette*, December 22, 1763.
7. University of Michigan, William L. Clements Library, Jeffrey Amherst Papers, Vol. 6. For the first time in publication, the complete roster of Major Trent's 1763 militia detachment is listed in Appendix H of this book.
8. HSP, Orderly Book of Captain William Trent, 1.
9. PMHB, Vol. 37, No. 2, 154.
10. Mississippi Valley Historical Review (MVHR), Vol. 11, No. 3, 394.

His officers and militiamen loaded their guns and posted all around the bastions. They were to keep a sharp eye out. Nothing appeared out of the ordinary outside the fort walls until a scouting party returned with their report of the perimeter later that evening. They reported there were King's horses stolen and two dead just a mile down the Ohio. The soldiers had been scalped, and the bloody tomahawk used in their demise[11] was left stuck above their massacred bodies.

The message was clear to both Ecuyer and Trent. Whoever had done this it was a declaration of war. An insurrection by the frustrated nations that Trent and Croghan both knew was inevitable since the policies from Amherst disrupted their trade and businesses in the Western country. For Ecuyer, the new commander barely six months at his post, it was something he had never experienced before. He feverishly wrote Bouquet in Philadelphia every day since the murder of Clapham, even admitting his lack of sleep and feeling anxious.[12] He also worried that Fort Pitt was slowly being surrounded and cut off by those Indian nations revolting against them.

"I tremble for the posts,"[13] he wrote to Bouquet, ending with a powerful line that eventually foreshadowed his methods in a few weeks: "Whatever happens, I shall do all in my power. Excuse haste as they say."[14]

The next day, on the 30th, Trent and the militiamen joined the other soldiers in working around the fort. They helped bring the oxen, cows, and horses closer to the fort walls while Ecuyer ordered all the inhabitants (those women, children, and invalids not in the militia) to leave the Upper and Lower Towns and enter inside the main curtains and protective bastions. Then, the drawbridge was lowered behind them.[15]

It was a wise defensive plan until Trent realized he must now abandon his store and bring all his goods, like blankets, skins, and provisions inside to the fort's storehouse, joining the goods of the King's Store. His barrels of powder marked "Trent and Levy & Co." upon them were stored in the King's Magazine[16] as well.

This alarming situation meant no merchant, trader or King's storekeeper had separate goods or provisions despite their branded insignias or logos. They were all Kings' goods now. Just like now, with his militia being interwoven with grenadiers and regulars until further notice. It's probably why Trent kept a journal since May 14th, to verify or keep a record once his remaining mercantile goods were lost, stolen, or, in this case, utilized throughout the fort. (The

---

11. Ibid.
12. BP, Vol. 6, 195.
13. Ibid.
14. Ibid., 196.
15. MVHR, Vol. 11, No. 3, 394.
16. BP, Vol. 6, 203.

author must note that originally when this journal was transcribed from its original format,[17] it was mistakenly identified as the daily writings of Fort Pitt's commander Simeon Ecuyer. But after careful examination, it was later correctly identified as the journal of militia commander Major William Trent).

The next night, on the 31st, Trent marched the militia back inside the fort to the parade ground[18] as he had five more men join his large company. On the 1st of June, he added another sergeant when trader Thomas Calhoun returned hastily from the town of Tuscarawas.[19] They returned (well, rather retreated to the fort) after he and thirteen others were attacked near Beaver Creek, and only he and two others escaped alive. Calhoun brought valuable intel that validated the fears in the garrison. Fort Detroit had been under siege since the 13th of May, but despite rumors of nobody left alive in the garrison, it was still being held. The next outpost at Sandusky was believed to have also met the same fate and was cut off from all directions for expresses to pass through.

He also confirmed six were presumed dead[20] after the capture of Hugh Crawford and a boy at the mouth of the Maumee River near the present site of Toledo, Ohio. Calhoun, however, did bring an important message from Lenape Kings Shingas and the Beaver. They condemned this murder attack on Clapham's plantation but insisted despite the Wolf's indiscretions; they had not gone to war with the English, saying, "The nations that have taken up the Hatchett against you are the Ottawas and Chepewas."[21]

Regardless of who was directly responsible, the danger was lurking closer. Two men returned after being sent by Ecuyer the day before to Fort Venango and only made it as far as three miles up the Allegheny before being attacked by several warriors. Around the village of Shannopin's Town, they were fired upon, and one was wounded in the leg.[22]

Meeting with his officers, including Trent, Ecuyer issued his next set of orders. The two hundred and fifty soldiers[23] in the garrison were divided up evenly and trusted with the task of demolishing all the houses in the Lower and Upper Towns. The houses taken down in the Lower Town were recycled for their timber and used for the newly constructed ovens and forge[24] built inside the fort walls along the perimeter of the parade ground. As for the Upper Town, all the houses toward the "hill" above the point were set aflame and burned

---

17. See Fort Pitt and Letters from the Frontier by Mary Carson Darlington (1892) when it was transcribed and incorrectly identified as the 1763 journal of Simeon Ecuyer.
18. HSP, Orderly Book of Captain William Trent, 2.
19. The Tuscarawas village was found near the present site of Bolivar, Ohio.
20. MVHR, Vol. 11, No. 3, 392.
21. Ibid., 396.
22. Ibid., 395. BP, Vol. 6, 202.
23. BP, Vol. 6, 202.
24. Ibid.

The present-day view looking out over the original ruins of the flag bastion of Fort Pitt, one of the original five bastions toward the city of Pittsburgh. (Author photo.)

to the ground. Ecuyer, with the assistance of Trent, wanted to make sure no building was left standing to aid the enemy in protection from the fort's guns.

"Conquer or die" was the motto[25] of the hour as they worked into the following day outside the fort. On June 2nd, Trent watched the smoke rise into the sky from all the houses on the hill over the flag bastion,[26] only to see newer, larger flames beyond those. Then they all heard the loud yells as they spied through their pocket telescopes, several Indians with burning torches. Trent recognized they were burning the house of his friend William Thompson,[27] a half mile away.

---

25. Ibid.
26. Today a plaque commemorates where the flag bastion stood, whose traces can still be seen today in Point State Park in Pittsburgh, Pennsylvania.
27. MVHR, Vol. 11, No. 3, 397.

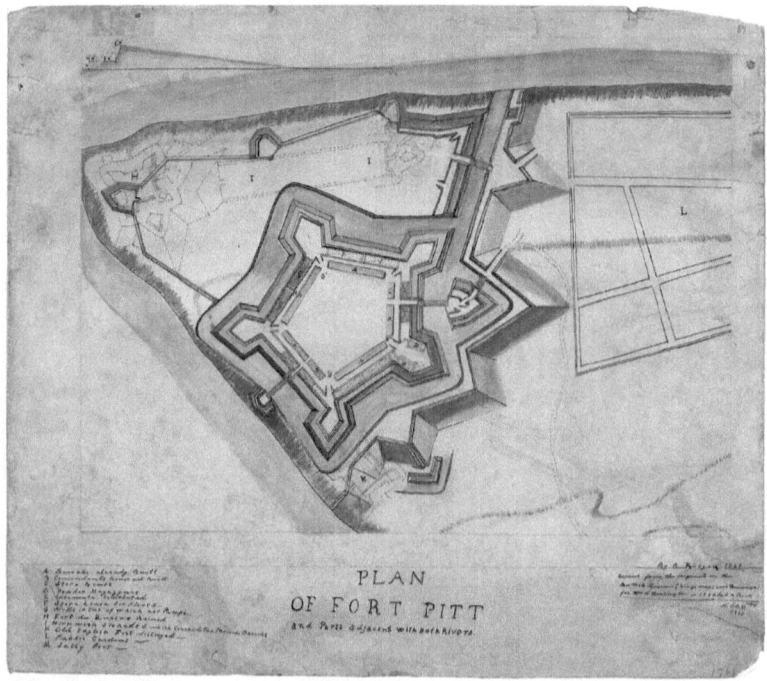

Copy of the original 1761 plan of Fort Pitt by Bernard Ratzer and found in the Darlington Digital Library. Letter L shows the King's Gardens and the Lower Town were closer to the shoreline of the "Point closer to Letters H and I on the drawing. Courtesy of Public Domain.

Ecuyer ordered the drums to sound the alarm, and everyone returned inside to their posts. Trent assembled his militia into columns, issued full cartridges[28], and made sure they each had spare flints and musket balls.[29] The other officers were then ordered to open the barrels of tomahawks marked with the Trent and Levy & Company stamp. Eighty-four tomahawks were issued[30] to those inhabitants or militiamen who were in want of them. They also use the remaining bear and deer skins[31] from Trent's store to camouflage the vulnerable overhead where those individuals could shoot atop the walls.

After casks of water were placed in the five bastions around the fort in case of fire and beaver traps were placed along the exterior ramparts for protection,[32] they seemed to be ready now to face the potential attack. For two days,

---

28. HSP, Orderly Book of Captain William Trent, 3.
29. BP, Vol. 6, 202.
30. Public Archives of Canada, Crown to Levy, Trent and Company 1763. For the complete inventory list, see Appendix I of this book.
31. Ibid. BP, Vol. 6, 203.
32. BP, Vol. 6, 203.

they stood on alarm with nothing out of the ordinary, and it was then perhaps Ecuyer thought the assumption of his superiors was correct. Both Bouquet and Amherst were not sharing his concerns, stating that "No Indians will dare attack you openly"[33] and that "this Alarm will End in Nothing more than a Rash Attempt of what the Senecas had been threatening which We have heard of for some time past."[34]

But on June 7th, Trent and Ecuyer received an alarming account from an express from Presque Isle. A lieutenant of the Queen's Rangers named Abraham Cuyler was attacked at the mouth of the Detroit River[35] and lost half his detachment of one hundred. Fleeing to Sandusky, he found it destroyed, as well as the outpost of Presque Isle, which was now cut off from communication. Well, except for this note that made its way through with a Mr. Wilkins and his wife[36], who were able to arrive at Fort Pitt unmolested. It was only a matter of time before this seemingly "invisible" foe set their sights on the outpost at the Forks of the Ohio, so all they could do was anxiously wait to repel them.

On the 9th, two expresses were sent to Fort Venango[37] and its commander, Lieutenant Francis Gordon, to hear their daily report from up the Allegheny River. It was also the same day smoke was spotted towering high in the sky several miles up the Allegheny River. Trent could only assume the Indian nations had continued their conquest of burning the surrounding residences to draw them all out of the fort, and his best guess now was they had possibly burned the house of his former partner Croghan.[38] At least for his friend's sake, he hoped not.

The next day the bad luck continued when the two itinerants arrived back at the fort, having little confidence to find their way in the blackest of night to Venango. That same morning and braving the lurking danger, Trent, with the permission of Ecuyer sent some of his militia under arms to put up fences[39] to keep the cattle and horses in. They had not been laboring for very long when guns fired at them from the trees. Quickly, they returned to the fort, but the alarm had been raised again. It seemed as the days went by, those harassing and burning the houses were moving closer to the outskirts of the fort. This proved true at dawn on the 11th when sentries spotted several warriors amongst the remnants of the Upper Town. Those manning the walls fired out at them and

---
33. Ibid., 208.
34. Ibid., 209.
35. MVHR, Vol. 11, No. 3, 398.
36. Ibid.
37. Ibid.
38. This was the house known as "Croghan Hall" opposite the mouth of Pine Creek across the Allegheny River. MVHR, Vol. 11, No. 3, 398.
39. Ibid.

forced them to scatter, but throughout the day, they stayed within the borders of the Upper Town. The sentries only fired when they came in the open because they were ordered not to fire "without being sure of seeing the Enemy before them."[40] Later that night, at about ten o'clock, the enemy approached with torches and let a pile of logs on fire left from a house. In response, Ecuyer ordered a howitzer to launch a shell at them. When they ran from the explosion flash, sentries posted on the Ohio Curtain spied a few of them now near the Lower Town.[41]

The next morning, after the guards reported no sightings, Trent sent a small party of his men out to guard the women selected to cut the long spelt with sickles from the field near the King's Garden.[42] As they filled their baskets so the grains could be dried, two Indians appeared near the garden, and some of the guards fired on them.[43] The women were told to return to the fort as soon as the male laborers grabbed the baskets and hurried back through the gate. Suddenly, the forest near the hill erupted with loud yells and cries, and the spelt guard realized they were outnumbered. When the war party slowly approached closer, a cannon roared from the walls. They immediately scattered and ran back to the trees, hollering and firing their guns. With all the recent activity outside the fort and expecting a much larger force of Native warriors as each report arrived, Trent found the time to write his wife, Sarah. The letter traveled east via John Armstrong[44] to Carlisle and, for the moment, gave Sarah some temporary relief to his well-being despite hearing horrific tales of incidents in the Western country.

Meanwhile, another attempt to cut the spelt was organized by Trent on June 15th. However, this time, the leader of the guard party, Sergeant Adam Miller,[45] tried a counteroffensive when they were fired upon. Miller and three others took off after the fleeing warriors into the forest, but before he could reach the hill crest of Grant's Defeat, he was struck down by a musket ball that killed him.[46] Luckily, as the warriors withdrew their knives to scalp Miller, shots from the remaining guards sent them retreating further.[47] The spelt guard carried his body back to the fort. It was the first casualty in Trent's militia company. Had Miller obeyed orders, he might probably be still alive. This unfortunate event led to Ecuyer addressing the garrison on June 16th, that no

---

40. HSP, Orderly Book of Captain William Trent, 5.
41. MVHR, Vol. 11, No. 3, 398.
42. Ibid. HSP, Orderly Book of Captain William Trent, 7.
43. Ibid. Ibid.
44. BP, Vol. 6, 223.
45. University of Michigan, William L. Clements Library, Jeffrey Amherst Papers, Vol. 6.
46. MVHR, Vol. 11, No. 3, 398.
47. Ibid.

The original outcropping of Trent's house (circa 1760) that still lies today in Carlisle, Pennsylvania on 7 N. East Street. (Author photo.)

officer or soldier could leave their guard party outside the fort without written permission.[48] (It didn't stop another militia man named James Thompson, who was scalped and killed near the fort[49] when looking for his horse just over a week later).

Now, wandering soldiers outside the fort was the least of his worries. Inside the fort, they had a much bigger problem. Despite the forage, Master Sgt. John Clark daily inspecting each inhabitant and soldier for disease[50], and the women washing in the Lower Town batteau shed,[51] smallpox reared its ugly head. Now, because of such tight quarters since the inhabitants moved inside the fort, this disease spread rather quickly. Ecuyer and Trent quickly established a makeshift hospital away from the garrison's population and vulnerability to musket fire or arrows. Ecuyer also ordered, "That nobody goes near any person that hath the smallpox, except the Doctor and the people

---

48. BP, Vol. 6, 232.
49. MVHR, Vol. 11, No. 3, 400.
50. HSP, Orderly Book of Captain William Trent, 4.
51. Ibid., 8.

attending them who are themselves to be very care full not go near any person that has not had them."[52]

Which brings us to the fateful day on June 24th, 1763. Assistant Deputy Agent Alexander McKee left the fort in the morning to meet Lenape warriors Turtles Heart and Mamaltee, who had wished to relay a message since they called out to him prior at midnight.[53] In their message was the announcement that the English outposts at Detroit, Sandusky, Presque Isle, Le Boeuf, Venango and now Ligonier were all destroyed. (They received an account of the burnings of Le Boeuf and Venango from the arrival of Ensign George Price of the Royal Americans the next day). They also said that Fort Pitt was the last outpost left standing, and since "great numbers of Indians were coming, out of regard to us, they had prevailed on 6 Nations not to attack us but give us time to go down the country and desired we would set off immediately."[54]

Apparently, like the Shawnee's speech on the 16th, they too blamed the bloody tomahawk at the sawmill and the recent hostilities towards them at the fort on the Six Nations. When he finished hearing their speech, McKee told them to wait while he gave this message to his commander, Ecuyer. After Ecuyer received this "warning," he told McKee to thank them and "let them know that we had everything we wanted, that we could defend it against all the Indians in the Woods, that we had three large Armies marching to Chastise those Indians that had struck us."[55] McKee delivered this response to Turtles Heart and Mamaltee, but what happened next needs to be discussed in detail.

As was contrary to Indians who stopped at Fort Pitt, the two Lenape requested "Of little Provisions and Liquor"[56] to take back to their town. However, this time, the gifts they received in return were subject to much controversy that even today is talked about with any mention of the late Indian War or the history of Fort Pitt.

So, let's first look at the controversial entry in Trent's 1763 journal dated June 24th that followed Ecuyer's reply.

Trent wrote: "Out of our regard to them we gave them two blankets and a handkerchief out of the smallpox hospital. I hope it will have the desired effect."[57]

Breaking it down further, there is no denying this is definitive proof that the English (including Trent) purposefully gave smallpox blankets and a

---

52. Ibid., 39.
53. MVHR, Vol. 11, No. 3, 400.
54. Ibid.
55. Ibid.
56. BP, Vol. 6, 262.
57. MVHR, Vol. 11, No. 3, 400.

handkerchief with the intent to infect their towns. But Trent used "we" instead of "I," meaning the garrison as a whole or usually when he was aware of what Ecuyer (referred to as their Commanding officer in his journal) was doing. In other words, it was not solely involving just Trent and Ecuyer but other officers as well during the current siege. Now, the next line does use "I" (as in Trent's perspective) but is much like an entry in the journal of his former partner George Croghan, who stated rather sarcastically his opinion toward Amherst's policy to stop giving presents to the Indian nations in the Western country. It's a known fact that Trent dryly jousted with the Natives (the letter to Colonel Bouquet dated June 5, 1758, where he accepted a shirt from the Cherokees of Fort Loudoun, is a fine example),[58] so knowing how Turtles Heart or Mamaltee might react, he more than likely didn't comment about this moment maliciously but rather sarcastically as Croghan did. But regardless of the malicious or possibly sarcastic intent of the entry, we cannot really know for certain except for the apparent evidence.

Which raises questions concerning this incident. Was Trent the "mastermind" behind this attempt of biological warfare conducted at Fort Pitt? Or was somebody else responsible for this malicious attempt to put an end to this insurrection throughout the Western country? The following evidence suggests this heinous act extended further beyond Trent's cynical journal entry and description. Scholars also pointed to an incriminating note discovered in "The Crown's Account to Levy, Trent, and Company." Written in August of 1763, it clearly says, "To Sundrys got to Replace in kind those which were taken from people in the Hospital to Convey the Smallpox to the Indians."[59]

Once again, this was proof of the British garrison's intent, but this note, along with the rest of the account, was not written by Trent. It was also not written by Trent's partner Levy either because the Wyandots captured him on May 20th. This time, Ecuyer himself wrote the account. Further proof appeared just a few lines after the note, with the signature "S. Ecuyer Commandt."[60]

Once Ecuyer ordered the Lower Town to be demolished on June 1st, all the goods, including blankets, weapons, and powder, were placed in the King's Store and Magazine inside the fort. Which meant they were all under one entity now, the British Crown. It also meant Trent had no choice but to let them use his goods. Refusal meant insubordination or treason. So, when items were taken from the storehouse (hence, in Trent's case, the eighty-four tomahawks, thirteen

---

58. BP, Vol. 2, 37.
59. Public Archives of Canada, Crown to Levy, Trent and Company 1763. For the complete inventory list, see Appendix I of this book.
60. Ibid.

bearskins, blankets, handkerchiefs, and linens from the smallpox hospital under the drawbridge),[61] Ecuyer used them with the intention to reimburse those individuals who own the items he "borrowed" to help His Majesty's troops. Ecuyer even admitted later he used most of the traders' goods from Trent and Levy since, until the hostilities began, they had the largest mercantile store at Fort Pitt, not named the King's Store. (See also Appendix I for the 1763 Crown Ledger from Ecuyer and Gage to Levy and Trent).

But did Trent have a motive to commit this atrocity? In other words, after he had to end credit accounts with his Indian customers, was he so frustrated enough that he resorted to any means of evil design to avenge his potential financial loss? The answer, unfortunately, is not so cut and dry and could easily be yes and no.

Like Ecuyer, Trent had no way of knowing if the Native's report of Fort Pitt being the last standing outpost in the Western country was true, so at this point of the siege, all the officers had reached their point of desperation. It was no secret that Trent, by himself, had the most to lose. So, something had to be done to potentially end the siege if no others were coming to their support, and so the "gifts" were the climax of this drastic measure.

However, shifting to the other side of the argument, Trent's majority of customers and sales *were* the Native population. He and Levy had sold or traded "Indian" goods at the Lower Shawnee Town, Detroit, Sandusky, and, of course, at their large store at Fort Pitt. So, when the "no gift" policy took effect, and the insurrection began, losses at these outposts or towns were substantial. Trent and Levy were not only cut off from communication from these towns but had no way to retrieve their goods until the hostilities were over. Notwithstanding, if his evil plan was to "wipeout" or, as Amherst later described to Bouquet as, "extirpate"[62] and in his response to Trent's letter on June 25th, "Recovering what may belong to His Majesty's Subjects, out of the Hands of the Barbarians,"[63] then he was forcing his own business and himself into financial ruin.

Even Trent's personal feelings toward the Indian nations were nothing like his superiors, Bouquet, Amherst or even Ecuyer. For almost twenty years, he had conducted business with them or attended treaties since his first council at Lancaster in 1744 and hoped to continue this budding relationship after this insurrection ended. He also witnessed scalpings outside Fort Clinton in 1747, saw the horrific aftermath of Pickawillany in 1752, and suffered his larger financial losses in 1754, but not once did Trent ever address them with disrespect or,

---

61. Ibid.
62. BP, Series 21634, 161.
63. HSP, Frank M. Etting Collection, Revolutionary Papers, Jeffrey Amherst to William Trent, June 25, 1763.

like Bouquet and Ecuyer use the derogatory term "savage." Also, at this time, an article appeared in the *Aberdeen Journal* that was described as a letter from William Trent dated June 28th but only contained one actual quote and the rest of the article was submitted with Bouquet's opinion of the insurrection, using the word savage throughout.

Trent's level of respect toward them was probably why, nine years ago, he had the Half-King lay the first log of Fort St. George so they both could establish a successful outpost among those involved. His business and profit may have taken precedence at times, but he was the true embodiment of the Ohio Company's motto, "Pax et Commercium," which meant "Peace and Commerce." He knew commerce could not work without the other. Basically, after much consideration, Trent, though guilty in many ways of what conspired that day, should not be the only surname synonymous with this terrible means of warfare. Yes, he did write the "smoking gun" journal entry that incriminated him and others, but this was a group act.

Surprisingly, if Trent's journal or the Crown's account of him weren't discovered, there was no evidence this incident even happened. Perhaps he recorded it privately, so what transpired that day had to be remembered. Contrast that to Assistant Deputy Agent Alexander McKee, who dictated Ecuyer's description of that same day a bit differently: "The above provisions were granted to them & they set off home about 2 o'clock that Night."[64]

A rather mild description of a controversial plot suggests McKee tried to leave his commander's actions out of the original report. So, if Ecuyer was behind this distribution plan, who had originally grabbed the blankets and handkerchief from the smallpox hospital and given Turtles Heart and Mamaltee the items in the first place?

The accomplice to Ecuyer's plot was not only retrieving these items but was putting himself in great jeopardy of possibly contracting the disease as well. Colonel Bouquet, who agreed with Amherst's detrimental suggestion to spread smallpox among the Indian population, shared this same fear in July after the incident at Fort Pitt.

"I will try to inoculate the Indians," Bouquet wrote on July 13, 1763, "With some blankets that may fall in their hands and take care not to get the disease myself."[65]

Besides, the last thing Ecuyer wanted was to have someone spread the disease in the garrison like wildfire after building an isolated hospital. Not unless this person had been inoculated or had already survived having it. Now it is

---

64. BP, Vol. 6, 262.
65. Ibid., Series 21634, 215.

known Ecuyer was not immune (his orders to not have anyone in the hospital except those doctors or inoculated was a testament to this), and neither was Trent. This means that based on the primary evidence, the most likely candidate to be Ecuyer's accomplice was none other than Trent's second-in-command, Lieutenant Josiah Davenport. Though Trent or Ecuyer did not mention him in any of their letters or entries for June 24th, Davenport was commissioned by Pennsylvania on July 22, 1761,[66] to replace John Langdale as both an Indian trade agent and Keeper of the King's Store.[67] In fact, by the time clerk James Kenny departed Fort Pitt on May 29th,[68] he was the only storekeeper and representative of the King's Store who remained. What is important for this argument is that Davenport was a former baker on Third Street in Philadelphia during the height of the smallpox outbreak in 1757[69] and witnessed his infant daughter contract the disease. In his uncle Benjamin Franklin's will dated April 28, 1757, Ben offered support for Davenport's child, "Which likely had the misfortune of losing its sight by the smallpox."[70] So, if Davenport hadn't directly contracted smallpox from his child, he and the rest of his family were probably inoculated from it to prevent this.

Furthermore, he was the only individual of authority (other than Ecuyer) with direct access to use any of the goods (for example, blankets, linens, etc.) in the King's storehouse and walk into the smallpox hospital. Then he could grab the infected blankets and handkerchief, bundle them in linens and join McKee outside that evening to give Turtles Heart and Mamaltee the "gifts." Another key point to support this theory is that Davenport was the only high-ranking officer of the militia who received a promotion in August.[71] It is quite possible he was rewarded by Ecuyer and appointed by Bouquet on August 18th because of his proven duties on June 24th.

But after all this, did the plot work and affect the Lenape? Unfortunately, there was no plausible way to determine this conclusion. Smallpox appeared sporadically over the next two months in the garrison. (Trent's own Sgt. John Bond, the former Pennsylvania Provincial doctor, succumbed to the disease on August 15, 1763),[72] but on July 22, 1763, Ecuyer saw two familiar foes he probably shouldn't have if the infected blankets had fulfilled their intended purpose. Trent wrote on that day that Lenape's Gray Eyes and Wingenum were joined by Turtles Heart and Mamaltee[73] as they came across the river to meet

---

66. Ibid., Vol. 5, 700.
67. Ibid., Vol. 6, 390.
68. PMHB, Vol. 37, No. 2, 199.
69. *Pennsylvania Gazette*, April 7, 1757. Colonial Records of Pennsylvania, Vol. 7, 517.
70. Franklin Institute, Last Will and Testament of Benjamin Franklin, April 28, 1757.
71. HSP, Orderly Book of Captain William Trent, 33.
72. University of Michigan, William L. Clements Library, Jeffrey Amherst Papers, Vol. 6.
73. MVHR, Vol. 11, No. 3, 406.

in council. Seeing how the latter was the first to accept the "gifts" on the 24th of June. Clearly, the blankets did not affect either of them. As for their town, Shinango[74] or any of the others in the Western country, the results were still inconclusive. Mainly because smallpox was already rampant this time in the summer, so there was no way to prove their people or any other nations had contracted it specifically from the Fort Pitt blankets or the handkerchief.

About a week later, the garrison experienced the worst part of the so-called siege. On the 27th of July, about sixty warriors were seen by the wheat fields, and after Ecuyer boasted to them they had provisions and ammunition to hold them off for three years (Trent estimated three months at best),[75] they were fired upon all day until two o'clock in the afternoon the next day.

With this alarm being raised again, Trent had initially warned his men not to stray past the King's Garden.[76] When his men returned to the fort after exchanging fire near the trees, a perfidious assault came throughout the afternoon and into the evening hours. Arrows soared into the fort, forcing those like Trent and Ecuyer watching from their curtains and respective bastions to seek cover. After the first barrage of arrows, Trent saw four had fallen,[77] including his superior, Ecuyer. Fortunately, Ecuyer was only hit in the leg and was fine. Two others, a corporal and a private, were struck in the head, so their fate was sealed as Trent described them as "mortal" wounds.[78]

The next day, on the 29th, the assault upon the fort continued, but this time, Ecuyer, still nursing a flesh wound, ordered a return fire among all who posted upon the walls. Officers, including Trent, fired their short arms[79] from the curtains and bastions. When several warriors appeared in canoes on the adjacent rivers, one of the six-pound cannons spat several rounds of round ball in their direction.[80] The first did not hit its mark, but the loud splash near them, when it landed, sent them diving out of their canoes. As they tried to climb into another passing by, a second cast iron ball found its target, splitting the birchbark canoe and one of the Indians in two.[81] The current was stained a crimson red.

Later that night, the garrison faced another aerial assault when fiery arrows were launched toward the walls. Wary of the grapeshot[82] and round ball this

---
74. Shinango or Shenango Town was near the present site of West Middlesex, Pennsylvania.
75. MVHR, Vol. 11, No. 3, 408.
76. Ibid.
77. Ibid.
78. Ibid.
79. Ibid., 409.
80. Ibid.
81. Ibid.
82. Grapeshot were smaller caliber round ball in a canvas bag that resembled a bunch of grapes and fired from an artillery piece.

time, several of the arrows were fired from a longer distance and could only reach the ditches just outside the walls.[83] Though a few did manage to set the Governor's house and barracks ablaze,[84] he and the rest of the garrison spent most of the night using the cask of water to put it out. The insides of both buildings were unscathed, but their roofs were badly damaged.[85]

Trent feared another attack on the 30th, but it never materialized. The next few nights, they faced sporadic firings, which they responded by having the grenadiers toss their grenades[86] at them in the ditches outside the walls.

Good news was on the horizon, however, when three expresses arrived[87] from Colonel Bouquet, who had left Fort Ligonier with a detachment to come to their support. Yet by August 8th, Bouquet and his detachment still hadn't arrived, and Trent feared they'd been attacked on their way to them.[88] Two days later, Private Miller[89], whom Trent sent to find Bouquet, returned and brought an account that Bouquet's detachment was attacked on the 5th. About a mile from Bushy Run, he spent two days fending off the attack[90] until they were able to drive the enemy away. It was reported Bouquet's men suffered fifty killed and sixty wounded.[91] Their Native adversaries suffered at least that many or even more.

The next day, on the 11th, Bouquet presented himself at Fort Pitt to confirm this victory in driving the Native parties off. He first addressed his appreciation and thanks to those in the fort "who have so bravely defended the post, against the repeated attacks of Barbarians and Malicious Enemies."[92] Then, he extended his appreciation from General Amherst to Ecuyer for "his firm and prudent conduct."[93]

Bouquet also had special praise for Trent. He made mention on the parade ground that he "takes a particular pleasure in Expressing to Major Trent how agreeable his Services, and those performed by the brave Militia command under his Command are to him and returns him his sincere thanks for the ready assistance he is constantly given to the Commanding officer desiring the will inform his Officers & Men of his grateful Sense that the Col. has of their behavior."[94]

---

83. MVHR, Vol. 11, No. 3, 409.
84. Ibid.
85. Ibid.
86. Ibid.
87. Ibid., 411.
88. Ibid., 410.
89. There were two Private Millers, either Patrick Miller or Christian Miller.
90. MVHR, Vol. 11, No. 3, 410.
91. Ibid.
92. HSP, Orderly Book of Captain William Trent, 26.
93. Ibid., 27.
94. Ibid.

This commendation came on the eve that the inhabitants could return to their settlements or the outpost to the east the next day. Some of Trent's men attached themselves to this guard[95] under Major Campbell[96] back to Forts Ligonier and Bedford, but by September 1st, most of his militia had been discharged from their service.

With his orders at Fort Pitt highly reduced now to picket duties and retrieving coal across the Monongahela River,[97] Trent began his focus on tallying losses suffered during the late Indian War. On September 5th, he compiled a list of those merchants and traders (like his partner Levi A. Levy) who were captured, taken, or killed[98] during this dark time. The list was eventually sent to General Amherst, along with the final return dated October 26, 1763,[99] of all the militia officers, subalterns, and one hundred and thirteen privates who served under his command so they could receive their eventual pay.

Several of them later became part of Pittsburgh and Pennsylvania lore. Smithfield Street and Girty's Run[100] near Pittsburgh were named in honor of Privates Devereaux Smith and Thomas Girty. While Thomas's brothers George and his infamous sibling Simon Girty joined Alexander McKee in defecting to the British cause and led raids across the frontier during the American Revolution. Finally, let's not forget two other privates under Trent's command, James Smith and Robert Black, the former who notoriously led a band of raiders in 1765 that included this Robert Black from the area of present-day Mercersburg, Pennsylvania, in a movement later known as the "Black Boys Rebellion."

Now, October 26, 1763, was also the date of the last time Trent signed his name as commander of the militia at Fort Pitt. His captains and subalterns followed, signing below him as well as his superiors, Simeon Ecuyer and Col. Henry Bouquet.[101]

When he finally returned home to Carlisle, his wife Sarah could rejoice that he made it safely home to her and his three daughters. The homecoming was short-lived, however, as usual. He was home for just a couple weeks before his presence was requested in Philadelphia with eleven others[102] who had suffered

---

95. MVHR, Vol. 11, No.3, 411.
96. John Campbell eventually laid out the four-block grid of Pittsburgh in 1764. In 1773, he and business partner John Connolly purchased four thousand acres in Kentucky in what was later known as Louisville.
97. MVHR, Vol. 11, No. 3, 412.
98. BP, Vol. 6, 412–13.
99. University of Michigan, William L. Clements Library, Jeffrey Amherst Papers, Vol. 6.
100. Smithfield formerly Smith's Field Street that runs from Liberty Avenue to Carson Street including the Smithfield Street Bridge in downtown Pittsburgh is named for Devereaux Smith. Girty's Run named for Thomas Girty empties into the Allegheny River near Millvale, Pennsylvania.
101. University of Michigan, William L. Clements Library, Jeffrey Amherst Papers, Vol. 6.
102. The twelve men who appeared at the Indian Queen Tavern were as follows: David Franks, Jeremiah Warder, Samuel Burge, George Croghan, John Coxe, Abraham Mitchell, William Trent, Robert Callender, Joseph Spear, Thomas McKee, Philip Boyle, and Samuel Wharton.

Portrait of Colonel James Smith by an unknown artist about 1800-1810. (Courtesy of the Warren J. Shonert Americana Collection and Eva G. Farris Special Collections, in the W. Frank Steely Library at Northern Kentucky University and Public Domain.)

devastating losses during the French and Indian War and now from the latest Indian War.

So, on the 7th of December 1763, as he trotted east on Market Street, Trent turned his horse down Fourth St. to the various stalls[103] after he rode under the wooden sign that read "Indian Queen Tavern." The "public house" owned by John and Grace Little[104] had the reputation of being one of the finest inns in all of Philadelphia. Where he entered, a servant wearing a bright livery[105] took his coat, and he proceeded to walk into one of the large meeting rooms the Indian Queen Tavern offered on the first floor. There, he immediately recognized Croghan and other suffering traders, such as his partner David Franks and his cousin and Philadelphia saddler Samuel Burge.[106] The group then extended

---

103. *Pennsylvania Gazette*, January 3, 1776.
104. The former Grace Nicholson shared ownership of the tavern with her late husband William Nicholson as early as 1757.
105. A livery is a special uniform or coat worn by the servants.
106. Samuel Burge was the son of William Burge and the nephew of Mary Burge, the first wife of Trent's father.

Present-day site of the Indian Queen Tavern in Philadelphia, now the Fox 29 Station building at the corner of Fourth Street and Market (High) Street. (Author photo.)

on to Moses Franks (the older merchant brother of his partner in London) and George Croghan, a memorial to orate before the Board of Trade to compensate or relieve those gentlemen present representing themselves or others for their recent "depredations."

Each man present, including Trent, was told to advance Franks and Croghan a sum of two hundred and ten pounds[107] for their trouble. When all except Jeremiah Warder agreed, an essay of the memorial was suggested by Croghan to be immediately drawn up for the Lords of Trade by six o'clock the next evening.[108] Naturally, Trent was chosen to draft this essay, along with the long-nosed thirty-one-year-old Quaker named Samuel Wharton. Wharton, a merchant himself, was one-third of the trading firm with John Baynton and junior partner George Morgan, which had

Wood engraving of merchant Samuel Wharton (circa 1770s). (Courtesy of the Emmet Collection of Manuscripts Etc. Relating to American History of the New York Public Library and Public Domain.)

---
107. Papers of William Johnson, Vol. 4, 264.
108. Ibid., 265.

suffered financial losses in investments throughout the Western country as well. Together, the two of them spent most of the evening sipping spirits in their glasses and writing this essay. After exhaustion finally overtook them, they indulged in the convenient lodgings up the staircase on the second or third floors.[109]

So, what began as a joint authorship to draft a short essay in Philadelphia seemingly transformed this group of "suffering" merchants and traders into something bigger. When the meeting concluded, and they all went their separate ways, Croghan sailed for London on the Baynton, Wharton, and Morgan ship the *Brittania* just before the new year.[110] Simply put, the hope for their restitution or relief rested squarely on Croghan and the memorial he carried with him. As for Trent and Wharton, this chance meeting was only the beginning of their lifelong vicarious partnership.

---

109. *Pennsylvania Gazette*, January 3, 1776.
110. The *Brittania* sailed on December 29, 1763, from Cape Henlopen, Delaware. Wainwright, 204.

Chapter 14

A Monumental Presence

Trent's mind was in a daze. And not because it was a little after one o'clock that early morning of the 29th of November 1764.[1] There was so much on his mind he had only heard part of the question from Rev. William Thompson as they all stood in his house on East Street in Carlisle.

Reverend Thompson asked again. "By what name shall we call the child?"

Trent looked over at his wife in bed, then at the small baby who was barely a few hours old. "Sarah, her name will be Sarah Trent."

Thompson then poured water across her tiny forehead. "I baptize thee in the name of the father and of the son, and of the Holy Ghost. . . . Amen."

It was William and Sarah's fourth daughter, and after Trent recorded her baptism in the family's Scottish Bible, he finally laid down to try to sleep.

With his family expanded by one, it probably made him think more and more about his and his family's financial future. Croghan's return from London left everything in doubt when he returned in late summer. Writing from his new residence at Monkton Hall[2] in the Northern Liberties, he informed Trent of the unfortunate news of his failure to receive royal approval or any compensation for their losses in 1763. Worse yet, the losses he and Trent suffered in 1754 weren't even considered by the Board of Trade but rather suggested to be addressed in future Parliamentary sessions. Trent couldn't fault Croghan for his efforts. Despite his best attempt at appearing as a scarlet-cloaked gentleman[3] from the American colonies, these high-ranking officials never accepted him as one or prioritized their financial losses now.

---
1. HSP, Family Bible Records, BrTr.
2. Monkton Hall was Croghan's country house along Poplar Lane in the Northern Liberties. Wainwright, 210.
3. Wainwright, 206.

Ten years earlier, there was little doubt in receiving this approval, but Great Britain had bigger problems to worry about since the Seven Years War had finally ended. The war had cost the British Treasury over seventy million pounds and nearly doubled their national debt. In addition, the latest Indian War had forced the King's hand and he had to declare a Royal Proclamation Line[4] to forbid any settlers west of the Appalachian Mountains back in October of 1763. He also forbade any conducting of trade or selling of goods to the Indian nations of the Western country. This proclamation was to keep the Western country as land "reserved" for the Native people despite being the potential land that fell under the original land tract of Trent's semi-dormant employer, the Ohio Company.

Trent knew the settlers heading west still had not abided by this latest restriction. They hadn't obeyed the provincial government after the Burnt Cabins expedition, so why listen to a declaration across the ocean thousands of miles away? For some of Trent's acquaintances, the Proclamation of 1763 may just have been the opening act in Great Britain maintaining control over them. Most of them didn't realize this until the Sugar Act was being enforced in the colonies in late September of 1764. The Sugar Act, passed by the British Parliament initially on April 5, 1764, was to raise revenue for Great Britain for their "protection" of the colonies during the French and Indian War. It also forced both storefront and shipping merchants to raise their prices for molasses and rum quite considerably to justify the enforced tax. While it didn't affect Trent directly, it might soon be if those merchants and past creditors began demanding payments to counter the rates.

Up until this time, Trent spent a good part of 1764 with his family and managing his properties and sawmill[5] near Carlisle. While he "retired" from his military career he had been entrusted by Colonel Bouquet to compensate those forty-two individuals[6] under his command at Fort Pitt that still had not been paid for their service. Bouquet sent him a sum of two hundred and fifty-five pounds, eleven shillings, and ten pence[7] for this purpose, of which Trent himself received thirty-eight pounds ten shillings[8] for his service. Bouquet also sent him an additional sixty-four pounds, one shilling, and sixpence[9] for those militiamen who served with the garrison at Fort Ligonier in 1763. To remind those unpaid individuals he still held their payments in Carlisle, Trent

---

4. *Pennsylvania Gazette*, December 8, 1763.
5. Ibid., June 12, 1776, 3.
6. University of Michigan, William L. Clements Library, Thomas Gage Papers American Series, Vol. 17.
7. Ibid.
8. Ibid.
9. Ibid.

even placed an advertisement in the *Pennsylvania Gazette* on May 1, 1764, to "give Notice that the Money is lodged in the Hands of Captain William Trent and that all concerned are desired to apply to him, themselves (or by others properly empowered) for their Pay, before the first day of August."[10]

Meanwhile to earn some extra money, Trent took a job on May 5, 1764, for what he described as "security" for both the Baynton, Wharton, and Morgan firm and his partners Simon, Franks, and Levy. He protected the carriage of skins and goods while he and his friend James Foley led thirty horses[11] from Fort Pitt to Carlisle, Lancaster and then Philadelphia. Unfortunately, by the end of summer, Foley had pocketed the money despite he and Trent having a verbal agreement over the profits. When Trent confronted him and flat out refused to give him half of the earned revenue of two hundred and thirty-seven pounds, fourteen shillings and two pence,[12] Trent sent this problem to a high-profile lawyer and Attorney General for Pennsylvania, Benjamin Chew.[13] After hearing the details of Trent's case at Chew's frequent hangout at the London Coffee House on the corner of First and Market Street, Chew determined Trent was, in fact, a co-partner with Foley. Chew said that Trent was entitled to half[14] and should pay him his share or be arrested once he appeared again in Philadelphia. Trent suggested that Foley usually stayed at the "Indian Queen"[15] when he came to Philadelphia, but it was not known if Trent received what he was owed from him.

In the meantime, as the new year of 1765 began, Trent and his suffering traders group re-strategized their approach to receive their restitution and royal approval. It appeared they could no longer rely on General Amherst, who previously promised Trent that he "may be assured every method in my power shall be used for not only reducing them to reason but for recovering what may belong to His Majesty's subjects."[16] Amherst, whose controversial policy spawned the late Indian war, had left for England and was replaced as Commander-in-Chief of North America by Thomas Gage. So, this time, Trent and his suffering traders' group wrote to Gage in New York City and then sent a copy to Superintendent of the Northern Indian Department William Johnson. In their original memorial dated January 5, 1765, to Gage, they hoped for

---

10. *Pennsylvania Gazette*, May 10, 1764, 2.
11. Pennsylvania State Archives, MG 19, William Trent to Baynton, Wharton and Morgan, June 11, 1764.
12. Ibid.
13. Benjamin Chew (November 19, 1722–January 20, 1810) was a Philadelphia lawyer who represented the Penn family for six decades. He held a private practice from his house on Front Street in the city and after 1771 at his house on Third Street.
14. Pennsylvania State Archives, MG 19, William Trent to Baynton, Wharton and Morgan, June 11, 1764.
15. Ibid.
16. HSP, Frank M. Etting Collection, Jeffrey Amherst to William Trent, June 25, 1763.

reimbursement for losses suffered in 1763 and for his consideration that the authors of this memorial were to "obtain satisfaction from other Indian Nations, for the damages they giving up part of their Country for that purpose other manners as to your Excellency shall seem the most likely to procure us redress."[17]

The copy sent to Johnson on February 7, 1765, not only listed their estimated losses in 1763 but also wished Johnson to speak with the Six Nations at the next council about this "redress." In other words, these men like Trent weren't hoping for money from them but rather a large tract of land equal to this total amount of financial loss. According to the attached list for merchants and traders, total losses amounted to 80,862 pounds, twelve shillings and four and three-quarters pence (over $17 million today in American currency).[18] Trent, as a lone merchant "sufferer," lost about four thousand five hundred pounds (close to $1 million)[19] himself. But since he was also a partner with Simon, Franks and Levy, their losses were over twenty-four thousand pounds (about $5.2 million).[20] So, combined with his personal debts, Trent's losses in 1763 alone were over one-third of the total 80,862 pounds, twelve shillings, and four and three quarters. Unfortunately, the total amount did not remain constant either. By the time Johnson addressed this agenda to the several Indian nations who attended the council at his house[21] on May 2nd, the estimated losses for the "sufferers" of 1763 had increased rather gradually over the last few months.

This was due to his former partner Croghan and the Baynton, Wharton and Morgan firm being caught transporting goods such as knives, tomahawks, and powder that were in direct violation of the Royal Proclamation terms passed in the fall of 1763. While Trent wisely decided not to join this venture (or provide security for it like the previous year), his fellow sufferers had begun investing in the future by stockpiling goods at Fort Pitt to open trade eventually in the Illinois country, and it cost them dearly. While transporting eighty-one horses[22] containing twenty thousand pounds worth of goods past Sideling Hill (just west of Great Cove in Fulton County), the supply train was attacked by Trent's former militiaman James Smith and other men from Cumberland County (including Trent's other militiamen like Robert Black and others) who blackened their faces and disguised themselves like Indians. These "Black Boys" were worried if these Native populations in the Western country received these

---

17. Papers of William Johnson, Vol. 4, 631–32.
18. HSP, Frank M. Etting Collection, Ohio Company Papers.
19. Ibid.
20. Ibid.
21. His house was Johnson Hall in Johnstown, New York.
22. Wainwright, 216.

goods, then future atrocities might be committed on them or other inhabitants living near the proclamation line.

Croghan appraised the destruction and goods being burnt at over three thousand pounds (over $580,000)[23], and that didn't include the rest that were confiscated and taken to Fort Loudoun on the Forbes Road. Despite the setback and a reprimand for those involved from General Gage for transporting "illegal" goods, all hope was not lost for Trent and the rest of the sufferers group of 1763.

William Johnson sent word from the Mohawk Valley that the Six Nations had accepted their proposal of land for retribution and decided for a later time "about the King's desire that we should agree about a line between us and the English."[24] Also, at this meeting, they hoped the traders or possibly Johnson decided "how you intended the Line should go and how far."[25] One thing Johnson hadn't mentioned was retribution for those sufferers in 1754 because he felt the French were more at fault for those losses.

As for Trent and the others, they took this small victory and crucial first step. Now, to when or where this meeting with the Indian nations took place, not even Trent or Johnson knew. But as the summer of 1765 changed to fall in Pennsylvania, the group soon found themselves yet again with another obstacle to overcome. Effective November 1, 1765, Great Britain tried once again to reduce their national debt by requiring a tax stamp on all legal documents and printed materials throughout the American colonies. This levied tax, known as the Stamp Act, sent shockwaves and grumblings between his Philadelphia merchant counterparts. Then, about a week before the Stamp Act was officially enacted, merchants, lawyers and businessmen from Boston, New York and Philadelphia signed non-importation agreements in protest. This agreement stated not to import any British goods until the tax was repealed.

For Trent, this could not have come at a worse time. Though his signature was not among those on October 25, 1765 (mainly because he lived in Carlisle and not Philadelphia), several of his partners and fellow suffering traders did sign it, such as merchants Samuel Wharton, David Franks, Jeremiah Warder, Abraham Mitchell, lawyer Benjamin Chew and his saddler cousin Samuel Burge.[26] This did not bid well if they were to win over the Board of Trade[27] for their land retribution, but they all believed the Stamp Act might be repealed

---

23. Ibid.
24. Documents Relative to the Colonial History of New York, Vol. 7, 725.
25. Ibid.
26. HSP, Treasures Collection, Am. 340.
27. The Board of Trade was a British government body concerned with commerce and industry. Its full name was The Lords of the Committee of the Privy Council appointed for the consideration of all matters relating to Trade and Foreign Plantations.

once Great Britain saw how they all felt towards the "taxation without representation" in Parliament.

Despite the present boycott of British goods, suffering Philadelphia merchants of 1763 agreed to and trusted only Trent (since he was a respected member of both the suffering groups of 1754 and 1763) as power of attorney for the group as he began gathering affidavits of losses for those wishing to seek shares in the potential land retribution from the Six Nations once it came to pass.

This also came on the heels of his good friend George Mercer, who Trent had heard left Virginia rather abruptly for London in November. Mercer, the acting London agent for the Ohio Company, had written a memorial on the company's behalf on May 21, 1765, to hopefully extend the previous grant that expired during the French and Indian War. He had also been commissioned as the stamp distributor for the colony of Virginia, but as he faced much opposition in Williamsburg toward the tax and himself, he instead chose to resign his commission and return to London to lobby on the Ohio Company's behalf. Little did Trent or the others realize how Mercer's memorial for those wealthy Virginians impacted their future endeavors.

So, by the end of December 1765, Trent went to work in gathering affidavits of those suffering losses in 1763. He began the day after Christmas in his residence of Carlisle, acquiring first a power of attorney from Croghan's kinsman Thomas Smallman, then trader and friend Robert Callender.[28]

He also spent well into the year of 1766 land speculating, getting paid in hand eight pounds to survey three hundred acres[29] along the Little Juniata River on August 1, 1766, while also receiving similar affidavits from traders or merchants who wished him to receive compensation on their behalf. The written agreements he received (either at his house or in person elsewhere) didn't come with at least a mention of compensation for previous losses in the French and Indian War, which Trent knew now was not a priority. He asked those who inquired specifically about losses in 1754 and 1756 to be patient and wait until they could meet with the Six Nations or hear from London.

When a permanent boundary could be established between the colonies and the Indian hunting ground, he assured them, only then could he and the Six Nations discuss compensation and give those two groups of "sufferers" a rectifying answer. Speaking of 1754, his former partner Croghan, fresh from exploring the Illinois country and temporarily residing that spring of 1767 at Johnson Hall, wrote to Ohio Company Treasurer George Mason at Gunston Hall. Croghan had heard the Ohio Company was settling outstanding accounts,

---

28. Bailey, 180–81.
29. Library Company of Philadelphia, John A. McAllister Collection, Box 1, Folder 5.

so he felt obliged to investigate a particular bond. This bond was part of money recovered by factor William Trent in the Robert Dinwiddie suit he won previously in 1760, but it was not known how Croghan was specifically involved. Apparently, the Ohio Company could not find proof of this involvement either, because Mason had to consult Trent's lawyer for this case, John Mercer. After much consideration, they both declared that "Croghan is not entitled to any cash from the Ohio Company on this Account."[30] Any claim that Croghan requested was exclusive to the sum of eight hundred pounds[31] that Mercer had collected for Trent's trial in 1760.

In a related letter, member Thomas Cresap wrote to James Tilghman on May 20, 1767, that any discrepancy found in the company books, such as five hundred and sixty pounds, four shillings, and three and three-quarters pence for various sundries purchased by Trent in 1754, was accounted for in the 1753 and 1754 "Books kept by Capt. Wm Trent."[32] Coincidentally, the books referred to by Cresap's letter also listed Trent's given name of the Ohio Company Fort, "Fort St. George." These books are not known to survive today.

Trent, who had seemingly moved on from his former employer since the French and Indian War ended, did manage to sign one last receipt dated September 25, 1767, as "William Trent, Factor for the Ohio Company," to settle a 1750 transaction from Francis Wafer for £111.10.[33]

His next order of business was fulfilling a promise by writing to his friend and London liaison Benjamin Franklin to try and solicit restitution for those suffering losses during the French and Indian War. While he collected many affidavits from 1763, Trent had accumulated over twenty more (twenty-four including himself)[34] from 1754 and 1756. He and several others belonged to both groups, so it couldn't hurt to have Dr. Franklin lobby for the oldest "suffering" group while he waited on news from Johnson Hall for the latest one.

However, a bit of good news already arrived in Carlisle when the cries of a newborn filled the Trent house at ten o'clock in the morning of April 21, 1768[35] with the Rev. William Thompson once again overseeing the baptism. The Trents named their son John and recorded it in the family Bible. John was their last child and only son to survive into adulthood.

---

30. James, 240.
31. Ibid.
32. James, Appendix A, 242.
33. HSP, Frank M. Etting Collection, Ohio Company Papers.
34. The twenty-four were as follows: George Croghan, Thomas McKee, Hugh Crawford, Samuel Chambers, James Silvers, Arthur Auchmuty, Adam Terrence, John Fraser, Thomas Kinton, John Gray, Alexander Stevens, James Rankin, John Galbreath, Francis Campbell, James Young, Robert Callender, Michael Teaff, James Dunning, Paul Peirce, John Owens, William Blyth, Morris Turner, Alexander McKennet, and William Trent.
35. HSP, Family Bible Records, BrTr.

Less than a month later, the news they were waiting for arrived in May of 1768, and so William Johnson relayed a message from General Gage to Croghan, Trent, and the Baynton, Wharton, and Morgan firm. The potential boundaries for the Indian hunting ground were drawn up for the settlers not to encroach. According to General Gage, the Indian hunting ground ran down the Ohio River as far as the great Kanawha River. The tract of land or "the country between the River and the Sea, I understand, is to be coated by then to the English in general."[36]

It meant this tract of land was, in fact, their retribution for past losses suffered in previous conflicts. As Trent and Wharton planned to see Johnson and prepare for this important council, Gage gave them one final warning about this proposed line and its boundaries. "As to the line of Virginia terminating at the southwest corner of Pennsylvania," Gage said, referring to the Ohio country, "I apprehend that it be a Matter between the two Provinces."[37]

For Trent, this warning for the time being was lost in the saltwater spraying his face as he, Wharton, and Croghan traveled by sloop from Philadelphia to New York, then up the Hudson to Albany. Croghan was finalizing his latest investment in upstate New York along the mouth of the Susquehanna River and had Trent and Wharton tag along (and to spark their interest, no doubt) before they went and saw William Johnson.

While in Albany, Trent signed an investment of his own as he and Wharton spent the night at the King's Arms Tavern (today, the corner of Beaver and Green Streets) owned by Richard Cartwright. On June 6th, 1768, he drafted a contract for Christian Redebauch,[38] who bound himself under his own accord (and with the consent of his father-in-law Joseph Ackley) for eleven and a half years of indentured servitude under Trent. As an eventual servant in the Trent household in Carlisle, he helped with all the labor once they returned home since their family had grown to five children with the birth of young John. Redebauch also performed the labor at his plantation in Middleton Township since they no longer had the enslaved servant performing these duties. In return, Trent promised to teach him to read, write, and cipher and his freedom was granted when his contract expired.

The next morning, they met Albany Mayor Volkert Pietr Douw and, with the payments (or possibly bribe) of three pounds, six shillings, and eight pence,[39] had the former skipper guide them back down the Hudson River to New York

---

36. Papers of William Johnson, Vol.6, 212.
37. Ibid.
38. University of Delaware Library, Special Collections, Indenture between Christian Redebauch and William Trent, June 6, 1768.
39. HSP, Papers relating to Indian Losses 1766–1770.

City and then to Connecticut. Traveling by water had become dangerous now, with British customs officials patrolling the seaports for smugglers and illegal trade, so Trent trusted few to guide them without incident. There, they landed at Harris's Wharf in the seaport of New London, where Johnson requested him to meet him[40], and due to the state of his bad health, the "bathing in the sea" could calm "the violent disorder of his bowels."[41] They met Johnson for breakfast at the home of former New London Postmaster Joseph Chew, who had once been garrisoned with Trent at Fort Clinton during King George's War in 1747. Though Trent fought his way out of an ambush in April 1747 near Fort Clinton, Chew was not as fortunate two months later when he was captured and taken to Quebec as a prisoner on June 30, 1747.[42]

Trent made a note of the cost of sixteen shillings, sixpence[43] they paid for breakfast in cash, but still wanted to make sure that Johnson pressed the Indian nations at their next council to agree on the proposed boundaries of the grant and payment for lands they plan to relinquish to them. After Johnson assured them the Indian grant was made, he, Croghan, Trent, his servant Redebauch and Wharton left New London for New Haven.

Although Johnson was feeling better, Trent was suddenly feeling under the weather. Either his passage aboard the sloop from Albany up the coast had been disagreeable, or his intermittent illness was returning. Regardless, Trent began purchasing miscellaneous sundries to remedy what ailed him. Before he left New London, Trent dropped two shillings on oranges, then two shillings eight pence in New Haven for tea.[44]

Eventually, after stops in Fairfield, Norwalk, and Stamford and feeding their horses in Rye, New York, they arrived for the night at the renowned tavern of George Burns at the corner of Broadway and Thomas Street on Lower Manhattan Island. Burns's Tavern, or "coffeehouse," was not only the previous site where New York merchants protested British goods by signing non-importation agreements in 1765 but eventually became the meeting place of the riotous organization known as the Sons of Liberty. Here, the public house entertainment and rumors of British troops landing in Boston to restore order by the end of September enthralled them for at least two nights, where Trent purchased almonds for two shillings and had a woman launder their clothes for sixteen shillings five pence.[45]

---

40. Ibid.
41. Documents Relative to the Colonial History of New York, Vol. 8, 70.
42. Ibid., Vol. 6, 488.
43. HSP, Papers relating to Indian Losses 1766–1770.
44. Ibid.
45. Ibid.

A print showing the former Burn's Coffee House where Trent stayed in 1768, which today resided at the corner of Thomas Street and Broadway in Lower Manhattan of New York City. (Courtesy of the Miriam and Ira D. Wallach Division of Art of the New York Public Library.)

On the 6th day of July, they boarded a sloop for their five-day journey back to Albany, where they stayed once again at Cartwright's Tavern or, as he recorded it, the "King's Lodge."[46] In Albany, they purchased goods for Johnson Hall, and as Trent loaded them onto a wagon they acquired, he saw the decaying remains of Fort Frederick. Barely a hull of its former self, the abandoned fort was so dilapidated it's hard to believe he had once stayed inside its walls over twenty-two years before[47] as a British captain of one of the four independent companies from Pennsylvania during King George's War.

Later, on the evening of July 13th, Trent and the others stayed the night in Schenectady at the "Sign of the Cross Keys" owned by Robert Clench,[48] whose tavern stood at the midway point between Albany and Johnson Hall. It was also where, in 1782, General George Washington had dinner and greeted the town officials of Schenectady. The site of Clench's Tavern today in Schenectady lies within the boundaries of Liberty Park along State and Water Street.

---

46. Ibid.
47. Colonial Records of Pennsylvania, Vol. 5, 132–33.
48. HSP, Papers relating to Indian Losses 1766–1770.

"Sir William Johnson Presenting Medals to Chiefs of the Six Nations at Johnstown, N.Y. in 1772" by artist Edward Lawson Henry. (Courtesy of the Canadian Museum of History in Gatineau, Quebec, and Public Domain.)

Soon, by the end of July, they arrived at the large Georgian-style house of Sir William Johnson. Trent must been in awe of Johnson's house and the amount of acreage he owned in the vicinity.[49] At this point in his life, Trent owned about 7,500 acres in Pennsylvania, but nothing compared to the grants of Sir William. However, if everything fell into place with this council, Trent could pay off his creditors, obtain more wealth with his land retribution and secure his family's future.

So, by September, while Croghan surveyed additional land near his forty thousand acres near Lake Otsego, Trent, Wharton, and Johnson arranged for twenty boatloads of presents to arrive in time for the proposed Indian meeting to reset the boundaries. The council or "Congress" with the Indian nations was to meet on September 20th at Fort Stanwix,[50] whose abandoned fortification stood along the Oneida Carry in present-day Rome, New York. Commissioners had already been appointed back in August, and Trent recorded every one of them he saw in his brown and black marble-covered book he entitled, "Treaty with the Indians at Fort Stanwix 1768."[51]

From Burlington, New Jersey,[52] the New Jersey commissioners eagerly appeared with Chief Justice Frederick Smyth[53] and Trent's good friend and Royal

---

49. The tract his house was on, consisted of eighty thousand acres. By the time of his death in 1774, he owned about one hundred and seventy thousand acres, behind the Penn and Van Rensselaer families.
50. Fort Stanwix was a large bastioned fort built by the British to protect the portage between the Mohawk and Hudson Rivers called the Oneida Carry.
51. HSP, Frank M. Etting Collection, Vol. 12.
52. William Franklin's house in Burlington, New Jersey was called "Green Brook" and is now the present site of the Veteran on Foreign Wars building on Riverbank in Burlington, New Jersey.
53. Frederick Smyth (1732–1815) was the last royal chief justice of New Jersey and one of Governor William Franklin's most trusted allies.

Governor of New Jersey, William Franklin, arriving first at Johnson Hall. Since the Pennsylvania commissioners had yet to join them, Johnson, Trent, Wharton, and the New Jersey constituents began their four-day journey to Fort Stanwix on September 15th[54] in their five boats loaded with food and other goods.

Trent and the others arrived on the 19th, a day before the treaty hoped to begin and were surprised to see the two commissioners from Virginia were already there. There, Trent saw Doctor Thomas Walker of Albemarle County, co-founder of the Loyal Land Company with Peter Jefferson and Joshua Fry back in 1750 and Irish-born Colonel Andrew Lewis, whom Trent hadn't seen since Lewis left with Major Grant to reconnoiter Fort Duquesne and was captured by the French and sent to Quebec in September of 1758. Lewis no doubt was representing those former soldiers of the Virginia Regiment whose land was promised to them under Robert Dinwiddie's Proclamation of 1754.

Though, when the 20th came, only a small party of Tuscarora's, Oneidas and Mohawks had arrived. Johnson was told the Lenape, Shawnee, and Stockbridge had been delayed but were on the way. So, while Johnson waited for most of them to arrive, he told them they were not discussing any talk of the boundaries and cession until then.

The next morning, on the 21st,[55] five commissioners and gentlemen from Pennsylvania finally arrived at the fort. Trent recorded that these men Rev. Richard Peters, the former Secretary of the Land Office, Attorney General and Trent's former lawyer Benjamin Chew, Ohio Company attorney and now current Secretary of the Land Office James Tilghman, Chief Justice William Allen, and his son-in-law and Governor of Pennsylvania John Penn. Penn, whose father and uncles were solely responsible for "acquiring" Lenape land through the controversial Walking Purchase in 1737, had to tread carefully at Fort Stanwix once his surname was announced to be involved in this "Congress."

The five dignitaries arrived just in time at the fort to hear he and Samuel Wharton give their account of the trader's losses in 1763 and "their Power of Attorney for obtaining a retribution in Lands, pursuant to an Article in the Treaty of Peace in 1765."[56] Though Governor Penn and the others felt confident hearing Trent and Wharton's memorandum, some other Philadelphia associates were not. An opposing letter came by express from merchant John Cox (and influenced by his Lancaster partners and creditors Simon, Levy, and Franks). Cox and others unnamed from Pennsylvania sought to challenge the claims made by those present at this Congress who were indebted to him and the

---

54. Papers of William Johnson, Vol. 12, 617.
55. Ibid., 617–18.
56. HSP, Frank M. Etting Collection, Vol. 12.

others. In other words, creditors like Cox, who had lost ventures in 1754 and in the Illinois country, wanted compensation or at least a share in the proposed restitution from those who suffered in 1763 since several men (including Trent) owed Cox and other creditors from Pennsylvania.

Trent had to be smart in his response to this. He knew there were repercussions since word of this "Congress" reached his creditors, but he still had to exude confidence while Penn and his Pennsylvania counterparts perused over the legwork of their affidavits and documents. So, he wrote on September 30th to one of those businessmen, John Baynton, in Philadelphia, expressing reassurance:

> I am sorry to find you as well as the rest of our Friends have been so much Allarmed I really think if you have attended to a letter Mr. Wharton wrote abt the Virginia commissioners you must have been convinced that we are fully acquainted with every circumstance of the Affair which has given you all so much uneasiness and been the cause of this Express.[57]

Trent concluded the letter with no cause of concern or alarm toward this sudden opposition, adding, "As to Dr. Cox, he cannot hurt us."[58] This same bold confidence was expressed publicly in Trent and Wharton's rebuttal on October 5th at the fort to Cox's memorial from Philadelphia. Now, all they had to do was wait.

Also, by that first week of October, about eight hundred Indians[59] had arrived, but with the promise of more upper nations in New York still delayed (either by evil intentions or not) to join them. Hearing this, Johnson immediately sent out belts to them to announce the urgency of their presence. Unfortunately, one of the commissioners of Virginia was not so patient. Colonel Lewis left on October 12th[60], feeling that Virginia and those who bled the ground for its province were not going to be represented fully at this treaty if it ever happened. Not wishing to be detained any longer, Lewis headed south, leaving Dr. Walker behind as Virginia's lone representative.

The next day,[61] news came from Lieutenant Achilles Preston and Trent's friend, Hugh Crawford, that a large delegation of Indian sachems and warriors numbering about three thousand were set to arrive. Quickly, Johnson wrote to

---

57. Bailey, 186.
58. Ibid.
59. Documents Relative to the Colonial History of New York, Vol. 8, 112.
60. Papers of William Johnson Vol. 12, 606.
61. Ibid., 607–608.

merchant John Glenn in Schenectady requesting more supplies, estimating he needed enough pork and flour to feed three thousand Indians for three weeks.[62]

> You will send a large quantity of provisions up here as Soon as possible; otherwise, it must overset the design of this Congress as it cannot be Supposed that Hungry Indians can be kept there, or in any temper without a Bellyful.[63]

Meanwhile, the Pennsylvania commissioners made their decision on the Cox affair. After Tilghman met with Johnson, Penn and the rest of the Pennsylvania gentlemen agreed that the application made by Trent and Wharton was "reasonable" and "any other application (like the one declared by John Cox) for losses sustained during the French and Indian War, which had never before been mentioned to the Indians, might be disagreeable to them and might tend to obstruct the Proceedings."[64]

It was another small victory for Trent and Wharton, but as for the suffering traders of 1754, this was a devastating blow and basically shut tight what little window they had left to garner restitution. Since the 1754 application had been rejected in London, it was declared void and not included in the current 1763 application. The line had to be drawn somewhere and was the only way to have the Indian nations successfully cede this land.

With this "affair" in opposition finally settled, Penn, Allen, and Chew left for Philadelphia. They left Tilghman and Peters behind to be present at the treaty since business in the province of Pennsylvania could not wait any longer. By the 23rd of October, two thousand two hundred Indian sachems and warriors (not three thousand as originally thought) arrived from all parts and directions from Fort Stanwix, making the official total around three thousand one hundred and two Native people,[65] and the largest treaty at this time between them and the British Empire. According to Trent's counterpart Wharton: "So much fewer Women and Children than I ever saw of any Treaty before, occasioned by their staying at their Villages, to secure their corn."[66]

The Treaty of Stanwix, according to Trent's minutes, began officially on October 24, 1768. In addition to the commissioners from several provinces announcing their credentials, his former partner Croghan, Daniel

---

62. Ibid.
63. Ibid.
64. Ibid., 620.
65. Ibid., 628.
66. Papers of Benjamin Franklin (BF), Samuel Wharton to Ben Franklin, December 2, 1768.

Claus (son-in-law of Sir William)[67] and Guy Johnson (supposed nephew of Sir William)[68] were representing the Deputy Agents for the Indian Affairs Department under the Crown. Two others attended the treaty whom Trent was familiar with and could not avoid seeing or interacting with. From the Lenape tribe came sachem Turtles Heart, the very same individual who accepted the bundle of smallpox blankets from Josiah Davenport and Simeon Ecuyer at Fort Pitt on June 24, 1763. Although Trent probably had more animosity to the other attendee. Phillip Phillips (who joined interpreters John Butler[69] and Andrew Montour) was the half-Indian, half-Dutch interpreter who, with a small party of French in the spring of 1753, attacked Trent's hired hands near a place called Kentucky.[70]

So, after formalities were announced and condolences were offered to the Six Nations, Johnson went right down to business on October 26th. Holding up a wampum belt of the convent chain fifteen rows wide with human figures at each end, he told them this represented the union of friendship between the English and the Six Nations. Then, he wished to discuss the boundaries, which he wanted to show them by laying forth a map of the region. Over the next five nights and after much deliberation, whether privately amongst themselves or with Sir William, on November 1st, they returned with the most agreeable answer. For those waiting earnestly and in anticipation, they listened as "the greatest number of Indians that ever met any Treaty in America."[71] agreed "to begin a Deed of Cession to the King, but also drafted a copy to the Indian traders, who suffered by the Robbery of the Shawnese and Delawares in 1763."[72]

As the only acting attorney for these men who comprised the suffering traders of 1763, Trent received the copy of this first deed signed and sealed by those in attendance on November 3, 1768. The deed titled "An account of the grant from the Six United Nations to the sufferers of 1763 November 2, 1768" not only listed Trent as the sole party merchant for the sufferers of 1763 (being nominated and appointed as their lawful attorney and agent) but also described the newly revised boundaries at the Six Nations cession of land. The tract, later called "Indiana," was bounded by the Ohio River on the west, the Little

---

67. Daniel Claus (September 13, 1727–November 9, 1787) married Ann "Nancy" Johnson Weisenberg, the daughter of Sir William Johnson and Catherine Weisenberg.
68. Guy Johnson (1740–March 5, 1788) was an Irish military officer and was the son of either John or Warren Johnson, both younger brothers of Sir William.
69. John Butler (1728–1796) fought in the French and Indian War at Fort Ticonderoga under General James Abercromby and under John Bradstreet at Fort Frontenac in 1758. In 1759, he fought under Sir William at the Battle of Fort Niagara and then in 1760 under General Jeffrey Amherst at Montreal. He lived on twenty-six thousand acres called "Buttersbury" in New York.
70. Darlington, Christopher Gist Journals, 192–93. P.R.O. CO5 1065/5.
71. BF Papers, Samuel Wharton to Benjamin Franklin, December 2, 1768.
72. Ibid.

A Monumental Presence 265

The aerial photograph showing the full outline of Fort Stanwix in Rome, New York, and the path through the sally port the Natives took to receive their boatloads of presents in the fall of 1768. (Courtesy of Public Domain.)

Kanawha River on the south, the Laurel mountains, and the Monongahela River on the east and the southern boundary of Pennsylvania as extended to the Ohio River in the north. This cession covered approximately three and a half million acres equal in value to the 1763 trading losses that amounted to over eight-six thousand pounds or, by today's standards, almost fifteen and a half million dollars. The deed copy Trent held proudly in his possession was described by the Six Nations as an "Act of Justice"[73] for those who suffered at their hands or others. Later, in 1776, these sufferers were known as the "Indiana Company."[74]

Two days later, after the Indian sachems and warriors wished to receive their payment for the cession of land and cash "as the speediest payment which was agreed to,"[75] Johnson displayed the goods he promised them from the beginning on the parade ground of the fort. It was an impressive sight for Wharton (and most certainly Trent) the presents that arrived by over twenty boats and "consisted of the greatest Quantity of Indian Goods and Dollars"[76] Wharton or Trent ever saw.

Thousands of Indian warriors entered through the main gate to the parade ground, surrounded by goods on three sides, with Sir William and all the provincial commissioners standing around the newly drafted King's deed that lay upon a table with a goose quill and a standish of fresh ink. With those standing on the ramparts to see over the grounds and witness the signing between the

---
73. Ibid.
74. The company was not called or referred to as the "Indiana Company" until after Trent returned home from London in 1775.
75. Documents Relative to the Colonial History of New York, Vol. 8, 133.
76. BF Papers, Samuel Wharton to Benjamin Franklin, December 2, 1768.

commissioners and the chiefs of the present nations, Trent was among them finishing up his minutes of a historic treaty on November 5, 1768.

This deed of cession was the "conditional sale"[77] of the land to the King (as Wharton described later), but Trent's copy of the deed still needed to be recorded officially in either the capital of Pennsylvania or Virginia. When Trent reached Philadelphia on December 1st, he excitedly wrote to John Baynton his news of the large tract they all received from the Six Nations Cession. Now was not the time to be indifferent towards those agreeably indebted to the industry.

"The tract which I got from the Six Nations is the most valuable one," Trent wrote, "I shall write you with all the Openness and Candour of a Friend in this Matter, & Therefore I must and do expect the same from you."[78]

Despite rumored opposition from a group of familiar Virginians (and relations from the former members of the Ohio Company), like Colonel Washington and the Lee family, Trent and suffering traders of 1763 were so close.

With the deed of cession recorded in Philadelphia by William Parr, Trent and Wharton began the necessary preparations to embark for London. To solidify and execute this monumental grant, one last step was needed. As lobbyists now for "Indiana," Trent and Wharton needed only the final stroke of His Majesty's hand.

---

77. Ibid.
78. Bailey, 198.

Chapter 15

A New Colony

"Well accommodated indeed," Trent probably thought as the Bristol flying machine[1] shifted him tightly against the "genteel" glass of the coach. Like the advertisement for Captain Seymour Hood's ship, the *Betsy*[2] he previously took passage on, the travel on land now was anything but well accommodated for him.

The original newspaper ad for buying passage aboard the Betsy in Philadelphia to England. This appeared in the March 23, 1769, edition of the Pennsylvania Gazette. *(Author photo.)*

In fact, the first leg of the journey across the dark Atlantic Ocean was, as he described, "A very disagreeable passage"[3] the moment he left Thomas Clifford's wharf in Philadelphia. So much so the rough waters and wind forced the *Betsy*, all one hundred and twenty tons[4] of her, to seek port along the rugged western

---

1. A "flying machine" was the newly improved coach for those who could afford passage and look out its expensive windows called "genteel glass." It was lighter in weight, much faster and could travel from Bristol to London in two days.
2. *Pennsylvania Gazette*, March 30, 1769.
3. HSP, Cadwalader Family Papers, William Trent to George Croghan, June 10, 1769.
4. *Pennsylvania Gazette*, March 30, 1769.

coastline of Ireland. A week later, when the waters of the Celtic Sea calmed, they sailed finally to their destination, the English seaport of Bristol, England and arrived on May 25, 1769.[5]

Now he and three other passengers bounced around inside the "flying machine," the latest (and costly) coach that boasted to swiftly get to London along the Great Road in two days from Bristol. Yet it wasn't the rigorous travel that made him uneasy. Trent was risking everything by coming to London. With creditors once again breathing down his neck in Pennsylvania, he mortgaged his house and properties in Carlisle to George Croghan and Joseph Morris Jr.[6] Then he moved his wife, five children and indentured servant to New Jersey temporarily, until he returned with the grant royally approved. Trent also persuaded his mother, who in her advanced age[7] was still living by herself in Philadelphia and whom he also wished safe from bill collectors who might know of her residence in the city. As he helped them move into Trenton in the parsonage house that Sarah had paid the rent[8] previously, he entrusted his wife to handle any business matters he was unable to sign off on. In case he couldn't, he left his black trunk with ledgers and bundles of papers[9] in her care.

Five months. It was the time length he promised her and his uncle William Morris he was to be gone. It was also how long he estimated his expenses might last. While he arranged a trust for Sarah for twenty-five pounds a month[10] during the time he was away, he still needed expenses once he arrived there. So, after much deliberation (and influencing) with George Croghan and now Royal Governor of New Jersey William Franklin, he invested in some land on Croghan's Otsego Tract[11] with shareholders from Burlington, New Jersey. By joining the Burlington Company,[12] Trent had their support and their deep pockets in London.

Right before he set sail from Philadelphia, Trent agreed and signed an agreement to receive £500 in cash and another five hundred pounds by letters of credit.[13] Governor Franklin not only signed this agreement but suggested places for room and board during his stay in London. Governor Franklin had so much

---

5. HSP, Cadwalader Family Papers, William Trent to George Croghan, June 10, 1769.
6. HSP, Lamberton Scot-Irish Collection, Vol. 1, 92. Schaumann, 51 and 168.
7. His mother Mary Trent was about seventy-six years of age in 1769.
8. Hall, 315.
9. Bailey, 357.
10. HSP, Wharton Family Papers, William Trent to William Morris, May 24, 1771.
11. Trent's purchase of land in the Otsego Patent was along the south side of the Mohawk River in Albany County, New York.
12. The Burlington Company was a short-lived enterprise (1768–1770) comprised of eight investors that lived in and around Burlington, New Jersey. Shareholders included George Croghan, William Trent, Royal Governor of New Jersey William Franklin, and merchant William Cooper, father of author James Fenimore Cooper.
13. Bailey, 205–210.

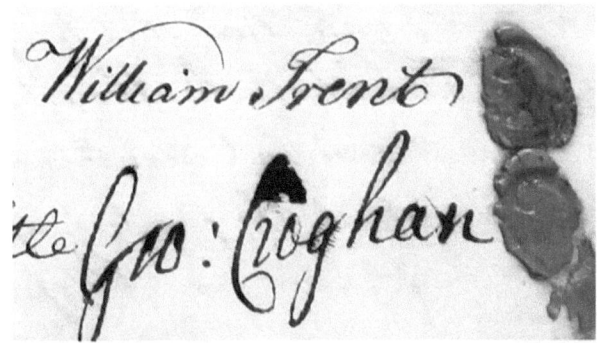

This is Trent and Croghan's signatures (circa January 1769) after joining the Burlington Company previously in 1768. Note this is the only time Trent used a business trademark in a wax seal, when he and Croghan used the silhouette of George III, which was the signature seal of the Burlington Company from 1768–1770. (Author photo.)

confidence in Trent receiving the royal approval for their grant he couldn't hide his optimism, writing from Burlington to his father on May 11, 1769:

> Captain Trent met with some unexpected Delays, but I suppose is by this time arrived in England. I hear that Sir William has a letter from Lord H mentioning that His Majesty entirely approves of all the transactions of the Treaty, so that I imagine Capt. Trent will meet with no Difficulty in his Application.[14]

A delay was an understatement. He lost over a week in Ireland, and it was not until the afternoon of May 27th did the coach pass Hyde Park[15], and he spied on the opposite side of the road, Buckingham House[16], across Green Park. Buckingham House was now called the "Queen's House" because it was the residence of Queen Charlotte after King George III complained that St. James Palace was not suitable for him and his new bride in 1762. The house, like the rest of Westminster, was drastically different since he roamed the streets as a young, ambitious merchant looking to make connections over twenty years before. Lamp posts adorned either side of Cockspur Street[17] now, the whale oil

---

14. BF Papers, William Franklin to Benjamin Franklin, May 11, 1769.
15. Hyde Park was originally created by King Henry VIII in 1536 for hunting. In the eighteenth century, it was the first road in London to be lit up to deter highwayman and a popular spot for duels. Today it's the largest of eight Royal Parks in Westminster, located between Kensington Palace in the west and Buckingham Palace on the right.
16. Originally a townhouse built for John Sheffield, 1st Duke of Buckingham, before being enlarged in the nineteenth century and becoming Buckingham Palace. Buckingham Palace sits today in the Royal Park of Green Park as it was named after 1746 when it was previously known as the Upper St. James's Park.
17. Borsay, 135.

"Charing Cross, with the Statue of King Charles I and Northumberland House" by artist Joseph Nickolls (circa 1750). This was what Trent saw when he arrived in Charing Cross in May of 1769. (Courtesy of the Yale Center for British Art and Public Domain.)

inside them ready to illuminate the side alleys of a once murky street at night. Trent felt the driver slow the coach, and the Bristol flying machine finally came to a halt. The door opened, and he could see the statue of Charles I demi-suited in armor atop a horse facing the street of Whitehall.

Trent was in the center of London called Charing Cross[18] and a short walk from his destination. Walking down the bustling street the Strand,[19] he turned right onto Craven Street, walked to the door marked #27,[20] and used the knocker. (Today, the townhouse is number 36). This was the boarding house of Margaret Stevenson and the residence of her chief renter, Dr. Benjamin Franklin. Here, Trent was received in the parlor by Franklin and joined by his lobbyist counterpart, Samuel Wharton. Wharton, who rented nearby in St. James Square, was most alleviated when Trent had arrived because, without the articles and minutes from the Treaty of Stanwix, Trent had in his possession as

---

18. A junction in Westminster, where six routes in the city intersect and was perceived as the center of London. A bronze equestrian statue of Charles I stands where a medieval monumental cross once stood since 1294 and was destroyed by Oliver Cromwell.

19. A major thoroughfare or road of central London and runs along the north side of the River Thames. Its name comes from the Old English "strand" that means "the edge of the river."

20. According to the Westminster Rate Books, Margaret Stevenson's residence was listed at No. 27 Craven Street. It was eventually renumbered to No. 36 after 1772 when ten houses were built at the southern end of Craven Street and is still numbered that today.

The present location of Franklin's Craven Street house now found at 36 Craven Street just off the Strand in London. (Author photo.)

power of attorney, the petition to ratify the grant had no ground. In fact, by the time Trent was able to leave Philadelphia, Wharton, who had been in London since February, wrote to George Croghan with much concern: "Captain Trent's unpardonably delaying to embark with me has been of great detriment otherwise we might have got the Business in some Forwardness."[21]

However, now, with his arrival, they could begin by utilizing the services of Henry Dagge,[22] their company attorney, who most likely solicited their petition before the Privy Council. Unfortunately, according to Wharton, concerns had already been raised even before Trent had arrived. The Board of Trade and

---

21. HSP, Cadwalader Family Papers, Samuel Wharton to George Croghan, April 3, 1769.
22. Henry Dagge, a London attorney became the trusted solicitor of their petitions sent before the King during the time of Trent's stay in London. He also published "Consideration on Criminal Law" in 1772 that was the quintessential guide of the time period on criminal law.

Plantations, a committee of the Privy Council, began questioning the proposed borders described in the 1768 grants, and if this invoked another Indian war, it was not something the mother country could afford to provoke. The Board of Trade led by their President and Secretary of State for the Colonies, Wills Hill, also known as the Earl of Hillsborough or Lord Hillsborough,[23] seemed to be their biggest opposition to ratifying their proposed grant.

Despite receiving the necessary papers, Lord Hillsborough had written to William Johnson and the Six Nations disapproving the proposed boundaries of the grant and, as Wharton described, "as ministerial intimidation."[24] towards those on the receiving end at Johnson Hall. Yet even with Trent and Wharton's persistent optimism towards this ratification, Parliament had not addressed any new business until after King George III's birthday, which fell on June 4th.[25]

In the meantime, Trent settled into his lodgings at the house of the Cranage brothers Thomas and George,[26] close to the River Thames and Hungerford Market on nearby Villiers Street.[27] The coal merchant house was only a few alleyways from Craven Court and the house of Margaret Stevenson and Doctor Franklin. He also began to purchase clothes, which he remarked was "the great expense" but he knew was necessary when strolling amongst London society and "waiting on those in public office and other great men whom Mr. Wharton has formed a surprising connection in order to carry our Business through."[28]

Trent was most impressed with Wharton's sudden reputation amongst men of the highest court. For every bit of gossip about Parliament members, Wharton heard it, which was good news for him and Franklin. Even until the King's birthday, Trent had barely seen his counterpart except as he described it, "Only early in the Morning when I called his lodgings, as he is visiting for Eleven o'clock till three o'clock and dines out every day with some of the Nobility, Members of Parliament &c."[29] This "living in a proper style" prompted Trent rather amusingly. It seemed to comment on the attire of Wharton, whose taste and fashion had risen since their first meeting in person at the Indian Queen in Philadelphia. "You would love to see him dressed," Trent wrote, "As he has not the least sign of a Quaker about him and wears his sword and with much ease as

---

23. Wills Hill, 1st Marquis of Downshire (May 30, 1718–October 7, 1793) was once known as the 2nd Viscount Hillsborough or Lord Hillsborough in 1742 until he was the Earl of Hillsborough in the Peerage of Ireland. From 1768 to 1772, Hillsborough was the Secretary of State for the Colonies and the President of the Board of Trade until he retired.
24. HSP, Cadwalader Family Papers, Samuel Wharton to George Croghan, May 28, 1769.
25. In the Old-Style Julian Calendar, he was born on May 24, 1738. But after 1752, Great Britain adopted the Georgian calendar, and it was then celebrated on June 4th annually. Trent referred to it as the "Birth Day."
26. Thomas and George Cranage were London coal merchants who worked in the ironworking industry. In 1766, they had patented their idea and new method to make wrought iron or bar iron from pig iron using a reverberatory furnace. The Cranage method was considered an important beginning of puddling in ironworking.
27. HSP, Cadwalader Family Papers, William Trent to George Croghan, June 13, 1769.
28. Ibid., August 10, 1769.
29. Ibid., June 10, 1769.

Present-day site of Villiers Street in London where Trent stayed a short time with coal merchants Thomas and George Cranage near the end of this street along the River Thames. (Author photo.)

if he had always done it."[30] Wharton and Franklin then visited the Court of St. James in their "finest silks" for the King's birthday while it was presumed Trent put his superior penmanship to the test by drafting several copies of petitions until it was suitable for solicitor Dagge to present before the Privy Council.

For the first week or two, he constantly drafted the words well into the night until his eyes hurt and the candle burned down to the wick bottom. In his opinion, the sooner the Indian grants were ratified, the sooner he could pay off his debts and return home.

It seemed he and Wharton weren't the only ones working into the early hours of the night. According to Trent, Dr. Franklin was "at the request of the House of Commons forming some Pipes & to keep a proper Degree of warmth allways in the House in winter, and is fixing wires, on St Paul's, the Royal Exchange &c."[31] Franklin's reputation for inventions from America preceded him because before the summer ended, he installed in the House of Commons along the Old Palace Yard with the similar heat insulation of his Franklin Stove prototype. As for the Cathedral of St. Paul's and the Royal Exchange, iron-cast lightning conductors were placed atop their roofs to prevent potential fires. Today, one such 1769 iron rod by Franklin survives and is on display at the Science Museum in London.

Finally, a week after the King's birthday, the men received their answer from their Privy Council. Dining with Franklin, Dagge, Wharton, and others, Trent found his petition on behalf of the Indian grantees was denied. Lord Hillsborough refused to budge on his discrepancy over the suggested boundaries for their proposed grant, and this news landed a vicious blow to not only their plan but also cut deep into the heart of Trent's confidence and ego. Apparently, his initial rejection was a moment of clarity for him after leaving everything behind across the water:

> I'm thoroughly convinced that all the Time Labor and Expense we have been at is Wholly last and both Mr. Wharton & myself are plunged into inevitable ruin and what is more distressing we have involved our Wives Friends and Children in it and reduced our families to Penury & Want.[32]

Once again, he let his blind ambition cloud his judgment of the situation, and now the guilt of leaving his family poured out of him like a gaping

---

30. Ibid.
31. Ibid.
32. Bailey, 230.

The dome of St. Paul's Cathedral was rebuilt by architect Christopher Wren after the Great Fire of 1666 and completed in 1710. Trent mentioned it in one of his letters written in June of 1769 that Dr. Franklin placed several lightning rods upon the top of the dome and the House of Commons in Parliament. The cathedral still survives today in London along Ludgate Hill. (Author photo.)

wound. Sarah, his poor wife, was virtually abandoned on her side of the water. Currently, she was reduced to much smaller confines of a Trenton parsonage house with meager payments to take care of their five children and his elderly mother while his larger plantation near Carlisle sat in solace.

He was right to move them; however, creditors in Pennsylvania like Joseph Simon or David Franks[33] knew already of his business in London, and once

---

33. Back in February 28, 1762, Trent gave to David Franks and Joseph Simon a mortgage for the 7,500 acres of land he owed in Cumberland County, Pennsylvania. He also owed Simon a separate account on a bond close to eight hundred pounds.

word got out of their rejection by the Privy Council, it forced those men to attack his character and what he loved the most. At one point, Trent felt they might even come to Carlisle to repossess his extravagant furnishings[34] and horses at his Middleton Township plantation if they weren't paid in full soon. He couldn't let that happen, so while he and his counterparts re-strategized in London, Trent pleaded with Croghan and Sir William to "make use of all your weight & Influence and turn your whole thoughts, immediately to the perfecting the Indian Grants."[35]

After less than three weeks in London, Trent was already desperate to do whatever was necessary to influence the Privy Council to ratify the grant. Calling himself "forever a Beggar,"[36] his written array of dramatics was on full display in another letter to Croghan:

> Just before We parted, you assured me That if my objections were started on this side the Water and that if it should Even be found necessary, that you would bring over 2 from each of the Six Nations or that you would do anything else that might be thought necessary to accomplish this unjust Affair & bring it to a happy conclusion.[37]

Clearly frustrated, Trent left Croghan and Johnson to hold up their end and convince Lord Hillsborough the land grant was a good investment for the Crown and the Six Nations. "I can write you no more," Trent concluded, "As you know Every Thing and that my fate is dependent on you and Sir William. Pray let Mr. Wharton & myself hear from you & have Sir Wm's Resolution as soon as possible, For we shall not have one Moments Rest Until we do."[38]

On either side of the water, both groups soon held up their end of the bargain. Three days later, a new plan was devised by Samuel Wharton along with MP and banker Thomas Walpole.[39] Walpole, a nephew of former Prime Minister Sir Robert Walpole and cousin to writer Horace Walpole, developed with Wharton "The idea of organizing a large land scheme with both England and American members for the purpose of speculating in American land."[40] By doing so, the enterprise was beneficial to both parties. The Englishmen (most

---

34. HSP, Cadwalader Family Papers, William Trent to George Croghan, August 10, 1769.
35. Bailey, 231.
36. HSP, Cadwalader Family Papers, William Trent to George Croghan, June 11, 1769.
37. Bailey, 231.
38. HSP, Cadwalader Family Papers, William Trent to George Croghan, June 11, 1769.
39. Thomas Walpole (October 6, 1727–March 1803) was MP for Sudbury 1754–1761, MP for Ashburton from 1761–1768 and MP 1768–1784 for Lynn. He also was Director of the East India Company from 1753–1754 and partnered in a booking firm from Robert Ellison in 1766 in London.
40. Lewis, 86.

of political influence like Walpole) had the opportunity to snag a profit with shares in the business, while men like Trent and Wharton got their grant ratified by the British Crown.

For the influential English shareholders, the organization had Lord President of the Privy Council Granville Leveson Gower (also known as Lord Gower), Secretary of State for the Northern Department (and eventually Southern Department) Lord Rockford, former Prime Minister George Grenville, Lord Chamberlain of the household Lord Hertford, Lord Camden, MP Thomas Pownall, Secretary for the Board of Trade John Pownall, Secretary for the Post Office Anthony Todd, and others. They joined those from the other side of the water from America: Samuel Wharton, William Trent, Benjamin Franklin, Joseph Galloway,[41] George Croghan, and others.[42] Together, the group was known as the Grand Ohio Company, and the executive committee consisting of chairman Benjamin Franklin, Thomas Walpole, Samuel Wharton, and banker John Sargent,[43] submitted their new petition to purchase the £10,460 for the 2,400,000 acres before the King by July 24, 1769 (the date it was read before the Privy Council).[44]

Though his name was not amongst the lobbyists comprising the executive committee, Trent left the main spotlight and shifted his duties to where he was valued more than any man in London. While they awaited the response from Lord Hillsborough, Trent acted as secretary for the Grand Ohio Company, keeping receipts and bills and drafting copies of letters for Wharton and others. Usually, he made six copies of one document and a dozen of another, day and night, until his eyes hurt.

Surprisingly, on December 20, 1769,[45] Lord Hillsborough was somewhat receptive to the new petition and hinted that they apply for an even bigger amount of land (more than twenty million acres, in fact), one that could lead to the formation of a new colony. This was the best news Trent had heard since arriving in London. So, a week later, the chairman of the Grand Ohio Company, Franklin, called a meeting for the shareholders near his townhouse on the Strand to discuss this latest development. The meeting was held secretly

---

41. Joseph Galloway (1731–August 29, 1803) first served on the Pennsylvania Provincial Council from 1756–1774, where for eight of them he was Speaker of the Assembly. In 1774, he represented the Pennsylvania delegates of the First Continental Congress and suggested to form a plan of union with Great Britain. When Congress did not adopt this plan, Galloway quit the Assembly and remained loyal to the King.
42. Lewis, 88.
43. John Sargent (1715–September 20, 1791) was originally a draper or storekeeper of cloth and dry goods and served as the Director of the Bank of England from 1753–1767.
44. Plain Facts (1781) by Samuel Wharton, Appendix 1, 149. Lewis, 90.
45. Lewis, 90–91.

Present-day site of the former Crown & Anchor Tavern which once stood at the corner of Arundel Street and the Strand. St. Clement Danes church still survives opposite the Strand in the background. (Author photo.)

at the Crown and Anchor Tavern,[46] a public house at the corner of the Strand and Arundel Street, right across from the baroque-style church St. Clement Danes. The large tavern had rooms to accommodate over two thousand five hundred people, so it was no wonder it was popular among political meetings.

Sixteen shareholders,[47] including Trent, attended this meeting as he took down the meeting minutes. On their agenda was the motion to expand shares in the Grand Ohio Company since now Wharton and Walpole wished to enlarge the original cession of land signed by Trent based on the "suggestion" by Lord Hillsborough. The current members unanimously accepted the motion after it was decided they purchased now about twenty million acres within the cession of land from Fort Stanwix. Also included in this grant was the land petition by Croghan and the land originally petitioned by the suffering traders since both fell within the proposed boundaries. The executive committee also voted to have

---

46. The Crown and Anchor Tavern was a public house built just before 1710 just off the Strand along Arundel Street. The famous composer George Frideric Handel premiered his first oratorio "Ester" there in 1732. It was notorious for meetings of political nature such as the Grand Ohio Company and later radical groups in the nineteenth century. It no longer stands today.

47. Bailey, 283.

Eighteenth century print depicting St. Clement Danes church on the left side of the Strand and the Crown & Anchor Tavern on the bottom right corner, a wooden sign displaying a crown and an anchor hangs above the entrance. (Courtesy of Public Domain.)

the company organized into seventy-two shares, having each member contributing two hundred pounds for each share. Thomas Walpole held eight shares, Wharton held five, and Trent held four.[48] Each of the remaining members who either held shares currently or purchased them later held one or two shares.

Before the meeting adjourned, it was decided they presented the revised petition before the treasury commissioners on January 4, 1770, including amongst this new petition the proposal for quit-rents of two shillings per every hundred acres of cultivated land after twenty years.[49] This quit-rent inclusion was meant to blockade any rival petitions that were submitted that might inhibit theirs.

By the spring of 1770, two such rival petitions emerged after word traveled across the water to Virginia of the Walpole Grant and its impediment to Virginia expansion. The first came from the Mississippi Company, whose members included Adam Stephen, several members of the Lee family, John Augustine Washington,[50] George Washington, and others. They were repre-

---

48. Lewis, 92.
49. Ibid., 92–93.
50. John Augustine Washington (January 13, 1736–January 8, 1787) was a Virginia planter and younger brother of George Washington. He resided at "Bushfield," a plantation located along Nomini Creek and the Potomac River about ninety-one miles southeast of Mount Vernon. His son Bushrod inherited Mount Vernon after Martha Washington's death in 1802.

sented by Arthur Lee, youngest son of the late Thomas Lee, who had been admitted to the Lincoln's Inn on March 1, 1770.[51] Their proposal was also to establish a new colony by petitioning the British Crown for two and a half million acres (some that overlapped the Walpole Grant) and what was later known as present-day Illinois, Kentucky, and Tennessee. Their other main rival to the Walpole Grant was a petition that rather hit home for Trent. This petition came on behalf of the bounty land claims from those soldiers under Robert Dinwiddie's Proclamation of 1754 (which Trent's men did not receive being first raised volunteers) and Trent's former employer, the Ohio Company who were still seeking a renewal of their grant from 1749. Ironically, the lone lobbyist for them was Trent's good friend George Mercer, who had been living on Holles Street near Cavendish Square[52] in the Marylebone district since he fled Virginia after the Stamp Act rioting.

With the Board of Trade considering this, Wharton and Walpole steered their attention in defeating their chief competition. Surprisingly, the tactic worked without much fighting. George Mercer, realizing he had no help from Virginia or other members of the Ohio Company, could not challenge the large Walpole Grant, and he withdrew his petition on May 7, 1770.[53] After failed attempts to receive the Ohio Company's claim and seeing his friend Trent's newest venture, Mercer signed articles of agreement on this same day to merge the Ohio Company into the Grand Ohio Company. The merger left the Ohio Company with two shares and Mercer with one while also including the two hundred thousand acres for those soldiers who still needed their bounty claims.

As for the Mississippi Company, their fate was sealed when the Privy Council rejected their petition before even hearing it. This also was the reason Mississippi Company member George Washington prompted a ride into the Ohio Country in October of 1770 to peruse those western lands. With his current venture being on the verge of complete failure, he feared the eventual approval of the Walpole Grant "If obtained will in my humble opinion, give a fatal blow to the interest of this Country."[54]

For Trent and the Grand Ohio Company, with their recent defeat of all conflicting claims and opposition from the colonies, all they had to do was wait for Lord Hillsborough and the Board of Trade to come forward and accept the petition. When Hillsborough's purposeful procrastination reached almost late summer without any definitive answer, none was more frustrated than Trent,

---

51. Middle Temple Register of Admissions, 377.
52. GMP, Mulkearn, 325.
53. Lewis, 98.
54. Library of Congress, Papers of George Washington, George Washington to Lord Botetourt, October 5, 1770.

"Wills Hill, the Earl of Hillsborough later 1st Marques of Downshire" by artist Pompeo Batoni (circa 1766). (Courtesy of the National Trust (U.K.) and Public Domain.)

who thought of his wife. This delay had left her in such a financial predicament, since his visit to London prolonged past a year instead of the five months he assured her was the maximum time he might be gone. These last few months, he had been pressed for cash but had more revenue once he convinced others to buy shares in the Grand Ohio Company.

As for Sarah, Trent approached the situation to keep his wife in the loop very cautiously. Their business in London was not to be discussed outside of the current members until finalized completely. When he did send a letter, it was only to Croghan, who at this time was conducting business for his land in New York with Sir William at Johnson Hall. But even then, he made sure to remind him not to show any of the letters to anyone, not even people from the Burlington Company like Governor Franklin. Until this grant was ratified, he could not have his creditors in Pennsylvania, (or in Governors Franklin's case) New Jersey, knowing his business or coming for his family in Trenton. He did, however, remind Croghan to check on his family when passing through Trenton via postscript: "I have not wrote Mrs. Trent if you get this at Philadelphia pray send that I am well."[55]

While months went by as Trent and the others sat idle in London, waiting for word from the Privy Council on the status of a new colony, he found himself once again worrying about her and their children in another letter to Croghan:

> I am almost distracted when I think of my poor Wife as I do not know how she is off her Money, I most earnestly intreat of you to fall on some Method to get her some as I cannot possibly conceive poor woman what she can do without you.[56]

By this time in 1771, he risked writing to Samuel Wharton's brother Thomas in Philadelphia and entrusted him to seek his uncle William Morris for them to enclose twenty-five pounds each in support of his wife. His uncle received the notice of this sum on May 24, 1771.[57]

As much as he wanted to write directly to his wife, it was a very precarious situation, and he couldn't risk anyone outside certain individuals knowing the whereabouts of his family while an ocean stood between them. So, for now, Sarah just received any news secondhand from him if the correspondence reached the trusted recipients. He and the rest of the members knew how dangerous it was to send letters directly through the post office in the city. With the Secretary to the London Post Office, Anthony Todd, being a shareholder now, it was no secret that any correspondence destined for the colonies was being intercepted and read. Which meant any letters found to not be in the best interest of the British Crown could be interpreted as treasonous. Trent's fear reached borderline paranoia, and even when he previously dined with Todd, Franklin, and Wharton on Friday, April 5, 1771, he chose his words carefully while indulging on salted fish and brandy.[58]

---

55. HSP, Cadwalader Family Papers, William Trent to George Croghan, December 5, 1769.
56. Ibid., September 1, 1770.
57. HSP, Wharton Family Papers, William Trent to William Morris, May 24, 1771.
58. BF Papers, Anthony Todd note dated April 5, 1771.

A picture of the original ground floor parlor at Dr. Franklin's Craven Street house in London where he entertained frequent visitors such as Trent, Wharton, and others. (Author photo.)

So, if Trent wanted to send any letters out now (at least to Croghan or Thomas Wharton with updates on the grant or his family), he did so by bribing the ship captains that ran the packet ships back and forth across the water. Trent eventually trusted his letters on the ships owned by merchant John Weatherhead,[59] whose packet sailed to New York harbor and was sent by horseback to Philadelphia or Johnson Hall. From there in the city, Croghan, Wharton, or Morris (when available) stopped by Trenton to update Mrs. Trent about her husband in London.

Unfortunately, this sum of fifty pounds delivered by his uncle William had been the first amount of any assistance that she had received since her husband

---

59. HSP, Cadwalader Family Papers, William Trent to George Croghan, March 7, 1770.

Present-day site of the former New Suffolk Street in London now called Nassau Street. Trent lived here briefly in the upper end at house No. 16 as did Dr. Franklin's son William in the final years of his life. (Author photo.)

left. Obviously, Croghan had been unable to send her any money or even make her aware of her husband's well-being or whereabouts. In fact, by this time, Trent had already moved from Villiers Street to the No. 16 house on New Suffolk Street (today known as Nassau Street)[60] with Wharton too at Argyle Street now only a few blocks away.

According to Sarah, though highly appreciative of the recent financial support, the fifty pounds already spent to satisfy "several small debts which I now am under a necessity to pay off."[61] She, of course, voiced her despair in his absence by telling Thomas Wharton, "Sir, I had five children to provide for; I have Received no money these fourteen months but what you Sent me."[62] Wharton

---
60. Ibid., September 1, 1770.
61. HSP, Wharton Family Papers, Sarah Trent to Thomas Wharton, September 9, 1771.
62. Ibid.

eventually sent her an additional fifty pounds from Philadelphia, which she received on December 28, 1771.[63]

At this point, the frustration for Wharton and Trent was boiling over. Lord Hillsborough seemed to be the only minister opposed to their grant, and now they were agreeing with Franklin that the only way this colony was ratified was if Hillsborough was no longer in office. Since the latter seemed unlikely, how long could both wait for the Privy Council to act? Wharton had already declared back in July that he wished to have ratification and sail home no later than November or December, but that deadline came and went. Trent, who must have also hinted at their business being completed by Christmas of 1771, wished for the same since his uncle William Morris expected his arrival in five or six weeks after the new year.[64]

After it was clear this was not going to happen, the frustration soon became resentment. In a letter to their newly shared acquaintance Sir Matthew Fetherstonhaugh, Wharton compared this business awaiting on the Privy Council as "the prays in of holding a candle to the Devil."[65] Fetherstonhaugh, a current MP for the borough of Portsmouth, had dined with both men when he frequently visited his townhouse on Whitehall called the "Dover House."[66] Sir Matthew and his wife Sarah (called Lady Fetherstonhaugh) enjoyed the company of both men, with Wharton writing him frequently from the city to Fetherstonhaugh's lavish estate called "Uppark."[67] Wharton always finished his letters by mentioning best regards or "compliments of the season"[68] to Sir Matthew and Lady Fetherstonhaugh from the "Major" referring to Trent. Fetherstonhaugh was a man of great influence in the city and, like Walpole, had expressed great interest with deep pockets.

So, in the early months of 1772, the prospect of the Walpole petition influenced Fetherstonhaugh enough to begin supporting them financially with the idea of purchasing a share in the company soon after it was ratified. Trent, knowing that all important memorialists, including himself, needed

---

63. Ibid., Thomas Wharton to Sarah Trent, December 28, 1771.
64. HSP, Cadwalader Family Papers, William Morris to Thomas Wharton, December 31, 1771.
65. British Library, MS 575, Grand Ohio Company Papers.
66. The Dover House was located on the site of the former Whitehall palace property that was mostly destroyed by a fire in 1698. Sir Matthew Fetherstonhaugh bought the lease of the property located near the "Cockpit" and commissioned architect James Paine to build his townhouse. Today the house still stands and is presently located at 70 Whitehall in the office for the Secretary of the State for Scotland.
67. Built around 1690, the house built atop the South Downs in West Sussex was originally the home of Ford Grey, the first Earl of Tankerville. It was sold to Sir Matthew Fetherstonhaugh and his wife Sarah in 1747 fir nineteen thousand pounds and had spent sixteen thousand six hundred and fifteen pounds on interior alterations like a mezzanine floor, tapestries, and several paintings by artist Pompeo Batoni. Despite a fire in 1989, Uppark still stands today with most of its original furnishings.
68. British Library, MS 575, Grand Ohio Company Papers, Samuel Wharton to Sir Matthew Fetherstonhaugh, December 22, 1773.

Uppark House (circa 1690) that was originally built for Ford Grey, the Lord of Tankerville but sold to Sir Matthew Fetherstonhaugh in 1747. Today the house is in South Harting, England in the district of West Sussex. (Courtesy of Public Domain.)

to eventually appear when summoned before the court to convince the Privy Council, realized he needed to purchase proper court attire. Though he had remarked rather amusingly at the fashion of Wharton and Franklin when he first arrived in London, ironically, it was this similar attire he needed to impress the members of the Cabinet and Privy Council. Trent needed a gentleman's court suit, a specific three-piece ensemble of a coat or jacket, waistcoat, and breeches. Originally, he could have had it made in France, but with the laws limiting any importation of foreign silks and the tight patrolling of smugglers, this was out of the question. Besides, Trent didn't have the time for it to be made and sent across the English Channel anyway.

So, instead, he left his lodgings along New Suffolk Street and the Middlesex Hospital[69] for the East End of London and the district known as Spitalfields.[70] This lowly reputed district was home to the silk weavers from Lyons, France, all of whom were Huguenot refugees who fled persecution from their homeland and established a booming fashion industry amongst the aristocrats. Their

---

69. Originally opened as the Middlesex Infirmary on Windmill Street in 1745 but later moved to Mortimer Street in 1757 where it remined until its closure in 2005. The present site lies in Fitzrovia district of London in Middlesex County between Nassau (formerly New Suffolk Street where Trent stayed briefly) and Cleveland Street along Mortimer.

70. Spitalfields was the center of the silk weaving industry during the eighteenth century. Most silk weavers were Huguenots, French protestant refugees who settled in the district by 1685. Today this area found within the East End of London and north of the Tower of London.

rococo style workmanship was the best in London, weaving floral patterns for suits and dresses for gentlemen and ladies alike, and this reputation was why Trent came there to have a suit designed and paneled for the tailors in Westminster.

When he arrived, Spitalfields, as of late, looked nothing like the place where his former master's sister Anne Shippen Willing once designed her elegant dress for her portrait in 1746.[71] Currently, Spitalfields's side streets off Brick Lane, like Fournier and Princelet, were no place for the upper class. Foot regiments have been ordered to stand guard, as well as daily patrols by the Bow Street Runners[72] to control the lawlessness and riotous violence that roamed in the East End. For almost seven years, weaver mobs rioted against low wages and long hours, even storming the Palace of St. James when he first arrived in the summer of 1769. This protest didn't end well, with two of the leaders being executed by hanging not too far away opposite the Salmon and Ball Pub on Bethnal Green[73] about a week before they all first met at the Crown and Anchor.

So, for the silk court suit, he spared no expense, having it designed in the spirit of the late silk designer Anna Marie Garthwaite[74] and her botanical brocades.[75] His underlying waistcoat was even more extravagant, a cream-colored silk with thirteen buttons covered in silver and blue metallic threads. Along the buttonholes and on the side pocket flaps were silk threads wrapped in silver foil and blue threads, warped and woofed to exuberate the beautiful blue flower stitchings.[76] Once the panels were sent to the tailor, they fit snugly around his six-foot-plus frame as they prepared to defend their petition before the committees of the Privy Council in 1772.

That spring, Lord Hillsborough, already openly defiant against their proposed colony, produced another opposing claim by the Council of Virginia on March 20, 1772.[77] This came as no surprise since it was apparent Hillsborough was making every effort to block their petition. Supposedly, this new Virginia

---

71. The Ann Shippen Willing portrait was an oil painting done by artist Robert Feke and is currently owned by the Winterthur Museum in Winterthur, Delaware. Her Spitalfields silk dress was made by silk weaver Simon Julins.

72. The "Bow Street Runners" were law enforcement officers of the Bow Street Magistrate's Court located near Covent Garden. Referred to as London's first police force, they were formed by renown author of "Tom Jones" and magistrate Henry Fielding in 1749.

73. John Doyle and John Valine were executed by hanging on December 6, 1769, in front of the Salmon and Ball Pub along Bethnal Green. Today it is found about three miles northeast of Charing Cross, opposite Victoria Park and along the south shoreline of the Regent's Council.

74. Anna Marie Garthwaite (March 14, 1688–October 1763) was an English textile designer on 2 Princelet Street renown for creating vivid floral designs for silk fabrics woven in the Spitalfields District of London. Many of her watercolor designs (over eight hundred fifty designs from the 1720s to the 1750s) still survive today and are found at the Victoria and Albert Museum in London.

75. Botanical brocades were decorative colored silks using brightly colored threads and specifically in this case, designs or floral patterns modeled after a botanical garden.

76. This description is found in the original paperwork of the 1719 William Trent House Museum in Trenton, New Jersey when the vest was taken for assessment at the Winterthur Museum on September 28, 1978.

77. Sosin, 201.

Present site of Fournier Street in Spitalfields, where Trent sought the expertise of the Huguenot silk weavers to design his court suit. (Author photo.)

opposition that emerged came from Council President William Nelson[78], along with support from new Royal Governor Lord Dunmore[79] and Commander-in-Chief Thomas Gage, who were all against the proposed colony. This all came a week before Trent and the others of the Grand Ohio Company were told to appear before the Commissioners of Trade on March 27, 1772,[80] to present any additional papers to their petition. Despite this last-minute development,

---

78. William Nelson (1711–November 19, 1772) was a Virginia planter who lived at the Nelson house built by his father Thomas "Scotch Town" Nelson, located in Yorktown, Virginia. Nelson served as governor of virginia from 1770–1771.

79. John Murray (1730–February 25, 1809) was the eldest son of William Murray, 3rd Earl of Dunmore. On September 25, 1771, he became Royal Governor of Virginia and began directing campaigns to attack the Shawnee who he thought posed threats to the Ohio country. In 1774 this conflict became known as Lord Dunmore's War. During the American Revolution, he was known for Lord Dunmore's offer of Emancipation which offered freedom to any slaves who left their Patriot masters and fought for the British. He continued to draw pay as Virginia's governor until 1783 when Great Britain officially recognized America's independence.

80. Sosin, 202.

A New Colony

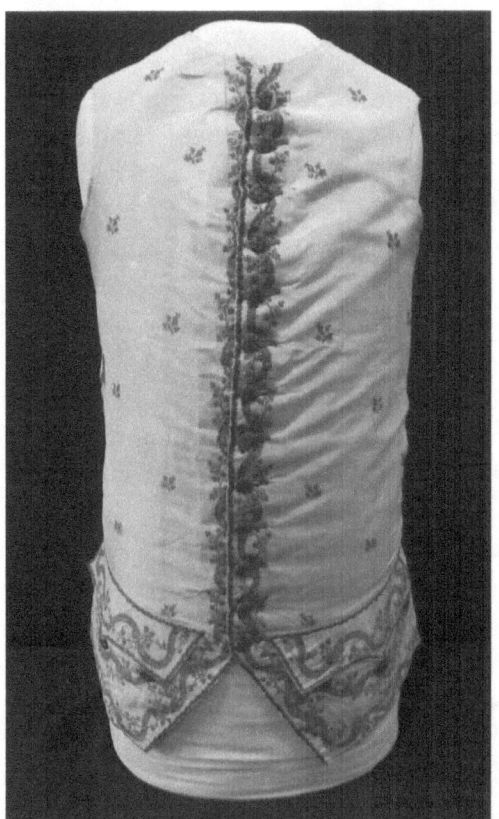

Major Trent's cream-colored silk court waistcoat with thirteen buttons is on display at the 1719 William Trent House Museum in Trenton, New Jersey.

This is a closeup of the side pocket of Trent's silk court waistcoat. It features botanical brocades, the stitching of silky blue threads wrapped in silver foil to form bright blue flowers. (Author photo.)

the Grand Ohio Company memorialists were confident their plan was solid and, therefore, as a group, decided to abstain from attending this meeting since nothing more was needed to be submitted to solicitor Dagge.

This decision taken by Trent and the others outraged Hillsborough, and he officially tried to conspire with other ministers to oppose and reject their petition before the report was submitted officially to the entire Privy Council. However, with two Secretaries of the Treasury, Thomas Bradshaw and Grey Cooper, and President of the Privy Council Lord Gower already shareholders of the Grand Ohio Company, this plot backfired and proverbially backed Lord Hillsborough into a corner he was not able to escape from.

Lord Gower eventually allowed evidence to support the Walpole petition, and the shareholders spent the next two months discussing the response or rebuttal for the Virginia claim. Even though Trent and the others discussed this as a group, the main authors of these "Observation and Remarks"[81] were Dr. Franklin, Thomas Walpole, and Samuel Wharton. Trent kept the minutes and outlined the suggested points for their proposed colony, but the finalized version was in Franklin and Wharton's hands.

So, on June 24, 1772, it was quite a spectacle when several coaches passed the equestrian statue of Charles I at Charing Cross and came down the road of Whitehall, where Trent and the most important memorialists stepped out in their finest silks and pasted shoe buckles. They walked up the narrow passage (site of 70 Whitehall today) to the octagonal structure and one of the last surviving buildings of the Whitehall Palace known as "the Cockpit." Built on the outskirts of St. James Park, the former house of entertainment (for cockfighting and theatrical plays) for King Henry VIII was now home to the various committees of the Privy Council and judicial purposes under the new Palace of St. James. Most letters by Trent or Wharton simply referred to it as the "Court of St. James,"[82] and it was here the gentlemen presented evidence to help promote their colony establishment in the Western country.

When the Committee for Plantation Affairs inquired about settlers currently within the boundaries of their proposed colony and the easiest route of transportation, Trent was the first to stand and address those present. He told them that between 1765 and 1767, by his estimate, no more than five thousand

---

81. The "Observation and Remarks" was a large pamphlet fully titled "Report of the Lords Commissioners for Trade and Plantations on the Petition of the Honorable Thomas Walpole, Benjamin Franklin, John Sargent, and Samuel Wharton, Esquires and their Associates for A Grant of Lands on the River Ohio in North America foir the purpose of Erecting a new Government" and printed in Piccadilly in 1772 by John Almon.

82. The present-day site of "the Cockpit" where Trent and the others presented their petition is 70 Whitehall in London. It is now the Cabinet Office, connecting to the Treasury buildings and adjacent to Downing Street where the Prime Minister resides.

families[83] had settled on the Monongahela River and were not subject to any laws. Which, in his opinion, was all more for a colony to be ratified so laws could be set in place to govern them, Trent probably pointed out.

His friend George Mercer further corroborated the evidence by also mentioning how far each capital of the neighboring provinces was to govern them. Williamsburg, Virginia, was over four hundred miles from Fort Pitt, aka Pittsburgh, and Philadelphia, over three hundred miles away.[84] Their point was that if the colony was approved, a new capital and center of government should be in the heart of their colony, and no place fit more geographically than Pittsburgh.

When the committee expressed doubt about the means of transportation toward establishing commerce with those settlers and Indian nations at this suggested capital in the Western country, the executive members allowed Trent and Mercer to argue their viewpoints once again. There were no two men in the room, or London for that matter, who knew the Western country better than Trent or Mercer. Both being former employees (or a member in Mercer's case) for the Ohio Company, they declared that if the wagons left near the former warehouse opposite Fort Cumberland (which goods sailed to Alexandria then up the Potomac to Fort Cumberland), a mere forty miles separated them from the mouth of Redstone Creek where the previous old road was around seventy miles.[85] From there, they could transport the goods by boats the remaining thirty-seven miles down the Monongahela to Pittsburgh. This new road to Redstone Creek was also cost-effective (saving them five shillings nine pence in carriage expenses)[86] , they declared to the committee, and more importantly, the shareholders in front of them could lead those supply wagons to Pittsburgh since they both knew it better than anyone. When this concluded Trent's part of the evidence in the Western country, Wharton spent the next few hours remarking on each objection made by Lord Hillsborough until the meeting ended, and the petitioners anxiously waited to hear the committee's decision.

After a week went by, the men returned to "the Cockpit" on July 1, 1772, and received the answer they had been finally hoping for. The Committee of Plantation Affairs had been thoroughly convinced by those men presenting on behalf of the Grand Ohio Company and, therefore, sent their approval of the petition for their new colony for the final process by the Privy Council.

---

83. Sosin, 203.
84. Ibid., 204.
85. Observation and Remarks, 71.
86. Ibid.

This announcement immediately spread across London. The very next day, on July 2, 1772, news of their approved petition appeared in the *Oxford Journal*:

> A Privy Council was held yesterday at the Cockpit, when the petition of the Honorable Thomas Walpole, Samuel Wharton, Esquires, and others, for a grant of a tract of country for a new Colony on the Banks of the Ohio and North America, was again taken into consideration, finally reported upon, in favor of the Petitioners.[87]

This news also sent shockwaves through Lord Hillsborough. Ultimately, his plan to block petitioners from America had self-destructed. Now, for whatever reason, he still refused to approve the grant and by refusing to do so, began internal fighting amongst those Lords in the Privy Council. When he realized the council was now going to approve this colony with or without his support, it left him with only one choice. On August 13, 1772, Lord Hillsborough resigned his positions as President of the Board of Trade and Secretary of State for the Colonies[88], and they named Prime Minister Lord North's half-brother, William Legge, the Second Earl of Dartmouth[89], as his successor. Ironically, a day after the resignation of Hillsborough, the Privy Council decisively gave their approval to the Walpole Grant and new colony on August 14, 1772.[90]

Finally, after all the deliberation (over three years, in fact) since Trent first arrived in England, the group had inescapably succeeded in what they were trying to accomplish. Rev. William Hannah[91], who went with Trent and the others that day, best described their victory in a letter to Sir William Johnson dated July 20, 1772: "This is looked upon here as the most extraordinary matter; And what no American ever so accomplished before."[92]

Yet the Grand Ohio Company members did not allow themselves to become idle. Almost immediately, Wharton and the others began to prepare and propose legislature for this new government and colony they named "Pittsylvania"[93] after former Prime Minister William Pitt the Elder. Trent wrote

---

87. *Oxford Journal*, July 4, 1772.
88. Sosin, 205.
89. William Legge (June 20, 1731–July 15, 1801) was the son of Viscount Lewisham and became the Viscount or 2nd Earl of Dartmouth or Lord Dartmouth as he was commonly referred to in 1732. He served as Secretary of State for the Colonies after Lord Hillsborough resigned on August 13, 1772, until 1775. He is also the namesake for today's prestigious college Dartmouth College, established in Hanover, New Hampshire in 1769.
90. Lewis, 120.
91. William Hannah (1738–1785) was born in Litchfield, Connecticut and was the first minister of Albany Presbyterian Church that stood along Beaver Street between Hudson and Grand streets in Albany, New York. He was an acquaintance of Sir William Johnson who suggested he become an Anglican minister, and he served the Anglican Church in Virginia and Maryland until his death in 1785.
92. Documentary History of the State of New York, Vol. 4, 297.
93. Sosin, 207. Lewis, 121.

EARL of DARTMOUTH.

Print of William Legge, 2nd Earl of Dartmouth (circa 1777). (Courtesy of the Miriam and Ira D. Wallach Division of Art, Prints and Photographs of the New York Public Library.)

copious letters every morning and evening, either updating his former partner Croghan or making copies of documents for the officers at Fort Pitt of their new colony.

Unfortunately, it was the same "feverish" ambition and the infrequency of packet ships that prevented Trent from receiving any news of his family from New Jersey over the next few months. Sadly, and unbeknownst to him, his mother, Mary Coddington Trent, passed away at an advanced age of seventy-nine in Trenton on December 15, 1772.[94] She was listed in the death registry of St. Michael's Church, and presumably meant she was placed next to her late husband, Judge Trent, in the Hopewell Churchyard,[95] Trenton's original burial ground before St. Michael's was built.

So, while he and the others hoped for Lord Dartmouth's charter for "Pittsylvania," Trent began planning to hopefully sail in the spring once the deal was done and they had favorable winds. In the meantime, the winter almost in full splendor, a hearty Trent hoped to sit back and for once marvel at London's grandeur during the holiday season.

The present site of the Hopewell Church burial ground, formerly Breese Farm and now on the grounds of the Trenton Psychiatric Hospital. It is believed that Judge Trent and his second wife Mary Coddington Trent are buried inside the brick wall structure. (Courtesy of Public Domain.)

---

94. In the archival records of St. Michael's Church, it lists in the registry, the death and burial of Mary Trent on December 15, 1772. Although they list her age at eighty-three years, this is incorrect because the Rhode Island Vital records kept by the Friends Meeting House of Newport list her birthdate as January 15, 1692/93 (or January 26, 1693, on the "New Style" or Gregorian Calendar) making her seventy-nine years old when she died.

95. According to Schuyler's "History of St. Michael's Church," burials were still common there at Hopewell Church burial yard at this time since St. Michael's Church member Samuel Tucker was buried there as late as 1789. This also supported the theory she may have wanted to be laid to rest next to her husband Judge William Trent who was believed to be interred there after he died on Christmas Day in 1724. As was mentioned earlier, the unmarked burial yard today is found on the property of Trenton Psychiatric Hospital.

Chapter 16

Restlessness and Mutiny

It was the middle of the day, and even with the bright sun beaming through the window, Trent struggled to read the note in his hands:

> Three months after Date, I promise to pay to William Trent Esqre. On order Three thousand pounds for Value received accts witness my Hand.
> Matthw. Fetherstonhaugh.[1]

Either way, he should have been overjoyed. With their petition being approved by the Privy Council, this was only the beginning. Now, the gates of interest had been opened, and each day, "genteels" or men of high reputation began trying to purchase a share in the Grand Ohio Company. First, it was Franklin's physician friend Edward Bancroft[2] who purchased a share and joined their elite circle. Next came their friend Sir Matthew Fetherstonhaugh, whose note he held in his hands, but Trent remembered it wasn't until he and Wharton met with him last fall did he finally "buy" into their grant. It was also when he realized something was wrong with his eyes.

Back in October of 1772, Sir Matthew and his wife Sarah wished to entertain them at their country estate of "Uppark" in West Sussex.[3] After graciously

---

1. British Library, MS 575, Grand Ohio Company Papers, March 25, 1773.
2. Edward Bancroft (January 20, 1745–September 7, 1821) was born in Westfield, Massachusetts. On July 14, 1763, he became a plantation doctor in the colony of Dutch Guiana or Suriname in South America. While there he studied torpedo fish and electric eels and in 1766 published an essay in London in 1769 titled, "An Essay on the Natural History of Guiana in South America." Later in 1777, he served under Dr. Benjamin Franklin as secretary to the American Commission in Paris, copying letters between America and France with his former schoolmaster Silas Deane.
3. "Uppark" is located in the village of South Harting, in the county of West Sussex. It is over sixty miles southwest of London.

"Sarah Lethieullier, Lady Fetherstonhaugh (1722-1788) with the branch of a Pear" by artist Pompeo Batoni. (Courtesy of the National Trust (U.K.) and Public Domain.)

"Sir Matthew Fetherstonhaugh (1714-1774), 1st Baronet, MP, with Wreaths of Fruit and Corn" by artist Pompeo Batoni. (Courtesy of the National Trust (U.K.) and Public Domain.)

accepting, it was there he and Wharton walked through the saloon across the mezzanine floor and admired the exquisite artwork he collected. Sir Matthew and Sarah had gone on a "Grand Tour" in 1752 throughout Europe and after visiting Italy, purchased several pieces of artwork to decorate the walls of Uppark. This included commissioning the artist Pompeo Batoni[4] to paint their likenesses, beautiful full-size portraits that still hung in the saloon. The only problem was Trent had issues seeing its vibrant colors. It was like his vision was distorted, and all objects in his sight were in a proverbial fog.

After they returned to Lippock[5] under the horses lent from Sir Matthew's extravagant stable and took a coach to London, Trent shared his secret with Wharton. It was decided then that after drafting volumes for their grant and recording receipts, accounts and ledgers, morning, noon, and night, it was time for him to rest the strain and stress on his eyes. But as the month went by, his eyesight had not improved. In fact, while trying to write on paper or read only

---

4. Pompeo Batoni (January 25, 1708–Frebruary 4, 1787) was a renown Italian painter who during the period of "Grand Tours," specialized in painting portraits of those in nobility, royalty, and even several popes like Benedict XIV and Clement XIII while residing in Rome, Italy. Batoni is still considered one of the most celebrated Italian painters of the eighteenth century.

5. Lippock or Liphook (as it is known as today), was a large village in Hampshire County and a major coach stop for those traveling from London to the seaport of Portsmouth.

a document, it had presumably gotten worse with only being able to see out of one eye.

So, in February of 1773, as he discussed accommodations to return home the next month as soon as they received the official charter, Trent came to terms with his questionable eyesight for those who wished to know his well-being. He also told Wharton, as he wrote to Croghan, to mention it openly. Wharton wrote in this letter dated February 4, 1773, that "Happy Americans? The Major was almost blind."[6]

On a positive note, while waiting on the official report from the King, talk began for the candidacy of a new governor for their colony. Wharton, whose influence amongst London's elite was unlike any who came from the other side of the water, seemed to be the most likely choice. In the same letter, he wrote Croghan about Trent's blindness. He also wished Croghan to inquire about the status of the governor's house at Fort Pitt and if it had been destroyed. Wharton planned to either reconstruct the previous governor's house at their proposed new capital or finance construction for two of the "best houses in Pittsburgh"[7] for his own use on the banks of the Monongahela and the Ohio Rivers. In fact, he was so confident in his possible governorship that he attached detailed blueprints of his two houses at the end of the letter with the promise to send seeds[8] from London to have a large kitchen garden beside these mansions.

Yet not all "Americans were happy," as Wharton described it. Croghan had unfortunately shown a few of Trent's correspondence to several at Fort Pitt who had then allowed Wharton's former disgruntled partner George Morgan to view them. Morgan, who had already threatened both Wharton and Trent for the exclusion of him and his father-in-law John Baynton[9] from the new Grand Ohio Company and proposed colony, became even angrier. "If you fly your country and escape to the Banks of the Ohio," Morgan wrote back on November 2, 1772, "For there I will pursue you."[10] Thankfully, a large body of water separated both Wharton and Trent from his idle threats, so for now, they could ignore his insults.

Besides, Trent had another problem on this side of the water involving his friend George Mercer. Like himself and Wharton, Mercer was in dire financial strain. The merger with the Grand Ohio Company and the lack of financial support from his former Ohio Company members in Virginia left him

---

6. HSP, Cadwalader Family Papers, Samuel Wharton to George Croghan, February 3, 1773.
7. Ibid.
8. HSP, Cadwalader Family Papers, Samuel Wharton to George Croghan, February 3, 1773.
9. George Morgan was married to Mary Baynton, daughter of John Baynton.
10. Pennsylvania State Archives, Baynton, Wharton, and Morgan Letter Books 1763–1775, George Morgan to Samuel Wharton, November 2, 1772.

in desperation to cover all living expenses. He had already petitioned the King for compensation for his military service from the French and Indian War, but rumors were rampant now that Mercer's insurmountable debts had plunged him into a debtor's prison called Marshalsea[11] that very spring of 1773.

> My Ruin dear Major is at length compleated- ten Minutes after I called on you to Day I was arrested on Account of that Thick Husband; and as I have no Probability of a Release, I presume all my other Affairs will be hurried in a upon- and God only knows what will be my exit.[12]

Trent promised to do what he could for Mercer in London while he got his brother James Mercer and Col. Washington to mortgage his lands in Virginia to cover the debts. For the time being, Mercer seemed to sulk in what he believed was a hopeless situation.

> Pray give our mutual good friend Wharton my best Wishes- in the utmost Anguish of my Soul I cannot forget his & your Friendship- Perhaps we may meet once more, and I enjoy full Liberty- Heavens- what I cannot write more- my Heart is so full- it overflows- God bless & protect you both from the dismal scene I see at present.[13]

This "dismal" scene saw some light, however, on May 6th, 1773, when the report of their grant was finally submitted to the King from the Lords of Trade. Almost two weeks later, the King approved the stipulated conditions and sent it to the Privy Council on May 19, 1773, for finalization. Not only were all prior claims honored within the boundaries of the grant, but included too was the 200,000 acres for the previous officers of Virginia (like George Mercer) who were promised land by former Lieutenant Governor Robert Dinwiddie on February 19, 1754. The purchase price also remained the same at 10,460 pounds sterling with a quick rent of two shillings for every one hundred acres of land leased, planted, or settled.

There were some minor changes to the new colony, however. The plan for government was a governor and the council appointed by the King like other royal colonies like Virginia or New Jersey. A court of justices was to be set up,

---

11. Marshalsea was a notorious prison just south of the River Thames in the Southwark District. Over half the population of England's prisoners during the eighteenth century were incarcerated because of debts. It was also used later in several of works by Charles Dickens such as "The Pickwick Papers," "David Copperfield," and "Little Dorrit." Today the site is found along Angel Place, just off the A3 below London Bridge.
12. Bailey, 359.
13. Ibid., 360.

along with the Church of England to be established in it. Now, for Wharton, this posed a problem since his devout Quakerism did not allow him to be an elected governor in partnership with the Bishop of London. It could also be why, despite being imprisoned, George Mercer was rumored to be the new governor as well. According to the *Virginia Gazette*: "Lord Dartmouth has nominated George Mercer Esquire, to be Governor of the new Colony on the Ohio which should be called Pittsylvania."[14]

Two months later, Mercer wrote to George William Fairfax, "I am not yet Governor, and a fresh objection, the best I hope they have to offer, has arisen against the policy of the grant, so far it is to relate to Britain."[15]

Despite the rumor mill churning in America, only the gentleman behind the scenes in London knew what was going on. By the time the King passed the report on to Solicitor General Alexander Wedderburn and Attorney General Edward Thurlow on July 3 to draft up the necessary papers for the charter, the name of the new colony had since changed from "Pittsylvania" to now "Vandalia." This, of course, was to gain more royal support by honoring the colony after Queen Charlotte, who, according to those at Buckingham House, "is descended from the Vandals,"[16] a Germanic tribe that inhabited southwestern Europe and northern Africa.

Now if there were any objections by these two royal officials, Trent did not hear of it until almost the end of the month. During the intolerable heat that breached the city, Trent had been confined to his new lodgings along Norton Street[17], fighting off a severe cold that unfortunately unleashed a "sudden relapse of his fever."[18] It was the second time Trent had been stricken with malaria, but this time, he was able to receive proper medicines to treat it. Unlike previously, in 1749, when he was not able to receive some, Trent began taking Peruvian bark to hopefully make a full recovery. The relapse, it seemed (and his blindness in one eye), was a direct side effect of his little treatment (or lack of) the first time. On July 31, Wharton updated their friend Sir Matthew that "the Major has fully recovered."[19]

It was also at this time he heard from Wharton that both Wedderburn and Thurlow had actually a few objections to the report on Vandalia they received. They both disputed the boundaries again and what were the specific

---

14. *Virginia Gazette*, September 23, 1773.
15. Rowland, 157, George Mercer to George Fairfax, December 2, 1773.
16. *Pennsylvania Gazette*, May 27, 1773. HSP, Wharton family Papers, Thomas Wharton to Samuel Wharton, June 18, 1773.
17. Norton Street today is called Bolsover Street in the parish of St. Marylebone in London's West End. HSP, Simon Gratz Collection, William Trent Will April 14, 1775. See also Appendix J of this book.
18. British Library, MS 575, Samuel Wharton to Sir Matthew Fetherstonhaugh, July 31, 1773.
19. Ibid.

"Charlotte of Mecklenburg-Strelitz (1744–1818)" by artist Allan Ramsay in 1762. (Courtesy of the Royal Collection (U.K.) and Public Domain.)

dimensions. Simply put, the description in their report by the Lords of Trade still seemed uncertain as it pertained to acreage or square mileage. Plus, they raised concerns about the potential collection of quit-rents and the issue of joint-tenancy.[20] If joint tenancy were issued without subgrants, then according to both officials, it was almost impossible even to collect the revenue of the quit rents,[21] let alone keep them secure to collect.

Meanwhile, trouble brewed again in America as once again Croghan had failed to be discreet with his letter from Trent. George Morgan, who seemed to become their formidable enemy, expressed his anger again at discovering Trent's

---
20. Sosin, 208.
21. Lewis, 130.

Present-day site of the former Norton Street in London where Trent stayed briefly until he departed for the American colonies in April of 1775. Today the street is now called Bolsover Street. (Author photo.)

real opinion of preferring Wharton over him or his father-in-law. On August 7, 1773, he lambasted Trent to Croghan: "Don't you think that if I have sufficient Spirit to ring Capt. Trent's Nose for writing this & such like to you I shall serve the Rascal as he deserves? I most ardently long for the Opportunity."[22]

Trent wisely chose not to be baited by Morgan and a week later, discussed their current agenda amongst the committee in pleasing both Wedderburn and Thurlow by delineating the boundaries of Vandalia and a solution for the quitrents. For those of the Grand Ohio Company like Trent, this was but one final obstacle before the grant became a reality. They all had risked too much and

---

22. Ibid., 134. Pennsylvania State Archives, Baynton, Wharton, and Morgan Letter Books 1763–1775, George Morgan to George Croghan, August 7, 1773.

came too far to be derailed now. Two of the more prominent members had even gone so far as to honor their residences after their future colony. Thomas Walpole began calling his rural Carshalton estate in Surrey the "Vandal house,"[23] while Sir Matthew began building a gothic tower to commemorate the colony's future establishment and naming it "Vandalia Tower."[24] Unfortunately, both faltered after the fate of the Vandalia colony was sealed with the outbreak of the American Revolution, with Walpole selling off Carshalton to pay off financial woes in 1785 and the Fetherstonhaugh family abandoning the tower after it became known as a "folly."

So, by the fall of 1773, member Lord Rochford, on behalf of the Grand Ohio Company (and Lord Dartmouth, who also agreed), brought forth a map drawn up with the Board of Trade to show their boundaries of Vandalia clearly. Together with the Archbishop of Canterbury and MP Richard Rigby on October 28, they told Wedderburn and Thurlow to draft the charter[25] and finally put this grant business to rest. It proved to make no difference. At this point, the incessant delay by both royal officials was now as deliberate as Hillsborough's previous attempts to halt their grant. The problem was, the more their grant sat idle here in the city with no great seal, the more problems it was making for them in America.

Croghan had since gathered the Indian nations in the Western country since the summer and by now wished to know when the shipment of presents was sent to him at Pittsburgh, along with the presence of future governor-elect Wharton. He had been forced to accommodate them since they heard the news of Vandalia in May with no support from Joseph Galloway or Governor Franklin, so he wished Wharton to help him out that November. Wharton and Trent could understand his frustration. Like Croghan, they had experienced intolerable suffering both financially and physically. Trent had made plans to sail back in March and Wharton in May or June, but when this "hasty scrawl"[26] by the "cursed attorney"[27] left still without the great seal in November, Wharton assured him the promise of a handsome present after the holidays. For now, all he could muster was a meager one hundred and fifty pounds to have Croghan reassure the Indian nations.

This delay also caused stress on Wharton's health. Wharton battled gout throughout the fall months and found his condition worsening when he slipped stepping into a coach and bruised his right leg and shin bone. "I am quite a

---

23. British Library, MS 575, Samuel Wharton to Sir Matthew Fetherstonhaugh, August 14, 1773.
24. Ibid. The ruins today of the "Vandalia Tower" are still visible on the Uppark property in South Harting.
25. Sosin, 209.
26. HSP, Cadwalader Family Papers, Samuel Wharton to George Croghan, November 3, 1773.
27. British Library, MS 575, Samuel Wharton to Sir Matthew Fetherstonhaugh, September 21, 1773.

Cripple," he remarked while also in postscript telling Sir Matthew about Trent saying, "He is invulnerable and as hearty as Ever, you know him."[28] This "indisposition" of his gout attacks left Wharton confined to his lodgings and, along with Trent's relapse of another undisclosed illness[29] in December, left the lobbyists with advancing their plan until after the rise of Parliament and after the new year. Their fate to receive "magnum sigillum"[30] for their colony was left in the hands of their attorneys, Richard Jackson and Henry Dagge[31], once the holidays were over.

Unfortunately, even more problems arose in America that threatened to doom their grant. With the newly enacted Tea Act by Parliament, tea ships were set to arrive that fall in Philadelphia and Boston to undercut the price of smuggling Dutch tea to the colonies. However, like the tax imposed on stamp distribution, protests and rioting broke out in these major seaports. The city of Boston had especially been recognized more than the Quaker capital when the Sons of Liberty, disguised themselves in Indian dress, destroyed and dumped three hundred and forty-two crates of tea[32] into Boston Harbor.

Thomas Wharton warned his brother Samuel that once Parliament or the Privy Council received news of the "tea parties" in both cities, the King would respond harshly toward the colonies and receiving the charter was almost impossible. Though, it was even worse for the Vandalia proprietors like Wharton and Trent. Just a little after the new year, alarming news arrived from Croghan. One of the recent Virginia leaders in the Vandalia opposition had begun to act on his own authority. Governor of Virginia Lord Dunmore had suggested a militia to be mustered and ordered them to seize the now abandoned Fort Pitt under the banner of Virginia. Even more shockingly, the commander of this Virginia militia company was none other than John Connolly,[33] nephew of Croghan, who immediately began carrying out Dunmore's plans to seize the Western country before Vandalia proprietors laid claim. He even renamed Fort Pitt as Fort Dunmore.

Dr. Franklin had warned Trent and Wharton over a year ago about the claims of Virginia, but this showed some pompous audacity. The only problem they faced currently was that Franklin was caught up in his own web of deceit with the attorney general and was of no service to them now. On January 29, 1774, Franklin was forced to appear in "the Cockpit" before the Privy Council

---

28. Ibid., November 13, 1773.
29. Ibid., December 22, 1773.
30. The Great Seal of England.
31. HSP, Cadwalader Family Papers, Samuel Wharton to George Croghan, December 22, 1773.
32. *Boston Gazette*, December 20, 1773.
33. Library of Congress, George Washington Papers, Vol. 2. November 22, 1770.

to answer for the publication of letters written by Andrew Oliver and Thomas Hutchinson, the colonial secretary and governor of Massachusetts, respectively. The letters had reached Franklin's hands in being the agent for them in London, but only a few among the Massachusetts Assembly were to see them. The result ended in them being leaked and published in the *Boston Gazette* in the June issue of 1773,[34] outraging Massachusetts politicians and London officials alike.

Franklin himself admitted to "transmission" and acquiring of the letters, so he faced ridicule and berating by the Attorney General Wedderburn who was the one person that stood blocking their way to establishing Vandalia. Discussing Franklin's "thievery and dishonor" and the mention of the "Boston Tea Party," Franklin was dismissed as Postmaster General while calls were made publicly for the removal of Thomas Hutchinson as governor. Hutchinson eventually sailed for London in May of 1774. This disheartening news seemed to pound nails into the coffin of the new colony of Vandalia and put Trent's world into a downward spiral. In March of 1774, he and Wharton's most trusted confidant and friend, Sir Matthew Fetherstonhaugh, had not recovered from his ailing illness and passed away at his house in White Hall.[35]

Worse yet, in response to the riots in Boston, the port city was closed under the Coercive Acts (called the Intolerable Acts in America)[36] and asserted more British control over the colonies. Speaking of control, Parliament also proposed the Quebec Act on June 22, 1774, which gave a bill of constitution to Quebec, meaning "all the country southwardly to the western Banks of the Ohio is annexed & made part of the province of Quebec."[37] This meant all land petitions then in the Western country, including their Vandalia colony, were considered void once officially enacted in America.

Trent was now at an impasse. He and Wharton could continue to pursue the lobbying for their colony, which, according to member Anthony Todd, was almost "one-half passed,"[38] but at what cost? It seemed that he was so caught up with the plans of Vandalia he had not written to Croghan to send an update to his wife and children in over a year. Now, if the smuggling of correspondence were risky three years ago, any effort for American correspondence was too dangerous with the recent acts of Parliament and their feelings toward the rebellious behaviors (Franklin's appearance at "the Cockpit" was an example of this) and admittedly treasonous acts in the colonies.

---

34. *Boston Gazette*, June 21, 1775.
35. His Whitehall townhouse was the Dover House.
36. Four acts were enacted by Parliament in 1773 in direct response to the "Boston Tea Party" and were called the Coercive Acts. Feeling the Coercive Acts were a direct violation of their rights, the colonists nicknamed them the "Intolerable Acts."
37. This Quebec Act of 1774 was not effective officially until May 1, 1775.
38. HSP, Wharton Family Papers, Samuel Wharton to George Croghan, March 17, 1774.

Thomas Wharton informed his brother that if Trent didn't find a way to correspond to Mrs. Trent for his long absence, she planned to set off to England by the next vessel[39] leaving Philadelphia to see for herself what he and Wharton were doing these last five years. Once again, his wife was desperate for money, even selling off their indentured servant Christian Redebauch on July 20, 1774, to Trenton ferry owner Elijah Bond for a sum of fifteen pounds.[40]

Though the response letter via Croghan or Wharton has not been found, before Trent finally sailed the following year in 1775, he received even more heartbreaking news from Trenton. His second oldest daughter, Martha, who was about fourteen years old, passed away while he was still in London. The only evidence suggesting her death was the last will and testament he deposed on April 14, 1775, before he left London. It gave no mention of her and only listed the division of his estate from his wife and children into only six shares[41] instead of seven. So, over those last few years, he had lost his mother and a daughter.

These bad signs seem to have little or no effect on Trent's counterpart, Wharton. Despite setback after setback, he assured Croghan to think of how this will all be worth it, "When we may ride, or stroll on the Verdant Banks of Ohio- or perhaps when sipping our Coffee or Tea, as now painful Twinges of the Gout while I fear, hereafter forbid our quassing the genomes Grape."[42]

Wharton also had a bit of luck along with Trent, as goods for the Indian nations at the future capital of Vandalia were finally being sent across the ocean. The invoice listed fifty bales of goods or merchandise[43] in all that was being shipped by Wharton's London friend Fountain Elwin (the former secretary for Governor Tryon)[44] and on the account of Sir Henry Fetherstonhaugh,[45] the son of the late Sir Matthew. The goods were sent on the *Rodger*, captained by James Phillips and were set to arrive in Georgetown, Maryland. This was the former site of one of the first Ohio Company warehouses[46] and seemed to be what the Grand Ohio Company wished to use to store sundries for Vandalia. Once the ship's cargo was cleared through each colony's newly established Committee of Safety, they could transport the goods up the Potomac River (since they

---

39. Lewis, 143.
40. University of Delaware Library, Special Collections, Indenture between Christian Redebauch and William Trent, June 6, 1768.
41. HSP, Simon Gratz Collection, William Trent Will April 14, 1775.
42. HSP, Cadwalader family Papers, Samuel Wharton to George Croghan, May 4, 1774.
43. British Library, MS 575, Grand Ohio Company Papers, June 24, 1774.
44. Ibid.
45. Ibid.
46. The first Ohio Company warehouse was at Rock Creek. It was first disregarded due to the nearly impassable waters of the falls of the Potomac and because the Virginia site at the mouth of Will's Creek (later named the New Store) was more efficient than its Maryland counterpart for transportation.

were past the falls) and land near Trent's former base of operations in Frederick County, Virginia, called the New Store. It was believed by then (since they paid twenty-five pounds, nine shillings for the rental of the Rock Creek warehouse for twelve months)[47] that Trent or Wharton (or both) might transport the goods personally to Pittsburgh.

Of course, this timeline only worked if they received their charter for Vandalia. So, one final attempt was made for Vandalia, as the Grand Ohio Company members sent a memorial on August 8, 1774. Accompanying this memorial was an additional plea by Croghan from the Western country that if the governor of the new colony were delayed any longer, the peace and commerce between the Indian nations and the current settlers might dissolve, and another war could result. (It was a foreshadowing of conflict between Virginia, the Shawnees, with other nations during Lord Dunmore's War).

While they did not hear from the Privy Council officials toward their latest memorial, Wharton and Trent continued to learn about the distress in America. The first of such came from their "frenemy" George Morgan, who once again lashed out at Wharton and Trent. Trent received the brunt of it as Morgan personally called him out, saying: "With regard to that contemptible Wretch Trent, my Treatment of him will depend on your Conduct; for of himself he is not worth giving a Kick in the Breech to, or a Pull by the Nose."[48]

Morgan, clearly still bitter over Trent's failure to ratify for the original suffering traders like Baynton or him, now blamed Trent and Wharton for the recent demise of his father-in-law back in June. According to Morgan, if the debts owed to the Baynton, Wharton, and Morgan firm had been repaid, then John Baynton might still be alive instead of his untimely demise due to their unfair treatment of him.

But in the fall of 1774, there were bigger things on the horizon than threats from Wharton's former partner. For over a month since September 5, 1774, delegates from twelve of the thirteen colonies met at Carpenter's Hall in Philadelphia to discuss the recent "Intolerable" Acts passed by Parliament. This group that formed became known as the First Continental Congress.

There was also word throughout London from Whartons' acquaintances that Lord Dartmouth had reprimanded Lord Dunmore for being "entirely ignorant of the claim of Mr. Walpole and his associates"[49] when he ordered Captain Connolly to seize Fort Pitt in the name of Virginia. What was even

---

47. British Library, MS 575, Grand Ohio Company Papers, June 24, 1774.
48. Lewis, 149. University of Illinois at Urbana-Champaign Library, George Morgan Letter Book 1774–1775, George Morgan to Samuel Wharton, September 1, 1774.
49. Plain Facts: Being an Examination Into the Rights of the Indian Nations (1781), 159.

more troubling was the newly elected Virginia justices of the peace for this region known as the West Augusta District. Two of them were relations to Croghan, with one being his brother (and Trent's former ensign at the Forks of the Ohio in 1754) Edward Ward and his cousin Thomas Smallman.

At this point, Trent was torn with uncertainty at the seams. The concern to stay in London by the early months of 1775 proved to be hopeless to him, especially now since Vandalia eventually fell under the jurisdiction of Quebec with the newly enacted bill. Even still, there had been no change in their colony being approved by the attorney general and the solicitor general, so before Trent left, he and Wharton adjusted their approach to Vandalia. Wharton used his London contacts to help Trent validate the legality of the previous land grants made by the Indian nations at Fort Stanwix in 1768 before he sailed home. Seeking advice from their company attorney Henry Dagge on March 20, 1775, he declared to Trent that:

> Upon the whole I am of opinion, that Mr Trent in his own right and as attorney for the traders, [hath a good, lawful and sufficient title] to the land granted by the said deed and conveyance, subject only the King's sovereignty over the settlements to be established thereon, and over the inhabitants, as English subjects.[50]

This also coincidentally came on the day that Dr. Franklin left London for America. Frustrated over their delays with the Privy Council for their colony and being accosted for his role in the Hutchinson letters affair, he had had enough of the responsive acts of parliament in a city he had called home for sixteen years.

"I suppose we've never had since we were a people so few friends in Britain," Franklin remarked, "The violent destruction of the tea seems to have earlier united all parties here against our province so that the bill now brought into Parliament for shutting up Boston as a Port till Satisfaction is made, meets with no Opposition."[51] He and his grandson "Temple" arrived back in Philadelphia on the night of May 5, 1775. The very next day, he was elevated as a member of the Second Continental Congress that was gathering in the city.

Meanwhile, Trent, having reaffirmed the validation of the land session and his rights as power of attorney for the sufferer's affidavits, called the final committee meeting for the Grand Ohio Company on April 11, 1775. At this meeting, Trent produced two legal opinions, one from John Dagge and the

---

50. Ibid., 100. Lewis, 149.
51. Lewis, 140. BF Papers, Benjamin Franklin to Thomas Cushing, March 22, 1774.

other from John Glynn, "that the title obtained from the Indians needed no validation by the Crown."[52] According to Wharton, "This is also the real opinion of every sound lawyer in Westminster Hall,"[53] and now could quite surely just be approved in Philadelphia after they spent six years away from their home and families to pursue it in London.

On this declaration, the executive committee of Thomas Walpole, John Sargent, and Samuel Wharton then granted power of attorney to Trent as acting agent for Vandalia once it was conveyed to them either in London or to Trent by Congress. He also carried these necessary papers along with several from Margaret Stevenson[54] to convey to Dr. Franklin once he arrived in Philadelphia. This empowerment now enabled him to give any authorization for any laws within the twenty-million-acre boundaries of Vandalia. In other words, Trent was given the task to dispose of and sell any land he could during a time of uncertainty in the Western country between the Crown and the colonies. That and their fear that the Act of Quebec was made soon, which they all knew might "declare all Purchases of the Nations made after the Act by private persons, illegal or void."[55]

Either way, a few days later, he began to put his final affairs in order before his eventual departure. On April 14, 1775, his friend George Mercer, despite his supposed financial ruin, offered a state of indebtedness to transfer £200 once he could finalize Vandalia in America or follow up on the sale of his Virginia lands in Fairfax County.

That very same day, Trent also drafted his last will and testament, the first of three he wrote in the latter half of his life. This one listed him as late of Pennsylvania because, temporarily, he did not own lands in New Jersey. (See also Appendix J for his complete 1775 will). In this will, he divided his estate into six parts, starting with his wife Sarah receiving one part. His youngest and only son, John (a week from his seventh birthday), received two parts in the promise of one hundred and fifty pounds yearly when he turned fifteen. His three other daughters, Sarah, Mary, and Ann, received their one part each as well with a promise of £50 each yearly.[56] Trent also made a declaration (probably in case of any controversy in lieu of his unexpected death) that the woman Sarah Wilkins, his wife, was indeed his wife when he left North America in 1769. He reasoned that the original wedding certificate of their union had been destroyed,[57] and if anything happened to him before he returned to her, she

---

52. BF Papers, Franklin, Thomas Walpole, Samuel Wharton, John Sargent: Power of Attorney to William Trent, April 11, 1775.
53. HSP, Cadwalader Family Papers, Samuel Wharton to George Croghan, April 17, 1775.
54. BF Papers, Margaret Stevenson to Benjamin Franklin, April 24, 1775.
55. HSP, Cadwalader Family Papers, Samuel Wharton to George Croghan, April 17, 1775.
56. HSP, Simon Gratz Collection, William Trent Will April 14, 1775.
57. Ibid.

could benefit from his estates in Pennsylvania and New York without it being disputed. When he finished the four-page will, he signed his name and wax seal, followed by witness signatures of Joseph Wharton Junior (Samuel's younger brother), Grand Ohio Company shareholder Dr. Edward Bancroft, and finally, Philadelphia merchant Henry Elwes.[58]

Soon after, he began his departure by traveling to the customs house along the Thames at the Key of Wool-Wharf[59] in the shadow of the Tower of London (Today just below Lower Thames St. around Tower Hill). There, he bought passage aboard the *Sally* docked nearby and took advantage, no doubt, of the fourteen beds in the ship's cabins.[60] Once aboard the ship, he also observed several passengers from afar that he recognized or crossed paths within the city. There was Lieutenant Patrick Moncrief and Ensign Lundy, both officers in His Majesty's troops whose regiments were stationed now in Quebec, but the last individual made him suspicious. His name was Major Phillip Skene,[61] and he lodged in London at 50 Margaret St., not too far from his lodgings along Norton St.

Skene, who, like Trent, came to London to petition for a new colony but in the Lake Champlain region, was also suspected by Wharton as being there in the city "for a servile and dishonorable Purpose."[62] It had probably had something to do with his title bestowed upon him back on January 28, 1775, by Lord Dartmouth. Major Skene had been appointed Lieutenant Governor of Ticonderoga and Crown Point, and rumors circulated he had the authority to raise a large contingent of His Majesty's troops "to subdue the rebels"[63] near his residence of Skenesborough where he wished to begin a new province.

Skene could also be spying or retaining information on certain persons going to and from England, so Trent had to be careful. Especially since amongst the necessary papers he kept in his coat when he strolled the docks of the ship were the Restraining Acts for Pennsylvania and New Jersey[64] that had yet to reach across the water officially in their respective provinces. This act, when enacted across his home province, was bad for business, limiting the export

---

58. Ibid.
59. Wool was the most productive source of revenue and principal export for England in the medieval period, so a wharf was built along the sandy island like shoreline called a key. Later in the 1380's, a custom house was built upon the wool-wharf, but it was destroyed during the Great Fire of 1666. Today a custom house built around 1814, lies just east upon the site of the original one. This is located along Lower Thames Street in the Tower Street Ward just below the Tower of London. *Kentish Gazette*, April 22–26, 1775.
60. *Kentish Gazette*, April 22–26, 1775.
61. Begor, 39.
62. BF Papers, Samuel Wharton to Benjamin Franklin, April 17, 1775.
63. Hadden's Journal and Orderly Books, 397.
64. This was the British Ministry's response to the boycott of British goods by the New England colonies, only allowing their trade with Great Britain and the British West Indies. Trade with non-British nations was strictly prohibited. After April of 1775, Great Britain learned of colonies Pennsylvania and New Jersey voicing their support for New England, they added them to the Restraining Acts, along with Virginia, Maryland, and South Carolina. It wasn't effective until July 1, 1775, and news of this restriction reached Philadelphia a month earlier with Trent carrying the announcement of this.

or import of any goods by way of Great Britain, Ireland, or the British West Indies. Unfortunately, Trent had to smuggle these documents, as well as others addressed to Dr. Franklin, through essentially the lion's den of British North America in Quebec to make his way back to Philadelphia.

So, the question remained: why did Trent choose to sail on a ship intended for Quebec instead of one that landed closer to his family in New Jersey, like New York? As discussed earlier in the chapter, perhaps Trent wanted to gain Governor Carleton's approval in Quebec before their grant fell under this jurisdiction anyway (the Quebec Act in America was enacted on May 1, 1775). But since his friends, Thomas Walpole and Henry Elwes, wrote to him on May 30th and 31st, 1775[65], expected him to be back home by then and wished him good fortune handling their grants, this was probably unlikely. It seems more feasible, however, that he left England as soon as he could, not wanting to wait several weeks or months before a packet to Philadelphia arrived. It also explained why he wrote his will with haste and sailed out just over a week later from London, hoping to reach America in sufficient time.

So, sailing down the Thames to open water, the *Sally* stopped first at the port cities of Margate and Deal[66], and then after they passed between the white cliffs of Dover and the distant shoreline of France, they arrived finally at Portsmouth on England's southern coast for a brief stop before the long trek across the ocean.

Though Wharton wasn't leaving for America with Trent, it was here he rode a coach to see him off when Trent arrived in Portsmouth. When Trent exited the ship, the port city was abuzz with the regiments of His Majesty marching up and down the streets. In London, talk amongst their counterparts spoke of how regiments in the mother country were being sent to support the King's troops in Boston to control the rioting and violence from its citizens. Now, he was seeing firsthand this was not just gossip.

Several of these professional soldiers were also filling a large magazine of their large six-rate frigate that stood tall in the harbor with twenty-eight guns and twelve half-pound swivels[67] gleaming in the sun. The King's colors flapped atop her heavy mast as three officers stood overseeing the baggage, whom both Wharton and Trent recognized as Viscount William Howe and generals John Burgoyne and Henry Clinton.[68] They were "waiting only for a favorable wind"[69]

---

65. HSP, Frank M. Etting Collection, Thomas Walpole to William Trent, May 30, 1775, and Henry Elwes to William Trent, May 31, 1775.
66. Margate and Deal were the two seaports located on the southeastern coast of England. Margate was located on the farthest point where the North Sea meets the River Thames. Deal was located just south of Margate along the coastline and only about nine miles north of Dover, the main port that offered passage to Calais, France.
67. *Caledonian Mercury*, December 9, 1758.
68. BF papers, Samuel Wharton to Benjamin Franklin, April 17, 1775.
69. Ibid.

"General John Burgoyne (1722–1792)" by artist Joshua Reynolds in 1766. (Courtesy of the Frick Collection in New York City and Public Domain.)

"Sir Henry Clinton (1730–1795)" by artist John Smart. (Courtesy of the National Army Museum in Chelsea and Public Domain.)

"Sir William Howe, 5th Viscount Howe (1729–1814)" by engraver Richard Purcell aka Charles Corbutt in 1777. (Courtesy of the Anne S. K. Brown Military Collection at Brown University in providence, Rhode Island.)

before these three British commanders boarded this ship, ironically named the *Cerberus*, for the three-headed dog in Greek mythology that guarded the entrance to the underworld across the river Styx. Currently, it was being loaded with the military stores of seventy chests of arms, money, and clothing[70] for the British Army in North America.

Nonetheless, with Portsmouth and the *Cerberus* soon behind them, luck was in Trent's favor on this voyage. Due to questionable or contrary easterly winds along the coast of Canada, the *Sally* was forced to veer off course and anchor near the banks of Newfoundland until they calmed down. While docked, an alarming report arrived in the hands of the *Sally*'s master, William Ansell,[71] and to Major Skene. On May 10th and 11th, 1775, militiamen from the New Hampshire grants under Ethan Allen and Benedict Arnold captured both British outposts, Forts Ticonderoga and Crown Point (the same posts that Skene was appointed governor of) and took Skene's son Andrew prisoner.[72]

When Skene asked about his home in nearby Skenesborough, it too had been seized along with his forty-ton schooner he had named after his wife, Katherine.[73] This enraged Skene so much that he demanded loudly (probably in front of Trent and others) to Captain Ansell that "he would March from Canada with five thousand men and recapture the area."[74]

So, instead of sailing toward the Saint Lawrence River, the *Sally* turned southwardly (Skene probably assumed toward Boston to join the thousands of King's troops already stationed there, including the *Cerberus* by now, and kept going. But much to the shock of Skene and his officers, they arrived in Philadelphia on June 7, 1775[75], not Boston. Apparently, Ansell, realizing the importance of his now belligerent passenger, decided to steer the ship where he knew (either by a suggestion from Trent or someone else) Skene and the other's information could be useful. After all, the brig was originally constructed in the Quaker city, and the captain probably knew Congress was meeting there.

When the *Sally* was docked at its wharf, those on board, like Trent, were ordered to remain on the ship until officers arrived to inspect the ship's cargo. It was only a few minutes before Trent saw certain individuals come aboard, but he knew they weren't customs officials. In fact, he might have even recognized

---

70. Begor, 9.
71. *Kentish Gazette*, April 22–26, 1775.
72. Begor, 9.
73. After patriots captured the "Katherine" it was renamed the "Liberty" on May 11, 1775. It was later used to take supplies to and from Ticonderoga and was usually docked near the birthplace of the American Navy at Skenesborough and later Whitehall, New York. Later it was captured and used by the British fleet until it became beyond repair in St. John's Quebec along the Richelieu River.
74. Begor, 38.
75. Library of Congress, Letters of Delegates to Congress 1774–1789, Diary of Robert Treat Paine, Smith, 456.

most of them as a large crowd of citizens gathered behind them on the wharf. The first to question the captain about this "dangerous partisan of administration"[76] who was on board was John Hancock, followed by Silas Deane, John Adams, and Thomas Mifflin.[77]

When the captain pointed Skene and his officers out to the members of the Congressional Committee, he immediately demanded his private papers. Skene denied he carried any but then after further interrogation, admitted he pitched most of them overboard before they anchored in Philadelphia. Unfortunately for Skene, the delegates had been meeting in the Pennsylvania State House for over a month now[78] and were tipped off (possibly by Wharton or a packet ship from London) that he was aboard this ship. So, Skene, Moncrief, and Lundy were arrested and being put under a guard, were sent until further notice along Second Street to the New Tavern. (The New Tavern, just built in 1773 near the former house where Trent once began his apprenticeship, soon became known as City Tavern, where it is a museum today). Eventually, the trio was dispatched to Connecticut under a guard of nineteen men.[79]

Relieved to be finally at his destination, Trent was able to deliver all his papers for Dr. Franklin now, who had been chosen to represent Pennsylvania in the Second Continental Congress. As much as he was glad to return home to see his wife and children after six long years in London, Trent was still worried about what he heard from Franklin as the former printer sat arguing amidst the spirited delegates at the State House last month. News from Wharton in London reported that on May 1, 1775,[80] Vandalia had finally been drafted by both the attorney general and the solicitor general but was not going to be chartered by the King until hostilities ceased in Massachusetts.

Hostilities? Trent probably asked him since he had only just learned of Ticonderoga and Crown Point a week or so ago. Since he was halfway across the Atlantic Ocean when it began, Trent finally learned now of General Gage's attempt this past April to have British troops secretly seize powder stores outside of Boston and arrest the two ringleaders behind this supposed "illegal" assembly of arms and ammunition. When Middlesex County militiamen[81] learned of this, they began forming in Lexington to show resistance. So, when the British couldn't find the powder or Sons of Liberty leaders Sam Adams and John

---

76. Haddon's Journal and Orderly Books, Appendix No. 16, 510.
77. Ibid.
78. The Second Continental Congress had been meeting since May 5, 1775.
79. Haddon's Journal and Orderly Books, Appendix No. 16, 510.
80. Plain Facts: Being an Examination Into the Rights of the Indian Nations (1781), Appendix 1, 159. Lewis, 151.
81. The Middlesex County militiamen nicknamed the "Minutemen" were led by French and Indian War veteran Captain John Parker who mustered his detachment by 2 am on April 19, 1775 upon Lexington (MA) Green to await the large British force marching to capture Samuel Adams and John Hancock and seize their ammunition stores.

Hancock (obviously since both men were in Philadelphia), the result of their meeting with the militiamen was deadly. On the early morning of the 19th of April 1775, shots were exchanged, and in a matter of minutes, eight militiamen or "Minutemen" lay dead on the town green at the hands of the King's troops. Eventually, more militiamen formed in the adjacent towns and successfully drove the British soldiers from Concord Bridge back to Charlestown.

So, with the militiamen besieging Boston to hopefully drive the redcoats from the city, Congress discussed their next move to support them. An army needed to be raised and someone to lead them as overall commander or commander in chief. Hearing this, Trent hoped there might still be a reconciliatory plan with Great Britain, but then he remembered back in Portsmouth and watching the thousands of His Majesty's troops board the *Cerberus* for Boston and possibly New York. Perhaps he was wrong. Maybe the day was coming for the ruin of the English nation, and if so, the end was near for both their colony and his future.

Chapter 17

The Internal Struggle

Trent had barely been home a month when he crumpled up the letter that arrived for him in Trenton and pitched it into the fireplace. Morgan! Just the mere mention of his name now made him infuriated. He'd been gone a long time, and yet this length of time did nothing to mend Morgan's opinion of him.

The notice that came from the corner of Elm and Third St.[1] in Philadelphia arrived in Trenton dated July 8, 1775:

> Captain William Trent, lately arrived from England, having been guilty of very dishonest & dishonorable Acts to the Prejudice of my late father-in-law John Baynton, dec'd, & having refused to give him any reason for his conduct & still refusing to give any satisfaction therein, I do hereby announce and declare the said Wm. Trent to be an infamous lyar and a Scoundrel.[2]

Almost immediately, he took out a piece of paper and dipped the quill in the ink well to write a response. Trent could no longer turn his cheek or ignore another verbal assault from George Morgan. He looked over at his black trunk, where he kept his personal papers, ledgers, and his Queen Anne-style pistol. Action spoke louder than words, and this time, Morgan had insulted his honor: "Mr. T desires Mr. Morgan will be so obliging to acquaint him of the Time and Place by a Line directed to Him to be left at the Indian Queen."[3]

---

1. *Pennsylvania Gazette*, February 15, 1775.
2. Papers Read before the Lancaster Historical Society XXIII, 182.
3. University of Illinois at Urbana-Champaign Library, George Morgan Letter Book 1774–1775, William Trent to George Morgan, July 10, 1775.

Trent did not mince words. He was imposing a challenge from Morgan to settle their dispute gentlemanly, possibly with a duel of pistols. In other words, once Morgan selected a time and place of his choosing, then he was to let Trent know at his favorite public house, the Indian Queen, a few blocks south on Fourth and Market.

He didn't have to wait long for an answer but the reply did surprise him. Morgan had changed his tone completely, possibly at the thought of dueling Trent (who was not only a veteran of three different conflicts but also pretty accurate with a pistol) or just letting his temper get the best of him and sent this immediate reply:

> Sir,
>
> Notwithstanding you have mistaken the meaning of my letter of the 1st Instant, I close in with your Sense of it & at 10 o'clock next Thursday will meet you at John Cadwaladers & from thence accompany you to Mr. Morris's July 11th.[4]

This meeting in the Northern Liberties[5] finally repaired the animosity that lasted almost six years between the two, and by the end of July, Trent, after reassurance with Morgan about the grant in the Western country, also gave his apology to him and John Baynton's widow.

> Let me request a Favor of you to make my Compliments to Mrs. Baynton and assure Her from Me that I'm extremely sorry that I should have done any Thing to give Her Uneasiness, and at some Time that I ask Her pardon between Me when I say that I shall at all Times be happy in rendering Her and Her family any Service in my Power.[6]

For Trent, as agent for Vandalia, it was his job to restore those business relationships that soured over the last six years and assure them they could still prosper once it was approved by Congress or finally by the King. For now, he didn't wish to divulge openly about Vandalia until more details came from London. It also meant reassurance under his roof as he explained to Mrs. Trent why he had been gone from her and the children all those years. He had explained to her the reason for his delay and now the prospect of boasting their fortunes once he met with former sufferers in the early fall in Pittsburgh.

---

4. Ibid.
5. The Cadwalader residence was along north Second Street between streets Spruce and Union.
6. University of Pittsburgh Archives, William Trent to George Morgan, July 28, 1775.

"View of the Attack on Bunker's Hill, with the Burning of Charles Town, June 17, 1775," by engraver John Lodge between 1781 and 1783. One of the British warships featured in the print is the Cerberus, the ship that Trent saw docked at Portsmouth in April of 1775. (Courtesy of the Library of Congress in Washington D.C.)

At this time, he also promised his wife they would leave the parsonage house in Trenton once the property was available. For the time being he was still cautious in returning anywhere in Pennsylvania until after the meeting in the Western country, especially since some he knew might be there who were creditors for his previous debts in Carlisle.

Before he left for the Western country, he did, however, write to update his friends in London on what was going on with the recent hostilities on this side of the water. Fighting had continued in Massachusetts since he arrived in Philadelphia that first week of June. Just over a week after he returned to Trenton, one of the three officers he saw in Portsmouth, Howe, partook in the siege of Boston. Most of the soldiers he saw aboard the *Cerberus* also participated, marching later under the tutelage of commanders Howe and Clinton when they laid siege to a colonial redoubt built on Breed's Hill in Charlestown, Massachusetts, on June 17, 1775.

Trent wrote to shareholder and London Postmaster Anthony Todd on August 1, 1775, and wondered about Parliament's reaction to this latest battle since "Bunker Hill"[7] was a rather "costly" victory for His Majesty's troops after they controlled the peninsula despite suffering over one thousand casualties.

---

7. Though known commonly as the "Battle of Bunker Hill," the battle itself actually took place on nearby Breed's Hill, the hill adjacent to Bunker Hill.

Trent informed Todd that despite these latest battles, there was still "an army of 80 battalions in pay and militia of 200,000 men embodied ready to support them."[8] He did hope it ended soon, though, because Trent insisted to Todd that here in America, "A reconciliation is wished for by every good man on this side of the water."[9]

This bold assumption by Trent, however, proved to be a bit of a stretch because as he was drafting this letter for a packet ship to London, the Second Continental Congress had already selected a Commander-in-Chief of colonial troops in America, and he had already arrived outside of Boston on July 2, 1775. It was also whom Trent wrote at his headquarters along the King's Highway at the House of John Vassall[10] in Cambridge, Massachusetts. On July 22, 1775,[11] Trent wrote his former comrade from the French and Indian War and now Commander-in-Chief, General George Washington to inquire about the sales of lands from his friend George Mercer. Washington, who didn't reply until August 4, 1775, still gave an honest reply despite being preoccupied with the task of raising a large colonial army and trying to supply them:

> As I have none of the Papers with me, I cannot, from Memory, recollect the particulars or give answers to the several queries you have propounded, but as I have before observed, a circumstantial account was transmitted to the Colonel before I left Virginia in May. His Estate, to the best of my recollection, sold for upwards of 14,000 pounds and was thought scarce sufficient to answer the Mortgages upon it in England & Virginia-.[12]

Unfortunately, Mercer's situation was like his lands in New York, meaning it was likely Trent never received any compensation for them. The two hundred pounds promised to him by Mercer for helping him in London was not spared due to the lavish debts he accumulated in London since 1765. As for Trent's lands he purchased within the Otsego Patent, they too faltered before he could do any sort of business with them. He found this out on his way to Pittsburgh,

---

8. Calendar of King George III Papers 1760–1775, Vol. 4, Number 1071, 380, William Trent to Anthony Todd, August 1, 1775.
9. Ibid.
10. The house was built in 1759 for loyalist John Vassall along the King's Highway in Cambridge, Massachusetts. In 1774, it was confiscated by Patriots and used as a temporary hospital after the battles of Lexington and Concord. George Washington, the newly elected Commander-in-Chief of the Continental Army moved into the house on July 16, 1775, didn't leave until April of 1776. Later it became the residence of poet Henry Wadsworth Longfellow, who wrote, "Paul Revere's Ride" and "the Village Blacksmith" and other works while living in the house.
11. This letter though mentioned in Washington's response, has never been found.
12. Library of Congress, George Washington Papers, George Washington to William Trent, August 4, 1775.

Present site of the land of Thomas Cresap and the ruins of his original house (circa 1740) in the foreground near Lock 70 just off Green Spring Road SE in Oldtown, Maryland. (Author photo.)

where he met the ailing Croghan near Warm Springs, Virginia (today Berkeley Springs, West Virginia)[13], who was trying to soothe his crippling gout.

Croghan told him that with the death of Sir William Johnson while he was in England, the distribution of New York, which he oversaw, had lost its appeal. With no one to sell the land to other than his son-in-law Augustine Prevost, he was forced to mortgage most of the land (including Trent's land) to their friends Governor Franklin and Thomas Walpole and a second mortgage to Samuels Wharton's brother Thomas. Later, it was sold to William Cooper, founder of Cooperstown and father of eventual author James Fenimore Cooper.

At least for Trent, he still had their grant in the Western country, and so he continued west from Warm Springs to Old Town, Maryland, and the home of Thomas Cresap by August 21st. There, he paid two pounds ten shillings to John Montour,[14] son of the late Andrew Montour (and another important figure in Trent's life who had died while he was in London), to purchase some goods at Colonel Cresap's. Trent also purchased some bullet molds, powder horns,

---

13. Berkeley Springs was originally called "Warm Springs" because it held mineral water springs whose warm pools were used for those suffering ailments such as George Croghan with gout and George Washington's older half-brother Lawrence when he suffered from consumption (tuberculosis). It was originally part of Berkeley County, Virginia hence its name in 1776 as "Berkely Springs." Today the town of Berkeley Springs lies in Morgan County, West Virginia.

14. Bailey, 336.

wampum, ruffled shirts, and large match coats[15] that he used as gifts for the chiefs of the Six Nations and others at Pittsburgh.

He arrived there on September 13th but realized how much had changed since he had last been to the Forks of the Ohio and Fort Pitt. The journey from Colonel Cresap's house was a bit more rugged than he remembered (he was, after all, in his mid-50s now) and seemed more desolate and "run down" than before. The town of Pittsburgh (if you could call it one) had sparsely 30 houses,[16] most of which were traders and artificers, nothing like when he once resided in the Lower Town. He also observed walking down to the Point how Fort Pitt kept its pentagonal shape but saw inside the abandoned ruins of the governor's house. This spot was going to be the mansion of his friend Samuel Wharton in the capital of Vandalia, but sadly, the door was closing on their long, arduous years laboring for a colony.

That evening of the 21st, he once again used his oratory skills to convince those in attendance in Pittsburgh what their end game really was for those wishing to reclaim their prosperous gains that made the Western country desirable in the first place. Trent was disappointed at the number of attendees, having only eight former "sufferers"[17] that first night, four of which were Croghan, Croghan's cousin Thomas Smallman, and friends Robert Callender and George Morgan. Joseph Simon, his former Lancaster partner had shown up too, no doubt to collect rather than hear what became of Trent's business in London. The remaining audience was current traders and previous ones during the booming days of Fort Pitt since he recognized all three: John Gibson, John Ormsby, and Joseph Spear. It was at this meeting that Trent informed these eight of the status of Vandalia, the larger colony he, Wharton and the other London elite had petitioned before the King and his council for six long years.

Before they adjourned until the following morning at 6 o'clock, he warned them of the secrecy of their plan and not to be discussed openly because "it may perhaps give an unfavorable idea of our right to the common people."[18] Truth be told, with the hostilities against the Crown, it was a dangerous time for anyone to form strong opinions against or for the Crown.

The next morning, Trent will produce the original minutes he kept of their meeting at the Crown and Anchor Tavern in London, and discussion began for most of the day over possible resolutions to establish the foundation of this grant now called "Indiana." Much to Trent's disappointment, the attendees

---

15. Ibid., 336–37.
16. Journal of Nicholas Cresswell, 65.
17. Bailey, 288.
18. Ibid., 288–89.

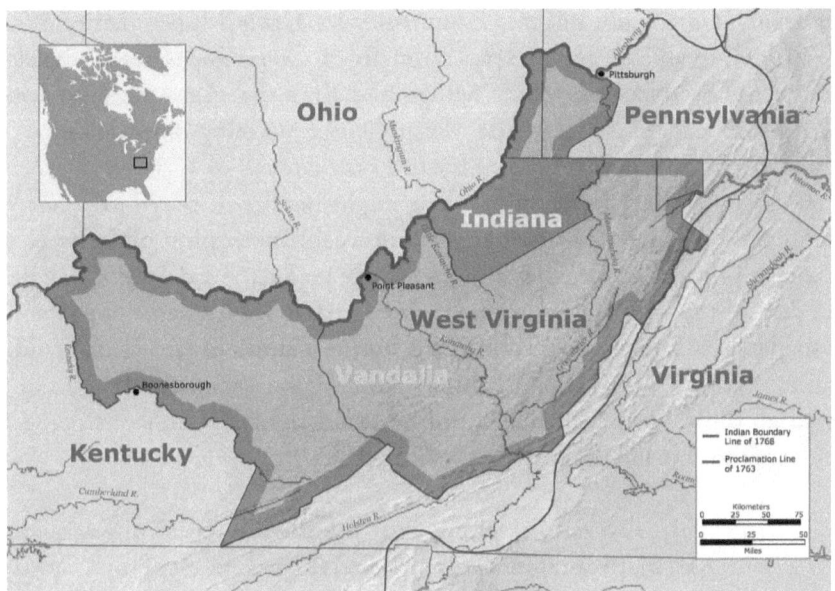

A map showing the boundaries of "Indiana" and "Vandalia". "Indiana" was land that fell under the guidelines of the Treaty of Stanwix in 1768 for the suffering traders of 1763, while "Vandalia" was the proposed fourteenth colony devised in London by members of the Grand Ohio Company in 1772. (Courtesy of Public Domain.)

agreed that unless something developed for London as of late, Vandalia had no precedent here amongst the current settlers or even with Congress. There was nothing official to prove its enacted charter, but if Wharton sent them the original deed from Fort Stanwix, their "Indiana" grant had some solidarity at least. This suggestion was only one resolution, but seventeen more were voted unanimously by Trent and other attendees at Fort Pitt. George Morgan was selected as the land officer for "Indiana" along with Trent, Gibson, and Smallman to be commissioners[19] to oversee the surveyors and chain bearers to mark the boundaries of this grant.

When the meeting officially ended, they agreed to spread the word to those potential members who wish to obtain shares in "Indiana" and to meet in Carlisle on the second Monday in November.[20] They also drafted their joint letter to Samuel Wharton that very same day to ensure this plan would immediately be set into motion and recorded in Williamsburg since, despite it being renamed back to Fort Pitt under new commanding officer John Neville, Virginia still had jurisdiction of their proposed grant boundaries. Just to be

---
19. Ibid., 292.
20. The second Monday in November was November 13, 1775.

safe, Trent, along with Virginia commissioners Lewis Morris, James Wilson and Thomas Walker, gave presents from Rock Creek and Cresap's house to chiefs of the Six Nations, White Mingo and Kiasutha. Kiasutha (also known as Guyasuta) was the Seneca chief whom George Washington once called "the Hunter" on his journey to Fort Le Boeuf in the late fall of 1753.

Those, including Trent, knew what might happen if they were "not very speedily fall on some measures to obtain peaceable possession of them, & permission to proceed in the Sales"[21] without any inadvertent delays. A few weeks later, that was exactly what they inevitably faced as Trent's name appeared in a newspaper headline that questioned his business dealings in London and his loyalties. Writing to his friend Edward Bancroft on October 15th, Trent neglected all duties with "Indiana" until he could rightfully clear his name. He even feared for his life because of it, telling Bancroft:

> The affair is so serious, although it is known to every one acquainted with Me, that I am so strongly attached to the Interest of my Country as any Man in it, that I shall be obliged immediately to go to the Congress at Philadelphia; To get the Affair cleared up in such a Manner as the Committee for all the different Countys in all the Colonies, may be acquainted with my political Opinions, otherwise I shall be murdered in the first Place I go to where I'm not known.[22]

The news came straight from Williamsburg, dated September 8, 1775, and was first printed in the *Hartford Courant* on September 25th and the *Maryland Gazette* on September 28th. This was just the first time he had heard of it now. The article deposed how Trent had recently returned from London and "had been interested by Lord North with the like sum of 40,000 pounds to see the Indians cut our throats."[23]

While in Pittsburgh, Trent brought the said Maryland paper before the court of the West Augusta District to clear his name and appeared before the Virginia committee on October 27, 1775. With Trent being the face of the grant in America, he wished to clear the air of any lies that questioned his character to potential buyers and "remove any bad impressions it may have made on such of his countrymen as are not acquainted with him."[24]

When Morris, Wilson, and Walker listened to his testimony, they also questioned him about where his allegiance was since he had resided in London

---

21. Bailey, 300.
22. P.R.O. CO 5/40, 116–18, William Trent to Edward Bancroft, October 15, 1775.
23. *Hartford Courant*, September 25, 1775. *Maryland Gazette*, September 28, 1775.
24. American Archives 4th Series, Vol. 3, 1205–1206.

since 1769. Trent, having experienced a trial before to defend his character, was prepared for this line of questioning, especially since one of the commissioners, Walker, had opposed their grant from the beginning at Fort Stanwix since 1768. To clear his name, he produced copies of letters written to Croghan and Thomas Wharton, gentlemen who corroborated he made claims "which breathe the strongest spirit of American freedom."[25] He also declared that the paragraph written about him was "false and scandalous and seems to be inserted with a design to ruin him in the opinion of his countrymen, and to saw dissensions amongst us."[26]

He didn't know this "unknown" gentleman that authored this "insidious publication"[27] but was sure it had to be those from Virginia opposing their grants., a possible fabrication to mask their anonymity. When Trent was cleared of any wrongdoing and proven "that of a true friend of American Liberty,"[28] he wished his slanderous author to be apprehended and sued. He also wished to publish a retraction of his tarnished reputation in the official paper of the Continental Congress, the *Pennsylvania Journal*, of which he was personally a subscriber. This request was sent on November 5, 1775, to the editor of the *Pennsylvania Journal*, William Bradford,[29] with the explanation that "I was suspected by Lord North before I left England, of coming into this Country to take up arms against them. I forewent some very considerable Advantages while there because I would not give Room to any of my countrymen to suspect my attachment to the Interest of America: Here I am suspected of being employed by Him against my Country."[30]

Two weeks later, more potential shareholders met in Carlisle to hear Trent's speech about "Indiana," but he was a no-show. Something was amiss, according to Trent's former store partner at Fort Pitt, Levi Andrew Levy. Levy had gone to Carlisle on Monday, November 13th, but didn't understand why the acting agent for Vandalia and "Indiana" hadn't found time to appear.

> I am Sorry you have not attended agreeable to your promise- it leaves room for a good deal of Suspicion you have ever Maintained the Character of an honest gentleman and I hope you Still Maintain the Same.[31]

---

25. Ibid.
26. Ibid., 1205.
27. P.R.O. CO 5/40, 116–18, William Trent to Edward Bancroft, October 15, 1775.
28. American Archives 4th Series, Vol. 3, 1205.
29. William Bradford (1719–September 25, 1791) was a publisher of the *Pennsylvania Journal*, a weekly newspaper in Philadelphia that began on December 2, 1742. He also operated the London Coffee House in 1754, a coffee house used for political activity and business advertisements. In 1774, Bradford was named the official printer for Congress, having been openly against the Stamp Act printing his opposition in several editions.
30. HSP, Bradford Family Papers, Bradford Correspondence William Trent to William Bradford, November 5, 1775.
31. Bailey, 303.

Apparently, though, Trent had good reason for his absence in Carlisle. Leaving Pittsburgh, he took a bad fall from his horse, the animal rolling over the top of him as he lay on the ground.[32] The accident was enough to warrant a cautionary stay in Pittsburgh till he felt able enough to ride. In fact, before he rode east, he hired the services of George and James Girty, his former militiamen, for £5 each[33] from Fort Pitt to transport supplies like blankets, axes, and rifles to Philadelphia. There in the city, he not only sold off those goods but also began to sell off shares in "Indiana" for any gentleman interested. For a voter's share of "Indiana," out of ten thousand acres worth lying on the River Ohio, Trent offered one thousand dollars (about $38,545). His first buyer was George Campbell of Keys Alley (today New Street), an attorney and the Keeper of Rolls in Philadelphia. Campbell authorized an obligatory bond with Trent for £300 and an additional £375 for a voter's share that totaled almost seven hundred pounds.[34]

Before the new year, he used the money toward the leasing of a large property in South Trenton and Burlington County, New Jersey, that became available in the last few weeks. Mrs. Trent, anxious to leave her smaller tenement, had alerted her husband to a plantation that "lies on the River Delaware, near Trenton at the Head of the Tide."[35] This messuage and land were first built by his parent's former Quaker neighbor Thomas Lambert II, and after staying in the Lambert family, was sold to "Sign of the Wheat Sheaf"[36] owner Elijah Bond in 1752. The property had almost seven hundred acres, including a large fishpond that held up to one thousand sturgeon, fruit orchards, a shad fishery on the Delaware, the former Lambert Burying Ground and a ferry landing built by Elijah Bond in 1773.[37] Bond's Ferry, despite having no royal patent, was only a mile or so from the former landing built by his half-brother James in 1726 and presently owned by relation Daniel Coxe.[38] (The landing with Bond's Ferry today is the present site of Marine Terminal Park in South Trenton, New Jersey).

Nonetheless, the "New Ferry" operated by Thomas Harvey ran successively for its first two years, offering rates of one man three pence (3d), a man and horse sixpence, and a four-wheeled carriage with two horses three shillings to

---

32. P.R.O. CO 5/40, 116–18, William Trent to Edward Bancroft, October 15, 1775.
33. Bailey, 338–39.
34. Ibid., 303–304.
35. Ibid., 304.
36. Boyer, 67.
37. HSP, Miscellaneous Collection, Box 5 A-B, Survey of Elijah's Bond land 1773.
38. Daniel Coxe (October 15, 1739–March 10, 1826) was a lawyer in Trenton, New Jersey and in Pennsylvania. He married Sarah Redman, daughter of prominent Philadelphia physician John Redman. Daniel was the grandson of Colonel Daniel Coxe who married Sarah Eckley, the half-sister of Mary Burge, Judge Trent's first wife.

View looking across the Delaware River to Pennsylvania from the former location of Trent's ferry called the Continental Ferry. Today his ferry was located in Marine Terminal Park just below Riverview Cemetery in Trenton, New Jersey. (Author photo.)

the Pennsylvania shore owned currently by John Thornton.[39] Though it wasn't quite clear as to why Bond relinquished his plantation and ferry to Trent at this time, he still lived in the vicinity of the property.[40] Based on the evidence, at least until the spring of 1777, he was leasing it to Trent until he bought it outright and began paying Bond a mortgage.

At this time, Trent probably also took the time to transport any appurtenances from his Carlisle houses before they were sold. This probably included the pier glass gilded frame mirrors and the tall case clock that the Girty brothers helped him put into his new Trenton house. So, with his family properly situated in South Trenton, he rode to Philadelphia after the new year to meet with shareholders for "Indiana." The group of proprietors was now reorganized as the "Indiana Company" on January 20, 1776, and as a joint stock organization, divided each member's shares equivalent to their 1763 trading losses. In other words, the total number of shares was 80,867, equal to the 80,867 pounds,[41] the total number of losses in currency that was accumulated back in 1763. Trent had the third most shares at 7,147 behind trader Robert Callender at 8,651

---

39. *Pennsylvania Gazette*, June 23, 1773.
40. Bond owned a lot and house along the Delaware River near the wharf owned by Moore Furman. See the 1777 survey of William Trent's land by John Watson Jr.
41. Lewis, 193. See also Appendix K of this book for the total list of shares for the Indiana Company.

shares and Samuel Wharton with 16,628 shares.⁴² (See also Appendix K for the complete list of Indiana shares). Unfortunately, also at this meeting came Alexander Lowrey demanding compensation for money owed to him by Trent, Croghan, and Samuel Wharton. Lowrey had gone so far as to issue a writ for the four thousand and twenty-six pounds eight shillings (about $809,000)⁴³ to Trent to pay immediately or be arrested for unpaid debts.

After consulting this legal matter to counsel in the city, it was understood that he or the other two did not have to pay any of this writ due to the existing conditions of the original bond that stated the sum only be paid "within four years after the ratification and confirmation by His Majesty or other unlawful authority in England."⁴⁴ However, since the "Indiana" grant fell under different conditions not relevant to Lowrey's bond, it was agreed to borrow one thousand five hundred pounds (just over $300,000)⁴⁵ from merchant David Franks with the understanding the rest be paid at the first sale of Indian lands.

On the last day of January, Trent had much to write and update his friend Wharton in London. In this informative letter, his attitude or views had changed drastically from several months ago. Despite Trent's wishful thinking that their "Affection for the People of England still glows strongly in the Beasts of the Americans,"⁴⁶ most now wished for independence from the Crown. According to Trent, the recent "ploys" of the Crown to assert their control over the colonies by closing the port cities and offering gifts to the Indian nations to destroy merchants like himself were not going to end well.

"Hatred & Revenge will take place," Trent explained, "All Hopes of a Reconciliation will vanish in a most horrid bloody War will ensue, to the Destruction of the Power of Great Britain and the great Distress of America."⁴⁷ With 53,000 more of His Majesty's soldiers set to arrive in America, the war for independence was fully upon them and only a matter of time before the conflict spilled into their respective backyards. It also meant on their end that any correspondence leaving the colonies or being delivered between provinces was intercepted and read by their designated committees of safety. This was bad news for New Jersey Royal Governor William Franklin who that January had one of his letters intercepted. Despite his father's support for the American cause and being a delegate of Congress, Governor Franklin had been caught

---

42. Ibid. Lewis, Appendix D, 316. See also Appendix K of this book for the total list of shares for the Indiana Company.
43. Lewis, 189. Bailey, 306–307.
44. Ibid., 306.
45. Lewis, 190.
46. Princeton University, Firestone Library, General Manuscripts Miscellaneous Collection, CO 140, Box 50, William Trent to Samuel Wharton, January 31, 1776.
47. Ibid.

This is the original residence (completed in 1764) of New Jersey Royal Governor William Franklin called the Proprietary House where he lived from 1774-1776. It is also the only proprietary governor's house of the original Thirteen Colonies still standing. Today it is found at 149 Kearney Avenue in Perth Amboy, New Jersey. (Author photo.)

"William Franklin (1730–1813)" by artist Mather Brown in 1790. (Courtesy of David A Schorsch-Eileen M. Smiles in Woodbury, Connecticut.)

leaking intelligence to the British. Though he was detained briefly, he was ordered to be confined to his residence in Perth Amboy.[48] This was fine for Trent, who had already ignored several letters from Franklin wishing for Trent, along with Croghan and Wharton, to repay him and the members of the Burlington Company back. The total amount for their expenses for London and the Otsego Patent was just over one thousand seven hundred pounds (over $341,000 today).[49]

Besides, in the spring, he had to get his new plantation in Nottingham Township up and running. Being that he just acquired new property, he and his

---

48. Known as the "Proprietary House," it is the only proprietary governor's mansion from the original Thirteen Colonies still standing. Completed in 1764, it was first occupied by Chief Justice Frederick Smyth from 1766–1773. Later from 1774–1776, it was occupied by Governor William Franklin even after his house arrest until he was later taken to Litchfield, Connecticut. Today the house stands at 149 Kearney Avenue in Perth Amboy.

49. American Philosophical Society, William Franklin Papers, William Franklin to William Trent, March 14, 1776.

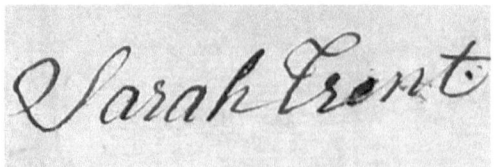

Original signature of Sarah Trent, wife of Major William Trent. (Author photo.)

new neighbor, Samuel Meredith, began discussing the boundaries that hugged the creek to the south. Apparently, Trent's new house stood atop the riverine bluff overlooking the lowland that annually flooded in the spring. His property had floodgates, but questions were still raised about who had ownership over the meandering banks.[50] Though he, Meredith and Randall Mitchell needed surveyor John Watson Jr to establish the answer officially, it had to wait for now.

In April, the Indiana Company submitted a petition for their grant to Williamsburg while Trent rode to Georgetown and Rock Creek to wait for their arrival of Wharton's shipment of goods from London that he hoped to give the Indian nations in the Western country that summer. Mrs. Trent also assisted in his shipments when she ordered ten gallons of Jamaican spirits[51] from merchant Michael Gratz and had it shipped in the care of Andrew Reed to their house from Philadelphia.

From Georgetown, Trent transported the bales to Pittsburgh, where he, Major Edward Ward, and Fort Pitt commander John Neville[52] sat in council with Captain Pipe and Kiasutha at Fort Pitt. Trent arrived there by July 6, 1776, to hear Kiasutha speak about his return from Fort Niagara. Kiasutha produced a belt of wampum that he offered to the Shawnee, Lenape, and other nations of the Western country in attendance to usher the peace between them. Then he told them he took no part in the war for independence and offered the others to do the same. Then Kiasutha looked over at Trent, Neville, and Ward, directing his next statement at them:

---

50. Trenton Free Public Library, Trentoniana Collection, MS 1776, Samuel Meredith to William Trent, March 18, 1776.

51. HSP, Frank M. Etting Collection, Gratz-Croghan papers, Vol. 1, 49, Sarah Trent to Michael Gratz, May 13, 1776.

52. John Neville (July 26, 1731–July 29, 1803) was a former soldier in the French and Indian War and in 1775 was appointed by the Virginia Provincial Council to take command of Fort Pitt that was temporarily called Fort Dunmore. He held that post until 1777, during which he fought in the American Revolution as a colonel. Later he was breveted to a brigadier general by the Continental Congress and soon accepted a job as Inspector of Revenue which he became directly involved in conflict when western Pennsylvania farmers refused to pay taxes on their distilled spirits. This uprising later known as the "Whiskey Rebellion" resulted in shots being fired at Neville and his house "Bower Hill" burned to the ground. This forced President George Washington to take drastic measures and lead a large military force to end the uprising. The area of Neville Island, Pennsylvania is named for General Neville and his second home "Woodville" still stands today in Heidelberg, Pennsylvania.

We will not suffer either the English or Americans to March an army thro' our Country. Should Either attempt it, we shall forewarn them three times from Proceeding, but should they then persist, they must abide by the Consequence.[53]

It's not exactly what Trent and the others of the Indiana Company wished to hear, but it beat the alternative. Kiasutha did not seem bothered by their proposed grant but rather by the main conflict affecting their homes and land. For now, Trent and even Neville could promise them neither might invade this Western country. But what if the war for independence ventured south from New England? It was only a matter of time.

That same month, while Trent returned from Pittsburgh, the town of Trenton came under fire just as he had forewarned to Wharton. In Philadelphia, Congress had drafted a resolution that declared the colonies independent from the Crown, and Thomas Jefferson presented the final revision to Congress on June 28, 1776. After several revisions, it was ratified on July 4, 1776, and just four days later, the first reading of it outside Philadelphia occurred in the center of Trenton upon the courthouse steps and once the land owned by his father, Judge Trent.

These "patriotic" words by Jefferson, no matter how stirring they may be, were not embraced by all in Trenton. The Rev. George Panton, who still wished to preach the offering of prayers from the "Book of Common Prayer" with no omittance or alteration of "King" or "Royal Family"[54] from its pages, decided along with the vestry and wardens to close the doors at Saint Michael's Church on King Street that Sunday, July 7, 1776. His reasoning was to avoid controversy and persecution between its members. (The church where his mother Mary once sat clutching her book of "Divine Meditation and Prayers by Joshua Smith"[55] for each sermon was suspended from public worship for seven years).

Much to their dismay, it had another use, however. The church itself became soldier barracks that December of 1776 for German auxiliaries hired by the Crown (men from the German provinces of Hesse-Cassel and Hesse-Hanau) called Hessians who arrived on December 14, 1776,[56] with their commander Colonel Johann Rall. Specifically, inside Saint Michael's Church, the main force of the Van Lossberg Fusilier Regiment used it as winter quarters as several of their artillery pieces aligned the adjacent burial yard outside. Throughout

---
53. University of Pittsburgh, Darlington Library, Meeting at Fort Pitt July 6, 1776.
54. Schuyler, 75.
55. State Archives of New Jersey, Rare Books and Manuscripts Collection 1652–1878, Box 1, Item 1.
56. Ewald and Tustin, 31.

St. Michael's Episcopal Church (where Trent once served as a vestryman in 1783) today resembles the two towers of Lambeth Palace in London and is found along 140 N. Warren Street in Trenton, New Jersey.

Trenton in all, over one thousand Hessians occupied its city limits under Rall while another thousand encamped at Bordentown almost ten miles to the south under Colonel Carl von Donop.

If there was ever a more dangerous time for Trent and his family, it was now. His newly acquired plantation at the "Lower Ferry" sat directly between these two large Hessian detachments, and the main route of communication between the two Hessian colonels was along Queen Street, the road that led to Crosswicks and Bordentown that passed over the northeastern corner of Trent's property. He and his family were trapped essentially, with no telling of how long the Hessian regiments remained in and out of Trenton. Like most of the residents of Trenton, he just wanted to remain neutral. Trent had seen three different wars and, quite frankly, was advanced enough in age not to be involved in a fourth.

Chapter 18

Choosing Sides

Just before sunrise on December 18, 1776, Trent and his wife awoke from their bed by a roaring boom in the distance. Was that thunder? When more booms followed quickly, he didn't hesitate and told Sarah to take their four children to the underground root cellar. By now, they were all too familiar with the routine, having done this once before on the 8th of December as Washington's army fled the Hessians across the Delaware and fired over a dozen artillery[1] to distract them.

Though he hadn't heard the loud resonating sounds in about thirteen years before this year, and since he commanded Fort Pitt, he couldn't mistake the noise now. It wasn't thunder they heard, but artillery, and judging by the slight echo across the Delaware, it was several cannons firing from the opposite shoreline in Pennsylvania. Soon, it subsided, and the next morning, he probably rode his horse up near Lamberton Road in the direction of the smoke rising from near the landing of his northern neighbor, Daniel Coxe. Coxe, a lawyer who pledged his loyalty rather openly to the Crown, had already fled two weeks before, on December 1st[2], with his family to Philadelphia, so something was not quite right.

From a safe distance, he saw the ferry house once built by his brother James was in smoldering ruins and even further, soldiers were stirring about near his boyhood home. Trent took out his pocket telescope to see better with his one good eye. At the home of his former residence (now owned by Dr. William Bryant)[3] were several groups of Hessian soldiers marching in line,

---

1. Ewald estimated about eighteen American guns. Ewald and Tustin, 27.
2. P.R.O. American Loyalist Claims 1776–1835, AO13, Series 11. Piece 002, 319.
3. Dr. William Bryant owned the Trent house from 1769–1778.

practicing their drill, and setting up pickets around the surrounding property and near Coxe's landing. It was probably the closest the enemy was since the First Battalion British Light Infantrymen were posted at his ferry landing[4] just less than ten days ago. According to ferry operator Thomas Janney, who was forced to flee during the explosions, the cannons across the Delaware in Pennsylvania were American artillery used to distract the Hessian pickets from a small detachment of American militia who came to raid the landing under a cover of darkness.

The ferry house, according to Daniel Cox's later claims for compensation, was burned by the Hessians to evade use by Washington's army. He later filed in 1784 that in addition to the said ferry house, the Hessians who took up residence on his property in December had destroyed his fences, barn, cider mill, press mill and other appurtenances amounting to about three thousand eight hundred and eighty-six pounds and four shillings.[5]

Despite their financial destruction in Trenton, the Hessian occupation barely lasted two weeks. On Christmas night, General George Washington and several detachments of his army crossed the Delaware undetected and, after marching almost nine miles south, launched an attack on the Hessians in Trenton. The attack was so demoralizing for the Hessian regiments the fighting was over in about an hour. The army under Washington, starving and naked, captured just over nine hundred Hessian soldiers, including officers[6], that morning, and the losses kept mounting for the enemy. Colonel Rall, the Hessian commander at Trenton, suffered a mortal wound at the battle and is believed to be buried in the First Presbyterian churchyard in Trenton near where Mrs. Trent once paid the parsonage rent. He joined the leader of the Knyphausen Regiment, Major Friedrich Von Dechow,[7] who also died from his wounds two days after the battle. Those Hessians who were able to escape the clutches of Washington's army, including most who encamped on the yard surrounding the former Trent house, totaled over three hundred (author David Hackett Fischer estimated it was around three hundred and sixty-eight)[8] and retreated to either Princeton or right past Trent's newest plantation toward Donop's detachment in Bordentown.

---

4. Tustin seemed to confuse the Trent ferry with the Falls Ferry. The Falls Ferry was just below the former Trent house (now Dr. Bryant's house) and the ferry to the south Ewald labeled as "Trent Ferry" was the former Bond ferry now owned by Major Trent. Ewald and Tustin, 27–29.

5. P.R.O. American Loyalist Claims 1776–1835, AO13, Series 11. Piece 002, 319.

6. The return of Hessian prisoners was 918.

7. Major Friedrich Ludwig von Dechow was a former officer in the Prussian army, who was previously wounded at the capture of Fort Washington in November of 1776. He was mortally wounded by the Assunpink Creek during the Battle of Trenton and died on December 27, 1776.

8. Fischer, 521.

For a week or so, Trenton and its surrounding areas were finally free of the Hessian army. Washington once again crossed into Pennsylvania to evade the rumored British army led by General Charles Cornwallis, only to appear in Trenton again before the new year. This time, by December 30, 1776, Washington made his headquarters on lower Queen Street at the House of John Barnes[9] in Trenton while the bulk of the army camped along the southern bank of the Assunpink Creek and built earthworks.

Now, at this time, Washington scoured the residents surrounding Trenton for provisions,[10] so it was more than likely Trent assisted Washington in what he could, being he was just over a mile south from their encampment. Though sources are limited as to what Trent gave to Washington and his army, primary evidence suggests he did encounter General Washington, most likely at this time before the Second Battle of Trenton rather than when they encamped in Trenton previously from December 3rd to the 8th. It was also known in a later letter dated May 29, 1780[11] Trent loaned his pocket telescope to General Nathaniel Greene at this time around the new year and possibly livestock to the army from his plantation, like some hogs or cattle.

On January 2nd, 1777, the Trent family had to weather another storm as Washington's army made its stand against Lord Cornwallis's detachment at night near his father's former mills on the Assunpink. From sunset to late into the night, they probably heard the distant volleys and artillery bombardments being exchanged. After the Americans repulsed the British that night and scored another victory the next morning at Princeton (much to the delight of many New Jersey residents, including himself), Howe's army removed themselves from most of New Jersey.

The war had finally left his doorstep, but for how long? General Howe was not going to go away that easily, even after a few defeats in the last couple of weeks. It was also at this moment Trent realized if he didn't start operating his business, he might foreclose on his mortgage. When word reached Trenton that Howe issued a November proclamation offering pardons to those who did not take up arms against the Crown, Trent was intrigued. He was too old to be fighting and was not a loyalist or a "tory," but simply wanted to be left alone from the Crown. Then, he could attend to his business by running a ferry and fishery, maintaining his plantation, and finally receive compensation for the large financial losses he had spent most of his life trying to obtain.

---

9. John Barnes's house was located near the Assunpink Creek in Trenton and along Queen Street, now called Broad Street today.
10. Library of Congress, George Washington Papers, George Washington to Robert Morris, December 30, 1776.
11. University of Michigan, William L. Clements Library, Nathanael Greene Papers, William Trent to Nathanael Greene, May 29, 1780.

So, on February 11, 1777, he wrote Brigadier General and Declaration of Independence signee Caesar Rodney stationed in Princeton to seek protection under Lord Howe's proclamation. When Rodney (who handled all business under Washington with suspected loyalists) asked the reason behind his request for a pardon, Trent declared being "in a bad state of health,"[12] referencing his recurring rheumatism and one blind eye. He also explained to Rodney that in addition, "to secure his Pardon and Property,"[13] he had faced much ridicule for his loyalty since he established himself in Trenton.

He even used the word "obnoxious" to describe it, saying:[14]

> He became obnoxious to his Resentment from the past he had taken in Favor of his Country and more so from the Representation of some of those Men who desired every Principle of Patriotism, took Commissions from Him, had made it their Business to represent Him as a dangerous Person.[15]

When the spring of 1777 came, Trent was able to finally get his plantation in Nottingham Township surveyed in its entirety. On March 31, 1777, Burlington County justice John Watson Jr. walked the outline of the five hundred and seventy acres[16] and then again the next day for an additional one hundred and ten acres of meadowland[17] he now owned along the Delaware River just over a mile south of Trenton, marking the property lines. Then, a few weeks after the survey, Trent no longer leased the property but, in fact, purchased it outright from previous owner Elijah Bond for six thousand pounds (about $1.1 million today)[18] with yearly mortgage payments to him for five years plus interest.

It proved to be quite a challenge for him to keep up the payments with no source of income coming in. Although fortunately for Trent, his extravagant purchase also included the landing and ferry he now operated, joining several ferries north and south of Trenton. To be profitable in such a competitive market (and to make ends meet), Trent offered a service no other ferry could. His Lower Ferry, now nicknamed the "Continental Ferry," offered reduced ferry rates to any active soldier in the Continental Army (a first-of-its-kind military discount) who wished to cross into Pennsylvania or back into New

---

12. HSP, Frank M. Etting Collection, Signers, Caesar Rodney to William Trent, February 24, 1777.
13. Ibid.
14. Despite the accusations, the certificate of protection from Howe arrived in Trent's hands from Rodney on August 23, 1777.
15. Ibid.
16. HSP, Miscellaneous Collection, Box 5 A-B, Survey of William Trent's land 1777.
17. Ibid.
18. Burlington County (New Jersey) mortgage Book A, Folio 247–249, April 23, 1777.

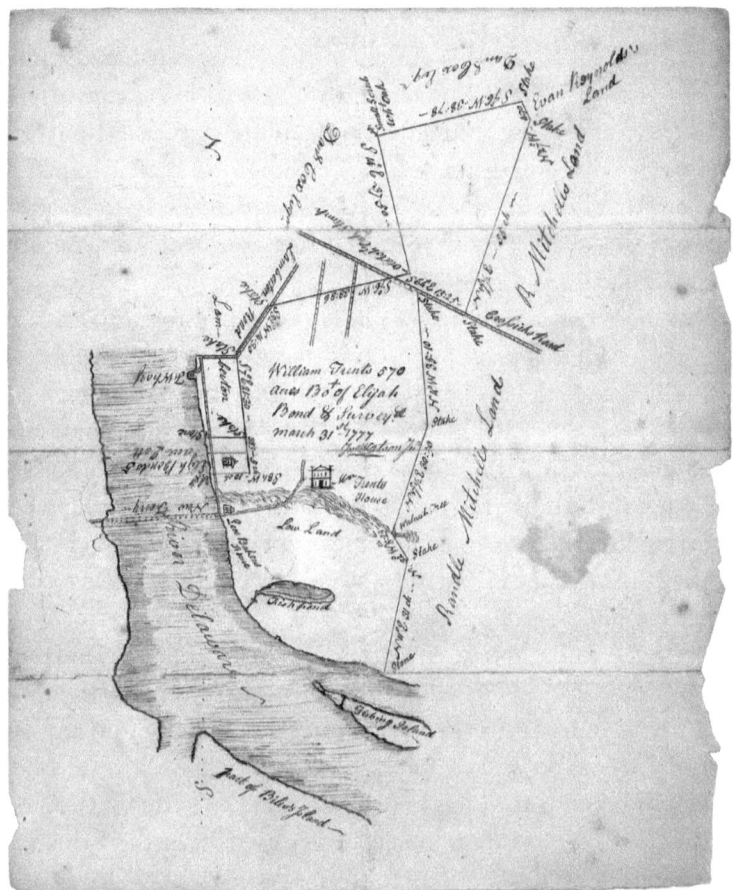

The original survey conducted by John Watson Jr. in 1777 of Trent's property in South Trenton that consisted originally of 570 acres along the Delaware River. (Courtesy of the Collection of the Historical Society of Pennsylvania.)

Jersey. This came full circle when in November of 1777, his plantation ferry was used to house a few of the officers serving under Major General Horatio Gates.[19] These men had recently returned from their decisive victory over the British at a place in New York most familiar to Trent. Not far from where he nearly died in an ambush outside Fort Clinton in 1747, officers General Enoch Poor[20] and others under General Gates took part in both the Battle

---

19. Bailey, 366–67. William Trent to Joseph Whitman, November 10, 1777.
20. Enoch Poor (June 21, 1736–September 8, 1780) served under General Amherst in 1755 during the French and Indian War. Living in Exeter, New Hampshire, he was colonel of the 2nd New Hampshire regiment at the beginning of the American Revolution. On February 21, 1777 he was named a brigadier general and joined General Horatio Gates at the Battle of Saratoga.

of Freeman's Farm and Bemis Heights[21] that forced the surrender of British General John Burgoyne and his entire northern army at Saratoga. Colonels Daniel Morgan and Richard Butler, with the rest of his rifleman regiment,[22] had also passed through but seemed more than intent to have Trent ferry them across the Delaware to reach the rest of Washington's army camped north of Philadelphia. Trent couldn't say *in Philadelphia* because he knew after the recent American defeats of Brandywine and Germantown, General Howe and the British had occupied Philadelphia.

This was most concerning to him because he had recently given a box of documents (old accounts and applications that were still pending) to Colonel Croghan[23] to take to Colonel Cresap's house in Old Town, but Croghan's health had detained him in Philadelphia just before the British took command of the Quaker city. Bedridden with gout, Croghan was confined to Monkton Hall under the careful watch of His Majesty's guards[24] sent by Lord Howe, with no way of meeting Trent. This meant if Trent's papers fell into the clutches of the British,[25] the pardon from Howe did not protect him from being thrown into the Walnut St. Gaol.[26]

Especially now with their former president of the Indiana Company, Joseph Galloway, pledging openly his allegiance to the Crown and joining Howe as the Superintendent of Police in the city. (His Indiana Company successor, David Franks, was also arrested for suspicion of being a loyalist on October 21, 1778).[27] Though his business papers were deemed safe by Croghan in the city, "Indiana" business was temporarily shut down while the British occupied Philadelphia and Congress moved to York, Pennsylvania. This also left the now vacant first floor of Carpenter's Hall (where Congress previously met), a temporary barracks for those British soldiers braving the winter of 1777-1778 and granted them free access to the larger second-floor lending library

---

21. Both were sites of battles that comprised the overall Battle of Saratoga in 1777. Freeman's Farm was located just four miles north of Saratoga and was one of the longest land battles of the Revolutionary War fought on September 19, 1777. Despite the British seizing the field, the Americans led by Benedict Arnold later captured a British redoubt near Bemis Heights, resulting in exposing the right flank of the British General John Burgoyne's army. On October 17, 1777, Burgoyne surrendered, and this became the turning point of the American Revolution.

22. Richard Butler (April 1, 1743–November 4, 1791) was one of several brothers who came from Dublin, Ireland to Lancaster, Pennsylvania then to Carlisle, Pennsylvania in 1760. It was there the Butler family opened a gun shop and manufactured long rifles, a shop that still stands today in Carlisle along High Street. On July 20, 1776, Butler was commissioned a major in the 8th Pennsylvania Regiment and serving under Daniel Morgan. Less than a year later on June 7, 1777, he was promoted to colonel of the 9th Pennsylvania Regiment, where he fought at Saratoga that year and later in 1778 at Monmouth Courthouse.

23. Wainwright, 301.

24. Ibid.

25. Byars, 166–67.

26. Walnut Street Gaol (Jail) was opened in 1773 to prevent overcrowding at the High Street jail and was located at streets Sixth and Walnut in Philadelphia. It began housing prisoners in 1776, including American prisoners when the British occupied Philadelphia in 1777. Today it resided along the north end of Washington Square Park.

27. Journal of Congress, Vol. 4, June 1, 1778–January 1, 1779, 610.

Choosing Sides

Carpenter's Hall was completed in 1775 and still stands today at 320 Chestnut Street in Philadelphia, Pennsylvania. (Author photo.)

founded by Dr. Franklin called the Library Company of Philadelphia.[28] It was during this time, while the British perused the library's catalog and before Howe's replacement, General Henry Clinton (whom Trent also saw board the Cerberus three years ago in Portsmouth) withdrew His Majesty's troops out of Philadelphia on June 18, 1778, did Trent's name become associated with a bit of the library's lore. In a newspaper article written in 1938 from Sydney, Australia, came this passage:

> When British troops occupied Philadelphia in 1777-1778, they made good use of the Public Library, when they left one book borrowed

---

28. The Library Company of Philadelphia was founded on July 1, 1731, by Dr. Benjamin Franklin and others, for those shareholders and eventually lenders to access books at their leisure. The earliest catalogue (1741) lists three hundred and seventy-five titles, consisting of historical works, geographies, literature, science related, religion, philosophy, and social sciences. The repository expanded and moved to the second floor of Carpenter's Hall in 1773, where it expanded privileges to those of the Continental Congress and acted as the Library of Congress until 1800. Today the Library Company lies at 1314 Locust Street and houses over half a million books and over seventy thousand miscellaneous items including the Mayflower Compact and major collections for the seventeenth, eighteenth, and nineteenth centuries.

by them-Cranz's History of Greenland (two volumes)- had not been returned. It had been borrowed by Major Trent. In 1876, however the library received from England the missing volumes.[29]

The article also mentioned that this was possibly a world record for the longest-overdue book. Later, it was also discovered the world record for the longest overdue book was by Colonel Robert Walpole, who borrowed a book in 1668 when he was an undergraduate at Trinity College, and it was finally returned on January 16, 1956, 288 years later.

So, during this time of British occupation from September 26, 1777-June 18, 1778, Trent either ventured to the city to borrow these specific volumes or somebody used his name on their behalf to borrow them. Now, it must also be mentioned that because the book was returned from England, it was initially assumed the "Major Trent" borrower was a British officer. However, since British Army service records do not list any high-ranking officers with this surname during this period in Philadelphia, it was quite clear that he was this person affiliated with the Library Company and since he could enter the city on business with that certificate of protection. Nonetheless, if Trent did visit the occupied city, it wasn't just to borrow a book. Perhaps the brief visit was to check on the ailing Croghan, retrieve his old papers or learn of any news from Wharton in London.

But the certificate of protection could only help him so much; for as long as the British stayed in Philadelphia, Trent could not conduct any business pertaining to the Indiana Company. He spent the spring of 1778 instead, finally making his plantation operational and donating once again to the patriot cause. The militia companies raised in Burlington County still needed supplies like food and clothing, so in March, Trent gave two horned cattle from his herd of forty[30] to the Superintendent of Cattle Adam Aulberger for their want of beef. He was also given a receipt for payment by a member of the Calvary and Commissary of Trenton, John Dickson, on March 17, 1778.[31]

Yet despite this constant neutrality for business and continued support for those locally fighting for liberty, it wasn't enough to avoid suspicion for his current loyalties. (The certificate from General Howe was a damaging example of this). It was a very dangerous time to be a merchant, especially one whose business associates for "Indiana" were being questioned or arrested for their loyalties to the Crown. As far as he knew, his friend and Governor William Franklin was

---

29. Petterson and Jensz, 1–2.
30. State Archives of New Jersey, Burlington County (New Jersey), Nottingham Township Tax List 1777.
31. HSP, Frank M. Etting Collection, Army Collection, Vol. 1, 49.

recently released from imprisonment at Litchfield Gaol in Connecticut (he was later released to New York City on November 1, 1778). Joseph Galloway was convicted of high treason and fled to England, and now Thomas Wharton Sr. who fled to Virginia after being accused of treason. This was why, on March 29, 1778, Trent finally chose a side and went before Burlington County Justice John Watson Jr., declaring that:[32]

> I do sincerely profess & swear that I Do Not hold my Bound to bear allegiance to the King of Great Britain & that I do and will bear true Faith and allegiance to the Government Established in this State under the authority of the people.[33]

His oath of allegiance had impeccable timing because three months later, General Clinton withdrew his army from the Pennsylvania capital on June 18, 1778. With the news that France was allying with America, Clinton was forced to consolidate his two detachments in New Jersey. It was there, while Clinton's army remained divided, that Washington attacked the rear guard at Monmouth Courthouse, eager to test their new training regime while encamped the past winter at Valley Forge. After the smoke cleared and the American army took possession of the battlefield, Clinton escaped with what was left of his beaten, heat-inflicted army to New York City.

The turning point of the Revolutionary War was obviously apparent in late summer, and this was good news for Trent and his associates. Business could resume for the Indiana Company, and now they could finally present their memorial to the Virginia Assembly, whose delegates led by his friend and former Ohio Company treasurer George Mason had alarmingly released an opposing resolution over the winter.

It stated: "No person or persons had just claimed to the unappropriated western lands of state, and every survey entry made into the western region under any title whatever was declared to be void."[34]

When Trent and the other members met in Philadelphia in September,[35] their discussion focused mainly on this response to the Virginia delegates. They no doubt needed evidence that their grant of "Indiana" in 1768 was given before Virginia laid claim to the Western country. Additionally, it then proved the

---

32. See also Appendix L for Trent's complete Oath of Allegiance.
33. Ibid., Gratz Collection, Colonial Wars, Case 4, Box 9. For Trent's oath of allegiance in 1778, see also Appendix L of this book.
34. Lewis, 212.
35. Ibid., Byars, 172.

former Ohio Company grant was outdated and had no jurisdiction over lands within the boundaries of "Indiana."

Besides, if they could produce to the delegates their original copy of the Treaty of Stanwix, then according to Trent, it showed Virginia approved of their grants since there was at least one witness and signature by Dr. Thomas Walker, a Virginia commissioner. When their meeting in September concluded, it was decided in the majority that Trent represented them on their behalf if they could request an audience before the Virginia Assembly in the city of Williamsburg. For his sake, he hoped it was sooner rather than later. Two years after the fighting spilled into Trenton and near his residence, Trent found himself once again in the same financial trouble that had plagued him in Carlisle. Being absent from his residence and unable to maintain the upkeep of his ferry and farm, Trent was having trouble paying the high mortgage payments to Elijah Bond. It also explained why, on September 11, 1778, he put his large property up for sale after only owning it outright for just over a year. In the *New Jersey Gazette,* he placed an advertisement hoping a potential buyer might be tempted to purchase:

> To be SOLD, the very valuable plantation wherein the continental ferry is kept, about one mile below Trenton; it contains between 6 and 700 acres, has a very great proportion of Meadow and a sufficiency of woodland. It has every requisite to recommend it to the gentleman or farmer, amongst which are in its pleasant situation, rich meadows, ferry, orchards, fishery, large fish pond wherein 1,000 sturgeon may be kept, and great front on the river Delaware, a part of which is very suitable for a town as it has beautiful high banks and lays below the falls. If the plantation is disposed of, all the stock and farming utensils with part of the household furniture, all new and very elegant, will be sold. For terms apply to the subscriber living on the premises.
> William Trent[36]

Riding back to his plantation in Trenton, Trent had hoped to arrange his papers and gather his finest clothes for the journey to Williamsburg, but his plans were delayed by an unfortunate chain of events at his home. When he walked his horse to the stable, he realized his enslaved servant boy Hughy[37] had neglected his duties, and now one of his best horses was missing. Worse yet, his wife Sarah and youngest daughter Sarah were confined to their beds "lying

---

36. Documents Relating to the Revolutionary History of the State of New Jersey, Vol. 2, 429–30 (1903).
37. Bailey, 374. State Archives of New Jersey, Burlington County (New Jersey), Nottingham Township Tax List 1777.

dangerously ill."[38] According to Trent, he was not riding to Virginia unless they recovered. Unfortunately for him, his wife did fully recover, but his daughter Sarah did not. Just two months shy of her fourteenth birthday, she was laid to rest in Trenton. Further evidence of her death was proven by no mention of her name in Trent's second will he drafted in 1782, after previously giving her a share of his estate in his 1775 will.

As the Trent family grieved their loss into 1779, Trent received word that the Virginia legislature agreed to hear their memorial about "Indiana" on the third Monday in May (May 17, 1779).[39] This was good news indeed, but he still had some work to do before the long ride to Williamsburg. First, on January 4, 1779, he discharged a daunting mortgage still lingering in Pennsylvania before he left for England that spring of 1769. This was former property in Cumberland County that amounted to 1,912 acres[40] that he conveyed to creditors and former partners Joseph Simon and David Franks. Next, he needed any and every piece of evidence to showcase their just claim in the Western country. He needed books about the Indian titles or a copy of the Treaty of Stanwix in 1768 that hopefully had been proven in Virginia by three witnesses. If this were not proven, he had to get three citizens of Virginia[41] to place their signatures upon it to make it valid. He also had his friend George Morgan send him several inhabitants living on their proposed grant so that he had current members for the Virginia Assembly.

When he acquired satisfiable evidence to support the company's claim, he devised a pamphlet to be printed by Morgan so that when he eventually presented in Williamsburg, each Virginia delegate had a copy of their validity in their hands as he spoke. Morgan had five hundred copies[42] printed of Trent's pamphlet before he left.

Trent also had time for one last bit of business before he rode south. At his favorite watering hole and place to conduct business in Philadelphia, Trent sold nine hundred shares to recently retired Colonel and former Washington aid-de-camp William Grayson[43] at the Indian Queen Tavern on May 1, 1779.[44] This transaction of sales for Trent earned him a sum of one thousand two hundred pounds (just about $254,000 today), which he definitely needed to offset the

---

38. Byars, 172.
39. Lewis, 214.
40. Pennsylvania Supreme Court, Gratz v. Phillips Case in January 29, 1822.
41. Bailey, 316.
42. Ibid.
43. William Grayson (1742– March 12, 1790) was born at Belle Aire Plantation in present-day Woodbridge, Virginia. He practiced law in Prince William County, Virginia, and other counties. During the American Revolution, he served as assistant secretary to General George Washington, then his aid-de-camp in August of 1776.
44. Bailey, 318–23.

Today this is the reconstructed Capitol building in Williamsburg, Virginia, the third one built on the grounds after the previous two were demolished by fire. It was still the original site where Trent, George Mercer, and George Morgan separately lobbied their petition for "Indiana." (Courtesy of Public Domain.)

mortgage payments for his plantation. It also didn't hurt that Grayson, a native of Dumfries and Prince William County, was a prominent Virginian who only helped sway the opposition against their grant before May 17th. A rather bold move by Trent as he rode into Williamsburg and appeared before the delegates of Virginia and other land agencies presenting their memorials.

Trent argued first the proven validity of the 1768 Indiana grant and how, even in London, lawyers John Glynn and Henry Dagge had written statements proving its legality. His final "smoking gun" was that the Treaty of Stanwix or grant for "Indiana" had already been approved by a delegate of Virginia on two separate occasions, such as when Dr. Walker signed the original treaty in 1768 and when those Virginia district justices like John Gibson and Thomas Smallman approved of it at Pittsburgh in September of 1775.

Virginia, on the other hand, had assembly member George Mason counter-argue their claim to the Western country over the "Indiana" grant. He declared as far back as the Treaty of Lancaster in 1744 that before these lands were part of "Indiana," they were ceded to Virginia that day on July 4, 1744. Mason also pointed out that even if the "Indiana" grant was made valid in November of 1768, there was no such record of it in the Western country or at very least in writing before these district justices of Augusta County, Virginia,[45] whom currently had authority in jurisdiction over these lands.

The Virginia delegates after hearing all the arguments, decided to give their decision on June 9, 1779.[46] Referring back to the notion and resolutions that no private person or company had the right to purchase lands within the boundaries of Virginia and that since 1744, Virginia had exclusive rights to any territory from the Indians, the legislator defeated the "Indiana" grants by a vote of fifty to twenty-eight.[47] The loss in votes officially made the "Indiana" tract from the Treaty of Stanwix in 1768 invalid and a failure in their attempt to achieve any confirmation from Virginia.

For Trent and the rest of the "Indiana" shareholders, there was one final option that could result in a confirmation for their grant. They took their case before Congress since they were the principal framework of government reigning supreme in wartime and could overrule the decision by the Virginia Assembly. Trent and Morgan planned that their memorial fell in accordance with the Articles of Confederation that was proposed as the colonies wished to declare themselves independent from Great Britain that summer of 1776. It was influenced heavily by Dr. Franklin's former Albany Plan of 1754 (and ironically, after he received word of Trent's men surrendering the Forks of the Ohio in the spring of 1754) that the colonies existed as a whole entity, in this instance, the United States ruled by one authority and this being Congress that sat once again in the colonial capital of Philadelphia. This was why George Morgan appeared first in Philadelphia to present a memorial on September 14, 1779,[48] to secure compensation for those sufferers of 1763 and to put a hold on Virginia's decision until Congress heard their memorial.

Also on this same day, Trent, dressed in his finest silks, entered the Pennsylvania State House (only the second time since he was a former member of the Pennsylvania Assembly in 1751) and presented a separate memorial (he had written three days earlier) on behalf of Vandalia, representing those Americans who comprised the Grand Ohio Company on this side of the water. Ironically, Trent was the lone representative under the Vandalia group since Dr. Franklin was residing in Paris along with his friend Samuel Wharton, who was forced to flee England due to his letters from London being intercepted only a

---

45. Lewis, 217.
46. Ibid., 221.
47. Plain Facts (1781) by Samuel Wharton, Appendix II, 165. Lewis, 221.
48. Lewis, 227. Journals of Congress 1774–1789, Vol. 15, 1063–1064.

few months ago in the spring. So, like what he and the others composed to King George III at one point when he was in London, Trent addressed Congress president John Jay[49] and others that he and his associates were more than willing to match the original sum of 10,460 pounds that the Crown paid in land in addition to any other obligations they had promised in England.[50]

Like his fellow associate George Morgan, Trent hoped to have "speedy consideration" for this petition since Virginia wished to take control of the Western country by October. Despite Virginia representatives on Congress opposing the two memorials (which no doubt were Francis Lightfoot Lee and his brother Richard Henry Lee), Congress president John Jay passed a motion to elect a committee to consider the land petitions on October 8, 1779. This was all Trent and the others wanted from the beginning, to just have them hear their petition and consider their grant. After George Morgan recovered from an illness and New Jersey representative John Witherspoon[51] returned to Congress on October 29, 1779,[52] a motion was carried that struck a blow to Virginia's original plans. Congress highly recommended that they reconsider opening a land office or issuing warrants in the Western country until the war had ended. Adding insult to injury, the Indiana Company decided to take advantage of this and send George Morgan to seek a repeat repeal of the previous decision to the "Indiana" grant in Williamsburg.

Trent, who returned home by November, felt confident in this favorable decision by Congress and had no doubt Morgan convinced those in Virginia to change their mind about their grant and issue them restitution. "That many who voted on the other Side," Trent wrote ahead of Morgan's arrival to Virginia Attorney General Edmund Randolph,[53] "Some from Conviction and Others from a Knowledge that all most every man in Congress, as well as out of Doors reprobate their Conduct, will probably alter their Sentiments."[54] Trent knew what strong opposition tried to crush them once and for all, and they needed an ally like the future governor and eventual Washington's cabinet member

---

49. John Jay (December 12, 1745–May 17, 1829) was a lawyer and member of the New York Committee of Correspondence that protested the Intolerable Acts before the outbreak of the American Revolution. He also served in the First and Second Continental Congresses, while serving later as President of the Second Continental Congress. Later he served as the ambassador to Spain from 1779–1782 and co-authored the Federalist Papers with Alexander Hamilton and James Madison.

50. Bailey, 329.

51. John Witherspoon (February 5, 1723–November 15, 1794) was born in Yester, Scotland becoming a minister in the Church of Scotland from 1758–1768. In 1768, he came to New Jersey and became the sixth president for the College of New Jersey later called Princeton University. He also personally taught courses in history and divinity, helping train ministers, and organizing the Nassau Presbyterian Church in Princeton, New Jersey.

52. Journals of Congress 1774–1789, Vol. 15, 1223.

53. Edmund Randolph (August 10, 1753–September 12, 1813) was born in the influential Randolph family in Williamsburg, Virginia and graduated from the College of William and Mary. He was the executor of his uncle Peyton's estate, aid-de-camp to General Washington and later mayor of Williamsburg.

54. Bailey, 333.

Randolph to support their memorial. There were also ones amongst the Assembly in Williamsburg that Trent pointed out could not be trusted.

> There are those who have their Suspicions, and it would be difficult to persuade them out of the Opinion that he ought to be placed at the Head of the Blacklist.[55]

Trent, who knew exactly which person might challenge Morgan and the "Indiana" memorial, made sure Randolph was aware of this certain individual as well. Though he didn't openly name him, he did, however, hint at "Mr. M" as the person in question. "Mr. M" was clearly George Mason, who from the beginning, opposed, ridiculed, and tried to blockade their grant ever since the Ohio Company had fizzled after the French and Indian War and they formed the Grand Ohio Company in London.

It was resentment Trent warned Randolph that Mason felt, even though he should support their grant because they had a just claim. "Our cause was good, he knew it, but would not own it," Trent explained to Randolph about Mason's reasoning to oppose their grant, "We have stopped every kind of Publication on our Parts in hopes that Virginia will see Her Interest in doing us Justice, it has been with the greatest Regret that we have done what we have and Nothing but the Necessity of procuring Justice, which was held from us by the artifice of a few design Men, could have induced us to take the Steps we have."[56]

Trent's words of advice for Randolph proved to be a correct prediction of George Mason's next move. Mason, along with Patrick Henry[57] and Robert Munford,[58] formed a three-person committee that highly opposed the early recommendation from Congress and, in response, drafted their protest against Congress having any jurisdiction above Virginia over the "Indiana" and Vandalia grants. Bearing the dates of December 14, 1779, this drafted refutation against "Indiana," and Vandalia arrived soon after in Philadelphia. As a result, with the upcoming holiday and the new year approaching, the debate became a standstill until further notice.

---

55. Ibid., 334. HSP, Frank M. Etting Collection, William Trent to Edmund Randolph, November 9, 1779.
56. Bailey, 334.
57. Patrick Henry (May 29, 1736–June 6, 1799) was born in Hanover County, Virginia, having attended the King's College in Aberdeen, Scotland. He was elected to the Virginia House of Burgesses in 1765 and strongly opposed the Stamp Act in 1765. In 1774, he served on the First Continental Congress and opposed Governor Dunmore's decision to seize counterfeiters in Pittsylvania County without judicial proceedings. In 1775, he became notorious for his quote, "Give me Liberty or Give me Death," that was directed toward British Acts in America. He also served two terms as Governor of Virginia from 1776–1779 and then 1784–1786.
58. Robert Munford (1737–1783) studied law under his cousin Peyton Randolph and served as magistrate in Mecklenburg County, Virginia and in the House of Burgesses in 1765. Munford was also a playwright, writing "The Candidates" and "The Patriots," the supposed first comedic plays written in America.

In the meantime, as the year became 1780, Trent's powerful address before Congress brought him into a new light with the state of New Jersey and his residential county of Burlington. Since he had all the accolades, a military veteran, a gentleman in good standing (at least for now) in his county, and a strong voice to sway Congress, he found himself being pursued relentlessly for a career in politics every time he rode to Trenton on business.

With his responsibilities to oversee his plantation, ferry landing and grafted orchards, there was little time to explore anything extracurricular. Yet ever the ambitious seeker, Trent placed his name upon the ballot for Burlington County anyway. It was the second time Trent ran for a Provincial Assembly, but hopefully, this time, if elected, his strong influence in New Jersey would eventually lead to the confirmation of their grant by Congress. At this rate, he could only hope so because his level of grandiose lifestyle depended on it.

Chapter 19

A Feverish Attempt

With the sun rising behind him, Trent lightly kicked the heels of his boots into the rib cage of his grey horse as he felt her hesitation on the frozen snowy path down to the bottom land. When her feet sunk into the accumulated snow, she immediately sprang into a gallop to stay above it. "Easy girl," he probably whispered as he pulled on the reins. "Little Girty,"[1] as Trent called her, was a wild one in personality, having wandered previously from his plantation when a thief stole his other ten-year-old bay horse last November[2] and left the stable open. Now, by late March of 1780, with all nine of his horses back in his possession, he could begin routinely checking his fields that his enslaved servant Hughy and other unnamed servants[3] were hopefully going to plow once the snow melted and the ground thawed.

This winter of 1779-1780 had been the worst on record that Trent had ever experienced, with the snow drifting so deep it had been just this March before he could see his fences again around his property. Unfortunately, due to the severe weather, he was behind on the spring planting. At this time, the bottom should have been cleared or harrowed already, with plans to grow maize, timothy grass, and turnips.[4] The latter was future feed for the horned cattle and hogs for the upcoming winter, all seeds he acquired from miller Joseph Penrose[5] in Philadelphia. Penrose, a former Colonel in the 10th Pennsylvania

---

1. Bailey, 374.
2. *New Jersey Gazette,* November 22, 1779.
3. State Archives of New Jersey, Burlington County (New Jersey), Nottingham Township Tax list 1780 listed two slaves.
4. Bailey, 374.
5. Ibid.

infantry[6] under General Thomas Mifflin,[7] was the grandson of Captain Bartholomew Penrose, a shipmaster of the *Diligence* and later named *Happy Union* co-owned by William Penn, James Logan, William Penn Jr, and Trent's father. It was also probably Penrose's country estate in Passyunk Township (called Penrose's Island) where he gathered grafted fruit branches and seeds[8] currently comprising the six hundred fruit trees on the southern end of his property where the soil was the richest of the bottom.

For Trent, traveling each time to this part of the property became an issue because he was beginning to no longer see these vast orchards clearly without riding "Little Girty" close to the edge of the first row of trees. In fact, lately, it was difficult for Trent to check on the health of the trees without squinting his one eye into focus against the piercing glare of the snow. Regrettably, he should have never lent his pocket telescope to General Nathanael Greene when he and the Continental Army were encamped briefly in town in those early months of 1777. Because not only had Greene not returned it, but Trent also needed the "glass" more than ever to counter his failing eyesight and see across his seven hundred acres. This three-year lapse of having no pocket telescope bothered Trent so much by early summer that he wrote Greene on May 29, 1780, and gave it to Colonel Richard Butler, who had come to his plantation for supplies that month:

> I request the Favor of you to deliver the Bearer Colonel Richard Butler the Pocket Telescope, which I lent you about three years since. The Situation in my plantation is such as I can almost as well do without my Eyes as without a pocket Glass; otherwise, I should not be so pressing for it.[9]

Though there is no evidence that Greene wrote back or even returned the pocket telescope, Trent had to conduct business without it throughout the summer. Fortunately, by the fall, travel received a boost in business when Colonel John Nielsen[10] paid 108 and 74/90 Dollars or forty pounds six shillings two pence to have Trent's services "for the privilege of the landing of his ferry seven

---

6. Leah, 31.
7. The 10th Pennsylvania Infantry fought at the Battles of Brandywine, Paoli, Germantown, and Monmouth Courthouse.
8. *Pennsylvania Gazette*, July 17, 1784.
9. University of Michigan, William L. Clements Library, Papers of Nathanael Greene, Vol. 5, William Trent to Nathanael Greene, May 29, 1780.
10. John Neilson (March 11, 1745–March 3, 1833) became a brigadier general after the Revolutionary War and became the Deputy Quartermaster General for New Jersey.

Bronze statue of General Nathanael Greene that stands currently near the entrance of the Upcountry History Museum in Greenville, South Carolina. In his hands is a pocket telescope that could have been based on the one loaned to him by Major William Trent in 1777. (Courtesy of Public Domain.)

months + 13 days from 25 October 1780 to 7 June 1781 at £50 per annum and for 15 cords wood furnished by him to the Ferryman."[11]

At the same time, his landing was bustling with soldiers, horses, and wagons, and Trent finally heard the results of the latest county election for the New Jersey Assembly. When the votes were tallied, two new elects were representing Burlington County. Joining with re-elect Major Thomas Fenimore was militia paymaster for Monmouth and Burlington Counties William Hough, and what was no surprise, himself, Major William Trent, on October 17, 1780.[12]

Trent wasted no time using his newly elected platform. On October 30th, his vote in the New Jersey Assembly first helped re-elect incumbent Governor William Livingston over running opponents Philemon Dickinson and David

---

11. Rutgers University, Nielson Family Papers, Receipt No. 8170.
12. Documents Relating to the Revolutionary History of the State of New Jersey, Vol. 5, 48.

Brearley.[13] Then he and George Morgan presented their memorials of Indiana and Vandalia seeking congressional jurisdiction once again because, as they stated before, the grants were "of infinite consequences to the American Union as well as to your Memorialists and that it ought to receive a speedy and solemn Decision."[14]

Though this rang true to some, the delegates of Virginia in Congress refused to accept the pretensions of Trent and his associates were beneficial to America or its colonies. When Trent still found their respective paths blockaded against authorization by Virginia, he did, however, seek public opinion for their memorials with the help of the revolutionary and author of the pamphlet, "The American Crisis," Thomas Paine.[15] Published by Philadelphia printer John Dunlap,[16] Paine's latest pamphlet, "Public Good," appeared in December of 1780, lobbying for those memorialists whose land companies like the Indiana Company were trying to patent grants in the Western country "claimed" by Virginia.

With such a favorable outlook toward their stance, by the end of the new year, Paine, like William Grayson, acquired shares in the Indiana Company. But as Paine once remarked during the outbreak of the American Revolution, "These are the times that try men's souls," and so too came this notion only a few days into 1781. In northern New Jersey, tensions boiled past their usual public notices when Trent's assistance was requested by his friend, Colonel Richard Butler and Butler's superior and commanding officer of the Pennsylvania Line, Colonel Anthony Wayne.[17]

After enduring yet another harsh winter, this time in Jockey Hollow near Morristown, New Jersey, soldiers of the Pennsylvania regiments took their arms and left without permission or disregard to their superior officers. Soon, they established a headquarters in Princeton, where they told Wayne they refused to abide by him or anyone else until their grievances were met. On January 5, 1781, General Washington had no choice but to contact Congress to meet

---

13. Minutes and Proceedings of the Council and General Assembly of the State of New Jersey, August 30, 1776 to October 29, 1799.

14. Lewis, 237. Papers of the Continental Congress, No. 77, 230–33.

15. Thomas Paine (February 9, 1737–June 8, 1809) on January 10, 1776, published *Common Sense*, a pamphlet on independence from Great Britain and it became the bestselling pamphlet in the colonies selling over a half million copies during the American Revolution and helped encourage recruitment for the Continental Army when enlistments were expiring.

16. John Dunlap (1747–November 27, 1812) was born in Tyrone, Ireland and apprenticed under his uncle William, a printer in Philadelphia in 1766. In 1771, he partnered with David C. Claypool and printed the *Pennsylvania Packet* that ran until 1800. After 1791, it was known as the *American Daily Advertiser*.

17. Anthony Wayne (January 1, 1745–December 15, 1796) was born in Chester County, Pennsylvania and raised the Pennsylvania Militia in 1775. During the American Revolution, he served in the ill-fated invasion of Quebec, the Battle of Brandywine, Paoli, Germantown, and Monmouth Courthouse. Wayne was the commanding officer of the Pennsylvania Line when they threatened to mutiny over pay and mistreatment.,

with these individuals about their "deplorable" conditions and send President of Congress Joseph Reed two days later to hear their grievances. When Reed decided their terms were favorable and justified, he arranged for those disgruntled Pennsylvania soldiers to be discharged with their compensation in Trenton if they wished to end their enlistment. That day, he also gave Trent a receipt for three pounds for furnishing him and the other commissioners with one ton of hay as they "adjusted the claim of the Pennsylvania Line."[18] Unfortunately for Trent, it was not the "compensation" he hoped for after depleting a rather large quantity of forage from his plantation's inventory.

Money was tight that late spring, but things were looking up after the fateful return of his friend Samuel Wharton to America. After hearing of their current opposition, Wharton wasted no time in lobbying for the Indiana Company when using Trent's detailed minutes, he anonymously printed an even bolder pamphlet than Paine's "Public Good." Printed by bookseller Robert Aitken[19] on Market Street in Philadelphia, this pamphlet was entitled, "Plain Facts: Being an Examination into the Rights of the Indian Nations of America to their respective Countries; A Vindication of the Grant from the Six United Nations of Indians the Proprietors of Indiana Against the Decision of the Legislature of Virginia."[20]

Unlike Paine's pamphlet, Wharton and Trent made sure it showcased all the specific evidence they compiled over the years, including the Treaty of Stanwix in 1768 and their lobbying in London before the King. It also provided propaganda to the public about the importance of their grants in America and how they deserved precedence over any opposition of Virginia.

Riding the heels of this pamphlet and its popularity, Trent, Wharton, and business associate Barnard Gratz[21] prepared a memorial to Congress on May 21, 1781.[22] This petition, written in Trent's hand, referred to not only the Fort Stanwix treaty and land cession but also the 200,000 acres conveyed to George Croghan in August of 1749, which, according to the deposed boundaries, also lay within the tract of "Indiana." This memorial also displayed (and hinted) Trent's impatience at a fair ruling, which they stated in this document

---

18. High Sheriff Joseph Inslee Duplicate Book No. 3, 147.
19. Robert Aitken (1734–1802) was a bookseller and published *The Pennsylvania Magazine*, which activist Thomas Paine contributed to. In 1781, he printed the first complete English bible produced in America and the "Aitken Bible" was the first and only edition of the bible authorize by Congress.
20. It was usually shortened to just *Plain Facts*.
21. Barnard Gratz (1738–1801) born in the Prussian Silesia region (Today it is Poland), he and his brother Michael established a mercantile firm after they arrived in Philadelphia. They protested the Stamp Act and helped pave the way for Jewish people to run for office. His niece was Rebecca Gratz, supposedly the inspiration for the heroine Rebecca in Sir Walter Scott's book, "Ivanhoe".
22. Papers of the Continental Congress, Memorials addressed to Congress, Vol. 10, 87–89.

should have already been "investigated and determined in a Court of Law or Equity."[23]

Congress's indecision came at an impromptu time for Trent as he received disheartening news from Trenton. His ferry landing, designated the "Continental Ferry," was about to lose potential business and a leg up on the rival ferries when he was told by the Deputy Quartermaster of New Jersey, Moore Furman, that this respected title was now being moved one mile north to his neighbor's landing. The reason was that those French scouts surveying the route ahead of advancing from Rhode Island preferred the access of two ferry boats and some sailboats[24] at this landing for their large detachment instead of Trent's landing in the bottom below his house. This, of course, was the same ferry his brother James formerly patented and now was operated by Hugh Runyon[25] on the forfeited lands of loyalist Daniel Coxe and just below his boyhood home owned currently by Colonel John Cox (now the 1719 William Trent House Museum).[26] As he initially feared the potential loss of business, the ferry just above his was, in fact, where Washington's large army, along with French forces under Comte Rochambeau,[27] crossed on their route from Newport, Rhode Island to Yorktown, Virginia, from August 31, 1781 to September 1, 1781.

This latest development (and bad luck), mixed with little or no shares from "Indiana" sold to potential shareholders, left him in a precarious situation financially. Per his 1777 agreement with Elijah Bond, he had drastically fallen behind on his yearly mortgage payments and the interest that had accumulated because of it. On June 3, 1781, Trent received his first notice of a potential eviction by Bond. "But as I now see no payment of your Complying with your engagement," Bond warned, "I must now inform you unless the interest is paid immediately, I shall be under the Necessity of Proceeding to the Recovery of the farm."[28] Yet he cast this note aside, having to return to Philadelphia with another memorial, this one revised to end their delay and ratify their grant on July 24, 1781. When this failed to reach any sort of conclusion, Trent rented a room on October 8, 1781, at the Indian Queen Tavern, making it the unofficial headquarters and meeting place while he conducted Indiana Company business.

---

23. Ibid., 89.
24. "Ferries across the Delaware," Nigh, 2007.
25. *Dunlap's Pennsylvania Packet*, October 6, 1781.
26. Colonel John Cox owned the former Trent house from 1778–1792.
27. Jean-Baptiste Donatien de Vimeur Comte de Rochambeau (July 1, 1725–May 10, 1807) was a veteran soldier during the War of the Austrian Succession and obtained the rank of colonel. During the Seven Year's War, he was promoted to brigadier general for his efforts at the Battle of Minorca in 1756. Later in 1780 he was given the rank of lieutenant general of over 7,000 French troops and sent to join General Washington in America. He landed at Newport, Rhode Island on July 10, 1780, but stayed there until the French fleet was no longer blockaded in Narragansett Bay. Finally in the fall of 1781, he and his detachment joined Washington's forces as they laid siege to Yorktown and the French Navy trapped the British forces under Charles Cornwallis from escaping by water.
28. Bailey, 371.

Though he wasn't sure of the proposed duration of his accommodation, he eventually paid Indian Queen Tavern proprietor Francis Lee fifty-six pounds five shillings for "20 weeks Boarding and Lodging from Octr. 8th 1781 to Feby 24th 1782."[29] Throughout this lengthy stay, Trent received word in the city of Washington's decisive victory at the battle of Yorktown and the capitulation and surrender of General Cornwallis's army.

The war was soon coming to an end, and with America being victorious, all lands, whether settled or not could be finally seated or adjudged to the future United States. This was favorable to Trent and Wharton's claims, and on November 3, 1781, they finally heard a report[30] from the committee about Virginia's "unlawful" cession of the Western country, which they submitted on October 28, 1781.[31] The congressional committee declared the grants to the Indiana Company and George Croghan at Fort Stanwix were, in fact, valid, and once the colonies became the United States officially, then under this single consolidated entity, their grants could finally be confirmed. Trent and his associates could finally chalk up a tally in the win column. Congress had the final say or jurisdiction of the Western country but could only authorize this ratification once America broke away officially from Great Britain. Virginia delegate James Madison knew this and did not give up so easily despite the opinion of Congress. He knew this was not official until a majority vote could be cast, so until then, he continued to lobby his opposition amongst delegates throughout the winter of 1781 and the spring of 1782.

In the meantime, Trent made use of his residency at the Indian Queen and of Congress's decision, diligently writing to prospective shareholders and the promise toward what he described to those interested as a sound investment. Up until February 24, 1782, he made sure those potential "investors" were compensated and well catered by using the company expenses to treat them "to Clubs at Diner and Super and Drinck at Sende Tines for Silf and Gentelmen."[32] In fact, it was going so well, according to receipts and bills from Trent to Francis Lee, this "dining" of investors will continue further until almost May 3, 1782.[33]

Everything was going according to plan for Trent until an unknown illness seized him violently the first week of March, and he was confined to his room at the Indian Queen. Pain and discomfort ached throughout his body, rendering him almost immobile. It was nothing like he had experienced before,

---

29. Ibid., Statement of Account by William Trent to Francis Lee.
30. Bailey, 335.
31. Lewis, 249.
32. Bailey, 372.
33. Ibid., 371.

not even when he was stricken with intermittent fever twice. When the illness did not wither, he sent immediately for the closest physician nearby. From the tavern, his messenger ventured south down Fourth Street, crossing Chestnut and Walnut Street, past Willing's Alley and finally to the corner of Locust and Fourth. It was the home of Dr. William Shippen Jr,[34] the nephew of his former master Edward Shippen III and husband of Alice Lee, daughter of one of the founding members of the Ohio Company, the late Thomas Lee. Shippen Jr, who was the former Director of Hospitals for the Continental Army, faced much controversy at this residence when it was rumored he and his assistants were "taking" those laid to rest in nearby Southeast Square[35] and dissecting them in the basement. Nonetheless, Shippen Jr. was his best solution, and the doctor recommended "sundry medicines and attendance 16 weeks."[36]

Since "sundry medicines" is quite nonspecific, being required to return the Shippen's house for sixteen weeks is not. In fact, at this time, only one type of medicine was prescribed for this lengthy amount of time. For Trent's severe rheumatism (he claimed he suffered aching in his ankle, back, and hand)[37], Shippen probably recommended Portland's Powder. The medicinal powder, named for William Bentinck, 2nd Duke of Portland (who suffered from gout), was a mixture of birthwort root, gentian root, the tops and leaves of the germander, ground pine and centaury.[38] Ground together into a fine powder, Trent took a dram[39] of it each morning with water, broth, tea, or wine. This continued the first three months with half to three-quarters of a dram the next three months to see if he experienced any change since it operated somewhat slowly.

While he tried to recuperate, he had his "relation" in Philadelphia, Tench Coxe,[40] handle some of his business affairs. On April 9, he had Coxe act as his attorney and pursue the money left on the six-thousand-pound bond that was due to him from merchant John Mitchell and now Philadelphia County Recorder of Wills, George Campbell.[41] Apparently, Trent chose to pursue this specific bond back from March 17, 1779, because his illness had not ceased its severity over the last month. By May, when he struggled to fulfill his attendance to see Dr. Shippen, he assumed the worst and began putting his affairs in order

---

34. The house of Dr. William Shippen was at 238 South 4th Street where it still stands today in Philadelphia.
35. Today it is called Washington Square.
36. Library of Congress, Dr. William Shippen Daybook, Book C, Box 28, 1776–1793, 107.
37. University of Illinois at Urbana-Champaign Library, George Morgan Papers, William Trent to George Morgan, July 8, 1782.
38. Theobald, 44.
39. A dram is 1/8th of an ounce.
40. Tench Coxe was the son of William Coxe, Trent's former friend and fellow apprentice under Edward Shippen III. William Coxe was the son of Daniel Coxe and Sarah Eckley, the half-sister of Judge Trent's first wife Mary Burge.
41. George Campbell was named Recorder of Wills on April 6, 1782.

Today the Shippen-Wistar house (built in 1750) still survives on 238 South 4th Street in Philadelphia, Pennsylvania. At the time of Trent's illness in 1782, it was here Trent went to see Dr. William Shippen Jr and received Duke of Portland's Powder over the sixteen weeks. (Author photo.)

at the Indian Queen. On May 13, 1782, he sat up in bed and began drafting his last will and testament, the second time he wrote one, superseding the one he wrote in London on April 14, 1775. In this will, he divided his estate into five parts, with his wife Sarah and daughters Ann and Mary getting one part and his son John receiving the remaining two parts. John, who had just turned thirteen last month, was of school age, and Trent recommended "giving to my Son the best Education this Country affords."[42] He also declared Tench Coxe to oversee the will as the attorney and hoped that Congress settled the dispute between "Indiana," Vandalia, and Virginia so his legatees (those individuals of the Indiana Company and others he owed money) were reimbursed finally for their shares pertaining to the Western country. Trent finished with his signature and wax seal along with three witnesses, Indian Queen Tavern owner Francis Lee, Westmoreland County (Pennsylvania) Prothonotary Michael Hufnagel, and merchant George Moore, who put their signatures beside his. (See also Appendix M for the complete 1782 will).

Now, while Trent was on his supposed deathbed, his poor wife received an unfortunate notice of trespass and ejectment from attorney and clerk to the New Jersey Supreme Court, William Churchill Houston.[43] Houston was representing plaintiff Elijah Bond, who was now suing Trent for his failure to pay the mortgage and interest on his seven-hundred-acre plantation just south of Trenton. The notice dated May 13, 1782 (the same day as his will) was for Trent to appear in Trenton with an attorney or face eviction from his plantation and property. This also came along with a writ from High Sheriff Jacob Phillips for twelve thousand pounds (almost $2.5 million today)[44] in debt he owed. Mrs. Trent, wary of her husband's unfortunate situation in Philadelphia, informed Associate Justice Isaac Smith of his severe illness and successfully postponed the hearing until the November term.[45]

Meanwhile, by late June, Trent miraculously survived his severe illness and recovered enough to return home despite aching still over most of his body. He even continued to rely on the Portland's Powder to lessen the pain. But the court date worried the Trent family, and if the court did remove them from their home, they had to take care of their youngest, whose future career might be in jeopardy because of it. In August of 1782, Trent gave fifty pounds[46] to the new grammar school in town on Fourth Street (today Academy Street and on the present site of the Trenton Free Library) called the Trenton School Company and, as a shareholder, entitled his son John to attend for free. Teenage

---

42. HSP, Simon Gratz Collection, Will of William Trent May 13, 1782. To view Trent's 1782 will, see also Appendix M of this book.
43. William Churchill Houston (1746–August 12, 1788) graduated from the College of New Jersey (Princeton University) and became a professor of mathematics and natural philosophy in 1771. From 1779–1781, the government of New Jersey sent him as a delegate to the Continental Congress. Later he studied law under Richard Stockton and was admitted to the bar in 1781. Eventually he opened a law office in Trenton and became Clerk to the New Jersey Supreme Court.
44. State Archives of New Jersey, Bond v. Trent 1782.
45. Ibid.
46. Dayton, 10.

This is the present-day location of the Trenton School Company also known later as Trenton Academy where Trent's son John attended and he was a trustee. The school formerly stood on the site of what is now the Trenton Free Library along Academy Street in Trenton, New Jersey. (Author photo.)

John learned arithmetic and, later that month, public speaking.[47] Together with other children in town, the young Trent was one of forty total scholars[48] and received a good education before an apprenticeship could be arranged for him.

However, as the first signs of fall began appearing, Trent received sad news from Philadelphia. His former on and off again business partner, confidant and friend George Croghan had passed away on the 31st of August 1782[49] in the city. His death was a shocking revelation for Trent. Croghan, who battled the last few years with serious gout due to his hard drinking and lifestyle, had finally succumbed to his deteriorating health. Like Trent, he had been bedridden his last few remaining months, and, that early summer had already drafted a will on June 12, 1782.[50] Two months later, he was dead, giving what property remained to his business colleagues Michael and Barnard Gratz to pay off debts he still owed. Any money left from his estate went to his daughter Susanna Prevost, and it covered enough expenses to have him laid to rest in the burial yard of Saint Peter's Church in Philadelphia.[51]

It put things into perspective for Trent as now he was one of the last surviving influential backcountry merchants. Christopher Gist died of smallpox on

---
47. Ibid., 9.
48. Ibid.
49. Wainwright, 310.
50. Philadelphia County Wills, Book S, 164.
51. Today a modern gravestone marks his interment and is located near the grave of artist Charles Wilson Peale.

The grave tablet of George Croghan lies within the burial yard of St. Peter's Episcopal Church on 313 Pine Street in Philadelphia, Pennsylvania. His modern gravestone resides next to the grave of artist Charles Wilson Peale. (Author photo.)

the road to Virginia on January 25, 1759.[52] Conrad Weiser, a year after him, on July 13, 1760.[53] His former lieutenant and friend John Fraser, on April 16, 1773,[54] in Bedford County, Pennsylvania, while he was lobbying in England. Sir William Johnson, Superintendent of Indian Affairs, at his home of Johnson Hall, from a stroke on July 11, 1774.[55] Then, on July 29, 1776,[56] it was Robert Callender in Carlisle, not much after he returned home, his mentor and father figure Edward Shippen III in Lancaster in September of 1781,[57] and now Croghan, who he knew for most of his adult life.

At this point, though, Trent continued to fight, whether it be for his lands in the Western country or his lands in South Trenton. While validation in the Western country had fallen to the wayside with the peace negotiations and separation from Great Britain, Trent shifted his efforts toward the hearing of his ejectment. On November 15, 1782, he appeared in court alongside his attorney Samuel Williams Stockton before Associate Justice Isaac Smith and

---

52. George Mercer Papers, 92. BP Series 21644, Letter from Captain James Gunn to Major John Tullekin, July 31, 1759, 216–17.
53. Weiser, 90.
54. Fraser died after serving as justice of the peace of Bedford County, Pennsylvania and residing in Bedford, Pennsylvania. Pennsylvania Archives, Third Series, Vol. 22, 1773 Bedford Township Tax List, 18.
55. Papers of Sir William Johnson, Vol. 3, xi.
56. Robert Callender's gravestone is in the Old Graveyard in Carlisle, Pennsylvania next to John Armstrong, hero of Kittanning and major general during the American Revolution.
57. Edward Shippen III is buried at St. James Episcopal Church along Duke Street in Lancaster, Pennsylvania and is buried next to his son Colonel Joseph Shippen and General Edward Hand.

The grave of Edward Shippen III is located in the burial yard of St. James Episcopal Church on 119 N. Duke Street in Lancaster, Pennsylvania. (Author photo.)

declared himself "not guilty" for the charges of trespassing and ejectment for his seven-hundred-acre plantation.[58] The plaintiff, Elijah Bond, deposed "that the value of the lands in controversy is above two Hundred Pounds Sterling further saith not."[59] After both parties made their statements, it was decided that Bond needed to present evidence he owned the title of the lease to this property Trent lived on, or the case was being thrown out. So, the trial resumed on the 3rd of April 1783, giving Bond ample time to produce this primary evidence if possible. On the other hand, it also gave Trent the opportunity, as the new year approached, to dispute it by the court date in the spring of 1783.

---

58. State Archives of New Jersey, Bond v. Trent November 1782.
59. Ibid.

After it officially became 1783, Trentonians rejoiced with the announcement that St. Michael's Church on King Street (it was not renamed to Warren Street until later) was no longer suspending service and reopened in the Evangelical doctrine of Episcopacy. Though the church needed repairs (it had been closed since July 7, 1776), an election was held and, on January 4, 1783, named churchwardens Rensselaer Williams and Isaac DeCow along with a dozen vestrymen.[60] One of these twelve vestrymen chosen was William Trent, and it was the first time a Trent was a vestryman since his brother James at St. Mary's of Burlington in 1727. He was also the second such Trent (after his father) with this old congregation since services were originally conducted at Hopewell Church.

In addition to his role as vestryman, Trent did his neighborly duty and helped Captain Thomas Ashmore conduct the inventory on February 6th, 1783,[61] for former "boatman" John Douglas, who died just over a week before. Trent and Ashmore valued Douglas's inventory at forty pounds, seventeen shillings, and nine pence.[62]

His notoriety in the Trenton community continued as he struck up a friendship with attorney Ebenezer Cowell Jr.[63] who resided on Pennington Road and who volunteered to help Trent fight his case of ejectment and trespass. Filing through the chancery court on March 24, 1783,[64] Cowell requested Elijah Bond submit the bill or debt for his client before these proceedings continued in April. This "injunction" successfully delayed the trial until at least November. It was exactly what Trent needed while he sent several futile requests out to his fellow "Indiana" shareholders for an emergency meeting. One such notice he sent to Barnard Gratz in Philadelphia:

> *Sir,*
>
> *Your attendance is desired in this city on Thursday, the first day of May next, as the proprietors of Indiana are specially to meet, at seven o'clock that evening of the Indian Queen Tavern, on affairs of great consequence.*
>
> *Your most humble servant,*
> *William Trent.*[65]

He sent another to his former partner Joseph Simon, following up almost a week later with a letter requesting he and his former Fort Pitt store co-owner

---

60. Archives of St. Michael's Church, Trenton, New Jersey.
61. Documents Relating to the Colonial History of New Jersey, Vol. 6, 1781–1785, 124.
62. Ibid.
63. State Archives of New Jersey, Burlington County Chancery Records.
64. Ibid.
65. Lussing, 473.

Levi A. Levy to forget (or at least temporarily) his financial obligations to them and attend the meeting. "If we lose our grant," Trent wrote, "Let those whose Penury have left no person to attend the Business blame themselves."[66]

He was trying to explain without upsetting his associates that he, Morgan, and Wharton were tired from doing all the main legwork to confirm their grant. In fact, ten days after he wrote Simon, Trent appeared before Congress in Philadelphia to submit another memorial for "Indiana." This time was an outright plea by Trent on behalf of those memorialists of "Indiana" representing New Jersey that they hear him out and what was "actually" being alleged by the legislature of Virginia. He reminded them in a three-page memorial that the cession of land at the Treaty of Stanwix in November of 1768 was not only approved by the British Crown, but also by New York and their main opposition, Virginia. Additionally, Trent and the rest of his associates were suffering "injustices"[67] for this long delay on this decision, never mind the "aged, distressed widows and helpless orphans"[68] who needed this grant. A decision needed to be made, Trent concluded, if "Justice between States do not interfere with justice which may be due to individuals."[69]

While he awaited Congress's response, he received a letter from General William Irvine[70] in Carlisle. Irvine, who owned shares in "Indiana," regretted to inform Trent he would not be able to attend the meeting due to being on active duty as the commander of the Western Department of the Continental Army, whose headquarters were at Fort Pitt. Irvine cast much doubt for the eventual confirmation of "Indiana" because he felt the Pennsylvania borders weakened much of Indiana's suggested tract and felt that even if Congress confirmed it, "the present possessors and claimants will never be dispossessed but by force nor pay a shilling to anybody or set of men"[71] like himself or any other proprietors.

Although Irvine made a good point, his reassurance to evict squatters by force had already failed a year earlier when he organized an expedition along the Sandusky River to drive out those Indian nations and loyalists who had spearheaded attacks on settlers in the Western country. The result led to a disastrous defeat and the torturous execution of his friend from the Forbes Expedition, William Crawford.[72]

---

66. University Archives, William Trent to Joseph Simon, April 7, 1783.
67. Papers of the Continental Congress, Vol. 10, Volume T–Z, 101.
68. Ibid.
69. Ibid.
70. William Irvine (November 3, 1741–July 29, 1804) came to America in 1763 and settled in Carlisle, Pennsylvania where he married Robert Callender's daughter Ann in 1772. On September 25, 1781, he was ordered by Congress to command the Western Department of the Continental Army, its headquarters at Pittsburgh, Pennsylvania.
71. HSP, Irvine Papers, William Irvine to William Trent, April 23, 1783.
72. Crawford was tortured and burned to death near Sandusky, Ohio on June 11, 1782, a retaliation for the Gnadenhutten Massacre on March 8, 1782.

Nevertheless, in case Irvine was right, on May 1st (delaying his meeting about a week),[73] Trent delivered a memorial about Vandalia, this time for Congress to consider, adding to the double-digit number of memorials he had submitted since 1779. Unfortunately, the only response he received was the rejection of the Vandalia one, having no apparent basis with the present separation from Great Britain.

On the night of May 8th, he had hoped to have better news for those in attendance at the Indian Queen, but he couldn't keep his associates waiting any longer. Those that came that Friday night, May 8, 1783, were as follows:

> William Trent
> William Pollard
> Samuel Wharton, trustee for deceased John Welch
> Michael Gratz
> Levi Hollingsworth
> Levi A. Levy
> Tench Coxe[74]

Since there was no update of Congress's report on private land dealings, those attendees wished to see their financial report and accounts withstanding. It was then Trent produced his expense account he "wrote off" his company business from when he housed, dined, and entertained current shareholders and potential ones for four years. The account he compiled amounted to three hundred and sixty-nine pounds, three shillings and ten pence.[75] Most of which were bills he accumulated while frequently Mr. Lee's public house, the "Indian Queen." After all, as he explained to Joseph Simon that spring, "Mr. Wharton & Myself have paid some attention to the business, but it cannot be expected we should give our time & payment over own expenses."[76] The rest of the Indiana Company did not see it that way, however. A motion was unanimously resolved that although" great Expenses may be incurred & became chargeable to the Company for want of a proper regulation, no proprietor or Shareholder nor any Attorney for a proprietor or shareholder shall be entitled to payment of any account or charge against the Company for transacting any business for the Company or for his Expenses."[77] If he must do so again in the name of the Indiana Company as he had done over the last four years, then he must sell off

---

73. Papers of the Continental Congress, Committee of the States 1784, Item #32, 473.
74. Bailey, 340.
75. Ibid., 341.
76. University Archives, William Trent to Joseph Simon, April 7, 1783.
77. Bailey, 341.

"one voter share of the Company's lands in order to pay off the set accounts."[78] After the meeting adjourned, more bad news came the following month when the congressional committee suggested a compromise to the legislature of Virginia, ignoring his memorials toward considering the tract of "Indiana."

Despite delegates from New Jersey apologizing for "troubling" Congress with so many applications (no doubt referencing Trent or Morgan without mentioning their names), Congress delayed their final report until the fall, which at this point favored the Virginia opposition led by James Madison. That summer, Trent covered the Indiana Company expenses he accumulated since 1779; however, when he sold three hundred shares of "Indiana" to Captain John Paul Jones on July 4, 1783, who in turn paid him 1000 Spanish milled dollars.[79] In 1783, one Spanish milled dollar or "piece of eight" was worth 90 pence in Pennsylvania, meaning Jones paid him ninety thousand pence or equivalent to 375 pounds (A little over $69,000 today), therefore covering the total company expenses declared by Trent.

Yet by the fall of 1783, his biggest obstacle still staring at him directly in the face was the trial for ejectment and trespassing. Throughout his entire life, Trent had faced much adversity with insurmountable debts and possible arrests by creditors, but always managed to evade jail or possible eviction. Unfortunately, in this specific case, luck finally ran out on Trent. So, hoping the court was lenient on him and his family, Trent pled guilty and confessed to the judgment of ejectment and trespass. Though the verdict wasn't clearly determined in the court records, Trent was ordered to pay back the recited obligation of six thousand pounds (just over $1 million today)[80] within a year to plaintiff Elijah Bond or be forced to vacate the premises indefinitely.

Realizing he only had one option to obtain such an exorbitant sum, he gave one last attempt to present his memorial of "Indiana" and went before the New Jersey legislature. He was hardly a public speaker or true politician, yet Trent gave a powerful speech about his grievances before the New Jersey House. "There must be hope for redress," he stated, "When he considered that the State against whom he's obliged much against his Inclination to complain of have or express possession in their Declaration of Rights, which could not have been Forgotten by them as the ink on the paper which conveyed these assurances to the people was scarcely day at the time they committed their atrocities act of Sequestering Private Property against the opinion of right."[81]

---

78. Ibid.
79. Indenture of William Trent to John Paul Jones, July 4, 1783, PMHB, Vol. 77, No. 2, 156–63.
80. State Archives of New Jersey, West Jersey deeds, Vol. AN, June 1, 1784, 187.
81. Bailey, 345.

"John Paul Jones (1747–1792)" by artist Charles Wilson Peale. (Courtesy of Independence National Historic Park and Public Domain.)

On behalf of himself and the Indiana company, Trent hoped for the New Jersey legislature to challenge the hostility of Virginia and restore the rights bestowed upon them by the Treaty of Stanwix in 1768. The legislature acknowledged his desperate plea and, on December 18, 1783,[82] appointed fellow New Jersey resident[83] and Indiana Company member George Morgan to present this memorial to Congress on behalf of New Jersey and the Articles of Confederation. Although this was good news, it was rather bittersweet because time was slowly slipping away from the aging Trent. Between overwhelming debts and now his deteriorating health, the possibility of receiving compensation for land in the Western country was growing thinner and thinner. Suddenly, the winter of 1783-1784 was fast approaching, and Trent realized there was a good possibility he may not live to see another one.

---

82. Lewis, 264.
83. George Morgan lived at "Prospect farm" in Princeton, New Jersey.

Chapter 20

The Poorest of Circumstances

After reading the express from Maryland, Trent tried desperately to dip the goose quill into the pewter standish when it fell from his fingers and splattered ink across the blank parchment. He couldn't hold a pen without his hand shaking or his fingers "seizing up" from the grip. This sudden movement allowed the nagging cough deep within his chest to return and made him almost double over. Coughing so harshly, he probably grabbed a spittoon and purged up some mucousy phlegm. Indian Queen owner Francis Lee had suggested to send for Dr. William Shippen Jr but he may have insisted the frigid ride had caught up with him.

But Trent was wrong. The Portland's Powder had worked for a time, but his rheumatism had returned worse than before and now, ever since the first month of 1784, he hadn't been feeling like himself. Each time he traveled just over a few miles on horseback, he could feel it in his lungs. Shortness of breath. The aching of his back and ankles. He just hoped it wasn't consumption.

It hadn't helped he had previously spent the entire month of January in Philadelphia, settling a few old accounts and retrieving what money he could from them. On the 12th,[1] he received a bill of exchange from Richard Barrington courtesy of Messr. Drummonds Bank in Charing Cross in London[2] for one hundred pounds sterling ($17,311). Then, on the 29th,[3] he authorized his longtime friend Samuel Wharton as power of attorney to collect the remaining balance from John Mitchell and George Campbell (dated March 17, 1779) because his former attorney, Tench Coxe, was pursuing his political ambitions.

---

1. Bailey, 495.
2. Drummonds Bank was located at 49-50 Charing Cross in Trafalgar Square in London.
3. LCP, John A. McAllister Collection, William Trent Papers, Box 1, Folder 29.

This is the present location of Drummond's Bank (founded in 1717) where Trent received a bill of exchange from Richard Barrington in 1784. The present building (circa 1887) lies on the site of the original bank at 49 Charing Cross in Trafalgar Square in London. (Author photo.)

However, when he finally returned home to Trenton the first week of February from the Quaker city, Trent found himself struggling to breathe in the icy, cold air. The sudden shortness of breath surprised him, and even though he dismissed it then as nothing more than exhaustion in his advanced age, he didn't leave his bed for a few days after.

Trent had to face the facts. Now, a month later, in March of 1784, back in Philadelphia, he was in his early 60s and couldn't brave the sickness and travel like he used to. Perhaps then or later, he felt dizzy, and his legs began to waver on him. Quickly, Trent probably staggered to the bed and lay down before he collapsed on the wooden floorboards. This time he had them send for somebody, but not Dr Shippen this time. "Nurse Watters," he probably uttered with a gasp that day. Mary Watters (sometimes spelled Waters) was reputed throughout the city after she assisted in several of the military hospitals set up for the Continental Army. She was also known by other names. Apothecary. Healer. Even fellow shareholder of the Trenton School Company, Continental Army doctor and Declaration of Independence signee Dr. Benjamin Rush[4] had a nickname for her and her "noble profession."[5] Watters was called a "doctoress" by him, an outstanding boost of respect amongst her male physician colleagues since the College of Physicians at the time excluded women. Later, the 1796 Philadelphia city directory even listed her occupation under this respected nickname.[6]

Trent had visited her previously after his two-year dependency on Portland's Powder proved to be too costly and found her treatments or remedies of healing prowess much more effective. Watters lived south of the Indian Queen on Willing's Alley near the old St. Joseph churchyard, just a street before Dr. Shippen's along Fourth Street[7] and a block south of Walnut Street. She also sold Huxham's Tincture of Bark[8] and other healing powders on credit, which Trent had to oblige until he secured more payments.

Now, his cash funds were low since just before he received the express, he purchased a rather unusual array of goods. From the warehouse of Michael and Barnard Gratz at the corner of Fourth and Market (today, it's the site of the Museum of Illusions), he acquired several yards of silk and calico fabrics along with stitching thread and three hundred bars of lead.[9]

Speaking of the express, the letter he received at the Indian Queen (just before he felt ill) was from his friend George Morgan with a report on their memorial with Congress meeting in Annapolis. About the first instant of March, Morgan had presented their memorial for "Indiana" along with the argument that Virginia (despite their supposed claims) had no jurisdiction in the Western country. This land, Morgan argued, was always the property of the Indiana Company shareholders in accordance with the Treaty of Stanwix back in November of 1768. Unfortunately, the concluding part of the letter and the stress of his reaction probably played its part in his sudden fit of

---

4. Benjamin Rush (January 4, 1746–April 19, 1813) studied at the College of New Jersey (Princeton University) and apprenticed under Dr. John Redman of Philadelphia. He also earned a degree from the University of Edinburgh and opened a medical practice in Philadelphia in 1769. During the American Revolution, Rush consulted on Paine's *Common Sense* and was a signee of the Declaration of Independence in the summer of 1776. Rush also accompanied the Philadelphia militia and crossed the Delaware on Christmas night. He was also with the army when they fought at Trenton and Princeton. He was later forced to leave the army after criticizing General Washington, but in 1783 was appointed to the staff of the Pennsylvania Hospital.

5. HSP, Benjamin Rush letter book, Vol. 82.

6. Stephen's 1796 Philadelphia Directory, 193.

7. Her house on Willing's Alley was located adjacent to the south end of St. Joseph's Catholic Churchyard.

8. This appeared as part of an advertisement by Mary Watters for her "worm cakes" in her son's publication, *The Weekly Magazine* in Volume 1 in 1798.

9. LCP, John A. McAllister Collection, Gratz-Franks-Simon-Papers (1752–1831), Box 2, Folder 63.

Present-day location of Willings Alley and close to the St. Joseph's Catholic Church where Trent visited the home of doctoress Mary Watters. (Author photo.)

coughing and aching body. In the letter, Morgan was straight to the point and told him that their final effort was in vain. A vote was taken, and the appeal to lay claim to those lands in and around the Ohio River in favor of the Indiana Company was denied.[10] Congress also declared it was not going to hear another appeal, memorial, or petition from them and recognized openly now that this grant could not be confirmed because this land indeed belonged to Virginia. Ultimately, their hope for a fourteenth colony and Trent's redemption in keeping his house and property in New Jersey by paying off his creditors was soundly defeated.

---

10. Lewis, 264–68.

After Trent finally felt well enough to travel, he returned home to his Trenton plantation and began to put all his affairs in order. With most of his Pennsylvania and New York lands already mortgaged to his former business associates or in foreclosure, Trent was set to sell his New Jersey plantation that early summer to help fulfill the court-ordered obligation he owed to Elijah Bond.

Trent was assisted by his cousin Israel Morris in preparing the plantation to be sold but felt the property, including the messuage, could be sold as is to be more marketable. This included any household or kitchen furniture[11] inside as soon as he passed over the recited indenture mortgage officially to Bond. It also was easier with his declining health so that once he officially notarized the selling of the indenture, he could just stay in Philadelphia and continue to monitor his illness. Besides, in Trenton with the recent passing of Dr. David Cowell last December,[12] nobody in town could provide his necessary medicine to lessen his ailments.

It did surprise Trent, however, that in the doctor's will, Cowell, a bachelor with no children, made Trent the executor of his estate on December 17, 1783, and left his teenage son John as residuary legatee.[13] After the specifics had been sorted out, John was left with Cowell's property and house in Trenton that he and his brother Ebenezer (Trent's former attorney) had once resided in during the Battle of Trenton. Trent probably resided there a few weeks before he, John, his wife Sarah, and daughter Mary (his eldest daughter Ann had since been married and moved just outside of Trenton) departed to Philadelphia around the end of May. (It was also probably why he eventually wrote in his 1784 will as "late of Hunterdon County"[14] instead of his former plantation in Burlington County and Nottingham Township).

Eventually arriving in the city, Trent and his wife headed to the lower corner of Black Horse Alley and Front Street at the home office of notary Assheton Humphreys[15] on June 1, 1784. Once notarized, the recited indenture of mortgage authorized Elijah Bond as Trent's power of attorney and entitled Bond "Peaceable and Quiet possession in Seiz'n"[16] of the property which he proposed to sell for the asking price of six thousand pounds (Just over $1 million today), only half the amount Trent owed Bond. To chip away at some of the principal debt of twelve thousand pounds (Today about $2.1 million),[17] he offered his

---

11. State Archives of New Jersey, West Jersey Deed, Volume AN, June 1, 1784, 187.
12. Documents Relating to the Colonial History of the State of New Jersey, Calendars of New Jersey Wills, Volume VI, 97.
13. History of the Presbyterian Church in Trenton, New Jersey, Hall, 292.
14. Philadelphia County Wills, Book T, 487. Trent's complete 1784 will is found in Appendix N of this book.
15. *Pennsylvania Gazette*, January 26, 1774, 3.
16. State Archives of New Jersey, West Jersey Deed, Volume AN, June 1, 1784, 187.
17. Ibid.

Today this is Black Horse Alley in Philadelphia and the former site for the office of notary Assheton Humphreys that once stood at the corner of this alley and Front Street, which is shown in the distance. (Author photo.)

remaining five thousand acres along the Mohawk River in New York that had been mortgaged to Thomas Walpole[18] in London years before. Sadly, there was no guarantee the property's worth equaled this remaining balance since the lands he once owned were in danger of foreclosure.

Bond wasted no time and published the advertisement for this sale of Trent's South Trenton plantation house and property on June 28, 1784, then had it appear sporadically in July in three different newspapers. On July 4, 1784, it appeared in the *Pennsylvania Gazette*, the next day on the 5th in the

---

18. HSP, Frank M. Etting Collection, January 7, 1784, Thomas Walpole to William Trent.

> **To be SOLD by the Subscriber,**
>
> At Public Sale, on TUESDAY, the 20th of July next: A VALUABLE Farm, on which Major William Trent lately lived, situated on the river Delaware, within two miles of Trenton, containing about 700 acres, 250 cleared, 100 of which is meadow of the first quality, two orchards of 600 trees, of the best grafted fruit, an excellent shad fishery, and the old accustomed ferry, known by the name of the Trenton Lower Ferry, with boats, also the frame of a large shallop. There is on the said farm, a large brick dwelling-house a kitchen, barn, stables, and other out-houses. One sixth part of the purchase money to be paid down, the remainder the purchaser may have a considerable time, upon paying the interest annually.
>
> Trenton, June 28. ¶ 1 w. ELIJAH BOND.

This is the original advertisement (submitted by Elijah Bond) that appeared in the July 14, 1784, edition of the Pennsylvania Gazette *to sell Trent's plantation in Trenton, New Jersey. (Author photo.)*

New Jersey Gazette and finally on the 17th in the *Pennsylvania Packet*. All three announced the public sale on July 20, 1784, and it was, in fact, purchased that day for four thousand five hundred pounds (About $780,000 today)[19] by Trenton resident and clothier to the Continental Army, Barnt De Klyn.[20] De Klyn resided there for little over a year when, on November 3, 1785, a fire destroyed Trent's former house,[21] and he built another a few years later he called "Bow Hill." Today, De Klyn's 2nd house (circa 1790) still stands and is used as a Ukrainian Cultural Center at 477 Jeremiah Avenue in Hamilton Township, just south of downtown Trenton, New Jersey.

For Trent, signing over this New Jersey property probably brought him mixed emotions. He and his family were sad to leave the city of Trenton where they had resided as a family longer than anywhere, but relieved to distance themselves from a place that brought them nothing but heartache and grief. Trent's mother, Mary, and two daughters, Martha and Sarah, had all died in that town, which had been nothing but a curse ever since he moved back to Trenton right before he left for London in the summer of 1769. Worse yet, he never stayed on track with the annual payments or the accrued interest, and it progressively brought him and his family into financial ruin.

---

19. Burlington County Deeds, Deed Book O part 2, 253–55.
20. Barnt De Klyn was born in Massachusetts to a family of French Protestants called Huguenots and lived in Philadelphia. During the American Revolution he sold woolen textiles to the Continental Army and became known as the "Clothier General", so they could have uniforms. Later he purchased the property and house formerly owned by Trent in 1784 but lost the house to a fire in November of 1785. He built a new house around 1790 he called "Bow Hill" that he rented to Napoleon's brother Joseph Bonaparte, the former King of Spain. Today the house is a Ukraine American Cultural Center on 477 Jeremiah Avenue in Hamilton Township.
21. *Dunlap's Pennsylvania Packet*, November 10, 1785.

On a positive note, they were able to arrange an apprenticeship for their son John. After attending Trenton School Company, the sudden vacancy of a physician in Trenton (with the death of Dr. Cowell) sparked some interest in young John's career choice. He learned the medical profession under the Surgeon General of Pennsylvania, Dr. James Hutchinson (also spelled Hutchison),[22] who had a practice now alongside Dr. William Shippen on Second Street in Philadelphia between Walnut and Spruce. To pay for his son's apprenticeship, Trent had the property formerly owned by Dr. Cowell[23] that was given to John and used as collateral. It proved to be the final land transaction Trent was ever involved in.

His health worsened, and he sought help physically and financially from any relations in the city he still had left. When his cousin Israel Morris could only help so much, Trent either stayed at the Indian Queen or stayed with his kinsman John Todd,[24] a Quaker schoolmaster who lived at the southwest corner of Fourth and Chestnut,[25] just across from his schoolhouse beside Carpenter's Hall. These lodgings were also a little closer in proximity to Willing's Alley and the house of "doctoress" Mary Watters, who probably checked on him frequently and provided him with medicines if he requested them. Unfortunately for Trent, his earlier bouts with intermittent fever (malaria) and poor diet had led to his partial blindness and the severe rheumatism that was crippling him. So, back when he was prescribed Portland's Powder, he developed a dependency on it, and this only made his condition worse. The bitters found inside the powder contained lycopodium, an unknown toxin at the time that, when ingested frequently by Trent over the last two years, resulted in the paralysis of motor nerves and led to only one certain outcome. He was dying, and there was nothing he could do about it.

Further proof of this medicine's toxicity was discovered later in the 1805 Volume II book *Medical Inquiries and Observations,* written by Dr. Benjamin Rush. In Rush's publication, he described the effects of ingesting "bitters" and asked the proverbial question, "Are bitters proper to prevent a return of this state of gout?"[26] He then mentioned "that the Duke of Portland's powder,

---

22. James Hutchinson (1752–1793) was born in Bucks County, Pennsylvania and apprenticed under druggist Moses and Isaac Bartram. He earned a medical degree from the College of Philadelphia in 1774 and worked as an apothecary at the Pennsylvania Hospital from 1773–1775. During the American Revolution, he served as the Surgeon General of Pennsylvania from 1778–1784. He was also a founder of the College of Physicians in 1787 and died of yellow fever while treating patients during the yellow fever epidemic in 1793.

23. State Archives of New Jersey, Ebenezer Cowell Papers, Box 2, Item #14, Deed of John Trent to Ebenezer Cowell, September 28, 1789.

24. The Trent family seems to be related to the Todd family through the Powell family. The Powell's married into John Todd Sr's line and also into the Morris family which was through Trent's mother Mary's line.

25. MacPherson's 1785 Philadelphia Directory, 73.

26. Rush, 292.

which is composed of bitter ingredients, excited a fatal gout in many people who used it for that purpose."[27] Rush, who preached the ineffectiveness of this medicine that Trent once took, described it as follows:

> I should as soon expect to see gold produced by the operations of fire upon copper or lead as expect to see gout prevented or cured by any medicine that acted upon the system without the aid of more or less of the remedies that have been mentioned.[28]

This was why, by early July, Trent, barely able to see, speak, or rid the fluid from his lungs, summoned his wife to gather certain relations and friends in the city to see him urgently. On July 6, 1784[29] and realizing the end could be near, Trent struggled past the aching of his fingers and deep coughs to draft his last will and testament. The document was just two pages long, a sad epiphany of the standing of his social status compared to his previous ones written in 1775 and 1782. No longer was he even land wealthy, having little property in Pennsylvania and no more in New York or New Jersey. The debt he amassed or tried to pay off in the last thirty years had truly daunted him, and now, with his waning health, he could no longer hide from creditors.

All Trent had left were a few personal items which he and Sarah stored in his precious black trunk before they moved permanently to Philadelphia. He had remaining in his possession a charger plate with the Trent coat of arms engraved in the center, his Spitalfields silk suit from London and over fifteen bundles, books, or loose papers[30] from his life as a backcountry merchant for over forty years since the Treaty of Lancaster in 1744.

The only other "assets" or wealth he had left were found in what remained of his 7,147 shares in "Indiana," which, since their latest defeat by Congress, was diminishing in value with each passing month. In his will, Trent left one share each in "Indiana" to Richard Wharton, John Todd Jr, and his brother James Todd.[31] Wharton, the son of his friend Samuel and John Todd Jr, the son of schoolmaster John Todd Sr, were both up-and-coming law school graduates who were awaiting their acceptance to the Pennsylvania Bar. They were also providing legal advice to him since he or Sarah could not afford a high-priced probate attorney to oversee his will.

---

27. Ibid., 292–93.
28. Ibid., 293.
29. Philadelphia County Wills, Book T, 487. Trent's complete 1784 will is found in Appendix N of this book.
30. LCP, John A. McAllister Collection, William Trent Papers, Box 1, Folder 31. For a complete inventory list of Trent's black trunk, see also Appendix O of this book.
31. Philadelphia County Wills, Book T, 487.

He next left one-half share of "Indiana" to his cousin Israel Morris for his assistance and in trust for Israel's four children, Susanna, Sarah, Phoebe, and William.[32] What meager cash he did have left, he set aside £10[33] for his nurse and visiting "doctoress" Mary Watters. Anything else left of his estate, a few hundred acres of land in Bedford County (Colerain Township),[34] Northumberland County (on Middle Creek)[35] and Cumberland County (Barree Township), and his beloved clock were either sold or divided amongst his wife Sarah, daughters Ann and Mary and his son John.

Despite having a minuscule estate, Trent designated four executors[36] in his will in case certain persons were not able to manage. He appointed his friend Samuel Wharton, the first executor, cousin, or "kinsman" Israel Morris the second, his daughter Mary the third, and relation John Todd Jr. the fourth. Trent omitted his wife Sarah as executrix because he knew what litigations and debts might come about once he died, so he didn't wish her to be caught up with that burden.

Finally, he weakly signed his name at the bottom with his seal and then allowed three witnesses who all lived nearby along Fourth Street to declare they saw him depose his last will and testament. Tailor John Martin signed first, his shop next door to the Indian Queen Tavern.[37] Next came schoolmaster John Todd[38] and finally James Birchall,[39] a grocer whose store lay between Martin's shop and the Todd house. The will was then recorded at the office of the Probate of Wills at the corner of Keys Alley[40] and Second Street. This was the home of the Recorder of Wills George Campbell, who ironically was the same individual on the bond that still owed money to Trent back in 1779.

This third will deposed by Trent was not only the final will he wrote but also the last known document by his hand before his death.[41] Though an inventory valuing his current estate has never been found alongside Trent's last will, there was a list compiled of the specific contents of his black trunk. This transcription of its contents was conducted by his relation, John Todd Jr, the current librarian at the Library Company of Philadelphia[42], which at that time resided inside Carpenter's Hall. Today, this document or list lies amongst the

---

32. Ibid.
33. Ibid.
34. *Freeman's Journal, Or, The North American Intelligencer,* March 9, 1791.
35. *Dunlap's Pennsylvania Packet,* August 20, 1789.
36. The four executors were: Samuel Wharton, John Todd Jr, Mary Trent, and Israel Morris.
37. MacPherson's 1785 Philadelphia Directory, 51.
38. Ibid., 73.
39. Ibid., 10.
40. Today this is New Street between Race and Vine.
41. See also Appendix N for the complete transcription of Trent's will.
42. John Todd Jr. was the librarian at the Library Company of Philadelphia from January 13, 1784–February 19, 1785.

Today the present-day site of where the house of schoolmaster John Todd once stood and one of the places Trent stayed briefly before his death on December 1, 1784. The house formerly stood at the corner of 4th and Chestnut Street in Philadelphia. (Author photo.)

thousands of other collections at the Library Company of Philadelphia at 1314 Locust Street, directly beside the Historical Society of Pennsylvania.[43]

Surprisingly, Trent survived the summer, and by the late fall of 1784, it is presumed with the state of his health, he did not venture far (if at all) from the Todd house or the Indian Queen Tavern along that stretch of Fourth Street between Market and Chestnut. In fact, if it weren't for a specific letter written by Quaker merchant Thomas Clifford on December 27, 1784, researchers might never have learned the exact date of Trent's death. (At one point it was always

---

43. See also Appendix O for the complete contents of Trent's black trunk.

This is New Street in Philadelphia and formerly called Keys Alley. It was on this street at the house and office of the Register of Wills George Campbell where Trent submitted his last will and testament dated July 6, 1784. (Author photo.)

mistakenly assumed he died the same year as his probated will in 1787). In this letter to London Postmaster and former Grand Ohio Company member Anthony Todd, Clifford wrote the only brief mention of Trent's passing and the only statement regarding the final minutes of his life:

> About the first Inst, William Trent Departed this life; he made a Will appointed Samuel Wharton, John Todd Junr, and others, His executors. Was, I believe, very low in Circumstances, having been helped in his Last Illness for sometime Past by his Friends, unless Congress

should decide in his favor respecting Considerable Quantity of Lands he claimed that lays on or near the Ohio River.[44]

The first day of December was the day he expelled his last breath, and there was no widespread announcement of his death, not even for an important figure who still considered himself a gentleman before he died. But because of the aforementioned low circumstances and no affiliation with a church in the city, Trent instead underwent the customary tradition of somebody who met his poverty-stricken end. His wife Sarah "laid" him out that night into the next day, wrapping him in a cloth shroud to be buried, probably using the yards of calico fabric her husband had purchased back in March. She may have also used the abundance of lead bars her husband purchased at that same time to take to a local ironmonger. There in his shop, the ironmonger or blacksmith could melt down the three hundred bars of lead (or whatever was left from the original quantity) for handles or grips upon the coffin and the rest for a possible deposition plate or "coffin" plate. This was usually a lead plate that was placed upon the coffin that displayed the decadence name along with the death date or age. It could even be removed from the coffin before the burial as a keepsake for the family of the deceased. However, this use of the lead bars is pure speculation since later, Trent's daughter Mary only suggested settling a return with ironmonger Benjamin Horner in the city and never mentioned what was exactly on the bill or the purpose for the lead bars. More than likely, the Trent family couldn't afford to have him placed in a coffin but just in the customary shroud. It made no difference because the weather was the deciding factor on where Sarah had him buried anyway. At first, she probably wished him interred in the Trenton churchyard of St. Michael's, but navigation on the Delaware River had been "impeded by ice" since the end of November, and it was reported was not "seldom practicable until the first week of March."[45]

So, without many options left in the city, Sarah had him probably taken to the closest burial yard to their location along Fourth Street, a place called "the Potters Field." Originally named Southeast Square and located just two streets over between Walnut and Spruce, it was one of the five original quadrants or "public squares" designed by surveyor general Thomas Holme in his plan of Philadelphia published in 1683. It was also the only square with a formal patent issued by William Penn on January 29, 1706, that made it "a common burying-place for the service of the city of Philadelphia for interring

---

44. HSP, Clifford Family Papers, Collection #0136, Thomas Clifford to Anthony Todd, December 27, 1784. See also the complete Thomas Clifford letter dated December 27, 1784 in Appendix N of this book.

45. *Independent Gazetteer*, January 1, 1785.

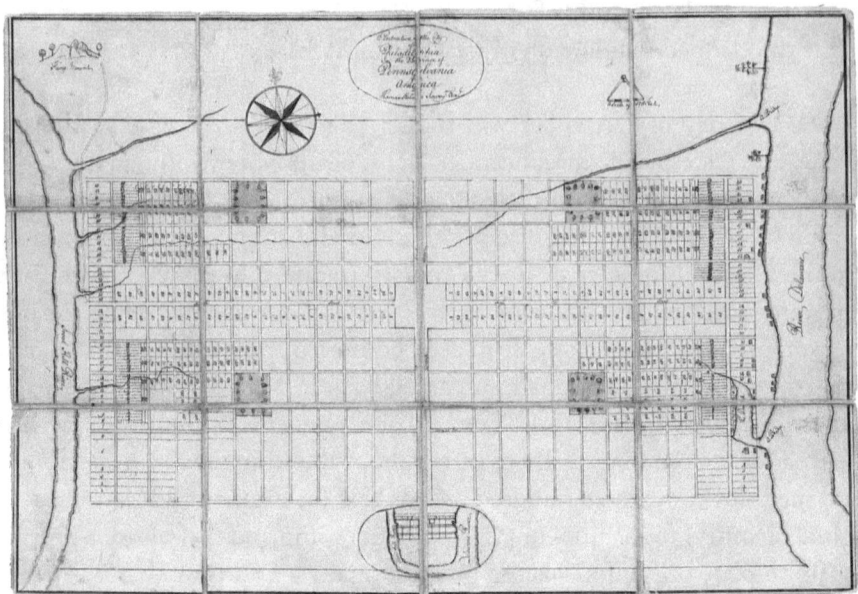

"A Portraiture of the City of Philadelphia in the Province of Pennsylvania in America" completed by surveyor-general Thomas Holme in 1683. There were five original squares with the bottom right square named Southeast Square and used as a potter's field. (Courtesy of the Historical society of Pennsylvania and Public Domain.)

the bodies of all manner of deceased persons whatsoever, whom there shall be occasion to lay therein."[46] Now, almost eighty years later, "the Potters Field" still acted as a large unmarked burial ground for those deceased who were once enslaved, paupers, prisoners from the nearby Walnut Street Gaol and unidentified persons. Most recently, it was even used to bury those soldiers who fought during the Revolutionary War. Perhaps Sarah even found this last detail most suitable for her husband and his final resting place since he was a veteran captain in three different wars. After all, there was no funeral procession for him to Southeast Square. Just a hole dug amongst the several coffins and shrouds already interred in the northern section of the square just below Walnut Street, and the shrouded Trent was placed down in, his feet toward the east and his head to the west. He was then covered up with dirt while a few of his friends and family looked on. Then, his unmarked grave was guarded over the next few nights to keep safe from a group of "body snatchers" or rather associates of Dr. William Shippen who used this burying ground rather frequently to

---

46. Pennsylvania Archives, Vol. 12, Hazard, 469.

Today this is the northern section of Washington Square Park (formerly Southeast Square) where it is believed Trent was laid to rest. (Author photo.)

retrieve the newly deceased for dissection[47] in Shippen's anatomical lectures at the College of Philadelphia.[48]

Yet after Trent's burial, something strange happened. Life in the city around the square continued without even the slightest remembrance of him in the New Jersey or Pennsylvania newspapers. It was like once Trent died, his story had faded and been extinguished, joining the thousands interred there before him and the thousands more a decade later after him who fell prey to the city's horrific yellow fever epidemic in 1793.

Even Southeast Square's name faded from existence when, on May 19, 1825,[49] an ordinance passed officially naming it as Washington Square honoring Trent's former friend and the First President of the United States, George Washington. Fortunately, over a century later, these unknown individuals who lay buried beneath the earth in Washington Square were finally remembered for their forgotten stories. In 1957,[50] a memorial was constructed and completed that stood in the square to honor these once-forgotten individuals with

---

47. Library of Congress, Shippen Family Papers, Letter from Dr. William Shippen to Thomas Lee Shippen, December 18, 1787.
48. The College of Philadelphia eventually became the University of Pennsylvania.
49. Cultural Landscape for Washington Square (2010). Section 1.45.
50. Ibid., Sections 1.117–18.

the Tomb of the Unknown Soldier from the American Revolution, an eternal flame, and a bronze statue of George Washington.

Today, though now a public park, Washington Square is hallowed ground for those unknown soldiers and the thousands like Trent who, in some way, could once tell a story of their sacrifice. For Trent, the first phrase engraved across the memorial could have easily been describing his own life and story: "Freedom is a light for which many men have died in darkness."

Those simple words spoke the truth. Toward the end of his life, it seemed he had slipped into darkness. He had failed veritably, countless times over, in pursuit of his ambitions, but it was not in vain. Because, like darkness, it was not permanent, and now William Trent's powerful story was finally coming into the light.

The eternal flame today in Washington Square Park along with a statue of George Washington and the words, "Freedom is a light for which many men have died in darkness." (Author photo.)

Postlude

One Last Chime

Trent's will was not proven until May 2, 1787, having much litigation between his creditors Joseph Simon, Silas Deane, Moses Franks, Edward Bancroft, Levi Andrew Levy, and others to receive any kind of retribution from his indentures, mortgages, or outstanding debts. Of Trent's creditors previously mentioned, friend Edward Bancroft (who also witnessed Trent's 1775 will in London) was worth mentioning for his exploits that made him infamous posthumously. In 1891, when British diplomatic papers were finally released, it was discovered that Bancroft was a double agent and spy for the British.[1] Since 1777, he had worked for the British Secret Service and reported to them the activities of Dr. Franklin and Silas Deane in Paris while serving under Franklin as the Secretary to the American Commission in France.[2] During this time Trent also exchanged correspondence with Bancroft until he died in 1784, all while having no indication Bancroft may have been updating the British Ministry with any of Trent's reports or memoranda from America. Bancroft was successful as a spy but could not prevent the alliance between America and France that ultimately sealed America's victory over Great Britain in the Revolutionary War.

As for the business side, Trent's name and the Indiana Company even continued to be involved in several Supreme Court cases by the turn of the century, with William Grayson v. Virginia in 1792 and Levi Hollingsworth v. Virginia in 1798.[3] The latter set a precedent in which the President of the United States had no formal power to amend the Constitution and that the 11th Amendment was binding on all cases already pending prior to its ratification.

---

1. Schaeper, 267–68.
2. Ibid., 89–97.
3. Marcus, 299.

Trent's former legal hire, John Todd Jr., joined the Pennsylvania Bar in 1785. He later operated a private law practice in 1791 from his house in the Society Hill neighborhood at 341 Walnut Street, not less than a block from his parent's former house. (Today, the Dolley Todd house still stands at that exact address and is run by Independence National Historic Park in Philadelphia). Unfortunately, Todd barely reached his thirtieth year when he succumbed to yellow fever in the fall of 1793 along with his infant son William Temple Todd and both his father, John Todd, the schoolmaster and mother, Mary Durborow Todd.[4] Todd's Quaker widow, the former Dolley Payne,[5] eventually married "Father of the Constitution" and Trent's "Indiana" rival James Madison on September 15, 1794, becoming the First Lady when Madison eventually became the Fourth President of the United States.

Trent's widow Sarah continued to live poorly in Philadelphia, but as her situation worsened, she found herself residing in a boarding house in the Northern Liberties District of the city[6] until late 1791 or early 1792. Clement Biddle's 1791 Philadelphia directory listed her as a widow at this boarding house located at No. 442 North Second Street.[7] Before yellow fever embraced the city in the summer of 1793, she moved back to New Jersey and lived out her final days in Trenton with one of her two children still residing in western New Jersey. Since personal correspondence doesn't exist between Sarah and her husband today, we can assume, like the eventual widow Martha Washington, Sarah made sure the words between her and her husband remained private. The "True American" newspaper in Trenton announced her death "in an advanced age on Thursday, March 26, 1801."[8]

Their eldest daughter, Ann, married Samuel Raymond, a former soldier in the 21st Massachusetts Regiment and a prestigious member in the Commander-in-Chief's Guard (also known as Washington's Life Guard) for eighteen months under adjutant Caleb Gibbs.[9] He continued to serve in the Continental Army until December of 1779, having probably been introduced to Ann when his regiment came with General Washington to Trenton. Later, he worked as a millstone maker[10] in Maidenhead and Lawrence Township in Hunterdon County, where he and Ann lived just outside of Trenton. They had no children,

---

4. John Todd Jr. and his son William Temple Todd succumbed to yellow fever on October 24, 1793. John Todd Jr's parents died earlier in October of that year. John Todd Sr the schoolmaster on October 2, 1793 and his mother Mary Durburow Todd on October 12, 1793.
5. John Todd Jr. married Dolley Payne on January 7, 1790.
6. 1790 Pennsylvania Census, Philadelphia County.
7. Clement Biddle's Philadelphia Directory 1791, 132.
8. *True American* (Trenton, New Jersey), March 31, 1801.
9. 1820 Pension Records Hunterdon County, New Jersey, Continental Massachusetts Service, Pension Number S.33, 527, Samuel Raymond, August 4, 1820, 3.
10. Ibid.

and Ann outlived her husband, passing away on September 12th, 1826,[11] a few weeks shy of her seventieth birthday.

Her brother John finished his apprenticeship with Dr James Hutchinson in 1789, after also taking classes for one year at the School of Medicine (Today known as the Perelman School of Medicine at the University of Pennsylvania in Philadelphia) in 1788. He lived three more years in Trenton but sold off his two lots in Trenton along Shabakunk Creek to his future brother-in-law Nathan Beakes in 1792[12] and then moved to Kershaw County, South Carolina, to begin his medical practice. In the spring of 1799, he married the former Mary Louisa DuBose in Camden, South Carolina and had five children: Isaac, Martha, John, Mary, and William Henry Trent. Dr. John Trent served as a practitioner of physick in Camden for sixteen years until his death at the age of forty-one on November 9, 1809.[13] Today, John, his wife Mary and four of his children are buried in the Old Presbyterian Cemetery on Meeting Street in Camden.

Trent's other daughter, Mary, became the lone executrix of her father's will and estate after the three other executors renunciated. By late December 1789, she was relieved to finally free herself of these duties and suggested she "shall not be liable to be called on in a future day."[14] She did, however, still retain most of her father's remaining possessions to make sure they stayed within his descendants. In early 1790, she married Trenton native Nathan Beakes, and they lived at the old Beakes plantation house, whose site today was at the corner of Beakes and Calhoun Street in downtown Trenton. It was also where she and her husband freed their enslaved servant, Caesar, on December 30, 1793.[15] Mary and Nathan had three children: Lydia, Nathan Jr, and Morgan Beakes. Mary Trent Beakes died at the advanced age of seventy-eight on December 20, 1840, "the last person that borne the name of Trent"[16] of her line.

Mary's granddaughter, Anna Rossell (the youngest daughter of Lydia Beakes and her husband, Adjutant General Zachariah Rossell),[17] was the one responsible for why a few items belonging to Major William Trent (her late great-grandfather) still survive today. She was said to be one of the last direct descendants of Major William Trent, residing on 228 West State Street in Trenton and became an honorary member of the Daughters of the American

---

11. *United States Gazette*, September 22, 1826.
12. Trenton Free Public Library, Trentoniana Collection, 1792 Deed John Trent to Nathan Beakes.
13. South Carolina Historical Magazine, Vol. 25–26, 49.
14. HSP, Gratz Papers, Mary Trent to Moses Franks, December 30, 1789.
15. State Archives of New Jersey, Manumission of Slaves Hunterdon County 1788–1836, 6.
16. Documents Relating to the Colonial History of the State of New Jersey, Volume XX. 1756–1761, 558.
17. Zachariah Rossell (November 14, 1788–July 21, 1842) was a distinguished officer during the War of 1812 under Colonel Zebulon M. Pike and was promoted to adjutant general after the war. He married Lydia Beakes on January 26, 1815. He is interred at Riverview Cemetery in Trenton, New Jersey alongside his wife Lydia Beakes and his two daughters, Mary Trent Rossell Higbee and Anna Rossell.

Revolution in Trenton. This chapter, named for her late great-grandfather, was, in fact, called the William Trent Chapter and was organized on January 24, 1895, holding meetings at the Old Barracks on Barrack Street.

On November 12, 1905, she donated to the Trent Chapter's collection three original pieces of pewter (two plates and one charger plate) dated 1760 with the Trent family coat of arms in the center and a familiar piece of original clothing framed behind glass. This was the vest from Trent's silk suit he had made in the Spitalfields District and the only remaining original garment from his six-year stint in London. Today, the Trent vest still survives, having been taken out of the frame, refurbished, and put inside a display case at the visitor center of his boyhood home. It is the only known piece of clothing in existence to be worn by Major Trent and is the heart of the 1719 William Trent House Museum, still standing in Trenton, New Jersey.

Now, as for Trent's beloved clock, it was passed from Mary Trent Beakes to her son Morgan (Grandson of Major William Trent) and then passed along to his daughter Mary Louisa, who married Daniel R. Furman of Ewing, New Jersey. After Mary Louisa Beakes Furman died in 1899, the clock became the property of Trenton native Emily Warren Roebling,[18] wife of Washington Roebling, co-engineer, and supervisor for the completion of the Brooklyn Bridge. Then, a month before she died, Roebling gifted the clock in January of 1903 to the National Society of the Colonial Dames of America in the State of New Jersey (NSCDANJ), to which she was a member, assuring its historical preservation. (Emily Warren Roebling died on February 28, 1903). It was under this stewardship that the Trent clock still survives today in West Hampton, New Jersey. The clock stands atop the stairs inside Historic Peachfield, a plantation house originally built in 1725 and currently used as the official headquarters for the National Society of the Colonial Dames of America in the State of New Jersey.

Though the William Trent clock no longer chimes today, it can be forever linked to Trent's legacy and be remembered even now as time goes by.

---

18. The Roebling family specifically Emily Warren Roebling and her husband Washington Roebling lived at 191 West State Street in Trenton, New Jersey. Today this is the site of the New Jersey State Museum.

Appendix A

Judge William Trent's and Mary Coddington's Wedding Certificate, dated July 22, 1710

Historical Society of Pennsylvania, James Hamilton Collection, Box 43, Folder 6.

This is the only known evidence of Judge William Trent and Mary Coddington's marriage. Despite Rev. George Ross officiating and witnessing their Anglican ceremony in Philadelphia, his parents' nuptials were only legal by going out of their native province and receiving a marriage license from New York/New Jersey Governor Robert Hunter because Trent's mother Mary was under the age of eighteen (She was seventeen) and was forbidden to marry outside her Quaker faith.

This is to certify all concerned that William Trent Merchant of Philadelphia & Mary Coddington were joined together in holy matrimony according to the Form of the Church of England by virtue of his Excellency Robert Hunter Esq. Governor in Chief of the Province of New Jersey, his license to that purpose on the twentieth day of July 1710. As Witnessed given under my hand this 22 of July 1710 at Philadelphia, I say to me.

George Ross

Appendix B

Captain William Trent's Return of his Company in September of 1746 and the Narrative of the Captivity of Nehemiah How in 1745–1747

Pennsylvania Archives Fifth Series, Volume 1, pp. 8-11 and The Narrative of the Captivity of Nehemiah How, p. 54.

In September of 1746, all four captains of the Pennsylvania companies were to submit their roster or "return" to Pennsylvania Governor George Thomas. This was the return Trent submitted of his men, listing their age, date of enlistment and their occupation. The following entry kept by captive Nehemiah How at the prison in Quebec was why, after the battle near Fort Clinton, New York, Trent was presumed dead.

Captain William Trent's Return of his Company, Specifying the Day of Each Man's Enlistment, &C., September 1746.

Soldier	Age	Place of Birth	Date of Enlistment	Occupation or Description
Adams, Emanuel	28	Ireland	Aug. 1	Woolcomber
Adams, John	25	Scotland	Aug. 18	Laborer
Armstrong, Joseph	23	Ireland	June 27	Laborer
Arnold, Joseph	40	England	July 16	Laborer
Atkins, William	–	–	July 11, deserted Aug. 7	–
Balls, Richard	–	–	July 7, died July 27	–
Baem, David	32	Ireland	July 17	Weaver
Bayman, Nathaniel	30	Ireland	July 1	Baker

Appendix B

Soldier	Age	Place of Birth	Date of Enlistment	Occupation or Description
Benn, Benjamin	27	England	July 1	Laborer
Black, William	23	Scotland	July 21	Weaver
Boardman, Matthew	28	Germany	Aug. 7	Laborer
Boyle, James	27	Ireland	Aug. 4	Laborer
Brooks, Robert	22	England	July 22	Laborer
Burch, Thomas	22	England	July 30	Laborer
Burn, Edward	24	Ireland	June 26	Laborer
Byrn, Charles	27	Ireland	July 21	Joiner
Cally, James	30	England	July 7	Gardener
Campbell, John	31	Scotland	June 27	Collier
Carpenter, William	25	Maryland	July 1	Cordwainer
Carson, Charles	36	Scotland	June 30	Tailor
Cheese, Richard	–	Jerseys	June 26	House Carpenter
Clark, John	30	England	July 19	Husbandman
Clawson, John	32	Pennsylvania	June 27	Cordwainer
Corbet, John	34	Ireland	July 9	Laborer
Crook, John	23	England	July 22	Laborer
Darling, Jeremiah	42	Pennsylvania	July 14	Sawyer
Davis, John	27	England	July 23	Flatsman
Dawson (Danvon), John	21	Pennsylvania	Aug. 5	Laborer
Dennahew, Florence	40	Ireland	July 7	Laborer
Dermott (Durmot), Matthew	28	Ireland	July 19	Carpenter
Drumming, John	21	England	June 30	Laborer
Dugan, John	23	Scotland	July 9	Laborer
Evans, John	25	Pennsylvania	July 3	Laborer
Fitzpatrick, Dennis	26	Ireland	July 23	Laborer
Flannigan, George	40	Ireland	July 16	Cordwainer
Fox, Adam	20	Germany	July 2	Laborer
Fox, Thomas	35	Ireland	July 20	Laborer
Fay, James	–	–	July 30, deserted Aug. 18	–
Fay, Matthew	40	Ireland	June 30	Laborer

Soldier	Age	Place of Birth	Date of Enlistment	Occupation or Description
Freburn, William	19	Pennsylvania	July 7	Smith
Gallagher, Henry	25	Ireland	June 27	Sawyer
Garrigue, Matthew	34	St. Christopher's	June 27	Tailor
Gethins, Daniel	28	Ireland	Aug. 7	Trader
Gollerthon, William	25	Virginia	Aug. 7	Laborer
Goodwin, John	30	England	July 14	Laborer
Grace, William	30	Ireland	July 21	Laborer
Grant, John	31	Ireland	Aug. 11	Clothier
Gray, Joseph	–	–	June 28, deserted July 12	–
Griffith, William	30	England	June 30	Shoemaker
Gunter, William	20	England	Aug. 19	Laborer
Harris, James	33	Ireland	July 13	Laborer
Hinds, John	23	England	July 7	Blacksmith
Hitchley, George	26	England	July 9	Laborer
Hooper, Thomas	–	–	June 28, deserted July 28	–
Irish, Richard	24	England	July 30	Laborer
Isles, James	22	England	June 27	Tanner
Jackson, Daniel	25	Pennsylvania	June 27	Laborer
Jenkins, Thomas	32	England	July 5	Laborer
Johns, Joseph	–	–	July 29	–
Johnston, John	–	–	July 11, deserted Aug. 1	–
Jones, Thomas	24	Pennsylvania	July 1	Sadler
Judge, Rowland	–	–	July 10	–
King, William	31	Barbados	Aug. 7	Mariner
Lalley, Thomas	–	–	July 3, deserted Aug. 31	–
Larey, John	21	Ireland	June 26	Laborer
Lindon, Patrick	35	Ireland	July 5	Laborer
Lorne, Charles	25	Ireland	July 21	Weaver
McCarty, Bartholomew	22	Ireland	Aug. 7	Laborer

Appendix B

Soldier	Age	Place of Birth	Date of Enlistment	Occupation or Description
McCarty, Cornelius	26	Ireland	July 10	Mariner
McCarty, John	24	Ireland	June 30	Laborer
McDonald, Minass	30	Ireland	Aug. 7	Laborer
McDonald, Peter	21	Scotland	June 29	Smith
McEldemar, John	–	–	July 1, deserted Aug. 19	–
McGee, Thomas	21	Ireland	Aug. 1	Laborer
McGoun, Patrick	35	Ireland	June 30	Laborer
McKee(Mckeis), William	26	Ireland	July 17	Laborer
McManus, James	20	Ireland	June 26	Laborer
Mahan, Owen	36	Ireland	Aug. 13	Laborer
Martin, Patrick	30	Ireland	July 19	Laborer
Merchant, Nicholas	30	England	July 18	Laborer
Meredith, John	25	Pennsylvania	July 1	Carpenter
Miller, George	22	Pennsylvania	July 30	Smith
Mooney, Michael	21	Ireland	July 7	Laborer
Morrison, James	19	Ireland	July 11	Laborer
Moses(Mosus), William	25	Pennsylvania	July 7	Blacksmith
Murphy, Archibald	40	Ireland	July 25	Sawyer
Natherland, William	32	England	July 3	Tailor
Neigle, James	21	Ireland	July 11	Tailor
Newman, Edward	26	Ireland	July 14	Laborer
Priscott, James	22	Ireland	July 11	Bricklayer
Randle, Warwick	38	England	July 7	Cordwainer
Raredon, Michael	37	Ireland	July 11	Weaver
Read, John	21	Ireland	July 9	Laborer
Reynolds, Edward	23	Ireland	July 30	Laborer
Reynolds, Patrick	35	Ireland	July 7	Laborer
Robertson, William	27	Ireland	July 1	Smith
Runnell, Peter	30	Ireland	Aug. 4	Laborer
Sammon, Dennis	–	–	July 18, deserted Aug. 5	–
Shea, Timothy	23	Ireland	July 23	Laborer

Soldier	Age	Place of Birth	Date of Enlistment	Occupation or Description
Snapes, Paul	28	Ireland	Aug. 2	Woolcomber
Stanly, Joseph	–	–	July 5, died July 25	–
Stephenson, Samuel	–	–	Aug. 12, deserted Aug. 27	–
Sullivan, Daniel	30	Ireland	July 14	Laborer
Swaney, Thomas	23	Ireland	July 7	Laborer
Swanson, Samuel	–	–	June 26, deserted Aug. 4	–
Tartum, William	23	Pennsylvania	June 26	Cooper
Tilt, John	21	England	July 18	Mariner
Tomey, John	32	Ireland	July 21	Laborer
Tulton, William	21	Ireland	Aug. 7	Laborer
Vaughe, Groves	–	–	July 9, deserted July 23	–
Warfield, William	–	–	July 30, deserted Aug. 14	–
Wasson, Robert	20	Ireland	July 30	Tailor
Windsor, Thomas	43	England	July 1	Laborer
Woodnought, Robert	30	England	July 29	Cordwainer
Yorgen, Dennis	20	Ireland	July 22	Laborer
Young, John Carsum	30	Denmark	June 26	Mariner

Howe's Narrative for April 26, 1747:

Three Men were brought to Prison, who were taken at Albany three Weeks before, and tell us that thirteen were kill'd, Capt. Trent, one of them, they were all Soldiers for the Expedition to Canada.

Appendix C

Hockley, Trent, and Croghan Tanyard Accounts 1752

Historical Society of Pennsylvania, Cadwalader Family Papers, Series 4, Box 202, Folders 15-24.

Before Croghan tried to transfer ownership by the "selling" of his tanning yard along the Conodoguinet Creek to his half-brother Edward Ward and his clerk Roger Walton in the summer of 1751, he and Trent had accumulated quite a large number of debts. This was the list of those accounts "outstanding" or not paid in full to the mercantile firm of Hockley, Trent, and Croghan. It was recorded most likely by clerk Roger Walton.

List of the Tan Yard Debts

Name	(£) Pound	(S) Shilling	(d) Pence
James Young	0	17	0
James Gibey	0	9	0
John Cockendal	3	19	9
Sanders McClair	0	9	4
John McClair Cautt	0	19	6
William Camble	0	7	3
Sam Calhoon	0	7	8
Saml Thompson	1	4	8
Caleb Lamb	0	9	0
Saml Simson	1	6	5
William Steel	0	4	9
John Redick	0	15	0
Robert Stewart	0	4	0

Name	(£) Pound	(S) Shilling	(d) Pence
Henry Paulin	2	5	7
John Poalk	1	8	0
Richard McAlister	1	13	6
John McCluer	0	11	0
Andrew Fobise Brother	0	10	6
James Farguson	2	7	11
Thos & Fran Baskins	1	12	0
Alexander Paterson	0	11	10
John Smith Conogogjg	9	10	4
Thomas Harris	1	15	6
Robert Thomson	0	11	6
John Nailer	0	12	0
Peter Rench	2	10	0
John Garner Senr.	0	11	0
Andrew Armstrong	1	2	7
Johnathan Holms	2	6	0
John McAlister	8	17	2
John Mitchel	1	15	11
Geo. Cowen	3	10	8
Robert Carothers	0	10	2
John Elder	0	11	10
Ezeachel Duning	2	6	6
Richard Tulton	0	5	1
Samuel Culberson	0	7	7
Joseph Wallice	0	7	6
Robert Miller	0	17	11
Daniel O'Cain	6	7	11
William Shephard	1	13	4
Tobias Hendricks	0	10	4
Willam Blyth	4	11	0
Patrick Laugherty	1	1	
James Bigam	0	8	0
John Miller	11	0	7

Appendix C

Name	(£) Pound	(S) Shilling	(d) Pence
Daniel Williams	1	0	2
John Hailough	0	18	0
Malken Miller	1	5	4
Callendar & Company	15	2	10
John Adams	1	3	8
Daniel Lawrence	30	0	7
William Trent	34	3	6
Robert Meeks	5	14	6
John McCluer	0	8	4
William Chesnott	2	2	1
Robert Callendar	10	14	0
Mary Lormose	0	8	0
Francis Weafer	0	7	0
William Farguison	0	12	0
Allen Robenett	0	7	0
Garret Pendergrass	0	10	8
James Brown	1	9	4
Widow Huff	1	13	0
Robert Denny	10	2	0
Adam Calhoon	0	18	10
John Vanleare	1	12	2
Thomas Wilson	4	12	8
George Croghan	44	15	3
Barny Hughs	9	11	1
Wm Dunlap	0	10	7
James Armstrong	1	0	0
Geo. Gilaskey	0	19	3
Lawrence Andrew	0	7	6
James Paterson	4	4	2
Joseph Tunkens	0	9	4
Andrew Montour	0	7	6
Michael Teaff	7	18	2
William Miller	1	1	6

Name	(£) Pound	(S) Shilling	(d) Pence
Jacob Pyatt	1	6	0
Widow Quigley	0	6	1
Geo. Moor	0	4	5
Widow Woods	1	12	1
James Brandon	4	10	0
John Marton Toad	0	10	8
Geo. Bradley	9	1	5
James Farguison	58	6	0
James Martin	8	8	0
John Scull	7	2	6
Hugh McHlhenny	34	4	0
Robert Hunter	11	13	1
John Moor	236	0	0
Thomas Ward	163	0	0
John Hays	50	0	0
Walter Boughanan	0	19	4
John Webb	1	7	10
Abraham Hendricks	1	9	0
William Adoare	1	19	2
Charles West	0	17	8
Patrick Nowlen	5	0	0
To the Stock in ye Yard	200	0	0
To a millhouse	13	0	0
To a Neagro Man	100	0	0
To a Courryer	40	0	0
To Sundry Household Bought of Widow Griffith	27	16	0
Sundry household good	10	0	0
Two cows at the Yard	7	10	0
To Sundry Youtensils Belonging to the yard	30	0	0
Sundrys at on Croghans House_____vizt			
A cart and two horse	35	0	0

Appendix C

Name	(£) Pound	(S) Shilling	(d) Pence
Sundry Sheep	7	0	0
5 Cows	17	0	0
Store goods			
Nine pcs of Garlix	27		
Three pcs of Shalloon	9		
One pc of Shroud	10		
One pc of Bleu Duffels	9	10	
One pc of ¾ cloth	6	0	
Two pcs of holland	12	0	
Two prs of Women's Shoes	1	0	
Three pcs Callicoe	2	10	
One Groce of knives	4	10	
Three Groce of Gartering	5	0	
Six Blankets	4	10	
Sundry other Small Goods	4	0	
Three Neagros	12	0	0
To Appurtinences Belonging To house, I live in	2	0	0

£250844

Appendix D

Commission of William Trent and Official Orders on January 26, 1754

Official Records of Robert Dinwiddie 1751-1758 Volume 1, pp. 55-57.

On January 16, 1754, Lt. Governor Robert Dinwiddie received his report from the young emissary George Washington, who had just returned from Fort Le Boeuf. After reading the French commandant's reply, Dinwiddie immediately suggested to the Governor's Council a captain's commission for William Trent to recruit one hundred men. The date of the official commission was January 26, 1754, and his official orders were delivered to Trent by Thomas Cresap at the mouth of Redstone Creek on February 10, 1754.

COMMISSION OF CAPTAIN WILLIAM TRENT

Rob't Dinwiddie Esq'r His Majesty's L't Gov'r Com'd'r in Chief and Vice Admiral of his Colony and Dom'n of Virg'a—

To WM. TRENT, ESQ'R:
Whereas certain Persons pretending to be Subjects of his most X'n Majesty the King of France, and that they act by his Como. have in a hostile Manner invaded the Territories of our Sovereign His M'y King George the 2d King of Great B. &c. and have comitted divers Outrages and Violences on the Persons and Goods of His M'y's Subjects, in direct violation and infract'n of the Treaties at present subsisting between the two Crowns, and Whereas these Acts of hostility and depredations have been perpetrated in that Part of His Majesty's Dom's w'ch are under my Gov't; In order therefore to the Preservation of the Peace and Good understanding between the two Crowns and the Preservation of our Sovereign's undoubted rights, and the Protection of his Subjects as much as in me lies, I have thought fit to appoint and by Virtue of the Power and Authority to me given as Com'd'r in Chief of this Colony, I do hereby constitute and

appoint You Wm. Trent Esq'r to be Com'd'r of such and so many of His My's Subjects not exceeding 100 Men as You can imediately raise and enlist, and with the s'd Comp'a and the Assist-ance of our good and faithful Friends and Allies the Ind's of the Six Nat's and such others as are in Amity with them and Us, to keep Possession of His M'y's Lands on the Ohio and the Water thereof and to dislodge and drive away, and in case of refusal and resistance to kill and destroy or take Prisoners all and every Person and Persons not Subjects of the King of G. B. who now are or shall hereafter come to settle and take Possess'n of any Lands on said River Ohio, or on any of the Branches or Waters thereof. And I do hereby require the s'd Men who shall so en-list themselves and every ――――― of them to obey You as their Com'd'r and Capt'n &c. and You are to constitute such and so many Officers under You as the Service shall require, not exceeding 1 Capt. and 1 Lieut't.

Given under my Hand and the Seal of the Colony at W'msburg this 26th Day of January in the 27 Year of His M'y's Reign, annoq Dom. 1754.

GOVERNOR DINWIDDIE TO WM. TRENT, ESQR.
SIR:
Y'r Letter of the 6th Curr't I rec'd from Maj'r Washington, from his report, Informat'n and Observat's I find the French intend down the Ohio to build Forts and take Possession of the Lands on that River, w'ch I w'd very earnestly prevent. And as You think You c'd '° this Winter, if properly impower'd to do so, I therefore inclose You a Capt's Com'o to raise 1oo Men in Augusta and in the exterior Settlem'ts of this Dom'n and a blank Com'o for You to choose a suitable Lieut. to Co-operate with You. Y'r Comp'a will be in the Pay of this Gov't agreeable to the Assembly. Maj'r Washington has a Com'o to raise 100 Men, with them he is to join You and I desire You may march Y'r Men out to the Ohio where a Fort is propos'd to be built. When You are there You are to protect and assist them in finishing the Fort and to be on Y'r Guard ag'st any Attempts of the French. I doubt not the Woodsmen You may enlist will be provided with Guns &c., I have appointed Maj'r Carlisle of Alexandria a Commiss'y of Stores and Provisions, he will supply You accordingly with what Necessaries You may want and in case of want of Guns I have sent some to his Care to be delivered to the Com'd'rs of either of these Compa's giving receipt accordingly for them. As You have a good Interest with the Ind's I doubt not You will prevail with many of them to join You in order to defeat the Designs of the French in taking their Lands from them by force of Arms. The Ho. of Burgesses are to meet the 14th

of next Mo. w'n I hope they will enable me to send out 400 more Men early in the Spring to Y'r Assistance. I wrote to the neighbouring Gov'rs for their Aid and Assistance on the present Emergency and I am in hopes they will supply a good Number of men &c. I have some Cannon come in—ten I send up to the Comissary at Alexandria—they carry four Pound shot—I fear there will be a difficulty in carrying them out—as You are acquainted with the Roads, I shall be glad of Y'r Advice therein, and comunicate the same to Maj'r Carlisle. You see the Confidence and good Opinion I have of Y'r Capacity and Diligence w'ch I hope You will Exert on this Occasion by keeping a good Comand and strongly engaging our friendly Ind's to be on the Active. Provisions will be difficult to send regular Supplies. Mr. Washington says one Mr. Frazier can provide large Qu'ty of Venison, Bear, &c. I desire You may write him to get what he can. When You have compleated Y'r Comp'a send me a List thereof and the time of their enlisting and the Places of their Aboad. I wish You Health and Success in the present Expedition and am Sincerely
S'r Y'r h'ble Serv't

Appendix E

Expense Account of the Government of Virginia to William Trent April 8, 1754

Virginia (Colony) Colonial Papers, 1630–1778, accession 36138, State Records Collection, Library of Virginia, Box 147, Folder 44.

On March 17, 1754, William Trent left his men at the Forks of the Ohio to return to the Inhabitants for more supplies and men. The following account by Trent, recorded on April 8, 1754, at the mouth of Will's Creek, listed the following expenses that began when Trent gathered presents for the Six Nations in Winchester, Virginia, in September of 1753.

For Carriage of Fourteen Horses loaded with Powder, Lead, and Flints from Col. Cresaps to Ohio River at 2 Pistoles, a Load is 20 Pistoles......a 21/6......&30.2.0
For Carriage of the Powder, Lead, and Flints from Winchester to the Col......7.0.0
For 12 Deer Skins......a3/......1.16.0
For 9 Doe Bear Skins......a6/......2.14.0......4.10.0
For 19 ¼ yards purple half thicks for Bags to put the Powder in......a 2/9 a yard......2.12.11 ¼
For 3500 Black Wampum a 40/per M......7.0.0
300 White ditto......a3/2 per Ct......0.9.6......7.9.6
{NB 3000 of the Black Wampum and the 300 White was used in one belt}
For one making the Belt and the Leather to make it with......2.0.0
For One Peice of Matchcoat to wrap the Powder with......7.10.0
For 1 Gun, 1 Pistol and Matchcoat gave to one of the Six Chiefs of the Six Nations who Came down from the Upper Towns, as he Came upon Business he brought no Arms with him, he said it was hard for him to go home without Arms as he should run a great Risque as he was Obliged to go through the French to Warn their People from Amongst them......3.15.0

For 1 Case of Neat Pistols gave to the Half-King and Monacatootha and 2 fine Ruffled Shirts and 2 plain Shirts for themselves and Wives Pistols 2.10/ Shirts 3.10.0......6.0.0
These given as a particular Present sent by the Governour to them
For and Express sent for Mr. Andrew Montour to come to me to Ohio to deliver the Speeches paid by Coll. Cresaps......2.12.0

Carried Over......72.11.5 ¼
Brought Over......72.11.5 ¼

NB. There is no Carrying out Powder without Skin Wrappers when I had them of my own I made no Charge these I was Obliged to buy I used two Pieces of Matchcoats for Inside Wrappers, one peice being the outside ones in the Bundles were damaged which I gave to the Indians and with which I charge the Government there is no Such thing as Carrying Powder without damaging without......
For four Pounds paid Coll. Cresap for his going Express with the Governours Letters to me at Red Stone Creek......4.0.0

76.11.5 ¼

Accepted this 8th April 1754

William Trent

Appendix F

Baptism Records found in the Trent Family Bible

Historical Society of Pennsylvania, Family Bible records, Book Br Tr.

In 1755, William Trent recorded the first of six of his children's births, listing each one on the inside cover of his Scottish bible, printed in Edinburgh by Adrian Watkins. It was listed as follows:

William Trent was born opposite the Mouth of Wills Creek in Virginia 28th May 1754 & was baptised by Mr. Hamilton Chaplin to the Regiment

Ann Trent was born at Lancaster the 20th October 1756 & was baptized by Mr Craig Minister for the Borough of Lancaster

Martha Trent was born at Lancaster the 24th October 1759 & was baptized by Mr Barton Minister for the borough of Lancaster

Mary Trent was born at Carlisle the 3rd December 1762 & was baptized by Mr Thompson of Carlisle

Sarah Trent was born at Carlisle the 29th November 1764 a little after 1 O'Clock in the Morning & baptized by Mr Thompson

John Trent was born at Carlisle the 21st April 1768 about 10 O'Clock in the Morning & was baptized by Mr Thompson

Appendix G

Commission to Trent to be Assistant Superintendent of Indian Affairs dated September 3, 1758

The letters and papers of Cadwalader Colden, Volume 5, pp. 258-259.

After Trent successfully prevented the Indians from raiding their commissary at Fort Loudoun in Pennsylvania in the summer of 1758 and to seek further council from Colonel Henry Bouquet, Trent was acknowledged for his services to keep their loyalties with the English. General Forbes knew if he was to avoid the previous blunder by General Braddock, he made sure Trent's expertise was utilized along the way with their Native allies if they were to successfully capture Fort Duquesne. This was his official commission in the fall of 1758.

Capt. Abraham Bosomworth's Orders to
Capt. Trent

[Sept. 3, 1758]
By Abraham Bosomworth Esq' Capt" of a Company in the 2n Batt R.A. Regt & Commandant of His Majestys Indian Allies
To Capt Trent
By Virtue of Powers derived to me from His Excell' Gen¹ Forbes Commander in Chief of the Southern Expedition & with the Approbation of Co¹ Hen Bouquet. Commanding His Majesties Forces for the time being on the Frontiers I do appoint you one of my Assistants
in Conducting & regulating the Indians going to War & you are hereby directed and required to obey such orders as you shall from time to time receive from me or in my absence any other Command" offi" at the [?] Post and to use your best endeavours in keeping the Indians under proper Regulations and preventing any abuse being Committed by making sale of their Goods wasting

their Provisions Ammunition, &c. for which you are to receive 12/ Pennsylva day & this shall be your sufficient Warrant
Given under my hand at the Camp at Rays Town
3 Sept. 1758

Appendix H

Roll of the Militia at Fort Pitt 1763

University of Michigan, William L. Clements Library, Jeffrey Amherst Papers, Volume 6.

When original militia commander Hugh Crawford was captured on May 4, 1763, Fort Pitt Commander Simeon Ecuyer chose the most experienced person he could find to lead the militia company composed from the residents of the Upper and Lower Towns at Fort Pitt. On May 29, 1763, he chose veteran captain, backcountry merchant, and Lower Town storeowner, William Trent. Trent was promoted to Major and immediately helped defend Fort Pitt during the Indian War known later as "Pontiac's Uprising or Rebellion." This complete roll or "return" of Trent and his men was found in a miscellaneous box in the Jeffrey Amherst Papers and was drafted on October 26, 1763. Being published for the first time it lists some various names like Simon Girty, and his brothers Thomas and George, along with eventual Black Boys Rebellion leader James Smith who all later played controversial roles before and after the American Revolution.

Roll of the Militia at Fort Pitt

Officers, Names and when appointed

William Trent Major . . . . May 29, 1763
Josiah Davenport Captain . . . . ditto
Alexander McKee Lieutenant
   & adjutant . . . . ditto
John Flemming ditto . . . . ditto
William Christie Captain . . . . ditto
John Grabiz Lieutenant . . . . ditto. . . . . quit the service the 27th of August
James Millikan Lieutenant . . . . ditto
Thomas Calhoun ditto . . . . June 1st . . . . sergeant till the 18th of August
John Bond Sergeant . . . . May 29, 1763 . . . . died on August 15th
William Campbell ditto . . . . ditto. . . . . private till 16th June
John Robertson Senr. Sergeant . . . . ditto

Appendix H 405

John Robertson Junr. ditto . . . . June 1st . . . . Deserted 27th August
                                                                  Private till 16th June
Richard McMahon Sergeant. . . . . . ditto. . . . . Discharged 13th August
Adam Miller Sergeant. . . . . ditto. . . . . killd the 15th August
James Harris Sergeant. . . . . ditto. . . . . Private till 10th August
Thomas Woods Sergeant . . . . ditto
Patrick Campbell Corporal. . . . . . . May 29, 1763
William Heath ditto. . . . . ditto
Joseph Ray ditto. . . . . ditto
John McDonald ditto. . . . . ditto. . . . . Private till 20th Sept

No.	Mens Names	When Raised	When Discharged	Died or Killed	Deserted
1	Daniel Aldrichs	May 29, 1763	ditto		
2	Philip Atkinson	ditto	ditto		
3	Barney Caggan	ditto	ditto		
4	Frederick Clingle	ditto	ditto		
5	Nathaniel Colbert	ditto	ditto		
6	John Doran	ditto	ditto		
7	William Dun	ditto	ditto		
8	Samuel Daviny	ditto	ditto		
9	John Donnald	ditto	ditto		
10	John Davis	ditto	ditto		
11	Samuel French	ditto	August 27th		
12	Archibald Gutterie Junr	ditto	13th		
13	John Gilmore	ditto	27th		
14	Jacob Good	ditto	13th		
15	Archibald Gutterie Junr	ditto	ditto		
16	William Gutterie	ditto	ditto		
17	John Gutterie	ditto	ditto		
18	John Harry	ditto	27th		
19	Neal McCollome	ditto	13th		
20	William Mitchel	ditto	ditto		
21	Martin McDonnald	ditto	ditto		
22	William McMahon	ditto	ditto		
23	Joseph Mitchel	ditto	27th		

No.	Mens Names	When Raised	When Discharged	Died or Killed	Deserted
24	Eneap McAllister	ditto	ditto		
25	John McAllister	ditto	ditto		
26	Jonathan Plumer	ditto	13th		
27	Christian Rodenbauke	ditto	ditto		
28	Vincent Switzgaver	ditto	ditto		
29	Casper Toub	ditto	ditto		
30	John Whitty	ditto	ditto		
31	Adam Torrence	ditto	27th		
32	Jeremiah Woods	ditto	ditto		
33	Valentine Whitehead	ditto	13th		
34	William Willcoxe	ditto	ditto		
35	Lenard Young	ditto	ditto		
36	John Barton	ditto			Aug 16th
37	William Turpin	ditto			ditto
38	Alexander McDonald	ditto			
39	William Tillery	ditto		Aug 16th	
40	George Stinkerhorn	May 31st		Killed July 20th	
41	James Thompson	May 29th		Killed June 22th	
42	George Beard	ditto	Aug 13th		
43	Moses Beard	ditto			
44	John Burbige	ditto			
45	William Bowlin	ditto			Sept 1st
46	Barnibus Boner	ditto			ditto
47	Abraham Bidler	ditto			
48	Robert Black	ditto			
49	Daniel Collit	ditto			
50	John Connor	ditto			
51	William Cochran	ditto			
52	William Doe	ditto			
53	Joseph Dunlap	ditto			
54	Dudley Dougherty	ditto			

Appendix H

No.	Mens Names	When Raised	When Discharged	Died or Killed	Deserted
55	Robert Eggar	Aug 10th			
56	Isaac Erwin	May 29th			
57	William Evans	ditto			
58	Daniel Eliott	Aug 10th			
59	James Flemming	May 29th	Sept 1st		
60	Simon Girty	ditto			
61	George Girty	May 29th	Sept 1st		
62	Thomas Girty	ditto			
63	Henry Gilmore	ditto			Sept 1st
64	Joseph Goldsney	ditto			
65	Marcus Hullins Junr	ditto			
66	William Herbert	ditto			
67	Charles Haus	ditto			
68	Marcus Hullins Senr	ditto			
69	Michal Hullins	ditto			
70	John Hope	ditto			
71	Alexander Holton	ditto			
72	Daniel Heart	ditto			
73	John Hopkins	ditto			
74	Alexander Jervis	ditto			Sept 1st
75	Daniel Hennaday	ditto			
76	Caleb Hennaday	ditto			
77	William Lumley	ditto			
78	Andrew McFarland	ditto			
79	John Meaner	ditto			
80	Patrick Miller	ditto			
81	James Medcalph	ditto			
82	Christian Miller	ditto			
83	Samuel McClure	ditto			
84	William Munday	ditto			
85	John Medcalph	ditto			
86	Robert McKinley	ditto			
87	Dennis McEllhinney	ditto			

No.	Mens Names	When Raised	When Discharged	Died or Killed	Deserted
88	James Milligan	ditto			
89	Patrick O'Flaugherty	ditto			
90	George Roseberry	ditto			
91	Joseph Rochell	ditto			
92	Acey Reeves	ditto			
93	James Smith	May 31st			
94	Samuel Shuttle	29th			
95	George Sly	ditto			
96	Philip Shoats	ditto			
97	John Smith	ditto			
98	Henry Smith	ditto			
99	Devereaux Smith	ditto			
100	Frederick Sheets	ditto			
101	Benjamin Sutton	June 5th			
102	Daniel Stie	May 29th			
103	Jacob Toub	ditto			Sept 1st
104	George Toub	ditto			
105	Garret Thomas	ditto			Sept 1st
106	John Wallace	ditto			
107	James White	ditto			
108	Samuel Young	ditto			
109	Robert Harris	ditto	Aug 13th		
110	William Thompson	ditto	Aug 27th		
111	John Coxe	ditto	June 11th		
112	Isaac Coxe	ditto	June 11th		
113	George Rodebauke	ditto	Aug 13th		

Wehereby certifie the within to be a just and true Roll of the Effective Officers and Men in the Fort Pitt Militia and that they served according to the time mentioned in the said Roll Fort Pitt October 26th 1763

William Trent Major
J.F. Davenport Captain
Wm. Christy Capt.

Appendix H

A McKee Lieut & Adjutant
Jn. Flemming Lt.
Jas. Milliken Lt.
Thos. Calhoun Lt.

This is to certifie that at the breaking out of the Present Indian War I formed the militia agreeable to the within rolls the better to enable me to defend this post against the savages, and they adjusted in repairing the Fortifications and did other equal duty with His Majesty's troops from the time they were raised to the Tenth of August 1763 which was during my command and the arrival of Colonel Henry bouquet at this post given under my Hand at Fort pit the 26th October 1763.

S. Ecuyer Capt. Commandr.

I certify that the militia of this post have continued to do duty to this day, and adjusted in escorts and works, has the rest of the troops. Given under my hand at Fort Pitt the 26th October 1763

Henry Bouquet Coll.

Appendix I

Ledger of the Crown to Levy, Trent & Company 1763

Public Archives of Canada, Ledger of Crown to Levy, Trent and Company, 1763.

Fresh off driving out the Indian nations near Bushy Run Station, on August 10, 1763, Colonel Henry Bouquet and his detachment arrived to relieve the garrison at Fort Pitt. It was here that Bouquet and Fort Pitt Commander Simeon Ecuyer drafted this invoice to reimburse William Trent and Levi Levy for using their sundry goods as the fort lay under siege from early June to August and until their duty ended in October of 1763. Trent and Levy were ordered to submit their entire inventory to the King's Store at the end of May of 1763 and were compensated for those items used by Capt. Commander Ecuyer and King's Store liaison Lt. Josiah Davenport. This also included the controversial items Ecuyer and Davenport and the others "gifted" the Native warriors outside the gates of the fort.

Dr. The Crown To Levy, Trent & Compy, for Sundries by Order of Col. Bouquet

1763 }To 4 Tin Kettles for use of the Militia @6/£1.4.0
SeptTo 1 Box Candles for the Guard @2/3£11.9.6
To 16 Bear Skins destroyed, being part of those
Sent, during the Attack the Indians made on £4.16.0
The Fort to make a Blind on the Ohio Curtain
which was Enfiladed. £17.9.6

To Sundries for Andrew the Indian Express
At different timevizt.
1Blanket2of1 shirt 12/6, 1 Canteen 3/£1.16.6
1 for Mockesons 7/6, 1 Looking Glass 5/£0.12.6

Appendix I   411

1 ct. tobacco 2/1, 1 Tinkettle 5/£0.7.0
<u>£2.10.0£5.6.0</u>
£22.15.6
<u>£17.9.6</u>
£5.6.0

I do hereby certify that the shone article
amounting to Twenty-two Pounds Fifteen Shillings
six pence Pennsylv. Currency were had for the uses mentioned.
Given under my hand at
Fort Pitt Oct 12th 1763
Henry Bouquet Col in the 60th Regiment

Endorsed & Accot No, Levy, Trent & Co.
for 22 pounds. 15. 6 certify'd by Col. Br.
Oct, 12th.
The within Accot. Not coming under any particular Department; except one charge for Candles for the garrison belonging to the His Majestys Seal/ Col. Bouquet will discharge the same paying the accustomed prices for the sent Articles making Deductions if any on Accot or the King's Horses employed, as on any other Accot. that may be just For the Col. will be repayed in his Acct.
Thos. Gage

Dr. The Crown to Levy Trent & Compy for Sundrys had by Order of Capt. Simeon Ecuyer
Commandant.

1763 }To Sundrys for the Militia vizt
June84 Tomahawks@10/£42.00
6 Large Tin kettles@10/£ 3.0.0£45.3.0
1 Canteen<u>0.3.0</u>
To Sundrys delivered the Following Expresses vizt.
Vosse and his Comrade
2 pairs Leggings@6/£0.12.0
1 Britch Clout£0.8.0
Cash£1.0.0£2.0.0
Yaxley 2 Dressed Deer Skins @15/2£1.10.0

1 Blanket 20/Cash 3/6£1.3.6£0.15.0
Thompson & Johnson 1 Dressed Deerskin 0.15.0
Issac and John Coxe
2 pairs leggings @6/ £0.12.0
2 Britch Clout 8/0.16.0
2 pair garters1/60.3.0
3 Linnen Handerkerchiefs@3/60.10.6
1 Dressed Deer Skins 0.15.0
2 Rifles 15.0.0 17.16.0
Abraham Bidler1 pair Mockasons 0.7.623.12.6
To 1 Box of Candles for the Guard@2/313.12.3
To Sundries got to replace the Kind those which were
Got from People in the Hospital to Convey the Small Pox to
The Indians Vizt.
2 Blankets @2/ £2.0.0
1 Silk Handkerchief10/1 Linnenditto¾0.13.6 2.13.6
Fort Pitt August 13th 1763
I do hereby Certifie that the above Articles amounting
to the £85.1.3 Pennsylvania Currency were had for the use
above mentioned.
S. Ecuyer Capt. Commandt.

1763}Dr. The Crown to Levy Trent & Company for Sundrys
June had for the use of the work by orders of Capt. Ecuyer vizt.

To 1037 Nails @2/6129.12.6
To 2 halfround 8 ½ Inch files@2/60.5.0
To 1 knife 5 Inch ditto 0.1.0
To 8 Padlocks @3/1.4.0
To 200 Sadle Nailes @9/0.1.6
Fort Pitt 131.4.0
August 13th 1763
I do hereby Certifie that the above Articles
Amounting to One Hundred and Thirty One Pounds
Four shillings Pennsylvania Currency were had for
the use shone mentiond
S. Ecuyer Capt. Commandt.

Deductd. For Carriage of skins down on the King's Horses 27.0.0
Lt. Ourry./

Endorsed Copy of Accounts
Levy, Trent & Co. Against the Crown
One of 131.4.0 Certified by Capt. Ecuyer No. 2
One of 85.1.3 Certfied by Capt. Ecuyer No. 1
One of 11.19.3 Certfied by Col. Bouquet No. 3
One of 22.15.6 Certified by Col. Bouquet No. 4
Oct 12th
Fort Pitt 1763
Nos 1& 4 of this Acct. to be discharged by Col Bouquet. Nos 2 &3 by the Chief Engineer to whom the last Numbers are delivered for that Purpose. The other two enclosed herein.
T.G.

Appendix J

First Will of William Trent 1775

Historical Society of Pennsylvania, Simon Gratz Collection, April 14, 1775.

Just before departing from London, Trent drafted his will for the arduous journey back to America. This will the first of three he wrote in his lifetime, was dated April 14, 1775.

In the Name of God Amen I William Trent late of the Town of Carlisle and County of Cumberland in the Province of Pennsylvania in North America; But now of the Parish of Saint Mary le Bone, in the City of Westminster, and County of Middlesex in the Kingdom of Great Britain, do make this my last Will and Testament revoking all other and former Wills, in Manner and From following--------Imprimis I do order that all my just Debts and Funeral Charges shall be paid. After my Debts and Funeral charges are paid I do give and bequeath all the Remaining Part of my Estate Whether real, personal or mixed in Manner and From following------That is to say, I give and bequeath unto my Wife Sarah, Her Heirs and Assigns forever One equal sixth Part thereof. Item I give and bequeath unto my Daughter Ann, Her Heirs and Assigns forever One other equal sixth Part thereof. Item I give and bequeath unto my Daughter Mary Her Heirs and Assigns forever One other equal sixth Part thereof. Item I give And bequeath unto my Daughter Sarah, Her Heir and Assigns forever the One other equal sixth Part thereof. To Prevent any Person or a Persons giving my Wife and Children any Trouble after my Decease by obliging Her to prove Her Marriage, And in Order to prevent any Person or Persons and every Person whatsoever laying Claim to the Whole or any Part or Parcel of my Estate to the Prejudices of my Wife and Children to whom I have bequeathed it, and that my Intention in giving and bequeathing my said Estate may not be frustrated I do declare, That Sarah Wilkins who lives with Me or did live with Me at the Time I left North America last, that is in the year 1769 is the Person who I call my Wife, and that the said Sarah Wilkins and the Children I have by the said Sarah are the Persons to whom I give and bequeath my Estate; And it is the more necessary for Me to make this Declaration as the Certificate of our Marriage is destroyed. Item it is my will and I do appoint my said Wife Sarah or the said Sarah Wilkins to be the Executrix of this my last Will and Testament. Item It is my Will and I do order (that yearly and every year a sum sufficient for the maintenance, Cloathing and schooling of my said Children shall be taken from their shares, that is each Child's Share shall pay in proportion to what He or Her has bequeathed to Him or Her) provided it does not exceed the Sum of fifty pounds lawful Money of Pennsylvania for each Girl and One Hundred Pounds for my Son until He comes to the Age of 15 years and then to be increased to One Hundred and fifty Pounds Yearly. Item it is my Will and I do order that no Division be made of my Estate until my eldest Daughter attains the Age of twenty-five years, or if she should happen to die, until that year of our Lord, had she lived, she would have arrived at that Age. Item It is my Will and I do order that that Part of my Estate which lays in Pennsylvania & New York shall be sold to pay my Debts & the Childrens Maintenance and my Funeral Expences, if it shall require the whole; if not, such Parts as my Executrix shall direct, And if there shall not be sufficient to answer the purpose, then so much, & such other parts of my Estate as my Executrix shell direct shall be sold to make up the Deficiency. Item it is my Will and I do order if my said Wife Sarah should Mary, that then & in such Case, she shall apply to the County Courts of the Province she shall happen to live in at the Time of said Marriage, provided she lives at such Time in North America, to chuse or a point two good Men to join with Her in the Execution of this my last Will and that the Sum of Twenty Five Pounds shall be allowed them out of any Estate at large, to make them Satisfaction for their Trouble. Item it is my Will And I do Order that regular and well attested Accounts be kept to be produced by my said Wife, & the two Persons appointed by the County of the Moneys expanded by them in the maintenance of my said Children. Item it is my Will & I do Order that if my said Wife should not live in America at the time she shall marry, that then the two Men directed to be chosen to assist her in the Execution of this my last Will Shall be chosen by the Supreme Court of the Province of Pennsylvania. Item it is my will & I do order that if my Wife Sarah should not marry that then she shall not be obliged to render any Account of the Expenditure of the Money in the Maintenance of my said Children. Item it is my Will, that such Parts of my Household Furniture as my Wife shall chuse to keep for Her own use, she shall be allowed to take at the Appraisement, allowing the Sum they

shall be appraised Or to be deducted out of Her Part of my Estate bequeathed Her. London April 14th 1775.
Signed, sealed, published & declared
by the Testator as his last Will and Testament in the Presence of Us}
The words(or She—five—my—and the two Persons appointed by the Court—there bring first intentions.)

Jos. Wharton jun. Edwd. Bancroft Henry Elwes.

Appendix K

Schedule of Indiana Company Losses and Shares [1776]

Rosenbach Museum, Philadelphia, AM 1079/10.

On January 20, 1776, the Indiana Company was formed into a joint stock organization with each member's shares equal to their losses suffered in 1763. This is the original schedule of losses and shares.

Proprietors Names	Pennsylvania Currency	No. of Shares
William Trent	£7147	7147
Robert Callender	8651	8651
David Franks	5730	5730
Joseph Simons	4822	4822
Levy Andrew Levy	3097	3097
The said William Trent David Franks, Joseph Simon and Levy Andrew Levy in right of Philip Boyle	784	784
Thomas Smallman and George Croghan	1584	1584
John Baynton's Executors and Devisees	8530	8530
Samuel Wharton	16628	16628
George Morgan	5400	5400
Samuel Wharton Administrator of John Welch	3000	3000
Edmund Moran Evan Shelby and Samuel Postlethwaite	1215	1215
John Gibson	1692	1692

Edward Cole	1208	1208
Dennis Croghan	430	430
William Thompson	306	306
Richard Neave	352	352
James Dundas	352	352
John Ormsby	1780	1780
William Edgar	546	546
William Franklin	5399	5399
Joseph Galloway	1125	1125
Thomas Wharton	1125	1125

Appendix L

William Trent's Oath of Allegiance 1778

Historical Society of Pennsylvania, Simon Gratz Collection, Colonial Wars, Case 4, Box 9.

With certain members of the Indiana Company and his business associates being arrested or questioned for staying loyal to Great Britain, Trent officially gave his oath of allegiance in New Jersey for the patriot cause to avoid suspicion that he too was a Loyalist.

I William Trent of the Township of Nottingham County of Burlington & State of New Jersey Do sincerely, profess and swear that I Do Not hold my Bound to bear allegiance to the King of Great Britain & that I Do & will bear true faith & allegiance to the Government Established in this State Under the Authority of the people.
William Trent

Sworn before me and of the Justices for the
County of Burlington the 29th May 1778-
John Watson Junr

Appendix M

Second Will of William Trent 1782

Historical Society of Pennsylvania, Simon Gratz Collection, May 13, 1782.

Since he returned from London in 1775, Trent's frequent traveling to Pittsburgh and Philadelphia from New Jersey did nothing to slow down his ailments that by 1782 had reached a new level of severity. When he chose to finally visit Dr William Shippen Jr, Shippen recommended sundry medicines like Portland's Powder and sixteen weeks' worth of visits to his house on Fourth Street .At this point, Trent's failing health concerned him enough to write this 1782 will from the Indian Queen Tavern in Philadelphia, the second of three wills he wrote.

In the Name of God Amen I William Trent of the Township of Nottingham, County of Burlington and State of New Jersey, being in Health And of sound disposing Mind and Memory do make this my last will and Testament revoking and making null and Void all other and former Wills Imprimis I do order and it is my will and Pleasure that my Funeral Charges and all my Debts be first paid by my Executors herein after named. Item I do give and bequeath unto my wife Sarah, one fifth Part of all my Estate as well real as Personal, and to her Heirs or Assigns forever to be disposed of as She pleases. Item I do give and bequeath unto my Daughter Ann Her Heirs or Assigns forever One other fifth Part Of all my Estate as well real, as Personal to be disposed of as She pleases. Item I do give and bequeath unto my Daughter Mary Her Heirs or Assigns forever One other fifth Part of all my Estate, as well real, as Personal To be disposed of as She pleases. Item I do give and bequeath unto my Son John his Heirs or Assigns forever Two other fifth Parts of all my Estate aswell real, as Personal To be disposed of by Him in such Manner as He pleases when He arrives at the Age of twenty one years and not before. I do appoint my Daughters Ann and Mary and my loving Friend and Relation Mr. Tench Coxe of the City of Philadelphia to execute this my last Will and Testament. I particularly recommend the giving to my Son the best Education this Country affords. I leave to my Executors to determine which Parts of my Estate will be most for the Benefit of my Family to sell to say my Debts & to maintain Them until my Son comes of the Age of Twenty one years; after which as soon as may be convenient I recommend a Division to be made and each One Share to be allotted Him or Her I depend much on the Prudence of my Daughters and recommend to them to rely much on the Judgement of Mr. Tench Coxe who is well acquainted with the Nature of my Estate and on whose Honor and Abilities I have the greatest Reliance, I also recommend to my Legatees, if Congress does the Justice in the Dispute of Indiana & Vandalia Companys have with Virginia to give unto my Friend Mr. Tench Coxe over & above what the Laws allow Executors One Thousand Acres of Land within one of the Grants of Indiana or Vandalia. Legatees Receiving more money for their proportion out of the Lands to be sold to maintain them until my Son comes of Age be settled when the Estate is divided. Philadelphia May thirteenth One Thousand Seven Hundred and Eighty two.

William Trent[Seal]

Signed, sealed, published and
declared by the Testators to be his
last Will and Testament
In the Presence of......

Francis Lee
Mich Huffnagle
George Moore

Appendix N

Last Will and Testament of William Trent 1784 and Trent's death announcement in 1784 Letter

Philadelphia County Wills, Book T, Page 487.

William Trent's journey to Philadelphia by June of 1784 proved to be his final one as his finances left him in poverty and his health left him near death. On July 6, 1784, he wrote his third and final will, realizing his death was imminent.

Be it Remembered that I William Trent late of the County of Hunterdon in the State of New Jersey now of the City of Philadelphia in the State of Pennsylvania Gentleman being of sound disposing mind and memory do you make and publish this my last Will and Testament in manner following to wit Imprimis I direct that all my Just Debts and funeral expenses be duly paid and satisfied by my Executors herein after named. Item I give and devise unto Richard Wharton John Todd Junr. and James Todd all of the City of Philadelphia One Share of my Lands in the Tract of Land called or known by the name of Indiana as a Share is known and distinguished by the Book of Minutes & orders kept by the said Company of Indiana To hold to the said Richard Wharton John Tod Junr. and James Todd their Heirs and Assigns forever to be equally divided between them as Tenants in Common and not as Jointenants. Item I give and devise unto my Kinsman Israel Morris his Heirs and Assigns In Trust for his four Children Susannah Sarah Phebe and William One half of a share of my Lands in the Tract of Land called or known by the Name of Indiana as one half of a share is known and distinguished by the Book of Minutes and orders kept by the said Company of Indiana To hold to the said Israel Morris his Heirs and Assigns In Trust for and to the only proper Use Benefit and Behoof of his said Children___Susannah Phebe and William their Heirs and Assigns to be equally divided between them as Tenants in Common and not as Jointenants. Item I give and bequeath unto Mary Watters the sum of Ten Pounds. lastly I give bequeath and devise All the rest and residuary of my Estate both real and personal wheresoever (situate lying and being) and whatsoever unto my Wife Sarah and to my three Children Ann Mary and John their Heirs and Assigns to be equally divided between them as Tenants in Common and not as Jointenants. Provided always that the Estate hereby devise to my Wife Sarah is in full Lieu and Bar of Dower and I do hereby nominate and appoint my friend Samuel Wharton Esquire my Kinsman Israel Morris my Daughter Mary and my Kinsman John Todd Junior Executors of this my last Will and Testament hereby Revoking all Wills buy one here tofore made and declaring this only to be my last Will and Testament In Witness whereof I have hereunto set my Hand and Seal the 6th day of July in the year of our Lord One Thousand seven hundred and eighty four.

Signed Sealed published and
declared by the above named
Testator as his last Will & Testament }William Trent
in the Presence of Us
John Martin John Todd James Birchall

* * * * *

Letter from Thomas Clifford to Anthony Todd December 27, 1784

Historical Society of Pennsylvania, Clifford Family Papers, Volume 7, p. 170.

Since no newspaper announced his passing, Trent's death was only mentioned once in a letter by Quaker merchant Thomas Clifford to London Postmaster Anthony Todd, speaking of his death and poor circumstances.

Philadelphia 27th Dec 1784

Respected Friend

Thy Favours of Sept 1st and Oct 6th Come duly two hand we sent thy Mortgage after being authenticated to Albany and had it put on record there and have received advise that tis the first on record And therefore is Valid and wile Secure so much Land but to obtain a fee in it and a clear title thereto the Bond maybe served out the Land sold and Purchases in on thy Account and take the Sheriffs deed for it this will be Attended with some further Expence I think the whole will not be great___

I do not known of any other way to obtain a Clear title and to enable thy attorneys to sell it for the however as nothing suffers I shale wait thy further orders. About the first Inst Willm Trent Departed life he made a Will appointed Saml Wharton John Todd Junr and Others his executors. was I believe very Low in Circumstances having been helped in his last Illness for sometime Past by his Friends, unless Congress should Decide in his favour respecting Considerable Quantity of Lands he Claimed that lays on or near the Ohio River___I see no Prospect of thy Getting anything more if they Should acknowledge his right good to those Lands and that Business be Properly Conducted thy Debt may yet be worth something I am ready to serve thee if in my Power in Conjunction with the Doctr and very respectfully

Thomas Clifford

please forward the enclosed
to our Mutual friend
Joseph Galoway Esqre.
TC

Appendix O

The Inventory of a Black Trunk, belonging to the Estate of William Trent

Library Company of Philadelphia, John A. McAllister Collection, William Trent Papers.

Over the course of his life, Trent frequently mentioned the use of a large black trunk. Inside he placed his most valuable papers, books, and journals he possessed for forty years of his mercantile career from the Treaty of Lancaster in 1744 until his death in 1784. Though the black trunk's whereabouts are still unknown, a list was conducted of its contents by Library Company of Philadelphia librarian John Todd Jr who was also an executor of Trent's estate. This inventory is undated but was no doubt conducted right after Trent's death on December 1, 1784.

A List of Books, Papers to being the contents of a Black Trunk, belonging to the Estate of William Trent deceased

1. Leather Covered Waste Book, Commencing at Carlisle he 24 February 1764 & ending the 10 January 1769.
2. Parchment Cover'd Waste Book, Commencing February 19 1776 & ending July 17 1783.
3. Marble Cover'd Invoice Book dated in London July 1 1774
4. Marble Cover'd Memordm Book
5. Marble do Sales Book Commencg. August 1775
6. do Relating to Indiana conveyances
7. do Memorandm Book
8. do do Small of Indian purchases
9. A few Copies of July in Sheets
10. Geo. Croghan on accot of losses on the Ohio River viz. by the French & Indians

11. A Journal & Copies of Officers Orders in War of 1763.
12. An Attested Book with the large seal of Pennsylvania with accot of losses of Indian Traders
13. Powers of Attorney from Sundry Persons to Willm, Trent with office Seal.
14. a Bundle of Papers containing the following viz:

Extract of a letter from Col. Washington to Lord Botetourt

State of South & North Virginia.

A Report of the Lords of Trade & Form of the New Government.

A list of Papers left with Governier Morris 1780.

Lord Dunmore's letter to Lord Dartmouth dated April 2nd 1774.

Lord Dartmouth's letter to Lord Dunmore dated Octo 5th 1774.

Transactions with the Lords commissioners of the treasury ratifies the Fort Stanwix treaty.

Part of a letter from President Nelson to the Earl of Hillsborough

Proclamation respecting the Virginia affairs-Minutes Respecting the Virginia officers claims-Remarks on the Deed from the 6 Nations datd at Lancaster July 18 1774.

Answers to Mr. Mercers Papers Called Facts-

Copy of Grants of Land made from April 1745.

Instructions to the governor of Canada a case on Indian titles.

State of the case with H, Campbell opinion Brother to the Earl of Marchmont.

The Assembly of Pennsylvania against the governor dated 1748 January 18

Advertisement relating to traders losses being certified by Thos. & John Walker.

Remarks in the Treaty held at Lancaster 1744.

Copy of Mr. Hoopers letter to Tho. Wharton Esq. 1773 January.

The King's Order in Council in August 1772 for Establishing a new Colony on the Ohio a Case with Respect to Virginia.

Lord Dartmouth's Letter 2 Lord Dunmore October 5th 1774.

A paper Containing parts of a Deed add the Lancaster Treaty & some other remarks

Some Accots & Receipts of Hugh Smith

Hugh Smith's accounts & papers

Thos. Girty's receipt May 2, 1776 £40.19. and his account.

Thomas Lunndalls Receipt

John Montours order in favour of Col Cresap.

A draft 4397 acres & 18 perches of land on the north & West Branch of Franks town creek.

A copy of a memorial to Congress on behalf of the Indiana Company.

Appendix O

Mr. Riots advertisement.
Sundry Mem concerning the Indiana compy
Mr. Collin's acct. of sundry other receipts.
A letter from the Hon. Thomas Walpole May 1775
Sundry papers Articles of Agreement Power of attorney relative to Mr. Jn. Ballindine, of Virginia.

A bundle containing following papers viz:
A list of the proprietors Vandalia
Copy of a letter from Mr. Nelson concerning the Treaty of Lancaster & Geo. Washington Transactions with Indians in 1753 & 54.
A list of receipts that Mr. Walpole signed Proposals for.

Bibliography

MANUSCRIPT COLLECTIONS

American Philosophical Society, Philadelphia, Pennsylvania
Benjamin Franklin Ledgers A and B
Burd-Shippen Papers
William Franklin Papers
Archives of Christ Church, Philadelphia, Pennsylvania
Vestry Minutes 1717–1760
Boston Public Library, Boston, Massachusetts
Norman B. Leventhal Map and Education Center Collection
British Library, London, England
Grand Ohio Company Papers-MS 575
Colonial Williamsburg Foundation, Williamsburg, Virginia
Corbin Family Papers
Cumberland County (Pennsylvania) Archives, Carlisle, Pennsylvania
Land Deeds
Tax Books
Franklin Institute, Philadelphia, Pennsylvania
Will of Benjamin Franklin, April 28, 1757
Gunston Hall, Lorton, Virginia
Papers of George Mason
Haverford College Quaker and Special Collections, Haverford, Pennsylvania
William Penn Charter School Archives
Friendly Association Papers
Historical Society of Pennsylvania/Library Company of Philadelphia, Philadelphia, Pennsylvania
Benjamin Rush Papers
Bradford Family Papers
Cadwalader Family Papers
Clifford Family Papers
Family Bible Record Collection
Frank M. Etting Collection
James Hamilton Papers
John A. McAllister Collection

Bibliography 429

Norris Family Papers
Penn Family Papers
Richard Peters Letter Book
Simon Gratz Collection
Treasury Collection
Wharton Family Papers
Hunterdon County (New Jersey) Hall of Records, Flemington, New Jersey
Hunterdon County Plea Minutes (1714–1908)
Hunterdon County Misc. Court Records (1713–1860)
Lancaster County Archives, Lancaster, Pennsylvania
Deed Book B
Library of Congress, Washington D.C.
Geographic and Map Division
George Washington Papers
Journals of the Continental Congress
Lancaster Historical Society Publications
Letters of Delegates to Congress 1774–1789
Marion S. Carson Collection 1656–1995
Records of the Society for the Propagation of the Gospel in Foreign Parts
    (1630-1901)
Shippen Family Papers
Library of Virginia, Richmond, Virginia
William Trent Account to Government of Virginia April 8, 1754
Maryland State Archives, Annapolis, Maryland
Prerogative Court Probate Records
Middle Temple Archives, London, England
Register of Admissions 1501–1975
National Archives of United Kingdom (U.K.), Kew, England
Audit Office 13: American Loyalist Claims
Calendar of King George III Papers 1760–1775
Colonial Office Records
Fulham Papers
Prerogative Court of Canterbury and Related Probate, Jurisdictions, Will
    Registers
National Society of the Colonial Dames of America in the State of New Jersey,
    Westampton, New Jersey
Peachfield Collection
New Jersey Historical Society, Newark, New Jersey
Manuscript Group 7 New Jersey Manuscript Collection 1669–1840
New York Historical Society, New York, New York
George Clinton Collection 1686–1761
Pennsylvania State Archives, Harrisburg, Pennsylvania
Baynton, Wharton, and Morgan Letter Book 1763–1775
Burd-Shippen Papers

Warrant Registers (1733–1957)
Philadelphia City Archives, Philadelphia, Pennsylvania
Philadelphia Deed Books
Philadelphia Wills
Philadelphia Museum of Art and Library, Philadelphia, Pennsylvania
Philadelphia City Directories
Princeton University Archives, Seely G. Mudd Manuscript Library, Princeton, New Jersey
CO 140, Box 150
Public Archives of Canada, Ottawa, Canada
The Crown to Levy, Trent and Company 1763
Rutgers University Archives, New Brunswick, New Jersey
Neilson Family Papers
State Archives of New Jersey, Trenton, New Jersey
Burlington County Court Chancery Court Records
Burlington County Clerk's Office (1712–1750)
Deed Books
Manumissions of Hunterdon County
Nottingham Township Tax Lists
Probate Records
Rare Books and Manuscript Collections
Supreme Court Records
State House of New Jersey, Trenton, New Jersey
Inventory of William Trent 1726
State Library of New Jersey, Trenton, New Jersey
Minutes and Proceedings of the Council and General Assembly of the State of New Jersey
Trenton Free Public Library, Trenton, New Jersey
1724 Mary Trent Disclaimer
1724 Samuel Bustill Attestation to James Trent
Trentoniana Collection
University Archives, Wilton, Connecticut
William Trent to Barnard Gratz April 7, 1783
University of Delaware Archives and Special Collections, Newark, Delaware
1768 Indenture between Christian Redebauch and William Trent
University of Illinois, Champaign, Illinois
George Morgan Papers
University of Michigan, William L. Clements Library, Ann Arbor, Michigan
Every Man His Own Physician by John Theobald
George Clinton Papers
Jeffrey Amherst Papers
Minutes of Conferences held with the Indians at Easton 1757
Nathanael Greene Papers
Native American Collection

Thomas Gage Papers
University of Pittsburgh Archives & Special Collections, Pittsburgh, Pennsylvania
Book of Common Prayer 1753
Burd-Shippen Papers (1717–1898)
Meeting at Fort Pitt July 6, 1776
Plain Facts by Samuel Wharton (1781)
Report to Lord Commissioners, Observation and Remarks (1772)
William Trent's Account of Proceedings with Six Nations of Indians and Allies (1753)
University of Virginia Library, Charlottesville, Virginia
Headquarter Papers of Brigadier-General John Forbes
Virginia Historical Society, Richmond, Virginia
Letter from William Trent to the Half-King, June 8, 1753
Westminster School Archives, London, England
1714 enrollment of James Trent
Yale University, New Haven, Connecticut
Benjamin Franklin Papers

NEWSPAPERS

Aberdeen Journal
Boston Gazette
Boston Post-Boy
Dunlap's Pennsylvania Packet
Freeman's Journal or North America Intelligencer
Hartford Courant
Independent Gazetteer
Kentish Gazette
Maryland Gazette
New Jersey Gazette
New York Gazette
Pennsylvania Gazette
True American
Virginia Gazette

PRIMARY SOURCES

Arnold, James Newell ed. *Vital Records of Rhode island 1636:1850: First Series: Births, Marriages and Deaths*. Providence: Narragansett Historical Publishing Co, 1895.

Bailey, Kenneth P. ed. *The Ohio Company Papers 1753–1817: Being Primarily Papers pf the Suffering Traders of Pennsylvania*. Arcata, California, 1947.

Bockstruck, Lloyd D. ed. *Virginia's Colonials Soldiers*. Baltimore: Genealogical Publishing Company, 1988.

Borsay, Peter. *The Eighteenth Century Town: A Reader in English Urban History 1688–1820*. New York: Taylor & Francis, 1990.

Browne, William Hand, ed. *Proceedings of the Council of Maryland 1698–1731.* Baltimore: Maryland Historical Society, 1905.

Burton, Kimberly, ed. *The Orderly Book of Captain William Trent at Fort Pitt 1763.* Philadelphia: Historical Society of Pennsylvania, 1–61.

Bush, Bernard, ed. *Laws of the Royal Colony of New Jersey 1703–1745.* Trenton: New Jersey State Library, 1977.

Byars, William V. ed. *B. and M. Gratz: Merchants in Philadelphia 1754–1798.* Jefferson City: Hugh Stephens Printing, 1916.

Clark, Murtie Jane, ed. *Colonial Soldiers of the South 1732-1774.* Baltimore: Genealogical Publishing Co, 1983.

Colden, Cadwallader, *The Letters and papers of Cadwallader Colden 1711–1775.* 9 Vols. New York: printed for the New York Historical Society, 1918–1937.

Cresswell, Nicholas, *The Journal of Nicholas Cresswell 1774–1777.* New York: The Dial Press, 1924.

Darlington, Mary C. ed. *History of Colonel Henry Bouquet and the Western Frontiers of Pennsylvania.* Pittsburgh: University of Pittsburgh, 1920.

———. ed. *Fort Pitt and letters from the frontier.* Pittsburgh: J.R. Weldin & Co, 1892.

Darlington, William M. ed. *Christopher Gist's Journals with Historical, Geographical and Ethnological Notes and Biographies of his Contemporaries.* Pittsburgh: J. R. Weldin & Co, 1893.

Ewald, Johann and Tustin, Joseph P. ed. *Diary of the American War: A Hessian Journal.* New Haven: Yale University Press, 1979.

Galbreath, Charles B. ed. *Expedition of Celoron to the Ohio Country in 1749.* Columbus: The F. J. Heer Printing Co, 1921.

Goodman, Alfred Thomas, ed. *Journal of Captain William Trent from Logstown to Pickawillany A. D. 1752.* Cincinnati: Robert Clark & Co, 1871.

Grenier, Ferdinand, ed. *Papiers Contrecoeur Et Autres Documents Concernant le Conflit Anglo-Français Sur L'Ohio de 1745 à 1756.* Quebec: Laval University Press, 1952.

Hadden, James M. *Hadden's Journal and Orderly Books: A Journal kept in Canada and upon Burgoyne's Campaign in 1776 and 1777.* Bedford, Applewood Books, 1884.

Hazard, Samuel, ed. *Pennsylvania Archives First Series Vol. 1.* Philadelphia: Joseph Severns & Co, 1852.

Hildeburn, Charles R. ed. *Baptisms and Burials from the Records of Christ Church, Philadelphia 1709-1760.* Baltimore: Clearfield Company, 1995.

Honeyman, A Van Doren. ed. *Documents Relating to the Colonial History of the State of New Jersey First Series XXX Volume II 1730–1750.* Somerville: The Unionist-Gazette Association, 1913.

How, Nehemiah and Paltsits Victor Hugo, ed. *A Narrative of the Captivity of Nehemiah How in 1745–1747.* Cleveland: The Burrows Brothers Company, 1904.

Kalm, Peter. *Travels into North America.* 2 Vols. London: John Reinhold Forster, 1771.

Kenny, James and Jordan, John W. *Journal of James Kenny 1761-1763.* Pennsylvania Magazine of History and Biography Volume 37. Issues No. 1 and 2, 1–47 and 152–201. (1913).

Bibliography

Kent, Donald H. and Stevens, Sylvester K. eds. *The Papers of Colonel Henry Bouquet*. 18 Vol. Harrisburg: Pennsylvania Historical Commission, 1940.

Lee, Francis B. *Documents Relating to the Revolutionary History of the State of New Jersey*. Trenton: John L. Murphy Publishing, 1903.

Linn, John B. and Egle, William H. eds. *Pennsylvania Archives Second Series*. Harrisburg: E. K. Meyers State Printer, 1890.

MacKinney, Gertrude, ed. *Pennsylvania Archives Eighth Series: Votes and Proceedings of the House of Representatives of the Province of Pennsylvania*. 8 Vols. Harrisburg, 1931–1935.

McIlwaine, Henry Read, ed. *Executive Journals of the Council of Colonial Virginia*. 6 Vols. Richmond: Virginia State Library, 1925.

———. *Journals of the House of Burgesses of Virginia 1619–1776*. 13 Vols. Richmond: Colonial Press, E. Waddey Co, 1905–1915.

Marcus, Maeva, ed. *The Documentary History of the Supreme Court of the United States 1789–1800, Vol. 5*. New York: Columbia University Press, 1985.

Marshe, Witham, *Lancaster in 1744: Journal of the Treaty of Lancaster in 1744 with the Six Nations*. Lancaster, 1744.

Mitchell, James T. and Flanders, Henry, eds. *The Statutes at Large of Pennsylvania Volume V 1744–1759*. Harrisburg: Wm. Stanley Ray, 1898.

Montgomery, Thomas L. ed. *Pennsylvania Archives Fifth Series*. Vol.1. Harrisburg: Harrisburg Publishing Company, 1906.

Montgomery, Thomas L. *Report of the Commission to Locate the Site of the Frontier Forts of Pennsylvania*. 2 Vols. Harrisburg: Wm. Stanley Ray, 1916.

Mulkearn, Lois, ed. *George Mercer Papers: Relating to the Ohio Company of Virginia*. Pittsburgh: University of Pittsburgh Press, 1954.

Nelson, William, ed. *Documents Relating to the Colonial History of the State of New Jersey Volume XI*. Press Printing and Publishing Co, 1894.

New Jersey Historical Society, ed. *The Papers of Lewis Morris 1738–1746*. New York: George P. Putnam, 1852.

O'Callaghan, E. B. *Documents Relative to the Colonial History of the State of New York*. Albany: Weed Parsons and Company Printers, 1855.

Palmer, William P. ed. *Calendar of Virginia State Papers and other Manuscripts*. 2 Vols. Richmond: R.F. Walker, Superintendent of Public Printing, 1875.

Penn, William, Logan, James, Logan, Deborah Norris and Armstrong, E. ed. *Correspondence between William Penn and James Logan, Secretary of the province of Pennsylvania and others 1700–1750: From the original letters in possession of the Logan Family*. Philadelphia, 1872.

Pennsylvania Provincial Council. *Colonial Records of Pennsylvania*. 16 Vols. Harrisburg: T Fenn & Co, 1831-1853.

Petterson, Christina and Jensz, Felicity, eds. *Legacies of David Cranz, Historie von Gronland*. Springer International Publishing, 2021.

Purdon, John, ed. *A Digest of the Laws of the Pennsylvania From the Year One thousand seven hundred to the Sixth Day of July, One thousand eight hundred and eighty-three*. Philadelphia: Kay and Brother, 1885.

Ricard, Frederick W. and Nelson, William, eds. *Documents Relating to the Colonial History of the State of New Jersey Volume IX 1757–1767*. Newark: Daily Advertiser Printer House, 1885.
Rowland, Kate, ed. *Life of George Mason*. New York: G. P. Putnam's Sons, 1892.
Rush, Benjamin. *Medical Inquiries and Observations Volume 2*. Philadelphia, 1805.
Rutland, Robert A. ed. *The Papers of George Mason 1725–1792*. 3 Vols. Chapel Hill: University of North Carolina Press, 2011.
Severns, Joseph, ed. *Minutes of the Provincial Council of Pennsylvania*. Vol. 5. Harrisburg: Theo Penn & Co, 1851.
Stobo, Robert. *Memoirs of Major Robert Stobo of the Virginia Regiment*. Pittsburgh: John S. Davidson, 1854.
Sullivan, James. *The Papers of Sir William Johnson*. Albany: The University of the State of New York, 1921.
Thwaites, Reuben G. ed. *Early Western Travels: Journals of Conrad Weiser (1748), George Croghan (1750-1765). Christian Frederick Post (1758) and Thomas Morris (1764)*. Volume 1. Cleveland: The Arthur H. Clark Company, 1904.
Toner, Joseph M. ed. *Journal of Colonel George Washington, commanding a detachment of Virginia sent by Robert Dinwiddie, Lieutenant Governor of Virginia, across the Allegheny Mountains in 1754, to build Forts at the Head of the Ohio*. Albany: Joel Munsell's Sons, 1893.
Vaughan, Alden T. gen ed. *Early American Indian Documents: Treaties and Laws*. 20 Vols. Washington D.C.: University Publications of America, 1979.
Volwiler, Albert T. ed. *William Trent's Journal at Fort Pitt 1763*. Volume 11, pp. 390-413, 1924.
Washington, George. *The Journal of Major George Washington: sent by the Hon. Robert Dinwiddie, Esq. His Majesty's Lieutenant Governor and Commander-in-chief of Virginia to the Commandant of the French Forces on Ohio*. Chicago: The Newberry Library, 1958.
Whitehead, William A. ed. *Documents Relating to the Colonial History of the State of New Jersey*. Newark: Daily Advertiser, 1882.

SECONDARY SOURCES

Alberts, Robert C. *Most Extraordinary Adventures of Major Robert Stobo*. Boston: Houghton Mifflin, 1965.
Bailey, Kenneth P. *The Ohio Company of Virginia and the Western Movement 1748-1792*. Glendale: Arthur H. Clark Company, 1939.
Bausman, Joseph Henderson. *History of Beaver County, Pennsylvania Volume 2*. New York: Knickerbocker Press, 1904.
Börjeson, Hjalmar, *Biogrfiska anteckningar am officerare vid* örlogsflottan *1600-1699*. Unpublished manuscript. 1935.
Boyer, Charles Shimer. *Old Inns and Taverns in West Jersey*. Camden: Camden, New Jersey Historical Society, 1962.

Brown, Lloyd Arnold. *Early Maps of Ohio Valley: A Selection of Maps, Plans, and Views Made by Indians and Colonials from 1673 to 1783*. Pittsburgh: University of Pittsburgh Press, 1959.

Burr, Nelson R. *The Anglican Church in New Jersey*. Philadelphia: Church Historical Society Publications, 1954.

Butchko, Joshua Burrow, Burrow, Ian, and Hunter, Richard W. *William Trent House Public Archaeology Program: Archaeological Investigations on the East Side of the House*. Trenton: Trent House Association, 2016.

Cassel, Daniel K. *Genea-Biographical History of the Rittenhouse Family*. Philadelphia: The Rittenhouse Memorial Association, 1893.

Cherry, Jason A. *Pittsburgh's Lost Outpost: Captain Trent's Fort*. Charleston: Arcadia Publishing, 2019.

Clark, William Bell. *A Forgotten investment of John Paul Jones Volume 77 No. 2*. Philadelphia: University of Pennsylvania Press, 1953.

Cooley, Eli F. *Genealogy of Early Settlers in Trenton and Ewing, Old Hunterdon County, New Jersey*. Trenton: W.S. Sharp Printing Co, 1883.

Dayton, William L. *Historical Sketch of Trenton Academy*. Trenton: John L. Murphy, 1881.

DeValinger Jr, Leon. *Colonial Military Organization in Delaware 1638–1776*. Wilmington, Delaware: Delaware Tercentenary Commission, 1938.

Dorr, Rev. Benjamin. *A Historical Account of Christ Church, Philadelphia From its Foundation A.D. 1695 to A.D. 1841*. New York: Swords, Stanford and Co, 1841.

Durant, P.A. and Richard, J. Fraise. *History of Cumberland and Adams Counties Pennsylvania*. Chicago: Warner, Beers & Co, 1886.

Fitzhugh, McMaster. *Soldiers and Uniforms: South Carolina Military Affairs 1670-1775*. Columbia: University of South Carolina Press, 1971.

Fleming, George Thornton. *History of Pittsburgh and Environs*. 2 Vols. New York and Chicago: The American Historical Society Inc, 1922.

Force, Peter. ed. *American Archives: Containing a Documentary History of the English Colonies in North America*. Six Series. Washington: M. St. Clair Clarke, 1840.

Glidden, William *The English Stone Fortress: Fort Frederick*. Plattsburgh: Lake Champlain Weekly, 2003.

Goebel, Julius and Naughton, T. Raymond. *Law Enforcement in Colonial New York: A Study in Criminal Procedure (1664–1776)*. Montclair: Patterson Smith, 1970.

Hain, Harry Harrison. *History of Perry County, Pennsylvania*. Harrisburg: Hain-Moore Company, 1922.

Hall, John. *History of the Presbyterian Church in Trenton, New Jersey*. Trenton: MacCrellish & Quigley Printers, 1912.

Hanna, Charles B. *The Wilderness Trail*. 2 Vols. New York: The Knickerbocker Press, 1911.

Hills, Rev. George Morgan. *History of the Church in Burlington, New Jersey*. Trenton: William S. Sharp, 1876.

Historical Society of Pennsylvania. *Pennsylvania Magazine of History and Biography*. 144 Vols. Philadelphia: Historical Society of Pennsylvania, 1900.

Hunter, Richard and Burrow, Ian. eds. *Petty's Run Archaeological Site Iron, Steel, Cotton, and Papers.* Trenton: Hunter Research Inc, 2014.

Hunter, William A. *Forts on the Pennsylvania Frontier 1753–1758.* Harrisburg, Pennsylvania Historical and Museum Commission, 1960.

James, Alfred P. *The Ohio Company: Its Inner History.* Pittsburgh: University of Pittsburgh Press, 1959.

Jenkins, Howard. *The Family of William Penn: Founder of Pennsylvania, Ancestry and Descendants.* London: The Author, 1899.

Kimball, Hoke P. and Henson, Bruce. *Governor's Houses and State Houses of British Colonial America 1607-1783.* Jefferson, North Carolina: McFarland and Co, 2017.

Klein, Randolph S. *Portrait of an Early American Family: The Shippens of Pennsylvania across Five Generations.* Philadelphia: University of Pennsylvania Press, 1975.

Landis, Charles Israel. *Captain William Trent, An Indian Trader.* (Papers Read before the Lancaster Historical Society Volume 23 No. 10). Lancaster, Pennsylvania: Lancaster Historical Society, 1919.

Leah, Josiah. *History of the Penrose Family of Philadelphia.* Philadelphia: William Fell Company, 1903.

Lee, Francis Bazley. *History of Trenton, New Jersey.* Trenton: J.L. Murphy, 1895.

Lewis, George E. *The Indiana Company 1763–1798.* Glendale: University of California-Los Angeles, 1941.

Lossing, Benson John. *The American Historical Record.* Philadelphia: Chase & Town, 1872.

Martin, J. H. *Bench and Bar of Philadelphia.* Philadelphia, 1883.

Moon, Robert C. *The Morris Family of Philadelphia: Descendants of Anthony Morris 1654–1721.* Vol.1. Philadelphia, 1898.

Morton, Doris Begor. *Philip Skene of Skenesborough.* Granville, New York: Grastorf Press, 1959.

Mulkearn, Lois. *Why the Treaty of Logstown, 1752.* Richmond: Virginia Magazine of History and Biography Volume 59, January 1951.

Myers, James P. *The Ordeal of Thomas Barton: Anglican Missionary in the Pennsylvania Backcountry 1755–1780.* Bethlehem: Lehigh University Press, 2010.

Nelson, William. *Beginnings of the Iron Industry in Trenton, New Jersey, 1723–1750.* Philadelphia: Historical Society of Pennsylvania, 1911.

Nigh, Gary. *Ferries across the Delaware.* Trenton: J.J. Prats and Historical Marker Database, 2007.

Paltsits, Victor Hugo. *Scheme for the Conquest of Canada in 1746.* Worcester, Mass: The Hamilton Press, 1905.

Pennsylvania Magazine of History and Biography. Vol. 8. No. 1 (March 1884), 82–105, University of Pennsylvania Press.

Pernot, Rhett. *1719 William Trent House Museum.* Lawrenceburg: R. L. Ruehrwein, The Creative Company, 2007.

Preston, David L. *Colonial Saratoga: War and Peace on the Borderlands of Early America.* Washington DC: Department of the Interior, 2018.

Ridner, Judith. *A Town Between: Carlisle, Pennsylvania and the Early Mid-Atlantic Interior.* Philadelphia: University of Pennsylvania Press, 2011.

Rupp, Israel D. *The History and Topography of Dauphin, Cumberland, Franklin, Bedford, Adams and Perry Counties [Pennsylvania].* Lancaster: Gilbert Hills Publishing, 1846.

———, Iscrupe, William L., and Iscrupe, Shirley G. *Early History of Western Pennsylvania.* Laughlintown: Southwest Pennsylvania Genealogical Services, 1847.

Schaeper, Thomas J. *Edward Bancroft: Scientist, Author, Spy.* New Haven: Yale University Press, 2011.

Schaumann, Merri Lou S. *A History & Genealogy of Carlisle, Cumberland County, Pennsylvania 1751-1835.* Carlisle: M.L.S. Schaumann, 1987.

Schuyler, Hamilton. *History of St. Michael's Church.* Princeton: Princeton University Press, 1926.

Severance, Frank H. *Publications of the Buffalo Historical Society Volume IX.* Buffalo: Buffalo Historical Society, 1906.

Shackleford, George Green. *Book Review-James Patton and the Appalachian Colonists by Patricia Givens Johnson.* Richmond: Virginia Magazine of History and Biography (January 1901) Volume 8.

Sipe, C. Hale. *The Indian Chiefs of Pennsylvania.* Butler, Pa: Ziegler Print Co, 1927.

Slick, Sewell Elias. *William Trent and the West.* Harrisburg: Pennsylvania Archives Publishing Company, 1947.

Snell, James P. *History of Hunterdon and Somerset Counties, New Jersey.* Philadelphia: Everts & Peck, 1881.

Sosin, Jack M. *Whitehall and the Wilderness: The Middle west in British Colonial Policy 1760-1775.* Lincoln: University of Nebraska Press, 1961.

Steele, Ian K. *Setting All the Captives Free: Capture, Adjustment, and Recollection in Allegheny Country.* Montreal: McGill-Queen's University Press, 2013.

Stevens, Christopher, White, Linda, Griswald, William and Brown, Margie Coffin. *Cultural Landscape Report and Archaeological Assessment for Victory Woods.* Saratoga: National Park Service, 2007.

Stewart, Irene. *Letters of General John Forbes relating to the expedition against Fort Duquesne in 1758.* Pittsburgh: Allegheny County Committee, 1927.

Stobo, Robert and Craig, Neville B. *Memoirs of Major Robert Stobo of the Virginia Regiment.* Pittsburgh: John S. Davidson Publishing, 1854.

Stotz, Charles M. *The Fort Pitt Museum.* Pittsburgh: The Western Pennsylvania Historical Magazine Volume 52, 1969.

———. *Outposts of the War for Empire.* Pittsburgh: Historical Society of Western Pennsylvania, 1985.

Stretch, Carolyn W. *Early Colonial Clockmakers in Philadelphia.* Philadelphia: Pennsylvania Magazine of History and Biography (July 1932) Vol. 56.

Toner, Joseph M. *Washington in the Forbes expedition of 1758.* Washington DC: Columbia Historical Society, 1897.

Trap, Paul. *Charles Langlade in the French and Indian War.* Kalamazoo: Master Thesis, 1980.
Trenton Historical Society. *A History of Trenton 1679–1929.* Trenton: Princeton University Press, 1929.
Virginia Historical Society. *Members of the House of Burgesses.* Richmond: Virginia Magazine of History and Biography (January 1901) Volume 8.
Wainwright, Nicholas B. *An Indian trade Failure: The Story of the Hockley, Trent and Croghan Company 1748–1752.* Philadelphia: University of Pennsylvania Press, 1959.
———. *George Croghan: Wilderness Diplomat.* Chapel Hill: University of North Carolina Press, 1948.
Webber, Mabel Louise. *The South Carolina Historical and Genealogical Magazine.* Volume 25. Charleston: South Carolina Historical Society. 1924.
Weiser, Clement Z. *The Life of Conrad Weiser, the German pioneer, Patriot and Patron of Two Races.* Reading, Pennsylvania: David Miller Publishing, 1876.
Whipple, Wayne. *The Story of the Liberty Bell.* Philadelphia: Henry Altemus Company, 1910.

Index

A

Abercromby, James (Gen.), 264
Aberdeen Journal, 242
Ackley, Joseph, 257
Adams, Emanuel, 386
Adams, John (Continental Congress), 313
Adams, John (soldier), 386, 393
Adams, Samuel (Continental Congress), 313
Adena (nation), 69
Adoare, William, 394
Aitken, Robert (printer), 351
Albany (New York), 45, 50, 54–60, 63–64, 68, 168, 257–59, 268, 292, 343, 390
   Cornbury Place (New York), 55
   Eagle Street (New York), 55
   Fort Frederick (Albany, New York), 55, 57–58, 259
   Green Street (New York), 257
   King's Arms Tavern (Albany, New York), 257
      Cartwright, Richard (innkeeper), 257, 259
   Steuben Street (New York), 56
Aldrichs, Daniel, 405
Alexandria (Virginia), 130, 154, 162, 164, 172, 179, 291, 397–98
Algonquin (nation), 121, 133, 190
   Conewango (nation), 133, 141–42
   Nanticoke (nation), 190
Aliquippa, Queen, 70–71, 119, 146
Allegheny River (Pennsylvania), 66, 69–70, 112, 136, 146, 159, 164, 210, 219, 222, 225–27, 231, 233, 236, 246
Allen, William (chief justice), 261, 263
Allison, William, 94
Almon, John, 290
Alrick, Hermanus, 94, 97
Amherst, Jeffrey (Gen.), 205, 226–27, 229–32, 236, 240–42, 245–46, 252, 264, 335
Anderson, Maurice (doctor), 174
Annapolis (Maryland), 367
   Maryland Gazette, 322
Ansell, William (Capt.), 312
   Sally, 309–10, 312
Armstrong, Andrew, 392
Armstrong, James, 393
Armstrong, John (Col.), 191, 201, 358
Armstrong, Joseph, 386
Arndt, Jacob, 185
Arnold, Benedict (Gen.), 312, 336
Arnold, Joseph, 386
Arrants, Jacob, 157, 167

Arsdale, Samuel, 86, 157, 164, 167
Ashmore, Thomas, 360
Askew, John, 15
Assheton, Ralph, 1
Asunepachla (Frankstown, Pennsylvania), 69
Atkin, Edmund (Superintendent of Indian Affairs), 191–92, 199
Atkins, William, 386
Atkinson, Philip, 405
Atkinson, Samuel, 11
   Atkinson, Ruth (Beakes), 11
Auchmuty, Arthur, 256
Aughwick (Shirleysburg, Pennsylvania), 176, 178, 185
Augustus, Prince William (Duke of Cumberland), 178
Aulberger, Adam (Superintendent of Cattle), 338

B

Baem, David, 386
Bailey's Exercises, 38
Ballindine, John, 414
Balliol College (Oxford University), 10
Bancroft, Edward, 295, 309, 322–24, 381
Barbados (Island of), 10, 24, 35, 388
Bard, Peter, 21
Barnes, John, 333
Barrington, Richard (aristocrat), 365, 366
Barton, John, 406
Barton, Thomas (Rev.), 218, 401
Bartram, Isaac (druggist), 372
Baskins, Thomas and Fran, 392
Batoni, Pompeo (artist), 281, 285, 296
Battle of Brandywine (Pennsylvania), 336, 348, 350
Battle of Breed's Hill (Bunker Hill) (Massachusetts), 317
Battle of Bushy Run (Pennsylvania), 245, 410
Battle of Culloden (Scotland), 103, 178, 191
Battle of Monmouth (New Jersey), 217, 336, 339, 348, 350
Bayman, Nathaniel, 386
Baynton, John (merchant), 248–49, 252–53, 257, 262, 266, 297, 301, 306, 315–16
Beakes, Morgan (grandson), 383–84
Beakes, Nathan (Jr.) (grandson), 383
Beakes, Nathan (son-in-law), 383
   frees enslaved servant Caesar, 383
   marries daughter of Major Trent, 383
Beard, George, 406
Beard, Moses, 406

Beard, Robert, 51
Beatty, Charles (Rev.), 210
Beaver Creek (Pennsylvania), 68, 71, 77, 87, 142, 149, 210, 233
Bedford (Pennsylvania), 94, 113, 183, 198, 204, 246
    Colerain Township (Pennsylvania), 374
Belestre, Francois-Marie Picote, 191, 192
Benezet, James, 186
Benn, Benjamin, 387
Bentinck, William (2nd Duke of Portland), 354
Bethlehem (Pennsylvania), 185, 189, 192
Beulah, 74, 75
Beverly, William, 41
Biddle, Clement, 382
Bidler, Abraham, 406
Bigam, James, 392
Big Sewickley Creek (Pennsylvania), 79, 86, 87, 228
Birchall, James (grocer), 374
Bizellion, Peter, 49
Black, Robert, 246, 253, 406
Black, William, 387
Blaine, Ephraim, 222
Blair, John, 135–36, 139
    Blair Company, 136
Blakeney, William (Lt. Gen.), 52
Bland, Elias, 75–76, 78–79, 88, 99
Blane, Archibald (Ens.), 207, 208
Blyth, William, 256, 392
Boardman, Matthew, 387
Bonaparte, Joseph, 371
Bond, Elijah, 305, 324–25, 332, 334, 340, 352, 356, 359–60, 363, 369–71
    Sign of the Wheat Sheaf (New Jersey), 324
Bond, John (Sgt.), 243, 404
Boner, Barnibus, 406
Boone, Daniel, 134
Bordentown (New Jersey), 330, 332
Bosomworth, Abraham (Col.), 198–99, 202, 205, 402
Boston Gazette, 16, 303–304
Boston Post-Boy, 58–59, 61
Botetourt, Norborne (Lord), 280, 413
Boughanan, Walter, 394
Bouquet, Henry (Col.), 203–209, 219–20, 222–27, 229, 230, 232, 236, 240–43, 245–46, 251, 402, 409–11
    Bouquet's Camp (Pennsylvania), 209
Boyle, James, 387
Boyle, Philip, 246
Braddock, Edward (Gen.), 134, 179, 181–83, 185, 191, 198, 204, 214, 217, 402
Bradford, William (printer), 107, 323
Bradley, George, 394
Bradshaw, Thomas, 290
Bradstreet, John (Lt.), 264

Brandon, James, 394
Bratt, (Ens.), 61
Brearley, David, 350
Brinley, Anne, 7
Bristol, England (U.K.), 33, 35, 41, 267–68, 270
Broeck, Dirck Ten, 60
Brooks, Robert, 387
Brown, James, 393
Bryant, William (doctor), 331–32
Budden, Richard (Capt.), 76
Bullen, Captain, 199, 200, 205
Burbige, John, 406
Burch, Thomas, 387
Burd, James (Col.), 168, 174, 178, 183–85, 198–99, 205–206, 208, 220, 227
Burge, Samuel (saddler), 22, 246–47, 254
Burge, William, 247
Burgoyne, John (Gen.), 310–11, 336
Burlington (New Jersey), 9, 17, 39, 260, 268
    Burlington Company, 268–69, 282, 327
Burn's Coffeehouse (New York), 258
Burney, Thomas (blacksmith), 84, 123–25, 128, 140, 144
Burnt Cabins (Pennsylvania), 95–96, 98, 134, 185, 218, 251
Bustill, Samuel, 17–18, 23, 30
Butler, John, 264
    Buttersbury plantation (New York), 264
Butler, Richard (Col.), 336, 348, 350
Byles, Daniel (Lt.), 50, 53
Byrn, Charles, 387

C

Cadwalader, John, 316
Caggan, Barney, 405
Calais (France), 310
Caledonian Mercury, 310
Calhoon, Adam, 393
Calhoon, Sam, 391
Calhoun, Thomas (Lt.), 233, 404, 409
Callender, Robert, 83, 113, 125, 128, 136–37, 165, 246, 255–56, 320, 325, 358, 361, 393
Cally, James, 387
Camble, William, 391
Cambridge (Massachusetts), 318
Campbell, Donald (Maj.), 222–23, 246
Campbell, Francis, 256
Campbell, George (Register of Wills), 324, 354, 365, 374, 376
Campbell, John, 387
Campbell, Joseph, 158
Campbell, Patrick (Cpl.), 405
Campbell, Thomas, 186
Campbell, William (Sgt.), 404
Canso (Nova Scotia), 40

Index

Cape Henlopen (Delaware), 249
Carlisle (Pennsylvania), 89, 92; 103–105, 113–14, 128, 149, 192, 198–99, 214, 221, 229, 237–38, 246, 250–52, 254–57, 268, 275–76, 317, 321, 323–25, 336, 340, 358, 361, 401, 412
    Treaty of Carlisle (1753), 128
Carlyle, John (Maj.), 154, 170, 397–98
Carothers, Robert, 392
Carpenter, Joseph, 2
Carpenter, Samuel, 13, 31
Carpenter, William, 387
Carson, Charles, 387
Carson, John, 88
Catawba (nation), 199, 202, 204–207
Cautt, John McClair, 391
Caw-caw-wi-chaw-kee. *See* Shawnee (nation): Kakowatcheky (chief)
Céloron (Céleron), Pierre Joseph (Capt.), 70, 78, 80–83, 103, 117, 119, 125–26
Celtic Sea, 268
Cerberus, 312, 314, 317, 337
Chamberlain, Lord, 277
Chambers, Benjamin, 94, 185
    Falling Spring (Pennsylvania), 94, 185
Chambers, Robert, 94
Chambers, Samuel, 256
Chambersburg (Pennsylvania). *See* Chambers, Benjamin: Falling Spring (Pennsylvania)
Charles, Robert, 108, 110
Charleston (South Carolina), 52, 191
Charlestown (Massachusetts), 314, 317
Chartier's (Shurtees) Creek (Pennsylvania), 69, 119, 135, 141, 143, 216, 224, 228
    Fort Hill (Pennsylvania), 134–35, 216
    Rocher e´crit (Written Rock), 119
Chartier's Old Town (Tarentum, Pennsylvania), 69, 71
Chattin, James (printer), 195
Chauvignere (Chauvgnere), Michel, 161
Cheese, Richard, 387
Cherokee (nation), 127, 191–92, 199–200, 202–203, 207, 240
    Blue Shadow (Chief), 127
Chesnott, William, 393
Chew, Benjamin (attorney), 252, 254, 261, 263
Chew, Joseph (merchant), 258
Chickasaw (nation), 163
Child, James (Capt.), 74
Chiningué. *See* Logstown (Baden, Pennsylvania)
Chippewa or Ojibwa (nation), 216, 231, 233
Christie, William (Capt.), 404, 408
Clapham, William (Col.), 228, 231–33
Clark, John (Pvt.), 387
Clark, John (Sgt.), 238
Claus, Daniel, 264

Clawson, John, 387
Claxton, James (innkeeper), 53–54
    Sign of the Bear (Frankford, Pennsylvania), 54
Claypool, Daniel C. (printer), 350
Clench, Robert (innkeeper), 259
    Sign of the Cross Keys, 259
Clifford, Thomas, 267, 375–77
Clingle, Frederick, 405
Clinton, George (Gov.), 55–57, 63, 65
Clinton, Henry (Gen.), 310–11, 317, 337, 339
Coates, Samuel, 75
Cock, Peter, 30
    Cannonball Farm (Carpenter's Island, Pennsylvania), 30
    Boon's Creek (Pennsylvania), 31
    Eagle Creek (Pennsylvania), 31
Cockendal, John, 391
Coddington, Mary (Howard) (grandmother), 7, 24
Coddington, Thomas (grandfather), 7
Coddington, William (Gov.), 7
Coercive Acts (1774). *See* Intolerable Acts (1774)
Colbert, Nathaniel, 405
Collit, Daniel, 406
Connolly, John (Capt.), 246, 303, 306
Connor, John, 406
Conodoguinet Creek (Pennsylvania), 44, 47, 49, 63, 66–67, 76, 79, 105, 156, 391
Cookson, Thomas, 68, 86, 91, 104, 110
Cooley, Eli F. (author), 16
Cooper, Grey, 290
Cooper, William, 268, 319
    Cooper, James Fenimore (author), 268, 319
Corbet, John, 387
Corbutt, Charles (engraver), 311
Cork (Ireland), 179
Cornwallis, Charles (Gen.), 333, 352–53
Council at Easton (Pennsylvania) 1757, 80, 192–93, 195, 196
Cowell, David (doctor), 369, 372
Cowell, Ebenezer (attorney), 360, 369
Cowen, George, 392
Cowper, Thomas, 68
Coxe, Daniel (Col.), 3, 17–18, 39, 324
    Coxe, Sarah (Eckley), 3, 18, 39, 324, 354
Coxe, Daniel (Trenton ferry owner), 324, 331, 352
Coxe, Isaac, 408
Coxe, John (Philadelphia), 246
Coxe, John (Trenton, New Jersey), 27
Coxe, Sarah (Redman), 324
Coxe, Tench (attorney), 354, 356, 365
Coxe, William, 39, 191
Craig, George (Rev.), 188, 401
Craik, James (doctor), 165, 174
Cranage, George, 272–73
Cranage, Thomas, 272–73
Cranz's History of Greenland, 338

Crawford, Hugh, 165, 222, 224–25, 230, 233, 256, 262, 404
Crawford, William (Col.), 361
Cresap, Thomas (Col.), 68, 77–78, 82–83, 91, 122, 133–34, 136, 138, 144, 151, 154–55, 159–160, 165, 184, 196, 256, 319–20, 322, 336, 396, 399–400, 413
    Skipton, 91, 122
Croghan, George (merchant-trader), 44–48, 52, 63–64, 66–69, 71–88, 90–94, 97–98, 101–107, 110, 112–20, 122–24, 133–37, 146, 149, 152–53, 156–59, 163, 165, 176, 178–81, 185–86, 190–95, 204, 209, 214–17, 219–20, 222–24, 226–32, 236, 240, 246–50, 253–58, 260, 263, 267–69, 271–72, 276–78, 282–84, 293, 297, 300–308, 319–20, 323, 326–27, 336, 338, 351, 353, 357–58, 391, 393–94, 412
    Monkton Hall (Philadelphia, Pennsylvania), 250, 336
    Pennsborough plantation (Mechanicsburg, Pennsylvania), 44, 47, 64, 66–68, 76, 78–80, 85–86, 91, 97–98, 103–104, 106, 110
Cromwell, William, 136, 152
Crook, John, 387
Crosswicks (New Jersey), 330
Culberson, Samuel, 392
Cumberland County (Pennsylvania), 44, 46, 85, 88, 91, 93–94, 97, 99, 103–106, 112, 133, 185, 224, 226, 253, 275, 341, 374
    Barree Township (Pennsylvania), 374
    Cumbria, England, 103
Cumberland Gap (Virginia), 134
Curran, Barnaby (Barney), 139, 150–51, 171
Cuttaway (Kentucky) River, 134
Cuyahoga River (Ohio), 44, 64, 66
Cuyler, Abraham, 236
Cuyler, Cornelius, 56, 60

D

d'Arnouville, Jean Baptist de Machault, 210
Dagge, Henry (solicitor), 271, 274, 290, 307, 342
Dagworthy, John (Col.), 191, 206
Darling, Jeremiah, 387
Dartmouth, Lord (Earl of Dartmouth), 292–94, 299, 302, 306, 309, 413
Davenport, James (baker), 225
Davenport, Josiah Franklin (Capt.), 225, 228, 231, 243, 264, 404, 408, 410
Davidson, John (trader), 164
Daviny, Samuel, 405
Davis, John, 387
Davis, John (Fort Pitt), 405
Davison, Thomas, 164
Dawson (Danvon), John, 387

Deane, Silas (Continental Congress), 295, 313, 381
de Contrecoeur, Claude-Pierre Pécaudy (Comdt.), 80, 153, 161, 165, 175
DeCow, Isaac, 360
De Klyn, Barnt (clothier to the Continental Army), 371
de La Galissonière, Roland-Michel Barrin (Gov.), 80
de La Mague, Paul Marin (Comdt.), 57
de La Mothe Cadillac, Antoine (Comdt.), 122
de Langlade, Charles Michel (trader), 124
Delaware (nation). *See* Lenape (nation)
Delaware River, 3, 10–11, 16, 21, 24, 30–31, 37, 52, 54, 71, 73, 324–25, 331–32, 334–36, 340, 367, 377
de Lignery, Francois-Marie Le Marchand (Comdt.), 192, 216
Dennahew, Florence, 387
Denny, Robert, 393
Denny, William (Gov.), 190, 192–94, 196, 215
Dermott, Matthew, 387
de Villiers, Louis Coulon (Capt.), 83, 153, 174–75
Dickens, Charles (author), 298
Dickinson, Philemon, 349
Dickson, John (commissary), 338
Diemer, John (Capt.), 49, 51–52, 57
Dill, Matthew, 93, 97
Dinwiddie, Robert (Lt. Gov.), 114–15, 117, 120–21, 123, 128, 130, 133, 137–40, 144–45, 147, 149–50, 152–57, 160, 162, 166–67, 170–73, 175, 177, 191, 196–197, 214, 221, 256, 261, 280, 298, 396–97
Dongan, Thomas (Gov.), 60
Donnald, John, 405
Doran, John, 405
Dougherty, Dudley, 406
Douw, Volkert Pietr (mayor), 257
Doyle, John, 287
Draper's Meadow (Blacksburg, Virginia), 114
Drumming, John, 387
Duché, Jacob (Rev.), 193, 195
Dugan, John, 387
Dunbar, Thomas (Col.), 183
Duning, Ezeachal (Ezekiel), 392
Dunlap, John (printer), 350
Dunlap, Joseph, 406
Dunlap, William, 393
Dunlap Creek (Pennsylvania), 153
Dunmore, Lord, 288, 303, 306, 345, 413
Dunning (Dinnen), James, 13, 40, 157, 256

E

Easdale, Samuel. *See* Arsdale, Samuel
Ecuyer, Simeon (Comdt.), 229–46, 264, 404, 409–11
Eggar, Robert, 407
Eghnisara. *See* Montour, Andrew

Index

Eliott, Daniel, 407
Elwes, Henry, 309–10
Elwin, Fountain, 305
Erwin, Isaac, 407
Eskippakithiki (Kentucky), 133
Evans, Evan (Rev.), 8
Evans, John, 387
Evans, Lewis (cartographer), 46, 121
Evans, Peter (sheriff), 1, 2, 4, 218
Evans, William, 407

F

Fairfax, George William, 147, 299
Fairfax, Lord Thomas, 64, 83, 91, 136, 147, 154
Fairfax, Sarah (Walker), 147
Fairfax, William (Col.), 138–40, 145, 149, 214
   Belvoir plantation (Virginia), 138
Farguison, James, 392, 394
Farguison, William, 393
Faulkner, John, 151
Faulkner, Joseph, 83
Fauquier, Francis (Gov.), 215
Fetherstonhaugh, (Lady) Sarah (Lethieullier), 285, 296
Fetherstonhaugh, (Sir) Matthew, 285–86, 295–96, 299, 302, 304–305
   Uppark House, 285–86, 295–96, 302
   Vandalia Tower, 302
   West Sussex, England (U.K.), 285–86, 295
Fetherstonhaugh, Henry, 305
Fielding, Henry, 287
Finley, James, 93
Finley, John, 94, 133–34, 139, 224
Fischer, David Hackett (author), 332
Fishkill (New York), 57, 59–62, 65
Fitzpatrick, Dennis, 387
Flannigan, George, 387
Flemming, James, 407
Flemming, John (Lt.), 404, 409
Fobise, Andrew, 392
Foley, James, 86, 112, 120, 158, 164, 221, 224, 252
Forbes, John (Brig. Gen), 113, 185, 198–99, 201–203, 205, 208–10, 212–13, 218–19, 228, 254, 361, 402
   Pittencrieff House, 210
Fort Allen (Weissport, Pennsylvania), 192
Fort Augusta (Sunbury, Pennsylvania), 228
Fort de Chartres (Prairie Du Rocher, Ilinois), 221
Fort des Miamis (Fort Wayne, Indiana), 83, 126
Fort Detroit (Detroit, Michigan), 80, 83, 122, 124–25, 221–24, 226–27, 231, 233, 239, 241
Fort Frontenac (Kingston, Ontario), 264
Fort Halifax (Halifax, Pennsylvania), 228

Fort Hunter (Harrisburg, Pennsylvania), 228
Fort Le Boeuf (Waterford, Pennsylvania), 57, 136, 141, 177, 220, 239, 322, 396
Fort Littleton (Lyttleton) (Fort Littleton, Pennsylvania), 200, 202, 204
Fort Loudoun (Fort Loudon, Pennsylvania), 199–201, 203, 240, 254, 402
Fort Loudoun (Vonore, Tennessee), 174
Fort Michilimackinac (Mackinac Island, Michigan), 61
Fort Necessity (Farmington, Pennsylvania), 174
Fort Niagara (Youngstown, New York), 161, 175, 215, 217, 264, 328
   Battle of La Belle-Famille, 161
Fort Presque Isle (Erie, Pennsylvania), 141, 161
Fort Prince George (Pennsylvania). *See* Pittsburgh (Pennsylvania): Fort St. George (Pennsylvania)
Fort Rea's Town. *See* Rea's Town (Raystown) Pennsylvania: Fort Bedford (Bedford, Pennsylvania)
Fort Saint-Frederic (Crown Point, New York), 58–59, 61, 80
Fort Saratoga. *See* Saratoga (Saraghtogue), New York: Fort Clinton (Schuylerville, New York)
Fort Stanwix (Rome, New York), 260–61, 263, 265, 278, 307, 321, 323, 351, 353, 413
   Treaty of Stanwix (1768), 263, 270, 321, 340–43, 351, 361, 364, 367
Fort Ticonderoga or Carillion (Ticonderoga, New York), 217, 264
Foulk, Charles, 185
Foulk, Charles, 185
Frankford Creek (Pennsylvania), 52
Franklin, Benjamin (Continental Congress), 8, 36, 51, 68, 106, 113, 168, 195, 225, 231, 243, 256, 263–65, 269–70, 272, 274–75, 277, 285–86, 290, 295, 302–304, 307–10, 313, 337, 343, 381
   Franklin Stove, 274
Franklin, Sarah, 225
Franklin, Temple, 307
Franklin, William (Gov.), 51, 68, 71, 106, 135, 146, 231, 243, 261, 268, 282, 319, 326–27, 338
   imprisoned in Connecticut, 339
   lives at "Green Brook", 260
Franks, David, 186, 218–20, 228, 246–48, 252–54, 261, 275, 326, 336, 341
Franks, Margaret (Evans), 218
Franks, Moses, 76, 381, 383
Fraser, Jane or "Jenny" (McClane), 183
Fraser (Frazier), John (Lt.) (gunsmith), 80–81, 136–37, 141–42, 14–46, 156, 163–64, 171, 181, 183, 208, 256, 358, 398
Frederick Town. *See* Winchester (Virginia)

French, Mary (Streate), 3
French, Nathaniel, 3, 30
Fry, Joshua (Col.), 171–72
Funk, John, 136
Furman, Daniel R., 384
Furman, Mary Louisa (Beakes), 384
Furman, Moore, 325, 352

G

Gage, Thomas (Gen.), 241, 252, 254, 257, 288, 313, 411
Galbraith, James, 94
Galbraith, John, 94, 256, 419
Galloway, George, 93
Galloway, Joseph, 193, 277, 302, 336, 339
Galloway, William, 93
Garrigue, Matthew, 388
Garthwaite, Anna Marie (silk designer), 287
Gates, Horatio (Gen.), 335
Georgetown (Maryland), 132, 305, 328
Germantown (Pennsylvania), 40, 52, 336, 348, 350
Gethins, Daniel, 388
Giahaga River. *See* Cuyahoga River (Ohio)
Gibey, James, 391
Gibson, John, 320–21, 342
Gilaskey, George, 393
Gilmore, Henry, 407
Girty, George, 324–25, 404, 407
Girty, James, 324–25
Girty, Thomas, 246, 404, 407, 413
Girty (Jr.), Simon, 94, 246, 404, 407
Girty (Sr.), Simon , 94
Girty's Run (Pennsylvania), 246
Gist, Christopher (trader), 69–71, 83, 87, 104, 115–16, 123, 134, 136, 144, 150–52, 157–60, 163, 171, 175, 198, 357
   Monongahela (Gist's Plantation), 136, 152, 175
   Wilkesboro (North Carolina), 115, 134
Glenn, John (merchant), 263
Glynn, John (attorney), 308, 342
Gnadenhutten (Ohio), 185, 361
Goldsney, Joseph, 407
Gollerthon, William, 388
Gooch, William (Gov.), 55
Goodman, Alfred T. (author), 4, 7
Goodwin, John, 388
Gordon, Harry (Capt.), 204, 208, 216–17, 236
Gower, Lord, 277, 290
Grabiz, John (Lt.), 404
Grace, William, 388
Grand Ohio Company, 277–78, 280–81, 285, 288, 290, 292, 295, 297, 301–302, 305–307, 309, 321, 343, 376
   Walpole Grant, 279–80, 292
Grant, James (Ensign), 207

Grant, James (Maj.), 206–10, 237, 261
Grant, John, 388
Gratz, Barnard (merchant), 351, 357, 360, 362, 367
Gratz, Michael (merchant), 328, 357, 362, 367
Gratz, Rebecca, 351
Gravesend, England (U.K.), 76
Gray, John, 256
Gray, Joseph, 388
Grayson, William, 341–42, 350, 381
   Belle Aire plantation (Virginia), 341
Great Conestoga Road (Pennsylvania), 99
   Swedesford Road (Pennsylvania), 99, 100
Green, Joseph, 27
Greene, Nathanael (Gen.), 333, 348–49
Grenville, George (Prime Minister), 277
Grey, Ford (Lord of Tankerville), 285–86
Griffith, Widow, 394
Griffith, William, 388
Grymes, Phillip (Receiver General), 130
Gunn, James (Capt.), 358
Gunter, William, 388
Gutterie, Archibald, 405
Gutterie, John, 405
Gutterie, William, 405
Guyasuta. *See* Kiasutha (Chief)

H

Hailough, John, 393
Haldeman's Island (Pennsylvania), 214
Half Moon (Waterford, New York), 59
Halkett, Peter (Col.), 183
Hall, David (printer), 195
Hamilton, Alexander (Secretary of Treasury), 344
Hamilton, Andrew (lawyer), 40
Hamilton, James (Gov.), 77–79, 86, 90, 92, 97, 133, 153, 163, 168
   Bush Hill plantation (Pennsylvania), 40
Hamilton, John (chaplain), 170–72, 401
Hammer, John (carpenter), 102, 132
Hanbury, Capel (merchant), 130
Hanbury, John (merchant), 130, 143, 220
Hanbury, Osgood (merchant), 130
Hancock, John (Continental Congress), 313–14
Hand, Edward (Gen.), 358
Handel, George Frideric (composer), 278
Hannah, William (Rev.), 292
Harris, James (Sgt.), 222, 388, 405
Harris, Robert, 408
Harris, Thomas, 392
Harris's Ferry (Pennsylvania), 44, 176
Harris (Jr.), John, 176
Harris (Sr.), John, 49, 176
Harrison, William (Rev.), 13–14, 17
Harris's Wharf (New London, Connecticut), 258

Harrow, Isaac, 27–28
Harry, John, 405
Hartford Courant, 322, 418
Harvey, Thomas, 324
Haslet, John (Capt.), 210
Haudenosaunee Confederacy. *See* Six Nations (Haudenosaunee Confederacy)
Haus, Charles, 407
Hayes, John, 72–73, 394
Heart (Hart), Daniel, 407
Hendricks, Abraham, 394
Hendricks, David, 133
Hendricks, James, 39
Hendricks, Tobias, 392
Hennaday, Caleb, 407
Hennaday, Daniel, 407
Henriques, Isaac Nunes, 219
Henry, Edward Lawson (artist), 260
Henry, Patrick (Continental Congress), 345
Herbert, William, 407
Herbin, Frederick Louis (Lt.), 61, 62
Hertford, Lord, 277
Hesse-Cassel (German province of), 329
Hesse-Hanau (German province of), 329
Higbee, Mary Trent Rossell, 383
Higbee, Sarah, 17, 383
Hillsborough, Lord (Wills Hill), 272, 274, 276–78, 280–81, 285, 287, 290–92, 302, 413
Hinds, John, 388
Hitchley, George, 388
HMS *Baltimore*, 197
Hoare, William (artist), 211
Hockley, Richard (merchant), 73–74, 76, 78, 86, 97, 99, 102–103, 105–106, 110, 112–14, 178, 180, 219–20, 224, 391
Hogue Creek (Virginia), 224
Hollingsworth, Levi, 362, 381
Holme, Thomas, 377–78
Holms, Johnnathan, 392
Holton, Alexander, 407
Hood, Seymour (Capt.), 267
  Betsy, 267
Hooper, Thomas, 388
Hopkins, John, 407
Horner, Benjamin (ironmonger), 377
Horsfield, Timothy, 185, 189, 191
Hough, William, 349
Houston, William Churchill (attorney), 356
How, Nehemiah, 62, 386
Howard, John, 18
Howe, William (Gen.), 310–11, 317, 333–34, 336–38
Hudson River (New York), 55, 57–60, 65, 257, 260
Huff, Widow, 393
Hufnagel, Michael, 356
Hughs, Barney, 393

Hullins, Michael (Michal), 407
Hullins (Jr.), Marcus, 407
Hullins (Sr.), Marcus, 407
Humphreys, Assheton (notary), 369, 370
Hunter, Robert, 394
Hunter, Robert (Gov.), 385
Hunter, William (printer), 128–29
Huron (nation). *See* Wyandot or Huron (nation)
Hutchinson, Thomas (Gov.), 304, 307
Hutchinson, Thomas (New Jersey), 13
Hutchinson (Hutchison), James (doctor), 372, 383
Hyam (Hyham), Thomas, 74, 76, 88

I

Indiana Company, 220, 265, 325–26, 328–29, 336, 338–39, 344, 350–53, 356, 362–64, 367–68, 381, 413–14
Indiana grant, 321, 326, 342–44, 361
Ingoldsby, Richard (Gov.), 13
Inhabitants (Cumberland, Maryland), 45, 71, 134, 163, 165–66, 171–72, 175–76, 399
  Emmanual Episcopal Church (Cumberland, Maryland), 180
  Fort Cumberland (Cumberland, Maryland), 179–84, 191, 198, 205, 220, 291
  Fort Mount Pleasant or Mount Pleasant (Cumberland, Maryland), 176, 178–79, 340
  Will's Creek (Cumberland, Maryland), 83, 134, 152, 165, 168, 170–72, 175, 178, 205, 305, 399, 401
Innes, James (Col.), 172, 175–77
Inslee, Joseph (sheriff), 351
Intolerable Acts (1774), 304, 306, 344
Irvine, William (Gen.), 361–62
Irwin, Luke, 83
Isdale, Samuel. *See* Arsdale, Samuel

J

Jackson, Daniel, 388
Jackson, Richard (attorney), 303
Janney, Thomas, 332
Jefferson, Peter (cartographer), 114, 261
Jefferson, Thomas (Continental Congress), 114, 215, 329
Jenkins, Thomas, 388
Jenkins, William, 171
Jervis, Alexander, 407
Johns, Joseph, 388
Johnson, (Sir) William, 55, 81, 190, 194, 196, 215, 217, 226–27, 230, 252–54, 257–58, 260–65, 272, 276, 282, 292, 319, 358
  Johnson Hall (Johnstown, New York), 253, 255–56, 259–61, 272, 282–83, 358

Johnson, Guy, 264
Johnston, John, 388
Join Or Die snake emblem, 168
Joncaire, Phillipe-Thomas de Chabert, 81, 161
Jones, John Paul (Capt.), 363–64
Jones, Thomas, 388
Jumonville, (Ens.) (Joseph Coulon de Villiers), 172, 174, 177
Jung, Leonhard or Lenard (baker), 224, 406
Juniata River (Pennsylvania), 68–69, 92–94, 204, 214, 255

K

Kalm, Peter (naturalist), 60
Kanawha River (West Virginia), 130, 257, 265
Keith, William (Gov.), 13–14
Kekionga. *See* Fort des Miamis (Fort Wayne, Indiana)
Kennedy, John, 158
Kenny, James (storekeeper), 225, 227–28, 231, 243
Kentish Gazette, 309
Kiasutha (Chief), 322, 328–29
King's College (Aberdeen, Scotland), 345
King Charles I, 270, 290
King George I, 10, 55
King George II, 40, 46–47, 55, 65, 80, 129–30, 173, 178, 186, 204, 396
KIng George III, 160, 269, 272, 318, 344, 416
King Henry VIII, 269, 290
King Louis XV, 40, 81, 195
Kinsey, John (attorney), 22
Kinton, Thomas, 256
Kiskiminetas River (Pennsylvania), 64, 69, 130
Kitatinny or Kitochtinney Mountains (Pennsylvania), 91–92, 94
  Blue Hills (Pennsylvania), 92–95, 97, 103, 134
Kittanning Path, 69
Knyphausen Regiment, 332
Kuskuskies or Kuskusky (New Castle, Pennsylvania), 68, 71–72, 77

L

Lalley, Thomas, 388
Lamb, Caleb, 391
Lambert, Thomas, 16, 30, 324
Lancaster (Pennsylvania), 40–43, 64, 67–68, 100, 112, 114, 116–17, 120, 178, 188–90, 192, 195, 212, 214, 218–21, 227–29, 241, 252, 261, 320, 336, 342, 358–59, 373, 401, 412–14
  Penn Square (Pennsylvania), 42, 218, 220
  Shaarai Shomayim Cemetery (Pennsylvania), 219
  Treaty of Lancaster (1744), 42–43, 64, 114, 117, 190, 342, 373, 412, 414

Landis, Charles Israel (author), 5
Larey, John, 388
Laugherty, Patrick, 392
Lawrence, Daniel, 393
Lawrence, Thomas (merchant), 88, 113
Lechauwitank. *See* Council at Easton (Pennsylvania) 1757
Lee, (Light Horse Harry) Henry, 64
Lee, Arthur, 280
Lee, Charles (Lt.), 217
Lee, Francis Lightfoot, 64, 344
Lee, Philip Ludwell, 142
Lee, Richard Henry, 64, 344
Lee, Thomas, 41, 64, 90–91, 104, 130, 143, 280
  Stratford Hall (Virginia), 64, 104, 142–43
Leech, Thomas, 108
Legge, William (2nd Earl of Dartmouth). *See* Dartmouth, Lord (Earl of Dartmouth)
Le Mercier, Francois (engineer), 141
Lenape (nation), 33–34, 41, 68–71, 94, 98, 118–20, 122–23, 135, 141–42, 144–46, 149, 158, 161–62, 188–94, 208, 214–15, 224, 230–31, 233, 239, 243, 261, 264, 328
  Beaver (Tamaqua), 118, 144, 149, 215–16, 218, 233
  Delaware George, 149, 213, 227, 231
  Gray Eyes , 243
  Hockhocken or French Margaret's Town, 100, 122
  Lapechkewe (chief), 122, 144, 194
  Maguck (Circleville, Ohio), 123
  Mamaltee (chief), 239–40, 242–43
  Pisquatomen, 149
  Pumpshire, John (Cawkeeponen), 193–94
  Shingas (Chief), 118–19, 135, 141–42, 144, 146, 149, 233
  Teedyuscung (Chief), 189–95
  Turtles Heart, 239–40, 242–43, 264
  Wingenum, 243
  Wolf, (the), 231, 233
Leonard, Nathaniel, 21
Le Peyronie, William (Ens.), 177
Lester, Thomas, 110
Letort, James, 103
Levy, Levi Andrew, 219–29, 231–32, 235, 240–41, 246, 252–53, 261, 323, 361–62, 381, 410–11
Levy, Mary (Simon), 219
Levy, Nathan (merchant), 76, 186, 218
Lewis, Andrew (Col.), 261–62
Lewis, Joseph (innkeeper), 53
Linch, Patrick, 51
Lindon, Patrick, 388
Liphook (Lippock) (England) (U.K.), 296
Little Pict Town. *See* Eskippakithiki (Kentucky)
Livingston, Henry (Capt.), 57, 61–63
Livingston, Robert, 60

Livingston, William (Gov.), 349
Lockhart, Alexander (constable), 18
Logan, James (merchant), 32–35, 38–41, 43, 73, 348
   Stenton house, 32–33, 52
Logan, William, 137
Logstown (Baden, Pennsylvania), 71, 73, 77–78, 80–82, 87, 112, 114–16, 119, 121–22, 125, 127, 133, 138–42, 144, 147, 149, 153–54, 158, 161, 164, 176–77, 194
   Treaty of Logstown (1752), 112, 149, 194
Lomax, Lunsford (Col.), 114, 121
   Portobago plantation, 114
London (England) (U.K.), 3–4, 15, 33, 36, 41, 46–47, 52, 54–55, 63, 65, 73–79, 86, 88, 90, 97–99, 102, 105, 107–108, 110, 113, 143, 145, 168, 171, 183, 185–86, 204, 215, 218, 220, 248–50, 252, 255–56, 258, 263, 265–77, 281–84, 286–87, 290–92, 294–99, 301, 304–10, 313, 316–23, 326–28, 330, 338, 342–45, 351, 355, 365–66, 370–71, 373, 376, 381, 384, 412
   Angel Place, 298
   Argyle Street, 284
   Arundel Street, 278
   Buckingham House , 269, 299
   Cavendish Square, 280
   Charing Cross, 270, 287, 290, 365, 366
   Cleveland Street, 286
   Cockpit, the, 285, 290–92, 303–304
   Cockspur Street, 269
   Cornhill Ward, 75
   Covent Garden, 287
   Craven Street, 270–72, 283
   Dover House, 285, 304
   Downing Street, 290
   Drummond's Bank, 365–66
   Fitzrovia (district), 286
   Fournier Street, 287–88
   Green Park, 269
   Holles Street, 280
   Hungerford Market, 272
   Hyde Park, 269
   Kensington Palace, 204, 269
   Key of Wool-Wharf, 309
   Lambeth Palace, 330
      Archbishop of Canterbury, 302
   Lincoln's Inn, 280
   Marshalsea Prison, 298
   Marylebone District, 280, 299
   Middle Temple, 10, 26, 220
   New Suffolk (Nassau) Street, 284, 286
   Norton (Bolsover) Street, 299, 301
   Piccadilly, 290
   Princelet Street, 287
   Salmon and Ball Pub along Bethnal Green, 287
   Spitalfields, 286–88, 373, 384
   St. Clement Danes Church, 278–79
   St. Paul's Cathedral, 274–75
   Strand, the, 270–71, 277–79
   Thames River, 76, 270, 272–73, 298, 309–10
   Trafalgar Square, 365–66
   Villiers Street, 272–73, 284
   Westminster, 26, 269–70, 287
   Westminster Abbey, 10
   Westminster School, 10
   Whitechapel Bell Foundry, 110
   Whitehall (White Hall), 270, 285, 290, 304
Longfellow, Henry Wadsworth, 318
Lormose, Mary, 393
Lorne, Charles, 388
Lower Shawnee Town (Portsmouth, Kentucky), 73, 77–78, 80, 82–83, 87, 123, 126–27, 144, 229, 231, 241
Lowrey, Alexander, 221, 223, 231, 326
Lowrey, James, 133, 158
Loyalhanna (Camp at the), 204–10, 213, 218, 239, 245–46, 251
   Fort Ligonier (Pennsylvania), 210, 245, 251
Lucas, Edward, 167
Lumley, William, 407
Lundy, (Ens.), 309, 313

M

Macclesfield, 99
Mackarall, John, 41, 64
MacKay, James (Capt.), 172–73
MacQuire (McGuire), John, 171
Madison, Dolley (Payne), 382
Madison, James (Continental Congress), 344, 353, 363, 382
Maguck (Circleville, Ohio), 123
Mahan, Owen, 389
Maidstone-on-the-Potomac (Falling Waters, West Virginia), 181–82, 214
Marshall, Edward, 34
Marshe, Witham, 41
Martin, James, 394
Martin, John (tailor), 97, 374
Martin, Patrick, 389
Martin, Thomas Bryan, 147
Mason, French, 198
Mason, George (Virginia delegate), 83, 138, 143, 196, 255–56, 339, 342, 345
   Dogue's Neck (Virginia), 198
   Gunston Hall (Virginia), 198, 255
Maxatawny Path, 192
Maxwell, William, 94
McAlister, Richard, 392
McAllister, Eneap, 406

McAllister, John, 406
McBriar (McBryer), Andrew, 84, 123, 125, 158
McCarty, Bartholomew, 388
McCarty, Cornelius, 389
McCarty, John, 389
McClair, Sanders, 391
McCluer, John, 392–93
McClure, Samuel, 407
McCollome, Neal, 405
McDonald, Alexander, 406
McDonald, John, 405
McDonald, Minass, 389
McDonald, Peter, 389
McDonnald, Martin, 405
McEldemar, John, 389
McEllhinney, Dennis, 407
McFarland, Andrew, 407
McGee, Thomas, 389
McGoun, Patrick, 389
McHlhenny, Hugh, 394
McIlvaine, David, 186
McKee, Alexander (Lt.), 214, 223, 239, 242–43, 246, 404, 409
McKee, Thomas, 194, 214, 256
McKee, William, 389
McKennet, Alexander, 256
McKinley, Robert, 407
McLaughlin, James, 142
McMahon, Richard (Sgt.), 405
McManus, James, 389
McVeigh, James (innkeeper), 53
Meaner, John, 407
Medcalph, James, 407
Medcalph, John, 407
Memeskia. *See* Miami Confederacy: Old Briton (Piankashaw Chief)
Mercer, George, 134–36, 216, 221, 255, 280, 291, 297–99, 308, 318, 342
Mercer, Hugh (Col.), 210, 212–14
Mercer, John (attorney), 134, 138, 196–97, 215, 256
    Marlborough house, 134, 196
Mercier, Peter (Lt.), 173, 174
Meredith, John, 389
Meredith, Samuel, 328
Mesnard, Stephen (Capt.), 88
Miami Confederacy, 66, 82, 125, 127–28
    Old Briton (Piankashaw Chief), 66, 82, 123–24, 126, 128
    Piankashaw (nation), 66, 82, 120, 123–24, 127–28, 144
        Assapausa (Chief), 123–24, 127–28, 144
    Pyangeacha, Ellanagea (Ellangoa), 128
    Turtle (Chief), 123–24, 128, 144
    Twightwee (Miami) (nation), 66–67, 82, 103, 117–18, 120–28, 138, 216–17, 230

Mifflin, Thomas (Continental Congress), 313, 348
Miller, Adam (Sgt.), 237, 405
Miller, Christian, 407
Miller, George, 389
Miller, John, 94
Miller, John, 392
Miller, Malken, 393
Miller, Patrick, 407
Miller, Robert, 392
Milligan, James, 408
Millikan (Milliken), James (Lt.), 404, 409
Mississippi Company, 279–80
Mitchel, John, 392, 405
Mitchell, Abraham (hatter), 44, 88, 93, 106, 246, 254
Mitchell, John (merchant), 354, 365
Mitchell, Randall, 328
Mitchell, Thomas, 222
Mohawk River (New York), 260, 268, 370
Moncrief, Patrick (Lt.), 309, 313
Monongahela River, 64, 66, 69–70, 79–80, 118, 136–37, 146, 151, 153, 156, 159, 163, 166, 168, 175, 208, 213, 219, 225, 227, 246, 265, 291, 297
Montgomerie, Archibald (Col.), 205
Montour, Andrew, 77, 92, 114, 120–23, 127, 146, 149, 153, 157–59, 173, 176, 215, 264, 319, 393, 400
Montour, John, 319, 413
Mooney, Michael, 389
Moor, George, 394
Moor, John, 394
Moore, George (merchant), 356
Moore, John, 2, 4
Moore, Mary, 2, 4, 218
Moreau, Jacob Nicolas (historiographer), 195
Morgan, Daniel (Gen.), 336
Morgan, George, 248–49, 252–53, 257, 297, 300–301, 306, 315–16, 320–21, 341–45, 350, 361, 363–64, 367–68
    Prospect farm, 364
Morgan, Mary (Baynton), 297
Morgan, Morgan, 147
Morgan, Zachquill, 147
Morris, Anthony (brewer), 2, 24–25, 37
Morris, Israel (cousin), 369, 372, 374
Morris, Lewis (Gov.), 54
Morris, Lewis (Virginia), 322
Morris, Phoebe, 374
Morris, Robert Hunter (Gov.), 159, 182, 185
Morris, Sarah, 374
Morris, Sarah (Dury), 24
Morris, Susanna, 374
Morris, William (uncle), 19, 24, 27, 29, 36, 54, 268, 282–83, 285
Morris (Jr.), Joseph, 268

Morrison, James, 389
Moses, William, 389
Mouth of the Conococheague Creek (Williamsport, Maryland), 181, 183–85, 214
Munday, William, 407
Munford, Robert, 345
Murphy, Archibald, 389
Murray, John. *See* Dunmore, Lord
Muse, George (Maj.), 172

N

Natherland, William, 389
Neave, Samuel, 186
Neigle, James, 389
Neilson, James, 27
Neilson, John (Gen.), 27, 348
Nelson, William, 42, 288, 413–14
Nennatchehan. *See* Lenape (nation): Delaware George
Neville, John (Col.), 321, 328–29
    Woodville plantation, 328
Newman, Edward, 389
Newport (Rhode Island), 2–3, 7, 294, 352
New Store Tract (Ridgeley, West Virginia), 83, 102, 131–34, 138, 143, 151–53, 155, 159, 163–64, 167, 174–75, 179–81, 188, 196, 306
Nicholas, Robert Carter (attorney), 197
Norris (Jr.), Isaac, 106, 108, 186, 190
Norris (Sr.), Isaac (merchant), 3–4, 10–13, 15, 21–22, 34, 37
    Fairhill plantation, 12
North, Lord, 322–23
Northern Neck (Virginia), 64, 83, 147
Nottaway (Nation), 206
Nowlen, Patrick, 394

O

Oglethorpe, James (Gen.), 174, 198
Ohio Company, 64, 78, 80, 82–83, 86–87, 89, 91, 101–102, 104, 112, 114, 122–23, 130–36, 138–40, 142–44, 146, 149–53, 155, 157, 159–60, 163, 166–67, 172, 175–76, 179, 181, 188, 196, 214–16, 218, 220–21, 242, 251, 255–56, 261, 266, 280, 291, 297, 305, 339–40, 345, 354
    proposes a town called Saltsburg, 141, 157
Oldtown (Maryland), 91, 122, 319
Oliver, Andrew, 304
Opessah's Town or Shawnee Oldtown. *See* Oldtown (Maryland)
Oriel College (Oxford University), 190
Ormsby, John, 224, 320

Oswegle Bottom. *See* Swiegly Old Town (Pennsylvania)
Otsego Patent (New York), 268, 318, 327
Otstonwakin (Ohio), 121
Ottawa (nation), 101, 125, 133, 217, 233
Ouchterlony, Patrick (Capt.), 99
Owen, Griffin, 106
Owens, John, 112, 120, 138, 140, 158, 256
O'Cain, Daniel, 392
O'Flaugherty, Patrick, 408

P

Paine, James (architect), 285
Paine, Thomas (author), 350–51
    Public Good, 350–51
Palmer, Charlton, 220
Panton, George (Rev.), 329
Parker, Hugh (trader), 34, 38–40, 43, 72–73, 77–78, 82–83, 89, 91, 101, 104, 130, 132, 139
Parker, John (Capt.), 313
Parnell Knob (Pennsylvania), 200
Parr, William, 266
Partridge, Richard, 168
Path Valley (Fannettsburg, Pennsylvania), 94–96
Patton, James (Col.), 114, 121, 139, 154
Paxtang (Harrisburg, Pennsylvania), 44, 49, 94, 176
Peale, Charles Wilson (artist), 357–58, 364
Pearis, Richard, 151, 224–25
Peirce (Pearce), Paul (trader), 157–58, 256
Pelham-Holles, Thomas (1st Duke of Newcastle), 46
Pemberton, Israel, 193
Pemberton, James, 99
Pendergrass, Garret, 393
Penn, John (Gov.), 261–63
Penn, Thomas (merchant), 47, 73–74, 76
Penn, William (colony founder), 1, 25, 30, 32–34, 37, 49, 74, 108, 377
    Pennsbury Manor (Morrisville, Pennsylvania), 11
Penn (Jr.), William, 348
Penrose, Bartholomew (Capt.), 348
Penrose, Joseph (miller), 347–48
Perry, Samuel (Capt.), 49, 52, 57, 94–97
Peruvian Bark, 77, 299
    cochina tree, 77
Peters, Richard (Provincial Secretary), 47, 68, 73–74, 77–80, 82, 85, 91–95, 97, 100, 102–103, 106, 180, 186, 261, 263
Pettit, Nathaniel, 27
Philadelphia (Pennsylvania), 43–44, 46–47, 49–56, 63, 68, 74–79, 85–86, 88, 90, 93, 100, 102, 106–10, 112–13, 160, 168, 171,

183, 186, 190–93, 195–96, 198, 204, 212–15, 217–20, 225, 232, 243, 246–49, 252, 254–55, 257, 261–63, 266–68, 271–72, 282–83, 285, 291, 303, 305–10, 312–15, 317, 322, 324–25, 328–29, 331, 336–39, 341, 343, 345, 347, 350–52, 354–58, 360–61, 365–67, 369–79, 382–83, 385, 412
American Daily Advertiser, 350
American Weekly Mercury, 16
Arch (Mulberry) Street, 37, 49–50, 74, 113
Black Horse Alley, 369–70
Bunch of Grapes Tavern, 225
Carpenter's Hall, 306, 336–37, 372, 374
Cedar Street, 39
Chestnut Street, 13, 29, 37, 106–107, 109, 337, 354, 372, 375
Christ Church (Pennsylvania), 1–4, 8–9, 11, 14, 51, 113, 193, 212–13, 217–18
College of Philadelphia (University of Pennsylvania), 113, 193, 219, 372, 379
College of Physicians, 367, 372
Dunlap's Pennsylvania Packet, 352, 371, 374
First Presbyterian Church (Pennsylvania), 35
Fishbourne's Wharf, 73
Freeman's Journal, 374
Garden Alley, 4
Gray's Alley, 225
Hamilton Wharf (Pennsylvania), 76
Indian Queen Tavern (Pennsylvania), 246–48, 252, 272, 315–16, 341, 352–53, 355–56, 360, 362, 365, 367, 372, 374–75
Lee, Francis (innkeeper), 353, 356, 365
Little, Grace (Nicholson) (innkeeper), 247
Little, John (innkeeper), 247, 256, 372
Nicholson, William (innkeeper), 247
Keys Alley (New Street), 324, 376
Locust Street, 337, 354, 375
Lodge's Alley, 37
Logan's Alley, 37
London Coffee-House, 107
Market (High) Street or "the Market", 1, 35–36, 68, 195, 247, 252, 351
Mulberry Street (Pennsylvania) (see: Philadelphia (Pennsylvania) - Arch (Mulberry) Street)
Norris Alley, 3, 13, 37
Pennsylvania Gazette, 29, 36, 50–51, 168–69, 252, 370–71
Pennsylvania Journal, 323
Pewter Platter Alley, 2
Plumsted's Wharf, 99
Saint Peter's Church (Pennsylvania), 357
Sansom Walk (Street), 37, 38
Shippen-Wistar house, 355
Sign of the Dial, 109
Slate-Roof House, 37

St. George and the Dragon Inn, 50, 85, 160
St. Joseph's Catholic Church (Pennsylvania), 367–68
Washington Square (formerly Southeast Square), 336, 354, 379, 380
  Potter's Field, 377–78
  Southeast Square, 354, 377–79
Weekly Magazine, 367
White Horse Alley (Bank Street), 35
Willing's Alley, 43, 112, 354, 367–68, 372
Phillips, Francis (Rev.), 1, 2, 4, 8–9, 218
Phillips, Jacob (High Sheriff), 356
Phillips, John, 4
Phillips, Philip, 133, 264
Pickawillany or "Pick Town" (Piqua, Ohio), 66, 68, 80, 82–84, 87, 120–28, 133, 137, 140, 157, 162, 202, 241
Pike, Zebulon (Col.), 383
Piscataway (nation). *See* Algonquin (nation): Conewango (nation)
Pittsburgh (Pennsylvania), 64, 66, 69–70, 146, 209, 212, 214–20, 223–24, 228, 234, 246, 291, 297, 302, 306, 316, 318, 320, 322, 324, 328–29, 342, 361
  Forks of the Ohio (Pittsburgh, Pennsylvania), 66, 69, 71, 78–79, 86–87, 112, 115, 119, 121, 142, 146, 149–53, 155–58, 161–68, 170–71, 175, 177, 182, 190–91, 195–96, 198, 201–202, 205, 208–10, 212, 216, 219, 221, 225, 236, 307, 320, 343, 399
  Fort Duquesne (Pittsburgh, Pennsylvania), 80, 158, 174–77, 181, 188, 191–92, 198, 205–10, 261, 402
  Fort Pitt (Pittsburgh, Pennsylvania), 58, 165, 204, 214, 220–21, 225–36, 239–46, 251–53, 264, 291, 293, 297, 303, 306, 320–21, 323–24, 328–29, 331, 360–61, 404, 408–11, 418
    Ayer's Hill, 219
    Fort Dunmore, 303, 328
    smallpox hospital, 239, 241–43
    the fort is under attack, 232, 240–42
  Fort St. George (Pennsylvania), 160, 210, 221, 228, 242, 256
  Trinity Church (Pennsylvania), 224
Pittsburgh's Lost Outpost, 44, 81
Plumer, Johnathan, 406
Plumsted (Plumstead), William, 219
Pollard, William, 362
Poor, Enoch (Gen.), 335
Portland's Powder, 354–56, 365, 367, 372
Potter, John (sheriff), 93, 186
Potts, John (ironmaster), 100
Pownall, John, 277
Prevost, Susanna, 357
Princeton (New Jersey), 210, 344, 350, 364, 367

Index

College of New Jersey (Princeton University), 344, 356, 367
Priscott, James, 389
Proctor, William (Lt.), 59, 63
Purcell, Richard (engraver), 311
Pyatt, Jacob, 68, 95, 97, 394

Q

Quebec Act (1775), 304, 310
Queen Charlotte of Mecklenburg-Strelitz, 269, 299–300
  descended from the Vandals, 299
Quigley, Widow, 394

R

Rall, Johann (Col.), 329–30, 332
Ramsay, Allan, 300
Randle, Warwick, 389
Randolph, Edmund, 344–45
Rankin, Hugh, 21
Rankin, James, 256
Raredon, Michael, 389
Ratzer, Bernard, 235
Raymond, Ann (Trent) (daughter), 188, 229, 308, 355, 369, 382, 401
Raymond, Samuel (son-in-law), 382
Rea's Town (Raystown) Pennsylvania, 94, 198–200, 204–206, 208–209
  Fort Bedford (Bedford, Pennsylvania), 204–205
Redebauch, Christian (Major Trent's indentured servant), 257–58, 305
Redick, John, 391
Redman, John (doctor), 324, 367
Redstone Creek (Brownsville, Pennsylvania), 134, 136, 151–56, 166, 170, 175, 291, 396
  Fort Burd (Brownsville, Pennsylvania), 153
  Le Hangard, 153, 175
Reed, Andrew, 328
Reed, Joseph, 351
Reeve, Peter (Capt.), 99
Reeves, Acey, 408
Reynell, John, 75
Reynolds, Edward, 389
Reynolds, Joshua (artist), 311
Reynolds, Patrick, 389
Robenett, Allen, 393
Robert and Benjamin, 34
Roberts, John (Lt.), 55
Roberts, Robert, 157, 164
Robertson, William, 389
Robertson (Jr.), John (Sgt.), 404–405
Robertson (Sr.), John (Sgt.), 404
Rochambeau, Jean-Baptiste (Comdt.), 352
Rocheblave, Phillippe Francois, 208

Rochell, Joseph, 408
Rochford, Lord, 302
Rodebauke, George, 408
Rodenbauke, Christian, 406
Rodger, 305
Rodney, Caesar (Continental Congress), 334
Roebling, Emily Warren (engineer), 384
Roebling, Washington (engineer), 384
Roseberry, George, 408
Ross, George (Rev.), 3–4, 385
Rossell, Anna (great-granddaughter), 383
Rossell, Lydia (Beakes) (granddaughter), 383
Rossell, Zachariah (Gen.), 383
Runnell, Peter, 389
Rush, Benjamin (doctor), 8, 367, 372–73
Rush, William (Ens.), 50, 53
Russell, William (Col.), 135, 136, 139–40, 149
Rutherford, John (Capt.), 177

S

Saint Mary's Church (Burlington, New Jersey), 19, 39
Sammon, Dennis, 389
Samuel, John (merchant), 11, 13, 17–18, 22–23, 30–31, 49, 74–75, 98–99, 102–103
Sanduskee (Sandusky, Ohio), 221, 223, 226, 233, 236, 239, 241, 361
Saratoga (Saraghtogue), New York, 45, 57–61, 202, 335, 336
  Anthony Kill (New York), 60
  Batten Kill (New York), 60
  Battle of Bemis Heights (New York), 336
  Battle of Freeman's Farm (New York), 336
  Fort Clinton (Schuylerville, New York), 57–59, 61–63, 65, 125, 241, 258, 335, 386
Sargent, John, 277, 290, 308
Sattelihu. *See* Montour, Andrew
Schuyler, Hamiliton (author), 3, 16, 89
Schuyler, Philip (Gen.), 59
Schuyler, Phillp Johannes, 59–60
Schuylkill River (Pennsylvania), 22, 30
Scioto River, 73, 82–84, 87, 123, 126
Shamokin Path, 121
Shannon, John (Capt.), 49, 52, 56, 57
Shannopin's Town (Lawrenceville, Pennsylvania), 69–70, 79, 139, 146, 233
Shawnee (nation), 69, 71–73, 77–78, 80–83, 87, 91, 98, 117, 120, 122–24, 126–27, 138, 144–45, 165, 188, 191, 194, 214, 224–29, 231, 239, 241, 261, 264, 288, 306, 328
  Kakowatcheky (chief), 71–72, 81, 117, 127
  Nucheconner (chief), 127, 144
  Opessah (chief), 122
Shea, Timothy, 389

Sheffield, John (1st Duke of Buckingham), 269
Shephard, William, 392
Shere, John, 39
Sherman's Creek (Pennsylvania), 94
Shinango (Shenango), 244
Shippen, Alice (Lee), 354
Shippen, Rebecca (Howard), 7
Shippen, Sarah (Plumley), 35
Shippen, Thomas Lee, 354
Shippen (Jr.), William (doctor), 354–55, 365–66, 372, 378–79
Shippen (Sr.), William (doctor), 39
Shippen I, Edward, 2, 7, 25, 33–34
Shippen III, Edward, 31–32, 35–36, 38–41, 43–44, 72–73, 75, 78, 88, 112–13, 137, 178, 180, 354, 358–59
    called "Neddy", 38
Shippensburgh (Shippensburg), Pennsylvania, 33, 41, 43–44, 89, 93–95, 97, 104, 184–85, 198–200, 202–203, 212
    Fort Morris (Shippensburg, Pennsylvania), 185
    Widow Piper's Tavern (Pennsylvania), 89, 94–95
Shirley, William (Gov.), 57
Shoemaker, Benjamin, 74–75, 186
Shoemaker, Samuel, 74, 186
Sieur de Montizambert, Pierre Louis Bouche Niverville, 142
Simon, Joseph (merchant), 219–21, 228–29, 252–53, 261, 275, 320, 341, 360–62, 381
Sims, Buckridge, 186
Simson, Samuel, 391
Six Nations (Haudenosaunee Confederacy), 41, 43, 64, 67, 72, 79–80, 87, 92–94, 97–98, 103–104, 115–20, 123, 125–27, 138–42, 144–46, 149–50, 152–53, 157–59, 175–77, 179, 188, 190, 214, 219, 226, 239, 253–55, 260, 264–66, 272, 276, 320, 322, 351, 399, 413
    Caha-ja-chanah (Broken Kettle), 97
    Canassatego, 43
    Carandawana, 121
    Cayuga (nation), 71, 81
    Half-King (Tanarisson), 72, 80, 87, 114, 116–20, 137–39, 141–42, 144–47, 149–50, 156–58, 160–61, 163, 165, 176–77, 219, 242, 400
    Mingo (nation), 124, 166, 230
    Mohawk (nation), 58, 60, 71, 261
    Oneida (nation), 68, 71, 121, 125, 260–61
        Scarouady (Monacatootha or Scaruneate), 68, 80, 87, 95, 125, 127, 141, 144
    Onondaga (nation), 71, 118, 120–21, 137
    Seneca (nation), 70, 81, 236
    Tuscarora (nation), 71, 206, 261
    White Mingo, 322
Skene, Andrew, 312–13, 423

Skene, Philip (Maj.), 309, 312–13
    Katherine, 312
Skenesborough, New York, 309, 312
Skip-pa-key-tahkey. *See* Eskippakithiki (Kentucky)
Slick, Sewell A, (author), 3, 5
Smallman, Thomas, 165, 231, 255, 307, 320–21, 342
Smith, Devereaux, 246, 408
Smithfield Street (Pittsburgh), 246
Smith, Henry, 41
Smith, Hugh, 413
Smith, Isaac (associate justice), 356, 358
Smith, James (Col.), 246–47, 253, 404, 408
Smith, Joshua, 329
Smith, Samuel (district justice), 94
Smith, Thomas, 174
Smyth, Frederick (justice), 260, 327
Snapes, Paul, 390
Sober, John, 23, 30
Spear, Joseph, 246, 320
Speightstown, Barbados, 24
St. Christopher (Island of), 51, 388
St. Clair, John (quartermaster), 200, 202
St. John's Episcopal Church (Carlisle, Pennsylvania), 114
St. Peter's College. *See* London (England) (U.K.): Westminster School
Stacy (Jr.), Mahlon, 10
Stacy (Sr.), Mahlon, 11
Stafford County Courthouse (Virginia), 78, 131, 215
Stamp Act (1765), 254, 280, 323, 345, 351
Standing Stone (Huntingdon, Pennsylvania), 68
Stanly, Joseph, 390
Stanwix, John (Gen.), 192, 212, 216–18
Steel, William, 391
Stephen, Adam (Gen.), 147, 174, 203, 279
Stephenson, Samuel, 390
Sterrett, Robert, 85, 91
Stevens, Alexander, 256
Stevens, Lewis, 43
Stevens, Nehemiah, 158
Stevenson, George, 97
Stevenson, James (merchant), 56
Stevenson, Margaret, 270, 272, 308
Steward, Henry, 171
Stewart, Robert, 391
Stewart, Robert (Capt.), 214
Stewart (Stuart), Issobel (grandmother), 2
Stie, Daniel, 408
Stinkerhorn, George, 406
Stockbridge (nation), 261
Stockton, Richard (attorney), 356
Stockton, Samuel Williams, 358
Story, Ann (Shippen), 24, 33, 37
Story, Thomas, 24, 33, 37

Stow, John, 111
Streate, Abigail, 3
Streate, Leonard, 3
Streate, Mary (wife of Leonard), 3
Stuart, Charles Edward (Bonnie Prince Charlie), 103
Stupart, Alexander (Capt.), 99
Sugar Act (1764), 251
Sullivan, Daniel, 390
Susquehanna River, 44, 46, 49, 85, 121, 186, 214, 257
Sutton, Benjamin, 408
Swaney, Thomas, 390
Swanson, Samuel, 390
Swiegly Old Town (Pennsylvania), 79, 86–87, 228, 231
Switzgaver, Vincent, 406

T

Taafe, Michael (trader), 83, 113, 125, 256, 393
Talbot, John (Rev.), 9, 17, 25
Tamaqua. *See* Lenape (nation): Beaver (Tamaqua)
Tanarisson. *See* Six Nations (Haudenosaunee Confederacy): Half-King (Tanarisson)
Tarachiawagon. *See* Weiser, Conrad (Johann)
Tartum, William, 390
Terrence, Adam, 256
The Hunter. *See* Kiasutha (Chief)
Thompson, James, 238, 406
Thompson, Samuel, 391
Thompson, William (Capt.), 199–200, 202, 222, 234, 408
Thompson, William (Rev.), 250, 256, 401
Thomson, Robert, 392
Thomson (Thompson), Charles (Continental Congress), 193
Thornton, John, 325
Threlfall, Fred (artist), 119
Thurlow, Edward, 299, 301, 302
Tilghman, James (attorney), 160, 196, 256, 261, 263
Toad, John Marton, 394
Todd, (Jr.), John (attorney), 373–74, 376, 382, 412
Todd, Anthony (London Postmaster), 277, 282, 304, 317–18, 376–77
Todd, James, 373, 412
Todd, Mary (Durburow), 382
Todd, William Temple, 382
Todd (Sr), John (schoolmaster), 372–75, 382
Tomey, John, 390
Torrence, Adam, 406
Tostee, Peter, 44
Toub, Caleb, 406
Toub, Casper, 406
Toub, George, 408

Toub, Jacob, 408
Treaty of Easton (1758), 193, 209, 215, 217–18, 226, 229
Treaty of Paris (1763), 187
Trent, Isaac (grandson), 383
Trent, James (half-brother), 3, 10–11, 17–24, 26–27, 29–30, 61, 89, 331, 360
   becomes the American Colonies' first Queen's Scholar, 10
   issued a patent for the Trenton Ferry, 21, 305
Trent, James (Jacob) (Capt.) (uncle), 3, 10
   Charles (Carl XI), 3, 10
Trent, John (doctor) (son), 256–57, 356–57, 369, 372, 374, 383, 401
   Old Presbyterian Church (Camden, South Carolina), 383
   serves as practitioner of physick in Camden, South Carolina, 383
Trent, John (grandson), 383
Trent, John (half-brother), 3, 11, 17, 19, 21, 26, 30
Trent, Martha (daughter), 218, 229, 305, 371, 401
Trent, Martha (granddaughter), 383
Trent, Mary (Burge) (Judge Trent's first wife), 3, 7, 18, 29, 39, 247, 324, 354
   dies from childbed fever, 3
Trent, Mary (Coddington) (mother), 2–4, 7, 11, 14, 17–18, 24, 30–31, 34, 37, 268, 293–94, 385
   buys Latin book for young William, 37
   listed in the death registry of St. Michael's Church in 1772, 293
   marries Judge William Trent in 1710, 3
   sues her stepson James to receive her dower in 1728, 22
Trent, Mary Louisa (Dubose) (daughter-in-law), 383
Trent, Maurice (great uncle), 3
Trent, Maurice (half-brother), 3, 11, 17, 19, 21, 24, 26–27, 30, 174
Trent, Sarah (daughter), 250, 308, 340–41, 371, 401
Trent, Sarah (Wilkins) (wife), 132, 152, 171–72, 181, 188, 212, 229, 237, 246, 250, 268, 275, 281–82, 284, 308, 328, 331, 340, 355, 369, 371, 373–74, 377–78, 382
   orders ten gallons of Jamaican spirits, 328
Trent, Thomas (brother), 8–9
Trent, William (judge) (father), 2–4, 7–18, 20, 25, 28–31, 34, 38, 385
   dies from a bout of apoplexy, 14
   Williamstadt manor, 22
   Yaff (enslaved servant for Judge William Trent), 21
Trent, William (Maj.), 2–3, 5, 7, 12–13, 20, 24, 27, 34–69, 71–81, 83–86, 88–91, 93–110, 112–47, 149–68, 170–212, 214,

216–310, 312–81, 383–84, 386, 390–91, 393, 396–97, 400–402, 404, 408, 410–13
admits to his own blindness, 297
arrives at Craven Street house in London, 270
becomes a vestryman as St. Michael's Church reopens, 360
becomes factor for the Ohio Company, 131
casts his vote for the Pennsylvania State House bell, 108
challenges George Morgan to a duel, 316
christens the outpost at the Forks of the Ohio, 160
Colonel Bosomworth commissions him on the western expedition in 1758, 205
commissioned a captain in 1746 during King George's War, 49
conducts inventory for John Douglas, 360
contracts intermittent fever for first time, 76
credited for spelling of "Kentucky", 134
Cresap delivers captain's commission to him at Redstone Creek, 154–55, 396, 400
dines with Anthony Todd and Benjamin Franklin, 282
Dr. Shippen recommends Portland's Powder for his illness, 354, 365
drafts his third and final will in July of 1784, 373
elected a district justice in Frederick County, Virginia, 147
elected as one of the first district justices in Cumberland County, Pennsylvania, 88
elected to New Jersey Assembly in 1780, 346
faces another relapse of intermittent fever in London, 196
George Morgan blames him for the death of John Baynton, 306
gets a court suit made in the East End of London, 286
gives cattle to Washington's army, 338
gives oath of allegiance to the American cause, 339
Grand Ohio Company names their new colony "Pittsylvania", 292, 294, 299
has a clock made in Philadelphia for his house, 108–109, 325, 374, 384
has a plantation built along Letort Spring, 91, 110, 229
has Lt. Governor Robert Dinwiddie arrested, 197
hears about the death of Old Briton at Pickawillany, 124
helps company members rename colony of Pittsylvania and call it Vandalia, 299
helps form the Hockley, Trent and Croghan firm, 73–76
Hughy (enslaved servant at his plantation in South Trenton), 347
learns arithmetic from Shippen during his apprenticeship, 35
leases a plantation and ferry in South Trenton, 324
loans his pocket telescope to General Greene, 333, 348
made executor of the David Cowell estate in 1783, 369, 372
meets Croghan for the first time in Shippensburgh, 44–46
meets William Johnson in New London, Connecticut, 258
newspaper article falsely accuses him of a deal with Lord North, 322
offers military discount for use of his Lower Ferry, 334
opens up largest mercantile store at Fort Pitt in 1760, 220
orders his artificers to build a cache at Redstone Creek, 153
Pennsylvania companies arrive in Brunswick, New Jersey in 1746, 54–55
purchased almonds for two shillings, 258
purchases a blunderbuss, 94
resolves the hostilities over goods at Fort Loudoun (Pennsylvania) in 1758, 202
rides on "Little Girty", 347–48
rumored to have died in an ambush in 1747, 62
sails to London to borrow money from Thomas Penn in 1748, 73
sends Croghan to check on his family while in London, 282
smuggles Restraining Acts for Pennsylvania and New Jersey out of London in 1775, 309
stays at Burn's Coffeehouse on Broadway, 258
stays on Villiers Street when he first arrives in London in 1769, 272–73
takes a flying machine from Bristol, 267
takes Peruvian Bark, 299
the Trent family crest from Scotland, 89–90
Thomas Clifford writes about his death from illness, 375–76
travels with Weiser, Croghan and William Franklin to the Ohio country, 68, 71–72
uses his illness to apply for a certificate of protection from Lord Howe, 334
visits the Cockpit with Wharton and Walpole, 290–92
visits Warm Springs in Virginia, (Berkeley Springs, West Virginia), 319
writes from the Wolgemuth Mill (Maryland), 183–84
writes journal entry about the smallpox blankets, 239
Trent, William (merchant of Inverness, Scotland (U.K.) (grandfather), 2
Trent, William (son to Major Trent), 171–72, 188, 401–402

Index   455

Trent, William Henry (grandson), 383
Trent's Hills or Trent's Mountains, 91
Trent's Town (Trenton), New Jersey, 11–13, 16–19, 21, 24, 26–30, 36, 47, 49, 54–55, 268, 275, 282–83, 287, 289, 294, 305, 315, 317, 324–25, 329–30, 332–35, 338, 340–41, 346, 351–52, 356–58, 360, 366–67, 369–72, 377, 382–84
    Assunpink Creek, 10–11, 19, 22, 27–28, 47, 54, 190, 332–33
    Breese Farm (New Jersey), 294
    Calhoun Street (New Jersey), 383
    First Presbyterian Church (New Jersey), 332
    Hanover Street (New Jersey), 24, 27
    Hopewell Church (New Jersey), 13–14, 17, 294, 360
    Hunters Research Inc. (New Jersey), 28
    King (Warren) Street (New Jersey), 27, 36, 329, 360
    Kingsbury House (Formerly Judge Trent's house) (New Jersey), 54
    New Jersey Gazette, 340, 371
    Petty's Run (New Jersey), 27, 28
    Queen (Broad) Street (New Jersey), 36, 54, 330, 333
    Shabakunk Creek (New Jersey), 383
    St. Michael's Church (New Jersey), 16, 27, 89, 294, 329, 360, 424
        Van Lossberg Fusilier Regiment stays inside St. Michael's Church, 329
    Trenton School Company (New Jersey), 356–57, 367, 372
Trenton Academy. *See* Trent's Town (Trenton), New Jersey: Trenton School Company (New Jersey)
Troupes de la Marine, 57, 61, 191
Tucker, Samuel, 115, 294
Tulton, Richard, 392
Tulton, William, 390
Tunkens, Joseph, 393
Turner, Morris, 256
Turpin, William, 406
Turtle Creek (Pennsylvania), 79–80, 146, 153, 156, 181, 208
Tuscarawas (Ohio), 233
Tuscarora Path, 68, 94, 95

V

Valine, John, 287
Van Braam, Jacob (Lt.), 177
Vandalia Colony, 301–308, 313, 316, 320–21, 323, 343, 345, 350, 356, 362, 414
Vanleare, John, 393
Vassall, John, 318
Vaughe, Groves, 390

Venango (Franklin, Pennsylvania), 69, 81, 141–42, 145, 158, 164, 168, 207, 210, 213–14, 216, 220, 233, 236, 239
    Fort Machault (Franklin, Pennsylvania), 145, 161, 210, 213, 216
    Fort Venango (Franklin, Pennsylvania), 233, 236
Vernon, Henry (attorney), 23
Von Dechow, Friedrich Ludwig (Maj.), 332
Von Donop, Carl (Col.), 330, 332

W

Wafer, Francis, 256, 393
Walker, Thomas (doctor), 261–62, 322–23, 340, 342, 413
Walker, William, 44
Walpole, Thomas (banker), 276–80, 285, 290, 292, 302, 306, 308, 310, 319, 370, 414
    Carshalton estate, 302
    Vandal House, 302
Walton, Roger (clerk), 68, 78, 105–106, 391
Ward, Edward (Capt.), 78, 105–106, 156–57, 160, 163–66, 168, 171, 201–202, 210, 307, 328, 391
Ward, Thomas (trader), 78, 394
Warder, Jeremiah, 186, 246, 248, 254
Warfield, William, 390
Warner, Edward, 108, 422
Warrior's Path, 134, 205
Washington, Bushrod, 279
Washington, George (Gen.), 70, 81, 83, 104, 136, 138, 150–52, 154–55, 157–58, 161–67, 170–77, 191–92, 195, 198, 205, 214, 217, 221, 259, 266, 279–80, 298, 318–19, 322, 328, 331–34, 336, 339, 341, 344, 350, 352–53, 367, 379–80, 382, 396–98, 413–14, 424
    Mount Vernon mansion (Virginia), 138, 198, 279
    Washington's Life Guard, 382
        Gibbs, Caleb (adjutant), 382
Washington, John Augustine, 279
    Bushfield plantation (Virginia), 279
Washington, Lawrence, 104, 130
Washington, Martha, 382
Wasson, Robert, 390
Watkins, Adrian (printer), 401
Watkins, Evans, 181–82
Watson (Jr.), John, 325, 328, 334–35, 339
Watters (Waters), Mary (doctoress), 366–68, 372, 374
    Huxham's Tincture of Bark, 367
    Worm Cakes, 367
Wayne, Anthony (Col.), 350
Weatherhead, John (Capt.), 283
Webb, John, 394
Wedderburn, Alexander (solicitor general), 299, 301–302, 304

Weisenberg, Catherine, 264
Weiser, Conrad (Johann), 66–72, 81, 92–95, 117–19, 135, 146, 165, 176, 185, 193, 358, 421, 425
    Womelsdorf, 66, 185
Welch, John, 362
Wenango. *See* Venango (Franklin, Pennsylvania)
West, Charles, 394
Wharton, Richard, 373
Wharton, Samuel (merchant), 246, 248–49, 252–54, 257–58, 260–66, 268, 270–72, 274, 276–80, 282–86, 290–92, 295–99, 301–10, 313, 319–21, 323, 326–29, 338, 343, 351, 353, 361–62, 365, 373–74, 376
    resides at Argyle Street, 284
Wharton, Thomas (merchant), 283–85, 299, 303, 305, 323, 339
Wharton (Jr.), Joseph, 309
Whitman, Joseph, 335
Whitty, John, 406
Willcoxe, William, 406
Williams, Daniel, 106, 393
Williams, Elizabeth, 158
Williams, Rensselaer, 360
Williamsburg (Virginia), 114, 121, 128–30, 138, 140, 145, 147, 152, 154, 156, 166, 197, 214, 220–21, 255, 291, 321–22, 328, 340–42, 344–45, 397
    Capitol building (Virginia), 156, 342
    College of William and Mary (Virginia), 114, 162, 344
    Duke of Gloucester Street (Virginia), 128
    Virginia Gazette, 299
Willing, Anne (Shippen), 287
Wilson, James, 322
Wilson, Thomas, 93, 393
Winchester (Virginia), 43, 83, 136, 138–40, 144–45, 147–51, 153, 164, 166, 191, 198–99, 214, 224, 399
    Fort Loudoun (Winchester, Virginia), 191, 214
    Treaty of Winchester (1753), 148
Windsor, Thomas, 390
Winterthur Museum (Delaware), 32, 287
Witherspoon, John, 344
Wolgemuth, Joseph (miller), 183
Wood, James (Col.), 172
Wood (Jr.), John (clockmaker), 108
Wood (Sr.), John (clockmaker), 108–109
Woodnought, Robert, 390
Woods, Jeremiah, 406, 424
Woods, Thomas (Sgt.), 405
Woods, Widow, 394
Wren, Christopher (architect), 275
Wyandot or Huron (nation), 71, 83, 87, 121, 144, 214, 216, 231, 240
    Muskingum, 121–22, 157
Wyoming Valley (Pennsylvania), 189, 191, 194

Y

Yadkin River (North Carolina), 104, 115, 134
Yorgen, Dennis, 390
York (Yorktown), Virginia, 197, 288, 352–53
Youghiogheny River (Pennsylvania), 70, 77, 79, 86–87, 136, 228
Young, Lenard. *See* Jung, Leonhard or Lenard (baker)

About the Author

A native of Butler, Pennsylvania and 2002 graduate of the University of Massachusetts, Jason Cherry has reenacted the French and Indian War for over 30 years portraying the group of volunteers hired under William Trent Jr in 1754, a unit known as Captain William Trent's Company. Currently he is the "research consultant" for the 1719 William Trent House in Trenton, NJ and works as an Assistant Group Supervisor for Stepping Stones Children's Center in Gibsonia, PA. His latest book *William Trent: Factor of Ambition* explores for the first time, the definitive life of William Trent and his forgotten place in eighteen century history. He also lives with his wife Emily and his two beautiful daughters Penny and Charlotte.

www.ingramcontent.com/pod-product-compliance
Lightning Source LLC
Chambersburg PA
CBHW030600230426
43661CB00053B/1782